BARRON'S

HOW TO PREPARE FOR THE

SAT II

MATHEMATICS
LEVEL IC

8TH EDITION

James J. Rizzuto
Director of College Counseling
Chairman, Mathematics Department
Hawaii Preparatory Academy
Kamuela, Hawaii

BARRON'S

To Shirley,
Rahna, Ticia, and Tony

All inquiries should be addressed to:
Barron's Educational Series, Inc.
250 Wireless Boulevard
Hauppauge, New York 11788
http://www.barronseduc.com

Library of Congress Catalog Card No. 99-11433

International Standard Book No. 0-7641-0770-4

Library of Congress Cataloging-in-Publication Data

Rizzuto, James J.
   Barron's how to prepare for the SAT II—mathematics level IC / James J. Rizzuto.—8th ed.
      p.   cm.
   Rev. ed. of: How to prepare for SAT II—mathematics, level I and IC. 7th ed. © 1996.
   Includes index.
   ISBN 0-7641-0770-4
   1. Mathematics—Examinations, questions, etc.   2. Universities and
colleges—United States—Entrance examinations—Study guides.
   3. Scholastic Assessment Tests—Study guides.   I. Rizzuto, James J.
How to prepare for the SAT II—mathematics level I and IC.
   II. Title.   III. Title: How to prepare for the SAT II—mathematics level IC.
QA43.r59   2000
510'.76–dc21   99-11433
                                                                                 CIP

PRINTED IN THE UNITED STATES OF AMERICA
9

CONTENTS

MODEL TESTS 371

APPENDIX   503

ALL ABOUT THE SAT II: MATH LEVEL IC EXAMINATION

CHAPTER

1

WHAT IS IT?

The SAT II Math Level IC test, like each of the 20 subject tests sponsored by the College Board, tests your knowledge of a particular subject—in this case, mathematics—and your ability to apply that knowledge. Unlike an aptitude test, a subject test is curriculum-based and is intended to measure how much you have learned rather than how much learning ability you have.

The subject tests are described, with sample questions, in a booklet prepared by the Educational Testing Service and available at secondary school counseling offices.

Registration forms for the tests are contained in the *Registration Bulletin for SAT I and II,* copies of which are also supplied to high schools. If your guidance or counseling office does not have a copy, write to:

College Board SAT
CN 6200
Princeton, New Jersey 08541-6200
or call whichever of the following is closer to you:
Princeton, NJ (609) 771-7600
Berkeley, CA (415) 849-0950

Subject tests are usually given on six Saturday mornings during the academic year, in October, November, December, January, May, and June, at hundreds of test centers around the country. Dates vary from year to year. For information on dates and test sites, write to the College Board Admission Testing Program at the address given above or visit your counseling office.

WHAT IS THE TEST FORMAT?

The SAT II: Mathematics Level IC test is one hour long, and you may take from one to three different subject tests at one sitting.

The test contains 50 multiple-choice questions, each having five possible answers. All questions count equally. The penalty factor to discourage random guessing is a score calculation of the total right minus one fourth of the total wrong (answers left blank are neither right nor wrong and receive no points added or subtracted).

Mathematical symbols are kept simple and are intended to be clear from the context of the problem. For example, the symbol *AB* may be used to denote "line *AB*," "segment *AB*," "ray *AB*," or "length AB."

HOW IS THE TEST USED?

Colleges use subject tests to predict an admission candidate's future success on the level of work typical at that college. Applicants to colleges use the test to demonstrate their acquired knowledge in subject areas important to their future goals.

Some colleges, especially the most selective, have found subject test results to be better predictors of success in related college courses than SAT I scores or even the high school record. Because grading systems, standards, and course offerings differ among secondary schools, a student's subject test score may provide the college with more and better information about what the student knows than a high school transcript does.

Colleges also use subject test results to place students in appropriate courses after they have been admitted.

High schools use subject tests to examine the success of the school's curriculum and to indicate strengths and weaknesses.

WHAT IS THE DIFFERENCE BETWEEN LEVEL IC AND LEVEL IIC?

Note first that the IC and IIC tests both require the use of a scientific calculator.

The *Level IC* test is a broad survey exam covering topics typical of 3 years of college-preparatory mathematics. It contains questions designed to determine knowledge (facts, skills, and processes), comprehension (understanding and applying concepts), and higher mental processes (solution of nonroutine problems, logical reasoning, and generalization of concepts).

Of the 50 questions on the test, the approximate number pertaining to each topic of high school math is as follows:

Topic	Percent	Number of Questions
Algebra	30	15
Plane geometry	20	10
Solid geometry	6	3
Coordinate geometry	12	6
Trigonometry	8	4
Functions	12	6
Statistics/Probability	6	3
Miscellaneous	6	3

The topic "functions" includes functional notation, composites, inverses, and the value of a function. Solid geometry includes space perception of simple solids (spheres, rectangular solids, pyramids, etc.), including their surface areas and volumes. The trigonometry questions deal primarily with right triangle trigonometry and basic relationships among the trigonometric ratios.

The *Level IIC exam* is intended for students who have had $3\frac{1}{2}$ or 4 years of college-preparatory math or an exceptionally strong 3-year math curriculum. The test involves more advanced work, with greater emphasis on trigonometry, elementary functions, and material that is prerequisite to calculus.

An important difference between Level IC and IIC is that plane Euclidean geometry is *not* directly tested on Level IIC. The geometry questions on IIC deal with two or three-dimensional coordinate geometry, transformations, solid Euclidean geometry and vectors. The trigonometry questions are concerned primarily with the properties and graphs of trigonometric functions, inverse trigonometric functions, identities, and equations and inequalities in trigonometry.

The approximate allocation of questions on Level IIC is as follows:

Topic	Percent	Number of Questions
Algebra	18	9
Solid geometry	8	4
Coordinate geometry	12	6
Analytical trigonometry	20	10
Functions	24	12
Miscellaneous	18	9

As to which test you should take, it is generally to your advantage to select Level IC if you have completed courses in elementary algebra and plane Euclidean geometry and are in the final stages of completing a third course in intermediate math that includes coordinate geometry and an introduction to functions and trigonometry. This is the normal situation in the spring term of your third year in a college-preparatory math program.

If, on the other hand, you have had sound preparation in analytical trigonometry, coordinate geometry of conic sections and elementary functions (including logarithmic and exponential functions) and have attained grades of B or better in your math course, you should take the Level IIC test. This is true also if you are enrolled in an introductory calculus or advanced placement calculus course.

If you are adequately prepared for Level IIC, do not make the mistake of choosing Level IC in the hope of receiving a higher score. Remember that the Level IC test deals primarily with more elementary topics, which you probably studied some time ago. Also, because Level IIC is elected by a more highly prepared group of candidates, the test scores are placed higher on the reported scale, a distinct advantage for qualified candidates.

For more guidance, we have included some Level IIC questions in sections of Chapters 23 through 31.

Finally, whichever level exam you select, keep in mind that you will not be expected to have studied every topic on the test, or be required to answer every question.

HOW SHOULD I PREPARE FOR THE TEST?

There are four important long-range steps:

1. Enroll in secondary school courses in elementary algebra, plane Euclidean geometry, and intermediate math (with trigonometry) in your first 3 years of high school.
2. Apply your best effort to these math courses to learn the material to best advantage.
3. Review thoroughly over a time period (several weeks or more) long enough to provide renewed mastery and understanding. Avoid "cramming," that is, a superficial, last-minute survey of a course undertaken in the shortest possible time.
4. Study sample testing material under exam conditions. In this way you will become familiar with what the actual test is like—the types of questions it contains, and how it is structured—and will thereby gain the confidence that comes from familiarity. You will learn how to use your time efficiently and will gain practice in problem-solving skills. You will diagnose your strong and weak areas and, through our explanations keyed to sections of the text, be directed to review sections designed to help you overcome weaknesses.

This book is designed to help you with the last two steps.

Here are some helpful last-minute tips:

1. Make dependable arrangements to get to the test center in plenty of time.
2. Have ready the things you will need: your ticket of admission, some positive form of identification, two or more No. 2 pencils (with erasers, or bring an eraser), calculator, watch (though test centers *should* have clearly visible clocks), and a simple twist-type pencil sharpener (so that you need not waste time walking back and forth to a pencil sharpener if your point breaks). No books, rulers, scratch paper, compasses, protractors, or other devices are allowed in the examination room.
3. The night before the test, spend a short time (no more than half an hour) reviewing important concepts or formulas. Then relax for the rest of the evening by doing something you enjoy—perhaps

reading, watching television, jogging, or chatting with friends.

4. Go to bed in time for a full night's rest.
5. On the day of the test, eat a moderate and balanced breakfast with adequate protein. Specifically avoid a sugary breakfast that may bring on feelings of anxiety when your blood sugar level drops rapidly an hour or two later.

WHAT DOES MY SCORE MEAN?

From your raw score, a scaled score is calculated. Scaled scores range from a low of 200 to a high of 800 with 570 the average of all Level IC scores. Sixty-eight percent of all Level IC scores fall between 480 and 660, and 84 percent are below 660. With your scaled score, you will receive a percentile ranking that shows what percentage of students scored below you and, by inference, above you.

For comparison purposes, the average for Level IIC is 640 and 68% of test-takers score between 540 and 730.

The College Board does not establish a passing grade. What constitutes "success" on the test depends on the college you wish to attend and your own personal aspirations. In general, you can be satisfied with any Level IC test score that is 50 or more points higher than your math SAT I score.

HOW SHOULD I USE THIS BOOK?

There is more here than the typical student will need. How much you need will depend on how much you already know. Proceed as follows:

1. Read the preceding sections of Chapter 1 (to familiarize yourself with the nature of the SAT II: Mathematics Level IC test), Chapter 2 (to familiarize yourself with calculator usage), and Chapter 3 (to learn successful methods that will help you answer multiple-choice mathematics questions).
2. Take and score the diagnostic test, and use the self-evaluation chart to pinpoint your weak areas.
3. Now turn to Chapter 5 and note the title and the topic headings. On the diagnostic test did you get all the arithmetic questions correct? If so, skim the chapter. Skip over the questions that you know you can answer. If, however, you are doubtful about any question, work out the answer and check it against the one recorded in the answer section. If your answer is wrong, read the discussion following the question.
4. When you have finished with Chapter 5, go on to Chapter 6. Again, if you answered all the real number questions correctly when you took the diagnostic test, skim the chapter and spend time only on problems about which you feel uncertain. If, however, you did poorly on questions dealing with real numbers, work through the chapter question by question, reading the discussion and doing the drill exercises for any problems you cannot solve correctly.
5. Review the remaining chapters in this manner.
6. When you have finished your review, turn to the six sample tests at the end of the book. After reading the discussion that precedes them, work through the tests one by one, analyzing the results by means of self-evaluation charts and reviewing topics on which you are still weak.

CHOOSING AND USING A CALCULATOR ON LEVEL IC

CHAPTER

2

OUR CALCULATOR SYMBOL

▣ Throughout this book, the calculator icon identifies calculator comments. We use this symbol to call your attention to calculator features, principles, and tactics. This chapter is entirely about calculator use; therefore, our first calculator icon asks you to consider a broad range of important concepts related to calculator use on Level IC.

TYPES OF CALCULATOR QUESTIONS ON LEVEL IC

About 60 percent of the questions on Level IC are "calculator inactive." For these 30 questions, the calculator provides no advantage and may even be a disadvantage (more about that later). The remaining 40 percent are either "calculator neutral" (they can be solved with or without a calculator) or "calculator active" (a calculator will be helpful, perhaps even necessary). However, all 50 questions test your knowledge of mathematical principles and your ability to apply them. No question specifically tests your ability to use a calculator. No question requires the use of a complicated calculator procedure, and only a few questions would be judged impossible to answer without a calculator. Therefore, the use of a calculator on Level IC is no substitute for a strong understanding of the mathematical principles tested. Because calculator use is relatively simple and secondary to the mastery of math skills, well-prepared students who have taken Level IC without a calculator have scored 700 or more. On the other hand, poorly prepared students armed with the most powerful instruments have scored well below average.

Your goals should be to: (a) understand mathematical principles and how they are applied, (b) acquire a reliable and dependable calculator with features you can operate with confidence, and (c) know how and when to use a calculator to help solve problems.

CALCULATOR TYPES AND FEATURES

Level IC allows the use of scientific and graphing calculators, including programmable calculators. The amount of help your calculator will be to you will depend on your experience with your calculator and the way you decide to use it.

When you choose a calculator to use on the Level IC test, what features will be important to you?

A basic scientific calculator will add, subtract, multiply, and divide integers and decimals, find powers and roots, provide values of logarithmic functions (natural or base 10), and find the values of trigonometric functions of entries expressed in degrees or radians. The calculator you choose should have those minimum features. (For more details, see the summary of calculator features at the end of this chapter.)

More sophisticated types of scientific calculators have other features you may find useful on the Level IC. Some will display rational numbers as fractions as well as decimals. Most will also allow you to insert parentheses to change the order in which calculations are performed. Others will calculate factorials and may have keys designated for the calculation of permutations, combinations, and means (averages).

Graphing calculators (also known as "graphics calculators") have more helpful features (even if you never use the graphing feature). Because the screen is larger, the graphing calculator will allow you to display all of the steps in your calculation. Having the steps displayed will aid you in finding errors. As further assistance in troubleshooting, some graphing calculators will point out a mistake if you have entered the information in a way the calculator cannot handle.

Graphing calculators will also display the graph of a function after you have entered its equation. From the graph, you will be able to see how the function behaves, determine its range and domain, and find its roots by using the solving feature of the calculator.

You are even allowed to use a programmable calculator, though you might honestly wonder what sorts of prepared programs would be useful on the Level IC. Some students program their calculators with important formulas they might expect to find on the test and think they might forget. Examples include formulas for slope, distance, midpoint, areas, circumferences, permutations, and combinations. Others program them with math facts, such as fundamental trigonometric identities (the triangle definitions of trigonometric functions, the Pythagorean and reciprocal relationships, etc.) You are, of course, much better off committing such rules to memory than taking time to search for them through the program menu of your calculator.

As of this writing, you are not allowed to use handheld or laptop computers. Banned, too, are electronic writing pads and other pen-input devices, as well as those with typewriter-style keypads or built-in paper-tape printers, You may not use a calculator that talks or makes noise, or one that must be plugged into an electrical outlet or similar external power source.

Test policies have changed several times in recent years, so you should check the registration materials in force at the time you sign up to take the SAT II.

YOUR BEST CALCULATOR CHOICE

With all of the possibilities, what level of calculator should you bring to the test to derive the greatest benefit?

Simply put, choose the most sophisticated (having the most features) calculator with which you are comfortable. But remember that there is no sense in having an instrument packed with complicated features you don't know how to use. It may, in fact, be a handicap to have a calculator that confuses you because it is too complicated for you.

If you are the typical Level IC student, you have had three years of high-school courses in which only basic scientific calculators were allowed. Because you have used these nongraphing calculators until they were familiar to you, they will probably be your greatest help. Be assured that they have all the features you will need. (Refer to the summary at the end of this chapter.)

On the other hand, you may already have a lot of experience with graphing calculators because you were allowed to use one in your intermediate math course, or you may be enrolled in an upper-level course such as precalculus where your teachers have encouraged the use of a graphing calculator. If so, you may be aided by its special features. Throughout this book, we will occasionally point out a graphing calculator technique; however, nearly every calculator comment in this book refers to a procedure that can be done on either a standard scientific calculator or a graphing calculator.

ELEVEN BASIC PRINCIPLES OF CALCULATOR USE

The first step in answering each Level IC test question is to decide how to solve the problem before deciding how (or even whether) to use the calculator. Over and over in your classroom instruction, you have heard the advice "think before you punch." In each section of the book, we'll help you decide what to think about.

Let's look at examples that illustrate eleven basic principles of calculator use,

1. If a direct calculator solution requires many keystrokes, there must be a shorter way.

EXAMPLE 1

$$\left(\frac{1}{2}\right)\left(\frac{3}{6}\right)\left(\frac{7}{14}\right)\left(\frac{15}{30}\right) = ?$$

(A) $\frac{1}{16}$

(B) $\frac{26}{52}$

(C) $\frac{2}{3}$

(D) $\frac{1}{4}$

(E) $\frac{3}{8}$

Should you just start entering parentheses, numbers, and operations? That will take at least 20 keystrokes, which is not only time consuming but leaves you with the unsettling possibility that the answer might be wrong because of an incorrect keystroke.

In this case, each fraction reduces to $\frac{1}{2}$, which you should be able to determine by inspection. Thus, the answer is $\left(\frac{1}{2}\right)^4$. Whether you now use the calculator to finish the calculation or recognize the result from your experience with numbers, the answer is $\frac{1}{16}$. Here, a calculator-only approach will take you longer and introduce many possibilities for error.

What's more, there is an added benefit to the insightful method: by seeing through the problem, you have more confidence in your answer because it makes more sense.

This has been an example of a question for which trying to use a calculator may be a disadvantage.

2. When an exact answer is not one of the choices, select the choice that best approximates the exact value.

EXAMPLE 2

Five percent of a shipment of 100 light-bulbs are defective. A bulb is selected at random and then a second is selected from the remaining 99. What is the probability that the first is defective and the second is not?

(A) .479

(B) .995

(C) .048

(D) .959

(E) .500

On the Level IC exam, the choices for some questions will be expressed to the nearest tenth, while on other questions they might be to the nearest hundredth or thousandth. For a given question, however, the choices are usually rounded off to the same number of decimal places. For this question, the answer is rounded off to the nearest thousandth.

When selections are made at random without replacement, as in this case, the probability of both things happening is found by multiplying the probabilities of each event.

The probability that the first is defective is 5%, or $\frac{5}{100}$. Once you have selected a bulb, there are 99 left. Of these, 95 are not defective, so the probability that the second is not defective is $\frac{95}{99}$. The total probability is $\left(\frac{5}{100}\right)\left(\frac{95}{99}\right) = .04797979\ldots$ or, to the nearest thousandth, .048.

3. A calculator is most likely to be useful for problems involving powers, roots, radicals, and decimals.

EXAMPLE 3

What is the length of the line segment with endpoints at the x- and y-intercepts of the line $x - y = \sqrt{5}$?

(A) 2.24

(B) 3.16

(C) 3.87

(D) 5.00

(E) 10.00

The intercepts of the line can be found at $(0, -\sqrt{5})$ and $\sqrt{5}, 0)$. The distance between these points can be found by the distance formula:

$$\sqrt{\left(\sqrt{5}\right)^2 + \left(\sqrt{5}\right)^2} = \sqrt{10} \quad \text{(approximately 3.16)}.$$

We did not use the calculator until we actually had something to calculate, $\sqrt{10}$. In fact, if the question had given the answer in radical form, we might never have used the calculator at all. For most test-takers, this would be a "calculator-neutral" question.

4. When a question involves algebraic expressions only, the calculator is not likely to be useful.

EXAMPLE 4

If p and q are positive integers and $p + q$ is odd, which of the following must necessarily be odd?

   I. $p - q$

   II. pq

   III. $(p - 1)(q + 1)$

(A) I only

(B) II only

(C) I and II only

(D) I and III only

(E) All

The question involves algebraic expressions only. You might approach it by testing particular even and odd integers, but even then, the calculations would be very simple. To select numbers to test, note that one must be even and the other odd. That's because if $p + q$ is odd, then only one of p and q can be odd (the sum of two odd numbers is even, and so is the sum of two even numbers). Trying

$p = 2$ and $q = 1$ will help you eliminate II and III. On the other hand, if you are unsure which numbers to use for testing, you can get the answer through reasoning, as follows. When you subtract any odd number from any even number, the result is odd. Therefore, $p - q$ is always odd and statement I must always be true. Multiplying by an even number always produces an even result. Therefore statement II is always even, which rules out a choice that includes II. Adding or subtracting 1 will change an odd to an even and an even to an odd. Therefore, regardless of which of p or q is even or odd, one of the numbers $p - 1$ or $q + 1$ must be even and the product must be even. This eliminates any choice that contains statement III. The answer is (A). This is another "calculator-inactive" question.

5. Use your calculator to perform tedious operations.

EXAMPLE 5

If $\sqrt[3]{x - 27} = .216$, then $4x = ?$

(A) 27.01008

(B) 27.60000

(C) 3.60000

(D) 3.01008

(E) 33.26198

This is a "calculator-active" question, because the calculator is very helpful and most test-takers would use it. We will, however, explore one effective way of getting the answer without a calculator.

To illustrate some special points about calculator use, we will compare four different approaches: estimation, paper and pencil, scientific calculator, and graphing calculator.

Estimation: The number on the right of the equation, .216, is the cube root of the difference between x and 27. If x were 28, the difference would be 1, for which the cube root, 1, is more than four times as big as .216. Therefore, you would probably be comfortable with an estimation between 27.0 and 27.3. The only answer in that range is (A). That's a neat, quick, noncalculator solution.

Pencil and paper: Solve the equation by cubing both sides to eliminate the cube root.

$$x - 27 = (.216)^3$$

Without a calculator, you would be faced with the tedious and time-consuming task of multiplying $(.216)(.216)(.216)$ by longhand. That task is too disagreeable and undesirable to pursue further.

Scientific calculator: Use the pencil-and-paper approach to get to a point where you actually have to do some calculating. Then raise .216 to the third power with the exponent key on your calculator.

$$x - 27 = (.216)^3$$
$$x - 27 = .010077696$$

Add 27 to both sides:

$$x = 27.010077696$$

Rounded off to five decimal places, the answer is closest to (A).

Graphing calculator: You may, of course, use the same scientific-calculator approach and ignore the special features of your graphing calculator. Or you might enter the function $\sqrt[3]{x - 27} - .216$ and use a "solve" feature. For example, you might ask your calculator first to graph the function. Then, with the graph displayed, you can estimate the solution by inspection or by moving a tracer point along the curve. Some calculators, such as Texas Instruments' TI-82, will calculate the solutions directly through one or more features. For example, the TI-82 has a solve feature (at $\boxed{\text{MATH}}$ 0) and a root option (at $\boxed{\text{CALC}}$ 2), either of which will produce the correct value.

When we used a TI-82 on this question, we got the answer but it actually took us nearly three times as long because of time needed to enter the full function, wait for the graph, and then go through the steps of the solving routine.

(Note: It is not our purpose in this book to persuade you to use a graphing calculator or to teach you how to use any of the dozens of different models available. Consult your calculator manual for guidance. As already mentioned, we will point out a few places where graphing-calculator methods might be appropriate but leave the procedural details for you and your calculator manual.)

As further guidance in test-taking, we want to note some special traps built into this question. A poorly prepared student may decide to distribute the cube root on the left side and therefore, change $\sqrt[3]{x - 27} = .216$ to $\sqrt[3]{x} - 3 = .216$. This incorrect procedure would yield $\sqrt[3]{x} = 3.216$. If you then cube both sides to remove the cube root, you get $x = 33.2619817$. Note that the question writer gave you an option near that one, (E), to make you pay the price for the error.

On the other hand, a very clever student might note that .216 is the cube of .6 and mistakenly decide to "eliminate the cube root" by rewriting the equation as $x - 27 = .6$. This error yields $x = 27.6$, an answer that would also make you pay the price for being too clever and too careless.

6. Practice with your calculator until you know the steps needed to perform the kinds of operations you can expect to find on the Level IC test.

EXAMPLE 6

A 20-foot ladder leaning against a vertical wall makes an 82° angle with the ground. How high up the wall does the ladder touch the wall?

(A) 6.26 feet

(B) 2.78 feet

(C) 142.31 feet

(D) 19.81 feet

(E) 16.40 feet

The Level IC test includes questions about trigonometry for which a scientific calculator is extremely helpful. In your high-school course, you probably worked with the values of trigonometric functions of special angles $(0°, 30°, 45°, 60°, 90°$ and their multiples) for which the values could be calculated from geometric facts. Your scientific calculator will give you the values of trigonometric functions of all angles, including the special angles, directly. In this question, once you have set up the trigonometric equation, the calculator will help you get the result even though the angle, 82°, is not a special angle:

$$\sin 82° = \frac{x}{20}$$
$$x = 20 \sin 82°$$
$$= 19.81 \text{ feet.}$$

But you are not home safe yet unless you know how to make your calculator perform the operations above. Calculators differ in the steps needed to enter the information. Some give you the correct answer if you enter the numbers and operations in the order shown. Others require you to start backward (for example, by entering 82, then $\boxed{\text{SIN}}$, then $\boxed{\times}$, then 20). For more details on the use of the calculator with trigonometric functions, see the summary at the end of this chapter.

7. Know what mode you are in and make sure the mode settings are appropriate to the problem.

If you chose answer (A) in the preceeding example, your calculator was set to radian mode rather than degree mode. Be sure you know how to identify the current mode setting of your calculator and change the mode to provide results in the form you require.

8. The calculator does not eliminate your need to learn mathematical principles.

If you chose answer (B) or answer (C) in the preceeding example, you used the wrong trigonometric function for your equation. To get answer (B) we used cosine, and for answer (C), tangent. Throughout our review sections we will emphasize the fundamental mathematical principles you are expected to know when taking the Level IC test.

The calculator will only do what you ask it to do and cannot compensate for erroneous information or mistakes in the way the information was entered. Remember to ask yourself if your answer is reasonable, which will help you avoid picking absurd answers such as (B) or (C).

9. Always check your results to see whether they make sense. A calculator has no way of knowing whether the information you entered is correct or not and the calculator can quickly turn your entry errors into improbable results.

EXAMPLE 7

If $2^x = 3$, then, to the nearest hundredth, $x = ?$

(A) .14

(B) .18

(C) .23

(D) 1.49

(E) 1.58

We are offering this example to illustrate the value of estimating your answer to avoid making improbable choices. Before using the calculator to find the correct decimal answer, let's estimate the result to see which answers might be reasonable. We'll do this by checking some simple values of x to see what the pattern looks like. You know that $2^1 = 2$ and $2^2 = 4$. Therefore, if $2^x = 3$, then x must be between 1 and 2. From this estimation alone, we can rule out all but (D) and (E) because the other values are too small.

In this case, the estimation alone nearly answered the question, but here's how to get the exact answer with your calculator:

$$2^x = 3$$
$$\log 2^x = \log 3 \quad \text{(log represents log base 10)}$$
$$x \log 2 = \log 3 \quad \text{by the exponential rule of logs}$$
$$x = \frac{\log 3}{\log 2}$$

If we use our calculator to divide $\log 3$ by $\log 2$ we get $1.584962501\ldots$

See the chapter summary for more details about using the log function of your calculator.

10. The calculator may help you find answers through trial and error.

EXAMPLE 8

If $0° < x < 90°$, then $\dfrac{\cos x \tan x}{-\sin x} = ?$

(A) -1

(B) 0

(C) 1

(D) $\sin x$

(E) $\sin^2 x$

Can your calculator help you find an answer when you don't remember the principle being tested? Here the answer could be found quickly if you remember that $\tan x = \dfrac{\sin x}{\cos x}$. When you substitute $\dfrac{\sin x}{\cos x}$ for $\tan x$ and simplify, the result is -1.

But suppose you forgot the relationship between $\tan x$, $\sin x$, and $\cos x$? You could then use your calculator to test several angles, say 30, 45, 60, etc., selected from the specified domain. Each value you try produces -1.

11. The more things you can do with your calculator, the more ways you will be able to use it and the more help it is likely to be.

EXAMPLE 9

In the following quadrilateral, if the ratio of a to b is $\sqrt{3}$ what is the measure of the greatest angle?

(A) $60°$

(B) $90°$

(C) $120°$

(D) $150°$

(E) $180°$

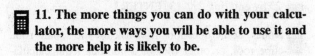

The answer can be found with or without a calculator. Draw the diagonal and you will see a pair of congruent triangles. Your experience with 30-60-90 triangles should suggest that the angle marked x measures $60°$. The largest angle will be $120°$ because the diagonal is the bisector.

To use the calculator, we set up the equation

$\tan x = \sqrt{3} = 1.732050808\ldots$

To solve for x, we need to know the relationship between "tan" and "tan⁻1", which are both accessed by

the same key on most calculators. To enter $\boxed{\tan^{-1}}$, you will probably need to use your $\boxed{\text{2nd}}$ function key (designated as the $\boxed{\text{inv}}$ key on some calculators). To proceed, you need to know that for $0° < x < 90°$,

$$\tan x = \sqrt{3} \text{ means}$$
$$x = \tan^{-1}\sqrt{3}$$

If you enter $\tan^{-1}\sqrt{3}$ in your calculator, it will display 60, which you will then convert to 120, as indicated above.

"Inverse trigonometric functions" such as $\tan^{-1}$ are not normally part of the syllabus for Level IC, and you may not have worked a problem on your calculator using an inverse trig function. On the other hand, the more things you can do with your calculator, the more ways you will be able to use it and the more help it is likely to be. The next question explores that principle further.

EXAMPLE 10

The minimum value of the function $f(x) = x^2 - 3x$ over the interval $1 \leq x \leq 4$ is ?

(A) 1

(B) -1

(C) -2

(D) -2.5

(E) -2.25

This question is a further illustration of Calculator Principle 11. This time, we will use a graphing calculator. Our discussion follows the procedure for a TI-82 calculator, but the steps would be similar on others. We'll begin by setting the standard viewing window for the calculator and then enter the function $x^2 - 3x$. We'll then press the $\boxed{\text{graph}}$ key and view the graph. From the graph displayed, we may now answer the question. If we were uncertain, we could get more help from the calculator by pressing $\boxed{\text{2nd}}$ $\boxed{\text{Calc}}$ and then electing option 3 "minimum." At that point, the calculator will ask for a lower bound (which we'll enter by moving the trace point to the left of the lowest point), then an upper bound (move the trace to the right of the lowest point) and a guess (which we'll ignore by pressing $\boxed{\text{ENTER}}$). The screen will quickly display the minimum value -2.25.

If you have had a lot of practice with similar calculations this will seem quick, easy, and uncomplicated. What's more, when you reach the answer, chances are you will be very confident in the result.

On the other hand, a well-prepared student can find the answer quickly without a graphing calculator. From the factored form of the function, $x(x-3)$, it can be seen to be a parabola that opens upward with x-intercepts at 0 and 3. The minimum point must be halfway between the intercepts at 1.5. Using a standard scientific calculator you can readily find the value of $(1.5)^2 - 3(1.5)$.

The way you answer any calculator-active (or, perhaps, calculator-neutral) question will depend on the features of the calculating device you bring with you and what you feel comfortable doing with it.

As you work through the sections in the chapters of this book, you will review mathematical principles and gain experience in deciding when to use your calculator.

Not all calculators accept and process information the same way. Therefore, in the summary below, we have also included some information to help you learn some important features of your calculator.

SUMMARY OF IMPORTANT CALCULATOR FEATURES

Decimal-place accuracy. Answer choices on the Level IC test are usually rounded off to the nearest tenth, hundredth, or thousandth. You seldom need more accuracy, even though your calculator will probably display answers accurate to eight or more decimal places. Many calculators allow you to change the number of decimal places displayed by changing a mode setting, but you should maintain the standard (8- to 12 place) setting to avoid confusion while taking the test. Some calculators round off the last digit displayed, while others don't. You can test your calculator by calculating 2/3, for which the decimal value is .6666... (the three dots mean the 6's repeat endlessly). The number of 6's displayed will tell you the number of decimal places your calculator displays. If the digit at the far right is 7, you know your calculator rounds off the last place. If the final digit is 6, the display merely stops the decimal.

Large-number display. When a number is too large to display, your calculator will switch to exponential notation. To test your display, enter 10 and then $\boxed{x^2}$. Your display should read 100. Now, enter $\boxed{x^2}$ again so your display reads 10000 (we have not placed a comma to mark thousands because your calculator doesn't). Enter $\boxed{x^2}$ again and your display will read 10000000. Enter $\boxed{x^2}$ again and your display will now read $1.^{16}$ or $1\,\text{E}\,16$ or 1×10^{16}. Familiarize yourself with how your calculator represents numbers too large to be displayed as a sequence of digits.

Arithmetic operations. Your calculator has keys for addition, subtraction, multiplication, and division. Don't confuse the subtraction key, $\boxed{-}$ with the additive inverse key, $\boxed{(-)}$. The division key may be represented by $\boxed{\div}$ or by $\boxed{/}$.

Carrying out calculations. Your calculator may carry out an operation as soon as you input the second number, or it may require you to press $\boxed{\text{ENTER}}$ or $\boxed{=}$ or $\boxed{\text{EXE}}$ or some other key. Test by adding 2 and 3.

Powers. On some Level IC tests, you will need to square or cube numbers. Your calculator will have a key designated $\boxed{x^2}$ and may also have one for $\boxed{x^3}$. The latter may require entering $\boxed{\text{2nd}}$ or $\boxed{\text{INV}}$ or $\boxed{\text{3rd}}$ to change the function of the key. These, and higher powers, can also be carried out with a special set of keystrokes. Check to see if your calculator has a key marked $\boxed{y^x}$ or $\boxed{x^y}$. Test the function of the key by entering 2 $\boxed{y^x}$ 3 and then $\boxed{\text{ENTER}}$ or $\boxed{=}$ or $\boxed{\text{EXE}}$. If the display shows 8, the key calculated 2^3. If the display shows 9, the key calculated 3^2. Be sure you know the correct keystroke order to find the calculations you require. Your calculator may also carry out exponentiation a different way, however. If your calculator has a key designated $\boxed{\wedge}$, use it to calculate 2^3 by entering 2 $\boxed{\wedge}$ 3 $\boxed{\text{ENTER}}$.

Roots. Some questions may ask for the square root, cube root, or other root of a number. Your calculator has a square root key, designated $\boxed{\sqrt{}}$, and may also have a cube root key. The latter might be accessed by first entering $\boxed{\text{3rd}}$ to access the third function level. If your calculator has an exponent key $\boxed{y^x}$, the same key may also calculate the xth root of a number. Examine your key panel to locate $\boxed{\sqrt[x]{y}}$. Check the order of your keystrokes by entering 3 $\boxed{\text{2nd}}$ 8. If your answer is 2, this sequence enters $\sqrt[3]{8}$.

Special constants. The only mathematical constant of special importance on Level IC is π. You will find π useful in answering questions related to areas and circumferences of circles or figures based on circles. On some calculators, the value of it is entered through the first function of a key. On others it may be the $\boxed{\text{2nd}}$ or $\boxed{\text{3rd}}$.

Special modes. The only mode of special importance on Level IC is degree mode. The trigonometric functions on this test are functions of angles in degrees. Learn how to set your calculator to degree mode and keep it in degree mode throughout the test. Most basic calculators display the message DEG to show that the calculator is in degree mode. If your calculator displays RAD your calculator is in radian mode and the values of trigonometric functions will be incorrect.

Reciprocal. Your calculator may have a special key to calculate the reciprocal of the number displayed. The key may be designated $1/x$ or x^{-1} . Calculating the reciprocal of a number may be useful when simplifying an expression, but it is also a step in the process of finding the reciprocal trigonometric functions.

Trigonometric functions. The Level IC test will contain questions about sine, cosine, and tangent but not secant, cosecant, and cotangent. When solving a problem, however, you might wish to use one of the latter functions, so it is desirable to know how to enter all six functions. The first three are entered with the keys marked sin , cos , and tan . The order in which you enter the function and the angle will vary from calculator to calculator Test your calculator by entering 30 sin . If the screen displays .5, this is the correct order. If not, enter sin 30 ENTER or = or EXE and the screen should now display .5. (If it displays -0.98803... it is in radian mode and must be changed to degree mode.) To find csc, enter sin 1/x . To find sec, enter cos 1/x . To find cot, enter tan 1/x .

When solving trigonometry problems, you may need to find an angle when you know the value of a trigonometric function. You do that with the inverse sine, cosine, and tangent keys. On most calculators, these values are found at the second function level. For example, to find $\sin^{-1}$, you must first 2nd or inv and then sin .

Counting aids. Some types of counting problems require computing the value of a factorial. For example, the number of ways six different books may be arranged on a shelf is 6! Your calculator may have a key $x!$ that is accessed by the second or third function. Test this key by entering 6, then the proper function exchange key (2nd , 3rd , inv), and then $x!$. Your screen

should display 720. Your calculator may also have keys for the permutations and combinations formulas, $_nP_r$ and $_nC_r$ respectively. Though these may prove helpful, don't be alarmed if your calculator does not have them. They are not essential, and you can do counting problems simply with your $x!$ and a knowledge of the formulas.

Parentheses. The parentheses key on your calculator operates the same way as the parentheses you use in algebraic expressions: it changes the order in which operations are done. For example, if a question asked you to find the slope of a line containing $(-2, 3)$ and $(4, -6)$, you would write the fraction $\dfrac{3 - (-6)}{-2 - 3}$. To carry out the operation on your calculator, you would probably have to use more parentheses than the algebraic expression shows—in other words, $\dfrac{(3 - (-6))}{(-2 - 3)}$. The extra parentheses are needed by the calculator to group the numerator and the denominator so the calculator can perform the division on the correct numbers. We did this by entering (3 − ((−) 6) / ((-) 2 − 3) ENTER .

Log keys. Your calculator may have both a key marked log and another marked ln . The log key represents log base 10, and we have already used it in an example for which we had to find an unknown exponent. The ln key represents natural logs. The log key is the only one you are likely to use on Level IC (though the example we gave would produce the same answer if we had used ln instead). Calculators differ in the way logs are entered, so check yours by entering 100 log . If the calculator displays 2, it requires you to enter the number before the log. Otherwise, enter log 100.

Mean (average). Your calculator may have a key to calculate the average of a set of numbers when you enter the set and press a designated key. Different calculators accept sets of numbers in ways too different to explore here. However, this feature is not likely to be useful on Level IC, because questions on the test generally involve weighted averages. If you do need to find the average of a set of numbers, use your calculator to add the members of the set and then divide the result by the number of members of the set. Often, this procedure is as quick as or quicker than the averaging feature programmed into the calculator.

ANSWERS

[1] (A)   [3] (B)   [5] (A)   [7] (E)   [9] (C)
[2] (C)   [4] (A)   [6] (D)   [8] (A)   [10] (E)

THIRTY-THREE STRATEGIES FOR ANSWERING MULTIPLE-CHOICE MATHEMATICS QUESTIONS

CHAPTER

3

Using actual multiple-choice test questions as examples, we'll explain problem-attack skills. Problem-solving skills are usually necessary to answer questions whose solutions have several steps. In several of our examples, we'll use more than one problem-solving technique to get the answer, but we'll focus on one method at a time in the discussion of each example.

1. Know what multiple-choice questions are like.

A multiple-choice question involves given information, operations (sometimes stated but usually unstated) by which the correct answer is found and five answer choices. Only one choice is correct. (We'll call the incorrect choices "distractors.") Regard the answer choices as part of the given information since they help you focus your effort.

EXAMPLE 1

For what values of x is the equation

$$x^2 - \left(\frac{1}{b} + b\right)x + 1 = 0$$

true?

(A) $2b, \dfrac{2}{b}$

(B) $-b, -\dfrac{1}{b}$

(C) $1, \dfrac{1}{b}$

(D) $b, \dfrac{1}{b}$

(E) $b^2, \dfrac{1}{b}$

The given information is the equation, the information that the desired result is the set of values of x that make the equation true, and the set of answer choices. All provide information about the type of answer desired.

Choice (D) is the correct answer, and the remaining choices are the distractors. Note that the distractors generally represent possible incorrect results that stem from common errors. Choice (B), for example, results from an error in sign; (A), from a misuse of the quadratic formula (failure to divide by 2). This means that, if you make a predictable error in working out a test question, you are likely to find a matching distractor, which may give you unwarranted confidence in your answer.

Answering the question correctly requires both mathematical knowledge (specifically, that in a quadratic equation the second coefficient is the negative of the sum of the roots) and some ingenuity in applying this knowledge quickly and simply.

A calculator is unlikely to be helpful, because the coefficients are not numerical.

A student who knows the concept can find the answer by inspection. A student who doesn't know the concept but can solve the quadratic equation (by any of several methods) will find the correct answer, but only after expending considerable time and effort. A student who knows only that the product of the roots is the final coefficient, 1, can eliminate choices (A), (C), and (E), but is forced to guess between (B) and (D), a somewhat risky business, though in this case better than just leaving the answer blank. (There will be more about guessing later.)

2. Use the answers.

Multiple-choice questions are particularly responsive to strategies because the answers are given. Therefore, it may be possible to answer a question correctly without knowing the mathematical procedure the test-maker used to derive the answer in the first place.

EXAMPLE 2

If $x^3 - x^2 - x - 2 = 0$, then $x =$

(A) 0

(B) 1

(C) 2

(D) -1

(E) -2

To answer this question, you don't need to know how to solve a cubic equation. You would, though, if it weren't a multiple-choice question. And even if you did know how to solve a cubic equation, you would still be able to find the answer more quickly by checking the choices given. (The answer is (C). Having your goal defined in advance allows you to work backward, a process we'll explain more thoroughly in further examples.

Even an equation-solving calculator may not get your answer faster.

3. Do no more work than you have to.

Unlike questions on classroom tests, College Board test items do not require complete solutions showing steps. You earn full credit by selecting the correct answer, not by showing work. Only the answer counts. Work carefully to avoid errors, but show only the steps *you* need to keep track of what you are doing. Painstakingly writing out elaborate procedures can waste time you need to answer other questions.

4. Recognize information implied by diagrams.

For most problems, some information is implied, not stated. Figures, for example, provide information about the relationships between points and lines. They are drawn accurately unless the problem states that the figure is *not* drawn to scale. Size relationships in accurately drawn figures are helpful in suggesting ways to proceed and in estimating answers, *but should not be the only reason an answer is chosen.*

In addition, all figures are plane figures unless the problem states that the figure is three-dimensional.

5. Recognize information implied by terms.

The values of a variable and the domain of a function are the set of all real numbers unless the question states otherwise. In some questions, however, special values *are* stated, especially the restriction of a domain to the set of *integers*. Therefore, it is extremely important to be familiar with the meanings of the terms "integer," "positive integer," "negative integer," "rational number," "real number" and "complex number." Furthermore, the meanings of all mathematical terms provide important implications you should use.

EXAMPLE 3

If a linear function has a graph with a positive slope and its y-intercept is also positive, then its x-intercept is

(A) Zero

(B) Negative

(C) Positive

(D) Equal to the y-intercept

(E) Greater than the y-intercept

To answer the question you need to know what is directly implied by the terms "linear function," "slope," "y-intercept" and "x-intercept."

You also need to know that a positive slope implies that the line (the "graph" of the "linear function") rises from left to right, which in turn implies that the x-intercept is negative in order to satisfy the given condition that the y-intercept is positive.

6. Know mathematical facts.

Although most test questions require more skill than just the knowledge of mathematical facts, many elementary test questions require nothing more.

EXAMPLE 4

$\sin x - \cos(90 - x) = ?$

(A) -1

(B) $-\dfrac{1}{2}$

(C) 0

(D) $\dfrac{1}{2}$

(E) 1

The relationship between sine and cosine is an elementary fact of trigonometry. Answering this question requires no higher level of problem-solving skill than knowing that the sine of an angle is the cosine of its complement. Because $90 - x$ is the complement of x, it follows that $\sin x = \cos(90 - x)$. Substitute and subtract. The result is 0.

EXAMPLE 5

Which of the following has a graph that is perpendicular to the x-axis and contains the point $(-2, 5)$?

(A) $x = 2$

(B) $x = -2$

(C) $y = -2$

(D) $x + y = 2$

(E) $x - y = 2$

A line perpendicular to the x-axis is a vertical line. The graphs and equations of vertical and horizontal lines are basic facts in the study of linear equations. To answer this question, you need know only that $x = -2$ is the equation of the vertical line containing all points having -2 as their first coordinate.

7. Know mathematical methods.

Some test questions require no more than the ability to apply routine algebraic processes to the given information.

EXAMPLE 6

If $\frac{2}{3}(x-1) \leq \frac{x+4}{6}$, then

(A) $x \leq \frac{5}{3}$

(B) $x \leq \frac{8}{3}$

(C) $x \leq \frac{5}{4}$

(D) $x \geq \frac{5}{3}$

(E) $x \leq 4$

The answer is found merely by applying routine steps of inequality solving. First, clear fractions by multiplying each side by 6:

$$6\left(\frac{2}{3}(x-1)\right) \leq 6\left(\frac{x+4}{6}\right),$$

This gives

$$4(x-1) \leq x+4,$$
$$4x-4 \leq x+4,$$
$$3x \leq 8,$$
$$x \leq \frac{8}{3}.$$

EXAMPLE 7

At what points do the graphs of $2x+y=6$ and $3x-4y=9$ intersect?

(A) $(0, 6)$

(B) $(1, 4)$

(C) $(6, 9)$

(D) $(3, -4)$

(E) $(3, 0)$

Solving systems of linear equations in two variables is a routine procedure of elementary algebra.

Before we show an algebraic solution, note that the problem can be quickly solved on a graphics calculator. To do so, you would solve both equations for y, enter them in y-form and then use the intersection feature of your calculator.

If $2x+y=6$, then $y=6-2x$. Substituting $6-2x$ for y in $3x-4y=9$ yields $-3x-4(6-2x)=9$, which simplifies to $x=3$.

Because $x-3$ and $y=6-2x$, it follows that $y=0$.

8. Draw inferences.

When you have carefully studied the given information until you are sure of what it says and what it asks, you will sometimes see a solving process immediately. If not, examine the given information to see what inferences might be drawn. Each inference is a potential starting point. The most important question a problem solver can ask him- or herself is, "What can I conclude?" Search your memory for everything you can remember about concepts of the type given.

EXAMPLE 8

If quadrilateral $ABCD$ is a parallelogram and the measures of angles A and B are $2x+4$ and $3x-4$, respectively, then $x =$

(A) 8

(B) 24

(C) 36

(D) 76

(E) 55

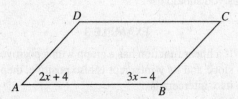

(Figure is not drawn to scale.)

There are dozens of implications that can be drawn from the fact that the figure is a parallelogram: (1) opposite sides are congruent, (2) opposite sides are parallel, (3) the diagonals bisect each other, (4) the opposite angles are congruent, (5) the adjacent angles are supplementary, etc.

Obviously, not all of these are useful in the solution of any one problem. In this problem it is clear that we need an inference about a pair of adjacent angles. We've noted that adjacent angles are supplementary, so the measures of angles A and B must add up to 180:

$$(2x+4)+(3x-4) = 180,$$
$$x = 36.$$

Suppose that you could not remember any of the angle relationships. From the fact that the figure is a parallelogram, you can infer that opposite sides are parallel. From the fact that opposite sides are parallel, you can infer that the angles noted in the following diagram have the same measure:

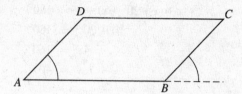

From the fact that the angles indicated have the same measure, you can infer that the adjacent angles are supplementary.

EXAMPLE 9

$PQRS$ is a parallelogram and angle T is a right angle. $RT = 5$, $ST = 12$. $PQ =$

(A) 13

(B) 17

(C) 7

(D) 11

(E) 15

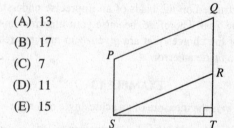

Because $\triangle RTS$ is a right triangle, you can conclude that $RS = 13$ from the Pythagorean Theorem:

$$
\begin{aligned}
RS^2 &= RT^2 + ST^2 \\
&= 5^2 + 12^2 \\
&= 25 + 144 \\
&= 169, \\
RS &= 13.
\end{aligned}
$$

 Use your calculator to find $\sqrt{169}$ if you forgot.

Because $PQRS$ is a parallelogram, you can conclude that both pairs of opposite sides are congruent. Hence $PQ = RS = 13$.

Sometimes the place to look for inferences is not just the given facts but also the goals. In other words, always examine the suggested answers before attempting to draw conclusions.

EXAMPLE 10

If $a = xy$ and $b = xz$, then $a - b =$

(A) $x(y - z)$

(B) $xy(1 - xz)$

(C) $xz(1 - y)$

(D) $z(x - y)$

(E) $y(x - z)$

All of the answers are in factored form; therefore you can infer that, when you do find an expression for $a - b$, you must factor it before comparing it with the choices given:

$$
a - b = xy - xz = x(y - z)
$$

9. Seek alternative approaches when you reach a dead end.

Is it possible to know too much relevant information? In the long run, probably not, but sometimes you may head off on the wrong track because you started with an unproductive inference.

EXAMPLE 11

If $Q(x)$ is any quadratic function and $f(x)$ is any linear function, then the number of possible solutions for $Q(x) = f(x)$ is

(A) 0

(B) 1

(C) 2

(D) None of these

(E) All of these

Since $Q(x)$ is a quadratic function, you can infer that it can be written in the form

(1) $\qquad Q(x) = ax^2 + bx + c.$

Similarly, a linear function $f(x)$ can be written in the form

(2) $\qquad f(x) = px + q.$

If $Q(x) = f(k)$, then

(3) $\qquad ax^2 + bx + c = px + q,$ and

(4) $\quad ax^2 + (b - p)x + (c - q) = 0.$

Equation (4) is complicated enough to be a dead end for many test-takers, who would then abandon this line of reasoning and start over.

Starting over with a different set of inferences, we can note that the graph of a quadratic function is a parabola with a vertical axis and the graph of a linear function is a line. Since $Q(x)$ represents the whole family of parabolas with vertical axes and a line can intersect a parabola in zero, one, or two points, the correct answer is (E).

In most cases, however, mathematical paths that start with the same concept tend to reconnect later on. That complicated "dead-end" equation (4) would lead to the right conclusion for a student who recognized that it was still a quadratic equation and that a quadratic equation may have zero, one, or two solutions.

Your mind may travel a different logical path to a solution, but if your inferences are correct, your conclusion will be the same.

EXAMPLE 12

If $AB = AC$ and $BM = AM = AN = NC$, then $x =$

(A) $20°$

(B) $25°$

(C) $30°$

(D) $40°$

(E) $60°$

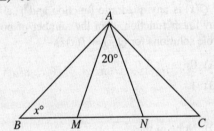

(Figure is not drawn to scale.)

Two different paths lead to the correct solution.

1. Because $AM = AN$, you may conclude that $\angle AHN$ and $\angle ANM$ have the same measure. Call this measure a; $a + a + 20° = 180°$ since the sum of the measures of the angles of a triangle is $180°$.

$$2a = 160°$$
$$a = 80°$$

The measure of $\angle BAM$ is x because $AM = BM$. Also, $\angle AMN$ is an exterior angle of $\triangle BMA$. Because an exterior angle is the sum of the two nonadjacent interior angles,

$$80° = x + x$$
$$80° = 2x$$
$$40° = x$$

2. A second approach is to note that $\angle BAM$ is x since $BM = AM$, $\angle C$ is x because $AB = AC$ and $\angle NAC$ is x because $AN = NC$.

Because the sum of the measures of the angles of $\triangle BAC$ is $180°$,

$$x + (x + 20° + x) + x = 180°$$
$$4x + 20° = 180°$$
$$4x = 160°$$
$$x = 40°$$

These two paths are not as different as they appear. One involves an inference that is a logical consequence of the other.

10. Correctly define your goal.

The goal of a multiple-choice question is more precisely defined than that of any other type of mathematical problem because the goal is given as a choice; you are not asked to discover an unknown. Nevertheless, the goal can be misunderstood. Remember that many distractors are constructed on the basis of an imprecise understanding of the goal. Therefore, because your incorrect answer is one of the choices that are given, you may not realize you have made an error.

EXAMPLE 13

If m is the measure of an acute angle of a right triangle and $\tan m = \dfrac{b}{2}$, then $\sin m =$

(A) $\dfrac{\sqrt{4 - b^2}}{b}$

(B) $\dfrac{b}{\sqrt{4 - b^2}}$

(C) $\dfrac{b}{\sqrt{4 + b^2}}$

(D) $\dfrac{\sqrt{4 - b^2}}{2}$

(E) $\dfrac{2}{\sqrt{4 + b^2}}$

In this problem, each of the distractors represents an error by confusing the meaning of "sine" or "tangent." The correct answer is (C). Answer (E) is the cosine. Answers (A) and (B) result from confusing the meaning of "tangent" with that of "sine."

By giving, say, the cosine when the question asks for the sine, you are really answering the wrong question through your own misunderstanding of the meanings of the terms. The only remedy for this type of error is to learn the meanings of terms and to double-check your work to make sure you are using them correctly.

Though your calculator computes sines and tangents, you still must know the definitions of the terms in order to solve calculator-inactive questions such as this one.

11. Try to restate the goal in your own words.

Such restatement helps clarify the meaning of the goal, although it can sometimes lead to errors if your restatement is not accurate.

EXAMPLE 14

If a polygon *ABCDEF* is a regular hexagon with perimeter $36p^2$ then the length of side $AB =$

(A) $6p^2$

(B) $6p$

(C) 6

(D) p^2

(E) p

Since a regular hexagon has six equal sides, the perimeter is six times the length of a side. Dividing $36p^2$ by 6 gives $6p^2$.

Had you confused the meaning of "perimeter" with "Area" (because $36p^2$ is a perfect square, which suggests area), you would be answering a far more complicated question.

EXAMPLE 15

If $x = \log_2 20$, then x is between what pair of consecutive integers?

(A) 0 and 1

(B) 1 and 2

(C) 2 and 3

(D) 4 and 5

(E) 16 and 32

The precise value of $\log_2 20$ is unnecessary in finding the answer. Since precise values of $\log_2 x$ are most readily determined when x is a power of 2, we can get all of the information we need by inspecting powers of 2 on either side of 20. Because $\log_2 16 = 4$ and $\log_2 32 = 5$, the correct answer is (D).

Your calculator gives values of $\log_{10}$ and $\ln$, from which you can calculate other logs by using the formula $\log_a b = \dfrac{\ln b}{\ln a}$.

12. Answer the right question.

Don't confuse the actual question with some other question suggested by the problem but not really asked.

EXAMPLE 16

The graphs of $x^2 + y^2 = 4$ and $x^2 = 4y$ intersect in how many points?

(A) 0

(B) 1

(C) 2

(D) 3

(E) 4

Look carefully and you will see that the question does not ask you to *find* the points of intersection but to tell *how many* there are. Perhaps you have had to find the points of intersection as part of your regular studies and on classroom tests. If so, you may rush into solving the system without realizing that it is unnecessary.

Because you can infer that the graph of the first equation is a circle with center at the origin and radius 2, and that of the second is a parabola with vertex at the origin, you can see by inspection that there are two points of intersection without ever working out what they are.

Answer (D), by the way, deserves special comment. Many students select it because they don't realize that the center of the circle is not a point of the circle.

13. Infer properties from the information in the question.

Sometimes, to solve a problem you must infer new properties you may never have known before.

 ### EXAMPLE 17

If the length of the side of an equilateral triangle is 10, then its area =

(A) 50

(B) 100

(C) 25

(D) 8.66

(E) 43.30

Chances are that you have not memorized the formula

$$a = \frac{\sqrt{3}}{4}s^2,$$

where *A* is the area of an equilateral triangle and *s* is the length of a side. Nor should you.

You can infer all of the information you need from the figure and the Pythagorean Theorem (or from the 30-60-90 triangle relationship). First draw a figure: an equilateral triangle ABC with altitude CD:

Altitude CD bisects AB, so $DB = 5$.

From the Pythagorean Theorem (or 30-60-90 triangle relationship), $CD = 5\sqrt{3}$.

From the formula for the area of a triangle,

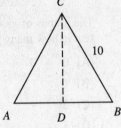

$$\text{area of } \triangle ABC = \frac{1}{2}(AB)(CD)$$
$$= \frac{1}{2}(10)(5\sqrt{3})$$
$$= 43.30$$

Through this logical sequence, you have inferred a new property, the area of an equilateral triangle, from other properties.

14. Infer properties from the answer choices.

As noted earlier, multiple-choice questions are sometimes most easily answered by working backward from the choices.

EXAMPLE 18

The set R includes p, q, r and s. Multiplication in the set R is defined by a table, part of which is given below:

×	p	q	r	s
p	s			
q		0		
r			r	
s				q

Which of the following is 1?

(A) p

(B) q

(C) r

(D) s

(E) None of these

The question becomes simple to answer once you realize that a property of 1 is $1 \times 1 = 1$. In the portion of the table given, each number is multiplied by itself, so we are looking for a number x such that $x \times x = x$. Since $r \times r = r$, the answer is (C). We discovered it by inferring properties about our goal, the number 1, and matching these properties with the given information.

15. Use trial and error effectively.

Working backward takes many forms. One of these, trying and discarding answer choices, was introduced in Example 2 and is reviewed here.

EXAMPLE 19

If $\sqrt{5x-4} + \sqrt{2x+1} = 7$, then $x =$

(A) -4

(B) 4

(C) 2

(D) 1

(E) 0

To answer the question by solving the equation involves a complicated and time-consuming procedure. Checking the answer choices in the equation takes only a few seconds, especially since the answer is (B).

16. Try specific cases.

Often it is helpful to rephrase the given information in terms of specific cases.

EXAMPLE 20

If $f(x)$ is a function for which

$$f(a+b) = f(a) + f(b),$$

which of the following must also be true?

  I. $f(a-b) = f(a) - f(b)$

  II. $f(4a) = 4f(a)$

  III. $f(ab) = f(a) \times f(b)$

(A) I only

(B) I and II only

(C) II and II only

(D) All

(E) I and II only

Direct methods exist for answering this question, but let us suppose you are unable to think of one. You can still get a "feel" for the problem by trying a specific case. The problem deals with a function that has a simple property. The simplest of the functions are linear functions of the form $f(x) = mx$. A quick check shows that $f(x) = mx$ does have the desired property since

$$f(a+b) = m(a+b)$$
$$= ma + mb$$
$$= f(a) + f(b)$$

Let us see what happens when we try I, II and III on $f(x) = mx$.

I. $\begin{aligned} f(a-b) &= m(a-b) \\ &= ma - mb \\ &= f(a) - f(b) \end{aligned}$

II. $\begin{aligned} f(4a) &= m(4a) \\ &= 4(ma) \\ &= 4f(a) \end{aligned}$

III. $\begin{aligned} f(ab) &= m(ab) \\ &\neq (ma)(mb) \\ &= f(a) \times f(b) \end{aligned}$

This special case shows that property III cannot be true and eliminates choices (C), (D), and (E) narrowing down the possibilities to (A) and (B).

Since $f(x) = mx$ is only one of many types of functions having the given property, we cannot assert that I and II must be true from working with this special case. But we can see that, for any function with the given property,

$$\begin{aligned} f(4a) &= f(a+a+a+a) \\ &= f(a) + f(a) + f(a) + f(a) \\ &= 4f(a) \end{aligned}$$

without looking at special cases.

Therefore the correct answer must be (B). We never really came to grips with property I; but then again, we never really had to in order to get the answer.

In some problems, there is nothing else you *can* do except try specific cases.

EXAMPLE 21

If x is an integer, then $\dfrac{x^2}{x-4}$ is a positive integer when $x =$

(A) 4

(B) −4

(C) 1

(D) 3

(E) 6

Unlike Examples 18 and 19, in which elementary algebraic processes do exist that will crank out an answer (despite the fact we chose not to use them), this example involves algebraic principles sufficiently unfamiliar to be a dead end for many students. You should, however, be able to check all of the answers within 10 to 15 seconds just by substituting them for x. That's less time than it may take even to begin searching for a different strategy.

17. Identify subgoals.

A subgoal is a step partway between the given information and the final answer. Setting up subgoals is a process similar to drawing inferences.

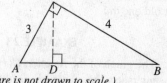

EXAMPLE 22

If $\triangle ABC$ is a right triangle with right angle at C, what is the length of altitude CD?

(A) 5

(B) 3.5

(C) 2

(D) 3

(E) 2.4

(Figure is not drawn to scale.)

This question can be answered by determining two subgoals: (1) finding the length of AB and (2) finding the area of the triangle. Then, (3), we'll combine the information from (1) and (2) to get the answer.

Subgoal (1): From the Pythagorean Theorem,

$$AB^2 = BC^2 + AC^2.$$

Therefore $AB = 5$.

Subgoal (2): The area of a right triangle is one-half the product of the legs, or

$$\frac{1}{2}(3)(4) = 6.$$

Then

$$\begin{aligned} \text{area} &= \frac{1}{2}(CD)(AB), \\ 6 &= \frac{1}{2}(5) \\ CD &= \frac{12}{5} \\ &= 2.4. \end{aligned}$$

Subgoals are determined as part of the process of deciding what can be inferred. Clearly, both the area of the triangle and the missing hypotenuse can be inferred from the given lengths and the fact that the figure is a right triangle. By itself, each inference is a dead end. Together, the inferences combine to reach the goal.

This example, by the way, is an excellent case where understanding the mathematics used is not enough to answer the question. Proficiency in problem-solving strategy is essential.

18. Break out of circles.

Your attempts to solve a problem may lead you around and around the same mental paths without reaching the desired conclusion. Either the inference you started with is not the basis of the answer, or the sequence of actions you are using won't lead to the answer. To break out of the circle, go back to the given information and look for other inferences. If you cannot see any other inferences, look for a different action sequence. Be aware, however, that you haven't really changed action sequences if your new one is merely a different way of doing the same thing your old one did.

EXAMPLE 23

The graph of the function $Q(x) = x^2 + bx + c$ intersects the x-axis in exactly one point. At that point, $x = r$. Therefore, $b =$

(A) r

(B) $2r$

(C) $\pm 2\sqrt{c}$

(D) $\dfrac{bc}{r}$

(E) $\dfrac{c}{r}$

At the point of intersection of the graph with the x-axis, $Q(x) = 0$. Your first approach might be to try to solve $x^2 + bx + c = 0$ to find an expression for the roots. Whether you do this by (1) factoring, (2) completing the square or (3) substituting the coefficients into the quadratic formula, you are on the same track, despite the differences in the methods used. All three are equivalent action sequences. All spin you around the same circle.

If you discover that you cannot find the answer along that path, you should try to break out of the circle. Since you started by trying to infer results from the equation, you can change procedures by inferring results from the solutions.

The graph intersects in exactly one point, so the quadratic equation has a single solution; therefore the discriminant, $b^2 - 4ac$, is zero. Since $a = 1$,

$$b^2 - 4c = 0,$$
$$b^2 = 4c,$$
$$b = \pm 2\sqrt{c}.$$

Note that the root itself plays no role in answering the question.

19. Use destructive processes to narrow down to an answer.

Simplifying expressions and solving equations are examples of what might be called "destructive" processes because they break down complex expressions and statements into increasingly simpler ones. In many test questions, the initial information is complex, the answer choices are simple and a destructive process leads directly to the correct conclusion.

EXAMPLE 24

If $f(x) = 7x - 4$, $g(x) = 2x + 8$, and $f(2a) = g(a)$, then $a =$

(A) -1

(B) 0

(C) 1

(D) -2

(E) $\dfrac{1}{2}$

From the given information,

$$f(2a) = 7(2a) - 4$$

and

$$g(a) = 2a + 8.$$

Since $f(2a) = g(a)$, the following equation is true:

$$7(2a) - 4 = 2a + 8.$$

This can be solved by elementary processes to get

$$a = 1.$$

Sometimes a destructive process need not be carried all the way to the solution set of the variable.

EXAMPLE 25

If x is an acute angle for which $\tan x = \dfrac{1}{3}$ and $\cos x = \dfrac{3\sqrt{10}}{10}$, then $\sin x =$

(A) 10

(B) $\dfrac{\sqrt{10}}{10}$

(C) $\dfrac{\sqrt{10}}{3}$

(D) $\dfrac{3}{10}$

(E) $\dfrac{10}{3}$

This question can be answered without carrying the solving process all the way to a value for x.

$$\tan x = \frac{1}{3}$$

$$\frac{\sin x}{\cos x} = \frac{1}{3}$$

$$\frac{\sin x}{\frac{3\sqrt{10}}{10}} = \frac{1}{3}$$

$$\sin x = \frac{1}{3} \times \frac{3\sqrt{10}}{10}$$

$$= \frac{\sqrt{10}}{10}$$

By calculator, you could find $x = \tan^{-1}\frac{1}{3}$ and then find the sine of the result, which is .31. You must then choose the answer closest to .31, which is not obvious because (B), (D), and (E) are all relatively close. Check each with your calculator.

EXAMPLE 26

If $5(1+b) - a = 4a + 5$, then $a =$

(A) 1

(B) 5

(C) $5b$

(D) b

(E) $\frac{b}{5}$

Breaking the equation down through solving processes gets the desired result, even though it does not produce a value for a or for b. (As you will see, no unique value exists.)

$$5(1+b) - a = 4a + 5$$
$$5 + 5b = 5a + 5$$
$$5b = 5a$$
$$b = a$$

20. Write an equation.

Often, information is given about two quantities that are equal. In that case the question can usually be answered by setting up an equation and solving it.

EXAMPLE 27

Two rectangular boxes have equal volumes. Their dimensions are $8, 3, h$ and $4, 4, (2h-1)$, respectively. Then $h =$

(A) $\frac{1}{16}$

(B) -1

(C) $\frac{4}{5}$

(D) 4

(E) 2

The volumes are found by multiplying the length times the width times the height, or:

Volume of the first box $= 8(3)(h)$

Volume of the second box $= 4(4)(2h-1).$

Since the volumes are equal,

$$8(3)(h) = 4(4)(2h-1),$$
$$24h = 32h - 16,$$
$$-8h = -16,$$
$$h = 2.$$

21. Use constructive processes to expand out to an answer.

When the initial information is expressed in simpler form than the requested expression, the answer can usually be found by developing the latter from the former.

EXAMPLE 28

If $a - 3 = b$, which of the following is the value of $|a-b| + |b-a|$?

(A) 0

(B) -3

(C) 3

(D) -6

(E) 6

The equation $a - 3 = b$ can be used to construct the expression $|a-b| + |b-a|$, thereby presenting the answer:

$$a - 3 = b,$$
$$a = b + 3,$$
$$a - b = 3 \quad \text{and} \quad b - a = -3,$$
$$|a-b| = 3 \quad \text{and} \quad |b-a| = 3.$$

Therefore $|a-b| + |b-a| = 3 + 3 = 6.$

22. Transform and combine.

It is helpful to change an expression from a form you are unable to recognize into one that is easier to work with. At times this process will even enable you to answer a question for which you do not have adequate mathematical background. The following example was chosen because it involves a topic most Level IC test-takers have not studied (and that is not part of the syllabus tested on Level IC), yet all should be able to answer by using a transformation.

EXAMPLE 29

What is the graph of the following set of parametric equations in the xy-plane?

$$x = 6t - 2$$
$$y = 9t^2$$

(A) A parabola

(B) A line

(C) A circle

(D) An ellipse

(E) A hyperbola

You may never have encountered "parametric" equations before, but this doesn't matter. Since you may be familiar just with the graphs of equations involving only x and y, transform the two equations by combining them into one that involves only x and y. From the first equation, $x = 6t - 2$, we get

$$x + 2 = 6t,$$
$$\frac{x+2}{2} = 3t.$$

Substituting for $3t$ in the second equation gives

$$\left(\frac{x+2}{2}\right)^2 = 9t^2,$$

and we get

$$\left(\frac{x+2}{2}\right)^2 = y.$$

Now you should see that the graph in the xy-plane is a parabola. This question was selected only to show you the power of the method. Questions involving parametric equations are not asked on the Level IC test. Transformations solve simpler problems as well.

EXAMPLE 30

If $(\sin x + \cos x)^2 = \dfrac{5}{4}$, then $\sin x \cos x =$

(A) $\dfrac{1}{2}$

(B) $\dfrac{1}{8}$

(C) $\dfrac{1}{5}$

(D) $\dfrac{1}{4}$

(E) $\dfrac{5}{4}$

Even though enough information is given to find values for x, you only have to find an expression involving x that can be found by transforming the left side of the equation.

$$(\sin x + \cos x)^2 = \frac{5}{4}$$
$$\sin^2 x + 2\sin x \cos x + \cos^2 x = \frac{5}{4}$$
$$1 + 2\sin x \cos x = \frac{5}{4}$$
$$2\sin x \cos x = \frac{1}{4}$$
$$\sin x \cos x = \frac{1}{8}$$

At first, this looks like a job for the calculator, but there really is no calculation to be done.

EXAMPLE 31

If $x + y = 1$ and $x^2 - y^2 = 6$, then $x - y =$

(A) 5

(B) −6

(C) 6

(D) −3

(E) 7

Transform $x^2 - y^2 = 6$ into

$$(x+y)(x-y) = 6.$$

Substitute 1 for $x + y$:

$$1(x - y) = 6.$$

Again, both x and y could have been determined from the given information by solving systems of simultaneous equations, but this was unnecessary since the desired result could be derived by transforming and combining.

EXAMPLE 32

If $\sin x = 3\cos x$, then $\tan x =$

(A) $\dfrac{\sqrt{3}}{2}$

(B) $-\dfrac{1}{3}$

(C) $\dfrac{1}{3}$

(D) $\sqrt{3}$

(E) 3

Since $\tan x = \dfrac{\sin x}{\cos x}$, transform the given equation into one involving $\tan x$ by dividing each side by $\cos x$:

$$\frac{\sin x}{\cos x} = 3 = \tan x.$$

23. Work both ends toward the middle.

As already noted, some problems are easily resolved by starting with the initial information and working toward the goal, while others are best handled by working backward from the goal. Still a third group is best resolved by simultaneously working forward and backward to meet halfway.

EXAMPLE 33

If x and y are positive integers and 4 is a factor of xy, then which of the following must always be true?

(A) 4 is a factor of x but not of y.

(B) 4 is a factor of y but not of x.

(C) 4 is a factor of both x and y.

(D) 2 is a factor of both x and y.

(E) 2 is a factor of at least one of x and y.

The complicating aspect here is the difference between what is "necessary" and what is "sufficient." The correct answer is (E). The number 2 must be a factor of at least one of x and y, though this is not sufficient to make 4 a factor of xy. In each of cases (A) through (D), 4 can be a factor of xy without requiring the answer choice to be true. Yet, in each case, if the answer choice is true, 4 will be a factor of xy. To work this out, you must be constantly considering the initial information and the conclusion to join them in a train of thought at a point somewhere between the start and the finish.

In other words, without the answer choices, the problem is not defined, and from the answer choices alone, the goal is not defined.

This situation is very different from questions like 30 through 32, in which the answer can be found without knowing the choices offered.

24. Use general cases.

Just as using special cases can point to a procedure, generalizing the problem is often helpful.

EXAMPLE 34

Which of the following points is on the line containing $(-1, 0)$ and $(1, 3)$?

(A) $(0, -1)$

(B) $(0, 3)$

(C) $\left(0, \dfrac{3}{2}\right)$

(D) $(0, 5)$

(E) $(0, -3)$

The equation of a line is a general condition satisfied by all points of the line. We can find the equation by first finding the slope of the line:

$$\frac{3-0}{1-(-1)} = \frac{3}{2}$$

Substituting the slope and one point into the point-slope form of the equation of the line gives us the general condition

$$
\begin{aligned}
y - 0 &= \frac{3}{2}\left[x - (-1)\right] \\
&= \frac{3}{2}(x+1), \\
&= \frac{3}{2}x + \frac{3}{2}.
\end{aligned}
$$

The points can now be checked quickly by letting $x = 0$, which produces (C).

EXAMPLE 35

The average of three numbers is $2a$. If two of the numbers are $-3a$ and $7a$, the third number is

(A) $4a$

(B) $-6a$

(C) $10a$

(D) a

(E) $2a$

In general, the average of three numbers, x, y, and z, is given by the equation

$$\frac{x+y+z}{3} = \text{average}.$$

In this case, we are given x, y, and the average, and we are asked to find z. Substituting into the general condition gives

$$\frac{-3a+7a+z}{3} = 2a,$$
$$\frac{4a+z}{3} = 2a,$$
$$4a+z = 6a,$$
$$z = 2a.$$

25. Represent the answer symbolically.

As we have already seen, representing the answer by a variable will help you set up equations, will suggest operations, and will enable you to keep track of results.

EXAMPLE 36

The largest of four consecutive odd integers is one less than twice the smallest. Which of the following is the largest?

(A) 7

(B) 21

(C) 11

(D) 13

(E) 5

Represent the consecutive odd integers by

$$x, x+2, x+4, \text{ and } x+6.$$

If the largest, $x+6$, is one less than twice the smallest, x, this fact can be represented symbolically by

$$x+6 = 2x-1,$$
$$6 = x-1,$$
$$7 = x.$$

Hence the integers are 7, 9, 11, and 13.

26. Use diagrams.

In most Level IC tests, if a diagram is helpful, it is provided. There are exceptions, however, and for these you should draw your own diagrams.

EXAMPLE 37

Two vertices of an equilateral triangle are contained in the x-axis, and the third in the y-axis. The sum of the slopes of the three sides is

(A) 0

(B) 1

(C) −1

(D) 3

(E) −3

First, draw a diagram showing the given information:

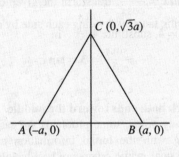

The diagram should suggest a number of possibilities. A plotting approach is to represent the coordinates of the vertices and, from these, the slopes of the sides. Let $A = (-a, 0)$ and $B = (a, 0)$. From the Pythagorean Theorem, or the 30–60–90 triangle relation, OC can be found to be $\sqrt{3}$, making $C = (0, \sqrt{3}a)$. Therefore the slopes of BC and AC are, respectively,

$$\frac{a\sqrt{3}}{a} = \sqrt{3} \quad \text{and} \quad \frac{a\sqrt{3}}{-a} = -\sqrt{3}$$

The slope of AB is 0, so the sum of all three slopes is 0.

An ingenious student noticing the y-axis symmetry of lines AC and BC would recognize that their slopes must be the negatives of each other and must add to 0, without doing any work.

Ah, well, there is no problem-solving tactic as valuable as ingenuity!

27. Substitution.

Many test questions (including some we've already discussed) are answered quickly and directly by substitution.

EXAMPLE 38

The points at which the line $x = 4$ and the circle $x^2 + y^2 = 25$ intersect are

(A) $(4, \pm 3)$

(B) $(4, 0)$ and $(-4, 0)$

(C) $(4, \pm 9)$

(D) $(4, \pm 16)$

(E) $(\pm 3, 4)$

Since $x = 4$, substitute 4 for x in

$$x^2 + y^2 = 25.$$

Then

$$\begin{aligned} 4^2 + y^2 &= 25, \\ y^2 &= 9, \\ y &= \pm 3. \end{aligned}$$

Substitution usually plays an important role in questions involving functional notation.

EXAMPLE 39

If $f(x) = (4 - x)^x$, then $f(6) =$

(A) 2

(B) 1

(C) 0

(D) 16

(E) 64

The value of $f(6)$ is found by substituting 6 for x in $f(x) = (4 - x)^x$:

$$f(6) = (4 - 6)^6 = 2^6 = 64$$

EXAMPLE 40

If $f(x) = ax$ and $f(f(x)) = 4x$, then $a =$

(A) ± 2

(B) ± 3

(C) 4

(D) $\dfrac{1}{2}$

(E) $\dfrac{1}{4}$

$$\begin{aligned} f(x) &= ax \\ f(f(x)) &= a f(x) \\ &= a(ax) \\ &= a^2 x \end{aligned}$$

Since

$$\begin{aligned} f(f(x)) &= 4x, \\ a^2 x &= 4x, \\ a^2 &= 4, \\ a &= \pm 2. \end{aligned}$$

EXAMPLE 41

If $f(x) = 2x - 1$ and $g(x) = x + 4$, then $f(g(x)) =$

(A) $3x + 3$

(B) $x - 5$

(C) $2x + 7$

(D) $2x + 3$

(E) $-x + 5$

To find $f(g(x))$, substitute $g(x)$ for x in $f(x) = 2x - 1$:

$$\begin{aligned} f(g(x)) &= 2(g(x)) - 1 \\ &= 2(x + 4) - 1 \\ &= 2x + 8 - 1 \\ &= 2x + 7. \end{aligned}$$

28. Carry out operations.

Many questions require merely the ability to carry out operations that are clearly stated in the given information.

EXAMPLE 42

$$\left(\frac{1}{x}\right)^4 + \left(\frac{2}{x^2}\right)^2 =$$

(A) $\dfrac{3}{x^4}$

(B) $\dfrac{5}{x^4}$

(C) $\dfrac{8}{x^2}$

(D) $5x^4$

(E) $3x^4$

The answer is found directly by raising each term to the indicated power and adding the results:

$$\frac{1}{x^4} + \frac{4}{x^4} = \frac{5}{x^4}.$$

EXAMPLE 43

If

$$\begin{vmatrix} a & b \\ c & d \end{vmatrix} = d(a-c) - c(b-d),$$

then

$$\begin{vmatrix} 1 & 2 \\ 3 & 4 \end{vmatrix} =$$

(A) 3

(B) 1

(C) 2

(D) −1

(E) −2

You need never have encountered the symbol $\begin{vmatrix} a & b \\ c & d \end{vmatrix}$ before to answer the question correctly. The symbol is well defined by the given information. Carry out the operations on $\begin{vmatrix} 1 & 2 \\ 3 & 4 \end{vmatrix}$ by substituting into the formula:

$$\begin{vmatrix} 1 & 2 \\ 3 & 4 \end{vmatrix} = 4(1-3) - 3(2-4)$$

$$= -2.$$

■ Practice using your parentheses keys.

29. Use ingenuity and insight.

For many test questions, even ones that seem relatively simple, no problem-solving tactic can completely replace ingenuity and insight, even though all problem-solving tactics are designed to help inspire these mental qualities. Perceptive mental traits are best developed by (1) mastering fundamental facts and skills, (2) developing an understanding of mathematical concepts, and (3) wrestling with problems that require ingenuity.

EXAMPLE 44

A pentagonal dodecahedron is a solid figure with 12 faces, each face having 5 sides. How many edges does this solid have?

(A) 60

(B) 30

(C) 45

(D) 17

(E) 48

Your first thought might be to multiply the number of faces, 12, by the number of sides of each face, 5, to get 60. But, if you visualize this solid in your mind, you'll realize that each edge of the solid is shared by 2 pentagons.

Therefore the answer you guessed first, 60, counts each side twice. The correct answer, then, must be half of 60, or 30.

EXAMPLE 45

If $f(x) = (x - a)^2 + (x - b)^2$, then the least value of $f(x)$ occurs when $x =$

(A) a

(B) b

(C) $a + b$

(D) $a - b$

(E) $\dfrac{a+b}{2}$

A bit of doodling with diagrams should help your insight. The functions defined by $(x - a)^2$ and $(x - b)^2$ have graphs that are parabolas opening upward with vertices on the x-axis and axes of symmetry at $x = a$ and $x = b$, respectively:

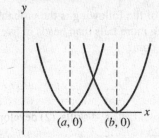

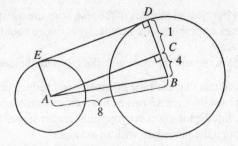

Their sum, $(x-a)^2+(x-b)^2$, is also a quadratic function, so it must also be a parabola, which also opens upward. Without drawing $M(x)$ you should be able to see from the symmetry of the drawing that the parabola that is the sum of the parabolas must have its axis of symmetry halfway between a and b—in other words, at $\frac{a+b}{2}$. Since this is the "bottom" of the parabola, it must be the point that gives the minimum value.

Such questions test insight far more than they test any specific mathematical fact. It would not be assumed, for example, that a test-taker had ever encountered the function $M(x)$ as such before.

 EXAMPLE 46

A belt is stretched tightly over two wheels having radii of 1 and 5 inches, respectively. If the centers of the wheels are 8 inches apart, what is the total length of the *straight* sections of the belt?

(A) 5.66

(B) 6.00

(C) 3.50

(D) 13.86

(E) 7.00

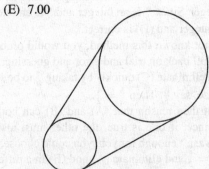

(Figure is not drawn to scale.)

After experimenting by drawing radii to various points of the figure, you might have the insight to produce the following figure:

In the figure, $ACDE$ is a rectangle since BD is perpendicular to DE because a radius and a tangent are perpendicular at the point of tangency, and AC is drawn perpendicular to BD. Because AE is 1, CD must also be 1 and BC is 4. Using the Pythagorean Theorem on triangle ABC gives:

$$\begin{aligned} AB^2 &= BC^2+AC^2, \\ 8^2 &= 4^2+AC^2, \\ 64 &= 16+AC^2, \\ \sqrt{48} &= AC \\ &\doteq 6.93 = DE. \end{aligned}$$

Therefore each of the two straight sections of belt has length of 6.93, for a total of $2(6.93) = 13.86$.

Besides a knowledge of the Pythagorean Theorem and of the fact that radii are perpendicular to tangents at the point of tangency, the only (!) other requirement is ingenuity. Knowledge of the facts, however, provides a major boost to your insight.

30. Guess efficiently.

Guessing is the ultimate problem-solving strategy—"ultimate" only because it is a last resort when all else has been tried unsuccessfully.

Trial-and-error methods sometimes result in the elimination of only one or two distractors, leaving you with three or four possible choices and no way to decide which is correct. When you cannot identify the correct choice but have eliminated one or more distractors, guessing may help your test score.

Efficient guessing procedures help you to save time and to keep track of which questions you have guessed on. Here is a procedure many students have found helpful.

If you decide to guess on a question, mark it as follows:

1. Place a question mark next to the question *in the test booklet* to remind yourself that you arrived at the answer by guessing.
2. In the test booklet (not on the answer sheet!) cross out the letters of the choices you feel are definitely incorrect (this avoids unnecessary pondering later).
3. In the test booklet (not on the answer sheet!) circle the response you wish to choose.
4. Postpone marking the answer sheet until the last few minutes of the test, or until you have completed all the questions you are sure of.

5. In the closing minutes of the test, scan the question-marked problems for new insights (more about that later).
6. Mark the answer sheet with the guessed choices.

Procedures that use time efficiently and reduce confusion are useful because two or three correct answers can have a significant effect on your final scaled score. Let's go through the procedure with an example.

EXAMPLE 47

Which of the following is the probability of obtaining more tails than heads in five tosses of a fair coin?

(A) .5

(B) .6

(C) .4

(D) .625

(E) .15625

Let's pretend the question is totally unfamiliar to you, which is most likely to be true if you, like many high school students, have studied no probability theory. That's why we chose this example for guessing.

Let's fumble our way through it as though we don't know much about probability but do have some experience with flipping coins. We'll suppose that all we know is that, when five coins are flipped, the possible outcomes are:

Tails	Heads
0	5
1	4
2	3
3	2
4	1
5	0

The bottom three lines show the situation described in the question, "more tails than heads," as the desired outcome, and the top three show "more heads than tails." Therefore the tossing of five coins seems to offer only two possibilities, more tails than heads and more heads than tails, with about the same results for each.

That's enough information to make us feel that answer choice (E) can be eliminated and that (A) is our best guess, even though it is not enough information to make us feel totally secure (it would if we were good students of probability).

We may want to think about this problem a little more before we commit choice (A) to the answer sheet, so we'll mark our test booklet as follows and return to the question in the closing minutes of the test.

47.   Which of the following is the probability of obtaining more tails than heads in five tosses of a fair coin?

(A) .5

(B) .6

(C) .4

(D) .625

(E) .15625

You might be interested to know, by the way, that 68% of a group of high school students who tried to guess the answer to this question by intuition alone (they knew nothing of probability) chose answer (B) and the remainder chose (C). Our guess, based on just a bit more than intuition, is correct.

Although the choices were expressed as decimals, the only "calculation" necessary was to convert $\frac{1}{2}$ to .5.

EXAMPLE 48

If $\frac{a}{b}$ is an integer, which of the following must also be an integer?

(A) $a+b$

(B) $a-b$

(C) $\frac{b}{a}$

(D) $\frac{5a}{b}$

(E) ab

The quick and simple way to answer this question is to recognize that the set of integers is closed for multiplication—in other words, an integer times an integer is an integer. Since $\frac{a}{b}$ is an integer and 5 is an integer, $5\left(\frac{a}{b}\right)$ is an integer and (D) is correct.

Had you not known this method, you would probably have had to fall back on trial and error and guessing.

You could eliminate (C) quickly by taking $\frac{a}{b}$ to be some particular case, say $\frac{6}{3}$. Then $\frac{b}{a} = \frac{1}{2}$.

You might then reason that (A) and (B) can both be eliminated since, if one is true, the other must also be true. If that wasn't enough for you, you could choose, say, $a = 1$ and $b = \frac{1}{2}$ and eliminate (A) and (B) in a different way. These same values would eliminate (E).

At this point, (D) is the only one left.

That's a different kind of guessing game from the one described in the answer to Example 47. Here our job was to guess values of a and b that would expose the right properties of the answers.

But suppose we had not thought to use fractional values of a and b. Then we would have had no other recourse but to eliminate only (C) and pick the best guess among the ones remaining.

Just how did we know to use fractional values for a and b? That's a result of our efforts to break out of a circle. Using integer values did not eliminate all distractors. Using other integer values kept us going around the same circle. To break it, we had to try a different set of numbers. Had we been especially adventurous, we might have tried irrationals such as $a = 2\sqrt{2}$ and $b = \sqrt{2}$.

Many different problem-solving strategies may prove useful in the same problem, as this example showed.

31. Don't eliminate distractors for the wrong reasons.

Here are four wrong reasons for eliminating distractors.

1. Don't just eliminate (or choose!) an answer because it is different in form or appearance from all the rest.

EXAMPLE 49

Each of x cartons contains y boxes. Each box contains z marbles. How many marbles are there in all?

(A) xyz

(B) $\dfrac{yz}{x}$

(C) $x+y+z$

(D) $\dfrac{xy}{z}$

(E) $\dfrac{xz}{y}$

Choices (B), (D), and (E) are similar in form, a "clue" to some unsuspecting test-takers that this is the form of the correct answer (by a vote of 3 out of 5). They would then concentrate on these answers. But the correct answer is (A).

2. Don't assume that the correct answer must be somewhere in the middle of the choices, with the incorrect answers at the extremes.

EXAMPLE 50

The points at which the graph of $2x - 3y = -4$ intersects the x-axis are

(A) $(-2,0)$

(B) $(0,0)$

(C) $(4,0)$

(D) $(2,0)$

(E) $\left(0, -\dfrac{4}{3}\right)$

The correct answer is (A), which is at the extreme left on the graph of the points.

3. Don't assume that there is any pattern to the answer choices. In other words, if you have marked answer choice (A) more often than any other throughout the test, this does not mean that the next answer is less likely (or more likely!) to be (A). Because positions for correct answers are selected at random, there *should* be approximately 10 of each choice, but there does not *have* to be. Certainly, if you have marked 20 answers as (A), you have reason to be concerned and should suspect that some of these are wrong. But there is no pattern by which you can determine which ones are incorrect.

4. Don't assume that there is always enough information but that you just don't know how to use it. Occasionally you will find a question for which one of the answer choices is "cannot be determined from the given information" and there really is not enough information given to get the answer. Such questions can be especially trying and time consuming. You always think you've forgotten something and hope it will come to you if you just persevere!

EXAMPLE 51

Given the figure with the center of the circle at P. If $a = 50°$, then $b =$

(A) 25°

(B) 20°

(C) 27.5°

(D) 22.5°

(E) Cannot be determined from the given information.

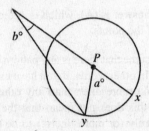

Several inferences can be drawn about arc XY, but no information will relate a to b definitively. Your temptation is to approximate the value of b from the figure and guess the measure that looks closest. In this case, guessing the choice that appears most obvious from the figure gives the wrong answer, even though it may actually *be* the correct measure!

Don't assume there is a way to "beat" the test—meaning to earn a satisfactory score without knowing a sufficient amount of mathematics. It is possible, unfortunately, to have a test score lower than it should be for a person of your mathematical skill because you have not been able to do your best work. But it is very unlikely that you can score higher than you should merely by using a system for eliminating distractors rather than your developed mathematical ability and knowledge.

32. Return later to difficult problems.

Rarely is it a good idea to continue working on a problem past a reasonable deadline of a few minutes, and you should go on to other questions rather than bogging down.

But leaving a problem is not the same as giving up on it. In fact, leaving it temporarily may be all you need to do to eventually solve it!

When you return to a problem after working on others for a while, you will sometimes see a new approach. Some psychologists have suggested that your subconscious mind continues to work on the problem as your conscious mind solves others. Other psychologists feel that you merely bring a different mind-set with you the second time around, your original associations with the problem having been broken up by the intervening mental activity.

Returning with a "fresh mind" succeeds often enough to be part of your test-taking strategy, but only if you are familiar with the subject matter of the question. Don't waste time by returning to problems that have a mathematical basis you don't understand.

After taking a multiple-choice mathematics test, several students were asked to give examples of questions they were unable to answer the first time around but correctly solved on returning later. The following are three of the examples given.

EXAMPLE 52

For what values of x is $\dfrac{|x|}{x} = 1$?

(A) $x = 0$

(B) $x \geq 0$

(C) $x \leq 0$

(D) $x > 0$

(E) $x < 0$

The student who selected this question said that her first attempt was to substitute values for x, which got her confused. This approach, by the way, would have worked had she been able to continue with it.

When she returned to the problem later, she immediately saw that the equation could be rewritten as $|x| = x$ (except for $x = 0$), which could be resolved quickly through the definition of absolute value. Within seconds, she had the correct answer, (D).

EXAMPLE 53

If $\dfrac{9a}{5} = 32$ and $\dfrac{9ab}{5} = 4$, then $b =$

(A) 4

(B) $\dfrac{1}{8}$

(C) $\dfrac{1}{4}$

(D) 16

(E) Cannot be determined.

The student who chose this question recognized that

$$\frac{9ab}{5} = \left(\frac{9a}{5}\right)(b)$$

and wrote the following for his scratch work:

$$\frac{9a}{5}(b) = 32(?) = 4.$$

He recognized that the missing number was the factor needed to produce 4 when multiplied by 32 but committed the simple mental lapse of thinking that 32 times 8 equals 4 rather than 8 times 4 equals 32.

Since 8 was not a choice, he left the problem temporarily. The second time around, this student made a new start and the error did not recur.

EXAMPLE 54

If $\log a = p$, then $\log 10a^2 =$

(A) $\log 2a$

(B) $2\log a$

(C) $1 + 2\log a$

(D) $10\log a$

(E) $20\log a$

This student explained that the question came early on the test before he had really settled down, and his own lack of ease with logarithms caused him to panic. After building up his confidence on questions he found to be much easier, he returned to this question with a relaxed mind, reviewed the properties of logarithms that he remembered, and then transformed the equation to

$$\log 10 + \log a^2$$

and next to

$$\log 10 + 2\log a.$$

By calculation, $\log 10 = 1$ in base 10 logs. Therefore, the answer is

$$1 + 2\log a$$

33. Remember your strategies.

We have summarized them in the list below for your reference.

- **Simplify** expressions that can be reduced, combined or altered by removing grouping symbols and by carrying out the operation of addition, subtraction, multiplication, or division.
- **Transform** expressions that can be written in a different form by factoring, using trigonometric or algebraic identities or replacing with equivalent expressions.
- **Expand** expressions that are powers of monomials or binomials.
- Look for **patterns** in the given information or in any expressions that result from your work on a question.
- **Substitute** given values or other values that you have calculated for unknowns.
- **Solve** equations that are given or that can be set up from the given information.
- **Try** the suggested answer choices to see how they fit your work and the known information.
- **Infer** properties and implications from the given information and the suggested answer choices.
- **Represent** unknowns by variables as an aid to setting up and solving equations.
- **Sketch** information that can be represented pictorially to aid the visual path of your mental processes.
- Try **alternative** approaches to finding the answer if your original method reaches a dead end.
- **Return** near the end of the test to questions you did not understand or could not answer the first time around.
- **Guess** only after **eliminating** at least one of the suggested answer choices.

ANSWERS

[1] (D)	[10] (A)	[19] (B)	[28] (E)	[37] (A)	[46] (D)
[2] (C)	[11] (E)	[20] (B)	[29] (A)	[38] (A)	[47] (A)
[3] (B)	[12] (D)	[21] (E)	[30] (B)	[39] (E)	[48] (D)
[4] (C)	[13] (C)	[22] (E)	[31] (B)	[40] (A)	[49] (A)
[5] (B)	[14] (A)	[23] (C)	[32] (E)	[41] (C)	[50] (A)
[6] (B)	[15] (D)	[24] (C)	[33] (E)	[42] (B)	[51] (E)
[7] (E)	[16] (C)	[25] (B)	[34] (C)	[43] (E)	[52] (D)
[8] (C)	[17] (E)	[26] (D)	[35] (E)	[44] (B)	[53] (B)
[9] (A)	[18] (C)	[27] (E)	[36] (D)	[45] (E)	[54] (C)

DIAGNOSE YOUR WEAKNESSES

PART

1

DIAGNOSTIC TEST

CHAPTER

4

Before outlining a plan of study for the Math Level IC examination, you should identify the areas in which you are weak and those in which you need little or no further preparation. In that way you can allot your time and focus your efforts to major advantage.

For this purpose the following diagnostic test has been provided. It is similar in number of questions, format, and subject matter to the actual test, but it is slightly more difficult.

Use your calculator as much as you wish, but don't expect it to be very helpful. We have specifically chosen our questions to illustrate mathematical principles and identify areas in which your mathematical understanding may be weak. In other words, these are some of the thoughts you need to be able to think before you punch.

Allow yourself 1 hour to take the test. Work steadily, without distractions. Answer as many questions as you can, but do not guess unless you can definitely eliminate at least one of the answer choices. If you need more time, make a note of where you were at the end of the hour and continue on until you have tried all questions. That way, you'll see how many questions you were able to answer

during "regulation" time and you'll also get a chance to try all of the questions to identify all of your weak areas.

When you have finished, turn to the answer key and the answer explanations. Place a check mark next to each correct answer, and an X beside each incorrect answer. Then, for each question you got wrong, read the explanation carefully.

Fill out the self-evaluation chart that follows the answer explanations, noting the areas in which you did poorly, and calculate your score:

total number of correct answers

$-\dfrac{1}{4}$ the number of incorrect answers

Finally, record your score on page 60 and evaluate your performance using the chart provided.

Note the following: All geometric figures are drawn as accurately as possible; unless otherwise specified, all figures lie in a plane.

You may assume that the domain of a function f is the set of all real numbers x for which $f(x)$ is a real number, unless the question indicates otherwise.

Now turn to the test.

DETERMINING YOUR COLLEGE BOARD SCALED SCORE

The College Board converts the raw score you achieve on the SAT II: Mathematics Level IC to a scaled score that ranges from 200 to 800. Use the following table to convert your raw score on the model test to a scaled score. Simply find your raw score in the left-hand column; the corresponding College Board scaled score is located next to it in the right-hand column. For example, a raw score of 29 corresponds to the scaled score of 580.

Model Test Score Conversion Table							
Raw Score	Scaled Score	Raw Score	Scaled Score	Raw Score	Scaled Score	Raw Score	Scaled Score
50	800	34	630	18	500	2	370
49	790	33	620	17	490	1	360
48	780	32	610	16	480	0	360
47	770	31	600	15	480	−1	350
46	760	30	590	14	470	−2	340
45	750	29	580	13	460	−3	330
44	740	28	580	12	450	−4	330
43	730	27	570	11	440	−5	320
42	720	26	560	10	440	−6	310
41	710	25	550	9	430	−7	300
40	700	24	540	8	420	−8	300
39	690	23	540	7	410	−9	290
38	680	22	530	6	400	−10	280
37	660	21	520	5	390	−11	270
36	650	20	510	4	390	−12	270
35	640	19	510	3	380		

ANSWER SHEET FOR DIAGNOSTIC TEST

Determine the correct answer for each question. Then, using a No. 2 pencil, blacken completely the oval containing the letter of your choice.

1. Ⓐ Ⓑ Ⓒ Ⓓ Ⓔ	18. Ⓐ Ⓑ Ⓒ Ⓓ Ⓔ	35. Ⓐ Ⓑ Ⓒ Ⓓ Ⓔ
2. Ⓐ Ⓑ Ⓒ Ⓓ Ⓔ	19. Ⓐ Ⓑ Ⓒ Ⓓ Ⓔ	36. Ⓐ Ⓑ Ⓒ Ⓓ Ⓔ
3. Ⓐ Ⓑ Ⓒ Ⓓ Ⓔ	20. Ⓐ Ⓑ Ⓒ Ⓓ Ⓔ	37. Ⓐ Ⓑ Ⓒ Ⓓ Ⓔ
4. Ⓐ Ⓑ Ⓒ Ⓓ Ⓔ	21. Ⓐ Ⓑ Ⓒ Ⓓ Ⓔ	38. Ⓐ Ⓑ Ⓒ Ⓓ Ⓔ
5. Ⓐ Ⓑ Ⓒ Ⓓ Ⓔ	22. Ⓐ Ⓑ Ⓒ Ⓓ Ⓔ	39. Ⓐ Ⓑ Ⓒ Ⓓ Ⓔ
6. Ⓐ Ⓑ Ⓒ Ⓓ Ⓔ	23. Ⓐ Ⓑ Ⓒ Ⓓ Ⓔ	40. Ⓐ Ⓑ Ⓒ Ⓓ Ⓔ
7. Ⓐ Ⓑ Ⓒ Ⓓ Ⓔ	24. Ⓐ Ⓑ Ⓒ Ⓓ Ⓔ	41. Ⓐ Ⓑ Ⓒ Ⓓ Ⓔ
8. Ⓐ Ⓑ Ⓒ Ⓓ Ⓔ	25. Ⓐ Ⓑ Ⓒ Ⓓ Ⓔ	42. Ⓐ Ⓑ Ⓒ Ⓓ Ⓔ
9. Ⓐ Ⓑ Ⓒ Ⓓ Ⓔ	26. Ⓐ Ⓑ Ⓒ Ⓓ Ⓔ	43. Ⓐ Ⓑ Ⓒ Ⓓ Ⓔ
10. Ⓐ Ⓑ Ⓒ Ⓓ Ⓔ	27. Ⓐ Ⓑ Ⓒ Ⓓ Ⓔ	44. Ⓐ Ⓑ Ⓒ Ⓓ Ⓔ
11. Ⓐ Ⓑ Ⓒ Ⓓ Ⓔ	28. Ⓐ Ⓑ Ⓒ Ⓓ Ⓔ	45. Ⓐ Ⓑ Ⓒ Ⓓ Ⓔ
12. Ⓐ Ⓑ Ⓒ Ⓓ Ⓔ	29. Ⓐ Ⓑ Ⓒ Ⓓ Ⓔ	46. Ⓐ Ⓑ Ⓒ Ⓓ Ⓔ
13. Ⓐ Ⓑ Ⓒ Ⓓ Ⓔ	30. Ⓐ Ⓑ Ⓒ Ⓓ Ⓔ	47. Ⓐ Ⓑ Ⓒ Ⓓ Ⓔ
14. Ⓐ Ⓑ Ⓒ Ⓓ Ⓔ	31. Ⓐ Ⓑ Ⓒ Ⓓ Ⓔ	48. Ⓐ Ⓑ Ⓒ Ⓓ Ⓔ
15. Ⓐ Ⓑ Ⓒ Ⓓ Ⓔ	32. Ⓐ Ⓑ Ⓒ Ⓓ Ⓔ	49. Ⓐ Ⓑ Ⓒ Ⓓ Ⓔ
16. Ⓐ Ⓑ Ⓒ Ⓓ Ⓔ	33. Ⓐ Ⓑ Ⓒ Ⓓ Ⓔ	50. Ⓐ Ⓑ Ⓒ Ⓓ Ⓔ
17. Ⓐ Ⓑ Ⓒ Ⓓ Ⓔ	34. Ⓐ Ⓑ Ⓒ Ⓓ Ⓔ	

Directions: For each of the 50 multiple-choice test questions, select the BEST answer among the five choices given. When the exact numerical value is not one of the choices, select the best approximation to the exact value. Mark your choice on the answer sheet by filling in the corresponding oval.

Notes:

1. Some questions (but not all) will require the use of at least a scientific calculator. Programmable and graphing calculators are also permitted. Calculator questions are not marked as such, so you will have to decide whether or not to use one on each question.

2. All angle measures are in degrees. Set your calculator to degree mode.

3. Some problems are accompanied by figures, which provide information useful in solving the problem. Figures are drawn accurately unless marked "Figure not drawn to scale." All figures lie in a plane unless the diagram clearly shows otherwise.

4. Except when stated otherwise, the domain of a function f is the set of real number values of x for which $f(x)$ is a real number.

5. Reference information consisting of volume and surface area formulas that may be useful in answering some questions on this test can be found below:

- Sphere with radius r.   Volume: $V = \frac{4}{3}\pi r^3$ Surface Area: $S = 4\pi r^2$
- Right circular cone with radius r and height h.   Volume: $V = \frac{1}{3}\pi r^2 h$
- Right circular cone with circumference of base c and slant height L.
  Lateral Area: $S = \frac{1}{2}cL$
- Pyramid with base area B and height h.   Volume: $V = \frac{1}{3}Bh$

---

1. Which of the following is NOT equal to $a(b+c)$?

    (A) $(b+c)a$

    (B) $(a+b)c$

    (C) $a(c+b)$

    (D) $ab+ac$

    (E) $(c+b)a$

2. If the product of $2ab^2$ and $-3a^3b$ is divided by $-12ab$, the result is

    (A) $2a^3b^2$

    (B) $\dfrac{a^3b^3}{-2}$

    (C) $\dfrac{1}{2}a^3b^2$

    (D) $\dfrac{2}{a^3b^3}$

    (E) $-2a^3b^3$

USE THIS SPACE FOR SCRATCH WORK

GO ON TO THE NEXT PAGE

3. If $x < 0$, then

   (A) $|x| < 0$

   (B) $-x < 0$

   (C) $x < -x$

   (D) $-x < x$

   (E) $x = |x|$

4. If a and b are any real numbers, then $a - b =$

   (A) $-(a+b)$ $a = 5$

   (B) $-(b+a)$ $b = 3$ $= 2$

   (C) $a - (-b)$

   (D) $b - (-a)$

   (E) $-b - (-a)$ $-3 + 5$

5. If $x < y$ and $c < -1$, which of the following must
   be true?

   I. $x + c < y + c$ $x = -5$

   II. $x - c < y - c$ $y = -3$

   III. $cx < cy$ $c = -7$

   (A) I only

   (B) II only

   (C) I and II only

   (D) III only

   (E) II and III only

6. The simplified form of

   $$\frac{x^2 - 3x + 2}{x^2 - 2x - 3} \times \frac{x^2 - x - 6}{x^2 - 4}$$

   is

   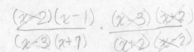

   (A) 1

   (B) -1

   (C) $x^2 - 1$

   (D) $\dfrac{x-1}{x+1}$

   (E) x

GO ON TO THE NEXT PAGE

7. In $\triangle ABC$ in Figure 1, $AB = BC$ and the measure of $\angle B$ is 70°. What is the measure of $\angle A$?

   (A) 70°

   (B) 110°

   (C) 60°

   (D) 35°

   (E) 55°

8. A number such that one fourth of its square root is 3 is

   (A) $2\sqrt{3}$

   (B) $\dfrac{\sqrt{3}}{2}$

   (C) 12

   (D) 36

   (E) 144

9. Which of the following has the graph shown in Figure 2?

   (A) $x < 2$ or $x > -2$

   (B) $x^2 < 2$

   (C) $|x| < 2$

   (D) $x \le 2$ and $x \ge -2$

   (E) $2 \le x \le -2$

10. In Figure 3, the center of the circle is at O and chord AB is 6″ long and 2″ from the center. In inches, the radius is

    (A) 3.0

    (B) 4.0

    (C) 4.5

    (D) 3.6

    (E) 5.6

USE THIS SPACE FOR SCRATCH WORK

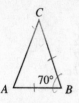

Figure 1

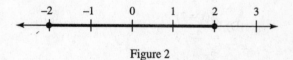

Figure 2

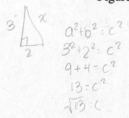

Figure 3

$a^2 + b^2 = c^2$
$3^2 + 2^2 = c^2$
$9 + 4 = c^2$
$13 = c^2$
$\sqrt{13} = c$

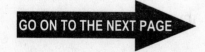

GO ON TO THE NEXT PAGE

11. If $\dfrac{a}{b} = \dfrac{c}{d}$, then each of the following is always true EXCEPT

(A) $\dfrac{a}{d} = \dfrac{c}{b}$

(B) $ad = bc$

(C) $ad = cb$

(D) $\dfrac{a+b}{b} = \dfrac{c+d}{d}$

(E) $\dfrac{a-b}{b} = \dfrac{c-d}{d}$

$\dfrac{5}{10} = \dfrac{1}{3}$

$\dfrac{5}{3} = \dfrac{1}{13}$

12. If $x = 2$ which of the following has a value of 4?

(A) $\dfrac{x-4}{3x}$

(B) $\dfrac{4x}{x-2}$

(C) $\dfrac{2x}{x-1}$

(D) $\dfrac{3(x-2)}{2x}$

(E) $\dfrac{2x^2}{3}$

13. When two numbers, x and y, are added, the sum is a. The larger number is b more than twice the smaller. The smaller is

(A) $\dfrac{a+b}{2}$

(B) $\dfrac{a-b}{3}$

(C) $a+b$

(D) $a-b$

(E) $\dfrac{a+b}{a-b}$

$x = 7$
$y = 14$
$a = 21$
$b = 0$

14. If $(y+1)(2y-3) = 25$, then $y =$

(A) -1 or 3

(B) 4 or 8

(C) 4 or $-\dfrac{7}{2}$

(D) 6 or 2

(E) 2 or $\dfrac{3}{2}$

$2y^2 - 3y + 2y - 3$
$2y^2 - y - 3 = 25$
$2y^2 - y - 28 = 0$
$(2y+7)(y-4)$
$y = -\dfrac{7}{2} \quad y = 4$

GO ON TO THE NEXT PAGE ▶

15. $\dfrac{3\sqrt{24}-2\sqrt{18}}{-\sqrt{2}} =$

(A) $6\sqrt{2}+6\sqrt{6}$

(B) $6\sqrt{6}-6\sqrt{2}$

(C) $\sqrt{6}$

(D) $24-12\sqrt{3}$

(E) $6-6\sqrt{3}$

Scratch work:

$(3)\,2\sqrt{6} - 2(3)\sqrt{2}$
$\overline{\qquad -\sqrt{2}\qquad}$

$\dfrac{6\sqrt{6} - 6\sqrt{2}}{-\sqrt{2}} \cdot \dfrac{-\sqrt{2}}{-\sqrt{2}}$

$\dfrac{6\sqrt{6} + 6\,(2)}{2}$

$\dfrac{6\sqrt{6} + 12}{2} = 6 +$

16. If $(a^3 b^{-2})^{-2}$ is simplified to a form in which all exponents are positive, the result is

(A) $\dfrac{b^4}{a^6}$

(B) $\dfrac{1}{a^2 b}$

(C) $\dfrac{a^6}{b^4}$

(D) $a^2 b$

(E) $\dfrac{a}{b^4}$

Scratch work: $a^{-6}b^4$ $\dfrac{b^4}{a^6}$

17. What angle is determined by the hands of a clock at 2 o'clock?

(A) $10°$

(B) $20°$

(C) $30°$

(D) $45°$

(E) $60°$

Scratch work: $\dfrac{2}{3}$ of $90° = 60°$

18. If a and x are any positive integers, which of the following is always an integer?

(A) $\dfrac{1}{x^{-a}}$

(B) x^{-a}

(C) $\dfrac{1}{x^a}$

(D) $\left(\dfrac{1}{x}\right)^a$

(E) $(x^{-1})^a$

GO ON TO THE NEXT PAGE

USE THIS SPACE FOR SCRATCH WORK

19. If each of the answers below is a pair of numbers that indicate the length of the base and the altitude to that base of a different isosceles triangle, which triangle has a vertex angle of degree measure different from each of the others?

(A) Base = 4, altitude = 6

(B) Base = 10, altitude = 15

(C) Base = 9, altitude = 12

(D) Base = 6, altitude = 9

(E) Base = 2, altitude = 3

20. Given that quadrilateral *ABCD* in Figure 4 is a parallelogram, which of the following statements would lead to the conclusion that *ABCD* is a rectangle?

(A) *AC* and *BD* are the perpendicular bisectors of each other

(B) *AB = CD*

(C) *AB = BC*

(D) ∠*DAB* and ∠*CBA* are supplementary

(E) ∠*DAB* and ∠*CBA* are equal in measure

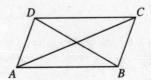

Figure 4

21. If the sum of the lengths of any three consecutive sides of a square is 9, the perimeter is

(A) 10

(B) 12

(C) 16

(D) 18

(E) Cannot be determined

22. In Figure 5, rays *BA* and *BC* are tangent to a circle with center at *O* and with *E* the point of tangency of *BA*. If the measure of ∠*EOB* is 30°, what is the measure of ∠*DBC*?

(A) 30°

(B) 45°

(C) 20°

(D) 60°

(E) 55°

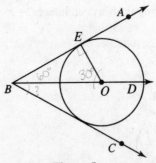

Figure 5

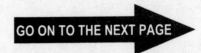

GO ON TO THE NEXT PAGE

23. If D and F in Figure 6 are the midpoints of the sides, then the ratio $\dfrac{\text{area of } \triangle ABE}{\text{area of } \square DEFC}$ is

   (A) $\dfrac{1}{2}$

   (B) $\dfrac{2}{3}$

   (C) $\dfrac{7}{8}$

   (D) 1

   (E) $\dfrac{3}{2}$

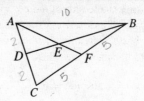

Figure 6

$\sim \dfrac{7.5}{10} \quad \sim.75$

24. If the radius, AB, of the circle in Figure 7 is 6 and $\angle BAC$ has degree measure 40, what is the area of the shaded region?

   (A) 18.85

   (B) 12.57

   (C) 6.28

   (D) 88.83

   (E) 9.42

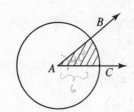

Figure 7

$\dfrac{40}{360} = \dfrac{1120.04}{113.04}$

25. If the sides of a triangle have lengths of 3, 4, and x, then

   (A) $0 \le x \le 4$

   (B) $0 < x < 7$

   (C) $1 < x < 7$

   (D) $3 < x < 4$

   (E) $1 < x < 12$

26. In Figure 8, segments AQ, BQ, and CQ lie in plane E and have respective lengths of 4.4, 4.5, and 4.6. PQ is perpendicular to E.

   Which of the following is an arrangement of PC, PA, and PB in order of length beginning with the shortest?

   (A) PB, PA, PC

   (B) PB, PC, PA

   (C) PA, PB, PC

   (D) PA, PC, PB

   (E) PC, PA, PB

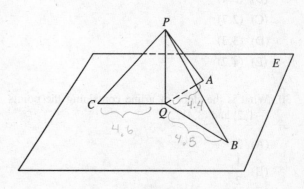

Figure 8

GO ON TO THE NEXT PAGE

27. If the radius of a sphere is r, then the ratio $\dfrac{\text{surface area}}{\text{volume}}$ is

    (A) $3\pi r$

    (B) π

    (C) πr

    (D) $\dfrac{3}{r}$

    (E) $9r$

28. If $\dfrac{i+2}{1-3i} = a+bi$, then $(a,b) =$

    (A) $(-1,7)$

    (B) $\left(\dfrac{1}{4},\dfrac{1}{4}\right)$

    (C) $\left(4,-\dfrac{1}{4}\right)$

    (D) $\left(-\dfrac{1}{10},7\right)$

    (E) $\left(-\dfrac{1}{10},\dfrac{7}{10}\right)$

29. If a ray is drawn from the origin through each of the following points, which ray makes the greatest angle with the nonnegative ray of the x-axis?

    (A) $(3,1)$

    (B) $(2,4)$

    (C) $(2,7)$

    (D) $(3,3)$

    (E) $(4,2)$

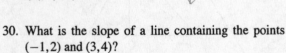

30. What is the slope of a line containing the points $(-1,2)$ and $(3,4)$?

    (A) 2

    (B) $\dfrac{1}{2}$

    (C) -2

    (D) $-\left(\dfrac{1}{2}\right)$

    (E) 1

GO ON TO THE NEXT PAGE

31. If the graph of $x^2 + y^2 = c$ contains the point $(-3,5)$, then $c =$

$9 + 25 = 34$

(A) 4

(B) 34

(C) $-\sqrt{34}$

(D) $\sqrt{-34}$

(E) -4

USE THIS SPACE FOR SCRATCH WORK

32. If an ellipse has foci $(0,2)$ and $(0,-2)$ and $(0,-4)$ is a point of the ellipse, then an x-intercept is

(A) 5

(B) $2\sqrt{3}$

(C) $2\sqrt{5}$

(D) 3

(E) $3\sqrt{2}$

33. A parabola has a vertical axis of symmetry and contains points $(0,0)$, $(1,12)$, and $(-3,108)$. Its equation is

(A) $y = 12x^2$

(B) $x = 12y^2$

(C) $y = -12x^2$

(D) $12y = x^2$

(E) $12y = -x^2$

34. If $y = |\sin x|$, then for all x the range of values of y is

(A) $-1 \le y \le 1$

(B) $0 \le y \le 1$

(C) $-\dfrac{\sqrt{2}}{2} \le y \le \dfrac{\sqrt{2}}{2}$

(D) $0 \le y \le \dfrac{\sqrt{2}}{2}$

(E) $y \ge 0$

35. If $x = \dfrac{\pi}{4}$, then $\sin x =$

.707106781

$45°$

(A) $\csc x$

(B) $\tan x$

(C) $\cos x$

(D) $\sec x$

(E) $\cot x$

GO ON TO THE NEXT PAGE

36. If $1 - 2\cos^2 x = 2\sin^2 x - 1$, then $x =$

    I. 0 only

    II. 45° only

    III. Any real number

    (A) None

    (B) I and II only

    (C) I only

    (D) II only

    (E) III only

37. If a central angle of a circle of radius 8 intercepts an arc of length $\dfrac{16\pi}{3}$, then its degree measure is

    (A) 30

    (B) 60

    (C) 90

    (D) 120

    (E) 150

38. How many angles of a quadrilateral may have negative cosines?

    (A) 0

    (B) 1

    (C) 2

    (D) 3

    (E) 4

39. If in $\triangle ABC$ the sine of $\angle A = .504$, $BC = 7$ and $AC = 5$, the $\sin \angle B$ is

    (A) .714

    (B) .360

    (C) .707

    (D) .504

    (E) .864

40. If $f(x) = -5x^2 - kx + 4$ and $f(-1) = 0$, then $k =$

    (A) −2

    (B) −1

    (C) 0

    (D) 1

    (E) 2

GO ON TO THE NEXT PAGE

41. If $f(x) = \dfrac{1}{|x| - 1}$, then the domain of f is

   (A) All real numbers

   (B) All real numbers except 0

   (C) All positive real numbers

   (D) All non-negative real numbers

   (E) All real numbers except 1 and -1

42. If $f(x) = \sqrt{x - 1}$ and $g(x) = x^2 - 3$, then $f(g(2\sqrt{3})) =$

   (A) $2\sqrt{3}$

   (B) $3\sqrt{2}$

   (C) $2\sqrt{2}$

   (D) 3

   (E) 4

43. If $\log x + \log 8 = \log 16$, then $x =$

   (A) 2

   (B) 4

   (C) 8

   (D) $\dfrac{1}{8}$

   (E) $\dfrac{1}{2}$

44. Which of the following functions is its own inverse?

   I. $f(x) = x$
   II. $f(x) = -x$
   III. $f(x) = x + 1$

   (A) I only

   (B) II only

   (C) I and II only

   (D) II and III only

   (E) I, II, and III

GO ON TO THE NEXT PAGE

45. If $\log_2 5 = M$, then $\log_2 10 =$

(A) 1

(B) $2M$

(C) $\dfrac{1}{M}$

(D) $1 + M$

(E) $M - 1$

46. If $3^{x+y} = \dfrac{1}{3}$ and $2^{x-y} = 1$, which of the following is (x, y)?

(A) $\left(-1, -\dfrac{1}{2}\right)$

(B) $\left(-\dfrac{1}{2}, -\dfrac{1}{2}\right)$

(C) $(-1, 0)$

(D) $(0, -1)$

(E) $\left(\dfrac{1}{2}, \dfrac{1}{2}\right)$

47. Arcs AB and DC in Figure 9 are semicircles with the same radius. Quadrilateral $ABCD$ is a square with sides of 4. The total surface area of the solid is

(A) 53.7

(B) 78.8

(C) 16

(D) 37.7

(E) 62.8

$16 + 12.56 +$

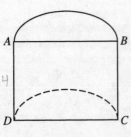

Figure 9

48. The seventh term in the expansion of $\left(1 - \dfrac{1}{m}\right)^{12}$ is

(A) $-\dfrac{792}{m^6}$

(B) $\dfrac{924}{m^7}$

(C) $-\dfrac{792}{m^7}$

(D) $\dfrac{924}{m^6}$

(E) $\dfrac{495}{m^8}$

GO ON TO THE NEXT PAGE

49. If $\frac{1}{2}, a, \frac{3}{8}$ is a geometric sequence, then $a =$

(A) $-\dfrac{\sqrt{3}}{4}$

(B) $\dfrac{3}{4}$

(C) $\dfrac{2}{5}$

(D) $\dfrac{7}{16}$

(E) $\dfrac{\sqrt{3}}{2}$

50. If an auto license is to have four symbols, the first two of which are letters and the remainder digits, how many different license plates can be made? (I and O cannot be used as letters, but 0 can be used in either place as a digit.)

(A) 642

(B) 57,600

(C) 49,680

(D) 46,200

(E) 6420

ANSWER KEY

1. B	11. A	21. B	31. B	41. E
2. C	12. C	22. D	32. B	42. C
3. C	13. B	23. D	33. A	43. A
4. E	14. C	24. B	34. B	44. C
5. C	15. E	25. C	35. C	45. D
6. D	16. A	26. C	36. E	46. B
7. E	17. E	27. D	37. D	47. A
8. E	18. A	28. E	38. D	48. D
9. D	19. C	29. C	39. B	49. A
10. D	20. E	30. B	40. D	50. B

ANSWER EXPLANATIONS

1. **(B)** Choices (A), (C), and (E) follow the Commutative laws of addition and multiplication. Choice (C) follows the Distributive law.

2. **(C)**
$$\frac{(2ab^2)(-3a^3b)}{-12ab} = \frac{-6a^4b^3}{-12ab}$$
$$= \frac{a^3b^2}{2}$$

3. **(C)** Since $x < 0$, it follows that $-x > 0$ so $0 < -x$.

4. **(E)** $a - b = -b + a = -b - (-a)$.

5. **(C)** Multiplying both sides of an inequality by a negative number reverses the inequality.

6. **(D)** In factored form the product is:
$$\frac{(x-2)(x-1)}{(x-3)(x+1)} \times \frac{(x-3)(x+2)}{(x-2)(x+2)}$$

When common factors are removed we get:
$$\frac{x-1}{x+1}$$

7. **(E)** Since the sum of the measures of the angles of a triangle is 180:
$$(\angle A)^\circ + (\angle C)^\circ + 70 = 180$$

But $(\angle C)^\circ = (\angle A)^\circ$ by the Isosceles Triangle Theorem, so:
$$(\angle A)^\circ + (\angle A)^\circ + 70 = 180$$
$$2(\angle A)^\circ = 110$$
$$(\angle A)^\circ = 55$$

8. **(E)** Let $x =$ the number, then:
$$\frac{1}{4}\sqrt{x} = 3$$
$$\sqrt{x} = 12$$
$$x = 144$$

9. **(D)** The graph consists of all points that have coordinates greater than or equal to -2 and less than or equal to 2. This is the meaning of (D).

10. **(D)** The "Distance" from a point to a line is the length of the perpendicular segment (in this case the $\perp$ segment from O to AB; label the point of intersection X). Thus $OX = 2$ and $XA = 3$ (any perpendicular segment from the center to a chord will bisect the chord). By the Pythagorean Theorem:
$$(OA)^2 = 3^2 + 2^2$$
$$OA = \sqrt{13}$$
$$\doteq 3.6$$

11. **(A)** If $\dfrac{a}{b} = \dfrac{c}{d}$, then $ad = bc$ by cross-multiplication. Dividing both sides of this second equation by d^2, we get:
$$\frac{a}{d} = \frac{bc}{d^2},$$

which contradicts (A).

For (D) and (E), divide the denominator into the numerator and remove the constant from both sides of the equation. For example:

(D) $\dfrac{a+b}{b} = \dfrac{c+d}{d} \rightarrow \dfrac{a}{b}+1 = \dfrac{c}{d}+1 \rightarrow \dfrac{a}{b} = \dfrac{c}{d}$

(E) $\dfrac{a-b}{b} = \dfrac{c-d}{d} \rightarrow \dfrac{a}{b}-1 = \dfrac{c}{d}-1 \rightarrow \dfrac{a}{b} = \dfrac{c}{d}$

12. **(C)** If $x = 2$, then $\dfrac{2x}{x-1} = \dfrac{2(2)}{2-1} = \dfrac{4}{1} = 4$.

13. **(B)** Let $x =$ the smaller, then:
$$x + y = a \quad \text{and} \quad y = 2x + b$$

Subtracting the second equation from the first, we get:
$$x = a - 2x - b$$
$$3x = a - b$$
$$x = \frac{a-b}{3}$$

14. (C) $(y+1)(2y-3) = 25$
$$2y^2 - y - 3 = 25$$
$$2y^2 - y - 28 = 0$$
$$(2y+7)(y-4) = 0$$
$$2y+7 = 0 \text{ or } y - 4 = 0$$
$$y = -\frac{7}{2} \text{ or } y = 4$$

15. (E) $\dfrac{3\sqrt{24} - 2\sqrt{18}}{-\sqrt{2}} = \dfrac{3\sqrt{24}}{-\sqrt{2}} - \dfrac{2\sqrt{18}}{-\sqrt{2}}$

$$= \dfrac{3\sqrt{4}\sqrt{3}\sqrt{2}}{-\sqrt{2}} + \dfrac{2\sqrt{9}\sqrt{2}}{\sqrt{2}}$$

$$= -6\sqrt{3} + 6$$

Calculator? Too many keystrokes? Written on the page, it looks like we have done a lot of work here, but much can be done in your head.

16. (A) $(a^3 b^{-2})^{-2} = (a^3)^{-2}(b^{-2})^{-2} = a^{-6} b^4 = \dfrac{b^4}{a^6}$

17. (E) The angle formed by the hands at 2 o'clock is $\frac{1}{6}$ of a rotation or $\frac{1}{6}(360°) = 60°$.

18. (A) $\dfrac{1}{x^{-a}} = x^a$, which will always be the product of a integers and hence an integer.

19. (C) The ratio of altitude to base for all except (C) is 3 to 2. For (C) it is 4 to 3. All of the triangles are similar except (C). Similar triangles have corresponding angles of equal measure. If the vertex angle in (C) *were* equal in measure to that of each of the others, the triangles would be similar by SAS, and the altitude-base ratio would have to be the same for all.

20. (E) Since $ABCD$ is a parallelogram, $AB \parallel CD$ and $\angle ADC$ is supplementary to $\angle BAD$. If they are also equal in measure as given in (E), they must be right angles.

21. (B) Let x be the perimeter, then $\frac{3}{4}x = 9$ and $x = \frac{4}{3} \times 9 = 12$.

22. (D) $\angle OEB$ is a right angle since OE is a radius drawn to tangent EB. Thus $(\angle EBO)° = 60$, since the sum of the measure of the angles of a triangle is 180. But $(\angle OBE)° = (\angle OBC)°$ since BE and BC are tangents and ray BD contains the center of the circle.

23. (D) Since $\triangle ABD$ and $\triangle CBD$ have equal bases (D is the midpoint) and equal altitudes (there is

exactly *one* perpendicular to AC from B), then:

$$\text{area } \triangle ABD = \text{area } \triangle CBD = \frac{1}{2}\text{area } \triangle ABC.$$

By similar reasoning:

$$\text{area } \triangle AFB = \text{area } \triangle AFC = \frac{1}{2}\text{area } \triangle ABC.$$

Thus the union of the triangular regions determined by $\triangle ADB$ and $\triangle AFB$ is equal in area to the union of those determined by $\triangle AFC$ and $\triangle BDC$. If we subtract the sum of the areas of $\triangle ADE$ and $\triangle BEF$ from each of the unions mentioned in turn, we get the area of $\triangle AEB$ from the first subtraction and the area of quadrilateral $CDEF$ from the second. These areas are thus equal.

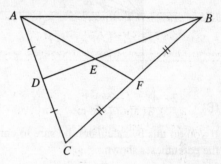

24. (B) With a radius of 6 the circle has an area of $\pi(6)^2 = 36\pi$. Since $\text{m}\angle BAC = 40$ and $\dfrac{40}{360} = \dfrac{1}{9}$, the area of the shaded region is

$$\frac{1}{9}(36\pi) = 4\pi \doteq 12.57.$$

25. (C) The length of a side of a triangle must be less than the sum of the lengths of the other two sides, but greater than the absolute value of their differences.

26. (C) If we were to rotate segments QB and QA around point Q and into the plane of $\triangle PQC$ we would get:

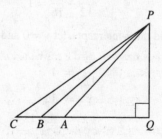

27. (D) Surface area $= 4\pi r^2$, volume $= \dfrac{4}{3}\pi r^3$

$$\dfrac{4\pi r^2}{\frac{4}{3}\pi r^3} = \dfrac{4\pi r^2}{4(\frac{1}{3})\pi r^2 r} = \dfrac{1}{\frac{1}{3}r} = \dfrac{3}{r}$$

28. (E) $\dfrac{i+2}{1-3i} = \dfrac{2+i}{1-3i} \times \dfrac{1+3i}{1+3i}$

   $= \dfrac{-1+7i}{1+9}$

   $= -\dfrac{1}{10} + \dfrac{7}{10}i$

29. (C)

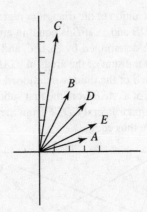

30. (B) $\dfrac{(2-4)}{(-1-3)} = \dfrac{-2}{-4} = \dfrac{1}{2}$

▨ If you do this by calculator, be sure to enter all of the parentheses shown.

31. (B) $(-3)^2 + (5)^2 = c$
   $9 + 25 = c$
   $34 = c$

32. (B)   Foci of $(0,2)$ and $(0,-2)$ indicate that the ellipse is centered at the origin with major axis on the y-axis and is of the form

   $$\dfrac{x^2}{b^2} + \dfrac{y^2}{a^2} = 1,$$

   where $(0,a)$ is the y-intercept and $(0,c)$ is a focus. Thus $c^2 = 4$, $a^2 = 16$ and $b^2 = a^2 - c^2$ (a relation which is true for all ellipses). So $b^2 = 16 - 4 = 12$ and the equation is thus:

   $$\dfrac{x^2}{12} + \dfrac{y^2}{16} = 1$$

   To find the x-intercepts, let $y = 0$ and solve for x.

   $$\dfrac{x^2}{12} = 1$$
   $$x^2 = 12$$
   $$x = \pm\sqrt{12}$$
   $$= \pm 2\sqrt{3}$$

33. (A)   If the axis is vertical then the parabola is of the form $y = ax^2$, which eliminates (B). The given point $(0,0)$ satisfies each of the others, but $(1,12)$ satisfies only (A).

34. (B)   Sin x has a maximum value of 1 and a minimum value of -1. Thus the absolute value of $\sin x$ varies from 0 to 1.

▨ Easy enough without a calculator. However, the graph of $y = |\sin x|$ can be displayed on a graphing calculator and the answer determined from the graph.

35. (C) $x = \dfrac{\pi}{4}$radians $= 45°$, and the trigonometric functions as calculated in section [12] of Chapter 23.

▨ A 45° angle creates an isosceles right triangle, so sine and cosine are equal. If you forgot that fact, your calculator would enable you to check each answer choice.

36. (E) $1 - 2\cos^2 x = 2\sin^2 x - 1$
   $2 = 2\sin^2 x + 2\cos^2 x$
   $1 = \sin^2 x + \cos^2 x$

   The last equation is a fundamental trigonometric identity.

37. (D)   Circumference $= \pi d = 16\pi$; thus, $\dfrac{16\pi}{3}$, the length of the arc, represents $\dfrac{1}{3}$ of the circumference, so its central angle is

   $$\dfrac{1}{3}(360°) = 120°.$$

38. (D)   For an angle of a quadrilateral to have a negative cosine the angle must be obtuse. Since the sum of the measures of the angles of a quadrilateral is 360, it may have as many as three obtuse angles but the final one must be acute (say $91°, 91°, 91°, 87°$).

39. (B)   In $\triangle ABC$, the Law of Sines states that:

   $$\dfrac{\sin \angle A}{BC} = \dfrac{\sin \angle B}{AC}$$

   Therefore:

   $$\dfrac{.504}{7} = \dfrac{\sin \angle B}{5}$$
   $$5(.072) = \sin \angle B$$
   $$.360 = \sin \angle B$$

▨ Note: You don't have to find angle B even though your calculator would if you asked it to.

40. (D) $f(-1) = -5(1)^2 - k(-1) + 4$
   $= -1 + k$

   Since $f(-1)$ was given as equal to zero,

   $$-1 + k = 0 \text{ and } k = 1$$

41. (E) When the domain of a function is not specified it is assumed to be all real numbers except those for which the function is meaningless. If $|x| - 1 = 0$, $(x = \pm 1)$, then f is undefined.

42. (C) $\begin{aligned} g(2\sqrt{3}) &= (2\sqrt{3})^2 - 3 \\ &= 12 - 3 \\ &= 9 \end{aligned}$

$\begin{aligned} f(g(2\sqrt{3})) &= f(9) \\ &= \sqrt{9 - 1} \\ &= \sqrt{8} \\ &= 2\sqrt{2} \end{aligned}$

If you are rusty with radicals, use your calculator to find $f(2\sqrt{3}) = 2.83$. Then check each answer choice.

43. (A) $\begin{aligned} \log x + \log 8 &= \log 16 \\ \log 8x &= \log 16 \\ 8x &= 16 \\ x &= 2 \end{aligned}$

Avoid the temptation to start tapping away on calculator keys. For this question, the calculator will slow you down.

44. (C) To find the inverse, $f^{-1}(x)$, replace $f(x)$ by x and x by $f^{-1}(x)$ and then solve for $f^{-1}(x)$. If $f(x) = x + 1$ as in III, then:

$$\begin{aligned} x &= f^{-1}(x) + 1 \\ f^{-1}(x) &= x - 1 \end{aligned}$$

On a graphing calculator, you can graph each option and look for symmetry with respect to the line $y = x$.

45. (D) $\begin{aligned} \log_2 10 &= \log_2(2 \times 5) \\ &= \log_2 2 + \log_2 5 \\ &= 1 + \log_2 5 \\ &= 1 + m \end{aligned}$

Your calculator can calculate logs of any base. For example,

$$\log_2 10 = \frac{\log 10}{\log 2} = 3.32$$

and

$$\log_2 5 = \frac{\log 5}{\log 2} = 2.32.$$

46. (B) If $3^{x+y} = \dfrac{1}{3}$, then $3^{x+y} = 3^{-1}$ and

(1) $\qquad\qquad x + y = -1$

If $2^{x-y} = 1$, then $2^{x-y} = 2^0$ and

(2) $\qquad\qquad x - y = 0.$

Adding (1) and (2), we get:

$$2x = -1 \text{ and } x = -\frac{1}{2} \text{ and } y = -\frac{1}{2}$$

47. (A) Area of square $ABCD = (4)^2 = 16$. Length of arc $AB = \dfrac{1}{2}$ (circumference of circle of diameter 4) $= \dfrac{1}{2}(4\pi) = 2\pi$, so area of curved surface $ABCD = $ height (4) times length of arc $AB(2\pi)$ or 8π. Area of each semicircular base is $\pi r^2 = 4\pi$. Total $= 16 + 12\pi$.

48. (D) $\begin{aligned} {}_{12}C_6(1)^6\left(-\frac{1}{m}\right)^6 &= \frac{12!}{6!6!}\left(\frac{1}{m^6}\right) \\ &= \frac{924}{m^6} \end{aligned}$

Here, a calculator with a factorial key or combinations key could be very useful.

49. (A) If $\dfrac{1}{2}, a, \dfrac{3}{8}$ is a geometric sequence, then

$$\frac{a}{\frac{1}{2}} = \frac{\frac{3}{8}}{a}$$

$$a^2 = \frac{3}{16}.$$

$$a = \pm\frac{\sqrt{3}}{4}$$

50. (B) The first symbol is a letter and may be chosen in any of 24 ways (I and O cannot be used). The second symbol may also be chosen in 24 ways. The third, being a digit from 0 to 9, can be chosen in one of 10 ways as can the fourth:

$$24 \times 24 \times 10 \times 10 = 57,600$$

SELF-EVALUATION CHART FOR DIAGNOSTIC TEST

SUBJECT AREA	QUESTIONS ANSWERED CORRECTLY	NUMBER OF CORRECT ANSWERS

Algebra 1
(15 questions)

1	2	3	4	5	6	8	11	12	13	14	15	16	18	49
✓	0	✓	✓	✓	✓	✓	✓	✓	✓	0	✓	✓	✓	✗

_____

Plane geometry
(11 questions)

7	9	10	17	19	20	21	22	23	24	25
✓	✓	✓	✓	✓	✗	✓	✓	✓	✓	✓

_____

Solid geometry
(3 questions)

26	27	47
✓	✓	✓

_____

Coordinate geometry
(6 questions)

29	30	31	32	33	46
✓	✓	✓	0	0	0

_____

Trigonometry
(5 questions)

34	35	36	37	39
0	✓	0	✗	0

_____

Functions
(6 questions)

40	41	42	43	44	45
✓	✓	✓	✓	✓	0

_____

Miscellaneous
(5 questions)

24	28	38	48	50
✓	0	0	0	0

_____

Total number of correct answers   34

Total number of incorrect answers   − 3

(Reminder: Answers left blank are not counted as correct or incorrect)

Raw score = (number correct) $-\frac{1}{4}$ (number incorrect)

To evaluate your performance, compare your raw score with the table below.

33.25

Evaluate Your Performance
Diagnostic Test

Excellent	760–800	46–50
Very Good	710–750	41–45
Good	640–700	35–40
Above Average	580–630	29–34
Average	530–580	22–28
Below Average	270–520	Below 22

STRATEGIES, REVIEW, AND PRACTICE—BASIC TOPICS

PART
2

ELEMENTARY CONCEPTS

CHAPTER

5

KEY TERMS

prime number	a number that is greater than 1 and has no other whole number factors except itself and 1. Examples: 5, 7.
least common multiple (LCM)	for two or more numbers, the smallest positive number in the set of common multiples. Example: For 4 and 5, the LCM = 20.
least common denominator (LCD)	for two or more fractions, the LCM of their denominators. Example: For $\frac{1}{3}$, $\frac{1}{4}$, and $\frac{1}{2}$, the LCD = 12.
reciprocal or **multiplicative inverse**	a number that, when used to multiply a given number, gives a product of 1. Example: $\frac{4}{5} \times \frac{5}{4} = 1$; $\frac{5}{4}$ is the reciprocal of $\frac{4}{5}$.
additive inverse	a number that, when added to a given number, gives a sum of zero. Example: $4 + (-4) = 0$; -4 is the additive inverse of 4.

In this chapter, you will review principles of arithmetic and practice how to do basic operations on your calculator.

FUNDAMENTALS OF ARITHMETIC

[1]   What is the value of

$$\frac{7+7+7+7+7}{5+5+5+5+5+5+5}?$$

(A) 0

(B) 1

(C) 5

(D) 7

(E) 35

A student planning to take the SAT II: Mathematics Level IC test should have a strong knowledge of the fundamentals of arithmetic. Throughout this chapter the emphasis will be on some of the less routine aspects of arithmetic and the way they relate to basic skills. We will point out many of the common errors that plague even some of the best-qualified students.

The question above illustrates not only some elementary arithmetic facts relating to addition and division, but also some of the devices test makers use to discover the student's level of mastery. Did you notice that the numerator is 5×7 (the sum of five 7's) and the denominator is 7×5 (the sum of seven 5's)? If you did, then you found the answer more quickly than the student who added all of the numbers and then divided.

TEST-TAKING TIP

Familiarity with underlying mathematical principles is part of what testers are looking for. Rarely does a test question require much computation. Most can be answered quickly, often with no pencil-and-paper work at all.

▣ To do this question by calculator would require 25 or more keystrokes—any one of which might be entered incorrectly.

DOING OPERATIONS IN THE CORRECT ORDER

[2]   Find the value of $4 + 7 \times 6 + 6 \div 2$.

(A) 69

(B) 49

(C) 45

(D) 36

(E) 25

The order of operations in a mathematical expression is an agreement among mathematicians about which steps are to be done first. One way to remember this order is to think of the order of the first letters in the phrase "*My Dear Aunt Sally.*" In other words, multiplication and division are carried out first, and addition and subtraction are done afterwards.

The expression above is really

$$4 + 42 + 3$$

since $7 \times 6 = 42$ and $6 \div 2 = 3$.

▣ Do this question on your calculator to see if it follows an algebraic order of operations. Then do the following both with and without the calculator that you will use on the Level IC test.

EXAMPLES

Find the value of each of the following mentally and by calculator:

1. $3 - 2 + 8 \times 7 - 4 \div 4 = 56$

2. $100 - 2 \times 36 + 12 - 6 = 34$

3. $10 \times 4 + 21 \div 7 = 43$

4. $36 - 9 \div 3 + 6 = 39$

5. $8 \div 2 \times 4 + 3 - 4 + 6 = 21$

[3]   Find the value of $9 - 2(5 - 1) + (5 - 1)$.

(A) 32

(B) 5

(C) 3

(D) 12

(E) 17

The order in which a series of operations is completed can be changed through the use of parentheses as grouping symbols. The operations enclosed in the parentheses are carried out first (using the MDAS order for operations inside the parentheses). Thus the preceding expression is really

$$9 - 2 \times 4 + 4 = 9 - 8 + 4 = 1 + 4.$$

Note the absence of a multiplication sign, $\times$, to designate the product of 2 and $(5 - 1)$. The multiplication sign is usually deleted when one or both multipliers are written in parentheses.

Check your calculator manual to be sure you know how to use the parentheses keys. Then find the value of each of the following with and without your calculator:

1. $(3 + 2)5 = 25$

2. $(2 + 3) - (5 - 2) = 2$

3. $4 - 2(3 - 1) = 0$

4. $(54 - 14 \div 7) \div 2 = 26$

FINDING THE LEAST COMMON MULTIPLE

[4]   What is the least common multiple of x and y if x and y are prime numbers?

(A) x

(B) y

(C) $x + y$

(D) xy

(E) $\dfrac{x}{y}$

A number is *prime* if it is greater than 1 and has no whole number factors except itself and 1. Examples of primes are 2, 3, 5, 7, 11, 13, 17, and so forth.

A number p is a *multiple* of q if $p \div q$ is a whole number $\{0, 1, 2, 3,$ etc. $\}$. Thus the multiples of 3 include $\{0, 3, 6, 9, 12, 15, \dots\}$, and the multiples of 5 include $\{0, 5, 10, 15, \dots\}$.

A *common multiple* of two numbers is a number that is a multiple of each.

Note that the common multiples of 3 and 5 include $\{0, 15, 30, \dots\}$. Thus 0 is a common multiple of every pair of numbers.

The *least common multiple* (LCM) of a set of two or more numbers is the smallest *positive* number in the set of common multiples. Therefore, the least common multiple of 5 and 3 is 15, and the least common multiple of 6 and 4 is 12.

One way to find the LCM is to write the first few members of the set of common multiples and choose the smallest positive number in this set. For example, the common multiples of 3 and 5 are $\{0, 15, 30, 45, \dots\}$, so the LCM is 15. A second method is sometimes quicker. To find the LCM of p and q, first write the prime factors of p and the prime factors of q. The LCM must contain each prime factor of p and each prime factor of q. The prime factors are each raised to a power equal to that of the greatest power of that prime factor in p or q, even if it appears in both.

For example, the prime factorizations of 12 and 45 are

$$12 = 2^2 \times 3,$$
$$45 = 3^2 \times 5.$$

The greatest powers of the primes are 2^2, 3^2 and 5 so the LCM is

$$2^2 \times 3^2 \times 5 = 180.$$

Note that 3 is a factor of both 12 and 45, but its greatest power in either is 3^2.

In the multiple-choice question above, x and y are both primes, so the LCM must be their product.

TEST-TAKING TIP

One way to discover this answer is to experiment with a few numbers as test cases. Using 2 and 3 (both are prime), for example, you can quickly see that 6 is the LCM, the product of 2 and 3. Test cases can be very helpful in understanding what an examination question means and how to answer it.

EXAMPLES

Verify the LCM given.

1. 2, 3 and 4, LCM = 12

2. 21, 30 and 54, LCM = 1890

3. 15 and 35, LCM = 105

4. 18 and 21, LCM = 126

FINDING THE GREATEST COMMON FACTOR

[5] Which of the following is the greatest common factor of 36, 27, and 24?

(A) 2

(B) 3

(C) 6

(D) 9

(E) 12

When two or more numbers are multiplied together, each is called a *factor* of the result. The number 30, for example, can be written as 6 times 5, 2 times 15, 3 times 10, or 1 times 30, so its set of factors is

$$\{1, 2, 3, 5, 6, 10, 15, 30\}.$$

If a number is a factor of each of two or more given whole numbers, it is called a *common factor* of the given numbers. Note that the numbers given in the factors question above have the following sets of factors:

$$36 \rightarrow \{1, 2, 3, 4, 6, 9, 12, 18, 36\},$$
$$27 \rightarrow \{1, 3, 9, 27\},$$
$$24 \rightarrow \{1, 2, 3, 4, 6, 8, 12, 24\}.$$

Thus the factors common to *all three* of the given numbers are

$$\{1, 3\}.$$

The greater of these is, of course, 3.

This question was easily answered by listing the common factors, but a more efficient method exists. Write it as a product in which all factors are prime numbers—the *prime factorization*. The *greatest common factor* (GCF) will be the product of the prime factors found in both. Each is used only as many times as it occurs in all of the numbers. The latter part of that statement is easily misinterpreted. Study the following prime factorizations:

$$27 = 3 \times 3 \times 3,$$
$$36 = 3 \times 3 \times 2 \times 2,$$
$$24 = 3 \times 2 \times 2 \times 2.$$

The first number has three 3's. Do they *all* have three 3's? No, the numbers 36 and 24 do not. The number 36 has two 3's. Do they *all* have two 3's? No, just 36 and 27 have. The number 24 has one 3. Do they *all* have one 3? Yes. Since only one 3 is common, and no other factors are common, 3 is the GCF.

What is the GCF for 24 and 60?

$$24 = 3 \times 2 \times 2 \times 2$$
$$60 = 5 \times 3 \times 2 \times 2$$

Therefore the GCF is $3 \times 2 \times 2 = 12$ since the factors listed are the ones common to both—in other words, the ones both have.

EXAMPLES

Verify the GCF given:

1. 8 and 28, GCF $= 2^2$

2. 6, 8 and 10, GCF $= 2$

3. 8, 12 and 18, GCF $= 2$

4. 24, 36 and 108, GCF $= 2^2 \times 3$

REDUCING FRACTIONS TO LOWEST TERMS

[6] If the fraction $\dfrac{9}{45}$ were expressed in lowest terms, what factor common to numerator and denominator would have to be removed?

(A) 3

(B) 5

(C) 9

(D) 15

(E) The fraction is already in lowest terms

A fraction is used to indicate that two numbers are to be divided; the number above the bar (the *numerator*) is to be divided by the number below the bar (the *denominator*). Two fractions that look very different may, in fact, indicate divisions having the same result. For example, $\frac{2}{5}$ and $\frac{4}{10}$ have the same result. This is so because

$$\frac{4}{10} = \frac{2 \times 2}{5 \times 2} = \frac{2}{5} \times \frac{2}{2} = \frac{2}{5} \times 1 = \frac{2}{5}.$$

The numbers 4 and 10 have the common factor 2, which has been removed by the process shown above.

The removal of common factors does not require the use of so many steps once the idea is understood. After the common factors have been identified, they may merely be crossed out:

$$\frac{9}{45} = \frac{1 \times \cancel{9}}{5 \times \cancel{9}} = \frac{1}{5}.$$

Thus $\frac{9}{45}$ and $\frac{1}{5}$ name the same number.

Fractions that name the same number are called *equivalent* fractions and the process of removing the common factors is called *reducing to lowest terms*.

Fractions may also be expressed as equivalent fractions in higher terms by reversing the process—in other words, by multiplying numerator and denominator by a common factor. Thus $\frac{2}{10}, \frac{3}{15}, \frac{4}{20}, \frac{5}{25}, \frac{6}{30}, \frac{7}{35}$, and so forth, are all expressions in higher terms for $\frac{1}{5}$.

TEST-TAKING TIP

The ability to express fractions in higher or lower terms is required in many kinds of test questions and should be learned thoroughly.

EXAMPLES

In lowest terms:

1. $\frac{4}{12} = \frac{1}{3}$

2. $\frac{25}{35} = \frac{5}{7}$

3. $\frac{27}{36} = \frac{3}{4}$

4. $\frac{100}{250} = \frac{2}{5}$

FINDING THE LEAST COMMON DENOMINATOR

[7] Find the least common denominator of the fractions $\frac{1}{60}$ and $\frac{5}{72}$.

(A) $\frac{6}{360}$

(B) $\frac{180}{360}$

(C) 12

(D) 360

(E) 6

The *least common denominator* (LCD) of two or more fractions is the same number that is the LCM of their denominators and, therefore, is found by the method described in section [4] of this chapter.

$$60 = 5 \times 3 \times 2^2$$
$$72 = 3^2 \times 2^3$$

$$LCD = 3^2 \times 2^3 \times 5$$
$$= 360$$

To verify that 360 is a common denominator, you may check this result by dividing 360 by each of 72 and 60 as follows:

$$360 \div 60 = 6,$$
$$360 \div 72 = 5.$$

TEST-TAKING TIP

When taking tests, always check to make sure you are answering the question being asked and not a different one also suggested by the given information but not explicitly asked. A suprisingly large number of students misinterpret the directions "Find the least common denominator" to mean "Change the fractions to equivalent fractions with the least common denominator." You are merely being asked to discover what the LCD is and not to alter the fractions to have this LCD.

EXAMPLES

For each of the following, verify the LCD.

1. $\frac{1}{2}, \frac{1}{3}, \frac{1}{6}$, LCD = 6

2. $\frac{1}{3}, \frac{1}{9}, \frac{1}{27}$, LCD = 27

3. $\frac{3}{8}, \frac{5}{28}$, LCD = 56

4. $\frac{5}{48}, \frac{7}{54}$, LCD = 432

[8] The value of $\frac{1}{2} - \frac{1}{3} + \frac{1}{4}$ is?

(A) $\frac{1}{3}$

(B) 5

(C) $\frac{1}{4}$

(D) $\frac{1}{9}$

(E) $\frac{5}{12}$

Familiarize yourself with how your calculator displays rational numbers (decimal form only? as a fraction or a decimal?). Then answer the question with and without your calculator.

Before a set of fractions can be added or subtracted, each fraction must be changed to an equivalent fraction with a denominator common to all. The LCD of $\frac{1}{2}$, $\frac{1}{3}$, and $\frac{1}{4}$ is 12.

$$\frac{1 \times 6}{2 \times 6} - \frac{1 \times 4}{3 \times 4} + \frac{1 \times 3}{4 \times 3}$$

Combining the fractions is completed by performing the indicated operations on the numerators and writing the result with the common denominator.

$$\frac{6 - 4 + 3}{12} = \frac{5}{12}$$

TEST-TAKING TIP

In listing answer choices, testers use incorrect answers resulting from common mistakes as "distractors." Don't assume that the answer you have found must be correct solely on the basis that it appears as one of the answer choices.

EXAMPLES

Verify the following calculations:

1. $\frac{1}{2} + \frac{9}{16} = \frac{17}{16}$

2. $\frac{3}{8} + \frac{1}{2} - \frac{27}{32} = \frac{1}{32}$

3. $\frac{7}{8} - \frac{3}{4} + \frac{2}{3} = \frac{19}{24}$

4. $\frac{5}{8} + \frac{11}{12} - \frac{13}{16} = \frac{35}{48}$

5. $\frac{1}{3} + \frac{5}{12} = \frac{3}{4}$

MULTIPLYING FRACTIONS

[9]   What is the value of $\frac{3}{8} \times \frac{4}{5} \times \frac{5}{6}$?

(A) $\frac{12}{19}$

(B) $\frac{1}{4}$

(C) $\frac{3}{8}$

(D) $\frac{3}{16}$

(E) 3

⌨ Don't start punching keys until you have simplified.

$$\frac{3 \times 4 \times 5}{8 \times 5 \times 6} = \frac{60}{240}$$
$$= \frac{1}{4} \times \frac{60}{60}$$
$$= \frac{1}{4}.$$

Note that the final step consisted of removing a factor common to numerator and denominator. A much more efficient procedure is to remove common factors before the multiplication is done. A common factor of any numerator and denominator may be removed, even if it is in different fractions. The numbers 3, 4 and 5 are common factors.

$$\frac{\overset{1}{\cancel{3}}}{\underset{2}{\cancel{8}}} \times \frac{\overset{1}{\cancel{4}}}{\underset{1}{\cancel{5}}} \times \frac{\overset{1}{\cancel{5}}}{\underset{2}{\cancel{6}}} = \frac{1 \times 1 \times 1}{2 \times 1 \times 2} = \frac{1}{4}$$

Students frequently confuse the procedure for multiplication of fractions with that for addition of fractions and start by changing to common denominators. Such a procedure just introduces many common factors that must be removed before the multiplication can begin.

TEST-TAKING TIP

The result may be a number that does appear as an answer among the choices but is so different in form as to be unrecognizable at first glance. Therefore, when comparing your answer with the choices given, always consider the possibility that the correct answer is in a form different from the one you've calculated.

EXAMPLES

Verify each of the following:

1. $\frac{2}{5} \times \frac{5}{16} = \frac{1}{8}$

2. $\frac{7}{12} \times \frac{4}{5} = \frac{7}{15}$

3. $\frac{7}{12} \times 6 = \frac{7}{2}$

4. $\frac{24}{35} \times \frac{21}{32} \times \frac{2}{3} = \frac{3}{10}$

USING MIXED NUMBERS AND IMPROPER FRACTIONS

[10] $4\frac{1}{3} - \frac{2}{3} = ?$

(A) $3\frac{1}{3}$

(B) 3

(C) $3\frac{2}{3}$

(D) 5

(E) $\frac{5}{3}$

The number $4\frac{1}{3}$ is an example of a mixed number. When you enter a mixed number, remember that the operation relating the 4 and the $\frac{1}{3}$ is addition. Thus another way of writing it is

$$4\frac{1}{3} = 4 + \frac{1}{3} = \frac{4 \times 3}{1 \times 3} + \frac{1}{3} = \frac{12}{3} + \frac{1}{3} = \frac{13}{3}.$$

When a mixed number is written in fractional form, the numerator of the resulting fraction is always greater than the denominator, making it an *improper fraction*.

For changing mixed numbers to improper fractions, there is a shorter procedure than the one just described. Multiply the whole number by the denominator of the fraction and add the numerator of the fraction to this product. Then write this sum over the denominator of the fraction.

$$\frac{4 \times 3 + 1}{3} = \frac{13}{3}$$

EXAMPLES

Change to improper fractions and compare your calculator result:

1. $3\frac{2}{3} = \frac{11}{3} = 3.666\ldots$

2. $1\frac{1}{2} = \frac{3}{2} = 1.5$

3. $4\frac{3}{8} = \frac{35}{8} = 4.375$

4. $7\frac{1}{7} = \frac{50}{7} = 7.1428571\ldots$

[11] If $2\frac{1}{3}$ is divided by $\frac{2}{3}$, the result is?

(A) 2

(B) 3

(C) $3\frac{1}{2}$

(D) $\frac{1}{3}$

(E) 7

If the product of two numbers is 1, then each is called the *reciprocal*, or *multiplicative inverse*, of the other. For example, $\frac{2}{3}$ and $\frac{3}{2}$ are reciprocals since

$$\frac{2}{3} \times \frac{3}{2} = 1$$

Most scientific calculators have reciprocal keys (designated by $\boxed{1/x}$ or $\boxed{x^{-1}}$) that will convert a displayed number to its reciprocal.

Dividing by a given number produces the same result as multiplying by its reciprocal. Hence:

$$2\frac{1}{3} \div \frac{3}{2} = 2\frac{1}{3} \times \frac{3}{2}.$$

Before this division can be carried out, however, the number $2\frac{1}{3}$ must be changed from a mixed number to an improper fraction by following the procedure described in the preceding section.

$$2\frac{1}{3} = \frac{2 \times 3 + 1}{3} = \frac{7}{3}$$

$$\frac{7}{3} \times \frac{3}{2} = \frac{7}{2} = 3\frac{1}{2}$$

EXAMPLES

Divide by multiplying by the reciprocal of the divisor and compare your calculator result:

1. $\frac{1}{3} \div \frac{2}{3} = \frac{1}{2} = .5$

2. $2\frac{2}{3} \div \frac{8}{3} = 1$

3. $\frac{1}{5} \div 2\frac{2}{5} = \frac{1}{12} = .08333\ldots$

4. $1\frac{1}{2} \div 2\frac{1}{4} = \frac{2}{3} = .666\ldots$

CHANGING FRACTIONS TO DECIMALS

[12] If $\frac{3}{9}$ is written as a decimal, the result is?

(A) $.\overline{3}$

(B) $.3$

(C) $.9$

(D) $.\overline{9}$

(E) $.39$

When you answer this question, pay attention to how your calculator treats a repeating decimal.

To change a fraction into decimal form, divide the numerator by the denominator *after reducing the fraction to lowest terms.*

EXAMPLE 1

To change $\frac{6}{8}$ to a decimal by longhand, first reduce it to $\frac{3}{4}$ and then divide:

$$4\overline{)3.00} \quad .75$$

Therefore, $\frac{6}{8} = .75$.

Frequently the division cannot be completed because there is always a remainder. As the division is carried out, however, a pattern of repeating digits emerges.

EXAMPLE 2

To change $\frac{3}{11}$ to a decimal, divide 3 by 11.

$$
\begin{array}{r}
.2727 \\
11\overline{)3.0000} \\
2\,2 \\
\hline
80 \\
77 \\
\hline
30 \\
22 \\
\hline
80 \\
77 \\
\hline
3
\end{array}
$$

Note that this division cannot be completed, since remainders of 8 and 3 will continue to alternate forever at each step. The result is called a "periodic" or "repeating" decimal and is generally written by placing a bar above the digits that repeat.

$$\frac{3}{11} = .\overline{27}$$

Whenever a given counting number is divided by another counting number, the result will be a decimal that

terminates (meaning that the division is completed since a remainder of zero is reached) or repeats.

The fraction $\frac{3}{9}$ can first be reduced to $\frac{1}{3}$ and then changed to $.\overline{3}$ by division.

$$
\begin{array}{r}
.333 \\
3\overline{)1.000} \\
9 \\
\hline
10 \\
9 \\
\hline
10 \\
9 \\
\hline
1
\end{array}
$$

Your calculator can display a repeating decimal for only as many places as the screen will show, so you must learn to interpret your display. Does the calculator round off the last decimal place shown? (If so, it would display 2 ÷ 3 as .666667.) Or does it simply reach the edge of the window and stop? (In that case, it would display 2 ÷ 3 as .666666.)

All repeating decimals can be changed to fractions having whole-number terms; this procedure will be reviewed in the next chapter.

EXAMPLES

Write as a decimal and compare with your calculator result:

1. $\frac{2}{4} = .5$

2. $\frac{1}{6} = .1666\ldots$

3. $\frac{3}{7} = .4285714$

4. $\frac{9}{12} = .75$

[13] If the number $7 \cdot 10^3 + 6 \cdot 10^1 + 5 - 10^0 + 4 \cdot \frac{1}{10^2} + 3 \cdot \frac{1}{10^3}$ were written as a decimal, which of the following would be the result?

(A) 76.543

(B) 76.43

(C) 706.543

(D) 706.043

(E) 7065.043

Numerical representation in the decimal system is based on place value. The number represented by each digit depends on how far to the left or the right of the decimal point it appears. Each digit represents the result of multiplying the value of the digit by the power of 10 determined by the position of the digit. The value of each place can be seen from the following table, where the arrow indicates the position of the decimal. The table is incomplete, of course, since the values continue to get larger to the left and smaller to the right, unendingly.

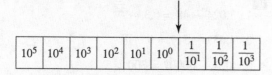

10^5	10^4	10^3	10^2	10^1	10^0	$\dfrac{1}{10^1}$	$\dfrac{1}{10^2}$	$\dfrac{1}{10^3}$

For example, the number 120.45 can be written as

$$1 \cdot 10^2 + 2 \cdot 10^1 + 0 \cdot 10^0 + 4 \cdot \frac{1}{10^1} + 5 \cdot \frac{1}{10^2}.$$

The latter form is called *expanded notation*. Negative exponents are sometimes used to simplify the writing of the terms on the right side of the decimal. The use of negative exponents will be reviewed later in this text.

EXAMPLES

Write in expanded notation:

1. $1.1 = 1 + 10^{-1}$

2. $101.101 = 10^2 + 10^0 + 10^{-1} + 10^{-3}$

3. $.032 = 3 \times 10^{-2} + 2 \times 10^{-3}$

4. $300.003 = 3 \times 10^3 + 3 \times 10^{-3}$

WORKING WITH DECIMAL NUMBERS

[14]   What is the value of $2.2 + .38 - 1.4$?

   (A)   1.18

   (B)   5.6

   (C)   4.6

   (D)   5.28

   (E)   2.4

A simple job for your calculator. To do this by long-hand, remember that addition and subtraction of decimal expressions are begun by first arranging the sum or difference vertically so that the decimal points are directly under each other in a vertical line. You may wish to annex zeros to the numerals being added so that each has the same number of decimal places.

$$
\begin{array}{r}
2.20 \\
+\ \ .38 \\
\hline
2.58 \\
-\ 1.40 \\
\hline
1.18
\end{array}
$$

EXAMPLES

Add or subtract as indicated mentally and by calculator:

1. $.023 + .4 - .05 = .373$

2. $2.5 - .13 + .0048 = 2.3748$

3. $1.624 + 1.369 - 1.9 = 1.093$

4. $.349 + 1.2 - .012 = 1.537$

[15] $.032 \times 1.85 = ?$

   (A)   .0592

   (B)   .5920

   (C)   5.92

   (D)   59.2

   (E)   592

Another simple job for your calculator, but wait. This is a good example of why you should scan the answer choices to discover what is being sought. Do you see that each of the choices has the same sequence of digits? This means that the multiplication need not be carried out to determine the correct answer. The question is really just "Where does the decimal point go?"

When multiplying two decimal numerals, the number of decimal places in the result is the sum of the numbers of decimal places in the two multipliers. Count the total number of places in the multipliers. Point this total off in the product, counting from right to left. If you run out of places before you have all you need, prefix as many zeros to the left side of the number as you need to get enough decimal places. In the event that the product ends in one or more zeros, these zeros should be recorded and counted along with the others. For example:

$$.02 \times .05 = .0010.$$

The result of this example may, of course, be written as .001, but this zero should not be discarded until *after* the decimal point has been positioned.

EXAMPLES

🖩 Carry out the multiplications by longhand and by calculator:

1. $2.07 \times 5.9 = 12.213$

2. $.49 \times 62 = 30.38$

3. $.380 \times .10 = .038$

4. $.35 \times .02 = .007$

[16] The quotient $3.84 \div 18.2$ is the same as the quotient $38.4 \div 182$ because the removal of the decimal points is equivalent to multiplication by:

(A) 100

(B) 10

(C) $\dfrac{10}{10}$

(D) $\dfrac{100}{100}$

(E) 1000

🖩 The question does not ask you to do the division, so your calculator may not help much.

To divide two decimal expressions, remove the decimal point from the divisor by shifting it as many places to the right as is necessary to make the divisor a whole number. Then move the decimal in the dividend (the number to be divided into) the same number of places to the right to compensate for the change you made in the divisor. The divisor and the dividend actually represent a fraction (dividend over divisor). The shift of the decimal point is the result of multiplying by a power of 10. The shift of the decimals in divisor and dividend is explained by the mathematical law that allows multiplication of the numerator and denominator of a fraction by a common factor. Thus:

$$3.84 \div 18.2 = \frac{3.84}{18.2}$$

$$= \frac{3.84 \times 10}{18.2 \times 10}$$

$$= \frac{38.4}{182}$$

$$= 38.4 \div 182.$$

Note that, to complete the division, the decimal point had to be moved only one place since the divisor contained only one decimal place.

$$18.2 \overline{)3.84}$$

It is not necessary to remove the decimal points from *both* dividend and divisor.

EXAMPLES

🖩 Divide mentally and by calculator:

1. $3.024 \div .48 = 6.3$

2. $4.653 \div .517 = 9$

3. $.021 \div .00007 = 300$

CHANGING PERCENTS TO DECIMALS

[17] If $\dfrac{1}{2}\%$ is written as a decimal, what is the result?

(A) .5

(B) .05

(C) .005

(D) .0005

(E) 5

🖩 Whether or not your calculator has a percent key, you still need to understand the underlying principle.

The term percent means "hundredths." A percent can be changed to a fraction by replacing the percent sign, %, with a denominator of 100. Thus:

$$5\% \text{ is } \frac{5}{100}, \quad 87.3\% \text{ is } \frac{87.3}{100} \quad \text{and} \quad \frac{1}{2}\% \text{ is } \frac{\frac{1}{2}}{100}.$$

Dividing a whole number or a decimal numeral by 100 is easily done by shifting the decimal point two places to the left. Hence:

$$\frac{5}{100} = .05 \quad \text{and} \quad \frac{87.3}{100} = .873.$$

When a fraction occurs in a percent, the new fraction that results when the percent sign is replaced by a denominator of 100 is a complex fraction. It can be simplified by first following the procedures of dividing fractions, and then by changing to a decimal through further division.

$$\frac{1}{2}\% = \frac{\frac{1}{2}}{100}$$

$$= \frac{1}{2} \div 100$$

$$= \frac{1}{2} \times \frac{1}{100}$$

$$= \frac{1}{200}$$

$$= .005$$

A simpler procedure is to change the fraction to a decimal and then shift the decimal point two places to the left.

$$\frac{1}{2}\% = .5\% = .005$$

EXAMPLES

Write as a decimal:

1. $3\% = .03$

2. $.6\% = .006$

3. $\frac{3}{8}\% = .00375$

4. $12\frac{1}{4}\% = .1225$

CHANGING FRACTIONS TO PERCENTS

[18] When written as a percent, $3\frac{2}{5}$ is which value?

(A) 34%

(B) 3.4%

(C) 340%

(D) .034%

(E) .34%

■ Your calculator probably does not display a percent sign, so you must learn how to interpret a decimal as a percent.

Since percent means "hundredths," annexing a percent sign to a number is the same as dividing the number by 100. To compensate for this division, the number must, in some way, be multiplied by 100. This multiplication is usually accomplished by moving the decimal point two places to the right. For example:

$$3 = 300\%,$$
$$.5 = 50\%,$$
$$.01 = 1\%.$$

If a fraction is to be changed to a percent, it is usually best to change the fraction first to a decimal. For example:

$$\frac{1}{2} = .5 = 50\%,$$
$$\frac{3}{8} = 375 = 37.5\%,$$
$$3\frac{2}{5} = 3.4 = 340\%.$$

In each case, annexing a percent sign (in effect, dividing by 100) is compensated for by shifting the decimal point two places to the right (multiplying by 100).

EXAMPLES

■ Write as percents after using your calculator to find the equivalent decimal:

1. $\frac{2}{5} = .4 = 40\%$

2. $2\frac{1}{4} = 2.25 = 225\%$

3. $\frac{7}{20} = .35 = 35\%$

4. $\frac{15}{7} = 2.142857\ldots = 214.2857\ldots\%$

SOLVING PERCENTAGE PROBLEMS

[19] What percent of p is q?

(A) 100%

(B) $q\%$

(C) $\frac{q}{p}\%$

(D) $\frac{100q}{p}\%$

(E) Not enough information is given

What percent of 5 is 3? Note that this question asks what fractional part of 5 the number 3 is, with the fraction being represented by use of the percent sign. The key idea to remember is that affixing a percent sign to a number is the same as dividing it by 100, so multiplication by 100 is necessary to counterbalance it.

$$\frac{3}{5} = \frac{3 \times 100}{5}\% = 60\%$$

The work on the example above was completed without resorting to decimals, since the decimal representation could not be given in the multiple-choice question we are preparing to answer. The procedure for the sample question is, therefore, identical.

$$\frac{q}{p} = \frac{q \times 100}{p}\% = \frac{100q}{p}\%$$

EXAMPLES

Answer the following after finding a decimal on your calculator:

1. What percent of 12 is 4? $33\frac{1}{3}\%$.

2. What percent of 4 is 12? 300%.

3. What percent of p is $\frac{1}{2}p$? 50%.

4. What percent of $5p$ is $3p$? 60%.

[20] 4.2 is 20% of what number?

    (A) 8.4

    (B) .84

    (C) .084

    (D) 21

    (E) 2.1

You'll need to set up an equation before performing a calculation.

All percents can be written as common fractions, using the principle that "percent" means "hundredths."

$$6\% = \frac{6}{100} = \frac{3}{50}$$

$$120\% = \frac{120}{100} = \frac{6}{5}$$

$$20\% = \frac{20}{100} = \frac{1}{5}$$

Thus many types of percentage problems can be solved by setting up a proportion—in other words, by writing an equation between two fractions. In the question above, let x be the missing number. Then

$$\frac{4.2}{x} = \frac{20}{100}.$$

The procedure for solving a proportion is discussed in depth in a later chapter, but we will describe it briefly here. In a proportion such as

$$\frac{a}{b} = \frac{c}{d},$$

the product ad equals the product bc regardless of what the numbers a, b, c, and d are as long as the equation relating the fractions is true. This means that

$$(4.2)(100) = 20x,$$
$$420 = 20x,$$
$$21 = x.$$

EXAMPLES

Answer the following by setting up an equation and using your calculator to divide decimals:

1. 5 is 20% of what number? 25

2. 6 is 200% of what number? 3

3. $\frac{1}{3}$ is 50% of what number? $\frac{2}{3}$

4. 4.4 is 4.4% of what number? 100

WORKING WITH SIGNED NUMBERS

[21] Which of the following is the additive inverse of $-\frac{1}{2}$?

    (A) -2

    (B) 2

    (C) $\frac{1}{2}$

    (D) $-\frac{1}{2}$

    (E) 0

Your calculator has separate keys for the subtraction sign and the signs for negatives (opposites, additive inverses, etc.). Learn which is which. On most calculators, the subtraction sign key is labeled with $\boxed{-}$ and the negative sign by $\boxed{(-)}$.

For each given real number there exists a number that when added to it results in a sum of zero. This number is called the *additive inverse* of the given number and is designated by prefixing a "−" to the given number.

The additive inverse of 3 is -3, because $-3 + 3 = 0$.

The additive inverse of $\frac{2}{3}$ is $-\frac{2}{3}$, because $-\frac{2}{3} + \frac{2}{3} = 0$.

The additive inverse of -5 is $-(-5)$, because $-(-5) + (-5) = 0$. But $5 + (-5) = 0$, so $-(-5) = 5$.

Note that the additive inverse of a positive number is always negative and the additive inverse of a negative number is always positive. Zero is its own additive inverse.

[22] Find the sum of $5+(-8)+(-2)$.

    (A) -5

    (B) -10

    (C) 5

    (D) 2

    (E) -2

Having a calculator does not eliminate your need to know the rules of signed numbers.

The rules of operations on signed numbers are expressed most simply in terms of the absolute value of the number. The *absolute value* of a positive number is the number itself. The absolute value of a negative number is its additive inverse. The absolute value of 0 is 0.

Absolute value is designated by a pair of vertical bars flanking the number.

$$|6| = 6$$
$$|32| = 32$$
$$|0| = 0$$
$$|-2| = 2$$
$$\left|-\frac{1}{2}\right| = \frac{1}{2}$$

Note that no absolute value can ever be negative.

To add signed numbers:

1. If the numbers have like signs, add their absolute values and prefix the common sign;

2. If the numbers have unlike signs, subtract the absolute values and prefix the sign of the addend with the greater absolute value.

EXAMPLES

To add $(-2)+(-4)$, add the absolute values, 2 and 4, then prefix the common "$-$" to get -6.

To add $(-5)+3$, subtract the absolute values, 5 and 3, to get 2, then prefix the "$-$" sign because it is the sign of the number with the greater absolute value, -5. The result is -2.

To add 7 and (-4), subtract the absolute values, 7 and 4, to get 3, then prefix the "$+$" sign because it is the sign of the number with the greater absolute value, 7. The result is 3.

Remember that in a chain of calculations involving more than one operation, the operations are performed in order from left to right by first doing multiplication and division in the order in which they occur, and then addition and subtraction in the order in which they occur. Hence

$$5+(-8)+(-2) = -3+(-2)$$
$$= -5.$$

TEST-TAKING TIP

Testers assume a thorough knowledge of signed numbers and the ways to add, subtract, multiply and divide them. Distractors are frequently made from common errors in the use of signs.

EXAMPLES

Find the value of each of the following mentally and then check with your calculator:

  1. $-3+(-7) = -10$

  2. $4+(-8) = -4$

  3. $(-18)+3 = -15$

  4. $(-5)+(-3) = -8$

[23] Find the value of $3-(-2)-4$.

    (A) -5

    (B) -3

    (C) 3

    (D) 1

    (E) -1

By calculator, you must be able to use both the subtraction and negative keys, but you still need to know the principles by which subtraction of signed numbers is carried out.

To subtract a signed number, add its opposite. In other words, convert the problem from one of subtraction to one of addition and then follow the procedure outlined in the preceding section.

$$5-(-3) = 5+3 = 8$$
$$-7-2 = (-7)+(-2) = -9$$
$$-4-(-4) = -4+4 = 0$$
$$-5-(-2) = -5+2 = -3$$

Again, in a chain of operations, work from left to right, completing the operations in order.

$$3-(-2)-4 = 3+2+(-4)$$
$$= 5+(-4)$$
$$= 1$$

EXAMPLES

Verify the values of each of the following:

1. $-3 - 7 = -10$

2. $4 - 8 = -4$

3. $-18 - (-3) = -15$

4. $-5 - 3 = -8$

[24] Find the value of $(3 - 7)(1 - 4)(-\frac{1}{2})$.

(A) 3

(B) −4

(C) −6

(D) 12

(E) 6

Does your calculator have parentheses keys? Practice using them here and then review the properties of multiplication for signed numbers.

To multiply signed numbers, multiply their absolute values and prefix a positive sign if the factors have like signs or a negative sign if the factors have unlike signs. In other words, the product of like signs is always positive; the product of unlike signs is always negative.

EXAMPLES

$$(-2)(-3) = 6$$
$$(-8)\left(\frac{1}{2}\right) = -4$$
$$(3)\left(-\frac{1}{3}\right) = -1$$

In the multiple-choice question, the operations inside the parentheses must be completed first, as explained in section [3] of this chapter; then the multiplication is carried out in order from left to right.

$$
\begin{aligned}
(3 - 7)(1 - 4)\left(-\frac{1}{2}\right) &= (-4)(-3)\left(-\frac{1}{2}\right) \\
&= (12)\left(-\frac{1}{2}\right) \\
&= -6
\end{aligned}
$$

EXAMPLES

Verify the values of each of the following mentally and then by calculator:

1. $(-2)(3 - 6) = 6$

2. $4(1 - 3) - 3(-3 + 2) = -5$

3. $(25)(-3) + (25)(-1) = -100$

4. $\left(-\frac{3}{4}\right)\left(-\frac{2}{3}\right)\left(\frac{2}{5}\right) = \frac{1}{5} = .20$

[25] Find the value of $(-3) \div \left(-\frac{3}{2}\right) \div \left(-\frac{1}{8}\right)$.

(A) −36

(B) −16

(C) $\frac{9}{16}$

(D) $-\frac{9}{16}$

(E) 12

Here's more practice for your parentheses and division keys.

The rules of signs for division of signed numbers are the same as those for multiplication; like signs give a positive quotient, unlike signs give a negative quotient. The first step in the problem above is to divide -3 by $-\frac{3}{2}$. The like signs indicate that the solution is positive, so the procedure is merely to divide 3 by $\frac{3}{2}$; inverting the divisor and multiplying gives 2 as the result. To divide this result, 2, by $-\frac{1}{8}$, first determine the sign. Since the signs are unlike, the result must be negative; inverting and multiplying yields -16.

EXAMPLES

Verify each of the following with and without your calculator:

1. $7 \div \left(-\frac{1}{7}\right) = -49$

2. $-121 \div (-11) \div (-11) = -1$

3. $\left(-\frac{1}{3}\right) \div \left(-\frac{2}{3}\right) = \frac{1}{2}$

4. $(-.4) \div (-4) \div (.04) = 2.5$

[26] If $\frac{2}{3}x = 0$, then $\frac{2}{3} - x =$

(A) $\frac{2}{3}$

(B) 0

(C) $\frac{1}{3}$

(D) $\frac{4}{9}$

(E) 2

This question is far simpler than it seems at first sight. It involves no computation with fractions at all and takes only the realization that a product can be zero only if a factor is zero. Therefore, x must be zero and subtracting x from $\frac{2}{3}$ leaves the number unchanged.

The answer, therefore, is $\frac{2}{3}$

Think before you punch.

[27] A jar contains three colors of candies. Two-fifths are red, $\frac{1}{3}$ are green and the remaining 4 are yellow. How many candies are in the jar?

(A) 10

(B) 12

(C) 15

(D) 18

(E) 30

Calculators aside, skill with fractions can be a major factor in successfully applying algebraic concepts. This problem is readily solved by representing the unknown number of candies in the jar with a variable, then solving the equation. Solving that equation requires skill with arithmetic of fractions.

Let x = the number of candies in the jar.

Then $\frac{2}{5}x$ is the number of red and $\frac{1}{3}x$ the number of green. The equation, therefore, is

(# of red) + (# of green) + (# of yellow) = (# in jar)

$$\frac{2}{5}x \quad + \quad \frac{1}{3}x \quad + \quad 4 \quad = \quad x$$

Solve the equation by changing $\frac{2}{5}$ and $\frac{1}{3}$ to common denominators ($\frac{6}{15}$ and $\frac{5}{15}$), adding them ($\frac{11}{15}$) and subtracting $\frac{11}{15}x$ from both sides:

$$4 = \frac{4}{15}x.$$

Now multiply both sides by $\frac{15}{4}$ (the reciprocal of $\frac{4}{15}$) and you find that there are 15 candies in the jar.

An easier way to solve the equation is to multiply both sides by 15, the lowest common denominator. The resulting equation will no longer have fractions, and you may find it easier to solve.

$$6x + 5x + 60 = 15x \quad \text{(combine like terms)}$$

$$11x + 60 = 15x \quad \text{(subtract 11 from each side)}$$

$$60 = 4x \quad \text{(divide each side by 4)}$$

$$15 = x$$

TEST-TAKING TIP

Because choices are given, this question is a good example of how the correct solution can be found simply by working backward. Since there must be a whole number of candies, that number must be divisible by both 5 and 3, the two denominators of the fractions. So you have narrowed your answers down to 15 and 30. Thirty won't work because one-third of it, 10, plus two-fifths of it, 12, when added to 4 yields 26, not 30.

TEST-TAKING TIP

Afraid of word problems? The bad news is you can count on finding a half dozen or so on each Level IC test. The good news is they are seldom complicated or hard to understand. You may be accustomed to encountering challenging word problems, often poorly worded, in your textbooks or classroom exercises. The ones on the Level IC test are usually phrased succinctly and clearly.

DRAWING CONCLUSIONS ABOUT ODD AND EVEN NUMBERS

[28] If a and b are odd numbers, c is an even number and $x = a + bc$, which of the following must be true of x?

(A) x is always odd.

(B) x is always even.

(C) x is even when a, b, and c are positive and odd when they are negative.

(D) x is even when all of a, b, and c are negative and odd when they are all positive.

(E) Nothing can be determined about whether x is odd or even.

Arithmetic with signed numbers follows a simple pattern:

$$\text{odd} + \text{odd} = \text{even}$$
$$\text{odd} + \text{even} = \text{odd}$$
$$\text{even} + \text{even} = \text{even}$$
$$\text{odd} \times \text{odd} = \text{odd}$$
$$\text{odd} \times \text{even} = \text{even}$$
$$\text{even} \times \text{even} = \text{even}$$

In the multiple-choice question, b is odd and c is even, so bc is even. Because a is odd and bc is even, $a + bc$ is odd.

WORKING WITH ABSOLUTE VALUES

[29] If $a + 5 = b$, then which of the following is

$$|b - a| + |a - b|?$$

(A) 0

(B) 10

(C) 5

(D) −5

(E) Cannot be determined

Since $a + 5 = b$, it follows that

$$b - a = 5 \quad \text{and} \quad a - b = -5,$$

by subtracting the appropriate expressions from each side. Therefore both $|b - a|$ and $|a - b|$ are 5.

Test yourself:

1. Is $|b-a| = |a-b|$ always true?

2. Is $|a-b|^2 = (a-b)^2$ always true?

3. Is $-(a-b) = b-a$ always true?

All of 1, 2, and 3 are true.

WORKING WITH REMAINDERS

[30] When p is divided by 7, the remainder is 1. When q is divided by 7, the remainder is 2. What will the remainder be if the product pq is divided by 7?

(A) 1

(B) 2

(C) 3

(D) 5

(E) 7

TEST-TAKING TIP

You probably have never seen a question like this one before, and when you encounter questions relating to unfamiliar material on the Mathematics Level IC test, you may decide to skip them. Skipping unfamiliar questions in order to devote time to the familiar ones can be a wise procedure, but do not reject a question you have not read carefully. Quite often a simple approach will get the answer quickly, as is true in this case.

Certainly a great deal of mathematical machinery can be cranked up to work on the problem of remainders after division by prime numbers. The development of theories about such things may be the life's work of a theoretical mathematician, but only a bit of common sense is needed on this one.

Choose a pair of numbers that satisfy the requirements for p and q; for example, 8 and 9. The remainders are, respectively, 1 and 2. Their product is 72. Dividing 72 by 7 gives a remainder of 2. The question has been answered. Will the remainder always be 2? A more involved approach to the question proves that it will be. To satisfy the requirements, p must be of the form $7m+1$ and q of the form $7n+2$, where m and n are whole numbers. The product of these numbers is

$$(7m+1)(7n+2) = 49mn + 14m + 7n + 2$$
$$= 7(7mn + 2m + n) + 2.$$

The number in parentheses must be a whole number since it is composed of sums and products of wholes. Therefore the expression $7(7mn+2m+n)$ must be divisible by 7 since it clearly has a factor of 7. Hence, the remainder must be 2 no matter what p and q are.

How do you represent a remainder on your calculator? After dividing, subtract the whole number part of the quotient to leave only the decimal portion. Now multiply the decimal by the divisor. For example, $23 \div 7 = 3.285714286$. Subtract 3, which leaves .285714286. Then multiply by 7 to get 2.0000000002. This was an easy question, so you knew the answer was 2. But what about that extra 2 sitting in the tenth decimal place in some calculators? It's an accuracy error that results from the way some calculators carry out their results. A second strange thing can occur when you try this with some types of repeating decimals. Try $4 \div 3$. The result is 1.333333. Subtract the 1 to get .333333. Now multiply by 3 to change the decimal back to a whole number. This time the result is .99999...but you were expecting 1. The number 1 is the same as the infinitely repeating decimal .9999..., a fact that your calculator is using here.

EXAMPLES

Using the numbers 9 and 17 with a divisor of 5, verify the following statements about the remainders:

1. The sum of the remainders is not the remainder of the sum.

2. The product of the remainders is not the remainder of the product.

3. The quotient of the remainders is not the remainder of the quotient.

4. The difference of the remainders is not the remainder of the difference.

TEST-TAKING TIP

Have you noticed how our discussion has moved in a very interesting direction, even though the question that started it has already been answered? Interesting questions should stimulate interesting points for you to ponder, but your first goal when taking a subject test is to answer as many questions as quickly and accurately as possible. Some fine students have done poorly merely because they have devoted more time than necessary to mulling over the ramifications of questions they have already answered. By all means, explore the fascinating aspects of mathematical questions, but do it after the test is over.

[31] A jar contains 10 ounces of gumdrops, 3 ounces of licorice bits, and 2 ounces of jelly beans. How many more ounces of jelly beans must be added to make the assortment 50 percent jelly beans in weight?

(A) 2

(B) 3

(C) 6

(D) 11

(E) 60

Let $x =$ the number of ounces of jelly beans to be added.

Then the final weight of the jelly beans in the assortment will be $2 + x$.

And the total weight of all of the candies is

$$10 + 3 + 2 + x.$$

Therefore, the equation is

(# of oz. of
jelly beans) = (50% of total weight)

$$2 + x = .50(10 + 3 + 2 + x)$$

$$2 + x = .5(15 + x)$$

$$4 + 2x = 15 + x \qquad \text{(multiply each side by 2 to change .5 to 1)}$$

$$x = 11$$

In this question, you must do some calculations with a number expressed as a percent. We've changed it to a decimal, but we could just as readily have used the fractional equivalent. You should be so familiar with relations between percents, decimals, and fractions that you can easily transform a numerical expression from one form to another without computation.

TEST-TAKING TIP

The central idea in solving most word problems is to determine what two things are equal and then compose an equation relating the two equal quantities. Here, the two equal entities are both expressions for the same thing: the number of jellybeans in the final mixture.

TEST-TAKING TIP

Most of the answer choices given above either repeat numbers given in the problem (for example, 2 and 3) or are simple combinations of those numbers ($2 \times 3 = 6$ and $2 \times 3 \times 10 = 60$). The correct answer, 11, is none of these. If a question like this were to occur early in the test, the correct choice would probably be a repeat or simple combination. If, on the other hand, it occurred late in the test, it would most likely not be a simple combination of the given numbers.

---

[32] For what values of a could $(a - 1)(1 - a)$ be 1?

I. 0

II. 1

III. All negative real numbers

(A) I only

(B) II only

(C) III only

(D) All of I, II, and III

(E) None of I, II, or III

This question uses a favorite device of test makers:

$$(x - y) = -(y - x).$$

In the multiple-choice question, note that $a - 1$ is the opposite of $1 - a$. Except for zero, every number is opposite in sign from its opposite number. When two numbers of unlike signs are multiplied, the results is always negative. Therefore, $(a - 1)(1 - a)$ must always be negative and can never be 1.

If you did not recognize the principle at work here, you could answer this question easily by trying 0 and 1 for a. When $a = 0$, the product is -1 and when $a = 1$, the product is 0. This leaves (C) and (E) as your only options. Test any negative number you wish, say, -1 for a and you will see that it does not work. That will eliminate choice (C) and leave you with (E).

[33] If $.03636 = 3.636 \times 10^n$, $n = ?$

(A) -100

(B) -2

(C) -1

(D) 2

(E) 100

When you write a number in the form of this question, you are changing it to "scientific notation." Experience with scientific notation is helpful here, but you can answer the question readily without it.

$$.03636 = 3.636 \times .01$$
$$= 3.636 \times 10^{-2}$$

Therefore, $n = -2$, (B).

Learning a few rules can help you write numbers in scientific notation quickly.

A number is in scientific notation when it is written in the form $m \times 10^n$ where $1 \leq m \leq 10$ and n is an integer.

To find m, shift the decimal point until it is immediately to the right of the first non-zero digit. To determine n, count the number of places you shifted the decimal point. It you shifted it to the left, n is the number of places. If you shifted it right, n is the opposite of the number of places.

EXAMPLES

$$363.6 = 3.636 \times 10^2$$
$$36.36 = 3.636 \times 10^1$$
$$3.636 = 3.636 \times 10^0$$
$$.3636 = 3.636 \times 10^{-1}$$
$$.03636 = 3.636 \times 10^{-2}$$

[34] If p and q are even integers, which of the following must be odd?

(A) $p(q+1)$

(B) $(p-1)(q+1)$

(C) $q(p-1)$

(D) $pq-p$

(E) $p^2 - q^2$

Let's examine each choice:

(A) The factor $q+1$ must be odd because q is even. But multiplying $q+1$ by p must produce an even result because p is even.

(B) Both factors are odd because each is either one more or one less than an even number. The product of odd numbers must be odd.

(C) Because q is even, the product must be even.

(D) Factor $pq-p$ and the result is $p(q-1)$. The product is even because p is even.

(E) Factor $p^2 - q^2$ to get $(p-q)(p+q)$. Both factors are even because the sum and difference of two even numbers is even.

Can p or q be zero and does that affect the result?

Zero is an even number, which meets the given condition. Therefore, everything said in each discussion applies to zero. When in doubt, try it out. Substitute 0 for p and q as appropriate to see what happens.

WHAT YOU SHOULD KNOW

KEY CONCEPTS

Handling Decimal Numbers

1. *To add (or subtract) decimal numerals*, line up the decimal points above each other when writing the numerals and add (or subtract) digits in the same column.
2. *To multiply decimal numerals*, ignore the decimal points and multiply as though the numerals represented whole numbers. Then count up the number of decimal places in the multipliers and point off this total in the answer, counting from right to left. Prefix as many zeros as needed to fill out the total before placing the decimal point.
3. *To divide decimal numerals*, reposition the decimal point by transferring it to the right of the divisor. Then transfer the decimal point the same number of places in the dividend. Position the decimal point in the quotient directly above the decimal point in the dividend.

Handling Fractions

1. *To reduce a fraction*, first factor the numerator and the denominator. Then strike out common factors.
2. *To raise a fraction to higher terms*, multiply the numerator and the denominator by the number needed to produce the desired denominator. This multiplier can be found by dividing the given denominator into the desired denominator.
3. *To add (or subtract) fractions*, change to a common denominator, then add (or subtract) numerators.
4. *To multiply fractions*, multiply numerators and multiply denominators. If a factor is common to any numerator and any denominator, it may be removed before multiplying.
5. *To divide fractions*, invert the divisor and multiply as in item 4.

Handling Conversions

1. *To change a fraction to a decimal*, divide the numerator by the denominator.
2. *To change a decimal to a percent*, shift the decimal point two places to the right and annex the percent sign.
3. *To change a percent to a decimal*, shift the decimal point two places to the left and remove the percent sign.

Handling Percentage Problems

1. *To calculate a percent of a given number*, change the percent to a decimal and multiply this decimal by the given number.
2. *To answer the question "What percent of* a *is* b*?"* set up the proportion

$$\frac{x}{100} = \frac{b}{a}$$

and solve it for *x*.
3. *To answer the question "*a *is* b*% of what number?"* set up the proportion

$$\frac{a}{x} = \frac{b}{100}$$

and solve it for *x*.

Handling Signed Numbers

1. *To add signed numbers with like signs*, add their absolute values and prefix the common sign.
2. *To add signed numbers with unlike signs*, subtract their absolute values and prefix the sign of the number with the greater absolute value.
3. *To subtract signed numbers*, change the sign of the number to be subtracted; then proceed as in addition.
4. *To multiply signed numbers with like signs*, multiply their absolute values.
5. *To multiply signed numbers with unlike signs*, multiply their absolute values and prefix a negative sign to the product.
6. *To divide signed numbers with like signs*, divide their absolute values.
7. *To divide signed numbers with unlike signs*, divide their absolute values and prefix a negative sign.

KEY FORMULAS

1. To find what percent (*x*) one number (*b*) is of another number (*a*):
$$\frac{x}{100} = \frac{b}{a}.$$

2. To find of what number (*x*) another number (*a*) is a given percentage (*b* %):
$$\frac{a}{x} = \frac{b}{100}.$$

TEST-TAKING STRATEGIES

- When dealing with an arithmetic question involving signed numbers, examine the answer choices carefully so that you can eliminate any in which signs are obviously used incorrectly.
- When dealing with decimal numbers, check to be sure the decimal is in the correct place in your answer. Often, distractors may be eliminated because the decimal point is improperly placed.
- Correct answers are always reduced fractions unless otherwise specified. An unreduced fraction is almost always an incorrect choice and can usually be eliminated unless the question specifically asks for an unreduced fraction. Keep this in mind.
- When numerical calculations appear to be very complicated and time-consuming, reread the question and check the answer choices to see if a simpler, more insightful, approach will get the desired answer.

CALCULATOR SKILLS

 Before going further, you should be sure you know:

- The order in which your calculator carries out the operations of $+$, $-$, $\times$, and $\div$.
- How to insert parentheses to change the order of operations.
- How your calculator represents fractions.
- How to input negative numbers (know the difference between the subtraction and negative keys).
- How many digits your calculator displays and the accuracy with which it displays answers.
- Whether your calculator automatically rounds off the last digit displayed.
- How to change your displayed number from a decimal to a percent (multiply by 100) and from a percent to its decimal equivalent (divide by 100).

ANSWERS

[1] (B)	[7] (D)	[13] (E)	[19] (D)	[25] (B)	[31] (D)
[2] (B)	[8] (E)	[14] (A)	[20] (D)	[26] (A)	[32] (E)
[3] (B)	[9] (B)	[15] (A)	[21] (C)	[27] (C)	[33] (B)
[4] (D)	[10] (C)	[16] (C)	[22] (A)	[28] (A)	[34] (B)
[5] (B)	[11] (C)	[17] (C)	[23] (D)	[29] (B)	
[6] (C)	[12] (A)	[18] (C)	[24] (C)	[30] (B)	

THE REAL NUMBERS

CHAPTER

6

KEY TERMS

KEY TERMS

natural number	any number in the set $\{1, 2, 3, \dots\}$.
whole number	any number in the set $\{0, 1, 2, 3, \dots\}$.
integer	any number in the set $\{\dots, -3, -2, -1, 0, 1, 2, 3, \dots\}$.
rational number	any number in the set $\{$all numbers that can be written in the form $\dfrac{p}{q}$ where p and q are integers and q is not zero$\}$. Examples: $\dfrac{1}{3} = 0.333\dots, \dfrac{1}{4} = 0.25$.
irrational number	any number in the set $\{$all numbers that do not have repeating or terminal decimal representations$\}$. Examples: $\sqrt{2}, \sqrt{1}, \pi, -1010010001\dots$.
real number	any number in the set $\{$all rationals and irrationals$\}$.

Before beginning this chapter, learn how to use the radical key, $\boxed{\sqrt{x}}$ and how to raise a number to a power, x^y. Also, locate your $\boxed{\pi}$ key and learn how to display its value when needed. (Consult your calculator manual.)

NAMES FOR NUMBERS

[1]   Which of the following values of p is a counterexample to "$\sqrt{p}$ is irrational when p is an odd integer."

(A) 3

(B) 11

(C) 9

(D) 5

(E) 7

TEST-TAKING TIP

Test makers really do expect you to know the names of sets of numbers. If you can't tell an "irrational" number from an "integer," you'll miss easy questions like this one. The number 9 is an odd integer, but $\sqrt{9}$ is 3, a rational number. Besides being rational, the number 3 is, of course, also an odd integer. You must be sure you know how these terms apply to common numbers.

Natural numbers $= \{1, 2, 3, \ldots\}$.

Whole numbers $= \{0, 1, 2, 3, \ldots\}$.

Integers $= \{\ldots, -3, -2, -1, 0, 1, 2, 3 \ldots\}$.

Rational numbers $= \{$all numbers that can be written in the form $\frac{p}{q}$ where p and q, are integers and q is not zero.$\}$

Note that each of the sets just listed contains each of the sets that precede it. In the decimal form displayed on your calculator the rational numbers are readily recognized since they either repeat digits infinitely (as in $\frac{2}{3} = 0.666\ldots$ and $\frac{1}{7} = 0.142857142857\ldots$) or terminate $\left(\frac{1}{2} = 0.5,\ \frac{2}{5} = 0.4\right)$.

Does your calculator round off the last decimal digit displayed? If so, you need to interpret your display accordingly.

Irrational numbers $= \{$all numbers that do not have repeating or terminating decimal representations$\}$. Therefore the set of irrational numbers contains no natural numbers, whole numbers, integers, or rational numbers.

Examples of irrationals are $\pi = 3.14159\ldots$ and $\sqrt{2} = 1.4142\ldots$.

Real numbers $= \{$all rationals and irrationals$\}$.

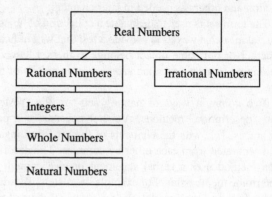

EXAMPLES

Give an example of:

1. a whole number that is not a natural number

2. an integer that is not a natural number

3. a rational number that is not an integer

4. an integer that is irrational

5. an irrational number that is real

Answers:

1. 0

2. $-1, -2, -3, \ldots$

3. $\frac{1}{2}, \frac{2}{3}, \frac{3}{4} \ldots$

4. none are irrational

5. all are real

WORKING WITH SET THEORY

[2]   If $P = \{x : x = 1\}$, Q is the set of all numbers which are equal to their squares, $R = \{0, 1\}$, $S = \emptyset$ and $T = \{0\}$, then which of the following is true?

(A) $P = Q$

(B) $Q = R$

(C) $R = S$

(D) $S = T$

(E) $P = R$

To discuss much of intermediate math in contemporary terms we must first establish some of the fundamentals of set theory. We will review a few facts about sets in this section and others as needed in later chapters.

The term *set* is used to designate a collection of objects named in such a way as to provide a test that will indicate whether or not some object belongs to the set. Objects belonging to a set are called *elements* or *members* of the set.

Two common ways of naming sets are the "roster" and "description" methods. A roster consists of a pair of braces, { }, with the elements of the set listed inside and separated from each other by commas. The description method uses a verbal statement precise enough to determine membership. For example the roster {Tuesday, Thursday} and the description "the set of all days of the week that have '*T*' as their first letter" both refer to the same set. Two sets, such as these, that have exactly the same elements are called *equal* sets.

A third procedure for naming a set is a combination of the roster and description types and makes use of the *set-builder* notation. For example, $\{x : x = 1\}$ is read "the set of all x such that x equals 1" and is just another way of describing $\{1\}$.

Whenever we use the roster or set-builder and the elements of the set are too numerous for all to be written out, we write as many elements as are necessary to show the pattern intended and then insert three dots, ..., read "and so on," to show that the pattern continues. If the set is finite (can be counted with the counting coming to an end) we are careful to place the final element to the right of the three dots as in $A = \{1, 2, 3, 4, \ldots, 100\}$. If no element appears to the right of the dots, it indicates that the set is infinite and, therefore, continues on in the same pattern, as in $B = \{1, 2, 3, 4, \ldots\}$.

Note that sets A and B above are not equal (symbolized by $A \neq B$).

If a set contains no elements, we call it the *empty set* and use the symbol $\emptyset$ or { }. Note that $\{0\} \neq \emptyset$, since $\{0\}$ contains the element 0 and $\emptyset$ contains no elements.

If every element of a set A is also an element of a set B, then we say that A is a *subset* of B. Further, we agree to consider $\emptyset$ to be a subset of every set. For example, the subsets of $A = \{a, b, c\}$ are $\emptyset$, $\{a\}$, $\{b\}$, $\{c\}$, $\{a, b\}$, $\{a, c\}$, $\{b, c\}$, $\{a, b, c\}$. Note that the last of these is A itself.

To answer the multiple-choice question above, use the given information to write a roster for each set: $P = \{1\}$, $Q = \{0, 1\}, R = \{0, 1\}, S = \{\ \}, T = \{0\}$; then the correct answer becomes obvious.

TEST-TAKING TIP

To answer comparison questions, it is usually helpful to put all items to be compared into the same form.

APPLYING THE FIVE LAWS OF ADDITION

[3]   Each of the following equations is true for all real numbers a, b, and c, EXCEPT

(A) $a + (b + c) = (a + c) + b$

(B) $a + (b + c) = (a + b) + c$

(C) $a - (b - c) = (a - b) - c$

(D) $a - (b - c) = (c - b) + a$

(E) $a - (b + c) = a - (c + b)$

The fundamental procedures of elementary algebra can be derived from a relatively few basic assumptions about the operations of addition and multiplication. In this and the next several sections we will review eleven elementary statements that we will accept as the basic laws of the real numbers.

We are using the names of the laws throughout the chapter for ease of reference. Knowing the names is not essential to complete the problems. However, you need to know how the laws apply to mathematics.

I.   CLOSURE LAW OF ADDITION
     If a and b are real numbers, then $a + b$ is a real number.

II. COMMUTATIVE LAW OF ADDITION
     If a and b are real numbers, then $a + b = b + a$.

III. ASSOCIATIVE LAW OF ADDITION
     If a and b are real numbers, then $(a + b) + c = a + (b + c)$.

Closure asserts that the sum of any two real numbers will always be a real number. The Commutative law says that the result of addition does not depend on the order in which the terms are added.

The Associative law says that regrouping the sum of three numbers does not change the sum. By definition the sum of three numbers, $a + b + c$, is the sum of the first two added to the last. It is thereby written $(a + b) + c$ since parentheses indicate operations that are to be performed first. In effect Law II guarantees that the sum of $a + b + c$ is $a + (b + c)$ as well as $(a + b) + c$.

Law II guarantees the truth of (A) and (E) above, since it says the order in which addition is carried out doesn't change the result. Law III directly states the equation given in (B). Therefore, you need to choose between (C) and (D). If your algebraic simplification skills fail you, try substituting 3, 2, and 1 for a, b, and c. You'll discover that (C) isn't true.

EXAMPLES

1. $(2+3)+4 = 2+(3+4)$, by III

2. $(2+3)+4 = 4+(2+3)$, by II

3. $(2+3)+4 = (3+2)+4$, by II

4. $(2+3)+4 = (4+3)+2$, by II and III

[4] If $x - 3(1-x) = 3(x-1) - 3$, then $x =$

(A) 0

(B) -1

(C) 2

(D) -3

(E) -2

The world of the "minus" sign is a quagmire that has swallowed up many unwary wanderers. By the time you have finished three years of high school math, however, you should have learned to recognize the safe pathways. The major rules of signs are reviewed below.

IV. **ADDITIVE INVERSE LAW**
For every real number b there exists a number $-b$ (called the additive inverse of b) such that $b + (-b) = 0$.

V. **ADDITIVE IDENTITY**
For every real number a, $a + 0 = a$.

We define the difference $a - b$ to be that number x such that $b + x = a$.

With subtraction defined in this way we can prove that

6-1 If a and b are real numbers, then

$$a - b = a + (-b).$$

For example:

$$3 - 2 = 3 + (-2) = 1$$

$$7 - 10 = 7 + (-10) = -3$$

$$-4 - 5 = -4 + (-5) = -9$$

Stated in words, Law 6-1 says, "To subtract a number, add its opposite."

Law V helps simplify expressions containing both subtraction and additive inverses.

6-2 If a and b are real numbers, then

$$a - (-b) = a + b.$$

Law 6-2 is really a slightly different way of writing, "To subtract a number, add its opposite." In this form the law makes subtraction of negative numbers easier to visualize.

6-3 If a and b are real numbers, then

$$(-a) + (-b) = -(a+b).$$

In words, Law 6-3 says, "The sum of the opposites of two numbers is the opposite of their sum."

If the equation in question [4] has mired you down, try changing all of the subtractions to addition.

$$x + (-3)(1 + [-x]) = 3(x + [-1]) + (-3)$$

Then distribute the multiplications (if you have trouble with the rules of multiplication, the next section is for you).

$$x + (-3) + 3x = 3x + (-3) + -3$$

Each side has the expression $-3 + 3x$ as an addend. Add its additive inverse to each side and you get

$$x = -3$$

EXAMPLES

Practice your ability to add and subtract signed numbers in your head and with your calculator:

1. $5 - 3 = 2$

2. $5 - (-3) = 8$

3. $-5 - 3 = -8$

4. $-5 - (-3) - 2$

5. $-(5 - 3) = -2$

6. $-(-5 - (-3)) = -8$

APPLYING THE FIVE LAWS OF MULTIPLICATION

[5]   Each of the following equations is true EXCEPT

(A) $(ab)\left(\dfrac{1}{b}\right) = a\left(b \cdot \dfrac{1}{b}\right)$ if $b \neq 0$

(B) $(ab)\left(\dfrac{1}{b}\right) = a$ if $b \neq 0$

(C) If $(ab)\left(\dfrac{1}{b}\right) = 0$, then $a = 0$

(D) $(ab)\left(\dfrac{1}{b}\right) = 0$ if $b = 0$

(E) $(ab)\left(\dfrac{1}{b}\right) = 0$ if $a = 0$

The following five laws of multiplication are similar to the assumptions already made for addition in the preceding section.

Again, we are listing them by name and number for ease of reference. Their names are not used on the Level IC test, but you need to know how to use the laws.

VI. CLOSURE LAW OF MULTIPLICATION
If a and b are real numbers, the product of a and b, written ab, is a real number.

VII. COMMUTATIVE LAW OF MULTIPLICATION
If a and b are real numbers, then $ab = ba$.

VIII. ASSOCIATIVE LAW OF MULTIPLICATION
If a, b, and c are real numbers, then $(ab)c = a(bc)$.

Note that the product of three numbers is defined as the product of the first two multiplied by the third. Law VIII guarantees that the result of multiplying the first by the product of the second and third is the same as the defined product, which verifies answer choice (A).

IX. MULTIPLICATIVE INVERSE
For every nonzero real number, a, there exists a number, $\dfrac{1}{a}$, called the multiplicative inverse of a, such that $a\left(\dfrac{1}{a}\right) = 1$. This verifies choice (B).

X. MULTIPLICATIVE IDENTITY
For every real number a, $a \cdot 1 = a$.

We will agree that when addition, subtraction, multiplication and division of any numbers are done to both sides of an equation, the result is another equation.

The property denoted 6-4 below is important in the solution of equations by factoring.

6-4   If a and b are real numbers and $ab = 0$, then
$$a = 0 \quad \text{or} \quad b = 0.$$

This property will be used in sections that review how to solve quadratic equations. It is the reason choice (C) is true—note that $b(\frac{1}{b}) = 1$.

Finally, an obvious rule included for completeness:

6-5   If a is a real number, then $a(0) = 0$.

In question [5], each of the choices seems to be an example of one of the properties just reviewed, but look closely at (D). It's impossible for b to be 0 if $\frac{1}{b}$ exists. And if $\frac{1}{b}$ does not exist, the left side of the equation is meaningless.

APPLYING THE DISTRIBUTIVE LAW

[6]   Each of the following equations is true EXCEPT

(A) $a[b + (-b)] = a[(-b) + b]$

(B) $a[b + (-b)] = (ab) + (-b)$

(C) $a[b + (-b)] = 0$

(D) $a[b + (-b)] = ab + a(-b)$

(E) $a[b + (-b)] = [b + (-b)]a$

The Distributive law completes the set of eleven assumptions from which the properties of the real numbers derive. This law involves both addition and multiplication and provides the justification for much of the multiplication and factoring of algebraic expressions.

XI. DISTRIBUTIVE LAW
If a, b, and c are real, then

(1) $a(b + c) = ab + ab$.

Many texts include a second statement,

(2) $(b + c)a = ba + ca$,

as part of XI. Statement (2), however, can be derived from statement (1). We will use the term "Distributive law" to include both (1) and (2).

In question [6], (A) and (D) are direct applications of the Distributive law. Choice (B) is an incorrect use—a is not multiplied by the second term. Do you recognize the Additive Inverse law in (C) and the Commutative law of Multiplication in (E)?

Law XI can be generalized to apply to multipliers of more than two terms.

EXAMPLES

Verify the following equations:

1. $x(x + x^2) = x^2 + x^3$

2. $(a + b)(c + d) = (a + b)c + (a + b)d$

3. $bc - bd = b(c - d)$

4. $a^2 + a + ab + b = (a + b)(a + 1)$

DERIVING LAWS OF SIGNS

[7] If a is a positive number and b is negative, which of the following is also negative?

(A) $-(ab)$

(B) $(-a)b$

(C) $a(-b)$

(D) $a - b$

(E) ab

The laws of signs for the multiplication of positive and negative real numbers can be derived from some of the preceding discussions in this chapter. These laws should be familiar to students of even the most elementary algebra but are included here for reference.

In the multiple-choice question, since a is positive and b is negative, the number ab [choice (E)] is negative. Since ab is negative, the number $-(ab)$ [choice (A)] must be positive. Since $-a$ is negative and b is negative, $(-a)b$ [choice (B)] is positive. Since a is positive and $-b$ is positive, $a(-b)$ [choice (C)] is positive. Choice (D) gives the greater number, a, minus the lesser number, b, so $a - b$ must be positive.

Two more multiplication properties for signed numbers are very useful:

6-6   If a is a real number, then $a(-1) = -a$.

6-7   If a and b are real, then $a(-b) = -(ab)$.

EXAMPLES

By the time you take the Math Level IC test, calculation with signed numbers should be second nature to you. Practice the following in your head and verify the results with your calculator:

1. $5 - 6 - (-7) - 1 = 5$

2. $9(7 - 3) - 2(-5) = 46$

3. $(-2)^3(2)^2 = -32$

4. $(-1) + (-1)^2 + (-1)^3 + (-1)^4 = 0$

5. $(10 - 5) - 3 = 2$

6. $-2(3)(-8) = 48$

7. If $x = -3$ then $(x + 3)^2 - 6x = 18$

8. $\dfrac{-2(-8)}{(-2 + (-8))} = -1.6$

9. If $a = 2$ and $b = -1$ then $\dfrac{a - b}{a + b} = 3$

10. $6 - \dfrac{4(4 - 9)}{5} = 10$

11. $(4 - 3)(2 - 3)(2 - 1)(1 - 2) = 1$

12. The arithmetic mean of -9, -8, 8, and 9 is 0.

DEALING WITH INVENTED OPERATIONS

[8] The symbol $\odot$ is defined as follows: $A \odot B = 2A + 2B$, when A and B are real numbers. Each of the following is true EXCEPT

(A) $A \odot B = B \odot A$

(B) $A \odot (B \odot C) = (A \odot B) \odot C$

(C) $A \odot 0 = 2A$

(D) $A \odot B$ is always a real number

(E) $A \odot B + B \odot A = 2A \odot 2B$

TEST-TAKING TIP

The operation $\odot$ is one that you have not encountered before, since it was defined specifically for this question in order to test your general understanding of the properties of operations in number systems. Questions like this are frequently used by test-makers.

(A) Is $A \odot B = B \odot A$? According to the definition of $\odot$ as given, $A \odot B = 2A + 2B$ and $B \odot A = 2B + 2A$. Since $2B + 2A = 2A + 2B$ by the Commutative Property of Addition, it follows that $A \odot B = B \odot A$.

(B) Is $(A \odot B) \odot C = A \odot (B \odot C)$?

$$(A \odot B) \odot C = 2(2A + 2B) + 2C$$
$$= 4A + 4B + 2C$$

$$A \odot (B \odot C) = 2A + 2(2B + 2C)$$
$$= 2A + 4B + 4C$$

(C) Is $A \odot 0 = 2A$?

$$A \odot 0 = 2A + 2 \cdot 0 = 2A$$

(D) $A \odot B$ is defined by a series of applications of addition and multiplication. Since these basic operations are closed in the real number system, so must $\odot$ be.

(E) $A \odot B + B \odot A = 2A + 2B + 2B + 2A$
$\qquad\qquad = 2(2A) + 2(2B)$
$\qquad\qquad = 2A \odot 2B$

TEST-TAKING TIP

Note that part (E) is quite complicated but the calculation is a waste of test time. Because choice (B) has already been judged to be the answer, no further work needs to be done. On a multiple-choice test, once you have found the correct response, go on to the next question. Return to such questions only if you complete the test early and wish to double-check your work by examining the answer choices you didn't analyze the first time.

EXAMPLES

If $A = 1$ and $B = -1$, verify the values of each of the following expressions with invented operations:

1. $A \odot B = \dfrac{A + B}{AB} = 0$

2. $A * B = (A - B)^2 = 4$

3. $A \triangle B = A + \dfrac{1}{B} = 0$

4. $\boxed{AB} = A + AB = 0$

5. $A \top B = A^B = 1$

SOLVING EQUATIONS INVOLVING ABSOLUTE VALUES

[9]   If a is a negative real number, then which of the following is NOT true?

    (A) $|a| = -a$

    (B) $|a| = a$

    (C) $-|a| = a$

    (D) $|a|^2 = a^2$

    (E) If $x^2 = a^2$, then $|x| = |a|$

For every real number, a, except 0, either a or $-a$ will be a positive number. Note that $-a$ is a positive number when a is negative.

The *absolute value* of any number a, symbolized by $|a|$, is always the nonnegative choice of a or $-a$. If a is positive or zero, then a is its own absolute value.

(1) $|a| = a$ when a is positive or zero. [This contradicts choice (B).]
If a is a negative number, then $-a$ is positive and is thereby the absolute value of a.

(2) $|a| = -a$ when a is negative. [This verifies choice (A).]
Statement (2) is difficult for many students to grasp because, at first glance, it appears to say that a certain absolute value is negative. However, remember that when a is negative, $-a$ is positive!

EXAMPLES

In each of the following a is positive and b negative. Verify that only 1. and 2. are negative.

1. ab

2. $|a||b|$

3. $|ab|$

4. $a|b|$

5. $|a|b$

6. $a + |b|$

7. $|a| - b$

[10] Which of the following sets contains all of the real values of x for which $|2x + 1| = 3$ is true?

(A) $\{1\}$

(B) $\{1, -1\}$

(C) $\{-1\}$

(D) $\{1, -2\}$

(E) $\{1, 2\}$

A simple result of the definition of absolute value is that when a is nonnegative and $|x| = a$, then x has the two values a and $-a$.

6-8   If $|x| = a$, then $x = a$ or $x = -a$.

This consequence is useful in solving equations involving absolute values.

EXAMPLE

Find y if $|3y - 2| = 4$.

SOLUTION: Since $|3y - 2| = 4$, then

$$
\begin{array}{rclcrcl}
3y - 2 &=& 4 & \text{or} & 3y - 2 &=& -4, \\
3y &=& 6 & \text{or} & 3y &=& -2, \\
y &=& 2 & \text{or} & y &=& -\frac{2}{3}
\end{array}
$$

The set of values that makes the equation true is $\{2, -\frac{2}{3}\}$.

In the multiple-choice question, since $|2x + 1| = 3$, it follows that

$$
\begin{array}{rclcrcl}
2x + 1 &=& 3 & \text{or} & 2x + 1 &=& -3, \\
2x &=& 2 & \text{or} & 2x &=& -4, \\
x &=& 1 & \text{or} & x &=& -2, \\
&& & \{-2, 1\}. &
\end{array}
$$

▨ To solve this absolute value equation on a graphing calculator, enter $|2x + 1| - 3$ in your $y =$ menu and then find the points at which the graph crosses the x-axis.

EXAMPLES

1. If $|x| = 3$, then $x = \pm 3$.

2. If $|2x| = 5$, then $x = \pm \frac{5}{2}$.

3. If $|x - 3| = 6$, then $x = 9$ or -3.

4. If $|4x - 1| = 7$, then $x = 2$ or $-\frac{3}{2}$.

CONVERTING REPEATING DECIMALS TO FRACTIONS

---

[11] If $x = .\overline{51}$, where the bar indicates that the digits under it repeat without stopping, write x as a fraction.

(A) $\dfrac{51}{100}$

(B) $\dfrac{5}{9}$

(C) $\dfrac{51}{99}$

(D) $\dfrac{510}{100}$

(E) No fraction is possible

In section [1] of this chapter we defined a rational number as any number that could be written as the ratio of two integers p and q where q is not zero. At the same time we mentioned that rational numbers can be written as decimals that terminate or in which a block of digits repeats interminably. When a rational number appears as a decimal, it is frequently useful to convert the decimal to its fractional form. Doing this in the case of a terminating decimal is easy since the position of the decimal indicates the denominator, as in:

$$.5 = \frac{5}{10} = \frac{1}{2}, \quad .51 = \frac{51}{100}, \quad \text{and} \quad 4.581 = \frac{4581}{1000}.$$

For repeating decimals the procedure is shown by the following examples:

EXAMPLE 1

Convert $.\overline{51}$ to a fraction.

SOLUTION: Let $x = .\overline{51}$; then $100x = 51.\overline{51}$ (we chose 100 as a multiplier because we wanted to shift the decimal point two places, two being the number of repeating digits).

$$
\begin{array}{rcl}
100x &=& 51.\overline{51} \\
x &=& .\overline{51} \\
\hline
\text{therefore} \quad 99x &=& 51 \quad \text{by subtraction} \\
x &=& \dfrac{51}{99}
\end{array}
$$

▨ This is answer choice (C) above. Check it and each of the other choices on your calculator.

EXAMPLE 2

Convert $3.2\overline{164}$ to a fraction.

SOLUTION: Let

$$x = 3.2\overline{164};$$

then

$$1000x = 3216.4\overline{164}$$

(we chose 1000 because we wanted to shift the decimal three places).

$$
\begin{aligned}
1000x &= 3216.4\overline{164} \\
x &= 3.2\overline{164} \\
\hline
999x &= 3213.2 \\
x &= \frac{3213.2}{999} \\
&= \frac{32132}{9990} \\
&= \frac{16016}{4995}
\end{aligned}
$$

EXAMPLES

1. $.\overline{3} = \dfrac{1}{3}$

2. $.0\overline{3} = \dfrac{1}{30}$

3. $2.0\overline{35} = \dfrac{2015}{990}$

4. $3.6\overline{831} = \dfrac{36795}{9990}$

WORKING WITH SIMPLE RADICALS

[12]   Each of the following is an irrational number EXCEPT

(A) $.1010010001\dots$

(B) $\sqrt{3}$

(C) $\sqrt{8}$

(D) $\sqrt{\sqrt{4}}$

(E) $\sqrt{-4}$

Most irrational numbers encountered in elementary algebra involve the radical sign. This sign, $\sqrt{}$, is used to denote the nonnegative square root of a nonnegative real number. In other words, if x and y are *positive*, then $\sqrt{x} = y$ if $x = y^2$. Furthermore $\sqrt{0} = 0$.

In other words, $\sqrt{}$ is always used to indicate a number that is positive or zero. Though it is true, for example, that -2 is *a* square root of 4, it is not the square root represented by the radical sign, and the statement $-2 = \sqrt{4}$ is *not* true.

We have previously defined rational numbers as ratios of integers and pointed out that they have repeating or terminating decimal equivalents. Decimals that do not either terminate or repeat represent irrational numbers. Answer (A) above is an example of a decimal for which no block of digits will repeat as long as the pattern indicated continues. Such nonrepeating, nonterminating decimals cannot be represented as the ratio of two integers and hence are nonrational. Merely being nonrational does not automatically make a number irrational.

Choice (E) is not rational but, certainly, cannot be found among any numbers we have mentioned. If a real number x were equal to $\sqrt{-4}$, then $x^2 = -4$. But the product x^2 always involves the multiplication of real numbers with like signs and can result only in a positive real number.

Know that $\sqrt{x}$, where x is a positive integer, is irrational as long as the prime factors of x (other than 1) do not all occur in pairs. It follows that (B) and (C) are irrational since (B) has only the prime factor 3 and the prime factorization of (C) is $2 \cdot 2 \cdot 2$ with the 2's not all in pairs. (D) is just another name for $\sqrt{2}$ (since $\sqrt{4}$ can be replaced by 2) and hence is irrational.

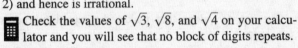 Check the values of $\sqrt{3}$, $\sqrt{8}$, and $\sqrt{4}$ on your calculator and you will see that no block of digits repeats.

TEST-TAKING TIP

Do not select or reject an answer choice merely because it is not in the same form as all of the others. Choice (A) for example, does not have a radical sign and the others do. Choice (D) has two radical signs, one inside the other. Nevertheless, all of the choices (A) through (D) satisfy the conditions of the question (they are irrational), and (E) is the correct response.

EXAMPLES

True or False?

1. $\sqrt{4} = 2$

2. $\sqrt{16} = \pm 4$

3. -3 is a square root of 9.

4. $-\sqrt{4} = -2$

(Only 2 is false.)

[13] Each of the following is equal to $2\sqrt{6}$ EXCEPT

(A) $\sqrt{6}+\sqrt{6}$

(B) $\sqrt{3}+\sqrt{3}$

(C) $\sqrt{24}$

(D) $\sqrt{3}\sqrt{8}$

(E) $\dfrac{\sqrt{96}}{2}$

Your calculator provides decimal approximations for numbers expressed as radicals. Even with this help, you will find the algebra of radicals to be useful for simplifying expressions.

> **6-9** If a and b are positive real numbers, then
>
> $$\sqrt{ab} = \sqrt{a}\sqrt{b}.$$

Using this law to simplify radical expressions, we attempt to write the number as the product of a perfect square and some other integer.

EXAMPLES

1. $\sqrt{18} = \sqrt{9\cdot 2} = \sqrt{9}\sqrt{2} = 3\sqrt{2}$

2. $\sqrt{12} = \sqrt{4\cdot 3} = \sqrt{4}\sqrt{3} = 2\sqrt{3}$

3. $\sqrt{2}\sqrt{3} = \sqrt{2\cdot 3} = \sqrt{6}$

4. $\sqrt{2}\sqrt{8} = \sqrt{16} = 4$

A frequent error is to apply a similar law for addition and to conclude that "the sum of the roots is the root of the sum." To verify that this is *not* true, note that such a "law" would have us believe that $\sqrt{16}+\sqrt{9} = \sqrt{25} = 5$, which is certainly not true since $\sqrt{16} = 4$, $\sqrt{9} = 3$ and $4+3 = 7$, not 5.

5. $\sqrt{6}+\sqrt{6} = 2\sqrt{6}$

6. $\sqrt{3}+\sqrt{3} = 2\sqrt{3}$

7. $\sqrt{24} = \sqrt{4\cdot 6} = \sqrt{4}\sqrt{6} = 2\sqrt{6}$

8. $\sqrt{3}\sqrt{8} = \sqrt{24} = 2\sqrt{6}$

9. $\dfrac{\sqrt{96}}{2} = \dfrac{\sqrt{16\cdot 6}}{2} = \dfrac{\sqrt{16}\sqrt{6}}{2} = \dfrac{4\sqrt{6}}{2} = 2\sqrt{6}$

EXAMPLES

Simplify and verify your result with your calculator:

1. $\sqrt{27} = 3\sqrt{3}$

2. $\sqrt{20} = 2\sqrt{5}$

3. $\sqrt{99} = 3\sqrt{11}$

4. $\sqrt{8}+\sqrt{18} = 2\sqrt{2}+3\sqrt{2} = 5\sqrt{2}$

Multiply and then simplify where necessary:

5. $\sqrt{27}\sqrt{3} = \sqrt{81} = 9$

6. $(3\sqrt{7})^2 = 9\cdot 7 = 63$

7. $(5\sqrt{6})(4\sqrt{3}) = 20\sqrt{18} = 20\cdot 3\sqrt{2} = 60\sqrt{2}$

8. $\sqrt{2}(\sqrt{32}-3\sqrt{2}) = \sqrt{2}(4\sqrt{2}-3\sqrt{2})$
$= \sqrt{2}(\sqrt{2})$
$= 2$

[14] Which of the following is equal to $\dfrac{3}{\sqrt{3}}$?

(A) $\sqrt{3}$

(B) $3\sqrt{3}$

(C) 3

(D) 9

(E) $\dfrac{\sqrt{3}}{3}$

A result of 6-9 follows:

> **6-10** If a and b are positive real numbers, then
>
> $$\sqrt{\dfrac{a}{b}} = \dfrac{\sqrt{a}}{\sqrt{b}}.$$

This property provides one method for answering the question above:

$$\dfrac{3}{\sqrt{3}} = \dfrac{\sqrt{9}}{\sqrt{3}} = \sqrt{\dfrac{9}{3}} = \sqrt{3}.$$

Other examples of its use in simplification follow:

EXAMPLES

1. $\sqrt{\dfrac{4}{9}} = \dfrac{\sqrt{4}}{\sqrt{9}} = \dfrac{2}{3}$

2. $\sqrt{\dfrac{32}{9}} = \dfrac{\sqrt{32}}{\sqrt{9}} = \dfrac{4\sqrt{2}}{3}$

3. $\sqrt{\dfrac{5}{4}} = \dfrac{\sqrt{5}}{\sqrt{4}} = \dfrac{\sqrt{5}}{2}$

4. $\dfrac{\sqrt{50}}{5} = \dfrac{\sqrt{50}}{\sqrt{25}} = \sqrt{\dfrac{50}{25}} = \sqrt{2}$

EXAMPLES

Simplify each of the following as far as possible and verify your result with your calculator:

1. $\sqrt{\dfrac{27}{4}} = \dfrac{3\sqrt{3}}{2}$

2. $\dfrac{\sqrt{125}}{5} = \dfrac{5\sqrt{5}}{5} = \sqrt{5}$

3. $\sqrt{\dfrac{49}{50}} = \dfrac{7}{5\sqrt{2}} = \dfrac{7\sqrt{2}}{10}$

RATIONALIZING DENOMINATORS THAT CONTAIN RADICALS

[15] If $\dfrac{\sqrt{10} - \sqrt{5}}{\sqrt{10}}$ were transformed to an expression with a rational denominator, the result would be:

(A) $\dfrac{\sqrt{10} - \sqrt{5}}{\sqrt{10}}$

(B) $\dfrac{2 - \sqrt{2}}{2}$

(C) $\dfrac{1}{2}$

(D) $\dfrac{\sqrt{10} + \sqrt{5}}{10}$

(E) $\dfrac{5}{10 + 5\sqrt{2}}$

We'll review fractional expressions later, but an elementary property is useful here:

> **6-11** If a, b, c, and d are real numbers, neither b nor d being zero, then
> $$\frac{a}{b} \times \frac{c}{d} = \frac{ac}{bd}.$$

Property 6-11, along with the Multiplicative Identity and Multiplicative Inverse laws, provides the means for transforming many expressions that have irrational denominators to expressions with rational denominators.

> **6-12** If a and b are positive real numbers, then
> $$\frac{\sqrt{a}}{\sqrt{b}} = \frac{\sqrt{ab}}{b} = \frac{1}{b}\sqrt{ab}.$$

EXAMPLES

1. $\sqrt{\dfrac{1}{2}} = \dfrac{\sqrt{1}}{\sqrt{2}} = \dfrac{1}{\sqrt{2}} = \dfrac{1}{\sqrt{2}} \cdot \dfrac{\sqrt{2}}{\sqrt{2}} = \dfrac{\sqrt{2}}{2}$

2. $\dfrac{\sqrt{2}}{\sqrt{3}} = \dfrac{\sqrt{2}}{\sqrt{3}} \cdot \dfrac{\sqrt{3}}{\sqrt{3}} = \dfrac{\sqrt{6}}{3}$

3. $\dfrac{5}{\sqrt{5}} = \dfrac{5}{\sqrt{5}} \cdot \dfrac{\sqrt{5}}{\sqrt{5}} = \dfrac{5\sqrt{5}}{5} = \sqrt{5}$

4. $\dfrac{\sqrt{10} - \sqrt{5}}{\sqrt{10}} = \dfrac{(\sqrt{10} - \sqrt{5})\sqrt{10}}{\sqrt{10}\sqrt{10}}$

   $\qquad = \dfrac{\sqrt{10}\sqrt{10} - \sqrt{5}\sqrt{10}}{10}$

   $\qquad = \dfrac{10 - \sqrt{50}}{10} = \dfrac{10 - 5\sqrt{2}}{10}$

   $\qquad = \dfrac{5(2 - \sqrt{2})}{5(2)} = \dfrac{2 - \sqrt{2}}{2}$

5. $\dfrac{\sqrt{2} + \sqrt{\pi}}{\sqrt{\pi}} = \dfrac{(\sqrt{2} + \sqrt{\pi})\sqrt{\pi}}{\sqrt{\pi}\sqrt{\pi}} = \dfrac{\sqrt{2\pi} + \pi}{\pi}$

(Note: In this example, even though we have removed the radical, the denominator is still irrational because π is an irrational number.)

EXAMPLES

Write each of the following with a rational denominator:

1. $\dfrac{2}{\sqrt{11}} = \dfrac{2\sqrt{11}}{11}$

2. $\dfrac{6\sqrt{3}}{\sqrt{8}} = \dfrac{6\sqrt{3}}{2\sqrt{2}} = \dfrac{3\sqrt{6}}{2}$

3. $\dfrac{xy}{\sqrt{y}}, y$ is positive $= \dfrac{xy\sqrt{y}}{y} = x\sqrt{y}$

[16] If $\dfrac{\sqrt{10}}{\sqrt{10} - \sqrt{5}}$ were transformed to an expression with a rational denominator, the result would be:

(A) $\dfrac{2 + \sqrt{2}}{5}$

(B) $2 + \sqrt{2}$

(C) $\dfrac{\sqrt{10}}{5}$

(D) $\sqrt{2}$

(E) $\dfrac{\sqrt{10}}{15}$

The procedure needed to answer this question is based on the following rule:

6-13   If x and y are real numbers, then
$$(x - y)(x + y) = x^2 - y^2.$$

This principle is useful here because the squares on the right side of the equation will remove radicals that appear as terms in the factors on the left. For example:

$$(\sqrt{2} + \sqrt{3})(\sqrt{2} - \sqrt{3}) = 2 - 3 = -1$$

$$(\sqrt{10} - \sqrt{5})(\sqrt{10} + \sqrt{5}) = 10 - 5 = 5$$

To assist in using this principle with radicals, we will rewrite it as:

6-14   If a and b are positive integers, then
$$(\sqrt{a} - \sqrt{b})(\sqrt{a} + \sqrt{b}) = a - b.$$

Property 6-14 provides a method for rationalizing denominators that are sums with radicals.

EXAMPLES

1. $\dfrac{1}{\sqrt{2} + \sqrt{3}} = \dfrac{1}{\sqrt{2} + \sqrt{3}} \cdot \dfrac{\sqrt{2} - \sqrt{3}}{\sqrt{2} - \sqrt{3}}$

$= \dfrac{\sqrt{2} - \sqrt{3}}{2 - 3}$

$= \sqrt{3} - \sqrt{2}$

2. $\dfrac{4 + \sqrt{7}}{4 - \sqrt{7}} = \dfrac{4 + \sqrt{7}}{4 - \sqrt{7}} \cdot \dfrac{4 + \sqrt{7}}{4 + \sqrt{7}}$

$= \dfrac{16 + 8\sqrt{7} + 7}{16 - 7}$

$= \dfrac{23 + 8\sqrt{7}}{9}$

To answer the multiple-choice question, note the following:

$$\dfrac{\sqrt{10}}{\sqrt{10} - \sqrt{5}} = \dfrac{\sqrt{10}(\sqrt{10} + \sqrt{5})}{(\sqrt{10} - \sqrt{5})(\sqrt{10} + \sqrt{5})}$$

$$= \dfrac{10 + \sqrt{50}}{10 - 5}$$

$$= \dfrac{10 + 5\sqrt{2}}{5}$$

$$= 2 + \sqrt{2}$$

EXAMPLES

Rationalize the denominators of the following fractions:

1. $\dfrac{2}{1 - \sqrt{5}} = \dfrac{2(1 + \sqrt{5})}{1 - 5} = \dfrac{(1 + \sqrt{5})}{-2}$

2. $\dfrac{2 - \sqrt{5}}{3 - \sqrt{5}} = \dfrac{(2 - \sqrt{5})(3 + \sqrt{5})}{(3 - \sqrt{5})(3 + \sqrt{5})}$

$= \dfrac{1 - \sqrt{5}}{9 - 5}$

$= \dfrac{1 - \sqrt{5}}{4}$

3. $\dfrac{1 - \sqrt{7}}{\sqrt{7} - 1} = \dfrac{-(\sqrt{7} - 1)}{\sqrt{7} - 1} = -1$

[17] When a is divided by 7, the remainder is 1.
      When b is divided by 7, the remainder is 2.
      What is the remainder if ab is divided by 7?

   (A) 3

   (B) 1

   (C) 2

   (D) 6

   (E) No remainder

The question looks much more complicated than it really is. You could spend a lot of time working up a general argument based on all numbers that fit the given information. However, you really only need to select a convenient pair of numbers that fit and then see what happens to their product. Use 8 (because its remainder is 1 after dividing by 7) and 9 (for which the remainder is 2). The product, 72, has a remainder 2, so the answer is (C).

Does answer choice (E) pose a threat? After all, you did not consider all possible numbers. There might be other pairs for which the products produce different remainders. If this question came early in the test, you could feel confident in your choice merely because the early questions are simpler and more straightforward.

For a later question, you might want to explore additional pairs to gain more confidence in a pattern.

If this were among the last few questions on the test, you would want to feel very secure that a wild card answer such as (E) could be eliminated.

For 100% relief from worry, the prescription might look like this. Let $a = 7x + 1$ to represent all numbers with a remainder of 1 after division by 7 and $b = 7x + 2$ to represent all those with remainders of 2. Then $ab = 49x^2 + 21x + 2$. Each of the first two terms is divisible by 7 so the last term, 2, is the remainder.

[18] How many solutions are there to the equation
      $3x + 6y = 25$ if both x and y are positive integers less than 25?

   (A) 0

   (B) 1

   (C) 6

   (D) 25

   (E) Cannot be determined

Not enough given information? That's a common reaction to questions with boundaries that are disguised in some way. So it's no surprise that the most common incorrect answer to this question is (E).

To remove the disguise, transform the equation. Divide both sides by 3 and the result is $x + 2y = \frac{25}{3}$. Sums and products of integers must always result in integers. No

integral values of x and y can combine to produce the non-integral result $\frac{25}{3}$; therefore, the correct answer is (A).

When an equation can be transformed, it is usually a good idea to do so. The fact that 3 and 6 are both multiples of 3 begs for action. The rest is just properly interpreting the result, which, in this case, means knowing what an integer is. By now, the term should be a comfortable fact for you and immediately call to mind the set $\{\ldots -3, -2, -1, 0, 1, 2, 3, \ldots\}$.

[19] If the operation $\dfrac{p \mid q}{r \mid s}$ is defined to give the
      same result as $ps - qr$, find the value of
      $\dfrac{-1 \mid 1}{3 \mid 0}$.

   (A) -4

   (B) -3

   (C) 3

   (D) 4

   (E) 2

You say you must not have been there the day the teacher taught your class that symbol? The good news is that no one was. The better news is that questions like these are self-explanatory, no matter how odd they may look.

The creation of unfamiliar symbols is a common testing device because the symbols are intended to be unfamiliar to everyone who takes the test. This symbol was made up specifically for this question, and you will certainly find other, equally unfamiliar, constructions on just about every Level IC test.

The test maker is presenting you with something new, explaining what it means and then asking you to show that you understand the meaning of this novelty.

In this case, all you need to do is identify the values of p, q, r, and s from their places in the table, substitute them into the formula and then carry out the calculation.

$$ps - qr = (-1)(0) - (1)(3) = -3, \text{ answer (B).}$$

Some students are simply scared off by the unfamiliarity, but these can really be some of the easiest questions on the Level IC test because everything you need to know is given to you in the question.

[20] If $a^2 = b^2$, which of the following must always be true?

(A) $a = b$

(B) $a = -b$

(C) $a = |b|$

(D) $|a| = |b|$

(E) $a = \sqrt{b}$

Whether you square a or $-a$, the result is a^2. The same is true for b^2, which results from squaring either b or $-b$. The given fact that $a^2 = b^2$ means that $\pm a = \pm b$.

Where is that message among the choices given?

Choices (A), (B), and (C) actually contradict it. (A) insists that $a = b$ but a actually could be $-b$. (B) says that $a = -b$, but a could really equal b. (C) tells us that a must always be non-negative because it is the absolute value of b. The given information, however, allows a to be negative. (E) is just plain incorrect (unless b is either 0 or 1).

So we are left to hope that (D) is true. Of course, by process of elimination it must be true but the math supports it too. Suppose, for example, $a = -3$ and $b = 3$. Then $a^2 = b^2$ because $9 = 9$ and $|a| = |b|$ because $3 = 3$.

[21] If 5% of x is 3.3, what is 15% of x?

(A) 1 . 1

(B) 3 4

(C) 9.9

(D) 16.5

(E) .33

Stop. Don't start tapping on your calculator keys. The question involves no tedious calculations. (As a matter of fact, it doesn't even involve percents!)

15% is three times 5%. Therefore, x is 3 times 3.3 or 9.9, which is answer (C).

Remember that Level IC questions are intended to test your knowledge of mathematical principles, not your ability to use a calculator.

This question could be changed slightly, however, to test both your knowledge of math principles and your facility with finding calculator keys.

Suppose the question asked for 16.5% of x rather than 15%. Then you would use your calculator to divide 16.5 by 5 and multiply the result by 3.3. Note that we ignored the percent signs (assume you multiplied both numbers by 100 to eliminate them). With that simple change, the problem becomes one in which a calculator is extremely useful, if not essential.

[22] A car dealer has 180 cars for sale. If x represents the number of different colors in stock and the dealer has the same number of cars in each color, which of the following cannot be x?

(A) 9

(B) 25

(C) 30

(D) 36

(E) 45

The number of cars, 180, must be a multiple of x, the number of colors. Therefore, the number of colors must divide evenly into 180 with no remainder. You can determine the correct answer by testing each. Numbers like 9, (A), and 30, (C), are easily checked in your head. The others can be tested with your calculator.

Choice (B), 25, does not divide evenly, which may have come to you quickly without a calculator. Once you find it, you need not check the others because you have already answered the question.

On the other hand, you may have decided to start by checking the larger numbers rather than the smaller numbers, beginning with 45 (E) and 36 (D). A bit of luck in where you started saves a few seconds that you can apply to more complicated questions. It is always a good idea to scan the answers first to get a feel for them before deciding which to test first. In this case, a knowledgeable scan would have spared you from having to check (D) and (E).

[23] A loom weaves 516 yards of cloth every 9 hours. How many yards will it weave in 12 hours?

(A) 344

(B) 520

(C) 612

(D) 644

(E) 688

To use a routine procedure, let $x =$ the number of yards in 12 hours and set up the proportion

$$\frac{9}{12} = \frac{516}{x}$$

Then solve for x.

If you were going to do the calculation mentally, you would probably reduce the $\frac{9}{12}$ to $\frac{3}{4}$ and then divide 3 into 516 to make your final calculation a matter of multiplying 172 by 4.

Use your calculator and you will not need to simplify the fraction $\frac{9}{23}$ or remove common factors to make your work easier. The calculator works no harder or easier if you enter simple numbers or more complex numbers. Multiply 516 by 12 and then divide the result by 9 to get 688, (E).

Even using tricks of mental calculation won't get an answer in less time than the calculator. Capitalize on that fact by getting comfortable using your calculator to solve proportions.

[24] Alice enters a walkathon to raise money for charity. She earns $18 for participation and $1.15 for each mile she walks. If she raises $31.80, how far did she walk?

    (A) 8

    (B) 9

    (C) 10

    (D) 12

    (E) 15

We'll use this as an example of how test makers use the same basic format to construct problems of many levels of difficulty.

In its present format, it is a two-step question similar to those found among questions 6–15. First, subtract $18.00 from $31.80 to get $13.80, the amount she earned for her mileage. Then divide $13.80 by $1.15 to get 12, the number of miles she walked (a long morning's trek, but for a good cause!). That's answer (D).

With only a slight change, the question could become a simple, one-step problem of the type found among the first five on the test. Change the last sentence to "If she raises $31.80, how much money did Alice earn for the miles she walked?" All you would then need to do is subtract: $31.80 − $18.00.

With a different change, it could become a three-step problem of the type found in questions 16–25. Change the last sentence to "If she raised $31.80 and walked steadily at the rate of three miles an hour, how long did Alice walk?" Now you carry out the two steps we explained in paragraph two and then finish by dividing 12 (the number of miles walked) by 3 (her walking rate) to get 4, the length of time she walked.

Another change makes it a four-step problem, similar in difficulty to those in questions 26 through 35. "If she raised $31.80 and walked steadily at the rate of three miles an hour, how much would Alice have raised by walking one mile an hour faster during the same time?" Now you go through the three steps of the preceding paragraph to get her walking time, 4 hours. Because she is walking one mile an hour faster for 4 hours, multiply the 4 by $1.15 to get $4.60 and add that to the $31.80 she earned at her present walking rate.

Note that the math itself did not get more difficult. (It is still merely adding, subtracting, multiplying, or dividing numbers with your calculator.) But the fact that you must work through more steps changes both what is being tested and your ability to deal with more complicated levels of reasoning.

[25] A 352,000 gallon solution of cleaning fluid is 2.8% alcohol and 5.4% ammonia. If the rest is water, how many gallons (to the nearest thousand) of water does it contain?

    (A) 323,000

    (B) 342,000

    (C) 333,000

    (D) 300,000

    (E) 29,000

First, find the percentage of water by adding the percentage of alcohol, 2.8%, to the percentage of ammonia, 5.4%, and subtracting the result, 8.2%, from 100. You now know that the solution is 91.8% water.

Change the 91.8% to the decimal .918 and multiply that by 352,000 to get 323,136 gallons, which rounded to the nearest thousand give you answer (A). Be sure you know how to change percents to decimals. One good way to remember this is to think about "%" as meaning "divided by 100."

When you affix a percent sign, you are dividing by 100 so you must compensate by multiplying the number by 100 (which is the same as shifting the decimal point two places to the right to make the number 100 times larger).

When you remove a percent sign, you are multiplying by 100 so you must compensate by dividing the number by 100 (which is the same as shifting the decimal point two places to the left to make the number 100 times smaller).

[26] If x is a number from column x, y is a number from column y, and $a \neq 0$, which of the following statements are true?

   I. xy always equals a value of y.

   II. $x + y$ never equals a value of y.

   III. $\dfrac{y}{x}$ always equals a value of y.

x	y
-1	a
0	0
1	a

(A) none

(B) II only

(C) III only

(D) I and II only

(E) I, II, and III

Rapidly check all values of xy in your head. You will quickly see that the result is always $-a$, 0, or a. Even though $xy \neq y$, every xy is a value of y. That means I is true.

Now rapidly check values of $x + y$. Do you see that $0 + 0 = 0$? Even though $x + y \neq y$. There is a value of $x + y$ that equals a value of y. Therefore, II is not true.

Now consider all values of $\frac{y}{x}$. At first, you may be tempted because $\frac{-a}{-1} = a$ and $\frac{a}{-1} = -a$. That only tells you that the rule is sometimes true—that $\frac{y}{x} =$ a value of y. But what about $\frac{a}{0}$?

Division by zero is not defined for any real number. Remember that division is defined in terms of multiplication. The equation $\frac{a}{0} = x$ means that $x(0) = a$. But $x(0)$ is always 0, which contradicts the given information $a \neq 0$. So III is sometimes true, but not always. Therefore, the answer is (D).

WHAT YOU SHOULD KNOW

KEY CONCEPTS

Mastering the Basic Laws of Real Numbers

1. **Closure Law of Addition:** If a and b are real numbers then $a + b$ is a real number.

2. **Closure Law of Multiplication:** If a and b are real numbers, then ab is a real number.

3. **Commutative Law of Addition:** If a and b are real numbers, then $a + b = b + a$.

4. **Commutative Law of Multiplication:** If a and b are real numbers, then $ab = ba$.

5. **Associative Law of Addition:** If a and b are real numbers, then $(a + b) + c = a + (b + c)$.

6. **Associative Law of Multiplication:** If a and b are real numbers, then $(ab)c = a(bc)$.

7. **Additive Inverse Law:** If a is any real number, then there exists a number $-a$ such that $a + (-a) = 0$.

8. **Multiplicative Inverse Law:** If a is any real number except 0, then there exists a number $\dfrac{1}{a}$ such that $a\left(\dfrac{1}{a}\right) = 1$.

9. **Additive Identity Law:** If a is any real number, then $a + 0 = a$.

10. **Multiplicative Identity Law:** If a is any real number, then $a(1) = a$.

11. **Distributive Law:** If a, b, and c are any real numbers, then $a(b + c) = ab + ac$.

12. **Multiplication Property of Zero:** If a is any real number, then $a(0) = 0$.

13. **Addition, Subtraction, Multiplication, and Division Properties of Equality:** If a, b, and c are any real numbers and $a = b$, then:
$$\begin{aligned} a + c &= b + c, \\ a - c &= b - c, \\ ac &= bc, \\ \frac{a}{c} &= \frac{b}{c} \quad \text{when } c \neq 0. \end{aligned}$$

14. **Multiplication Property of –1:** If a is any real number, then $-a = (-1)a$.

Handling Real Numbers

1. *To subtract any real number,* add its opposite: $a - b = a + (-b)$ or $a - (-b) = a + b$.

2. *To obtain the opposite of a sum,* add the opposites: $-(a + b) = (-a) + (-b)$.

3. *To obtain the absolute value of a number a,* take the nonnegative choice of a or $-a$. In other words,

$$|a| = a \text{ when } a \text{ is zero or positive,}$$

and

$$|a| = -a \text{ when } a \text{ is negative.}$$

Handling Radicals

1. A square root of a number x is a number y for which $y^2 = x$.

2. The nonnegative square root of x is denoted by $\sqrt{x}$ and is called the "principal" square root.

3. For any positive number x,

$$a\sqrt{x} + b\sqrt{x} = (a + b)\sqrt{x}.$$

4. *To simplify a radical expression,* identify the largest perfect square factor, a, of the radicand, and then apply the rule

$$\sqrt{ab} = \sqrt{a}\sqrt{b}.$$

5. *To multiply radicals,* apply the rule

$$\sqrt{a}\sqrt{b} = \sqrt{ab}.$$

Handling Fractions Whose Denominators Contain Radicals

1. *To rationalize the denominator of a fraction of the form* $\dfrac{a}{\sqrt{b}}$, multiply by $\dfrac{\sqrt{b}}{\sqrt{b}}$ to get the result, $\dfrac{a\sqrt{b}}{b}$

2. *To rationalize the denominator of a fraction of the form* $\dfrac{a}{\sqrt{b} + \sqrt{c}}$, multiply by $\dfrac{\sqrt{b} - \sqrt{c}}{\sqrt{b} - \sqrt{c}}$ to get $\dfrac{a\sqrt{b} - a\sqrt{c}}{b - c}$.

CALCULATOR SKILLS

Consult your calculator manual to be sure you know how to:

- Use the radical key to approximate square roots (remember that your display may be rounded off at the last decimal place).
- Use your exponentiation key to raise a number to a power.
- Input the value of π.
- Convert a decimal to a fraction if your calculator has this feature.

TEST-TAKING STRATEGIES

- When you encounter a problem involving a specially defined operation, deal with it, within the framework of the definition, according to the basic rules for operations in number systems.
- Convert radicals to the simplest radical form and use common radical factors that may occur.
- Different texts sometimes use different names for basic laws of algebra. For example, the Identity

Law of Multiplication is also known as the Multiplicative Identity Property. Rarely, however, will the exact wording of the name be a factor in determining the correct answer. Do not be confused by differences in nomenclature.

- Remember that all positive numbers have *two* square roots—one positive and the other negative. The negative root may lead to a correct answer when the positive root doesn't.
- Because College Board Tests are short-answer exams, you'll never need to do a proof. On the other hand, keep in mind that some questions are devised to find out whether you know how proofs are done.
- To ensure that you are able to recognize answers that are the same, be sure to rationalize any expressions with denominators that involve radicals.
- The most common errors made on simple algebraic questions result from incorrect calculations with signs. If you cannot find your answer among the choices, look for a sign error in your calculations.
- The Multiplication Property of Zero is a basic tool in solving equations of second degree or higher. When confronted with such an equation, factor the polynomial and determine the numbers that make each factor zero.

ANSWERS

[1] (C)	[6] (B)	[11] (C)	[16] (B)	[21] (C)	[26] (D)
[2] (B)	[7] (E)	[12] (E)	[17] (C)	[22] (B)
[3] (C)	[8] (B)	[13] (B)	[18] (A)	[23] (E)
[4] (D)	[9] (B)	[14] (A)	[19] (B)	[24] (D)
[5] (D)	[10] (D)	[15] (B)	[20] (D)	[25] (A)

POLYNOMIALS AND FACTORING

CHAPTER

7

KEY TERMS

monomial   an algebraic expression that is either a numeral, a variable, or the product of
numerals and variables. Examples: 5, *y*, *xy*.

polynomial   an algebraic expression that is the sum (or difference) of two or more monomials.
Examples: $3xy - 5$, $4x^2 - 6x + 3$.

like terms   two terms of a polynomial that have the same variables, with each variable having the
same exponents. Example: y^3 and $4y^3$.

IDENTIFYING POLYNOMIALS

[1] If $3x^3 + 6x$ is subtracted from the sum of $8x^2 + 1$ and $-5x + 6x - 3$, the result is:

(A) $3x^3 - 3x^2 + 2$

(B) $-3x^2 + 3x - 2$

(C) $-3x^3 + 3^2 - 2x$

(D) $-3x^3 + 3x^2 - 2$

(E) No result is possible

Polynomials may be added, subtracted, multiplied, and divided by means of the properties of the real numbers.

ADDING AND SUBTRACTING POLYNOMIALS

Addition and subtraction are carried out through the process known as "combining like terms." "Like" terms are terms that have the same variables raised to the same power.

EXAMPLE 1

Add $x^2 + 5x + 3$ and $3x^2 - 4x + 5$.

SOLUTION:

$$(x^2 + 5x + 3) + (3x^2 - 4x + 5)$$
$$= x^2 + 3x^2 + 5x - 4x + 3 + 5$$
$$= (1 + 3)x^2 + (5 - 4)x + (3 + 5)$$
$$= 4x^2 + x + 8$$

EXAMPLE 2

Add $4x^3 + 5x^2 - 6$ and $2x^2 + x$.

SOLUTION:

$$(4x^3 + 5x^2 - 6) + (2x^2 + x)$$
$$= 4x^3 + 5x^2 + 2x^2 + x - 6$$
$$= 4x^3 + (5 + 2)x^2 + x - 6$$
$$= 4x^3 + 7x^2 + x - 6$$

Before discussing subtraction of polynomials remember:

7-1 If a and b are real numbers, then

$$-(a + b) = (-a) + (-b).$$

EXAMPLE 3

1. $-(x^2 + 2x) = -x^2 - 2x$

2. $-(x^2 - 2x) = -x^2 + 2x$

3. $-(-x^2 + 2x) = x^2 - 2x$

7-2 If a, b, and c are real numbers, then

$$a - (b + c) = a + [-(b + c)]$$
$$= a + (-b) + (-c).$$

This theorem tells us how to remove parentheses when they are preceded by a negative sign: we apply the negative sign to each term in the parentheses when the parentheses are removed, thereby changing the sign of each term in the parentheses. Therefore a difference such as

$$(x^2 + 5x + 3) - (3x^2 - 4x + 5)$$

can be found by changing the signs of the terms of the second polynomial and adding the new terms to like terms in the first polynomial.

$$(x^2 + 5x + 3) - (3x^2 - 4x + 5)$$
$$= x^2 + 5x + 3 + (-3x^2) + 4x + (-5)$$
$$= -2x^2 + 9x - 2$$

The multiple-choice question can be restated and simplified as follows:

$$(8x^2 + 1) + (-5x^2 + 6x - 3) - (3x^3 + 6x)$$
$$= 8x^2 + 1 - 5x^2 + 6x - 3 - 3x^3 - 6x$$
$$= -3x^3 + 3x^2 - 2.$$

EXAMPLES

Verify the following:

1. $(x^2 + 2) + (9x^2 + 7x - 5) = 10x^2 + 7x - 3$

2. $(x^2 - x + 2) - (x - 3) = x^2 - 2x + 5$

3. $(14x^3 - 21x^2 + 49x) + (6x^4 - 8x^3 + 10x) = 6x^4 + 6x^3 - 21x^2 + 59x$

4. $(18x^2 + 10x - 5) - (2x^4 + 4x^3 - 8x^2 + 6x) = -2x^4 - 4x^3 + 26x^2 + 4x - 5$

MULTIPLYING POLYNOMIALS

[2] Each of the following is a term in the polynomial which is the product of $(x + 1)$, $(3x^2 + 6x)$ and $(2x^2 + 6x - 1)$ EXCEPT

(A) $6x^5$

(B) $36x^4$

(C) $63x^3$

(D) $-6x$

(E) -1

Multiplying polynomials can be accomplished through repeated use of the Distributive Law as shown below:

EXAMPLE

$(2x^2 + 6x - 1)(3x^2 + 6x)$
$= (2x^2 + 6x - 1)3x^2 + (2x^2 + 6x - 1)6x$
$= (2x^2)(3x^2) + (6x)(3x^2) - (1)(3x^2) + (2x^2)(6x)$
$\quad + (6x)(6x) - (1)(6x)$
$= 6x^4 + 18x^3 - 3x^2 + 12x^3 + 36x^2 - 6x$
$= 6x^4 + 30x^3 + 33x^2 - 6x$

But such a procedure is exceedingly lengthy, and we seldom do it this way in practice. We note instead that the above multiplication is the sum of the products of each term of one polynomial with each term of the other polynomial. A method that accomplishes this with less trouble follows. Note that each term of the lower polynomial in the arrangement below is multiplied by each term of the upper polynomial, forming two partial product polynomials. These partial products are written so that vertical columns contain the same powers of x. This arrangement allows ready addition of partial products.

$$
\begin{array}{r}
2x^2 + 6x - 1 \\
3x^2 + 6x \\
\hline
12x^3 + 36x^2 - 6x \\
6x^4 + 18x^3 - 3x^2 \\
\hline
6x^4 + 30x^3 + 33x^2 - 6x
\end{array}
$$

You could answer the multiple-choice question by performing the following operations:

$$
\begin{array}{r}
3x^2 + 6x \\
x + 1 \\
\hline
3x^2 + 6x \\
3x^3 + 6x^2 \\
\hline
3x^3 + 9x^2 + 6x \\
3x^3 + 9x^2 + 6x \\
2x^2 + 6x - 1 \\
\hline
- 3x^3 - 9x^2 - 6x \\
18x^4 + 54x^3 + 36x^2 \\
6x^5 + 18x^4 + 12x^3 \\
\hline
6x^5 + 36x^4 + 63x^3 + 27x^2 - 6x
\end{array}
$$

But take note of the following tip:

TEST-TAKING TIP

Rarely would a College Board question involve so much calculation, and most questions can be answered with no calculation at all. There is usually an insightful way of arriving at an answer with little pencil-and-paper work. So it is with this question. Since x is a factor of $3x^3 + 6x$, it will be a factor of each term in the product of the three polynomials. Therefore, without doing *any* calculation, you should be able to see that (E) cannot be a term of the product.

EXAMPLES

Verify the following multiplications:

1. $(a^2 + 7a - 2)(3a^2 - 2a + 5)$
   $= 3a^4 + 19a^3 - 15a^2 + 39a - 10$

2. $(2x + 3)(5x^3 + 6x^2 - 8)$
   $= 10x^4 + 27x^3 + 18x^2 - 16x - 24$

3. $(x^2 - x + 2)(x^2 + x + 1)$
   $= x^4 + 2x^2 + x + 2$

DIVIDING POLYNOMIALS

[3]   If $2x^4 - 7x^2 - 1 - 3x^3$ is divided by $3x - 1 + x^2$ which of the following is the remainder?

(A) $-9x^3 - 5x^2$

(B) $-9x^3 - 5x^2 - 1$

(C) $22x^2 - 9x - 1$

(D) $-75x + 21$

(E) $25x - 7$

If a polynomial P_1 is divided by a second polynomial P_2, then P_1 is called the dividend and P_2 the divisor. We carry out the division by a process similar to long division.

Step 1 Arrange both of P_1 and P_2 in decreasing order of the powers of some variable found in both P_1 and P_2. Replace any missing power with a term of that power having a coefficient of 0.

Step 2 Divide the highest degree term of P_1 by the highest degree term of P_2 to find the highest degree term of the quotient.

Step 3 Multiply P_2 by the first term of the quotient and write the product under P_1, keeping like powers in the same column. Then subtract this product from P_1 to get a remainder.

Step 4 If P_1 has more terms than P_2, bring down the next term and use the sum of this term and the previous remainder (from step 3) as your new dividend. Repeat these four steps until the highest degree of the remainder is less than the highest degree of the divisor.

Applying this procedure to the question above, we first rearrange terms in descending powers of x to get:

divisor: $x^2 + 3x - 1$,

dividend: $2x^4 - 3x^3 - 7x^2 + (0)x - 1$.

We can now set up the division.

$$
\begin{array}{r}
2x^2 - 9x + 22 \\
x^2 + 3x - 1 \overline{) 2x^4 - 3x^3 - 7x^2 + (0)x - 1} \\
\underline{2x^4 + 6x^3 - 2x^2} \\
-9x^3 - 5x^2 + (0)x \\
\underline{-9x^3 - 27x^2 + 9x} \\
22x^2 - 9x - 1 \\
\underline{22x^2 + 66x - 22} \\
-75x + 21
\end{array}
$$

Consequently the quotient is $2x^2 - 9x + 22$ with a remainder of $-75x + 21$.

Verify each of the following divisions:

1. $(x^2 + 3x - 5) \div (x - 2) = x + 5, R = 5$

2. $(x^3 - 6x^2 + 12x - 8) \div (4 - 4x + x^2) = x - 2$

FACTORING POLYNOMIALS

[4]   If a and b are integers, which of the following represents the factored form of $ax - bx + ay - by$ over the integers?

(A) $ax - bx + ay - by$

(B) $(a-b)x + (a-b)y$

(C) $(a-b)(x+y)$

(D) $(\sqrt{a} + \sqrt{b})(\sqrt{a} - \sqrt{b})(x+y)$

(E) $(\sqrt{a} + \sqrt{b})(\sqrt{a} - \sqrt{b})(\sqrt{x} - i\sqrt{y})$
      $(\sqrt{x} + i\sqrt{y})$

A polynomial is in "factored form" over a set of numbers, S, if it is expressed as the product of other polynomials whose coefficients are all members of S. Factoring involves repeated use of the generalized distributive property mentioned in section [6] of Chapter 6.

$$a(b + c + d + \ldots) = ab + ac + ad + \ldots$$

When read from right to left, this property provides a way of writing a sum of n terms:

$$\underbrace{ab + ac + ad + \ldots}_{n \text{ terms}}$$

as a product of a common factor, a, and a second factor of n terms:

$$\underbrace{a(b + c + d + \ldots)}_{n \text{ terms}}$$

The first step in the factoring of any polynomial is the factoring out of common multipliers if any exist. Other steps will be discussed in subsequent sections.

EXAMPLE 1

Factor $3ax^2 + 9a^2x$ over the integers if a is an integer.

SOLUTION: After noting that each term has a factor of $3ax$, we write the above expression as:

$$3ax(x + 3a).$$

We can always check for errors in factoring by multiplying the factors to see if their product is the original expression.

EXAMPLE 2

Factor $y^3 - y^2 - 3y + 3$ completely over the integers.

SOLUTION: There is no factor common to all terms, but grouping the terms in pairs gives

$$(y^3 - y^2) - (3y - 3),$$

with each group being factored to get

$$y^2(y - 1) - 3(y - 1).$$

Each of the two new terms, $y^2(y - 1)$ and $-3(y - 1)$, has $(y - 1)$ as a factor. Applying the Distributive Law again, we get

$$(y - 1)(y^2 - 3),$$

which can be verified by multiplying this indicated product.

You may have noticed that each answer choice of the multiple-choice question [4] is a step in the factoring of $ax - bx + ay - by$ over the "complex" numbers, a system to which we will later devote an entire chapter. In (A) no factoring has been done. In (B) the expression has been grouped in pairs, with common factors recognized in each group, but the expression is still an indicated sum. In (C) the factoring over the *integers* has been completed. In (D) the factors are over the reals and in (E) over the complex numbers. (D) and (E) will be discussed further in later sections.

TEST-TAKING TIP

Suppose that you did not understand how to answer this question, but you did recognize that $\sqrt{a}$ is not always an integer when a is an integer. You would then be able to eliminate (D) and (E). Having ruled out two choices, you would have increased your chances of guessing correctly and might improve your test score by making your best choice of (A), (B), and (C). Since (C) is the only one of these choices that is "factored," (written as a product) it would be a likely guess—and it is, in fact, the correct answer. You can verify this "guess" by working backward; multiply the two binomials in (C) and you will get the given expression.

EXAMPLES

Factor over the integers:

1. $10abx + 15b^2x = 5bx(2a + 3b)$

2. $x + xy - x^2y = x(1 + y - xy)$

3. $12x^4y^3 - 18x^3y^3 + 36x^3y^4 = 6x^3y^3(2x - 3 + 6y)$

4. $x^2 - 2x + 3x - 6 = (x + 3)(x - 2)$

---

[5]   If $32x^4 - 2y^8$ were factored completely over the integers, each of the following would be one of the factors EXCEPT

(A) 2

(B) $2x - y^2$

(C) $2x + y^2$

(D) $4x + y^4$

(E) $4x^2 - y^4$

We have noted that factoring results from the application of the Distributive Law from *right to left* whereas its application from *left to right* involves multiplication. In this way factoring can be thought of as "undoing" multiplication, and, as a matter of fact, we have verified our factoring by re-multiplying the factors. Multiplication also provides the means for the discovery of other laws of factoring. For example, property 6-13,

$$(x - y)(x + y) = x^2 - y^2,$$

suggests the factors for expressions involving the difference of squares.

EXAMPLES

1. $x^2 - 4 = (x - 2)(x + 2)$

2. $x^2 - y^4 = (x - y^2)(x + y^2)$

3. $16a^2 - 25b^2 = (4a - 5b)(4a + 5b)$

4. $16 - x^4 = (4 - x^2)(4 + x^2)$
   $= (2 - x)(2 + x)(4 + x^2)$

5. $x^2y + x^2 - 4y - 4 = x^2(y + 1) - 4(y + 1)$
   $= (x^2 - 4)(y + 1)$
   $= (x - 2)(x + 2)(y + 1)$

TEST-TAKING TIP

Remember that, in all factoring, common factors should be considered first.

To answer the multiple-choice question, note the following:

$$32x^4 - 2y^8 = 2(16x^4 - y^8)$$
$$= 2(4x^2 + y^4)(4x^2 - y^4)$$
$$= 2(4x^2 + y^4)(2x - y^2)(2x + y^2).$$

Note that (E), $4x^2 - y^4$, is a factor at the third step, but it can be factored further. The question states that the expression is completely factored.

EXAMPLES

Factor:

1. $1 - x^4 = (1 - x)(1 + x)(1 + x^2)$

2. $9x^2 - 81 = 9(x - 3)(x + 3)$

3. $x^2 - (y + 1)^2 = (x - y - 1)(x + y + 1)$

4. $4x^2 - 64 = 4(x - 2)(x + 2)(x^2 + 4)$

FACTORING TRINOMIALS

[6] If $a^2x^2 + bx + c^2$ is the square of a binomial, which of the following is the correct relationship among a, b, and c?

(A) $b = ac$

(B) $b^2 = a^2c^2$

(C) $b = 2ac$

(D) $b = 4ac$

(E) $4b^2 = a^2c^2$

If a binomial, a polynomial of two terms, is squared, the result is a polynomial of three terms, a trinomial. The clues to the recognition and factoring of perfect square trinomials are provided by squaring the binomial $ax + c$:

$$(ax + c)^2 = a^2x^2 + 2acx + c^2.$$

Therefore the second coefficient, b, equals $2ac$. The coefficient of the center term is, thus, twice the product of the roots of the coefficients of the first and last terms.

EXAMPLES

1. $x^2 + 2x + 1 = (x + 1)^2$

2. $16x^2 - 24x + 9 = (4x - 3)^2$

3. $x^2 + 6x + 9 = (x + 3)(x + 3)$

4. $25x^2 - 30x + 9 = (5x - 3)^2$

5. $9x^2 - 12xy + 4y^2 = (3x - 2y)^2$

[7] If $2x^2 + 7x + 6$ is factored over the integers, which of the following is a factor?

(A) $x + 6$

(B) $2x - 6$

(C) $2x - 3$

(D) $x + 1$

(E) $x + 2$

Many trinomials that are not squares of binomials are factorable. Developing the ability to factor them is a necessary preparation for solving some types of quadratic equations and for simplifying rational expressions. The simplest of these trinomials is the kind for which the coefficient of the second-degree term is 1,

$$(x + m)(x + n) = x^2 + (m + n)x + mn.$$

To factor we need only find a pair of numbers whose product is the final term and whose sum is the coefficient of the first-degree term.

EXAMPLES

1. $x^2 - 5x + 6 = (x - 3)(x - 2)$

2. $x^2 + 8x + 15 = (x + 3)(x + 5)$

3. $y^2 - 5y - 14 = (y - 7)(y + 2)$

Factoring trinomials with leading coefficients other than 1 is more difficult and involves trial and error. As we can see from:

$$(px + m)(qx + n) = pqx^2 + (mq + pn)x + mn,$$

we must find four numbers, p, q, m, and n, such that two are factors of the first coefficient while the other two are factors of the last term. The middle term must be the sum of certain products of these factors, and finding just what products are needed is accomplished by trial and error. We must first list the possible factors of the first and last terms and then try summing various products until we discover the ones that yield the middle term.

EXAMPLE

Factor $3x^2 + 11x - 4$ over the integers.

SOLUTION: The first term can only be factored into $3x$ and x (or their negatives, but these we will take into consideration by listing the negatives of the final term). The last term yields the three possibilities 2 and -2, 1 and -4, and -1 and 4. The possible factorings these yield are therefore:

1. $(3x + 2)(x - 2)$,

2. $(3x-2)(x+2)$,

3. $(3x+1)(x-4)$,

4. $(3x-4)(x+1)$,

5. $(3x-1)(x+4)$,

6. $(3x+4)(x-1)$.

If we multiply out each of these, we get six different tri-nomials but only number (5) is $3x^2+11x-4$.

Since this procedure may require numerous multipli-cations, we need a rapid way of multiplying binomials mentally. The FOIL device provides such a procedure. The diagram below indicates names for pairs of terms in the product of two binomials.

To multiply binomials, multiply the terms indictated in the order First, Outer, Inner, Last. The sum of the O and I terms gives the mid-dle term of the trinomial and is a quick check for which of the possible factorings works. You should develop the ability to factor trinomi-als mentally.

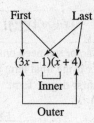

To answer the multiple-choice question,

$$2x^3+7x+6 = (2x+3)(x+2).$$

EXAMPLES

Factor:

1. $x^2-10x-75 = (x-15)(x+5)$

2. $81x^2+144x+64 = (9x+8)^2$

3. $-x^2-4x+77 = -1(x+11)(x-7)$

4. $4x^2+28x+48 = 4(x+3)(x+4)$

5. $36x^2+12x-35 = (6x-5)(6x+7)$

6. $7x^2-30x+8 = (7x-2)(x-4)$

FACTORING THE SUM OR DIFFERENCE OF CUBES

[8]   Which of the following is true?

(A) $x^3-8 = (x-2)^2$

(B) $x^3+8 = (x+2)^3$

(C) $x^3-8 = (x^2+4)(x-2)$

(D) $x^3+8 = (x+2)(x^2-2x+4)$

(E) $x^3-8 = (x-2)(x^2+4x+4)$

We sometimes find it useful to be able to factor the sum and difference of two cubes. The factors of each of a^3+b^3 and a^3-b^3 are not obvious but may be verified by carrying out the following multiplications:

$$\begin{aligned}(a+b)(a^2-ab+b^2) &= a^3+b^3,\\ (a-b)(a^2+ab+b^2) &= a^3-b^3.\end{aligned}$$

EXAMPLES

1. $x^3+8 = (x+2)(x^2-2x+4)$

2. $x^3-y^3 = (x-y)(x^2+2xy+y^2)$

3. $8x^3-27y^3 = (2x-3y)(4x^2+6xy+9y^2)$

4. $x+x^4 = x(1+x^3) = x(1+x)(1-x+x^2)$

5. $a^3+27b^3 = (a+3b)(a^2-3ab+9b^2)$

6. $x^3-1 = (x-1)(x^2+x+1)$

7. $16+2a^3 = 2(2+a)(4-2a+a^2)$

8. $64x^4-27x = x(4x-3)(16x^2+12x+9)$

WHAT YOU SHOULD KNOW

KEY CONCEPTS

Adding, Subtracting, Multiplying, and Dividing Polynomials

1. *To add polynomials,* add the coefficients of like terms.
2. *To subtract polynomials,* subtract the coefficients of like terms.
3. *To remove parentheses enclosing a polynomial when the parentheses are preceded by a positive sign,* merely remove the parentheses.
4. *To remove parentheses enclosing a polynomial when the parentheses are preceded by a negative sign,* remove the parentheses and change the signs of all terms within the parentheses.
5. *To multiply two polynomials,* multiply each term of one polynomial by every term of the other polynomial and combine like terms.
6. *To divide one polynomial by another,* first arrange both polynomials in descending order of the powers of a common variable and then proceed as in long division.

Factoring Polynomials

1. *To factor a polynomial,* first look for a common factor and remove it by using the generalized Distributive Law:

$$ab + ac + ad + \ldots = a(b + c + d + \ldots).$$

2. A trinomial of the form $a^2x^2 + 2abx + b^2$ can be factored as

$$(ax + b)(ax + b) = (ax + b)^2.$$

3. Trinomials of the form $ax^2 + bx + c$ may be factored into expressions of the form $(mx + n)(px + q)$, where $mp = a, nq = c, mq + np = b$. The values of m, n, p, and q must be found by trial and error.

KEY FORMULAS

1. To factor the difference of two squares:

$$a^2 - b^2 = (a + b)(a - b).$$

2. To factor the sum or difference of cubes:

$$a^3 - b^3 = (a - b)(a^2 + ab + b^2),$$
$$a^3 + b^3 = (a + b)(a^2 - ab + b^2).$$

CALCULATOR SKILLS

Most of the calculator skills you will use on Level IC have already been identified. A few more will appear in later chapters.

TEST-TAKING STRATEGIES

- In factoring, consider common factors first.
- When working with polynomials, always put them in standard form to facilitate comparisons and operations.
- When subtracting polynomials, check your work to be sure all terms of the subtrahend polynomial are subtracted—not just the first term.
- When working with polynomials, if no insightful way of answering a question comes to you, try looking at the factors of the polynomial. For example, if two polynomials are to be divided, factoring may show common factors that can be removed first, simplifying the division process.
- When dividing polynomials, take the extra time to do each step carefully and fully. Polynomial division involves all polynomial operations, thereby creating numerous opportunities for small errors.
- Factoring of polynomials is a skill basic to most types of algebra questions. Before taking a Math Level IC test, master fully the factoring of all types of second degree polynomials.
- On a Math Level IC test, you will never be asked to give the meanings of terms like "trinomial" and "binomial," but be aware that these words may be used in questions in ways that will require your knowledge of their meanings.

ANSWERS

[1] (D)   [3] (D)   [5] (E)   [7] (E)
[2] (E)   [4] (C)   [6] (C)   [8] (D)

INEQUALITIES

CHAPTER

8

KEY TERMS

degree of an inequality   the degree of an inequality is determined by the highest power of the variables involved. Thus a "second-degree inequality" has a second-degree term as its highest power.

equivalent inequalities   inequalities that have the same set of solutions.

THE MEANING OF INEQUALITY SIGNS

[1]   If $a < b < c$ and $a < 0$, which of the following
  must be true?

  (A) $b < 0$

  (B) $b > 0$

  (C) $c > 0$

  (D) $c - b > 0$

  (E) $a - b > 0$

If a positive number p is added to any real number a,
the result is a different real number, b, that is greater than
a. We formalize this intuitive idea in the following definition:

> If a and b are real numbers and $a < b$ (*read:*
> "a is less than b"), there exists a positive
> number p such that $a + p = b$. Furthermore,
> $a < b$ if and only if $b > a$ (*read:* "b is greater
> than a").

Because of this definition, when a lesser number is subtracted from a greater number, the result must be a positive number. For example, in (D) of the multiple-choice
question, $c - b$ must be positive since $b < c$. In choice (E),
on the other hand, $b - a$ must be positive so $a - b$ must be
negative. We will also make the following assumption:

> 8-1   If a and b are any real numbers, then one and
> only one of the following is true:
>
> $$a < b, \quad a = b, \quad \text{or} \quad a > b.$$

APPLYING THE TRANSITIVE
PROPERTY OF INEQUALITY

An immediate consequence of the definition is the
"Transitive Property of Inequality."

> 8-2   If a and b are any real numbers and if
>
> $$a < b \quad \text{and} \quad b < a,$$
>
> then
>
> $$a < c.$$

We sometimes write "$a < b$ and $b < c$" as $a < b < c$.

EXAMPLE

If $x < 0$, arrange $\frac{1}{2}x$, $x - 1$, and x in order from least to
greatest.

SOLUTION: For all x, the number $x - 1$ is always less
than x. (Use the definition of "$<$" at left. If you add $p = 1$
to $x - 1$, the result is x.)

(1)   Therefore, $x - 1 < x$.

Also, $\frac{1}{2}x + \frac{1}{2}x = x$, so

$$\frac{1}{2}x = x + \left(-\frac{1}{2}x\right)$$

Because $-\frac{1}{2}x$ is a positive number when $x < 0$, it follows from the definition of "$<$" that

(2) $x < \frac{1}{2}x.$

The Transitive Property of Inequality combines (1) and
(2) in the following order:

$$x - 1 < x < \frac{1}{2}x.$$

If this order does not make sense, test a negative number, say -4. Using -4 produces $-5 < -4 < -2$, which
should make you feel better about the relationship.

[2]   If $3 - 2x < -5$, then which of the following
  is true of x?

  (A) $x < -8$

  (B) $x < 4$

  (C) $x < -4$

  (D) $x > 4$

  (E) $x < 8$

APPLYING THE ADDITION PROPERTY

Our definition of "$<$" and the rules of signs for the
multiplication of real numbers allow us to deduce two
properties that will aid us in the solution of inequalities.

> 8-3   If a, b, and c are real numbers, then $a < b$ if
> and only if $a + c < b + c$.

EXAMPLES

1. $x + 5 < 6$

   $x < 1$ (By adding -5 to both members)

2. $-x - 6 < -4$

   $-2 < x$ (By adding $x + 4$ to both members)

APPLYING THE MULTIPLICATION PROPERTY

8-4 If a and b are real numbers and if $a < b$, then:
1. $ac < bc$ when c is positive,
2. $ac = bc$ when c is zero, and
3. $bc < ac$ when c is negative.

Thus, if each side of the inequality $2 < 4$ is multiplied by 3, the resulting inequality, $3 \cdot 2 < 3 \cdot 4$, has the same sense, but if the inequality is multiplied by -3, the result, $-3 \cdot 2 > -3 \cdot 4$, has the opposite sense.

EXAMPLE 1

If $5 - x > 9$, then $-x > 4$ and $x < -4$.

EXAMPLE 2

$$-(x + 2) \leq 2x + 5$$
$$-x - 2 \leq 2x + 5$$
$$-x \leq 2x + 7$$
$$-3x \leq 7$$
$$x \geq -\frac{7}{3}$$

In the multiple-choice question,

$$3 - 2x < -5.$$

Adding -3 to each side gives

$$-2x < -8.$$

Dividing each side by -2 (and reversing the inequality sign) gives

$$x > 4.$$

EXAMPLE 3

If $x < 3$, which of the following is NOT true?

(A) $3 + x < 3 + 3$

(B) $x - 3 < 3 - 3$

(C) $x(3) < 3(3)$

(D) $3 - x < 3 - 3$

(E) $\dfrac{x}{3} < \dfrac{3}{3}$

Choices (A) and (B) are true by direct application of the Addition Property of Inequality (adding 3 and -3, respectively). Choices (C) and (E) are true by the Multiplication Property (multiply by 3 and $\frac{1}{3}$, respectively). Choice (D) is false because it results in $x > 3$ if you first subtract 3 from both sides and then multiply by -1.

EXAMPLES

Solve each of the following inequalities:

1. If $7 - 4x > 15$, then $x < -2$.

2. If $4x - 3 < 2x + 7$, then $x < 5$.

3. If $3(x - 4) \geq 12$, then $x \geq 8$.

4. If $8 - 2(1 + 2x) \leq 1 + x$, then $x \geq 1$

INEQUALITIES USING "AND" AND "OR"

[3] If $x - 1 \leq -3x + 2 \leq x + 6$, then which of the following is true of x?

(A) $-1 \leq x \leq \dfrac{3}{4}$

(B) $\dfrac{3}{4} \leq x \leq -1$

(C) $-1 \leq x$

(D) $x \leq 4$

(E) No simpler equivalent statement is possible

The statement $a \leq b$ is equivalent to

$$a < b \quad \text{or} \quad a = b.$$

As with all statements connected by *or*, it is true whenever one of its composing statements is true.
The statement $a < b < c$ is equivalent to

$$a < b \quad \text{and} \quad b < c.$$

As with all statements connected by *and*, it is only true when *both* of its composing parts are true. Thus

$$5 < x \quad \text{and} \quad x < 6$$

is true when x is replaced by any number between 5 and 6 but is untrue for any other.

Inequalities of the form $a < b < c$ are often best handled by rewriting in the equivalent form and then applying properties 8-3 and 8-4.

EXAMPLE 1

Find the values of x for which

$$-3 < 2x - 1 < x + 4.$$

SOLUTION: Rewrite as:

$$-3 < 2x - 1 \quad \text{and} \quad 2x - 1 < x + 4.$$

Separate simplifications on both parts yield

$$-1 < x \quad \text{and} \quad x < 5,$$

which can be recombined to get

$$-1 < x < 5.$$

No special rearrangement is necessary to solve inequalities of the form $a \le b$.

EXAMPLE 2

Solve for x: $3x - 5 \le 4x$.

SOLUTION:

$$
\begin{aligned}
3x - 5 &\le 4x \\
-x &\le 5 \quad &\text{(By adding } 5 - 4x \\
& &\text{to both sides)} \\
x &\ge -5 \quad &\text{(Remember to change the} \\
& &\text{direction of the inequality sign} \\
& &\text{when multiplying both sides} \\
& &\text{by negatives.)}
\end{aligned}
$$

In the multiple-choice question,

$$x - 1 \le -3x + 2 \le x + 6,$$

so

$$x - 1 \le -3x + 2 \text{ and } -3x + 2 \le x + 6.$$

Adding $3x$ to each side of both inequalities gives

$$
\begin{aligned}
4x - 1 &\le 2 \quad \text{and} \quad 2 \le 4x + 6, \\
4x &\le 3 \quad \text{and} \quad -4 \le 4x, \\
x &\le \frac{3}{4} \quad \text{and} \quad -1 \le x.
\end{aligned}
$$

Therefore $-1 \le x \le \dfrac{3}{4}$.

Solve:

1. If $4 - (x - 1) > -(5 - 3x)$, then $x < \dfrac{5}{2}$.

2. If $-10 \ge 2 + 3x$, then $x \le -4$.

3. If $2 \le 8x - 1 \le -6$, then there is no solution.

4. If $4x \le 6 - 2(1 - x) < 3x + 2$, then $x \le 2$ and $x > 2$, hence no solution.

FACTORING SECOND-DEGREE INEQUALITIES

[4]   Which of the following is equivalent to

$$-2 < x < 3?$$

(A) $x^2 - x - 6 < 0$

(B) $3(x - 2) < 0$

(C) $x^2 < 9$

(D) $x^2 - 5x + 6 < 0$

(E) $x^2 < 6x$

All of the inequalities given as choices are of second degree (except (B)), which can be readily eliminated using techniques already reviewed.

Second-degree inequalities can be factored and the number line can be used to find solutions. As examples we will work out all of the above choices.

(A)

$$
\begin{aligned}
x^2 - x - 6 &< 0 \\
(x - 3)(x + 2) &< 0
\end{aligned}
$$

The zeros, -2, and 3 break the number line into three pieces.

Test a number in each section to determine which piece satisfies the inequality.

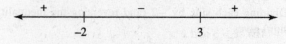

$-2 < x < 3$.

(B) does not involve a quadratic and is solvable by methods previously developed.

(C)
$$x^2 < 9$$
$$x^2 - 9 < 0$$
$$(x-3)(x+3) < 0$$

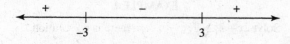

$$-3 < x < 3.$$

(D) simplifies to $2 < x < 3$.

(E)
$$x^2 < 6x$$
$$x^2 - 6x < 0$$
$$x(x-6) < 0$$

$$0 < x < 6$$

EXAMPLES

Solve:

1. If $x^2 - 5x - 6 < 0$, then $-1 < x < 6$.

2. If $3x^2 - 7x - 6 \leq 0$, then $-\dfrac{2}{3} \leq x \leq 3$.

3. If $3x^2 < 9x$, then $0 < x < 3$.

SOLVING SECOND-DEGREE INEQUALITIES

[5] If $3x^2 - 7x - 6 > 0$, then which of the following is true for x?

(A) $x < -\dfrac{2}{3}$ and $x > 3$

(B) $x < -\dfrac{2}{3}$ or $x > 3$

(C) $-\dfrac{2}{3} < x < 3$

(D) $-\dfrac{2}{3} < x$ or $x < 3$

(E) $x > 3$ and $x > -\dfrac{2}{3}$

This inequality differs from the last one discussed since the quadratic expression is greater than zero rather than

less than zero. Again, the technique for finding solutions involves factoring, but a different law of signs is applied.

To answer the multiple-choice question, perform the following steps:

$$3x^2 - 7x - 6 > 0,$$
$$(3x+2)(x-3) > 0.$$

Locate the zeros, $-\dfrac{2}{3}$, and 3 on the number line and test a number in each section.

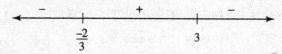

To do problems like these with a graphing calculator, enter the quadratic polynomial in the "$y=$" menu, graph the function and record the values of x for which the polynomial is above the axis (greater than 0) and below the axis (less than 0).

$$x > 3 \quad \text{or} \quad x < -\dfrac{2}{3}.$$

EXAMPLES

Solve:

1. If $x^2 - 5x - 6 > 0$, then $x > 6$ or $x < -1$.

2. If $3x^2 - 7x - 6 \geq 0$, then $x \geq 3$ or $x \leq -\dfrac{2}{3}$.

3. If $3x^2 > 9x$, then $x > 3$ or $x < 0$.

SOLVING INEQUALITIES INVOLVING ABSOLUTE VALUES

[6] Which of the following statements is equivalent to $|2x - 1| < 5$ for all x?

(A) $x < 3$

(B) $x > -2$ or $x < 3$

(C) $x > -2$ and $x < 3$

(D) $x > 3$ or $x < -2$

(E) $x > 3$ and $x < -2$

The solution of inequalities involving absolute value is a topic of intermediate math, even though the major applications of such statements are in higher math. In this and the next section we will introduce, without proof, two properties that aid the solution process.

8-5   If $a > 0$ and x is any real number, then $|x| < a$ if and only if $-a < x < a$.

8-6   If a is any real number and $|x| > a$, then

$$x > a \quad \text{or} \quad x < -a.$$

*Note that if $a \leq 0$ and $x \in R$, there is no value for which $|x| < a$ can be true.

To answer the multiple-choice question, note that if $|2x - 1| < 5$, then

$$-5 < 2x - 1 < 5.$$

Adding 1 to each of the three members, we get

$$-4 < 2x < 6.$$

Dividing each member by 2 gives

$$-2 < x < 3.$$

EXAMPLE 1

Solve $|x + 3| > 7$.

SOLUTION:

$$|x + 3| > 7$$
$$x + 3 > 7 \quad \text{or} \quad x + 3 < -7$$
$$x > 4 \quad \text{or} \quad x < -10$$

EXAMPLE 2

Find all values of x if $|2x - 1| > x + 1$.

$$|2x - 1| > x + 1.$$
$$2x - 1 > x + 1 \quad \text{or} \quad 2x - 1 < -x - 1$$
$$x > 2 \quad \text{or} \quad 3x < 0$$
$$x > 2 \quad \text{or} \quad x < 0$$

TEST-TAKING TIP

At first glance, this answer, $-2 < x < 3$, does not appear to be among the choices given, but that is only because it is in a slightly different form. You must be familiar with the many different forms an answer may have in order to be able to select correct responses.

EXAMPLE 3

Solve $|x| \geq x + 1$.

$$x \geq x + 1 \quad \text{or} \quad x \leq -(x + 1)$$
$$0 \cdot x \geq 1 \quad \text{or} \quad x \leq -x - 1$$
$$0 \quad \text{or} \quad 2x \leq -1$$
$$0 \quad \text{or} \quad x \leq -\frac{1}{2}$$
$$x \leq -\frac{1}{2}$$

EXAMPLE

If $|-3x - 4| \leq 3$, then:

$$-3 \leq -3x - 4 \leq 3,$$
$$1 \leq -3x \leq 7,$$
$$x \leq -\frac{1}{3} \text{ and } x \geq -\frac{7}{3},$$
$$-\frac{7}{3} \leq x \leq -\frac{1}{3}.$$

EXAMPLES

Solve:

1. If $|2x - 5| < 4$, then $\frac{1}{2} < x < \frac{9}{2}$.

2. If $|4x - 1| \leq 15$, then $-\frac{7}{2} \leq x \leq 4$.

[7]   If $|x| \geq x + 1$, then:

(A) x is no real number.

(B) x is any real number.

(C) x is zero only.

(D) $x \geq 1$ or $x \leq \frac{1}{2}$.

(E) $x \leq -\frac{1}{2}$.

EXAMPLES

Find the sets of values that satisfy the conditions:

1. If $|7x + 2| \geq 12$, then $x \geq \frac{10}{7}$ or $x \leq -2$.

2. If $|x| > x$, then $x < 0$.

3. If $|5 - 2x| > x - 1$, then $x < 2$ or $x > 4$.

[8] Which of the following is the graph of

$$|x - 1| < 2?$$

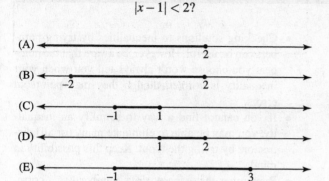

(A)

(B)

(C)

(D)

(E)

When combined with an expression involving absolute value, the inequality sign can be used to define a geometric interval of radius, r, centered on a given number, c.

If $|x - c| < r$, then

$$-r < x - c < r$$

and

$$c - r < x < c + r.$$

Geometrically, this inequality describes a segment on the number line that goes from $c - r$ to $c + r$ and has a midpoint at c.

For the inequality of the question, $|x - 1| < 2$, this means that x goes from $1 - 2 = -1$ to $1 + 2 = 3$, which has $x = 1$ at its center. That's choice (E).

The idea is very useful in advanced math and is essential to the study of limits and calculus. The geometric interpretation helps make these advanced ideas a bit easier to visualize. For that reason, inequalities involving absolute value are more important than they may seem when first encountered.

Any time a concept of intermediate math has special significance in higher math, it is good grist for the testing mill.

[9] If $|b| < |a|$, which of the following could be true?

I. $b = a$

II. $b < a$

III. $b > a$

(A) II only

(B) III only

(C) II and III only

(D) I, II, and III

(E) None of I, II, or III

Test makers like these three-statement questions because they test several different levels of understanding within the same item.

For example, statement I tests only your ability to make a distinction between "=" and "<" Only a very poorly prepared student would feel that a could equal b if a and b differed in absolute value.

Statement II will seem obvious to anyone who understands the absolute value symbol in its most elementary use. If two numbers are both positive, the lesser number has the lesser absolute value.

Statement III increases the level of the question a bit because it asks for a more sophisticated degree of understanding. To see that this statement is true, you must understand the absolute value of negative numbers and, thereby, the absolute value of numbers that differ in sign.

For example, suppose $b = 1$ and $a = -10$. Then $b > a$ even though $|b| < |a|$. The correct answer is (C).

Usually, these three-part questions contain a statement that is quite easy to resolve (usually statement I), a second statement that is a bit more difficult (usually statement II), and a third statement with some form of wrinkle. To correctly interpret the third statement, you usually have to look beyond the obvious.

WHAT YOU SHOULD KNOW

KEY CONCEPTS

1. If $a < b$, then $a + p = b$ for some positive number p.
2. If $a < b$, then $b > a$.
3. If $a < b < c$, then $a < b$ and $b < c$.
4. If $ab > 0$, then $a > 0$ and $b > 0$ or $a < 0$ and $b < 0$.
5. If $ab < 0$, then $a > 0$ and $b < 0$ or $a < 0$ and $b > 0$.
6. If $a > 0$ and x is any real number for which $|x| > 0$, then $-a < x < a$.
7. If $a > 0$ and x is any real number for which $|x| > 0$, then $x > a$ or $x < -a$.

KEY PROPERTIES

1. If a and b are any real numbers and if $a < b$ and $b < c$, then $a < c$. (Transitive Property of Inequality.)
2. If a, b, and c are real numbers, then $a < b$ if and only if $a + c < b + c$.
3. If a and b are real numbers and if $a < b$, then:
   (1) $ac < bc$ when c is positive,
   (2) $ac = bc$ when c is zero, and
   (3) $bc < ac$ when c is negative. (Multiplication Property.)

TEST-TAKING STRATEGIES

- If your solution to an inequality problem does not appear to be among the choices offered, try to recast your answer in a different form.
- Most of the rules for solving inequalities are identical to corresponding rules for solving equations. The major difference occurs when you must multiply or divide each side of an inequality by a negative number. When you do this, remember to change the direction of the inequality sign.

- Checking solutions to inequalities by trying numbers can be useful. However, be aware that the numbers you choose won't always tell you when your inequality is correct, though they may point out errors.
- If you cannot find a way to simplify an inequality, you may be able to eliminate many (or all) distractors by trying them out. Keep this possibility in mind.
- Remember that each positive number has a corresponding negative number with the same absolute value. Be sure to consider both when answering questions involving absolute value.
- Study the graphing of linear inequalities until it becomes second nature to you. Graphing helps you picture solutions, thereby providing a visual method of deciding which answer is correct.
- The product rules for inequalities parallel the laws of signs for multiplication, which may help you remember them. For example, the rule "If $ab > 0$, then $a > 0$ and $b > 0$ or $a < 0$ and $b < 0$" says that a product can be positive only if both factors are positive or if both factors are negative. Apply this relationship where appropriate.

CALCULATOR SKILLS

- Know how to represent negative numbers on a calculator.
- If you are using a graphing calculator, be sure you know how to graph a polynomial and find its zeros. By determining where the parabola is above the axis and where below, you can tell when the polynomial is greater or less than zero.

ANSWERS

[1] (D)

[2] (D)

[3] (A)

[4] (A)

[5] (B)

[6] (C)

[7] (E)

[8] (E)

[9] (C)

RATIONAL EXPRESSIONS

CHAPTER

9

KEY TERMS

rational expression   a fraction whose numerator and denominator are polynomials.

Examples: $\dfrac{1}{4}, \dfrac{2}{y}, \dfrac{x^2-5}{x}$.

reduce   to remove common factors from the numerator and denominator of a fraction.

EVALUATING RATIONAL EXPRESSIONS

[1] What is the value of $\dfrac{x-2y}{\frac{1}{2}+xy}$ when $x=1$ and $y=-\dfrac{1}{2}$?

(A) 0

(B) 1

(C) −1

(D) 2

(E) No real number

Any expression that is the quotient of two polynomials is a *rational expression*. For example,

$$\frac{x^2+1}{x}, \quad \frac{xy+3x^2}{2x+y}, \quad \frac{3}{x}.$$

The simplest of the polynomials are the integers, so the most elementary rational expressions are the rational numbers. For example,

$$\frac{1}{2}, \quad \frac{10}{3}, \quad \frac{-4}{5}.$$

To deal with division by zero, as in the multiple-choice question, we need to refer to the definition of division: If a and b are real numbers, then the quotient, $a \div b$, is the real number x for which $bx = a$.

Since this definition expresses division in terms of multiplication, the properties of division are consequences of those already assembled for multiplication, and this fact helps us to understand division by zero.

In the question above the substitution of 1 for x and $\frac{1}{2}$ for y yields $2 \div 0$. But if there exists some real number q that is the quotient $2 \div 0$, then by the definition of division,

$$q \times 0 = 2.$$

Since the product of 0 and every real number is 0, there can be no quotient $2 \div 0$.

Suppose the numerator had also been 0. By definition $0 \div 0 = x$ such that

$$0 \times x = 0,$$

and therefore x can be any real number.

Our conclusion: division by zero does not fit the definition of division and is thus undefined.

How does your calculator respond to division by zero? Some devices simply display an "error" message. Others will tell you what the error is. A graphing calculator might show a graph of the function and not indicate a break in the curve. Become familiar with this aspect of your calculator.

SIMPLIFYING RATIONAL EXPRESSIONS

[2] The simplest form of $\dfrac{-14a^3y^4}{-35a^3y^2}$ is:

(A) $\dfrac{-2y^4}{-5y^2}$

(B) $\dfrac{2y^4}{5y^2}$

(C) $\dfrac{2y^2}{5}$

(D) $\dfrac{5y^2}{2}$

(E) $\dfrac{-2y^2}{-5}$

9-1 If a, b, c, and d are real numbers and neither b nor d is zero, then

$$\frac{a}{b} \times \frac{c}{d} = \frac{ac}{bd}.$$

In future sections we will be using this principle to write products and quotients of rational expressions, but our immediate concern is in simplifying them. A rational expression is not in simplified form unless the numerator and denominator have no common factor other than 1. The principle by which we can remove common factors follows:

9-2 If a, b, and c are real numbers and neither b nor c is zero, then

$$\frac{ac}{bc} = \frac{a}{b}.$$

Note that c has been removed because it is a common (meaning that it appears in both numerator and denominator) factor (meaning it is *multiplied* by a and b).

This principle is the basis for reducing fractions by removing common factors:

EXAMPLES

$$\frac{3}{6} = \frac{1 \cdot 3}{2 \cdot 3} = \frac{1}{2}$$

$$\frac{10}{25} = \frac{2 \cdot 5}{2 \cdot 5} = \frac{2}{5}$$

$$\frac{x^2 y}{xy^2} = \frac{x \cdot xy}{y \cdot xy} = \frac{x}{y}$$

The expression in the multiple-choice question at the beginning of this section,

$$\frac{-14a^3 y^4}{-35a^3 y^2},$$

can be written as

$$\frac{(-7a^3 y^2)(2y^2)}{(-7a^3 y^2)(5)}.$$

With the common factor $-7a^3 y^2$ removed, the simplified form is $\frac{2y^2}{5}$.

EXAMPLES

Find the value of x for which the fractions in each of the following pairs are equal:

1. For $\frac{1}{2}$ and $\frac{2}{x}$, $x = 4$

2. For $\frac{3}{4}$ and $\frac{x}{16}$, $x = 12$

3. For $\frac{3a^2}{2b^2}$ and $\frac{3a^2 x}{2b^2 a^2}$, $x = a^2$

4. For $\frac{7p}{8q}$ and $\frac{21pq^2}{8qx}$, $x = 3q^2$

MULTIPLYING AND DIVIDING RATIONAL EXPRESSIONS

[3]   If $\frac{a}{x}$ is multiplied by $\frac{a}{x^2}$ and the product is divided by $-\frac{a^2}{x^3}$ the result is:

(A) 1

(B) -1

(C) 0

(D) a

(E) $-\dfrac{a}{x}$

We have agreed that the product of two rational expressions is a third rational expression whose numerator is the product of the original numerators and whose denominator is the product of the original denominators. With this property and the definition of division, we can prove the following property for the quotient of two rational expressions.

9-3   If a, b, c, and d are real numbers such that none of b, c, and d is zero, then

$$\frac{a}{b} \div \frac{c}{d} = \frac{a}{b} \times \frac{d}{c}.$$

This results in a familiar law: "When dividing fractions, invert the divisor and multiply."

EXAMPLE 1

1. $\dfrac{1}{2} \div \dfrac{1}{2} = \dfrac{1}{2} \cdot \dfrac{2}{1} = 1$

2. $\dfrac{2}{3} \div \dfrac{3}{4} = \dfrac{2}{3} \cdot \dfrac{4}{3} = \dfrac{8}{9}$

3. $\dfrac{a^2 b}{xy^2} \div \dfrac{ab^2}{x^2 y} = \dfrac{a^2 b}{xy^2} \cdot \dfrac{x^2 y}{ab^2} = \dfrac{ax}{by}$

EXAMPLE 2

$$\left(\frac{3xy^2}{5w^2 v} \cdot \frac{4x^2 y}{35wv} \right) \div \frac{24x^5 y^6}{175w^3 v^2} = ?$$

SOLUTION: We use property 9-3 to rewrite the above as

$$\frac{3xy^2}{5w^2 v} \times \frac{4x^2 y}{35wv} \times \frac{175w^3 v^2}{24x^5 y^6} = \frac{2100x^3 y^3 w^3 v^2}{4200x^5 y^6 w^3 v^2}.$$

After removing common factors we get

$$\frac{1}{2x^2y^3}.$$

To answer the multiple-choice question,

$$\frac{a}{x} \cdot \frac{a}{x^2} \div \left(-\frac{a^2}{x^3}\right) = \frac{a}{x} \cdot \frac{a}{x^2} \cdot \left(-\frac{x^3}{a^2}\right)$$

$$= -\frac{a^2x^3}{a^2x^3}$$

$$= -1.$$

EXAMPLES

Carry out the indicated operations:

1. $\dfrac{4xy^3}{7x^2y} \times (7x^2y) = 4xy^3$

2. $\dfrac{44a^4b^4}{7x^2y^2} \div \dfrac{8a^4b^3}{21xy^2} = \dfrac{33b}{2x}$

3. $\dfrac{7a}{x^2y^2} \times \dfrac{9xy}{a^3} \div \dfrac{3a}{xy} = \dfrac{21}{a^3}$

ADDING AND SUBTRACTING RATIONAL EXPRESSIONS

[4] If $\dfrac{-63a^3b^2}{-9a^2}$ is added to $\dfrac{81ab^3}{27a}$ and this sum is simplified, the result is:

(A) $\dfrac{18a^4b^5}{18a^3}$

(B) ab^5

(C) $\dfrac{81ab^3 - 63a^3b^2}{-27a^2}$

(D) $\dfrac{9b^3 + 7a^2b^2}{3a}$

(E) $7ab^2 + 3b^3$

We begin by defining addition for rational expressions.

If a, b, and c are real numbers and c is not zero, then

$$\frac{a}{c} + \frac{b}{c} = \frac{a+b}{c}.$$

Note that though we have only defined the sum of two expressions that have the *same* denominator, we are not really hampered since property 9-2 enables us to change any expression to any denominator desired.

EXAMPLE 1

Add $\dfrac{x+9}{9}$ to $\dfrac{x}{9} + 9$.

SOLUTION: Since we can rewrite $\dfrac{x+9}{3}$ as

$$\frac{x+9}{3} \times \frac{3}{3}$$

and 9 as

$$9 \times \frac{9}{9},$$

we can write the above as

$$\frac{3(x+9)}{9} + \frac{x}{9} + \frac{81}{9}.$$

Now that the denominators are all the same, the sum is

$$\frac{3(x+9)+x+81}{9} = \frac{4x+108}{9}.$$

EXAMPLE 2

Simplify $1 + \dfrac{1}{a} + \dfrac{1}{a^2} + \dfrac{1}{a^3} + \dfrac{1}{a^4}$.

SOLUTION: Change the above so that all fractions have a^4 as denominator:

$$1 \cdot \frac{a^4}{a^4} + \frac{1}{a} \cdot \frac{a^3}{a^3} + \frac{1}{a^2} \cdot \frac{a^2}{a^2} + \frac{1}{a^3} \cdot \frac{a}{a} + \frac{1}{a^4},$$

and get

$$\frac{a^4}{a^4} + \frac{a^3}{a^4} + \frac{a^2}{a^4} + \frac{a}{a^4} + \frac{1}{a^4}.$$

Our sum is

$$\frac{a^4 + a^3 + a^2 + a + 1}{a^4}$$

Property 9-4 below shows a similar principle for subtraction.

9-4   If a, b, and c are real numbers, and c is not zero, then

$$\frac{a}{c} - \frac{b}{c} = \frac{a-b}{c}.$$

EXAMPLE 3

1. $\dfrac{1}{2} - \dfrac{1}{2} = \dfrac{1-1}{2} = \dfrac{0}{2} = 0$

2. $\dfrac{2}{3} - \dfrac{1}{3} = \dfrac{2-1}{3} = \dfrac{1}{3}$

3. $\dfrac{3}{4} - \dfrac{7}{4} = \dfrac{3-7}{4} = \dfrac{-4}{4} = -1$

4. $\dfrac{a^3 b}{xy} - \dfrac{ab^3}{xy} = \dfrac{a^3 b - ab^3}{xy}$

5. $\dfrac{a^2}{b^2} - 1 = \dfrac{a^2}{b^2} - \dfrac{b^2}{b^2} = \dfrac{a^2 - b^2}{b^2}$

Fractions can sometimes be reduced before adding, as in the multiple-choice question:

$$\dfrac{-63a^3 b^2}{-9a^2} + \dfrac{81ab^3}{27a}.$$

Each fraction can be reduced:

$$\dfrac{(-9)(7)(a^2)(ab^2)}{-9a^2} + \dfrac{(27a)(3b^3)}{27a} = 7ab^2 + 3b^3$$

[choice (E)].

EXAMPLES

Perform the following operations:

1. $\dfrac{2}{a} + \dfrac{4}{b} + \dfrac{6}{c} = \dfrac{2bc + 4ac + 6ab}{abc}$

2. $\dfrac{3}{xy} - \dfrac{x}{zy} = \dfrac{3z - x^2}{xyz}$

3. $\dfrac{a}{4z} - \dfrac{5b}{12xy} = \dfrac{3axy - 5bz}{12xy}$

4. $\dfrac{19}{a-b} + \dfrac{7}{b-a} = \dfrac{12}{a-b}$

SOLVING SIMPLE EQUATIONS

[5]   If $ax^2 = 3y$, then $\dfrac{a}{y} = ?$

(A) 3

(B) $3x^2$

(C) $\dfrac{3}{x^2}$

(D) $\dfrac{x^2}{3}$

(E) x^2

An aid in solving simple equations involving rational expressions is the Cross-Multiplication Property.

> **9-5** *The Cross-Multiplication Property* If a, b, c, and d are real numbers and neither b nor d is zero, then
>
> $$\dfrac{a}{c} = \dfrac{c}{d} \quad \text{if and only if} \quad ad = bc.$$

EXAMPLES

1. If $\dfrac{x}{2} = \dfrac{3}{4}$, then $4x = 6$ and $x = \dfrac{3}{2}$.

2. If $\dfrac{2}{5} = \dfrac{7}{x+3}$, then $2(x+3) = 35$ and $x = \dfrac{29}{2}$.

3. If $ax^2 = 3y$, then $\dfrac{a}{y} = ?$

In order for the cross-multiplication property to produce the result $ax^2 = 3y$, the original equation must be

$$\dfrac{a}{y} = \dfrac{3}{x^2}$$

4. If $2\dfrac{3}{8} = 1 + \dfrac{x}{24}$ then $x = ?$

$$1\dfrac{3}{8} = \dfrac{x}{24}$$
$$\dfrac{11}{8} = \dfrac{x}{24}$$
$$\dfrac{33}{24} = \dfrac{x}{24}$$
$$x = 33$$

TEST-TAKING TIP

We began this solution by planning to use cross-multiplication but then saw a shortcut: making the denominators match. Test questions are often constructed to provide shortcuts.

EXAMPLES

Solve each of the following:

1. If $\dfrac{2}{3} = \dfrac{x}{6}, x = 4$

2. If $\dfrac{x+4}{4} = \dfrac{x}{2}, x = 8$

3. If $\dfrac{3}{x} = \dfrac{x}{12}, x = \pm 6$

4. If $\dfrac{7x}{6x} = \dfrac{7}{6}, x = $ any real number

[6] If the numbers $\frac{13}{23}, \frac{11}{15}$, and $\frac{13}{19}$ were written in order from least to greatest, which of the following arrangements would result?

(A) $\frac{13}{23}, \frac{11}{15}, \frac{13}{19}$

(B) $\frac{13}{19}, \frac{11}{15}, \frac{13}{23}$

(C) $\frac{11}{15}, \frac{13}{19}, \frac{13}{23}$

(D) $\frac{13}{23}, \frac{13}{19}, \frac{11}{15}$

(E) $\frac{13}{19}, \frac{13}{23}, \frac{11}{15}$

With your calculator you can answer this question easily by converting the fractions to the decimals .565, .733, .684, respectively (to the nearest thousandth). The choice is obvious—unless you lose track of which decimal goes with which function. However, you should also be able to use the following property:

> 9-6 If $a, b, c,$ and d are integers and both b and d are positive, then
>
> $$\frac{a}{c} < \frac{c}{d} \quad \text{if and only if} \quad ad < bc.$$

*Note that the numerators a and c remain on their original sides of the inequality sign and the denominators are positive.

By 9-6 we can determine that $\frac{13}{23}$ is less than $\frac{13}{19}$ since $13 \times 19 < 23 \times 13$ and $\frac{13}{19}$ is less than $\frac{11}{15}$ since $13 \times 15 < 11 \times 19$.

[7] If $\frac{3}{a} + \frac{7}{2} = -\frac{15}{2a}$, then $a = ?$

(A) -3

(B) 3

(C) $-\frac{9}{7}$

(D) $\frac{9}{7}$

(E) $\frac{3}{7}$

Two closely related procedures may be used to solve equations involving rational expressions:

1. carry out the additions and/or subtractions of both sides of the equation to get one rational expression on each side and then apply 9-6 or

2. multiply both sides of the equation by the lowest common denominator of all rational expressions

appearing in the equation. The resulting equation will have no rational expressions.

As always you should check your solutions by substitution into the original equation; quite often the process of multiplying both sides of an equation by an expression involving a variable introduces solutions that do not satisfy the original equation.

EXAMPLE

Solve: $\frac{2}{3x} + 5 = \frac{1}{2x}$.

SOLUTION: We will use method (1) and rewrite the above as:

(1) $$\frac{2 + 15x}{3x} = \frac{1}{2x},$$

(2) $$30x^2 + 4x = 3x,$$

(3) $$30x^2 + x = 0,$$

(4) $$x(30x + 1) = 0.$$

Since the product of two numbers can be 0 only when one or both of the numbers is 0, the solution becomes

(5) $$x = 0 \quad \text{or} \quad 30x + 1 = 0.$$

Consequently,

(6) $$x = 0 \quad \text{or} \quad x = -\frac{1}{30}.$$

Only $-\frac{1}{30}$ is an acceptable result, since substitution of 0 for x in the original equation leads to division by 0.

In the multiple-choice question,

$$\frac{3}{a} + \frac{7}{2} = -\frac{15}{2a}.$$

The least common denominator of the three fractions is $2a$. By method (2) we get:

$$2a\left(\frac{3}{a} + \frac{7}{2}\right) = 2a\left(-\frac{15}{2a}\right),$$

$$2a\left(\frac{3}{a}\right) + 2a\left(\frac{7}{2}\right) = 2a\left(-\frac{15}{2a}\right),$$

$$2(3) + a(7) = -15,$$

$$7a = -15 - 6$$

$$7a = -21$$

$$a = -3.$$

EXAMPLES

Solve for x.

1. If $\frac{1}{x} = 5$, then $x = \frac{1}{5}$

2. If $3 - \frac{1}{x} = \frac{1}{2}$, then $x = \frac{2}{5}$

3. If $\dfrac{1}{x} + \dfrac{1}{2x} = \dfrac{1}{3x}$, then no value of x is possible.

SOLVING INEQUALITIES

---

[8]   If $\dfrac{3}{x} < 1$, then which of the following conditions describes the values of x?

   (A) $x > 3$

   (B) $x < -3$

   (C) x is any number

   (D) $x > 3$ or $x < 0$

   (E) $x < 0$

To solve an inequality involving rational expressions: (1) find the least common denominator of all of the expressions; (2) separate the solving process into two cases based on when this common denominator is positive and when negative (it can't be zero); and (3) for each case multiply both sides by the common denominator to clear the inequality of rational expressions. *Be sure to change the direction of the inequality in the case for which the common denominator is negative.*

EXAMPLE 1

If $\dfrac{3}{x} < 1$, then x satisfies what condition?

SOLUTION:

Case 1: When $x > 0$, then $3 < x$.

Case 2: When $x < 0$, then $3 > x$, but $3 > x$ for all $x < 0$, so all $x < 0$ is in the set of solutions.

Hence the condition on x is

$$x > 3 \quad \text{or} \quad x < 0.$$

EXAMPLE 2

Solve: $\dfrac{8}{x-1} + 3 < x$.

SOLUTION: The least common denominator is $x - 1$.

Case 1: $x - 1 > 0$ (in other words, $x > 1$).

$$
\begin{aligned}
8 + 3(x-1) &< x(x-1) \\
0 &< x^2 - 4x - 5 \\
0 &< (x-5)(x+1)
\end{aligned}
$$

The solutions are therefore $x < -1$ or $x > 5$ (see Chapter 8, section [5]). But only $x > 5$ is acceptable for this case since our initial restriction was $x > 1$.

Case 2: $x - 1 < 0$ (in other words, $x < 1$). Therefore

$$8 + 3(x-1) > x(x-1).$$

(Note that we changed the direction of the inequality since $x - 1$ is negative.)

$$0 > x^2 - 4x - 5.$$

Consequently the solutions are

$$1 < x < 5.$$

But the domain of this case is $x < 1$ so it contains no solutions.

We conclude that the solutions contributed by both cases include all x such that $x > 5$.

EXAMPLES

Solve for x.

1. If $\dfrac{1}{x} < 1$, then $x > 1$ or $x < 0$.

2. If $\dfrac{1}{x} < -1$, then $-1 < x < 0$.

3. If $\dfrac{1}{x} < x$, then $x > 1$ or $-1 < x < 0$.

4. If $\dfrac{1}{x+1} > x - 1$, then $-1 < x < \sqrt{2}$ or $x < -\sqrt{2}$.

REDUCING COMPLICATED EXPRESSIONS

---

[9]   Which of the following reduces to $x + 4$?

   (A) $\dfrac{x^2 - 16}{x + 4}$

   (B) $\dfrac{x^2 + 8x + 16}{x - 4}$

   (C) $\dfrac{x^2 - 8x + 16}{4 - x}$

   (D) $\dfrac{x^2 + 8x + 16}{x^2 - 4}$

   (E) $\dfrac{-x^2 - 8x - 16}{-x - 4}$

In preceding sections we have already reviewed the techniques necessary to answer questions [9], [10], and [11]. The only new wrinkle here lies in the application of these techniques to numerators and denominators of many terms. Our experience is that students have more difficulty with this type of expression because they lose sight of the meaning of *reduce*. To *reduce* means to remove common *factors* from numerator and denominator. Many students indiscriminately "cancel" everything that looks the same in numerator and denominator regardless of whether these common entities are factors. We frequently see students who cancel the 2's in $\frac{2x+1}{2x-1}$ to get $\frac{x+1}{x-1}$ even though 2 is not a factor of either $2x+1$ or of $2x-1$. Agreed, 2 is a factor of $2x$, but $2x$ is just a term of the numerator and is not the entire numerator.

The first step in reducing complicated rational expressions is to rewrite the expression with numerator and denominator in completely factored form. Any factor that appears in both should then be struck from both numerator and denominator. Remember that 1 is always a factor of any expression and, if all other factors are removed from either the numerator or the denominator, the factor 1 will remain. To illustrate we will work each of the answers above:

(A) $\dfrac{x^2-16}{x+4}=\dfrac{(x+4)(x-4)}{(x+4)\cdot 1}=\dfrac{(x-4)}{1}=x-4.$

(B) $\dfrac{x^2+8x+16}{x-4}=\dfrac{(x+4)(x+4)}{(x-4)}$; no common factors.

(C) $\dfrac{x^2-8x+16}{4-x}=\dfrac{(x-4)(x-4)}{-1(x-4)}$

$=\dfrac{(x-4)}{-1}$

$=4-x.$

(D) $\dfrac{x^2+8x+16}{x^2-4}=\dfrac{(x+4)(x+4)}{(x-4)(x+4)}=\dfrac{(x+4)}{(x-4)}.$

(E) $\dfrac{-x^2-8x-16}{-x-4}=\dfrac{-1(x+4)(x+4)}{-1(x+4)\cdot 1}=x+4.$

EXAMPLES

Reduce:

1. $\dfrac{2a^2-5a+3}{2a^2-a-3}=\dfrac{a-1}{a+1}$

2. $\dfrac{2a^3+a^2-15a}{8a^3-125}=\dfrac{a(a+3)}{4a^2+10a+25}$

3. $\dfrac{2a-3b+1}{4a^2+4a-9b^2+1}=\dfrac{1}{2a+3b+1}$

[10] Which of the following equals $a-8$?

(A) $\dfrac{2a+5}{4a^2-14a+12}\times\dfrac{8a^3-27}{2a+5}$

(B) $\dfrac{2a^2-5a+3}{9-a^2}\times\dfrac{a^3-3a^2-a+3}{2a^2-a-3}$

(C) $\dfrac{a^2-4}{a+8}\div\dfrac{a^2-4}{a^2-64}$

(D) $\dfrac{21ab-28a}{14ab^2-14b^2}$

$\div\dfrac{15ab-20a-21b+28}{21-a-10a^2}$

(E) $\dfrac{a^3+64}{a+4}\times\dfrac{1}{a^2-4a+16}$

TEST-TAKING TIP

A question in which the answer choices are this complicated would rarely (if ever) appear on a test. We have constructed this question to present a large number of mathematical problems to resolve.

Factor each numerator and denominator completely before carrying out any operation. You may choose to write the product or quotient as a single rational expression or remove common factors *before* doing so, always bearing in mind where these factors will occur in the product or quotient. Use the techniques of the preceding section to reduce the product or quotient and, finally, multiply together the remaining factors. To illustrate we will work out each of the answers above, beginning with their factored forms.

(A) $\dfrac{(2a+5)}{2(2a-3)(a-2)}\times\dfrac{(2a-3)(4a^2+6a+9)}{(2a+5)}$

$=\dfrac{4a^2+6a+9}{2a-4}$

(B) $\dfrac{(2a-3)(a-1)}{-1(a-3)(3+a)}\times\dfrac{(a-1)(a+1)(a-3)}{(2a-3)(a+1)}$

$=\dfrac{(a-1)^2}{-(3+a)}$

(C) $\dfrac{(a+2)(a-2)}{(a+8)}\times\dfrac{(a+8)(a-8)}{(a+2)(a-2)}=a-8$

(D) $\dfrac{7a(3b-4)}{14b^2(a-1)}\times\dfrac{(7-5a)(3+2a)}{-1(7-5a)(3b-4)}$

$=\dfrac{3a+2a^2}{2b^2-2ab^2}$

(E) $\dfrac{\cancel{(a+4)}\cancel{(a^2-4a+16)}}{\cancel{(a+4)}(a-4)} \times \dfrac{1}{\cancel{a^2-4a+16}}$

$$= \dfrac{1}{a-4}$$

EXAMPLES

Simplify:

1. $\dfrac{a^2-8a}{a-5} \times \dfrac{a^2-25}{a^2-64} = \dfrac{a(a+5)}{a+8}$

2. $\dfrac{3a^2}{6b+42} \div \dfrac{a}{b^2-49} = \dfrac{a(b-7)}{2}$

3. $\dfrac{a^2-16}{a^2+2a-8} \div \dfrac{a^2-8a+16}{a^2+3a-10} = \dfrac{a+5}{a-4}$

4. $\dfrac{2a^2-14a+12}{a^3-4a^2} \div \dfrac{a^2+a-2}{a+2} = \dfrac{2(a-6)}{a^2(a-4)}$

FINDING THE LEAST COMMON DENOMINATOR

---

[11] If $\dfrac{6x}{x^2-3x}$ is subtracted from the sum of $\dfrac{3}{5x-15}$ and $\dfrac{x+3}{x-3}$, the result is:

(A) $-\dfrac{2}{3}$

(B) $\dfrac{x+2}{x-3}$

(C) $\dfrac{-5x}{x^2-3x}$

(D) $\dfrac{5x-12}{5x-15}$

(E) $\dfrac{x^2+2x}{x-3}$

We will begin with a few comments about common denominators. The product of the denominators of two rational expressions will always be a common denominator, though not necessarily the least common denominator (LCD). To find the LCD, factor the given denominators completely. The LCD will contain every factor that occurs in either denominator, and the power of each factor is the same as its higher power in either given denominator. For example, the LCD for

$$\dfrac{1}{a^2(a-2)(a-3)^3} \quad \text{and} \quad \dfrac{1}{ab(a-2)^3}$$

must be $a^2b(a-2)^3(a-3)^3$. Note that both b and $a-3$ are factors of the LCD though they are factors of only one of the given denominators. Note also that the power of $a-2$ in the LCD is 3 since its higher power in either denominator is 3.

Remember that when changing the denominator of a fraction you are actually multiplying the fraction by 1; to ensure this, you must multiply the numerator by the same expression by which you multiplied the denominator. For example, to change $\frac{1}{2}$ to fourths, multiply the $\frac{1}{2}$ by $\frac{2}{2}$; the value of the fraction is unchanged since multiplication by 1 cannot change it.

To write $\frac{x+3}{x-3}$ with denominator $5x(x-3)$, multiply the fraction by $\frac{5x}{5x}$.

$$\dfrac{x+3}{x-3} \cdot \dfrac{5x}{5x} = \dfrac{5x(x+3)}{5x(x-3)}.$$

To answer the multiple-choice question, simplify

$$\dfrac{3}{5x-15} + \dfrac{x+3}{x-3} - \dfrac{6x}{x^2-3x}$$

In factored form the denominators are

$$5(x-3), x-3, \text{ and } x(x-3),$$

so the LCD is $5x(x-3)$. Convert each fraction to the LCD as follows:

$$\dfrac{3}{5x-15} = \dfrac{3}{5(x-3)} = \dfrac{3}{5(x-3)} \cdot \dfrac{x}{x} = \dfrac{3x}{5x(x-3)},$$

$$\dfrac{x+3}{x-3} = \dfrac{x+3}{x-3} \cdot \dfrac{5x}{5x} = \dfrac{5x(x+3)}{5x(x-3)},$$

$$\dfrac{6x}{x^2-3x} = \dfrac{6x}{x(x-3)} = \dfrac{6x}{x(x-3)} \cdot \dfrac{5}{5} = \dfrac{30x}{5x(x-3)}$$

Therefore:

$$\dfrac{3x}{5x(x+3)} + \dfrac{5x(x+3)}{5x(x-3)} - \dfrac{30x}{5x(x-3)}$$

$$= \dfrac{3x+5x^2+15x-30x}{5x(x-3)},$$

$$\dfrac{5x^2-12x}{5x(x-3)} = \dfrac{x(5x-12)}{5x(x-3)}$$

$$= \dfrac{5x-12}{5x-15}.$$

EXAMPLE

Simplify: $\dfrac{3a-2}{4-4a+a^2} - \dfrac{a+8}{4-a^2} + \dfrac{9}{2+a}$.

SOLUTION: The denominators in factored form are $(2-a)^2$, $(2-a)(2+a)$, and $(2+a)$ so the LCD is $(2-a)^2(2+a)$.

$$\left[\frac{3a-2}{(2-a)^2} \times \frac{2+a}{2+a} \right] - \left[\frac{a+8}{(2-a)(2+a)} \times \frac{2-a}{2-a} \right]$$
$$+ \left[\frac{7}{2+a} \times \frac{(2-a)(2+a)}{(2-a)(2+a)} \right]$$
$$= \frac{(3a^2+4a-4) - (16-6a-a^2) + (28-7a^2)}{(2-a)^2(2+a)}$$
$$= \frac{-3a^2+10a+8}{a^3-2a^2-4a+8}$$

EXAMPLES

Simplify:

1. $\dfrac{1}{a} + \dfrac{1}{b} + \dfrac{1}{c} = \dfrac{bc+ac+ab}{abc}$

2. $\dfrac{2}{(a+b)c} - \dfrac{5}{(a+b)d} = \dfrac{2d-5c}{(a+b)cd}$

3. $\dfrac{2a}{-a-b} + \dfrac{2b}{a-b} - \dfrac{2}{a^2-b^2} = \dfrac{4ab-2a^2+2b^2-2}{a^2-b^2}$

[12] Simplify: $\dfrac{\dfrac{x^2-4}{x^2-x-6}}{\dfrac{x^2+x-6}{x^2-9}}$.

(A) 1

(B) $x-3$

(C) $x+2$

(D) $x-2$

(E) $x+3$

A fraction whose numerator and denominator are rational expressions can be treated as an indicated division. For example, we may rewrite the above as:

$$\frac{x^2-4}{x^2-x-6} \div \frac{x^2+x-6}{x^2-9}$$
$$= \frac{x^2-4}{x^2-x-6} \times \frac{x^2-9}{x^2+x-6}$$
$$= \frac{(x-2)(x+2)(x-3)(x+3)}{(x-3)(x+2)(x-2)(x+3)}$$
$$= 1$$

EXAMPLES

Simplify:

1. $\dfrac{\dfrac{x^3y^4}{18}}{\dfrac{x^4y^3}{36}} = \dfrac{2y}{x}$

2. $\dfrac{\dfrac{x^2+3x}{x^2+7x+10}}{\dfrac{x^3-9x}{x+2}} = \dfrac{1}{(x+5)(x-3)}$

[13] Simplify: $\dfrac{1+\dfrac{1}{x}}{1-\dfrac{1}{x}}$.

(A) 1

(B) -1

(C) x

(D) $x+1$

(E) $\dfrac{x+1}{x-1}$

A mixed expression is the sum of a polynomial and a rational expression. To simplify a fraction in which either the numerator or denominator (or both) is a mixed expression, rewrite the mixed expressions as rational expressions and then apply the techniques of the preceding section.

EXAMPLE 1

$$\frac{x-\dfrac{4}{x}}{1-\dfrac{2}{x}} = \frac{\dfrac{x^2-4}{x}}{\dfrac{x-2}{x}} = \frac{x^2-4}{x} \times \frac{x}{x-2} = x+2$$

EXAMPLE 2

$$\frac{\dfrac{1}{a}-\dfrac{1}{b}}{\dfrac{a-b}{ab}} = \frac{\dfrac{b-a}{ab}}{\dfrac{a-b}{ab}} = \frac{b-a}{ab} \times \frac{ab}{a-b} = -1$$

To answer the multiple-choice question, multiply numerator and denominator by x and clear fractions:

$$\frac{x\left(1+\dfrac{1}{x}\right)}{x\left(1-\dfrac{1}{x}\right)} = \frac{x+1}{x-1}.$$

We picked x to multiply by because x is the LCD of the fractions that make up the terms of the complex fraction. This is an alternative method to the one explained above.

EXAMPLES

Simplify:

1. $\dfrac{\dfrac{1}{a}+1}{a+1} = \dfrac{1}{a}$

2. $\dfrac{x-2}{\dfrac{1}{x}-\dfrac{1}{2}} = -2x$

3. $\dfrac{\dfrac{1}{a}+\dfrac{1}{b}}{\dfrac{1}{a}-\dfrac{1}{b}} = \dfrac{b+a}{b-a}$

4. $\dfrac{\dfrac{z-y}{z}+\dfrac{z-y}{y}}{\dfrac{z-y}{y}-\dfrac{z-y}{z}} = \dfrac{y+z}{z-y}$

[14] If $\dfrac{1}{x-1} = x-1$, what does x equal?

(A) 1

(B) 0

(C) 1 or 0

(D) 2

(E) 0 or 2

Applying the technique of section [7], we multiply both sides of the equation by the LCD, solve this simpler equation, and then check all solutions—discarding any that may have been introduced by the multiplication step.

EXAMPLE 1

$$\frac{1}{x-1} = x-1$$
$$1 = x^2 - 2x + 1$$
$$0 = x^2 - 2x$$
$$0 = x(x-2)$$

Therefore $x = 0$ or $x = 2$, both of which satisfy the original equation.

EXAMPLE 2

Find a if $\dfrac{1}{a} + \dfrac{2}{a+1} = \dfrac{5}{6}$.

SOLUTION: The LCD is $6a(a+1)$.

$$6a(a+1)\left(\frac{1}{a}+\frac{2}{a+1}\right) = 6a(a+1)\left(\frac{5}{6}\right)$$
$$6(a+1)+12a = 5a^2+5a$$
$$18a+6 = 5a^2+5a$$
$$0 = 5a^2 - 13a - 6$$
$$0 = (5a+2)(a-3)$$

Therefore $5a+2 = 0$ or $a-3 = 0$. The solutions are $-\frac{2}{5}$ and 3, both of which satisfy the original equation.

EXAMPLES

Solve:

1. If $\dfrac{1}{x-1} + \dfrac{2}{3} + \dfrac{2}{x-1} = \dfrac{13}{6}$, then $x = 3$.

2. If $\dfrac{15}{2x-1} = x$, then $x = 3, -\dfrac{5}{2}$.

3. If $7 - \dfrac{7x}{x+2} = \dfrac{3}{x+5}$, then $x = -\dfrac{64}{11}$.

THE OPPOSITE OF $x - y$

[15] Find the value of $\dfrac{a^2 - b^2}{b^2 - a^2}$.

(A) -1

(B) 1

(C) 0

(D) $a+b$

(E) $a-b$

What is the additive inverse of $(x-y)$? Note that

$$-(x-y) = (-x)-(-y)$$
$$= -x+y$$
$$= y-x$$

This important fact, $-(x-y) = y-x$, is frequently used in simplification of rational expressions, and it occurs in the question above. A useful way of dealing with it is to think of factoring out -1.

$$(x-y) = (-1)(y-x)$$

Therefore

$$\frac{a^2-b^2}{b^2-a^2} = \frac{a^2-b^2}{(-1)(a^2-b^2)} = \frac{1}{(-1)} = -1$$

EXAMPLES

Simplify each of the following:

1. $\dfrac{5-2}{2-5} = -1$

2. $\dfrac{x-y^2}{-x+y^2} = -1$

3. $\dfrac{a^2-b^2}{b^2-2ab+a^2} = \dfrac{a+b}{a-b}$

RESOLVING A FRACTION INTO A PAIR OF FRACTIONS

---

[16] Find the value of A if

$$\frac{2}{(x-5)(x+3)} = \frac{A}{x-5} + \frac{B}{x+3}$$

(A) 1

(B) 3

(C) 5

(D) -5

(E) $\dfrac{1}{4}$

Procedures for combining rational expressions are a standard part of the study of intermediate math. A question like the one above, however, asks not how to *combine* fractions but how to *resolve* a fraction into a pair of fractions for which the given fraction is the sum.

This can be done by using the techniques already learned for combining fractions. What is the result of adding $\frac{A}{x-5}$ and $\frac{B}{x+3}$? The LCD is $(x-5)(x+3)$, so the result is

$$\frac{A(x+3)}{(x-5)(x+3)} + \frac{B(x-5)}{(x-5)(x+3)}$$
$$= \frac{Ax+3A+Bx-5B}{(x-5)(x+3)}$$
$$= \frac{(A+B)(x)+(3A-5B)}{(x-5)(x+3)}.$$

In order for the last rational expression to be equal to the given expression,

$$\frac{2}{(x-5)(x+3)},$$

the numerators must be equal. Therefore

(1) $\qquad 2 = (A+B)x + (3A-5B).$

Since the left side has no x term, the coefficient of any x term must be zero.

(2) $\qquad A+B = 0$

Since the constant term, 2, must equal the constant term, $(3A-5B)$, we get

(3) $\qquad 3A-5B = 2.$

Solving the system composed of equations (2) and (3) simultaneously will give us the desired information. We begin by solving (1) for B,

$$B = -A,$$

and replacing B with $-A$ in equation (3):

$$3A-5(-A) = 2,$$
$$8A = 2,$$
$$A = \frac{1}{4}.$$

We could continue to find B, but the additional work is unnecessary since only A is requested.

If the left side of equation (1) had included a term involving x, we would have set $A+B$ equal to the coefficient of x in that expression and proceeded in the same way. For example, to resolve

$$\frac{3x-1}{x(x-1)} = \frac{A}{x} + \frac{B}{x-1}$$

we first write

$$\frac{A}{x} + \frac{B}{x-1} = \frac{A(x-1)}{x(x-1)} + \frac{Bx}{(x-1)x}$$
$$= \frac{(A+B)x-A}{x(x-1)}$$

Therefore

$$3x-1 = (A+B)x - A.$$

For this equation to be true, both of the following must hold:

$$A+B = 3,$$
$$-A = -1.$$

All that remains is to determine A and B; this is left as an exercise.

EXAMPLES

Find A and B if:

1. If $\dfrac{2x+1}{x(x+1)} = \dfrac{A}{x} + \dfrac{B}{x+1}$, then $A = 1$, $B = 1$.

2. If $\dfrac{7}{6x^2+x-2} = \dfrac{A}{3x-2} + \dfrac{B}{x+1}$, then $A = \dfrac{21}{5}$, $B = -\dfrac{7}{5}$.

[17]   For all $x < 0$, $\dfrac{(3x^2 - 15x)}{(5x - 25)} = ?$

(A) $\dfrac{3x}{5}$

(B) $\dfrac{3x-3}{-25}$

(C) $\dfrac{12x}{25}$

(D) $\dfrac{x-1}{8}$

(E) $\dfrac{3x^2-3}{-20}$

When you simplify rational expressions, avoid the temptation to become a mad slasher (one who crosses out anything in the denominator that looks remotely like something in the numerator).

Remember that only common factors may be "canceled." That means you must first factor the numerators and denominators. For this problem, the steps look like this:

$$\frac{3x^2 - 15}{5x - 25} = \frac{3x(x-5)}{5(x-5)} = \frac{3x}{5}, \text{ (A)}.$$

The factor, $x - 5$, can be removed for all values of x except 5. Note that $x = 5$ presents no problem because the domain specified was $x < 0$, which excludes 5.

As with most Level IC questions, a condition stated in the question (in this case, $x < 0$) removes a complication rather than adding one.

Regarding "canceling," remember to factor first, and then remove (cancel) only expressions that are common factors.

[18]   If $x = \dfrac{p-3}{p^3}$ and $y = \dfrac{p+3}{p^3}$, then $x + y = ?$

(A) $\dfrac{3}{p^2}$

(B) $\dfrac{2}{p^3}$

(C) $\dfrac{6}{p^3}$

(D) $\dfrac{2}{p^2}$

(E) $\dfrac{3}{p^3}$

The problem looks far more complicated than it really is. The simple form of all of the answers suggests that the process can't be very alarming. Add the two expressions, combine the fractions, and then reduce. For this problem, the steps look like this:

$$
\begin{aligned}
x + y &= \frac{p-3}{p^3} + \frac{p+3}{p^3} \\
&= \frac{(p-3)+(p+3)}{p^3} \\
&= \frac{2p}{p^3} \\
&= \frac{2}{p^2}, \text{ (D)}.
\end{aligned}
$$

At first, the question appears to involve solving a system of two equations in three unknowns. Instead, it is a routine problem of combining and then simplifying. The question itself, $x + y = ?$ is actually a set of directions designed to set you off in the right direction.

[19]   Find a if $\dfrac{1}{(x+2)(x-5)} = \dfrac{a}{x+2} + \dfrac{b}{x-5}$

(A) -3

(B) -10

(C) $-\dfrac{1}{7}$

(D) $\dfrac{2}{7}$

(E) 10

A question like this would be unfamiliar to most students who have only completed intermediate math. Therefore, it almost certainly presents a new situation to you. Test makers like to present unfamiliar questions among the final items on the test.

So what do you do when you are in a new situation? Try different things.

This is an equation with fractions, so start by multiplying both sides by the lowest common denominator, $(x+2)(x-5)$.

Now your equation looks like this:

$$1 = a(x-5) + b(x+2).$$

Definitely simpler, but the value of a is still not obvious.

Let's try something else now. Substitute -2 for x to make the right term drop out.

Now you have $1 = a(-7)$ and the value of a is easily seen to be $-\frac{1}{7}$, answer (C).

If the idea of substituting $x = -2$ didn't come to you, try something else—say, transforming the equation by collecting like terms.

That would give you

$$1 = (a+b)x + (-5a+2b).$$

That means $a + b = 0$ (because the left hand side of the equation has no x term, which is another way of saying the coefficient of x is 0) and $-5a + 2b = 1$. Solve the two equations for a by substituting $b = -a$ (from the first equation) into the second equation and you are done.

WHAT YOU SHOULD KNOW

KEY CONCEPTS

Handling Fractions

1. *To compare two fractions,* multiply the numerator of each by the denominator of the other and compare the products. The greater product contains the numerator of the greater fraction.
2. *To simplify a complex fraction,*
   a. express it as the division of the numerator by the denominator, then invert and multiply, *or*
   b. multiply the numerator and denominator of a complex fraction by the LCD of all the fractions that appear in either the numerator or the denominator.
3. *To solve an equation in which both members are fractions,* cross-multiply.

Handling Rational Expressions

1. *To simplify a rational expression,* first factor the numerator and the denominator, then remove common factors.
2. *To multiply rational expressions,* multiply the numerators and multiply the denominators.
3. *To divide rational expressions,* invert the divisor and multiply.
4. *To convert a rational expression to a different denominator,* multiply by $\dfrac{c}{c}$, where c is the factor needed to produce the desired denominator.
5. *To add (or subtract) rational expressions,*
   a. with the *same* denominator, add (or subtract) numerators and write the result with the common denominator.
   b. with *different* denominators, first change to the same denominator (see item 4 above) and then add (or subtract) (see 5a above).
6. *To solve an equation involving rational expressions,* clear fractions by multiplying all terms by the lowest common denominator (LCD).
7. *To gain additional opportunities to remove common factors,* replace the expression $a - b$ by the equivalent form $(-1)(b - a)$.

KEY PROPERTY

If a, b, c, and d are real numbers and neither b nor d is zero, then

$$\frac{a}{b} = \frac{c}{d} \quad \text{if and only if} \quad ad = bc.$$

(Cross-Multiplication Property)

TEST-TAKING STRATEGIES

- Reducing a fraction means removing common factors from the numerator and denominator. This operation can best be carried out by thinking of the three words "remove common factors" as telling you what to do in reverse order. First *factor*. Then identify factors that are *common*. Then *remove* these common factors.
- Cross-multiplication is an extremely useful way of comparing fractions and solving simple fractional equations. At first, it may look like a gimmick that has no reason for being true. Study the proof given in this text to assure yourself that cross-multiplication is well supported by mathematical theory.
- Complex fractions look nastier than they really are. Simply multiply the numerator and denominator of a complex fraction by the LCD of all of the fractions of which it is composed. The result is always a simple fraction that is easy to work with.
- Don't overlook the simplification potential in knowing that $x - y$ and $y - x$ are opposites. In most applications, one can readily be converted into the other by a simple algebraic manipulation. By doing so, you can often markedly reduce the number of steps necessary to get an answer.
- Finding LCDs and reducing fractions requires the ability to factor quickly and accurately. Be sure to master your factoring skills before taking the Math Level IC test.

CALCULATOR SKILLS

- Know how your calculator treats and displays division by zero.
- Know how to convert fractions to decimals and decimals to fractions so that you can determine which number is greater and operate with the numbers they represent.

ANSWERS

[1] (E)   [5] (C)   [9] (E)   [13] (E)   [17] (A)
[2] (C)   [6] (D)   [10] (C)   [14] (E)   [18] (D)
[3] (B)   [7] (A)   [11] (D)   [15] (A)   [19] (C)
[4] (E)   [8] (D)   [12] (A)   [16] (E)

LINES AND PLANES

CHAPTER

10

KEY TERMS

A **point**   has no width or thickness, only position.

A **line**   is a set of points, has no thickness, is straight, and continues infinitely in two directions.

A **plane**   is a set of points, is flat, has no depth (thickness), and continues infinitely in all directions.

A **ray**   has no thickness, has one endpoint, and extends infinitely in one direction.

A **postulate** is an agreement about the properties of algebraic or geometric elements.

Calculators are useful in solving some types of geometry problems but not others. The calculator can help with numerical geometry problems, which may involve area, perimeter, circumference, arc length, proportional parts, and angle measure. On the other hand, the calculator will probably not be helpful in answering questions about the relationships between lines, planes, and the congruence of figures. In this chapter, for example, all of the questions are calculator inactive.

IDENTIFYING INTERSECTIONS AND UNIONS

[1]   Each of the following sets of points could be the intersection of a line and a plane EXCEPT

(A) the empty set

(B) a single point

(C) a line

(D) a plane

(E) the intersection of two lines

The basic terms of geometry are *set, point, line,* and *plane*.

Texts vary in just what postulates they agree on at the outset, but the resulting theory derived from them is substantially the same. In general we will rely more on the motivation for each postulate than on its exact wording.

Lines are "straight" and extend infinitely in two directions. Points have no thickness or depth. Planes are flat, with no thickness, and extend infinitely in all directions.

Two sets *intersect* when they have at least one point in common. The *intersection* of two sets is the set of points that belong to both. Consequently, if a point X belongs to the intersection of two sets, A and B, then X must belong to B, and X must belong to A. If two sets do not intersect, their intersection is the empty set. Therefore, if a line L does not intersect a plane P, then $L \cap P = \emptyset$.

If a line pierces a plane but does not also lie in the plane, this intersection contains only a single point. If the line does lie in the plane, their intersection is the entire line, since every point of the line belongs to both.

Answer (E) above is tricky. The intersection of a pair of lines can be either a single point, the empty set, or (in the case where the lines coincide) a line. All of these are also possible intersections of a line and a plane, so only choice (D) will answer the question.

A point X belongs to the *union* of sets A and B if and only if it belongs to A *or* it belongs to B (or both). As long as it belongs to at least one of these sets it is in their union.

WORKING WITH LINES, SEGMENTS, AND RAYS

[2]   In the figure, points A, B, and C are collinear as drawn. If the length of $AB = 3x - 15$ and the length of BC is one-third the length of AB, the length of AC is?

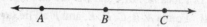

(A) $2x - 10$

(B) $2x - 20$

(C) $4x - 20$

(D) $4x - 10$

(E) $2x + 5$

A set of points is *collinear* if there is one line that contains every point of the set. Note that two points are always collinear, but three points need not be. That's why the testers specifically stated that the given points are collinear in this question. In a few minutes, we will use the fact they are collinear to help us set up an equation.

Your high school math text probably fussed over the differences in symbols used to differentiate between lines, segments, rays, and the lengths of segments. Different textbooks use different symbols. Sometimes different authors even use the exact opposite of the notation you learned in your geometry course, which can cause great confusion.

Therefore, test makers bend over backward to be clear in their use of notation.

To answer this question, first note that B is between A and C. From this you can conclude,

$$AB + BC = AC,$$

an equation math texts usually call the "definition of between."

Since BC is one-third the length of AB, the length of BC is $x - 5$. Therefore,

$$(3x - 15) + (x - 5) = AC$$
$$= 4x - 20.$$

UNDERSTANDING "STRAIGHTNESS" OF LINES

[3]   If A and B are two different points that lie on line CD and also on line EF, which of the following statements must be true?

    I.   Lines AC, BF, and ED are all parallel.

    II.   Points A, B, C, D, E, and F all lie on the same line.

    III.   Points A, B, C, and E all lie in the same plane.

    (A)   I only

    (B)   I and II only

    (C)   II only

    (D)   II and III only

    (E)   III only

Lines in Euclidean geometry are "straight" and have no bends.

Because straightness is fundamental, geometers don't take it for granted. Instead, they guarantee it by an agreement so basic to geometry that it is usually designated "Postulate 1."

Postulate 1 *If A and B are different points, there is one and only one line that will contain both.*

To see that this actually does disallow a "nonstraight" line, draw two points and then a line that contains both. Now try to draw a different line that also contains both. Unless you have allowed your second line to bend (or represented your original points by very fat dots) you cannot draw a second line.

Can a pair of different lines intersect in more than one point? Suppose they did intersect in two (or more) points. Then these two points would be contained in both lines, which contradicts Postulate 1. We have just used an informal argument to deduce the following:

> 10-1   Two different lines will intersect in exactly one point (if they intersect at all).

To answer the multiple-choice question, note that, in order for both line CD and line EF to contain points A and B, line CD and line EF must be the same line.

TEST-TAKING TIP

Look back at the format of this question. Some descriptive information is given. Three statements, each designated by a Roman numeral, are given. You must decide which must be true. There are really eight different outcomes or combinations of possible outcomes: I only; II only; III only; I and II; I and III; II and III; I, II, and III; and none. The test makers eliminate three possibilities and ask you which of the remaining five choices is correct.

This format is used in several questions on each Level IC exam.

Occasionally, as in this case, the truth of one statement guarantees the truth of another. Because all of the points lie on the same line (statement II), they all lie in the same plane (statement III). Also, the truth of one statement may guarantee the falsity of another. Because the points lie on the same line, lines connecting them in pairs cannot be parallel as required by statement I. Test makers prefer, however, not to give you these "two for one" opportunities. As much as possible, they construct statements that are independent of each other.

UNDERSTANDING "FLATNESS" OF PLANES

[4]   If A, B, C, and D are any four distinct points of a plane P, which of the following must be true?

    I.   Line AB must intersect line CD.

    II.   Line AB can contain a point not in plane P.

    III.   Any point of intersection of any of the pairs of lines containing A, B, C, and D must lie in plane P.

    (A)   I only

    (B)   I and II only

    (C)   II and III only

    (D)   II only

    (E)   III only

Here's more practice with the format discussed in the last section—as well as more experience with the idea of guaranteeing a geometric property by agreeing to a postulate.

We want our planes to be "flat" and extend in all directions. It takes two postulates to make this happen. And these two postulates lead us to a conclusion.

Postulate 2 *Any plane that contains two distinct points of a line must contain every point of the line.*

Postulate 2 provides the necessary restriction for "flatness."

Postulate 3 *The intersection of two distinct intersecting planes is a line.*

Among other things, Postulate 3 asserts that planes extend infinitely in all directions since lines extend infinitely in two directions.

A line, therefore, cannot intersect a plane in more than one point unless it lies in the plane, according to Postulate 2. We state this as a theorem:

> 10-2 The intersection of a line and a plane contains no more than one point (unless the line lies in the plane).

Statement I is incorrect since lines *AB* and *CD* could be parallel. Statement II disagrees with Postulate 2. Statement III is a consequence of Postulate 2.

> ### TEST-TAKING TIP
> You may have been misled into thinking statement I was true by drawing a figure in which the lines intersected. Drawing diagrams is, of course, very useful—but only if the figures consider all possibilities. You must always ask yourself, "What other possibilities satisfy the given information?" In this case, the given information allows both possibilities: parallel lines and intersecting lines.

IDENTIFYING PLANES

[5] A set of points is said to "determine" a plane if there is exactly one plane that contains all of the points. Which of the following does not determine a plane?

(A) A triangle

(B) Any three points

(C) A line and a point not on the line

(D) A pair of intersecting rays

(E) A pair of intersecting lines

> ### TEST-TAKING TIP
> In this question type, you are given a term and its definition and then asked to apply the meaning of that term. Sometimes, as in this case, the term is familiar. The idea of points "determining" a plane was probably discussed very thoroughly in your geometry classes. When the term is a common one, the testers are giving you the meaning to refresh your memory.
>
> Sometimes, however, you will be given an unfamiliar term and asked to use it to pick the correct answer. Testers use such questions to see how well you can understand a definition and apply it. The best preparation for this is the practice you receive with new terms introduced in your regular classroom lessons.

We will formalize an agreement already mentioned informally:

Postulate 4 *There exists at least one plane that contains any three points. There is at most one plane that contains any three noncollinear points.*

Thus three noncollinear points will determine a plane. A triangle also determines a plane since the three vertices of a triangle determine a plane, and this plane contains the sides by Postulate 2. Three collinear points do not determine a plane since infinitely many planes may contain all of them. Since a set containing two points of a line and a point not on the line is a set of three noncollinear points and since this line must lie in any plane that contains two of its points, we can conclude that (C) determines a plane. Both (D) and (E) involve the same idea. Let *X* be the point of intersection of the two sets and let *Y* and *Z* each be another point of each of the sets. These noncollinear points determine a plane that then contains the rays or lines by Postulate 2.

[6]   If a line is contained in a plane, the two sets of points of the plane that do not lie on the line may be called "sides" of the line. Each of the following statements is true about S_1 and S_2 if they are the two sides of a line L in a plane M, EXCEPT

   (A)   if P and Q lie in S_1, then every point of segment PQ lies in S_1

   (B)   if P lies in S_1, and Q lies in S_2, then segment PQ must intersect line L

   (C)   the union of S_1 and S_2 is plane M

   (D)   the intersection of S_1 and S_2 is the empty set

   (E)   there exists at least one line completely contained in S_1

This question gives you continued practice with: (1) the EXCEPT format, (2) test items that rely on terms whose meanings are part of the given information, and (3) using diagrams to help you visualize the given information.

In some texts the sides of a line are called "half-planes." We will occasionally use the notion of sides to help define more complicated regions of planes.

TEST-TAKING TIP

Representing geometric information by diagrams is extremely helpful. Often the diagram alone is enough to suggest an answer or a problem-solving method.

The following diagrams are useful in illustrating the information in several answer choices:

(A)

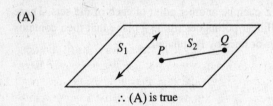

$\therefore$ (A) is true

(B)

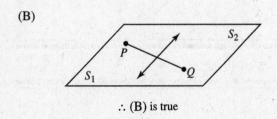

$\therefore$ (B) is true

(E)

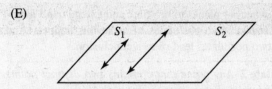

(C) cannot be true since line L by definition is not contained in either S_1 or S_2. (D) is true since L makes a boundary between S_1 and S_2. (E) is true—any line parallel to L will satisfy this condition.

[7]   The figure represents a trapezoidal prism with $BC \parallel AD$.

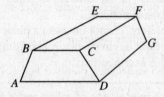

The intersection of plane BEG and plane EFD is line

   (A) BD

   (B) BG

   (C) DE

   (D) AF

   (E) AE

The Level IC test includes questions about geometry in three dimensions. Most questions about three-dimensional objects require little more than the ability to visualize the object as a figure with length, width, and depth. In other words, no special laws of three dimensions must be known.

This question becomes much easier to understand once you realize that plane BEG is also plane $BEGD$ (remember that you only need three points to determine a plane) and plane EFD is plane $EFDA$. Just from the duplication in letters in the symbols for these two planes (the points E and D appear in both) you can recognize that line DE must be the correct line of intersection.

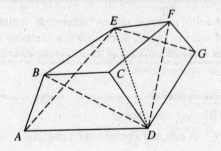

WHAT YOU SHOULD KNOW

KEY CONCEPTS

Handling Points and Lines

1. The *intersection* of sets A and B is the set of points that belong to both A and B.
2. The *union* of sets A and B is the set of all points belonging to either A or B.
3. A set of points is *collinear* if all are contained in the same line.
4. A set of points is *coplanar* if all are contained in the same plane.
5. A point B is *between* points A and C if and only if $AB + BC = AC$.
6. A point M is the *midpoint* of segment AC if and only if it is between A and C and

$$AM = CM = \frac{1}{2}AC.$$

7. Two different points are contained in exactly one line.
8. If two different lines intersect, their intersection is a point.

Handling Planes

1. If two points of a line lie in a plane, the line lies in the plane.
2. If two planes intersect, their intersection is a line.
3. If a line intersects a plane and does not lie in the plane, the intersection is one point.
4. Any three points lie in a plane; any three noncollinear points lie in exactly one plane.
5. A set of points "determines" a plane if there is one and only one plane containing all points of the set.
6. A plane is determined by (a) three noncollinear points, (b) a line and a point not on the line, and (c) a pair of lines intersecting at exactly one point.

7. A line lying in a plane separates the plane into two sets (neither of which includes the points of the line) called *half-planes* or *sides* of the line. The half-planes are *convex*. If a point A is in one half-plane and a point B is in the other, segment AB must intersect the given line.

KEY THEOREMS

1. Two different lines will intersect in exactly one point (if they intersect at all).
2. The intersection of a line and a plane contains no more than one point (unless the line lies in the plane).

TEST-TAKING STRATEGIES

- If a question dealing with lines and planes does not provide a diagram to show relationships, draw your own diagram to represent the information given.
- Definitions and postulates of geometry vary a great deal from textbook to textbook. SAT II Math Level IC tests are intended to test the ideas presented and not the wording used in any particular approach. For example, terms like "half-plane" and "convex" are not universally used in geometry tests, so it is unlikely that you will see them on the SAT II Math Level IC tests. We've used them here because they help you visualize the concepts they present and make other definitions easier to understand. Do not be confused by varying terminology.
- SAT II Math Level IC tests avoid using particular symbols to name rays, line segments, and lines. Instead, be aware that they use the terms "ray," "line," and "line segment" to avoid any possibility of confusion.

ANSWERS

[1] (D) [3] (D) [5] (B) [7] (C)
[2] (C) [4] (E) [6] (C)

ANGLES

CHAPTER

11

KEY TERMS

angle	the union of two rays that have a common endpoint and are not contained in the same line.
vertex of an angle	the point common to the two rays.
measure of an angle	a number between 0 and 180.
right angle	an angle with a measure of 90.
acute angle	an angle with a measure between 0 and 90.
obtuse angle	an angle with a measure between 90 and 180.

Calculators are useful in solving some types of geometry problems but not others. The calculator can help with numerical geometry problems, which may involve area, perimeter, circumference, arc length, proportional parts, and angle measure. On the other hand, the calculator will probably not be helpful in answering questions about the relationships between lines, planes, and the congruence of figures. In this chapter, for example, all of the questions are calculator inactive.

UNDERSTANDING SOME BASIC ASPECTS OF ANGLES

[1] Which of the following statements about angles is NOT true?

(A) An angle of a triangle may have a degree measure of 180.

(B) An angle of a triangle may not have a degree measure greater than 180.

(C) Two angles may be complementary without having a common side.

(D) The degree measure of an angle does not depend on the lengths of its sides.

(E) A triangle cannot have two right angles

In this section we will review many elementary aspects of angles. By an *angle* we mean the union of two rays that (1) have a common endpoint and (2) do not lie on the same line:

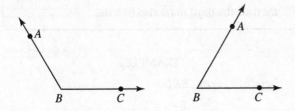

but neither

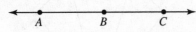

nor

Because an angle is the union of two rays, its sides cannot be segments. Therefore, answer (D) is true because the degree measure does not change as the lengths of the sides change. We will sometimes call the union of two segments an "angle" but what we will really mean is the angle whose sides contain the segments. When naming an angle we use the symbol ∠ followed by three capital letters. The first letter names a point on one ray, the second names the vertex (the common endpoint of the rays), and the third names a different point on the remaining side. (Thus the vertex of ∠ABC is B.) When only one angle has a given point as its vertex, we frequently use the symbol ∠ with just the letter labeling that vertex.

Two angles that (1) have a common vertex, (2) have a common side, and (3) have interiors that don't overlap are called *adjacent* angles. For example, ∠ABD and ∠DBC are adjacent, but not ∠ABD and ∠ABC, in the figure below:

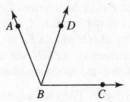

Your experience with measuring angles by protractor should prepare you to agree that every angle can be assigned a degree measure between 0 and 180 (but not either 0 or 180, since we have excluded "angles" with collinear sides). We formalize our agreements about angle measure in the following postulate.

Postulate 5 The Angle Postulate *To each angle we assign a number between 0 and 180 to be called its "degree measure." Given a point A on a line AB and a number m such that $0 < m < 180$, there is one and only one angle that can be constructed with (1) ray AB as a side, (2) m as its degree measure, and (3) its interior contained in a given side of line AB.*

As a result. answer (A) is NOT true and answer (B) is true.

When the sum of the measures of two angles is 180, we say these angles are *supplementary*. When their sum is 90, we call them *complementary* angles. Though we frequently encounter adjacent angles that are either supplementary or complementary, angles *do not* have to be adjacent to satisfy the definitions given.

Therefore, answer (C) is true.

If three points, A, B, and C, are not collinear, then the union of segments AB, BC, and AC is called a *triangle*.

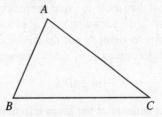

Answer (E) is true because sides forming two right angles would be perpendicular.

WORKING WITH THE MEASURES OF ANGLES

[2] If (1) point P is in the interior of $\angle LMN$, (2) point W is in the interior of $\angle XYZ$, (3) the measures of $\angle LMN$ and $\angle XYZ$ are equal, and (4) the measures of $\angle PMN$ and $\angle WYZ$ are equal, which of the following must be true?

   I. $\angle LMP$ and $\angle PMN$ are adjacent angles.

   II. The measure of $\angle LMN$ equals the sum of the measures of $\angle LMP$ and $\angle PMN$.

   III. The measure of $\angle ZYW$ = measure of $\angle LMP$.

   (A) I only

   (B) II only

   (C) I and II only

   (D) II and III only

   (E) I and III only

When a geometric question is as complicated as this one, it helps to draw a figure:

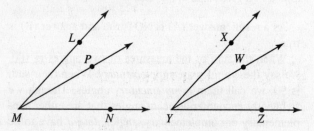

From the figure, you can see that I is true.

As a further aid, we can put the information given in more concise form. Abbreviations vary from text to text so writers of standardized tests avoid them and generally write out what they mean to avoid confusion. We will follow their lead in the formulation of questions but adopt a handy notation to simplify our discussions. When referring to the degree measure of $\angle ABC$ we will use

$$\mathrm{m}\angle ABC.$$

Thus, we can summarize the given information as:

$$\mathrm{m}\angle LMN = \mathrm{m}\angle XYZ$$

and

$$\mathrm{m}\angle PMN = \mathrm{m}\angle WYZ.$$

We will agree on the following:

Postulate 6 *If a point P is in the interior of $\angle LMN$, then:*

$$\mathrm{m}\angle LMN = \mathrm{m}\angle LMP + \mathrm{m}\angle PMN.$$

This agreement asserts the truth of answer II. It also leads us to conclude that:

$$\mathrm{m}\angle XYZ = \mathrm{m}\angle XYW + \mathrm{m}\angle WYZ.$$

We can also conclude that:

$$\mathrm{m}\angle LMN - \mathrm{m}\angle PMN = \mathrm{m}\angle LMP.$$

and, therefore, by substitution we deduce:

$$\mathrm{m}\angle XYW = \mathrm{m}\angle LMP,$$

which contradicts III.

We summarize these conclusions in the following theorem:

11-1   If D is in the interior of $\angle ABC$ and W is in the interior of $\angle XYZ$ then, when any two of

   (a) $\mathrm{m}\angle ABC = \mathrm{m}\angle XYZ$

   (b) $\mathrm{m}\angle ABD = \mathrm{m}\angle XYW$, and

   (c) $\mathrm{m}\angle DBC = \mathrm{m}\angle WYZ$

are true, the third must also be true.

EXAMPLES

If $\mathrm{m}\angle AEC = \mathrm{m}\angle BED$:

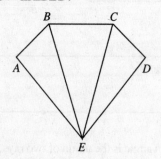

1. $\mathrm{m}\angle AEB + \mathrm{m}\angle BEC = \mathrm{m}\angle AEC$

2. $\mathrm{m}\angle BEC + \mathrm{m}\angle CED = \mathrm{m}\angle BED$

3. $\mathrm{m}\angle AEC - \mathrm{m}\angle BEC = \mathrm{m}\angle AEB$

4. $\mathrm{m}\angle BED - \mathrm{m}\angle BEC = \mathrm{m}\angle CED$

5. $\mathrm{m}\angle AEB = \mathrm{m}\angle CED$

[3] If in the figure $\angle COE$ and $\angle BOD$ are right angles and the measure of $\angle BOC$ is three times the measure of $\angle COD$, then the measure of $\angle AOB$ is

(A) 20°

(B) $22\frac{1}{2}°$

(C) 30°

(D) 45°

(E) 60°

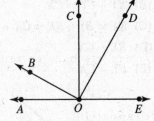

We will call a pair of angles such as $\angle DOE$ and $\angle DOA$ a "linear pair" and agree that:

Postulate 7 *The sum of the measures of the angles of a linear pair is 180.*

When the angles of a linear pair have the same measure, x, then the sum of their measures, $x+x$, is 180 and x must be 90. An angle with measure 90 is called a right angle. If a pair of lines intersect to form a right angle, we say the lines are perpendicular.

Let $y = m\angle COD$ in the figure above. Then

$$3y = m\angle COB$$

and

$$3y + y = 90,$$

since $\angle DOB$ is a right angle. Therefore

$$y = m\angle COD = 22\frac{1}{2},$$

and

$$3y = m\angle COB = 67\frac{1}{2}.$$

Because $m\angle COA$ is also a right angle,

$$m\angle BOA = 22\frac{1}{2}.$$

[4] If $\angle AOB$ is a right angle, decide whether you can conclude that $\angle AOD$ and $\angle BOC$ have the same measure. Which of the following justifies your conclusion?

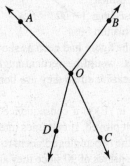

(Figure is not drawn to scale.)

(A) This conclusion cannot be justified from the information given.

(B) Complements of congruent angles are congruent.

(C) Supplements of congruent angles are congruent.

(D) Vertical angles are congruent.

(E) If two intersecting lines form one right angle, they must form four right angles.

TEST-TAKING TIP

When a figure is "not drawn to scale," it can be misleading. $\angle AOB$ is given to be a right angle but is acute in the diagram. When figures are not drawn to scale, it can be helpful to redraw them to avoid making incorrect inferences.

Answer (A) is correct, even though each of answers (B) through (E) is a provable geometric statement, which we will verify while showing why (A) is correct.

(B) and (C). If $\angle X$ and $\angle Y$ are any pair of angles such that $m\angle X = m\angle Y$, their complements and supplements must also be angle pairs of equal measure since

$$90 - m\angle X \text{ must equal } 90 - m\angle Y$$

and

$$180 - m\angle X = 180 - m\angle Y.$$

Our given information will not allow us to conclude that $\angle AOD$ and $\angle BOC$ are either complements or supplements of a pair of angles of equal measure.

(D) Two angles are vertical angles if their sides form two pairs of opposite rays. In other words, they are formed only by two intersecting lines. No such situation

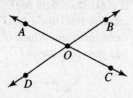

occurs above. If the figure had been as shown above, then ∠AOD and ∠BOC would be vertical angles. They must have the same measure since they are both supplements of ∠AOB.

The statement in (E) is a consequence of the vertical angle theorem just proved. If two lines intersect to form a right angle, then the two angles adjacent to the right angle must also have measures of 90 since they are supplements of the right angle. The nonadjacent angle forms a pair of vertical angles with the right angle. Again, the figure does not have a pair of intersecting lines so the correct answer is (A).

EXAMPLES

In the figure at right ∠DOB and ∠COA are right angles. BE and CF are lines.

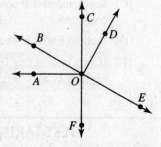

1. m∠COD = m∠BOA because both are complements of ∠BOC.

2. m∠BOC = m∠EOF because both are supplements of ∠COE or vertical angles are ≅.

3. m∠AOE = m∠DOF because both are supplements of ∠AOB and ∠COD, respectively, and (∠AOB)° = (∠COD)°.

[5] In the figure ∠AYB and ∠CXD are right angles, $AY = CX$, and $BX = DX = CY$. Each of the following is true EXCEPT

(A) $BX + XY = BY$

(B) $XY + CY = CX$

(C) $XY = BY - BX = CX - CY$

(D) $BX = CX$

(E) $BY = CX$

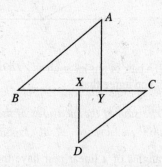

(Figure is not drawn to scale.)

The only information given above that is necessary to the solution of the problem is $BX = DX = CY$. (A) and (B) are conclusions that follow from the definition of "between." If we solve each of (A) and (B) for XY, we get statement (C). We can use part of (C),

(1) $$BY - BX = CX - CY,$$

along with part of the given information,

(2) $$BX = CY,$$

to get statement (E),

(3) $$BY = CX,$$

by the addition of (1) and (2). Since $BX = CY$, choice (D), $BX = CX$, must be incorrect.

By similar arguments we may verify the following:

11-2 If B is between A and C, and Y is between X and Z, then, whenever any two of

(a) $AB = XY$,

(b) $BC = YZ$, and

(c) $AC = XZ$

are true, the third must also be true.

EXAMPLES

In the figure at right

$AC = BD$,

$EF = GF$,

$BF = CF$,

$EH = DI$, and

$EA = DG$.

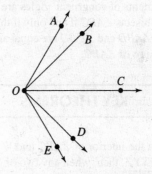

1. $AB = DC$

2. $EC = GB$

3. $AH = GI$

[6]   If ray BD is the bisector of $\angle ABC$ in triangle ABC, which of the following could be true?

I. If the measure of $\angle DBC$ is 50, then $\angle ABC$ is obtuse.

II. The bisector of $\angle ABE$ is perpendicular to ray BD.

III. The ray opposite to BD bisects $\angle EBF$.

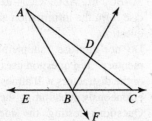

(A) I only

(B) II only

(C) III only

(D) none

(E) I, II, and III

I is true by definition since the measure of $\angle ABC$ must be 100 if ray BD is the bisector.

If a and b are the measures of the angles of a linear pair, then $\frac{1}{2}a$ and $\frac{1}{2}b$ must be the measures of the angles formed when the angles of the linear pair are bisected. But $a + b = 180$ since the angles of a linear pair are supplementary, and this means

$$\frac{1}{2}(a+b) = \frac{1}{2}a + \frac{1}{2}b = 90.$$

Thus the measure of the angle formed by the bisectors of a linear pair must be 90 and II must be true.

III is a consequence of the vertical angle theorem. Sketch in the ray opposite to BD and call it BX. By the vertical angle theorem,

$$m\angle FBX = m\angle ABD$$

and

$$m\angle EBX = m\angle CBD$$

The definition of angle bisector assures us that

(1) $m\angle ABD = m\angle CBD$

so we can conclude by substitution that:

(2) $m\angle FBX = m\angle EBX$

Statement (2) indicates that ray BX satisfies the requirements for an angle bisector.

If, in the figure below, ray OC bisects $\angle BOD$ and $(\angle AOB)° = (\angle DOE)°$,

1. $m\angle BOC = m\angle COD$ by Definition of angle bisector.

2. $m\angle AOB = m\angle BOC = m\angle AOC$ by Postulate 6.

3. $m\angle COD + m\angle DOE = m\angle COE$ by Postulate 6.

4. $m\angle AOB + m\angle BOC = m\angle COE$ by Substitution of Given and step (1) in step (3).

5. $m\angle AOC = m\angle COE$ by Substitution of step (2) in step (4).

WHAT YOU SHOULD KNOW

KEY CONCEPTS

1. Two angles are *adjacent* if they share a common side and their interiors do not intersect.
2. If two angles share a common side and their other sides form a line, then the angles are *supplementary* and the sum of their degree measures is 180.
3. Two angles are *supplementary* if and only if the sum of their degree measures is 180.
4. Perpendicular lines form right angles.
5. Two angles are *vertical* angles if their sides form two pairs of opposite rays.
6. Vertical angles are congruent.
7. Supplements of congruent angles are congruent.
8. Two angles are *complementary* if the sum of their degree measures is 90.
9. Complements of congruent angles are congruent.
10. Ray BD bisects $\angle ABC$ if and only if the degree measures of $\angle ABD$ and $\angle CBD$ are equal and each is half the measure of $\angle ABC$.

KEY THEOREMS

1. If D is in the interior of $\angle ABC$ and W is in the interior of $\angle XYZ$, then, when any two of

    (a) $m\angle ABC = m\angle XYZ$
    (b) $m\angle ABD = m\angle XYW$, and
    (c) $m\angle DBC = m\angle WYZ$

are true, the third must also be true.

2. If B is between A and C, and Y is between X and Z, then, whenever any two of

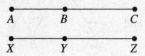

    (a) $AB = XY$
    (b) $BC = YZ$ and
    (c) $AC = XZ$

are true, the third must also be true.

TEST-TAKING STRATEGIES

- Whenever possible, use your knowledge of the symbols commonly used in geometry—$\angle ABC$, $\triangle ABC$, $m\angle ABC$, etc.—to express in more concise form the information about angles given in the question.
- Do not confuse "supplementary" with "complementary." If a question uses one of these terms, one of the distractors will almost always be the result of erroneously substituting the other term.
- Questions testing the ideas of angle measure reviewed in this chapter usually involve a figure with many different angles, some of whose measures are given. The question generally asks for one of the missing angles. Look for vertical angles first, then find supplementary or complementary angles. Having done so, you will almost always have found the measure of the missing angle.
- Though angles sharing a common side may be supplementary (or complementary), keep in mind that angles do not have to share a common side to be supplementary (or complementary).

ANSWERS

[1] (A)   [2] (C)   [3] (B)   [4] (A)   [5] (D)   [6] (E)

TRIANGLES

CHAPTER

12

KEY TERMS

triangle   a three-sided, closed figure whose sides are line segments.

isosceles triangle   a triangle with two sides of equal length.

equilateral triangle a triangle whose three sides are of equal length.

median of a triangle a segment connecting a vertex of the triangle to the midpoint of the opposite side.

altitude of a triangle   a segment that contains the vertex of one angle of the triangle and is perpendicular to the opposite side.

IDENTIFYING CONGRUENT TRIANGLES BY CPCTC, SAS, ASA, AND SSS

[1]   If $\triangle ABC \cong \triangle PQR$ and $\triangle PQR \cong \triangle XYZ$, then which of the following is true?

(A) Every side of $\triangle ABC$ has the same length as every side of $\triangle XYZ$.

(B) There is at least one angle of $\triangle ABC$ for which no angle of $\triangle XYZ$ has the same measure.

(C) $\triangle ABC \cong \triangle XYZ$.

(D) All three triangles must lie in the same plane.

(E) Each of the three triangles must have a right angle.

When we say two triangles are *congruent* we are expressing the intuitive idea that they have the same shape and size, or, in other words, that one of them can be fitted over the other in such a way that all of the sides and angles match exactly. What we mean by congruence between triangles, then, is a particular correspondence between the vertices of the triangles for which all of the matching ("corresponding") pairs of sides are equal in length and the corresponding pairs of angles have the same measure. As a shorthand notation to indicate which vertices we want to correspond to each other in a given congruence, we write the letters for the vertices in corresponding order. Thus if $\triangle ABC \cong \triangle XYZ$ we will assume that A corresponds to X, B to Y, and C to Z. We summarize all this in the following definition of congruent triangles. which we will refer to with the letters CP.

Definition of congruent triangles (CPCTC or simply CP):

$\triangle ABC \cong \triangle XYZ$ if and only if

$$\begin{aligned}
m\angle A &= m\angle X, \\
m\angle B &= m\angle Y, \\
m\angle C &= m\angle Z, \\
AB &= XY, \\
BC &= YZ, \text{ and} \\
AC &= XZ.
\end{aligned}$$

Do you see that answer (A) would mean that the lengths of all six sides of the two triangles would be the same number? To make this a true statement strike out the second "every," replace it with "the" and add "to which it corresponds" to the end of the sentence. (B) directly contradicts CP while (C) follows directly from CP.

The definition does not restrict congruences to triangles in the same plane so (D) is false. Finally, though the given information would be true if each were a right triangle, it can also be true if none is.

[2]   We can conclude that $\triangle ABC \cong \triangle XYZ$ from the information given in each of the following EXCEPT

(A) All pairs of corresponding sides have the same lengths and all pairs of corresponding angles have the same measures.

(B) $AB = XY$, $BC = YZ$, and $\angle B$ and $\angle Y$ have the same measure.

(C) $AB = XY$, $BC = YZ$, and $AC = XZ$.

(D) The measure of $\angle A$ equals that of $\angle X$ and of $\angle B$ equals that of $\angle Y$, $AB = XY$.

(E) All pairs of corresponding angles have the same measures.

Start with a given angle, $\angle A$, and then mark off a pair of segments, AB and AC, on the sides of the angle as at right.

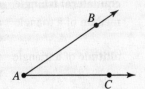

How many different segments can you draw that will complete a triangle that has the three parts mentioned? Do you see that only one such segment, BC, is possible? Thus the given information uniquely determines the size and shape of a triangle. (When two sides of a triangle lie on the sides of an angle, as in this case, we say the sides "include" the angle.) The experiment above encourages us to make the following agreement:

Postulate 8 (SAS) *If two sides and their included angle of one triangle are equal in length or measure to the corresponding parts of a second triangle, the two triangles are congruent.*

Now start with a given segment AB and draw a pair of angles with vertices at A and B.

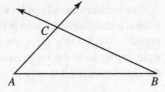

Do you see that the given information defines exactly one point, C, that can be the third vertex of a triangle having the given parts?

(In such a case we say that $\angle A$ and $\angle B$ "include" segment AB.) We agree as follows:

Postulate 9 (ASA) *If two angles and their included side of one triangle are equal in measure or length to the corresponding parts of a second triangle, then the two triangles are congruent.*

As a final experiment, take three sticks; tape them together at their ends, two sticks to a joint. The wooden triangle formed is "rigid" in a plane, meaning that it cannot be distorted into a different triangle in the same plane having the same dimensions. We agree then that the size and shape of a triangle are fixed when the lengths of the sides are fixed.

Postulate 10 (SSS) *If all three sides of one triangle are equal in length to the corresponding sides of a second triangle, then the two triangles are congruent.*

In the multiple-choice question:

(A) is true by the definition of congruent triangles,

(B) is true by SAS,

(C) is true by SSS,

(D) is true by ASA,

(E) is false as shown by the diagram below, in which the corresponding angles are all congruent but the triangles are not.

 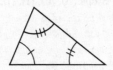

EXAMPLES

1. Segments AB and CD intersect at M, their common midpoint. $\triangle AMC \cong \triangle BMD$ by SAS.

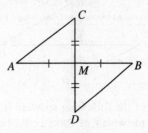

2. A, B, C, and D are four coplanar points such that B and D lie on different sides of line AC, $BC = AD$, and $DC = BA$. $\triangle ADC \cong \triangle CBA$ by SSS.

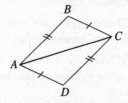

3. Segment AC is perpendicular to segment BD with C being the point of intersection, $(\angle CAD)° = (\angle CAB)°$. $\triangle ABC \cong \triangle ADC$ by ASA.

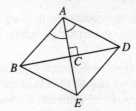

[3]   *E* is the midpoint of both segments *AB* and *CD*, which are also perpendicular to each other. We can prove that *AD* = *BC*.

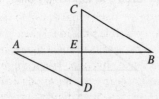

If each of the following answers is a step in this proof, which of these could be left out with the remaining answers still constituting a proof?

(A) *AE* = *BE* and *CE* = *DE* by definition of midpoint.

(B) ∠*CEB* and ∠*DEA* are right angles by definition of perpendicular.

(C) ∠*CEB* and ∠*DEA* have the same measure since vertical angles are equal in measure.

(D) △*AED* ≅ △*BEC* by Side-Angle-Side.

(E) *AD* ≅ *BC* by definition of congruent triangles.

In your geometry course you learned how to demonstrate the validity of various geometric statements in a formal way.

In a formal proof we attempt to gather and organize logical evidence to support the statement we hope to justify. Each statement of evidence we set down must in turn be supported by some previously established theorem, definition, or postulate. The hypothesis (or "if" part) of this theorem, definition, or postulate must name a category into which some earlier step of the proof fits. For example, statement (D) satisfies the hypothesis of the definition of congruent triangles used to support step (E). The conclusion (or "then" part) provides a category into which the statement of the same step must fit. For example, the conclusion of the reason in (E) is that all pairs of corresponding parts of congruent triangles are equal in measure or length, while the statement in (E) is that a pair of corresponding sides have the same length.

Merely assembling a collection of justified statements does not constitute proving a theorem. Each of these must in some way help to support the hypothesis of the final reason, even if only indirectly. For example, choice (A) is used to help justify (D) and, therefore, indirectly supports (E) since (D) supports (E). Accordingly, any step (except the final one) which does not justify a later step is unnecessary to the proof. Note that (B) though valid and correctly justified, does not contribute to any later step and can be omitted.

As a further example of how steps are interrelated, suppose we had inserted a step B between (B) and (C) which stated "∠*CEB* and ∠*DEA* are equal in measure since all right angles have the same measure, 90." Do you see that we could then omit step (C)?

EXAMPLE

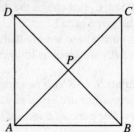

Given: *ABCD* is a square (meaning that all of its angles are right angles and all sides are the same length).

PROOF: △*ADP* ≅ △*BCP*.

(a) m∠*DAB* = m∠*CBA* = m∠*ADC*
              = m∠*BCD* = 90
     Definition of right angle.

(b) *AD* ⊥ *DC*, *BC* ⊥ *CD*   Definition of perpendicular.

(c) △*ADC* is a right triangle   Definition of right triangle.

(d) *AD* = *BC*   Definition of square.

(e) *AB* = *DC*   Definition of square.

(f) *AD* = *DC*   Definition of square.

(g) △*DAB* ≅ △*CBA*   SAS.

(h) m∠*CAB* = m∠*DBA*   CP.

(i) m∠*CBD* = m∠*DAC*   Postulate 6.

(j) m∠*DPA* = m∠*CPB*   Vertical angles.

(k) m∠*ADC* = m∠*BCD*   All right angles are equal in measure.

(l) *DC* = *DC*   Identity.

(m) △*ADC* ≅ △*BCD*   SAS.

(n) m∠*BDC* = ∠*ACD*   CP.

(o) m∠*ADB* = m∠*BCA*   Postulate 6.

(p) △*ADP* ≅ △*BCP*   ASA.

Steps (b), (c), (f), (j), and (k) can be omitted.

IDENTIFYING ISOSCELES TRIANGLES

[4] If, in the accompanying figure, $AD \perp DC$, $AD \perp BD$, and $DC = BD$, which of the following statements is NOT necessarily true?

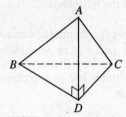

(A) $\angle DBC$ and $\angle DCB$ are equal in measure.

(B) $\triangle ADB \cong \triangle ADC$.

(C) $AB = AC$.

(D) $\angle ABC$ and $\angle ACB$ are equal in measure.

(E) $\angle BAC$ and $\angle BDC$ have the same measure.

A triangle is *isosceles* if and only if it has a pair of sides of equal length.

> 12-1 (ITT) Two sides of a triangle have the same length if and only if the angles opposite these sides have the same measure.

We will refer to this as the Isosceles Triangle Theorem because it is true of isosceles triangles, even though it never mentions the word *isosceles*.

To verify it, we use the figure at right, a triangle to which we have added a segment from one vertex, A, to the midpoint, M, of the opposite side. We know such a segment (called a *median* of the triangle) exists since the two points A and M determine a line by Postulate 1.

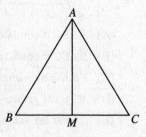

From the definition of midpoint we conclude that $BM = CM$. Of course, $AM = AM$. If we were given that $AB = AC$, do you see that $\triangle ABM \cong \triangle ACM$ by SSS and therefore m$\angle B =$ m$\angle C$ by CP?

TEST-TAKING TIP

At first the figure seems to make no sense. The right angles don't look like right angles. Therefore, you may suspect that it is not drawn to scale or represents an impossible situation. When you view the diagram as a three-dimensional figure, however, it does depict a real situation. When a figure doesn't seem to make sense, be sure to consider the possibility it represents three dimensions. Note that if the figure were two-dimensional, the two adjacent right angles would make BDC a straight line and it would have to coincide with the dotted line BC.

Suppose our given information had not been $AB = AC$, but m$\angle B =$ m$\angle C$. Consequently $AB = AC$ by a similar proof.

In the multiple-choice question answer

(A) is true by ITT,

(B) is true by SAS,

(C) is true by CP,

(D) follows from ITT, and

(E), though possible, is not necessarily true.

EXAMPLE

Given that $BC = ED$ and $AB = AE$, verify the reasons for the proof that $\triangle ACD$ is isosceles:

1. $BD = BC + CD$, $CE = CD + DE$ Definition of between.

2. $BC + CD = CD + DE$ Addition of CD to both sides of given equation.

3. $BD = CE$ Substitution.

4. m$\angle B =$ m$\angle E$ ITT.

5. $\triangle ABD \cong \triangle AEC$ SAS.

6. m$\angle ACD =$ m$\angle ADC$ CP.

IDENTIFYING ALTITUDES

[5]   Given that C lies in plane E, D lies in plane F, the intersection of the planes is line AB, $AC = BC$, $AD = BD$ and ray DX bisects $\angle ADB$.

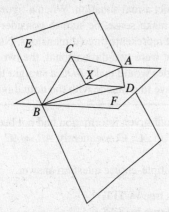

Which of the following must be true?

   I. Ray CX bisects $\angle ACB$.

   II. Segment CX is a median of $\triangle ACB$.

   III. Segment CX is an altitude of $\triangle ACB$

   (A) All of I, II, and III

   (B) I and II only

   (C) II and III only

   (D) I only

   (E) II only

TEST-TAKING TIP

We hope you will never see a figure this complicated on a Level IC exam. We have included it to stretch your ability to see three-dimensional figures. Once you visualize the two planes receding away from you, the figure really isn't complicated after all.

We have already reviewed "median" and "angle bisector." In order to be an *altitude* segment CX must be perpendicular to side AB. In $\triangle ADB$ we conclude that $m\angle ADX = m\angle BDX$ by the definition of angle bisector so $\triangle ADX \cong \triangle BDX$ by SAS and $AX = BX$ by CP. It follows that $\triangle AXC$ is congruent to $\triangle BXC$ by SSS: This means $\angle ACX$ and $\angle BCX$ must have the same measure so ray CX is the bisector of $\angle ACB$. We have already shown $AX = BX$ so X is the midpoint of segment AB and thus segment CX is a median of $\triangle ACB$.

Because $\angle AXC$ and $\angle BXC$ are a linear pair the sum of their measures is 180. But $m\angle AXC = m\angle BXC$ since

they are corresponding parts of the congruent triangles AXC and BXC. We conclude that each has a measure of 90 and consequently segment CX is an altitude.

Therefore CX is a median, an altitude, and an angle bisector.

EXAMPLES

Verify each of the following:

1. If a segment is a median and an angle bisector of a triangle, it must also be an altitude.

2. If it is an altitude and an angle bisector, it must also be a median.

3. If it is an altitude and a median, it must be an angle bisector.

IDENTIFYING EQUILATERAL TRIANGLES

[6]   If $\triangle ABC$ lies in plane E, $AC = BC$ and the measures of $\angle A$ and $\angle C$ are the same, which of the following is NOT true?

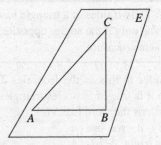

   (A) $\triangle ABC$ is equilateral.

   (B) $\triangle ABC$ is equiangular.

   (C) $\angle B$ is a right angle.

   (D) AC is not greater than AB.

   (E) $\angle A$ has the same measure as $\angle B$.

If we apply ITT to the statement $AC = BC$ we can conclude that $m\angle A = m\angle B$, so answer (E) is true. We were given $m\angle A = m\angle C$; hence all of the angles have the same measure and (B) is true. We now know that every pair of angles has the same measure, so every pair of sides must have the same length by ITT.

The line of reasoning used above allows us to deduce that every equilateral triangle is equiangular and every equiangular triangle is equilateral.

The process of verification of (A) and (B) has also demonstrated the truth of (D) and (E). As for (C), if $\angle B$

is a right angle, and, as we have just seen, it has the same measure as $\angle A$, then we have two perpendiculars from point C to line AB. How many should there be? Why? (We will review the number of perpendiculars from a point to a line in a later section of this chapter. From a point to a line, there is exactly one perpendicular.)

EXAMPLE

If in the figure the measure of $\angle AVE$ is $2x$ and all three triangles are equilateral, find the measures of all other angles.

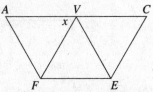

All triangles are congruent by SSS and all pairs of angles are congruent by CP, so each acute angle has measure x. If A, V, and C are *collinear*, then $3x = 180$ and $x = 60$. Thus the acute angles are $60°$ and the obtuse are $120°$.

WORKING WITH TRIANGLES THAT ARE PARTS OF OTHER FIGURES

[7]   Given that quadrilateral $MNOP$ lies in plane E, $MN = PO$, $MP = NO$, and $PX = NY$. Which of the following must be true?

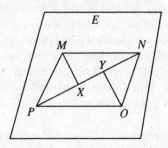

(A) $MX = OY$

(B) $\angle PMN$ is a right angle

(C)   Ray PN bisects $\angle MPO$

(D)   Segment MX is perpendicular to segment OY

(E) $\angle PMN$ is obtuse

For example, $\triangle MPN \cong \triangle NOP$ by SSS and this makes $\angle MPN$ and $\angle ONP$ corresponding parts of congruent triangles. But these angles are also corresponding parts of $\triangle PMX$ and $\triangle NOY$. Thus $\triangle PMX \cong \triangle NOY$ by SAS and $MX = OY$ by CP.

EXAMPLE

Given that $BE = AD$ and $BC = AC$, we can prove three pairs of triangles to be congruent. List them and indicate the congruence postulate that is their justification.

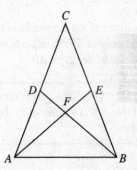

SOLUTION: $\triangle DAB \cong \triangle EBA$ by SAS, $\triangle CEA \cong \triangle CDB$ by SSS or SAS, $\triangle DFA \cong \triangle EFB$ by ASA.

WORKING WITH PERPENDICULAR BISECTORS

[8]   If L_1 and L_2 are the perpendicular bisectors of segments XY and YZ, which of the following must be true?

I. $AX = AY = AZ$

II. A, X, and Z are collinear

III. L_1 and L_2 lie in the plane determined by X, Y, and Z

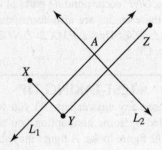

(A) I only

(B) I and II only

(C) I and III only

(D) II and III only

(E) III only

A line L is the *perpendicular bisector* of a segment AB if and only if line L is perpendicular to and contains the midpoint of segment AB.

12-2   If L is the perpendicular bisector of segment AB and X is a point of L, then X is equidistant from A and B.

12-3   If X is equidistant from points A and B, then X lies on the perpendicular bisector of segment AB.

In the figure below, no matter what point X is of line L, the following must hold:

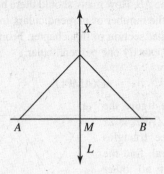

(a) $XM = XM$.

(b) $\angle XMA$ and $\angle XMB$ are right angles.

(c) $AM = BM$.

(d) $\triangle XMA \cong \triangle XMB$ (by *SAS*), and

(e) $XB = XA$ (by CP).

If in the figure above we know only that $XA = XB$ and $MA = MB$, we can conclude that $\triangle XMA = \triangle XMB$ by SSS ($XM = XM$, of course). Thus, no matter where X is in the plane, and as long as $XB = XA$, we know that $\angle XMA$ and $\angle XMB$ must be right angles since they are supplementary and equal in measure. Therefore the line that contains X and M is the perpendicular bisector of segment AB. Can there be more than one perpendicular bisector of AB? In other words, can there be more than one line passing through M and perpendicular to L? The answer is "no" if we limit the figure to a given plane; it is "yes" if we do not specify a plane figure. To visualize the latter case, ask yourself how many lines you can draw on the floor that will intersect the line formed by the joining of two walls. Thus L_1 and L_2 do not have to lie in plane XYZ and III is false. We will review this further in the next section.

In the figure segments XY and YZ appear to be perpendicular but the information given does not require this.

TEST-TAKING TIP

Remember that you cannot assume congruence, perpendicularity, or parallelism from the way a figure is drawn. If, however, line segments *look* congruent, parallel, or perpendicular, they may be so. Look for corroborating information that may suggest a way of solving the problem.

If XY and YZ were perpendicular, we would be able to prove that II is true. We summarize 12-2 and 12-3 in the following statement: the perpendicular bisector of a segment is the set of all points of a plane that are equidistant from the endpoints of the segment. Thus $AX = AY = AZ$, so I is true.

EXAMPLE

Given that L_1, L_2, and L_3 are three of the perpendicular bisectors of segment AB, $AZ = 4$, $AY = 3$, and $XB = 5$. Find BZ, BY, and AX.

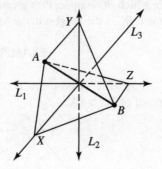

SOLUTION:
$BZ = 4$, $BY = 3$, $AX = 5$.

IDENTIFYING CONGRUENT TRIANGLES BY AAS AND HL

[9] If $\angle CDB$ and $\angle ABD$ have the same measure, and if $\angle DCB$ and $\angle BAD$ are right angles, then:

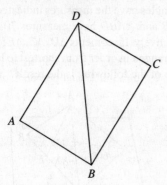

(A) All points of the figure must lie in the same plane

(B) The measure of $\angle DBC$ is twice the measure of $\angle ADB$

(C) $AD = DC$

(D) $\angle ADB$ and $\angle CDB$ have the same measure

(E) $AB = DC$

In this and the next section we will add to our list of congruence "postulates" for triangles.

Postulate 11 (AAS) *In a given triangle if a pair of angles and one of their nonincluded sides have the same measures or length as the corresponding parts of a second triangle, the two triangles are congruent.*

By AAS we can conclude $\triangle DCB \cong \triangle BAD$ and answer

(E) is correct. The figure may not at first appear to suggest this, but if you make a scale drawing and fold the paper along line DB, you should be able to visualize how perspective foreshortens $\triangle DAB$ to give the appearance shown. Imagine that the figure is a pyramid with points A, B, and C in its base and point D above the base.

[10] If in $\triangle ADC$ we know that $\angle ADC$ is a right angle, with $AB = AC$, then:

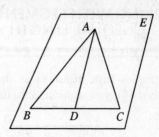

(A) $AB > AC$

(B) $\angle BAD > \angle DAC$

(C) $BD < DC$

(D) $AC = BD$

(E) $\triangle ABD \cong \triangle ACD$

Postulate 12 (HL) *If the hypotenuse and one leg of a given right triangle have the same lengths as the corresponding parts of a second right triangle, then the two triangles are congruent.*

In a right triangle the *hypotenuse* is the side opposite the right angle. The other two sides are called *legs*. From the figure, $\angle ADC$ may not appear to be a right angle unless you realize that plane E is not the plane of the page.

Answer (E), $\triangle ABD \cong \triangle ACD$, is correct by HL since the triangles are right triangles and they have congruent hypotenuses ($AB = AC$) and a pair of congruent legs ($AD = AD$).

EXAMPLES

In the figure

$m\angle ADC = m\angle ACD,$

$m\angle ABD = m\angle ABC = 90.$

Verify the reasons for each of the following:

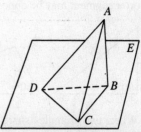

(a) $AD = AC$ ITT.

(b) $\angle ABD$ and $\angle ABC$ are right angles Definition of right angle.

(c) △ABD and △ABC are right triangles   Definition of right triangle.

(d) $AB = AB$ Identity.

(e) △ABD ≅ △ABC   HL.

(f) $DB = BC$ CP.

(g) m∠BCD = m∠BDC   ITT.

WORKING WITH SEGMENTS OF UNEQUAL LENGTH

[11] If the angles have measures as indicated, which is the longest segment in the drawing?

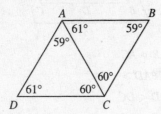

(A) BC

(B) AB

(C) AC

(D) Both BC and AC since $BC = AC$

(E) Cannot be determined

In a triangle, if two sides are not congruent, then the angles opposite them are not congruent and the greater angle is opposite the longer side. Furthermore, if two angles are not congruent, the longer side is opposite the greater angle.

> 12-4 In a △XYZ, $XY > YZ$ if and only if ∠Z > ∠X.

When applying this theorem, be sure to realize it relates to parts of *one* triangle. In two different triangles, a shorter segment may be opposite a greater angle:

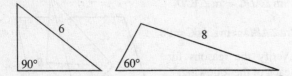

When two triangles share a common side, as in the multiple-choice question, comparing other parts with the common side may help you to determine the longest (or shortest) side in the figure.

If we apply 12-4 to the question we see that AC is the longest side of △ACD. But AC is also a side of △ABC in which BC is opposite a greater angle. Conclusion: segment BC is the longest in the figure.

EXAMPLES

If ray CX bisects ∠ACB, verify the reasons for the proof of $BC > BX$.

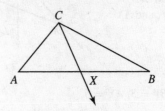

(a) m∠ACX = m∠BCX, by definition of angle bisector.

(b) m∠CXB > m∠ACX, by 12-4.

(c) m∠CXB > m∠BCX, by substitution.

(d) $BC > BX$, by 12-4.

[12] Segment AC is perpendicular to plane E. The angles have the measures indicated while ∠ADB and ∠ABD have measures 70 and 50 respectively. If segments AD, AC, AE, and AB are arranged in order from shortest to longest, which of the following is the result?

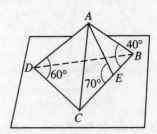

(A) AE, AD, AB, AC

(B) AE, AB, AC, AD

(C) AC, AB, AE, AD

(D) AC, AB, AD, AE

(E) AC, AE, AD, AB

A line is perpendicular to a plane at a point B if and only if it is perpendicular to every line in the plane that passes through B. Thus we can assume ∠ACD and ∠ACB are right angles. Therefore AC must be less than any of the segments in the figure since it is always a side of a triangle that is opposite a lesser angle of the triangle. Certainly $AE < BE$ since the angle opposite BE in △AEB is 110° while the angle opposite AE is only 40°. But what of AB and AD? In △ABD, AB is opposite the greater angle.

WORKING WITH THE TRIANGLE INEQUALITY LAW

[13]   If A, B, and C are any three points of a plane for which $AB = 5$ and $BC = 7$, which of the following can be the length of AC?

(A) 0

(B) 1

(C) 2

(D) 13

(E) 15

The following theorem is frequently referred to as the "triangle inequality."

> 12-5   If A, B, and C are three points of a plane, then $AB + BC \geq AC$.

Therefore we can eliminate answers (D) and (E) because $AB + BC = 12$, which is not greater than or equal to (D) and (E).

In the case for which B is between A and C (and, therefore, the points are collinear), $AB + BC = AC$ by the definition of "between." This means that $AB + BC \neq AC$ when B is not between A and C.

There is one further case to mention. Suppose C were a point of AB that was not between A and B. As you can see, $AC + BC$ is still greater than AB.

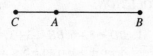

To answer the multiple-choice question draw a segment BC of 7 units and then a circle with center at B and radius 5. Do you see that the points of the circle are the only possible points that will do for A?

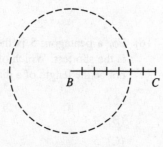

The intersection of the circle and the segment gives a location for A for which $AC = 2$, $AB = 5$, and $BC = 7$.

[14]   If $AB = BD$, then two of the following four statements about the figure are contradictory. Which two are they?

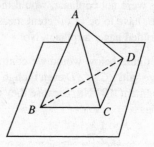

I. $AD = BC$

II. $\angle ABC > \angle DBC$

III. $\angle BAD$ is not less than $\angle BDA$

IV. $AC = DC$

(A) I and II

(B) II and III

(C) III and IV

(D) I and III

(E) II and IV

In the figure (below) points are coplanar and $AP_1 = AP_2 = AP_3$. What appears to be the relationship between P_1B, P_2B, and P_3B?

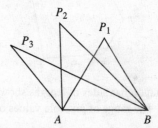

Certainly as the angle, $\angle BAP_n$, gets greater the side opposite it becomes longer and, conversely, as BP_n gets longer $\angle BAP_n$ gets greater.

Postulate 13 *When two sides of a triangle have the same lengths as the corresponding sides of a second triangle, then the included angle of the first pair is greater than the included angle of the second pair if and only if the remaining side of the first triangle is greater than the remaining side of the second triangle.*

Do you see that this means statement II must contradict statement IV?

In the multiple-choice question, $\triangle ABC$ and $\triangle DBC$ have two pairs of congruent sides, $AB = BD$ and $BC = BC$. Since $\angle ABC > \angle DBC$ in statement II, then $AC > DC$, which contradicts IV.

EXAMPLES

1. If in the figure on the preceding page, P_1, P_2, and P_3 were not coplanar, would the three angles, $\angle P_n AB$, have to be of different measures? (Visualize a folded paper airplane). No.

2. In the figure below would we contradict Postulate 13 if we said $\angle C > \angle D$ even though both are opposite segment AB? No, because they are in different triangles.

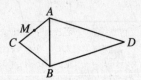

3. If $\triangle ABC$ is isosceles with $AB = BC$ and M is the midpoint of segment AC, use Postulate 13 to show that ray BM is the bisector of $\angle ABC$.

SOLUTION: If $\angle ABM > \angle CBM$, then $AM > CM$ by Postulate 13. If $\angle ABM < \angle CBM$, then $AM < CM$ by Postulate 13.

[15]

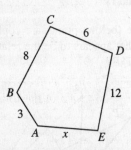

A pentagon has sides of lengths shown in the figure. The range of possible values of x is?

(A) $0 < x < 29$

(B) $11 < x < 18$

(C) $3 < x < 12$

(D) $6 < x < 8$

(E) $0 < x < 20$

TEST-TAKING TIP

A key to successful problem-solving is the ability to apply familiar principles to unfamiliar situations. This question may be unlike any you ever attempted in a geometry class. Yet its solution uses: (1) a basic property, the triangle inequality reviewed earlier in this chapter, and (2) a standard diagrammatic technique, the introduction of auxiliary line segments.

Draw segments AC and CE. You will then see three separate triangles.

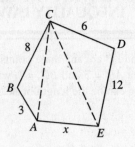

The triangle inequality law says that the length of a side of a triangle must be less than the sum of the lengths of the other two sides. Therefore:

$$AC < 3 + 8 \quad \text{and} \quad CE < 6 + 12$$
$$\text{Since } x \; < \; AC + CE,$$
$$x \; < \; 29.$$

Of course, x must also be greater than 0 or the "pentagon" will only have four sides.

EXAMPLES

See if you get the same result for x in the figure above if instead of drawing segments AC and CE, you introduce

1. BE and BD

2. BD and AD

SOLUTION:

1. $BD < 8 + 6$, $BE < 3 + x$: therefore, $12 < BD + BE < 8 + 6 + 3 + x$, so $-5 < x$. Since the length of a side must be nonnegative, $0 < x$.

2. By a process similar to 1, $-23 < x$ so $0 < x$.

[16] For a pentagon, 5 is the longest side and 2 is the shortest. Which of the following could not be the length of a diagonal?

(A) 3

(B) 4

(C) 5

(D) 7

(E) 11

You think this is a question about pentagons, but it is really about triangles. Draw a pentagon roughly in proportion to the given information and then draw one of its diagonals. Each diagonal forms a triangle with two sides. Consider the diagonal that forms a triangle with the two longest sides. Suppose both are 5, which would be the longest pair possible with the given information. Any side of a triangle must be less than the sum of its two other sides. That would mean the longest diagonal must be less than 10. That eliminates 11 (E).

But here is another line of thinking that is far less complicated. The only objection to the length of a diagonal would be that it would be too long or too short. That means the only objectionable answers would be (A) (in case it was too short) or (E) (in case it was too long).

Let's pretend we don't already know the right answer and look at the too-short possibility first. The pentagon could actually be as skinny as you wanted it to be. For an example of a thin pentagon that fits the given info, imagine one with sides of 5, 2, 3, 2 and 2.000001. The first two combine to give 7 and the last three combine to give 7.000001. Stretch that decimal out as far as you like and you see that the diagonal would really have to be 0 to be too short. So it has to be the upper boundary that is violated by the correct answer.

[17] If the sides of the inscribed triangles have the measures shown and PQ is a diameter, what is the value of $a^2 + b^2$?

(A) 25

(B) 4

(C) 10

(D) 29

(E) 100

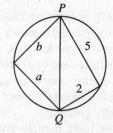

Few test items are solely about triangles, or circles, or solving mathematical equations. After all, test makers have to explore your knowledge of three years of high school math using only 50 questions!

For example, this question tests your knowledge of three principles: (1) if an angle is inscribed in a semicircle it is a right angle, which tells you that the two triangles in the figure are right triangles, (2) in a right triangle, the sum of the squares of the shorter legs is equal to the square of the longest (one version of the famous Pythagorean Theorem), and, (3) things equal to the same thing are equal to each other.

The first principle tells you the two triangles are right triangles. The second principle tells you that the square of the diameter equals both $2^2 + 5^2$ and $a^2 + b^2$ and the third says you can equate them to $a^2 + b^2 = 2^2 + 5^2 = 4 + 25 = 29$, choice (D).

[18] Three lines intersect at the points A, B, and C. What is the sum of the degree measures of the six marked angles?

(A) 180

(B) 270

(C) 360

(D) 540

(E) Cannot be determined

The question tests the most basic fact about angle relations (when two lines intersect, the vertical angles are equal) and the most basic fact about angles in triangles (the sum of the degree measures of the angles of a triangle is 180). These two relationships are tested on every Level IC exam, often in tandem as they are in this question.

In this triangle, both the interior angles and their vertical angle equivalents total 180, which provides an overall sum of 360, (C).

The most attractive incorrect answer for a test audience trying this question was (E) because not enough information is given to determine the measures of any of the individual angles. It really does not matter what the individual angles measure. The total will always work out to 360.

[19] If it is given that an altitude of a triangle bisects its base, which of the following can be proved?

(A) the triangle is isosceles

(B) the triangle is equilateral

(C) the triangle is a right triangle

(D) the triangle has an obtuse angle

(E) the triangle has three acute angles

The multiple-choice format of the Level IC exam provides ways to test your knowledge of geometric proofs, even though it prevents questions for which a fully developed proof is the answer.

Here's an example of a proof-but-not-a-proof question that is based on one of the most common proofs in elementary geometry.

To see what is going on, start by drawing a horizontal segment, BC, and then erecting a perpendicular at its midpoint, M. That gives you segment AM that is both an altitude and the bisector of the base of the triangle ABC.

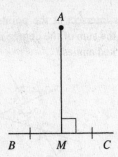

Now complete the diagram by adding segments AB and AC.

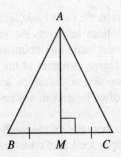

From the given information, you may conclude that triangle ABM is congruent to triangle ACM by Side-Angle-Side. Therefore, $AB = AC$, which makes the triangle isosceles and (A) true.

The triangle might also be equilateral (B), but the given information does not require it. It also might have a right angle or an obtuse angle at A [choices (C) and (D)], but neither is guaranteed by the given information (which is shown by the fact that it could have either). Since one angle can be obtuse or right, (E) must be wrong.

[20] If $ABCD$ is a rectangle with $AB = 4$ and $BC = 2\sqrt{3}$, and M is the midpoint of CD, find $b - a$.

(A) 15°

(B) 20°

(C) 30°

(D) 45°

(E) 90°

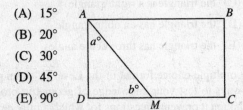

Often the principles being tested are disguised in some way. Ultimately, this question requires your knowledge of the relationship between the sides of a 30-60-90 triangle. But before you get to that step, you need to know the simple fact that the opposite sides of a rectangle are congruent (which makes $AD = 2\sqrt{3}$ and $DC = 4$) and the other simple fact that the midpoint of a segment bisects the segment (which makes $DM = 2$).

Now you know that for triangle ADM, $\angle D$ is a right angle and the sides are $DM = 2$ and $AD = 2\sqrt{3}$. Therefore, it is a 30-60-90 triangle with $b = 60°$ and $a = 30°$, (C).

The 30-60-90 triangle relationship is tested on every Level IC exam so be sure you know it cold. Your clue

that it might be in play is that you are given a right triangle with a leg for which $\sqrt{3}$ is a factor.

[21] For the figure shown, what information must be given to prove that CF bisects $\angle ACB$?

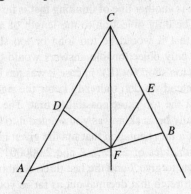

(A) $CD = CE$ and $DF = EF$

(B) $AD = EB$ and $CD = CE$

(C) $AD = BE$ and $DF = EF$

(D) $DF = EF$ and $\angle DFA = \angle EFB$

(E) $AF = BF$ and $DF = EF$

As already noted, you cannot really escape from a knowledge of geometric proofs just because the multiple-choice format of the Level IC exam prevents questions for which a fully developed proof is the answer.

Here's another example of a proof-but-not-a-proof question that is based on one of the most common proofs in elementary geometry.

The most basic triangle proof involves using given information about the corresponding parts (sides and/or angles) of two triangles to prove the triangles congruent and then using the fact of the triangle congruence to show that the remaining pairs of corresponding parts are also congruent.

Sometimes the "congruence" is slightly disguised. In this case, for example, the statement to be proved is that CF bisects $\angle ACB$, which is just another way of saying that $\angle ACF$ is congruent to $\angle BCF$.

Another disguising factor is the use of extra lines in the figure to misdirect the eye. For example, triangles ACF and BCF are clearly not congruent to each other so using them is not going to be helpful.

Concentrate on triangles DCF and ECF instead. Note that CF is a common side to both triangles so you can prove the triangles are congruent if the remaining pairs of sides are congruent. That is precisely the information given in answer choice (A). All of the other choices involve parts of triangles other than the two significant triangles, $\triangle CDF$ and $\triangle CEF$.

WHAT YOU SHOULD KNOW

KEY CONCEPTS

Handling Congruence

1. Two triangles are *congruent* if and only if all six pairs of corresponding sides and angles are congruent (abbreviated: CPCTC).
2. Two triangles are *congruent* if:
   (a) two pairs of corresponding sides and their included angles are congruent (SAS),
   (b) two pairs of corresponding angles and their included sides are congruent (ASA), *or*
   (c) all pairs of corresponding sides are congruent (SSS).
3. Two triangles are *congruent* if:
   (a) two pairs of angles and a pair of corresponding sides *not* included in the angles are congruent (AAS), *or*
   (b) the triangles are right triangles and the hypotenuses and a pair of corresponding legs are congruent (HL).
4. If two sides of a triangle are congruent, the triangle is isosceles.
5. If two sides of a triangle are congruent, the angles opposite the sides are congruent (ITT).
6. If two angles of a triangle are congruent, the sides opposite the angles are congruent.

Handling Medians and Perpendicular Bisectors

1. The median to the base of an isosceles triangle bisects the vertex angle and is perpendicular to the base.
2. A line is the perpendicular bisector of a segment if it is perpendicular to the segment and contains its midpoint.
3. The perpendicular bisector of a segment is the set of all points equidistant from the endpoints of the segment. In a plane the perpendicular bisector is a line. In space the perpendicular bisector is a plane.
4. If two points of a line are each equidistant from the endpoints of a segment, the line is the perpendicular bisector of the segment.

Handling Perpendicular Lines

1. If point P is on line L in plane E, there is exactly one line in plane E that is perpendicular to L at P.
2. If a point P is *not* on line L and both are in plane E, there is exactly one line in plane E that is perpendicular to L and contains P.

Handling Inequalites

1. The measure of an exterior angle of a triangle is greater than the measure of either of its remote interior angles.
2. If two sides of a triangle are not congruent, the angles opposite them are not congruent and the greater angle is opposite the longer side.
3. If two angles of a triangle are not congruent, the sides opposite them are not congruent and the longer side is opposite the greater angle.
4. The hypotenuse of a right triangle is the longest side.
5. The shortest segment from a point to a line is the perpendicular segment.
6. The sum of the lengths of two sides of a triangle is greater than the length of the third side.
7. If two pairs of corresponding sides of two triangles are congruent and their included angles are *not* congruent, the longer side is opposite the greater angle.

KEY THEOREMS

1. Two sides of a triangle have the same length if and only if the angles opposite these sides have the same measure. (Isosceles Triangle Theorem)
2. In a $\triangle XYZ$, $XY > YZ$ if and only if $\angle Z > \angle X$.
3. If A, B, and C are three points of a plane, then $AB + BC \geq AC$. (Triangle Inequality Theorem)

TEST-TAKING STRATEGIES

- If line segments appear to be congruent, parallel or perpendicular in a given diagram, look for information that may corroborate this possibility and thereby suggest a solution to a triangle problem.
- When it is given that two sides or angles of a triangle are congruent, the Isosceles Triangle Theorem is almost always needed to answer the question. Master this theorem and its application.
- If two triangles in a given figure share a common side, try comparing other parts with this common side as an aid in determining the longest (or shortest) side of the figure.

- Questions involving triangle inequalities often require the ability to distinguish between a plane figure and a two-dimensional representation of a three-dimensional figure. Whenever a drawing is given, you may assume the points all lie in the same plane unless the directions say otherwise. Furthermore, familiarize yourself with the way three-dimensional objects are shown in two dimensions; this will help you visualize drawings that carry the qualifier "All points are not necessarily in the same plane."

ANSWERS

[1] (C)

[2] (E)

[3] (B)

[4] (E)

[5] (A)

[6] (C)

[7] (A)

[8] (A)

[9] (E)

[10] (E)

[11] (A)

[12] (E)

[13] (C)

[14] (E)

[15] (A)

[16] (E)

[17] (D)

[18] (C)

[19] (A)

[20] (C)

[21] (A)

PERPENDICULARS AND PARALLELS

CHAPTER

13

KEY TERMS

quadrilateral	a plane figure with four sides.
trapezoid	a quadrilateral with one and only one pair of parallel sides.
parallelogram	a quadrilateral for which one of the following is true:

    a. both pairs of opposite sides are parallel,
    b. both pairs of opposite sides are congruent,
    c. a pair of opposite sides is parallel and congruent,
    d. all pairs of consecutive angles are supplementary,
    e. both pairs of opposite angles are congruent, *or*
    f. the diagonals bisect each other.

rectangle	a parallelogram with four right angles.
square	a rectangle with all sides congruent.
rhombus	a parallelogram with all sides congruent.

WORKING WITH PERPENDICULARS

[1]   Points *A*, *B*, *C*, and *D* lie in plane *F*. Segment *CD* is the perpendicular bisector of segment *AB*. Segment *ED* is perpendicular to plane *F*. Which of the following gives a segment and the plane to which it is perpendicular?

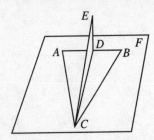

(A)   *EC*, plane *F*

(B)   *CD*, plane determined by *A*, *D*, and *B*

(C)   *CD*, plane determined by *E*, *D*, and *B*

(D)   *AD*, plane determined by *E*, *C*, and *B*

(E)   *ED*, plane determined by *A*, *E*, and *C*

By definition, a *line is perpendicular to a plane* at a point *B* if and only if it is perpendicular to every line lying in the plane and containing *B*. This definition is very useful when we are given a line perpendicular to a plane and are asked to draw conclusions.

> 13-1   A line is perpendicular to a plane at a point *B* if it is perpendicular to any two lines lying in the the plane and containing *B*.

In the figure above ∠*EDB*, ∠*EDC*, and ∠*EDA* are all right angles by definition of "a line perpendicular to a plane." ∠*CDB* and ∠*CDA* are right angles by definition of "perpendicular bisector." Thus *CD* is perpendicular to both line *ED* and line *DB*, so *CD* is perpendicular to the plane determined by *E*, *D*, and *B* by 13-1.

TEST-TAKING TIP
From the way the figure is drawn, you may think that *ED* is perpendicular to plane *F*, but there is not enough evidence to support this. You would need to know that *ED* is perpendicular to both *AB* and *CD* to conclude that it is perpendicular to the plane that contains them.

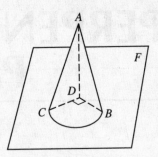

In the figure above *B*, *C*, and *D* are points of plane *F*. ∠*ADB*, ∠*CDB*, and ∠*ADC* are right angles, and *X* is any point of arc *BC*.

1.   What is the relationship between segment *AD* and plane *F*? Perpendicular by 13-1.

2.   What is the relationship between segment *AD* and segment *DX*? Why? Perpendicular by definition.

3.   Does your answer to part 2 depend on the fact that ∠*CDB* is a right angle? No.

[2]   If in the figure below all of the triangles shown are equilateral, then:

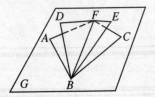

(A)   *EF* ⊥ plane G

(B)   ∠*E* is a right angle

(C)   *DF* > *EF*

(D)   *BF* ⊥ plane containing *A*, *C*, *D*, and *E*

(E)   ∠*DFA* is a right angle

A plane is the *perpendicular bisecting plane of a segment* if and only if (1) it contains the midpoint of the segment and (2) it is perpendicular to the segment.

13-2   Plane E is the perpendicular bisector of segment AB if and only if every point, X, of E is equidistant from A and B. In other words, $AX = BX$ for all X in E.

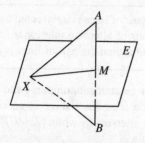

TEST-TAKING TIP

Questions involving parallel and perpendicular lines and planes in space can be quite confusing. Most Level IC tests contain several in some form. The questions we have included in this review are designed to give you experience with visualizing three-dimensional objects on paper, which is two-dimensional. The better you can see the object in your mind and sketch it on paper, the easier such questions will be.

Statement 13-2 is more easily remembered as: "The set of all points equidistant from the end points of a segment is the perpendicular bisecting plane of the segment."

In the multiple-choice question above, because the triangles are equilateral, all of points A, D, E, and C are equidistant from B and F so the plane containing A, D, E, and C is the perpendicular bisecting plane of BF.

[3]   Given a point P, a line L containing a point Q, and a plane E containing a point M. If P, L, and E do not intersect, then which of the following is false?

(A)   There is exactly one plane perpendicular to L at Q

(B)   There is exactly one line perpendicular to L at Q

(C)   There is exactly one line containing P and perpendicular to E

(D)   If segment PM is perpendicular to plane E, then $PM < PX$, where X is any other point of E

(E)   Any two lines that are perpendicular to E are coplanar

Geometry presents few surprises; in general, points, lines, and planes behave the way our intuition wants them to behave.

To represent the given information in a diagram, note that L must be parallel to E if they do not intersect. Remember that it is usually extremely helpful to represent information by a drawing whenever possible.

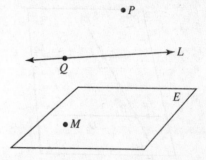

(A) is true. Your intuition should persuade you that there is at *least* one plane that satisfies this. If there were two, their intersection could only be a single line (two different planes can intersect in at most one line) and yet each plane is the set of *all* lines perpendicular to L at Q. (B) is false. There is a plane that is perpendicular to L at Q and this plane contains an infinite set of lines perpendicular to L at Q. (C) is true. You can visualize it by letting your line be a piece of string with a weight at one end. If you tie the other end to the ceiling, gravity will pull the string into a single position perpendicular to the floor. (D) is true. No matter where X is in plane E, $\triangle PMX$ will be a right triangle and PX will be the hypotenuse. (E) can be visualized by noting that for any pair of exactly vertical objects (such as telephone poles or fence posts) you can move into a position where the nearer one lines up with the farther. The plane here is the one determined by the two poles.

WORKING WITH PARALLELS

[4]   If lines $L_1, L_2,$ and L_3 lie in plane P, for which of the following must L_2 and L_3 be parallel?

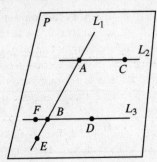

    I. L_2 and L_3 are both perpendicular to L_1.

    II. $\angle BAC$ has the same measure as $\angle EBD$.

    III. $\angle BAC$ has the same measure as $\angle DBA$.

(A) I only

(B) II only

(C) III only

(D) II and III only

(E) I and II only

Two lines are *parallel* if and only if they are contained in the same plane and do not intersect. Two lines in the same plane and perpendicular to a given line must be parallel; if they intersected, they would determine a triangle having two right angles.

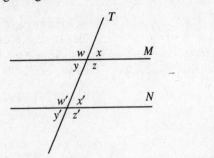

If two lines, M and N, are intersected by a third line, T, as in the figure, then T is called a *transversal* and the angle pairs, $x \to x',\, y \to y',\, z \to z',$ and $w \to w'$ are called *corresponding angles*, while the pairs $y \to x',\, z \to w'$ are called *alternate interior angles*.

If any pair of corresponding angles, say x and x', have the same measure, then lines M and N cannot intersect.

13-3   If a pair of lines is intersected by a transversal and a pair of corresponding angles have the same measure, then the pair of lines is parallel.

13-4   If a pair of lines is intersected by a transversal and a pair of alternate interior angles have the same measure, then the pair of lines is parallel.

The foregoing statements support I and II. You can see that III must be false since there is no contradiction in allowing L_2 to intersect L_3 while $(\angle BAC)° = (\angle DBA)°$.

EXAMPLES

1. If a pair of corresponding angles have the same measure, will each of the other pairs of corresponding angles also be equal in measure? Yes.

2. Would (E) have been true if we had been given $\angle BAC$ and $\angle DBA$ as supplementary? Yes.

3. In space, if two lines are each perpendicular to a third, must the first two be parallel? No.

4. If a pair of corresponding angles are equal in measure, must a pair of alternate interior angles also be equal in measure? Yes.

[5]   Given a plane containing the lines $L_1, L_2,$ and L_3. L_1 intersects L_2 at a point P and L_3 intersects neither L_1 nor L_2. Which of the following must be true?

(A) $L_1 \perp L_2$

(B) L_1 and L_2 are two distinct lines that are both parallel to L_3

(C) L_1 and L_2 are the same line

(D) L_3 is contained entirely in the inteior of an angle with vertex at P

(E) $L_1 \parallel L_2$

This question would not be a fair test question, but we chose to include it since it clearly illustrates the point we are trying to get across in this section. If you, like almost every other high school student, have studied only geometries based on Euclid, you will probably see no ambiguity and conclude that answer (C) is correct. No matter what geometry you've studied, you will automatically exclude (E) because we were given that L_1 and L_2 intersect and (A) because no restrictions, direct or indirect, were placed on angle measure. But what of (B)? You may recall a statement that restricted the number of lines passing through a point and parallel to a given line. Euclid (and many geometers following him) tried to prove that only one such parallel existed because his intuition told him that only one should exist. No one who tried to prove this succeeded.

But Euclid wanted his points, lines, and planes to behave the way he felt they should so he postulated the existence of only one parallel. Some geometers tried to prove this statement by assuming that it was false and then attempting to find a contradiction. Their failure to do so set others thinking about the consequences of systems of postulates that did not have the same "parallel postulate" as Euclid's. One such non-Euclidean geometry postulates a statement much like the one in (B). For this particular type of geometry we can actually prove that (D) is true!

You should be aware that other geometries besides the one you have studied are possible, and you should realize that these are formed by making up different postulates about the behavior of figures. Since our purpose is to review intermediate math, we have reminded you of the existence of non-Euclidean geometries; but we will continue to base our geometry on Euclid.

TEST-TAKING TIP
The plane geometry tested on the Mathematics Level IC test is Euclidean only. This test does not cover concepts of non-Euclidean geometries.

Postulate 14 *If point P does not lie on line L, then there is exactly one line in the plane of L and P that passes through P and is parallel to L.*

[6] If $L_1 \parallel L_2$ and L_3 intersects both L_1 and L_2 while the measure of $\angle 2 = 89°$, then:

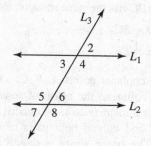

(A) $\angle 8$ is 89°

(B) $\angle 7$ is 91°

(C) $\angle 5$ is 89°

(D) $\angle 6$ is 91°

(E) $\angle 8$ and $\angle 2$ are supplementary

TEST-TAKING TIP
Know thoroughly the relationships between the measures of angles formed when parallel lines are intersected by a transversal. All Level IC tests include questions using these relationships.

In this section we will review the converses of the statements of section [4]. In that section we started with some statements about lines and angles that proved certain pairs of lines to be parallel. In this section we start with the information that the lines are parallel and review conclusions we can reach about pairs of angles.

13-5 If a pair of parallel lines is intersected by a transversal, then each pair of alternate interior angles is equal in measure.

13-6 If a pair of parallel lines is intersected by a transversal, then each pair of corresponding angles is equal in measure.

13-7 If three lines lie in a plane and two of them are parallel to the third, then all are parallel to each other.

13-8 If L_1, L_2, and L_3 lie in a plane and $L_1 \parallel L_3$ while $L_2 \perp L_1$, then $L_2 \perp L_3$.

In the multiple-choice question, $\angle 2$ and $\angle 4$ are supplementary because they are a linear pair. Also, $\angle 4$ and $\angle 8$ are congruent, because they are corresponding angles. Therefore $\angle 8$ and $\angle 2$ are supplementary (choice (E)). Note that $\angle 5$, $\angle 7$, and $\angle 8$ are 91° and $\angle 6$ is 89°.

EXAMPLE

Using the figure below: If the measure of $\angle 1$ is $50°$, find the measures of $\angle 2, \angle 3, \angle 4, \angle 5,$ and $\angle 6$.

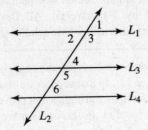

SOLUTIONS:

1. $\angle 1 = \angle 2 = \angle 4 = \angle 6 = 50$
2. $\angle 3 = \angle 5 = 130$

[7] If lines AD and BC are parallel and $\angle EAC$ is $40°$ while $\angle B$ is $60°$, what is the measure of $\angle EAB$?

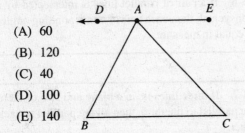

(A) 60

(B) 120

(C) 40

(D) 100

(E) 140

In the figure above m $\angle DAB = 60$ by 13-5. But the sum of the measures of $\angle DAB, \angle BAC,$ and $\angle EAC$ must be 180 since $\angle DAC$ and $\angle EAC$ are a linear pair. Therefore m $\angle BAC = 80$, and $\angle BAE = 120$.

> 13-9   The sum of the measures of the angles of a triangle is $180°$.

EXAMPLES

Using the figure above and just the information that $DA \parallel BC$, we conclude:

1. m $\angle DAB +$ m $\angle BAC + \angle CAE = 180$ since $\angle DAC$ and $\angle CAE$ form a linear pair.
2. m $\angle DAB =$ m $\angle CBA$ and m $\angle EAC =$ m $\angle BCA$ by 11-5.
3. m $\angle CBA +$ m $\angle BAC +$ m $\angle BCA = 180$ by substitution of 2. in 1.

EXAMPLES

1. If two angles of a triangle have the same measures as the corresponding angles of a second triangle, verify that the remaining pair of angles are equal.
2. Verify that the sum of the measures of the acute angles of a right triangle is $90°$.

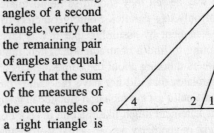

3. In the figure above, m $\angle 2 = 180 -$ m $\angle 1$, because linear pairs are supplementary. $\angle 2 = 180 -$ m $\angle 3 +$ m $\angle 4$, by 13-8. An exterior angle of a triangle is the sum of its remote interior angles.

[8] In the figure, $AB \parallel CD$, $AD \parallel BC$, and $DC \neq BC$. Which of the following is NOT a correct conclusion?

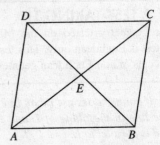

(A) $\triangle ADC \cong \triangle CBA$

(B) $\angle DCA$ has the same measure as $\angle BCA$

(C) $\angle ADC$ has the same measure as $\angle CBA$

(D) $AD = BC$

(E) $DE = BE$

Given four coplanar points $A, B, C,$ and D, no three of which are collinear, the union of segments $AB, BC, CD,$ and DA is a *quadrilateral*. A quadrilateral is a *parallelogram* if and only if both pairs of opposite sides are parallel. The figure above is thus a parallelogram. Furthermore, m $\angle DCA =$ m $\angle BAC$ since these are alternate interior angles of the parallel lines DC and AB with transversal AC. m $\angle DAC =$ m $\angle BCA$ since these are alternate interior angles of the parallel lines AD and BC with transversal AC. Thus $\triangle ADC \cong \triangle CBA$. In general, a diagonal of a parallelogram separates it into two congruent triangles. Therefore $DC = AB$ and $AD = BC$ by CP. Both pairs of opposite sides of a parallelogram are equal in length. m $\angle ADC =$ m $\angle CBA$ by CP. Both pairs of opposite angles of a parallelogram are equal in measure.

m∠*BDC* = m∠*DBA* because these are alternate interior angles of the parallel lines *DC* and *AB* with transversal *DB*. Consequently △*DEC* ≅ △*BEA* by ASA and both *DE* = *EB* and *AE* = *EC* by CP. The diagonals of a parallelogram intersect each other at the midpoint of both. We have now supported all of the answers except (B). If (B) were true, this fact, along with our knowledge that *DE* = *EB*, must make △*CED* ≅ △*CEB* and thereby, *DC* = *BC*, which contradicts the given information.

[9] If the statement "ABCD is a parallelogram" means *AB* ∥ *CD* and *BC* ∥ *AD*, then which of the following statements will NOT lead to the conclusion that *ABCD* is a parallelogram?

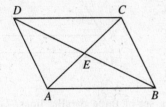

    (A) *AB* = *CD* and *AD* = *BC*

    (B) *ED* = *EB* and *AE* = *CE*

    (C) *AB* = *CD* and *AB* ∥ *CD*

    (D) *DC* = *AB* and *AD* ∥ *BC*

    (E) *AD* = *BC* and *AD* ∥ *BC*

At first glance this question may appear to duplicate number [8]. But in [8] we were given a parallelogram and asked to draw conclusions about its parts, whereas here we are given information about the parts of a quadrilateral and asked whether this information will lead to the conclusion that the quadrilateral is a parallelogram.

If *AB* = *CD* and *AD* = *BC*, then △*ADC* ≅ △*CBA* by SSS since *AC* = *AC*. Consequently, m∠*DCA* = m∠*BAC* and m∠*BCA* = m∠*CAD* by CP. Therefore both *DC* ∥ *AB* and *AD* ∥ *BC* because their pairs of alternate interior angles are equal in measure. In general, if both pairs of opposite sides of a quadrilateral are equal in length, the quadrilateral is a parallelogram.

If *DE* = *EB* and *AE* = *EC*, then △*DEC* ≅ △*BEA* by SAS since ∠*CED* and ∠*AEB* are vertical angles. Accordingly, m∠*EDC* = m∠*EBA* by CP so *DC* ∥ *AB*. Similar reasoning on △*DEA* and △*BEC* will yield *AD* ∥ *BC*. In general, if the diagonals of a quadrilateral bisect each other, the quadrilateral is a parallelogram.

If *AB* = *CD* and *AB* ∥ *CD* then m∠*DCA* = m∠*BAC* and m∠*CDB* = m∠*DBA* since they are alternate interior angles of parallel lines. Consequently, △*EDC* ≅ △*EBA* by ASA and *DE* = *BE*, *AE* = *CE* by CP. Thus *ABCD* is a parallelogram since its diagonals bisect each other. In general, if a pair of sides of a quadrilateral are parallel and equal in length, then the quadrilateral is a parallelogram.

We have supported all of the answers except (D). Does the figure at right satisfy the information in (D)?

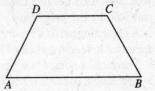

Figures like the one above are called trapezoids. A quadrilateral is a *trapezoid* if it has one and only one pair of parallel sides. It is an *isosceles trapezoid* if the nonparallel sides are equal in length.

EXAMPLES

If in the figure at right both *ADEF* and *BCEF* are parallelograms, we can prove that *ABCD* is a parallelogram. Verify the reasons:

    (a) *AD* = *EF*

    (b) *AD* ∥ *EF*

    (c) *BC* = *EF*

    (d) *BC* ∥ *EF*

    (e) *AD* = *BC*

    (f) *AD* ∥ *BC*

    (g) *ABCD* is a parallelogram

SOLUTIONS:

(a)–(d) Opposite sides of a parallelogram

(e)–(f) Substitution

(g)   It is a quadrilateral with a pair of opposite sides parallel and equal in length

[10] Which of the following is (are) true?

    I. A square is a parallelogram.

    II. A square is a rectangle.

    III. A square is a rhombus.

    (A) I only

    (B) II and III only

    (C) All of I, II, and III

    (D) I and II only

    (E) II only

If a parallelogram *ABCD* has one right angle, say ∠*A*, then it must have four, since m∠*A* = m∠*C* because they are opposite angles and both m∠*A* + m∠*B* = 180 and m∠*A* + m∠*D* = 180 since these are pairs of consecutive angles. A parallelogram is a *rectangle* if and only if it has a right angle. We have just shown that having one right angle means that all four angles will be right angles.

A parallelogram is a *rhombus* if and only if a pair of sides that contain the same vertex have the same length. Will all of the sides of a rhombus be equal in length? See part 1 of the example below.

A parallelogram is a *square* if and only if all of its sides are equal in length and all of its angles are right angles.

Therefore a square is a parallelogram by definition, it is a rectangle because it has four right angles, and it is a rhombus because all sides are congruent.

EXAMPLES

1. Is a rhombus equilateral? Yes.

2. Is a rectangle a rhombus? a square? a parallelogram? No, no, and yes.

3. Is a square a rhombus? a rectangle? a parallelogram? Yes, yes, and yes.

4. Is a rhombus a square? a rectangle? a parallelogram? No, no, and yes.

[11] If in quadrilateral $ABCD$ we know that $AE = EC$, $DE = EB$, $DE \perp AC$, and $DB = AC$, which of the following most completely describes $ABCD$?

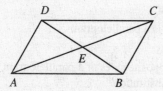

(Figure is not drawn to scale.)

(A) Trapezoid

(B) Parallelogram

(C) Rhombus

(D) Rectangle

(E) Square

The information that $AE = EC$ and $DE = EB$ (in other words, that the diagonals bisect each other) tells us that $ABCD$ is a parallelogram as we have seen in section [9]. If, in addition, $DB \perp AC$, then $\triangle AED \cong \triangle CED$ and $AD = DC$ by CP. In general, if the diagonals of a parallelogram are perpendicular, the parallelogram is a rhombus.

If $AC = BD$ along with the other information, then $\triangle DAB \cong \triangle CBA$ and m$\angle DAB =$ m$\angle CBA$ by CP. But these two angles are supplementary so they are right angles. If the diagonals of a quadrilateral bisect each other, are perpendicular, and are equal in length, the quadrilateral is a square.

EXAMPLES

1. If the diagonals of a quadrilateral have the same length, must it be a parallelogram? No, it could be an isosceles trapezoid.

2. Suppose they are also perpendicular? No, it could be a kite.

3. Suppose one diagonal also bisects the other? No, it could be a kite.

[12] In the figure $AB \parallel XY$, $DC \parallel XY$, $XD = 3(XA)$, and $CY = 6$. Find BC.

(A) 9

(B) 8

(C) 7

(D) 6

(E) 3

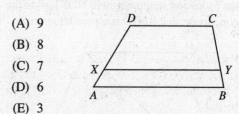

Suppose a set of three parallel lines, L_1, L_2, and L_3 is intersected by a transversal, T_1, and cuts off segments of equal length, $XY = YZ$, in the figure below. If T_2 is a transversal parallel to T_1, then what is the relationship of AB to BC?

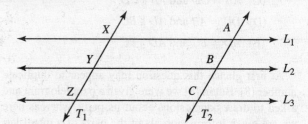

Certainly $XABY$ and $YBCZ$ are parallelograms, so $XY = AB$ and $YZ = BC$. Thus $AB = BC$, since $XY = YZ$. In general, if a set of parallel lines cuts off segments of equal length on one transversal, it will cut off segments of equal length on any parallel transversal.

Suppose T_2 is not parallel to T_1. Then through X and Y we can construct lines parallel to T_2 as in the figure below.

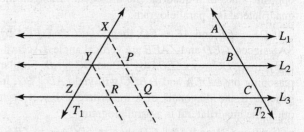

We know that $XY = YZ$ and can demonstrate that m$\angle XYP =$ m$\angle YZR$ as well as m$\angle XPY =$ m$\angle YRZ$. Consequently $\triangle XYP \cong \triangle YZR$ by SAA and $YR = XP$ by CP. But $AB = XP$ and $BC = YR$ because these are opposite sides of a parallelogram. We conclude that $AB = BC$

and state that, in general, if a set of parallel lines cuts off segments of equal length on one transversal, then it will cut off segments of equal length on *any* transversal.

To answer the multiple-choice question above, draw in two more lines that are parallel to AB and intersect segment XD between X and D to cut off segments of equal length

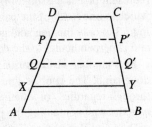

$(DP = PQ = QX)$. Since $XD = DP + PQ + QX = 3(XA)$, then $CY = CP' + P'Q' + Q'Y = 3(YB)$. Hence $YB = 2$ and $CB = 8$.

[13] Points $A, B, C,$ and D all lie in the same plane. If AB and CD are both perpendicular to AC but not to BD, which of the following must be true?

  I. Line AB is parallel to line CD

  II. $BD > AC$

  III. $AB = CD$

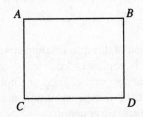

(Figure is not drawn to scale.)

(A) I only

(B) I and II only

(C) I and III only

(D) II and III only

(E) I, II, and III

This question tests three different principles relating to parallel and perpendicular lines and the distance between parallel lines.

When two lines in the same plane are perpendicular to the same line, they must be parallel to each other, so I is true.

The perpendicular segment connecting two parallel lines is shorter than any other segment connecting them. Therefore II is true.

Because AB and CD are not perpendicular to BD, the latter cannot be parallel to AC. Therefore, $ABCD$ cannot be a parallelogram.

Segments AB and CD could only be equal if $ABCD$ were a parallelogram. Therefore III is false and the correct answer is (B).

Note that the three statements, I, II, and III, differ in complexity, with statement III presenting the most challenge. That is often the case with questions written in this format.

Note, also, the diagram is not drawn to scale. It is drawn to look like a rectangle. If you tried to answer the question solely from the way the diagram looks, you would select choice (C), which was the most popular incorrect answer in our test group.

[14] Segments AD and BC are parallel and congruent. Segments AC and BD intersect at E. Which of the following is(are) true?

  I. $AB = CD$

  II. $AC = BD$

  III. $AE = CE$

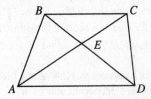

(Figure is not drawn to scale.)

(A) I only

(B) I and II only

(C) II and III only

(D) I and III only

(E) I, II, and III

The question tests three relationships within various types of quadrilaterals.

Because AD and BC are parallel and congruent, quadrilateral $ABCD$ is a parallelogram. Therefore, AB and CD are also parallel and congruent, which makes I true.

The diagonals of a parallelogram are congruent when the parallelogram is a rectangle, but not otherwise. The given information includes nothing from which you can conclude the angles measure 90°. Because it is not a rectangle, II is false.

The diagonals of a parallelogram bisect each other, so III is true. Therefore the correct answer is (D).

Be sure to know all of the relationships relating to parallelograms, rectangles, trapezoids, squares, and rhombuses as reviewed in these chapters, summarized at the ends of the chapters, and gathered in the appendix of principles, relationships, and formulas.

[15] If *ABCD* is a rectangle, $AB = 8$, $AD = 4$, and *P*, *Q*, *R*, *S*, *E*, *F*, *G*, and *H* are the midpoints of the segments drawn, find the area of *EFGH*.

(A) 32

(B) 16

(C) 24

(D) 4

(E) 8

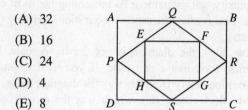

Even though this figure abounds with segments, drawing a few more helps direct you to the correct answer.

Draw segment *PR*, which you can easily see to be equal to *AB* because *ABPR* will be a parallelogram. *EF* and *HG* are segments connecting the midpoints of the sides of triangles *PQR* and *PSR*, respectively. Therefore $EF = HG = (\frac{1}{2})PR = 4$.

Similarly, draw segment *QS* and follow the same line of reasoning to show that $EH = FG = (\frac{1}{2})AD = 2$.

Therefore, *EFGH* is a rectangle with sides 2 and 4 and area 8, (E).

[16] Line *l* is in plane *m*. How many planes contain *l* and are perpendicular to *m*?

(A) none

(B) one

(C) two

(D) three

(E) more than three

Questions like this test your ability to see abstract three-dimensional objects in your head.

Visualize the situation in terms of familiar objects and then make the necessary adjustments to turn the real objects into idealized abstractions.

Plane *m* is the floor of a room. Line *l* is the bottom edge of one wall (the line formed where the wall meets the floor). The wall contains *l* and is perpendicular to the floor, *m*.

Other planes are also perpendicular to the floor—the other walls, for example—but only one wall contains *l*. At this point, the answer looks like (B), but wait, there may be more.

Other planes contain *l*, but they aren't perpendicular to the floor (imagine a flimsy house with wobbly walls).

Now it is easy to see why only one plane fits the situation, choice (B).

This visualization may not have occurred to you, but others might.

For this problem, for example, visualize a textbook, instead. Imagine that the book is lying open on the desk with the pages fanned out. The desk is plane *m*. The pages represent planes passing through the binding of the book, which is line *l*. All of the pages represent planes containing *l*, but only the one sticking straight up goes through *l* and is perpendicular to the desk.

Still another visualization. Picture a door hinged to a door jamb. The jamb is line *l*, which the door will pass through regardless of whether it is open or closed. Plane *m* is the wall containing the jamb. When the door is open to the point it is perpendicular to the wall, the conditions of the problem are met. In any other position, the conditions are not met. So there is only one position, one plane, that does the trick.

[17] Find *x* if lines L_1 and L_2 are parallel and the angle measures are as shown.

(A) 12

(B) 24

(C) 120

(D) 10

(E) 60

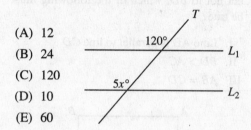

Some variation of this question appears on nearly every Level IC test. It combines knowledge of an important geometric fact about parallel lines, an important algebraic principle about the use of equations, and the ability to solve a basic algebraic equation.

If parallel lines are cut by a transversal, eight pairs of angles are congruent (some wag once simplified the rule by saying that "all angles that look congruent are congruent," which may help you if you can't keep straight names such as "corresponding angles," "alternate interior angles," and "alternate exterior angles").

In this case, the angles marked $5x°$ and $120°$ form one of four pairs of corresponding angles. Because they are congruent, you may write that fact in the equation:

$$5x = 120.$$

Then solve it by dividing both sides by 5 to get $x = 24$, (B).

This would be considered one of the elementary "warm-up" questions easy enough to be included among the first five.

The problem could be made slightly harder by shifting the $5x$ to a different location for which the angle relationship might be less apparent. Any other of the three locations where *T* and L_2 cross would make the question more complicated, enough to push it into the range of questions 6 to 15.

The question might be made more difficult if both angles were represented in terms of x, say $x^2 - 20$ and $10x + 4$. That change produces the equation

$$x^2 - 20 = 10x + 4$$
$$x^2 - 10x - 24 = 0$$
$$(x - 12)(x + 2) = 0$$
$$x = 12 \text{ or } x = -2$$

Now it is in the 16 to 25 range because of the level of algebra involved.

Test makers could move it up a notch further in difficulty by asking for the measure of the angle rather than the value of x. This adds one more step by making you convert x into the appropriate angle measure.

They could also up the ante just a bit more by removing the condition that the lines are parallel and replacing an answer choice with "cannot be determined" to see if you are paying attention. If the lines aren't given as parallel you cannot make any assumption about the measures (beyond the fact that they are numbers between 0 and 180).

The point here is that you need to pay attention because questions that look familiar might have variations that could catch you napping.

[18] In the figure, line L_2 is perpendicular to line L_4. P is a point on lines L_2, L_3, and L_4. If $a = b$, which of the following must be true?

I. $L_1 \perp L_3$
II. $L_1 \parallel L_2$
III. $L_1 \perp L_4$

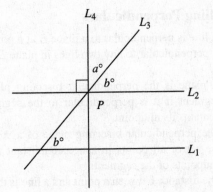

(A) I only

(B) I and II only

(C) II and III only

(D) I and III only

(E) I, II, and III

Let's see where the fact that $a = b$ takes us. If $a = b$, then $a = 45°$ and $b = 45°$. That should do it.

Because $b = 45°$, lines L_1 and L_3 do not meet at a right angle so they can't be perpendicular. Therefore I is false.

Because L_1 and L_2 are both crossed by L_3 to form congruent corresponding angles with measure $b°$, $L_1 \parallel L_2$ and II is true.

Because L_1 and L_2 are parallel and L_2 is perpendicular to L_4, they must both be perpendicular to L_4, so III is true. Therefore, the answer is (C).

WHAT YOU SHOULD KNOW

KEY CONCEPTS

Handling Perpendiculars

1. A line is perpendicular to a plane E at a point B if it is perpendicular to any two lines in plane E at point B.
2. A plane is the perpendicular bisecting plane of a segment if it is perpendicular to the segment and contains its midpoint.
3. The perpendicular bisecting plane of a segment is the set of all points in space equidistant from the endpoints of the segment.
4. The distance between a point and a line is the length of the perpendicular segment.
5. The diagonals of a rhombus are perpendicular.

Handling Parallels

1. Two lines are parallel if and only if they lie in the same plane and do not intersect.
2. Parallel lines are everywhere equidistant.
3. If two parallel lines are intersected by a third line (a "transversal"), then:
   a. all pairs of corresponding angles are congruent,
   b. both pairs of alternate interior angles are congruent, *and*
   c. interior angles on the same side of the transversal are supplementary.
4. If two lines are intersected by a transversal, the following conditions will guarantee that the lines are parallel:
   a. a pair of corresponding angles is congruent,
   b. a pair of alternate interior angles is congruent,
   c. interior angles on the same side of the transversal are supplementary, *and*
   d. the lines are each perpendicular to the transversal.
5. Two lines that are parallel to a third line are parallel to each other.

6. If a quadrilateral is a parallelogram, then:
   a. both pairs of opposite sides are parallel,
   b. both pairs of opposite sides are congruent,
   c. both pairs of opposite angles are congruent,
   d. all pairs of consecutive angles are supplementary, *and*
   e. the diagonals bisect each other.
7. If a set of three or more parallel lines intercepts congruent segments on one transversal, it will intercept congruent segments on any transversal.

KEY THEOREMS

1. The sum of the measures of the angles of a triangle is 180.
2. The measure of an exterior angle of a triangle is equal to the sum of the measures of its remote interior angles. (Exterior Angle Equality Theorem)

TEST-TAKING STRATEGIES

- When a question involves possible perpendiculars, try to visualize the relationships involved in terms of familiar vertical objects, such as trees, that are perpendicular to the ground.
- Though seemingly facetious, a handy way of remembering all of the angle relationships for parallel lines cut by a transversal is to remember that when parallel lines are cut by a transversal, all of the angles that look congruent are congruent. Keep this in mind.
- In working with rectangles, rhombuses, and squares, remember that all are parallelograms so all of the parallelogram relationships apply to them. For example, opposite angles are congruent, adjacent angles are supplementary, and the diagonals bisect each other.

ANSWERS

[1] (C)	[4] (E)	[7] (B)	[10] (C)	[13] (B)	[16] (B)
[2] (D)	[5] (C)	[8] (B)	[11] (E)	[14] (D)	[17] (B)
[3] (B)	[6] (E)	[9] (D)	[12] (B)	[15] (E)	[18] (C)

RATIO, PROPORTION, AND SIMILARITY

CHAPTER

14

KEY TERMS

proportion   an equation in which both sides are ratios.

sequence   a set of numbers arranged in a prescribed order.

geometric mean   the nth root of the product of n numbers. Examples: the geometric mean of 9 and 4 is 6; the geometric mean of the numbers a and b is the number $\sqrt{ab}$.

WORKING WITH RATIOS

[1]   If the ratio of the lengths of two segments measured in yards is $\dfrac{m}{n}$, then which of the following is the ratio of the lengths measured in inches?

(A) $3\left(\dfrac{m}{n}\right)$

(B) $12\left(\dfrac{m}{n}\right)$

(C) $36\left(\dfrac{m}{n}\right)$

(D) $\dfrac{m}{n}$

(E) $\dfrac{1}{36}\left(\dfrac{m}{n}\right)$

The ratio of p to q is the quotient $\frac{p}{q}$, where p and q are real numbers and $q \neq 0$. Representing ratios as fractions enables us to apply some of the ideas already reviewed. Specifically, we will use the following principle to answer this question.

> 14-1   If a, b, and c are real numbers and neither b nor c is zero, then
>
> $$\frac{ac}{bc} = \frac{a}{b}$$

Let us assume that the ratio $\frac{m}{n}$ in the question is in unsimplified form; in other words, that the length of one segment is m yards and of the other is n yards. Of course, this does not have to be the case, since if $m = 2$ and $n = 6$, the ratio is $\frac{1}{3}$, but we will consider this possibility later.

If the lengths are m and n yards, then they are $36m$ and $36n$ inches. Thus the ratio in inches is

$$\frac{36m}{36n} = \frac{m}{n}$$

Suppose $\frac{m}{n}$ was the simplified form. Then some common factor k has been removed from the numerator and denominator such that the original lengths were km and kn yards. This gives $36km$ and $36kn$ inches, which yields the ratio $\frac{36km}{36kn}$ — the latter also reduces to $\frac{m}{n}$

EXAMPLES

 Use your calculator as needed.

1. What is the ratio of boys to girls in a school of 500 boys and 625 girls?

$$\frac{500}{625} = \frac{4}{5}$$

2. Find two numbers that have the ratio $\dfrac{9}{4}$ if their sum is 39. 27 and 12.

3. What must be true of x and y if their ratio is $\dfrac{2}{3}$? $2y = 3x$.

WORKING WITH PROPORTIONS

[2]   If $\dfrac{9}{10} = \dfrac{x}{15}$, then $x = ?$

(A) 14

(B) $13\dfrac{1}{2}$

(C) 13

(D) $12\dfrac{1}{2}$

(E) 12

An equation in that both sides are ratios is called a proportion. From 14-1 we conclude that when two fractions are equal it must be possible to find some number k that, when multiplied by the numerator and denominator of one fraction, yields, respectively, the numerator and denominator of the other. For example, in the question above we see that $15 = 10(\frac{3}{2})$ so x must equal $9(\frac{3}{2})$. A second process for finding an answer here is to use the Cross-Multiplication Property.

> 14-2   If a, b, c, and d are real numbers and neither b nor d is zero, then:
>
> $$\frac{a}{b} = \frac{c}{d} \text{ if and only if } ad = bc.$$

Using 14-2, we can rewrite $\frac{9}{10} = \frac{x}{15}$ as $9 \cdot 15 = 10x$. Thus $135 = 10x$ and $x = 13.5$.

EXAMPLES

1. If $\dfrac{3}{4} = \dfrac{9}{x}$, then $x = 12$.

2. If $\dfrac{2x}{9} = \dfrac{3x}{4}$, then $x = 0$.

3. If $\dfrac{x+1}{8} = \dfrac{1}{9}$, then $x = -\dfrac{1}{9}$.

4. If $3\dfrac{(x-1)}{x} = \dfrac{2}{x-2}$, then $x = 3$ or $x = \dfrac{2}{3}$.

[3]   If the sequence 5, x, y is proportional to the sequence x, 20, 32, which of the following is y?

(A) 10

(B) 12

(C) 14

(D) 16

(E) 18

A *sequence* is a set of numbers arranged in a prescribed order. Two sequences,

(1) $a, b, c, \ldots$ and

(2) $a', b,' c', \ldots,$

are *proportional* if and only if there is some real number k such that:

(3) $a = ka',$ $b = kb',$ $c = kc', \ldots$

Equation (3) can be rewritten as

(4) $\dfrac{a}{a'} = k,$ $\dfrac{b}{b'} = k,$ $\dfrac{c}{c'} = k, \ldots$

Since equation (4) indicates that each of the ratios given is equal to the same number, k (called the "proportionality constant"), we conclude:

(5) $\dfrac{a}{a'} = \dfrac{b}{b'} = \dfrac{c}{c'} = \ldots$

Note that equation (5) (called a "proportionality") is equivalent to the separate equations:

(6) $\dfrac{a}{a'} = \dfrac{b}{b'}$ and $\dfrac{b}{b'} = \dfrac{c}{c'}$ and $\dfrac{a}{a'} = \dfrac{c}{c'}$, etc.

EXAMPLE

If the sequence x, y, 3 is proportional to 4, 5, 2, then what are x and y?

SOLUTION: We conclude:

$$\frac{x}{4} = \frac{y}{5} = \frac{3}{2},$$

which means

$$\frac{x}{4} = \frac{3}{2} \text{ and } \frac{y}{5} = \frac{3}{2},$$

so

$$2x = 12 \text{ and } 2y = 15.$$

Thus $x = 6$ and $y = 7\frac{1}{2}$.

In the multiple-choice question,

$$\frac{5}{x} = \frac{x}{20} = \frac{y}{32}.$$

Because $\frac{5}{x} = \frac{x}{20}$, by cross-multiplying we get

$$x^2 = 100,$$
$$x = \pm 10.$$

Because $\frac{5}{10} = \frac{y}{32}$, by cross-multiplying we get

$$10y = 160,$$
$$y = 16.$$

[4]   If $\dfrac{a}{2} = \dfrac{b}{3}$, then $\dfrac{b+3}{3} = ?$

(A) $\dfrac{a+3}{3}$

(B) $\dfrac{a+2}{2}$

(C) $\dfrac{a+3}{2}$

(D) $\dfrac{a+3}{6}$

(E) $\dfrac{a+2}{6}$

A proportion is an equation and thereby is subject to the addition and subtraction properties of equality. Consequently, if

$$\frac{x}{y} = \frac{z}{w}, \text{ then}$$

$$\frac{x}{y} + 1 = \frac{z}{w} + 1 \text{ and } \frac{x}{y} - 1 = \frac{z}{w} - 1.$$

Hence

$$\frac{x}{y} + \frac{y}{y} = \frac{z}{w} + \frac{w}{w} \text{ and } \frac{x}{y} - \frac{y}{y} = \frac{z}{w} - \frac{w}{w},$$

$$\frac{x+y}{y} = \frac{z+w}{w} \text{ and } \frac{x-y}{y} = \frac{z-w}{w}.$$

We state these results formally in the following:

14-3   If x, y, z, and w are real numbers such that $y \neq 0$ and $w \neq 0$, and if $\dfrac{x}{y} = \dfrac{z}{w}$, then

$$\frac{x+y}{y} = \frac{z+w}{w} \quad \text{and} \quad \frac{x-y}{y} = \frac{z-w}{w}.$$

You may recall that theorem 14-3 has applications to similar triangles, which we will review in a later section. Therefore, if $\frac{a}{2} = \frac{b}{3}$, then $\frac{a+2}{2} = \frac{b+3}{3}$.

EXAMPLES

1. If $\dfrac{x}{3} = 2$, then $\dfrac{x+3}{3} = 3$.

2. If $\dfrac{x}{y} = \dfrac{4}{3}$, then $\dfrac{x-y}{y} = \dfrac{1}{3}$.

3. If $\dfrac{x}{y} = \dfrac{4}{3}$, then $\dfrac{x-3}{y} = \dfrac{4y-9}{3y}$.

[5]   If $\dfrac{a}{b} = \dfrac{c}{d}$, then $\dfrac{a}{c} = ?$

(A) $\dfrac{a}{d}$

(B) $\dfrac{c}{d}$

(C) $\dfrac{b}{d}$

(D) $\dfrac{d}{b}$

(E) bd

14-4   If $\dfrac{a}{c} = \dfrac{c}{d}$, where $b \neq 0$ and $d \neq 0$, then

$$\frac{a}{c} = \frac{b}{d} \quad \text{and} \quad \frac{d}{b} = \frac{c}{a}.$$

Thus, in a proportion, we may interchange either numerator with the denominator of the other term, and the resulting equation will still be a proportion.

EXAMPLE

If $\dfrac{1}{2} = \dfrac{3}{6}$, switch the 2 and 3 to get $\dfrac{1}{3} = \dfrac{2}{6}$.

Or, switch the 1 and 6 to get $\dfrac{6}{2} = \dfrac{3}{1}$. Do you see that all three equations are true?

[6]   If $\dfrac{1}{2} = \dfrac{x}{4} = \dfrac{3}{6} = \dfrac{x+4}{y}$, find y.

(A) 9

(B) 10

(C) 11

(D) 12

(E) 13

14-5   For all a, b, c,... and a', b', c',..., such that none of the latter is zero,

$$\frac{a}{a'} = \frac{b}{b'} = \frac{c}{c'} = \cdots = \frac{a+b+c+\dots}{a'+b'+c'+\dots}.$$

This rule does not look as if it should be true, but consider these cases:

$$\frac{1}{2} = \frac{2}{4} = \frac{3}{6} = \frac{4}{8} = \frac{1+2+3+4}{2+4+6+8} = \frac{10}{20}$$

or,

$$\frac{1}{3} = \frac{2}{6} = \frac{3}{9} = \frac{4}{12} = \frac{5}{15} = \frac{1+2+3+4+5}{3+6+9+12+15} = \frac{15}{45}$$

Note that the numerator of the final term in the proportionality of the multiple-choice question is the sum of the numerators of the other terms, so the denominator must be the sum of the denominators.

Therefore

$$2+4+6 = y.$$

EXAMPLES

1. $\dfrac{x}{y} = \dfrac{z}{w} = \dfrac{2}{3}$; therefore $\dfrac{x+z}{y+w} = \dfrac{2}{3}$.

2. $\dfrac{2}{x} = \dfrac{5}{4} = \dfrac{7}{x+4}$

FINDING THE GEOMETRIC MEAN

---

[7]   If $x = \sqrt{ab}$, then $\dfrac{x}{a} = ?$

(A) $\dfrac{b}{x}$

(B) $\dfrac{x}{b}$

(C) bx

(D) ab

(E) $x\sqrt{b}$

14-6 If $\dfrac{x}{a} = \dfrac{b}{x}$ when $x > 0$, then

$$x^2 = ab \quad \text{and} \quad x = \sqrt{ab}.$$

When x satisfies the requirements of 14-6, it is called the *geometric mean* between a and b. Note that, if

$$\frac{x}{a} = \frac{b}{x},$$

then

$$\frac{b}{x} = \frac{x}{a}.$$

EXAMPLES

Find the geometric mean between each of the pairs of numbers given. Use your calculator where needed.

1. 3 and 12

2. 2 and 8

3. 4 and 5

4. Find a pair of numbers, a and b, such that their geometric mean is equal to their arithmetic mean (the arithmetic mean is the average).

SOLUTIONS:

1. $GM = \sqrt{3 \times 12} = \sqrt{36} = 6$

2. $GM = \sqrt{2 \times 8} = \sqrt{16} = 4$

3. $GM = \sqrt{4 \times 5} = 2\sqrt{5}$

4. $\sqrt{ab} = \dfrac{a+b}{2}$ is only true when $a = b = 1$

WORKING WITH SIMILARITY

[8] If $\triangle ABC \cong \triangle XYZ$, then which of the following is NOT necessarily true?

(A) The corresponding sides are proportional.

(B) The corresponding angles are proportional.

(C) The triangles are similar.

(D) The triangles have the same area.

(E) The triangles lie in the same plane.

If we take a photograph of a painting, the photograph and the painting will show figures that are exactly the same shape but different in size. We refer to this relationship as a "similarity."

A correspondence between the vertices of two triangles is a *similarity* if and only if the lengths of all pairs of corresponding sides are proportional and all pairs of corresponding angles are equal in measure.

Thus, when we write $\triangle ABC \sim \triangle XYZ$, we mean:

$$\frac{AB}{XY} = \frac{BC}{YZ} = \frac{AC}{XZ},$$

and

$$\mathrm{m}\angle A = \mathrm{m}\angle X, \ \mathrm{m}\angle B = \mathrm{m}\angle Y, \ \mathrm{m}\angle C = \mathrm{m}\angle Z.$$

If a correspondence is a congruence, is it also a similarity? Certainly all pairs of corresponding angles are equal in measure and the sides are proportional (with 1 as proportionality constant). Only answer (B) is tricky: If $\angle A = \angle X$ and $\angle B = \angle Y$, then

$$\frac{\mathrm{m}\angle A}{\mathrm{m}\angle X} = 1,$$

$$\frac{\mathrm{m}\angle B}{\mathrm{m}\angle Y} = 1.$$

Therefore

$$\frac{\mathrm{m}\angle A}{\mathrm{m}\angle X} = \frac{\mathrm{m}\angle B}{\mathrm{m}\angle Y}$$

Hence all pairs of corresponding angles and sides *are* proportional (with proportionality constant 1) because they are congruent. Congruent triangles, therefore, are also similar triangles and have the same area, but they need not lie in the same plane.

[9] If $AY = BX$, $AX = 3$, $YC = 12$, and $XY \parallel BC$, find AC.

(A) 15

(B) 18

(C) 16

(D) 21

(E) 20

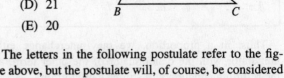

The letters in the following postulate refer to the figure above, but the postulate will, of course, be considered true for all triangles that have two sides intersected by a line parallel to the third side.

Postulate 15 *For any triangle ABC line XY intersects sides AB and AC and XY $\parallel$ BC if and only if*

(1) $$\frac{AB}{AX} = \frac{AC}{AY} = \frac{BC}{XY}.$$

In other words, the segments that are cut off are proportional to the sides that contain them. Are the segments cut off also proportional to each other? By 14-1, if (1) is true, then:

$$(2) \qquad \frac{AB - AX}{AX} = \frac{AC - AY}{AY}.$$

Since $AB - AX = XB$ and $AC - AY = YC$, we conclude:

$$(3) \qquad \frac{XB}{AX} = \frac{YC}{AY}$$

EXAMPLE 1

If $AX = 2$, $AB = 9$, $AY = 3$ in the figure in [9], find YC if XY is to be parallel to BC.

SOLUTION:

By Postulate 15, $\dfrac{AB}{AX} = \dfrac{AC}{AY}$, so $\dfrac{9}{2} = \dfrac{AC}{3}$ and $AC = 13\dfrac{1}{2}$.

Therefore $YC = AC - AY = 13\dfrac{1}{2} - 3 = 10\dfrac{1}{2}$.

EXAMPLE 2

Find m if $AX = 3m - 19$, $XB = m - 3$, $YC = 2m - 8$, and $AY = 8$, in the figure of the multiple-choice question.

SOLUTION:

$$\frac{3m - 19}{m - 3} = \frac{8}{2m - 8}$$
$$8m - 24 = 6m^2 - 62m + 152$$
$$0 = 6m^2 - 70m + 176$$
$$0 = 2(3m - 11)(m - 8)$$

Therefore $m = \dfrac{11}{3}$ or 8.

In the multiple-choice question,

$$\frac{AX}{BX} = \frac{AY}{CY}.$$

Let $BX = AY = m$. Then

$$\frac{3}{m} = \frac{m}{12},$$
$$m^2 = 36,$$
$$m = 6 = AY.$$

Since $AC = AY + YC$,

$$AC = 6 + 12$$
$$= 18.$$

[10] If $AB \parallel WX \parallel YZ \parallel CD$, $AW = 2$, $WY = 3$, $YC = 1$, and $BD = 12$, find BX.

(A) 2

(B) 3

(C) 4

(D) 6

(E) 8

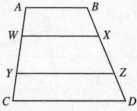

If a set of parallel lines crosses two or more intersecting lines, the corresponding segments cut off by the parallel lines are in proportion. For three parallel lines, the formal statement of this property is:

> 14-7   Lines L_1, L_2, and L_3 are parallel if and only if they intersect transversals T_1, and T_2 in points A, B, C and X, Y, Z respectively, such that
> $$\frac{AB}{BC} = \frac{XY}{YZ}.$$

A similar law can be proved for sets containing four or more parallel lines. In the question that begins this section, let $ZD = a$. Then $XZ = 3a$ and $BX = 2a$, so $a + 3a + 2a = 12$ and $a = 2$.

EXAMPLES

In the figure, lines l, m, and n are parallel.

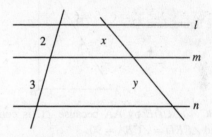

1. If $x + y = 10$, then $x = 4$, $y = 6$.

2. If $x + y = 50$, then $\dfrac{x}{y} = \dfrac{2}{3}$.

3. If $y = 36$, then $x = 24$.

[11] If line BC is parallel to line AD, find x when
$BC = x+1$, $AD = x+2$, $DE = x$, and $BE = 1$.

(A) 2
(B) 1
(C) 0
(D) 1.41
(E) 1.73

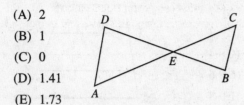

In a correspondence between two triangles for which two pairs of corresponding angles are equal in measure, will the third pair also be equal in measure? For any $\triangle ABC$ and $\triangle XYZ$, if $m\angle A = m\angle X$ and $m\angle B = m\angle Y$, then $m\angle A + m\angle B = \angle X + \angle Y$ and $180 - [\angle A + \angle B] = 180 - [\angle X + \angle Y]$. But $\angle C = 180 - [\angle A + \angle B]$ and $\angle Z = 180 - [\angle X + \angle Y]$, since the sum of the measures of the angles of a triangle is 180. Thus the third pair of angles, $\angle C$ and $\angle Z$, are equal in measure.

14-8 **(AA)** A correspondence between two triangles is a similarity if two pairs of corresponding angles are equal in measure.

EXAMPLE

In the figure, find AB.

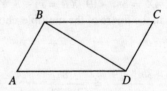

$\triangle ABC \sim \triangle CDE$ by AA because $\angle C$ is common to both and $\angle CED = \angle CBA = 90$.

$$\frac{AC}{CD} = \frac{4}{1}$$

$$\therefore \frac{AB}{DE} = \frac{4}{1} = \frac{x}{3}$$

$$\therefore x = 12$$

In $\triangle ABC$ the parallel lines give us two pairs of alternate interior angles of equal measure and thus the triangles are similar by AA. We need only solve the proportion:

$$\frac{x+1}{x+2} = \frac{1}{x}.$$

$$x(x+1) = 1(x+2),$$

$$x^2 + x = x+2,$$

$$x^2 = 2,$$

$$x = \pm\sqrt{2}.$$

$$\doteq \pm 1.41$$

The solution $-\sqrt{2}$ is extraneous, since x is the length of a segment, a positive number.

TEST-TAKING TIP

Often, as in this example, a solution of an equation will not fit the given information because the equation represents a more general situation than the original information allows. Always check your answers to see whether they make sense in terms of the given information as well as making the deriving equation true.

EXAMPLES

In each of the following indicate which triangles are similar by *AA*:

1. Given that $ABCD$ is a parallelogram.

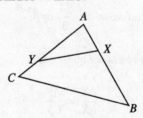

$$\triangle ABC \sim \triangle CDB$$

2. Given $m\angle AXY = m\angle C$.

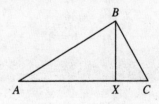

$$\triangle AXY \sim \triangle ACB$$

3. Given $AB \perp BC$ and $BX \perp AC$.

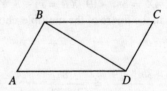

$$\triangle ABC \sim \triangle BXC \sim \triangle AXB$$

[12]   In the figure $AD = 16$, $AB = 12$, and $AC = 9$.
Both $\angle DAB$ and $\angle BAC$ have measures of 50.
$$\frac{DB}{BC} = ?$$

(A) $\dfrac{4}{3}$

(B) $\dfrac{16}{9}$

(C) $\dfrac{3}{4}$

(D) $\dfrac{9}{16}$

(E) Cannot be determined

If, in $\triangle PMQ$ and $\triangle XYZ$ below,

(1) $$\frac{PM}{MQ} = \frac{XY}{YZ}$$

and $m\angle M = m\angle Y$, we can prove the two triangles are similar. To do this we have copied $\triangle XYZ$ on $\triangle PMQ$ to get $\triangle X'Y'Z'$ and have added line L parallel to segment PQ.

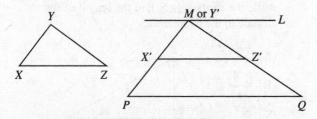

Since $X'Y' = XY$ and $Y'Z' = YZ$, we conclude:

(2) $$\frac{PM}{MQ} = \frac{X'Y'}{Y'Z'} \text{ by substitution in (1) above, and}$$

(3) $$\frac{PM}{X'Y'} = \frac{MQ}{Y'Z'} \text{ by 14-4}$$

Therefore

(4) $$\frac{PM - X'Y'}{X'Y'} = \frac{MQ - Y'Z'}{Y'Z'} \text{ by 14-3}$$

But $PM - X'Y' = PX'$ and $MQ - Y'Z' = QZ'$, so

(5) $$\frac{PX'}{X'Y'} = \frac{QZ'}{Y'Z'}.$$

The set of lines L, $X'Z'$ and PQ, therefore, cut off proportional segments on transversals PM and QM: this makes them parallel. This means $m\angle Y'X'Z' = m\angle P$ and, therefore, $m\angle XYZ = m\angle P$ so $\triangle XYZ \sim \triangle PMQ$ by AA. We have now proved the following:

14-9   *(SAS Similarity)* A correspondence between two triangles is a similarity if two pairs of corresponding sides are proportional and the included pair of corresponding angles are equal in measure.

In the multiple-choice question,

$$\frac{AD}{AB} = \frac{AB}{AC} \text{ since } \frac{16}{12} = \frac{12}{9}.$$

Because we are given that $(\angle DAB)° = (\angle BAC)° = 50$, it follows that $\triangle ADB$ is similar to $\triangle ABC$ by SAS. Therefore the ratio of DB to BC must equal the ratio of the given pairs of corresponding sides (16 to 12, which reduces to 4 to 3):

$$\frac{AD}{AB} = \frac{4}{3} = \frac{DB}{BC}$$

EXAMPLES

1. Are any two isosceles triangles similar? How many pairs of angles must be proved equal in measure? Will any pair of corresponding angles do?

2. Are any two equilateral triangles similar?

3. If AC bisects $\angle BAD$ (see the figure below), is $\triangle BAC$ ever similar to $\triangle CAD$? Suppose $AB = 1$, $AC = 3$, and $AD = 9$; can the triangles be similar?

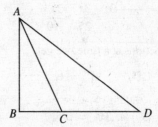

SOLUTIONS:

1. Similar only when vertex angles are congruent.

2. Yes.

3. Only when $AC \perp BD$; No.

[13] What must the values of x and y be if we are to conclude that $\triangle ABC \sim \triangle EDF$?

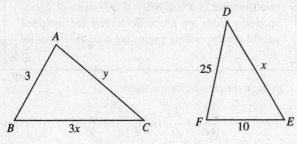

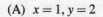

(Figures are not drawn to scale.)

(A) $x = 1, y = 2$

(B) $x = 2, y = 3$

(C) $x = 3, y = 4$

(D) $x = 4, y = 5$

(E) $x = 5, y = 6$

14-10 (*SSS Similarity*) A correspondence between two triangles is a similarity if all three pairs of corresponding sides are proportional.

In the question above we are given no information about the angles of the triangles and must apply 14-10 in order to conclude that they are similar. Thus we must find values of x and y such that

$$\frac{3}{x} = \frac{3x}{25} = \frac{y}{10}.$$

Using two fractions at a time, we get

$$\frac{3}{x} = \frac{3x}{25},$$
$$3x^2 = 75,$$
$$x^2 = 25,$$
$$x = \pm 5.$$

The solution -5 is extraneous since x is the length of a segment and must be a positive number. Using 5 for x in the above gives

$$\frac{3}{5} = \frac{y}{10},$$
$$\frac{3}{5}(10) = y,$$
$$6 = y.$$

EXAMPLES

If $BC = 3$, $AB = 2$, and $ED = 4$, find (to the nearest tenth):

1. AC

2. AE

3. AD

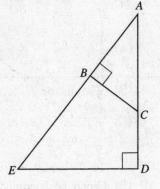

SOLUTIONS:

1. $AC^2 = BC^2 + AB^2 = 13, \therefore x = \sqrt{13} \doteq 3.6$

2. $\dfrac{AE}{AC} = \dfrac{AB}{ED}, \therefore \dfrac{AE}{\sqrt{13}} = \dfrac{3}{4}, \therefore AE = \dfrac{3\sqrt{13}}{4} \doteq 2.7$

3. $\dfrac{AD}{AB} = \dfrac{ED}{BC}, \therefore \dfrac{AD}{2} = \dfrac{4}{3}, \therefore AD = \dfrac{8}{3} \doteq 2.7$

[14] If the longest side of a right triangle is 13 while the shortest is 5, find the length of the altitude to the hypotenuse.

(A) 5

(B) $4\dfrac{8}{13}$

(C) 6

(D) $6\dfrac{5}{12}$

(E) $6\dfrac{5}{13}$

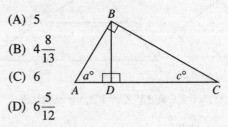

To answer this question we'll develop two formulas based on the similar triangles found in a right triangle. If a $\triangle ABC$ has a right angle at B and if $BD \perp AC$ while m$\angle A = a$ and m$\angle C = c$, what are m$\angle ABD$ and m$\angle CBD$? Since m$\angle BDA = $ m$\angle ABC$ and m$\angle BAD = $ m$\angle BAC$, we conclude that the remaining pair of angles in $\triangle ABD$ and $\triangle ACB$ are also equal in measure, so m$\angle ACB = $ m$\angle ABD = c$. By a like argument we conclude that m$\angle CBD = a$.

Put these measures, c and a, in the appropriate angles of the sketch above so you can keep track of the corresponding angles. You should now see that:

$$\triangle ABC \sim \triangle ADB \sim \triangle BDC$$

with the corresponding vertices given by the order of the letters.

The corresponding sides of $\triangle ABD$ and $\triangle BCD$ must be proportional so:

$$\frac{BD}{DC} = \frac{AD}{BD},$$
$$(BD)^2 = (AD)(DC), \text{ and}$$
$$BD = \sqrt{(AD)(DC)}.$$

14-11   The altitude BD to the hypotenuse AC in a right triangle $\triangle ACB$ is the geometric mean of the lengths of the segments AD and DC into which it separates the hypotenuse:

$$BD = \sqrt{(AD)(DC)}.$$

🖩 When the product of AD and DC is not a perfect square, use your calculator to approximate the square root.

The corresponding sides of $\triangle ABC$ and $\triangle ADB$ are proportional, so:

$$\frac{AB}{AD} = \frac{AC}{AB},$$
$$(AB)^2 = (AD)(AC),$$
$$AB = \sqrt{(AD)(AC)}.$$

Had we used $\triangle DBC \sim \triangle BAC$ we would have gotten:

$$BC = \sqrt{(DC)(AC)}.$$

14-12   A leg BC of a right triangle is the geometric mean of the hypotenuse AC and that segment of the hypotenuse DC cut off by the altitude and adjacent to the leg:

$$BC = \sqrt{(DC)(AC)}.$$

🖩 When $(DC)(AC)$ is not a perfect square, use your calculator to approximate the square root.

We will use both 14-11 and 14-12 to answer the question at the beginning of the section. If $AC = 13$, let $DC = x$ and $BC = 5$. By 14-12,

$$5 = \sqrt{13x},$$
$$\frac{25}{13} = x.$$

Thus the other segment of the hypotenuse is $13 - \frac{25}{13}$ or $\frac{144}{13}$. By 14-11 the altitude, BD, to the hypotenuse, AC, is the geometric mean of the two segments AD and DC, $\frac{25}{13}$ and $\frac{144}{13}$, respectively:

$$BD = \sqrt{\frac{25}{13} \times \frac{144}{13}}$$
$$= \frac{60}{13}$$
$$\doteq 4.61$$

EXAMPLES

🖩 Answer the following questions. Refer to the figure in question [14] and verify with a calculator.

1. $AD = 3$, $DC = 27$; find BD and BC.

2. $BC = 4\sqrt{3}$, $DC = 4$; find AC and BD.

3. $AD = \sqrt{5}$, $BD = \sqrt{5}$; find DC and BA.

SOLUTIONS:

1. $9, 9\sqrt{10}$ (approximately 28.5).

2. $12, 4\sqrt{2}$ (approximately 5.66).

3. $\sqrt{5}$ (approximately 2.24), $\sqrt{10}$ (approximately 3.16).

WHAT YOU SHOULD KNOW

KEY CONCEPTS

Handling Ratios and Proportions

1. If a, b, and c are real numbers and $c \neq 0$, then

$$\frac{ac}{bc} = \frac{a}{b}.$$

2. If $\frac{a}{b} = k$, then k is called the "constant of proportionality," and $a = kb$.

3. If two fractions are equal, their reciprocals are equal.

Handling Similar Triangles

1. Two triangles are similar if all pairs of corresponding angles are congruent and all pairs of corresponding sides are proportional.

2. If a line intersects two sides of a triangle and is parallel to the third, it cuts off segments proportional to the sides and forms a triangle similar to the original triangle.

3. Two triangles are similar if two pairs of corresponding angles are congruent (AA).

4. Two triangles are similar if two pairs of corresponding sides are proportional and their included angles are congruent (SAS).

5. Two triangles are similar if all pairs of corresponding sides are proportional (SSS).

Other

1. The segment connecting the midpoints of two sides of a triangle is parallel to the third and equal to half its length.

2. The altitude to the hypotenuse is the geometric mean between the segments into which it separates the hypotenuse.

KEY THEOREM

If a, b, c, and d are real numbers and

$$\frac{a}{b} = \frac{c}{d},$$

then

$$ad = bc.$$

The terms a and d are called the "extremes," and b and c are the "means." The above law is sometimes stated, using these terms, as "The product of the means equals the product of the extremes." (Cross-Multiplication Theorem)

TEST-TAKING STRATEGIES

- When you solve an equation in a similarity problem, check your answer to see that it not only satisfies the deriving equation but also fits the given information.

- Roughly speaking, similar triangles have the same shape, though they are not necessarily of the same size. (Triangles of the same size and same shape are not only similar, but they are also congruent.) If triangles appear to have the same shape, look for ways of determining if they are similar so you can set up proportions to find the missing sides. This generally means finding a way to show that two pairs of angles are congruent.

ANSWERS

[1] (D)	[5] (C)	[9] (B)	[13] (E)
[2] (B)	[6] (D)	[10] (C)	[14] (B)
[3] (D)	[7] (A)	[11] (D)	
[4] (B)	[8] (E)	[12] (A)	

CIRCLES

CHAPTER

15

KEY TERMS

circle	the set of all points in a plane that are the same distance (called the *radius*) from a fixed point (called the *center*) in the plane.
radius	a line segment joining the center and any point on the circle.
chord	a line segment joining any two points on the circle.
diameter	a chord that passes through the center of the circle.
arc	a part of a circle that consists of two points and the set of points on the circle between them.
secant	a line that intersects a circle in more than one point.
tangent	a line that intersects a circle in exactly one point.

WORKING WITH TANGENTS AND CHORDS

[1]   If line MN is tangent to the smaller circle at X, line PQ is tangent to the larger circle at Z, and $XZ \perp MN$, then which of the following is NOT necessarily true?

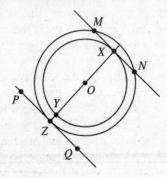

(A) $MX = XN$

(B) $PZ = QZ$

(C) $XZ \perp PQ$

(D) $MN \parallel PQ$

(E) $OX < OZ$

We can answer the multiple-choice question if we know the relationship of a tangent and the radius drawn to the point of contact.

> 15-1   A line, L, is perpendicular to a radius, segment OX, at a point X if and only if L is a tangent at point X to the circle with center O.

In the multiple-choice question above, XZ is therefore perpendicular to both of lines MN and PQ. $OM = ON$ because both are radii of the larger circle so $\triangle OXM \cong \triangle OXN$ by HL and $MX = NX$. In general:

> 15-2   A segment from the center of a circle that is perpendicular to a chord of the circle must bisect the chord.

In (B), though PZ looks equal to ZQ, P and Q can be any points of this line without contradicting the information that it is tangent.

1. Suppose we were given $XM = XN$ instead of MN tangent at X. Verify that $OX \perp MN$ and, thereby, MN tangent at X.

2. Can a line intersect a circle in more than two points? No, the center is not a point of the circle.

3. If a line L intersects a chord PQ of a circle at its midpoint M, must L contain the center, O, of the circle? Only if it is also $\perp PQ$.

[2] $\triangle ABC$ is equilateral with radius $OM \perp$ side AB, $OY \perp BC$, $OM = 6$, and $XM = 3$. Find the perimeter of quadrilateral $OYBX$.

(A) 10.4

(B) 6

(C) 12

(D) 16.4

(E) 15

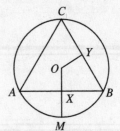

The *distance* from a point to a line is defined to be the length of the perpendicular segment from the point to the line.

> 15-3   Two chords of a circle are equal in length if and only if they are equidistant from the center of the circle.

In the multiple-choice question above, $AB = BC$ so $OX = OY = 3$. If we were to draw in radius OB we would get right triangle $\triangle OXB$ with hypotenuse of 6 ($OB = OM$ since both are radii) and leg OX of 3. To find XB, we need a relationship between the sides of a right triangle. We will informally introduce such a relationship here but postpone a more intense discussion until the next chapter.

If the sides of a right triangle have the lengths indicated in the figure at right, then $c^2 = a^2 + b^2$.

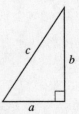

Thus

$$\begin{aligned} (OB)^2 &= (OX)^2 + (XB)^2, \\ 36 &= 9 + (XB)^2, \\ \sqrt{27} &= XB, \\ 3\sqrt{3} &= XB. \end{aligned}$$

Since $CB = AB$ and X and Y are the respective midpoints of the sides, we know that $YB = XB$ and we now have all the lengths of the sides of the quadrilateral in question.

 $6 + 6\sqrt{3} \doteq 16.4$

EXAMPLES

1. If CD is the altitude to AB, then: $a = ?$, $b = ?$, $y = ?$, $x = ?$ Since $x + y = c$, we can conclude $c = ?$ Therefore $c^2 = ?$

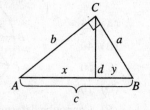

2. If a chord is 3 inches from the center of a circle of radius 5 inches, how long is the chord?

3. If a chord is 6 inches long and is 1 inch from the center of the circle, what is the radius?

4. If a chord is 8 inches long and the radius of the circle is 4 inches, how far is the chord from the center of the circle?

SOLUTIONS:

1. $\sqrt{yc}$, $\sqrt{xc}$, $\dfrac{a^2}{c}$, $\dfrac{b^2}{c}$, $\dfrac{a^2}{c} + \dfrac{b^2}{c}$, $a^2 + b^2$

2. 8

3. $\sqrt{10}$

4. Chord contains the center.

FINDING THE DEGREE MEASURES OF ARCS AND ANGLES

---

[3] Which arc in the figure has the greatest degree measure?

(A) AB

(B) BC

(C) AC

(D) DE

(E) GF

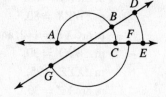

Do not confuse the "degree measure" of an arc with the "length" of the arc. To define degree measure we will first define "minor arc," "major arc," and "central angle."

An angle is a *central angle* of a circle if and only if its vertex is the center of the circle. For example, $\angle AOB$ is a central angle of the circle with center at O (right).

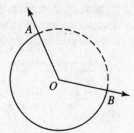

A *minor arc* of a circle is the set of all points of the circle that lie in the interior or on the sides of a given central angle. The dotted curve above indicates minor arc AB. Note that A and B are considered to be points of the arc.

A *major arc* of a circle is the set of points of the circle that lie in the exterior of, or on the sides of, a given central angle. The solid curve above, along with the points A and B, depicts major arc AB. Thus any given central angle determines two arcs, one minor and one major. When we write "arc AB" we will mean the minor arc.

The two arcs cut off by a diameter are called *semicircles* and include the endpoints of the diameter.

The *degree measure* of a minor arc is the degree measure of the central angle that determines it. The degree measure of a major arc is defined to be $360 - x$, where x is the degree measure of the determining central angle. The degree measure of a minor arc is always less than 180. The degree measure of a semicircle is 180. From the definitions above we can see that the total degree measure of a circle is 360.

In the multiple-choice question, arcs AB and GF are cut off by vertical angles and must each have the same degree measure. Arcs BC and DE also have the same measure because they are cut off by the same angle. Arc AC is a semicircle, and its degree measure must be greater than that of any minor arc.

EXAMPLES

Find the measures of each arc in the figure.

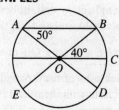

SOLUTIONS:

$BC = 40$,
$BD = 100$,
$CD = 60$,
$AE = 100$,
$AB = 80 = ED$.

[4] If both circles have centers at O and the degree measure of minor arc CB is 40, what is the degree measure of major arc DE?

(A) 220

(B) 215

(C) 210

(D) 205

(E) 200

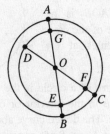

Since the degree measure of a minor arc is defined to be the degree measure of its central angle, two minor arcs determined by the same central angle must have the same measure no matter what circle contains them. Thus, in the above figure:

$$\text{m arc } CB = \text{m arc } FE.$$

Before proceeding we will postulate the following:

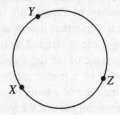

Postulate 16 *If* Y *is a point of an arc* XZ *(either major or minor), then:*

m minor arc XY + m minor arc YZ = m arc XYZ.

The use of the three letters in arc XYZ indicates the arc with endpoints X and Z that contains Y.

Postulate 16 could actually have been proved as a theorem, but the proof is tedious with several cases and the statement itself is straightforward.

Applying Postulate 16 to the above, we conclude

m arc FE + m arc FG + m arc GD = m major arc ED.

The measures of arc FE and arc DG are 40. Arc GE is a semicircle with measure 180, so arc GF contains $140°$. The answer requested is $220°$.

EXAMPLES

1. If two minor arcs are determined by central angles equal in measure, must the measures of the arcs be the same? Yes.

2. If A and B are two points of a circle, what is the intersection of major arc AB with minor arc AB? Points A and B. What is their union? The circle. What is the sum of their measures? 360.

3. If all points of a semicircle AB are removed from a circle, is the set of points that remain also a semicircle? No, it has no endpoints.

[5] If the measure of $\angle ABD$ is 50, what is the measure of $\angle ACD$?

(A) 25

(B) 40

(C) 50

(D) 100

(E) Cannot be determined

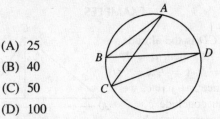

If X, Y, and Z are any three distinct points of a circle, then $\angle XYZ$ is called an *inscribed angle*. The arc determined by XZ and containing points of the interior of $\angle XYZ$ is called the *intercepted arc* of $\angle XYZ$. The arc determined by XZ and containing points of the exterior of $\angle XYZ$ is called the *inscribing arc* of $\angle XYZ$. $\angle XYZ$ is said to *intercept* the former arc and to be *inscribed* in the latter arc.

15-4 The measure of an inscribed angle is half the measure of its intercepted arc.

EXAMPLES

If m$\angle XYZ = 70$,
m$\angle WXZ = 15$, and
m arc $WX = 160$,
find the measures of
each arc and angle in
the figure.

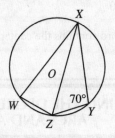

SOLUTIONS:

arc $WZY = 60$,

m$\angle ZXY = 15$,

m$\angle XWZ = 85$,

m$\angle WZX = 80$,

m arc $XY = 140$, and

m$\angle WXY = 30$,

m$\angle XYZ = 95$,

m arc $YZ = 30$.

[6]   If minor arc *AC* has the same degree measure as minor arc *AB*, which of the following CANNOT be true?

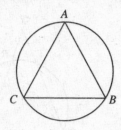

(Figure is not drawn to scale.)

(A) $AC = AB$

(B) $AC = BC$

(C) Segments *AC* and *AB* are equidistant from the center

(D) $\angle ACB$ is a right angle

(E) $\angle CAB$ is a right angle

As we have seen, a chord of a circle determines a major and a minor arc.

> **15-5** Two chords of a circle are equal in length if and only if their corresponding minor arcs are equal in measure.

In the multiple-choice question, $\angle ACB$ could not be a right angle. If it were, $\angle ABC$ would also be a right angle by the Isosceles Triangle Theorem, since $AB = AC$ because the chords have minor arcs of the same measure. Chord *AC* could equal *BC* since the three arcs can have the same degree measure. Chords *AC* and *AB* must be equidistant from the center of the circle since $AC = AB$. Though $\angle CAB$ need not be a right angle, nothing prevents it from being a right angle.

> **TEST-TAKING TIP**
>
> The figure suggests that $AC = BC = AB$, but the given information does not require this. Don't assume congruence from a figure alone.

[7]   If lines *AC* and *CD* are tangent to the circle with center at *O*, and if the measure of $\angle DBC$ is 70, what is the measure of $\angle DAC$?

(A) 70

(B) 65

(C) 60

(D) 55

(E) 50

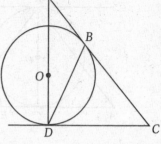

In the figure at right, rays *XA* and *XB* are tangent to the circle with center at *O*. $\angle XAO$ and $\angle XBO$ are right angles by 15-1. $AO = BO$ and $XO = XO$ so $\triangle XAO \cong \triangle XBO$ by HL.

We can now conclude each of the following:

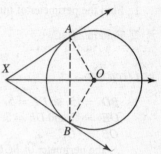

> **15-6** The ray from an external point *X* through the center of a circle bisects the angle formed by the tangent rays from *X* to the circle.

> **15-7** The tangent segments from a given external point to a circle are equal in length.

And, by ITT:

> **15-8** The angles formed by the two tangents from an external point with the secant connecting the points of tangency are equal in measure.

> **15-9** The measure of a secant-tangent angle is one-half the measure of its intercepted arc.

In the multiple-choice question, since m $\angle DBC = 70$, it follows that m $\angle BDC = 70$ and m $\angle C = 40$. Since $\angle ADC$ is a right angle, $\angle A$ must be the complement of $\angle C$ and m $\angle A = 50$.

EXAMPLES

Given that segments DB, DE, and EC are tangent to the circle, with $BD = 5$, $DE = 7$, $OB = 3$, and m arc $GB = 96$:

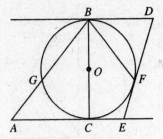

1. Find the perimeter of quadrilateral $BCED$.

2. Find m$\angle BAC$.

SOLUTIONS:

1. $BD = 5$, so $DF = 5$.
   $DE = 7$ and $DF = 5$, so $FE = CE = 2$.
   $OB = OC = 3$,
   $\therefore$ the perimeter of $BCED = 20$.

2. m$\angle BAC = \dfrac{1}{2}$ m arc $GB = 48$.

[8] Minor arc AB has degree measure 60 and $\angle CXD$ has degree measure 60. What is the degree measure of minor arc CD?

(A) 30

(B) 60

(C) 90

(D) 120

(E) 180

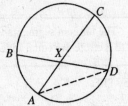

15-10 If two secants intersect in the interior of a circle, then the measure of any angle formed is one-half the sum of the measures of the arcs intercepted by the angle and its vertical angle.

EXAMPLES

Each of the following refers to the figure in the question above.

1. If m arc $AB = 40$ and m arc $CD = 50$, then m$\angle CXD = 45$.

2. If m$\angle BXA = 70$ and m arc $CD = 60$, then m arc $BA = 80$.

[9] Find the measure of $\angle CXD$ if the degree measures of minor arcs CA, AB, and BD are, respectively, 120, 40, and 80.

(A) 30

(B) 35

(C) 40

(D) 45

(E) 50

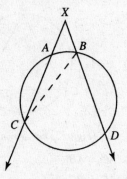

15-11 If two secants intersect in the exterior of a circle, then the measure of the angle formed is one-half the difference of the measures of the two arcs intercepted by the angle.

In the figure of the multiple-choice question:

(1) m$\angle CBD = $ m$\angle XCB + $ m$\angle CXD$
         by the
     Exterior Angle Equality Theorem,

(2) m$\angle XCB = \dfrac{1}{2}$ m arc AB, and

(3) m$\angle CBD = \dfrac{1}{2}$ m arc CD—both by the
     Inscribed Angle Theorem.

By substitution of (2) in (1) we get:

(4) $\dfrac{1}{2}$m arc $CD = \dfrac{1}{2}$m arc $AB + $ m$\angle CXD$, and

(5) $\dfrac{1}{2}$[m arc $CD - $ m arc AB] = m$\angle CXD$.

Substituting m arc $CD = 120$ and m arc $AB = 40$, we obtain

$$\dfrac{1}{2}(120 - 40) = \dfrac{1}{2}(80) = 40.$$

EXAMPLES

Each of the following refers to the figure in the multiple-choice question.

1. If m arc $AB = 30$ and m arc $CD = 120$, then m$\angle CXD = 45$.

2. If m$\angle CXD = 30$ and m arc $CD = 110$, then m arc $BA = 50$.

3. If m$\angle CXD = 40$ and m arc $AB = 10$, then m arc $CD = 90$.

[10] If the measures of minor arcs *AD*, *AB*, and *BC* are, respectively, 30, 40, and 50, find the measure of ∠*Y*.

(A) 170

(B) 160

(C) 150

(D) 145

(E) 140

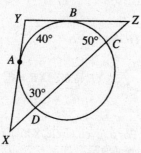

(Figure is not drawn to scale.)

15-12 If two tangents intersect, the measure of the angle formed is half the difference of the measures of the intercepted arcs.

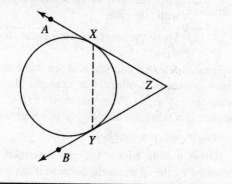

In the multiple-choice question,

$$\text{m major arc } AB = 360 - (\text{minor arc } AB)$$
$$= 320,$$
$$\text{m}\angle Y = \frac{1}{2}(320 - 40)$$
$$= \frac{1}{2}(280)$$
$$= 140.$$

You need not memorize the theorems—drawing the auxiliary segments should suggest the proper relationships. Test yourself by doing the following:

15-13 If a tangent and a secant intersect at a point in the exterior of a circle, then the measure of the angle formed is half the difference of the measures of the intercepted arcs.

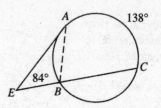

To find m∠*AEB*, construct *AB* as shown.

$$\text{m}\angle EAB = \frac{1}{2}(84) = 42 \quad \text{by 15-9}$$
$$\text{m}\angle ABC = \frac{1}{2}(138) = 69 \quad \text{by 15-4}$$
$$\text{m}\angle AEB = 69 - 42 \quad \text{because}$$

the measure of exterior angle ∠*ABC* is the sum of the measures of interior angles ∠*EAB* and ∠*AEB* for △*AEB*.

EXAMPLES

Segments *XZ*, *ZV*, and *XS* are tangent to the circle. Segment *TV* is a secant. If m∠*YXT* = 80, m∠*YZW* = 100, and m∠*WVU* = 70, find the measures of each of the minor arcs in the figure.

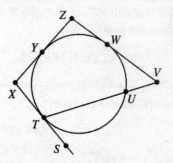

SOLUTION:
$$TY = 100, YW = 80, WU = 40, TU = 140.$$

HANDLING CHORD RATIOS

[11] If *CE* = 6, *CD* = 24, and *AE* = 4(*EB*), what is the length of *AB*?

(A) 8

(B) 12

(C) 10

(D) 26

(E) 9

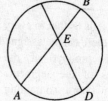

Let WX and YZ be two chords intersecting in a circle at a point E. Then

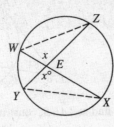

$$m\angle ZWX = m\angle XYZ$$

since both are inscribed angles that intercept arc XZ.

$$m\angle WEZ = m\angle YEX$$

since these are vertical angles. We conclude

$$\triangle WEZ \sim \triangle YEX \text{ by AA.}$$

Therefore:

$$\frac{WE}{YE} = \frac{ZE}{XE}$$
$$(WE)XE = (ZE)(YE)$$

15-14 If WX and YZ are two chords of a circle intersecting at a point E, then

$$(WE)(XE) = (ZE)(YE).$$

In the multiple-choice question,

$$(CE)(ED) = (AE)(BE),$$
$$(6)(18) = (4BE)(BE),$$
$$108 = 4(BE)^2,$$
$$27 = (BE)^2,$$
$$3\sqrt{3} = BE,$$
$$12\sqrt{3} = AE$$
$$AB = AE + BE = 3\sqrt{3} + 12\sqrt{3}$$
$$= 15\sqrt{3}$$

Use ▦ to find $15\sqrt{3} \doteq 26$

EXAMPLES

1. 15-14 tells us that to every point in the interior of a circle there can be assigned a positive number that is the product of the lengths of the segments of any chord containing the point. This number for the multiple-choice question above is $(CE)(ED) = 108$.

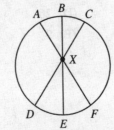

2. If $AX = 2$, $XE = 4$, and $CX = 6$, find XD, XB, and XF when the number described in 1. assigned to X is 12.

SOLUTION:

$$XF = 6, \quad XB = 3, \quad DX = 2.$$

[12] For a given circle, which of the following is greatest?

(A) The diameter

(B) The radius

(C) The circumference

(D) The perimeter of an inscribed polygon with 100 sides

(E) Twice the length of the longest chord

Scan the choices and you will see some that are obviously greater than others. For example, the diameter is twice the radius, so (A) is greater than (B). The circumference is π times the diameter so (C) is greater than (A).

Now it gets a bit tougher.

(D) is a little tricky, but any inscribed polygon is bounded by the circle itself, because it fits inside the circle (except for its vertices, which are points of the circle). So (C) is still greater than (D).

Now we only have (C) and (E) to compare. As noted, the circumference is π times the diameter, which is, itself, the longest chord. The number π is approximately 3.14, so π times the diameter is greater than 2 times the diameter. So (C) holds on to win.

The question tests your knowledge of the meaning of terms (radius, diameter, chord, circumference, inscribed, *pi*, and polygon), the formula for the circumference of a circle and that the diameter is the longest chord. It also tests your ability to visualize the relationship between an inscribed polygon and the circle itself.

Note that it is very easy to eliminate (A) and (B) from consideration. If a test-taker could go no further, guessing among the remaining three presents slightly better odds than just blindly guessing among all five choices. That is also part of the test-makers' plan to give test-takers some credit for knowing a few ideas even when they don't know them all. A student who could eliminate two answers on all 50 questions but could go no further would guess a third of them correctly, and earn 16 or 17 points minus 8 (that's roughly one-fourth of the 33 or 34 questions missed). The final raw score of 8 or 9 points is not magnificent. But it is not zero, either.

WHAT YOU SHOULD KNOW

KEY CONCEPTS

Handling Radii, Chords, Rays, and Tangents

1. A radius is perpendicular to a tangent at the point of tangency.
2. If a radius is perpendicular to a chord, then it bisects the chord.
3. Two congruent chords must be equidistant from the center of the circle.
4. Two chords have the same length if the degree measures of their minor arcs are equal.
5. If WX and YZ are two chords of a circle that intersect at a point E, then $(WE)(XE) = (ZE)(YE)$.
6. A ray from an external point X through the center of a circle bisects the angle formed by the tangent rays to the circle from X.
7. Tangent segments from an external point are congruent.

Handling Angles and Their Measures

1. A central angle of a circle is an angle whose vertex is the center of the circle.
2. The degree measure of a central angle is equal to the degree measure of its minor arc.
3. An inscribed angle is an angle with vertex on the circle and sides containing two other points of the circle.
4. The degree measure of an inscribed angle is half the degree measure of its intercepted arc.
5. The degree measure of a secant-tangent angle is half the measure of its intercepted arc.
6. If two secants intersect in the interior of a circle, the measure of each angle formed is half the sum of the measures of the arcs intercepted by the angle and its vertical angle.
7. If two secants intersect in the exterior of a circle, the measure of the angle formed is half the difference of the two arcs intercepted by the angle.

8. If two tangents intersect, the measure of the angle formed is half the difference of the measures of the intercepted arcs.
9. If a tangent and secant intersect at a point in the exterior of a circle, the measure of the angle formed is half the difference of the measures of the intercepted arcs.

KEY MEASURES

1. The degree measure of a *minor arc* is the degree measure of the central angle that determines it and is always less than 180.
2. The degree measure of a *major arc* is defined to be $360 - x$, where x is the degree measure of the determining central angle.
3. The degree measure of a *semicircle* is 180.
4. The total degree measure of a *circle* is 360.

TEST-TAKING STRATEGIES

- Take care not to confuse the "degree measure" and the "length" of an arc.
- Be sure to use the relationship between the measure of an angle and its intercepted arc when determining missing measures in a figure based on a circle.
- Always estimate the size of an angle to compare this number with the result you get by calculation. If an angle looks as if it measures 30 degrees and your calculation says it is 75 degrees, look for an error in your calculation.
- When given numerical information about parts of a figure, be sure to note this information in the appropriate place on your diagram. Often, this will immediately suggest the measures of missing parts.

ANSWERS

[1] (B)   [3] (C)   [5] (C)   [7] (E)   [9] (C)   [11] (D)
[2] (D)   [4] (A)   [6] (D)   [8] (B)   [10] (E)   [12] (C)

AREA, CIRCUMFERENCE, AND VOLUME

CHAPTER

16

KEY TERMS

altitude	the perpendicular distance from a vertex of a geometric figure to the opposite side, or from a side or face to a parallel side or face.
polygon	a closed figure with lines as sides. Examples: triangle, quadrilateral, hexagon.
sector	part of a circle bounded by two radii and an arc.
circumference	the distance around a circle; more formally, the limit of the perimeters of polygons regularly inscribed in a circle as the number of sides of the polygons increases endlessly.
prism	a solid figure determined by a pair of congruent polygons lying in a pair of parallel planes. Example: a cube.
circular cylinder	a solid figure determined by a pair of congruent circles lying in a pair of parallel planes.
pyramid	given a plane containing a polygon, P, and given a point, X, not contained in the plane: a *pyramid* is the union of all segments such that a. X is an endpoint, and b. the other endpoint lies within P.
cone	given a plane containing a circle, C, and a point, X, not contained in the plane: a *cone* is the union of all segments such that a. X is an endpoint and b. the other endpoint lies within C.
sphere	given a point O, and a positive number r: *sphere* consists of the set of all points in space that are r units from O.

WORKING WITH SQUARES AND TRIANGLES

[1]   A square and a triangle have equal areas. If one side of the square and the base of the triangle have length b, what is the relationship between b and the altitude, h, of the triangle?

(A) $\frac{1}{2}b = h$

(B) $2b = h$

(C) $b = h$

(D) $b = 2h$

(E) Cannot be determined

We will make three assumptions as the basis of our theory of areas.

Area Postulate 1 *Two triangles that are congruent have the same area.*

Area Postulate 2 *The area of a polygonal region is unique and is the sum of the areas of the polygonal regions that compose it.*

When we use AP-2 we must be careful to separate the original region into regions that do not overlap, but that use all of the points of the original region. "Unique" reminds us that each triangle has one and only one area regardless of how this area is correctly computed.

The next assumption is not obvious, but we select it from all of the possible "unit" postulates because it greatly simplifies our later work. The purpose of any "unit" assumption is to give meaning to the term "area" by providing the area of some simple figure as a basis for the computation of the areas of all other figures. The area of a square is the customary choice, but whereas few polygonal regions can be resolved into squares, all can be separated into triangles.

Area Postulate 3 *The area of a triangle is one-half the product of the length of any side and the altitude to that side.*

AP-3 yields the formula

$$A = \frac{1}{2}bh,$$

where A is the area of the triangle, b is the length of one side and h is the length of the altitude to that side. "Altitude" actually has two meanings: the altitude to a side is the segment from the opposite vertex drawn perpendicular to the line that contains the side and is also the length of this perpendicular segment.

For a right triangle the altitude to either one of the legs is the other leg (or the length of the other leg). Thus the area of a right triangle is one-half the product of the legs.

We will put the three assumptions together to derive the area of a square of side s.

Diagonal AC separates the square into two right triangles, the area of each of which is $\frac{1}{2}s^2$ by AP-3.

Since the area of a polygonal region is the sum of the areas of the composing regions (AP-2), the area of the square is

$$\frac{1}{2}s^2 + \frac{1}{2}s^2 = s^2.$$

The formula above can be used to solve the multiple-choice question. The area of the square is b^2, the area of the triangle is $\frac{1}{2}bh$ and the areas were given as equal.

Therefore

$$b^2 = \frac{1}{2}bh,$$

$$b = \frac{1}{2}h \text{ or } h = 2b.$$

EXAMPLES

If the area of a triangle, A_t, is $\frac{1}{2}bh$ and the area of a square, A_s, is s^2, find the missing elements of $\{A_s, A_t, s, b, h\}$ for each of the following.

1. $A_s = A_t$, $s = 5$, $h = 4$

2. $s = b$, $h = 2$, $A_s = 16$

SOLUTIONS:

1. $A_s = 25 = A_t$, $b = 12.5$

2. $s = 4 = b = A_t$

WORKING WITH RECTANGLES

[2]   If the area of a rectangle is doubled, but the length, b, of one side remains the same, what is the change in the length, a, of an adjacent side?

(A) Remains the same

(B) Quadruples

(C) Doubles

(D) Triples

(E) Cannot be determined

Using our area assumptions, we can compute the formula for the area of a rectangle in exactly the same way we computed it for the square.

In a rectangle $WXYZ$, diagonal WZ separates the polygonal region into two right triangular regions with sides of length a and b.

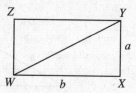

The area of each of these is $\frac{1}{2}ab$, so the area of the rectangle must be $\frac{1}{2}ab + \frac{1}{2}ab = ab$. Thus, if A is the area of a rectangle and a and b are the lengths of a pair of intersecting sides, then

$$A = ab.$$

To answer the multiple-choice question, solve for a to see how a relates to A and b:

$$a = \frac{A}{b}.$$

If A is doubled, the result is $2A$. Since

$$\frac{2A}{b} = 2\left(\frac{A}{b}\right) \quad \text{and} \quad \frac{A}{b} = a,$$

the new length of a is twice the original length.

EXAMPLES

Use your calculator when needed to find the missing element of $\{A, a, b\}$ if:

1. $a = 12, b = 17$

2. $A = 64, b = 8$

3. $A = 10, a = \sqrt{10}$

SOLUTIONS:

1. 204

2. 8

3. $\sqrt{10} \doteq 3.16$

WORKING WITH PARALLELOGRAMS

[3] Given parallelogram $ABCD$ with area X and $\triangle CDE$ with area Y, what is the relationship between X and Y?

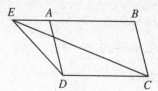

(A) $X = Y$

(B) $X = \frac{1}{2}Y$

(C) $X = 4y$

(D) $Y = \frac{1}{2}X$

(E) Cannot be determined

Diagonal PQ of parallelogram $PMQR$ separates it into two congruent triangles, $\triangle PMQ$ and $\triangle PRQ$. Since the distance, h, between 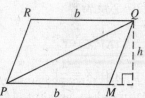 two parallel lines is constant, both triangles have the same altitude, h. The area of the parallelogram is the sum of the areas of the triangles. Both triangles have areas of $\frac{1}{2}hb$. Therefore the area, A, of the parallelogram is given by:

$$A = \frac{1}{2}hb + \frac{1}{2}hb$$
$$= hb,$$

where h is the distance between two parallel sides and b is the length of one of these parallel sides.

In the multiple-choice question, parallelogram $ABCD$ and $\triangle CDE$ have the same altitude (the distance between lines AB and CD) and the same base, CD. Since x, the area of the parallelogram, is the product of the altitude and the base, and y, the area of the triangle, is half the product of the altitude and the base,

$$y = \frac{1}{2}x.$$

EXAMPLES

🖩 If A is the area of a parallelogram, b is the length of one side, and h is the length of the altitude to that side, find the missing element of $\{A, h, b\}$ for each of the following (use your calculator when needed):

1. $A = 6$, $h = 4$

2. $h = 2$, $b = 5$

3. $A = \sqrt{2}$, $b = \sqrt{2}$

SOLUTIONS:

1. $\dfrac{3}{4}$

2. 10

3. 1

[4] If M is the midpoint of side CD of parallelogram $ABCD$, what is the relationship between the area, X, of $\triangle AMD$ and the area, Y, of $\triangle BCM$?

(A) $X = Y$

(B) $X = \dfrac{1}{2}Y$

(C) $X = 2Y$

(D) $X = \dfrac{1}{3}Y$

(E) $X = 3Y$

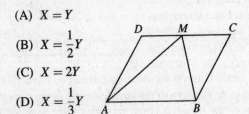

Since the area of a triangle is one-half the product of its altitude and base, two triangles that have equal altitudes and equal bases must have the same area. $\triangle AMD$ and $\triangle BCM$ have equal bases since $DM = MC$, because M is the midpoint of DC. They also have equal altitudes, since the length of the perpendicular from A to DC equals the length of the perpendicular from B to DC.

EXAMPLES

🖩 If L_1 and L_2 are parallel lines and points A, B, and C are on line L_1, while points M and N are on L_2, what is the relationship between the areas of $\triangle AMN$, $\triangle NBM$, and $\triangle CMN$?

SOLUTION: The areas are equal because the bases and altitudes are equal.

[5] In $\triangle ABC$, $BR \perp AC$, $CP \perp AB$, $CP = 18$, $AB = 16$, and $BR = 12$. What is the length of AC?

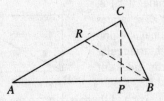

(Figure is not drawn to scale.)

(A) Cannot be determined

(B) 20

(C) 15

(D) 10

(E) 24

In AP-3 we construe "side" to mean *any* side. No matter which side of the triangle is selected as the base, the area is constant. For the multiple-choice question this means that

$$\frac{1}{2}(BR)(AC) = \frac{1}{2}(CP)(AB).$$

Substituting the given values into the equation produces

$$\frac{1}{2}(12)(AC) = \frac{1}{2}(18)(16),$$
$$6(AC) = 144,$$
$$AC = 24.$$

EXAMPLES

🖩 (Use your calculator when needed.)

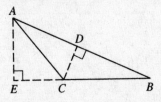

1. If $AE = 5$, $BC = 6$, and $CD = 3$, then $AB = 10$.

2. If $CD = 2$, $AB = 8$, and $AE = 4$, then $BC = 4$.

3. If $BC = 9$, $CD = 3$, and $AB = 9$, then $AE = 3$.

[6] Given parallelogram $ABCD$ with segment AF perpendicular to the line that contains segment DC, $DE \perp BC$, $AF = 7$, $CD = 9$ and $DE = 3$. Find BC.

(A) 20
(B) 22
(C) 19
(D) 23
(E) 21

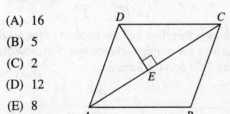

The area of a parallelogram is independent of the side chosen as base. The product of the length of any side and the altitude to that side must be the same as the product of the length of a different side and its respective altitude. In the question above, this means that

$$(DE)(BC) = (AF)(DC),$$
$$3(BC) = (7)(9)$$
$$= 63,$$
$$BC = 21.$$

EXAMPLES

1. If $AF = 12$, $BC = 5$, and $DE = 3$, then $AB = 20$.

2. If $DE = 5$, $AB = 10$, and $BC = 6$, then $AF = \dfrac{25}{3}$.

[7] If the area of parallelogram $ABCD$ is 64 and the length of diagonal AC is 8, what is DE if $DE \perp AC$?

(A) 16
(B) 5
(C) 2
(D) 12
(E) 8

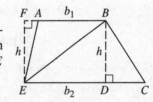

The diagonal of a parallelogram separates the parallelogram into two congruent triangular regions (SSS), which, therefore, have the same area. We can find the length of segment DE above by equating the area of $\triangle ACD$ as represented by $\frac{1}{2}(DE)(AC)$ with the area of $\triangle ACD$ as represented by one-half the area of the parallelogram:

$$\frac{1}{2}(DE)(8) = 32,$$
$$DE = 8.$$

WORKING WITH TRAPEZOIDS

[8] If the area of right triangle BCD is 12 and the lengths of the segments are as shown in the figure, what is the area of trapezoid $ABCE$ with $AB \parallel EC$?

(A) 30
(B) 21
(C) 42
(D) 63
(E) 84

The area of the trapezoid shown is the sum of the areas of $\triangle ABE$ and $\triangle EBC$.

$$\frac{1}{2}hb_1 + \frac{1}{2}hb_2 = \frac{1}{2}h(b_1 + b_2)$$

In the multiple-choice question the lengths of the bases are given but the altitude, BD, is missing. We can find this altitude since it is a leg of a right triangle whose area and other leg are given.

$$\frac{1}{2}(BD)(6) = 12$$
$$3BD = 12$$
$$BD = 4$$
$$\text{Area of } ABCE = \frac{1}{2}(4)(7 + 14)$$
$$= 2(21)$$
$$= 42$$

EXAMPLES

Find the areas of each of the trapezoids whose parts are given below (use your calculator when needed):

1. If $h = 2$, $b_1 = 3$, $b_2 = 3$, then $A = 6$.

2. If $h = 1$, $b_1 = 4$, $b_2 = 2$, then $A = 3$.

3. If $h = 3$, $b_1 = \sqrt{2}$, $b_2 = \sqrt{18}$, then $A = 6\sqrt{2} \doteq 8.5$.

[9] If the area of trapezoid $ABCD$ is 40 and $ABED$ is a parallelogram, find the area of $\triangle BCE$.

(A) 24

(B) 2

(C) 16

(D) 8

(E) 4

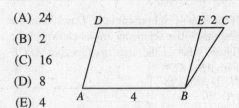

The area of a trapezoid is $\frac{1}{2}h(b_1 + b_2)$ and the opposite sides of a parallelogram have the same length. The latter fact tells us that the length of DC is 6, and this, with the trapezoid area formula, yields $h = 8$.

$$
\begin{aligned}
40 &= \frac{1}{2}(h)(4+6) \\
&= \frac{1}{2}(10h) \\
&= 5h \\
8 &= h
\end{aligned}
$$

Note that h is also an altitude of the parallelogram and the triangle. The area we seek is $\frac{1}{2}(2)h$.

$$
\begin{aligned}
A &= \frac{1}{2}(2h) \\
&= h \\
&= 8
\end{aligned}
$$

EXAMPLES

If the distance between parallel lines L_1 and L_2 is 3 and $AB = 5$, where B is the midpoint of AC, and if ED is also 5, find the areas of all triangles, parallelograms, and trapezoids in the following figure that have all vertices on line L_1 or L_2.

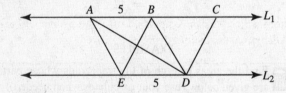

SOLUTIONS:

$$ABDE = 15,$$

$$ADE = EBD = ADA = ABE = BDC = 7.5,$$

$$AEDC = 22.5,$$

$$EDCB = 15 = ADC.$$

WORKING WITH RHOMBUSES

[10] If the area of a rhombus is 15 and the length of one diagonal is 7, what is the length of the other diagonal?

(A) $\dfrac{30}{7}$

(B) 30×7

(C) 15×7

(D) $15 \div 7$

(E) None of these

A rhombus is an equilateral parallelogram. The diagonals of a rhombus are perpendicular and bisect each other. We use these facts and our established pattern to develop a formula for the area of a rhombus in terms of its diagonals.

If $ABCD$ is a rhombus with diagonals $AC = a$ and $BD = b$, then $DE = BE = \frac{1}{2}b$ and $AE = CE = \frac{1}{2}a$. The diagonals form four right triangles with the sides, the area of each being

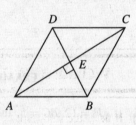

$$\frac{1}{2}\left(\frac{1}{2}a\right)\left(\frac{1}{2}b\right) = \frac{1}{8}ab.$$

The area of the rhombus is the sum of these four equal triangle areas:

$$4\left(\frac{1}{8}\right)ab = \frac{ab}{2}.$$

The area is therefore half the product of the diagonals.

To answer the multiple-choice question, substitute 15 for A and 7 for b in the formula:

$$
\begin{aligned}
A &= \frac{ab}{2}, \\
15 &= \frac{7b}{2}, \\
30 &= 7b, \\
\frac{30}{7} &= b.
\end{aligned}
$$

EXAMPLES

📱 Find the areas of the rhombuses that have the following as lengths of diagonals (use your calculator when needed):

1. 4, 2

2. $\sqrt{2}, \sqrt{2}$

3. $\sqrt{3}, 4$

4. $\sqrt{3}, \sqrt{2}$

SOLUTIONS:

1. 4

2. 1

3. $2\sqrt{3} \doteq 3.46$

4. $\dfrac{\sqrt{6}}{2} \doteq 1.22$

WORKING WITH TRIANGLES

[11] If M is the midpoint of side AC and the area of $\triangle ABM$ is 5, what is the area of $\triangle BMC$?

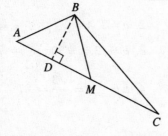

(A) $\dfrac{5}{2}$

(B) 5

(C) 10

(D) $\dfrac{7}{2}$

(E) Cannot be determined

In $\triangle ABC$ there is only one segment that can be drawn from point B perpendicular to the line that contains A and C. This is segment BD as shown, and must, therefore, be an altitude of all three triangles, $\triangle ABC$, $\triangle ABM$, and $\triangle BMC$. Since M is the midpoint of segment AC, it follows that $AM = MC$ and $\triangle ABM$ has a base equal to a base of $\triangle BMC$. With equal bases and equal altitudes, triangles ABM and BMC must have the same area.

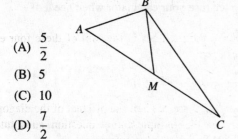

EXAMPLES

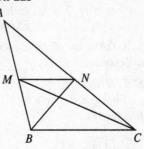

In the figure at right, if M and N are the midpoints of the sides that contain them, name all of the triangles that have the same area as $\triangle AMN$. (Is $MN \parallel BC$?)

SOLUTIONS:

MN is parallel to BC, therefore $\triangle AMN$, $\triangle MNB$, and $\triangle MNC$ have equal areas because they have MN as base and their altitudes are equal.

[12] If, in right triangle ABC, $BC = 12$ and $AC = 5$, what is the length of CD?

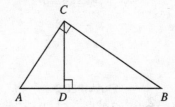

(A) $\dfrac{30}{13}$

(B) 120×13

(C) $\dfrac{120}{13}$

(D) $\dfrac{60}{13}$

(E) 120×13

We will find AB and then use the fact that a triangle has exactly one number as its area:

$$\frac{1}{2}(AC)(BC) = \frac{1}{2}(CD)(AB),$$

from which we can compute CD. To find AB we will use a theorem already introduced and proved.

> **16-1** *The Pythagorean Theorem.* A triangle is a right triangle if and only if the square of the length of its longest side is equal to the sum of the squares of the lengths of the remaining two sides.

Because of its importance, we'll review several more examples of the Pythagorean Theorem.

EXAMPLE 1

If the area of an isosceles triangle is 18, find its hypotenuse.

SOLUTION:

First use the area to find the leg.

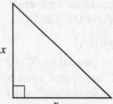

$$\frac{1}{2}x^2 = 18$$
$$x^2 = 36$$
$$x = 6$$

Then use the Pythagorean Theorem to calculate the hypotenuse.

$$x^2 + x^2 = 36$$
$$x^2 = 18$$
$$x = 3\sqrt{2}$$

EXAMPLE 2

If a right triangle has two sides of lengths 1 and $\sqrt{3}$, what are the possible lengths of the third side?

SOLUTION: If the given lengths are both legs, then the hypotenuse h can be found by the equation:

$$h^2 = 1^2 + (\sqrt{3})^2 = 4$$
$$h = 2$$

If 1 is a leg and $\sqrt{3}$ is the hypotenuse, then

$$(\sqrt{3})^2 = 1^2 + x^2$$
$$\sqrt{2} = x$$

Returning to the multiple-choice question, we see that $(AB)^2 = (BC)^2 + (AC)^2$ so AB is 13 since $BC = 12$ and $AC = 5$.

TEST-TAKING TIP

Questions involving the use of the Pythagorean Theorem appear in one form or another on every SAT II: Mathematics Level IC subject test.

EXAMPLES

If a and b are the lengths of the legs of a right triangle and c is the length of the hypotenuse, find the missing element of $\{a, b, c\}$ (use your calculator when needed):

1. If $a = 3$, $b = 4$, then $c = 5$.

2. If $a = 5$, $c = 13$, then $b = 12$.

3. If $a = \sqrt{2}$, $b = \sqrt{3}$, then $c = \sqrt{5} \doteq 2.24$.

4. If $c = \sqrt{2}$, $a = 1$, then $b = 1$.

[13] If $ABCD$ is a trapezoid and the lengths of the segments are as shown, then the area of $\triangle FCB$ is which value?

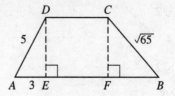

(A) 7

(B) Cannot be determined

(C) 4

(D) 14

(E) 28

The given lengths of AD and AE will yield 4 as the length of DE by 16-1. CF also equals 4. By 16-1 we conclude $FB = 7$. With CF, FB, and the area formula for right triangles we find the area of $\triangle CFB$ to be 14.

EXAMPLES

In each of the following, the given information is the length of the hypotenuse and one leg. Find the areas of the triangles by first using 16-1 to find the length of the missing leg (use your calculator when needed).

1. 6, 3

2. 2, $2\sqrt{2}$

3. 13, 5

4. 2, $\sqrt{3}$

SOLUTIONS:

1. $b = 3\sqrt{3} \doteq 5.2$, $A = \dfrac{9\sqrt{3}}{2} \doteq 7.8$

2. $b = 2$, $A = 2$

3. $b = 12$, $A = 30$

4. $b = 1$, $A = \dfrac{\sqrt{3}}{2} \doteq .87$

[14] What is the area of right triangle ABC if $\angle A$ and $\angle B$ both have measures of 45 while $AB = 5$?

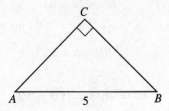

(A) Cannot be determined

(B) 25

(C) $\dfrac{25}{4}$

(D) 100

(E) 10

We can use 16-1 to develop an important relationship between the sides of an isosceles right triangle. If two sides of $\triangle ABC$, with right angle at C, have the same length, x, then the length of the hypotenuse, AB, is given by:

$$\begin{aligned} (AB)^2 &= x^2 + x^2 \\ &= 2x^2, \\ AB &= \sqrt{2x^2} \\ &= x\sqrt{2}. \end{aligned}$$

This relationship is of enough importance in the remaining work of intermediate math— especially trigonometry —that you should memorize the figure at right. We will use it to compute the other two sides when one side is given; the following examples show the procedure.

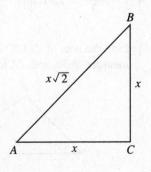

EXAMPLE 1

If a leg of an isosceles right triangle has length 4, what is the length of the hypotenuse?

SOLUTION: From the memorized figure, since $x = 4$ and the hypotenuse is $x\sqrt{2}$, the hypotenuse is $4\sqrt{2}$.

EXAMPLE 2

If the hypotenuse of an isosceles right triangle has length 5, what are the lengths of the legs?

SOLUTION: From the memorized figure the hypotenuse is $x\sqrt{2}$, so

$$x\sqrt{2} = 5 \quad \text{and} \quad x = \frac{5}{\sqrt{2}} \quad \text{or} \quad \frac{5}{2}\sqrt{2}$$

The results of Example 2 help us to answer the multiple-choice question by providing the lengths of the legs of the given right triangle. Since the area of a right triangle is half the product of the legs,

$$\begin{aligned} A &= \frac{1}{2}\left(\frac{5}{2}\sqrt{2}\right)\left(\frac{5}{2}\sqrt{2}\right) \\ &= \frac{1}{2} \cdot \frac{25}{4} \cdot 2 \\ &= \frac{25}{4}. \end{aligned}$$

EXAMPLES

If d is the length of the diagonal of a square and s is the length of each side, find the missing element of $\{d, s\}$ (hint: draw the diagonal and look for isosceles right triangles, and use your calculator when needed).

1. $s = 5$

2. $s = \sqrt{3}$

3. $d = 2\sqrt{2}$

4. $d = 3\sqrt{3}$

🖩 *SOLUTIONS:*

1. $d = 5\sqrt{2} \doteq 7.1$

2. $a = \sqrt{6} \doteq 2.45$

3. $s = 2$

4. $s = \dfrac{3\sqrt{3}}{\sqrt{2}} = \dfrac{3\sqrt{6}}{2} \doteq 3.67$

[15] If $\triangle ABC$ is equilateral with $BC = 6$, find the length of altitude CD.

(A) 5.2

(B) 3.0

(C) 1.7

(D) 0.6

(E) 3.5

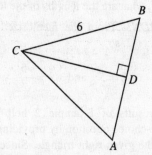

> 16-2 In a triangle whose angle measures are 30, 60 and 90, the length of the side opposite the 30° angle is half the length of the hypotenuse.

16-1 gives the length of the third side, CD, to be $a\sqrt{3}$. The figure at right puts together the relationships between sides and angles as proved. Memorize the figure for its use in later work.

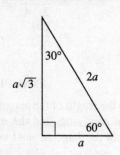

EXAMPLES

In each of the following, h is the length of the hypotenuse, t is the length of the side opposite the 30° angle, and s is the length of the side opposite the 60° angle. Find the missing elements of $\{h, t, s\}$ for each of the following:

1. Given $t = 5$:

   Since t is opposite the 30° angle it is half of the hypotenuse, h, so $h = 10$. The side opposite the 60° angle, s, is $t\sqrt{3}$, so $s = 5\sqrt{3}$.

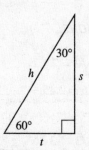

2. Given $h = 8$:

   Since t is opposite the 30° angle it is half of h, so $t = 4$. Again, $s = t\sqrt{3}$, so $s = 4\sqrt{3}$.

3. Given $s = 6$:

   Since $s = t\sqrt{3}$ we conclude $6 = t\sqrt{3}$ so $t = \dfrac{6}{\sqrt{3}}$ or $2\sqrt{3}$. Because $h = 2t$, we get $h = 4\sqrt{3}$.

To answer the multiple-choice question, note that $\triangle BCD$ is a 30-60-90 triangle with BC the hypotenuse and

CD the leg opposite the 60° angle. Using the 30-60-90 triangle relationship, we find that if

$$BC = 2a = 6,$$

then

$$BD = a = 3$$

and

$$CD = a\sqrt{3} = 3\sqrt{3} \doteq 5.2$$

EXAMPLES

Use the directions for the above examples in each of the following (use your calculator when needed):

1. $t = 7$

2. $h = 16$

3. $s = 6\sqrt{3}$

4. $s = 4$

SOLUTIONS:

1. $s = 7\sqrt{3} \doteq 12.12, h = 14$

2. $t = 8, s = 8\sqrt{3} \doteq 13.86$

3. $t = 6, h = 12$

4. $t = \dfrac{4\sqrt{3}}{3} \doteq 2.31, h = \dfrac{8\sqrt{3}}{3} \doteq 4.62$

[16] Find the area of $\triangle ABC$ if $BC = 4$, $\angle C$ has a measure of 30, and $\angle A$ has a measure of 45.

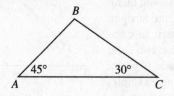

(A) $\dfrac{2 + \sqrt{3}}{2}$

(B) $2 + 2\sqrt{2}$

(C) 8

(D) $2 + 2\sqrt{3}$

(E) 4

In the figure above construct altitude BD. By the 30-60-90 triangle relationship, $BD = 2$ and $CD = 2\sqrt{3}$. $\triangle ABD$ must be an isosceles right triangle, so $AD = 2$ also.

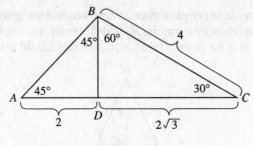

$$BD = 2$$

This yields $AC = 2 + 2\sqrt{3}$, and the area is

$$\frac{1}{2}(2)(2 + 2\sqrt{3}).$$

EXAMPLES

In each of the following, find the area of the triangle if a and b are the lengths of two sides and $\angle C$ is their included angle (use your calculator when needed):

1. If $a = 6, b = 5, \mathrm{m}\angle C = 30$, then $h = 2.5, A = 7.5$.

2. If $a = 6, b = 5, \mathrm{m}\angle C = 45$, then $h = \dfrac{5\sqrt{2}}{2} \doteq 3.54$,

    $A = \dfrac{15\sqrt{2}}{2} \doteq 10.61$.

3. If $a = 6, b = 5, \mathrm{m}\angle C = 60$, then $h = \dfrac{5\sqrt{3}}{2} \doteq 4.333$,

    $A = \dfrac{15\sqrt{3}}{2} \doteq 8.66$.

FINDING AREAS OF COMPOSITE FIGURES

[17] Which of the following is a formula for the area of the accompanying figure?

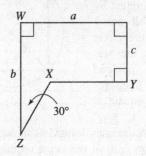

(A) $ac + \dfrac{(b-c)^2}{2\sqrt{3}}$

(B) ab

(C) $ac + (b - c)$

(D) $ac(b - c)$

(E) $\dfrac{ac(b-c)^2}{\sqrt{3}}$

The figure is composed of a rectangular region (with sides of a and c) and a right triangular region (with an angle of 30° and a side of length $b - c$). Draw in a dotted segment that extends XY to meet WZ. The length of the dotted segment must be $\frac{b-c}{\sqrt{3}}$ by the 30-60-90 triangle relations. The area of the figure is the sum of the area of the rectangle (ac) and the area of the triangle

$$\left[\frac{1}{2} \times \frac{b-c}{\sqrt{3}} \times (b-c)\right].$$

WORKING WITH INSCRIBED POLYGONS

[18] If the perimeter of a regular inscribed polygon of six sides (a hexagon) is 48, what is its area?

(A) $96\sqrt{3}$

(B) 384

(C) 288

(D) 96

(E) 200

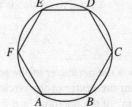

A polygon is *inscribed* in a circle if and only if the vertices of all of its angles lie on the circle. An inscribed polygon is *regular* if and only if all of its sides are equal in length and all of its angles are equal in measure.

To find the area of a regular inscribed polygon separate the figure into triangles by constructing all possible radii of the circle that intersect the vertices of the polygon as we have done for the inscribed square at right.

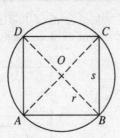

Each of the triangles formed is isosceles, since two of the sides are radii of the circle no matter how many sides the polygon contains. The triangles are all congruent, then, by SSS. Each triangle contains a central angle—each of which has the same measure as each of the others by CP. This measure is $\frac{360}{n}$, where n is the number of sides (and hence the number of central angles). With this measure, along with the fact that the sum of the measures of the angles of a triangle is 180 and by ITT, we can find the measures of $\angle OAB$, $\angle OBA$, etc. By adding the measures of the adjacent angles we can find the measures of the angles of the polygon. In general, if the measure of an angle of a polygon is x, then

$$x = 180 - \frac{360}{n}.$$

Returning to the multiple-choice question, we find that the measure of each angle of the hexagon is 120 and the length of each side is 8.

Each of the altitudes of the triangle drawn from O will equal each of the others. Call this length a. The area of the polygon then is

$$\underbrace{\frac{1}{2}as + \frac{1}{2}as + \cdots + \frac{1}{2}as}_{n \text{ terms}}.$$

(one for each of the n triangles)

The equation simplifies to

$$\underbrace{\frac{1}{2}a(s + s + \cdots + s)}_{n \text{ terms}}$$

But $s + s + \cdots + s$ is ns, which is the perimeter. Thus

$$A = \frac{1}{2}ap,$$

where p is the perimeter of the polygon and a is the altitude from the center of the circle; a is referred to as the "apothem" of the polygon.

For the hexagon on page 209, we can find the length of the apothem by using the 30-60-90 triangle relationship. If O is the center of the circle, consider $\triangle AOB$ below:

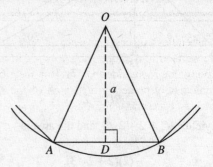

Since $AB = 8$, $BD = 4$, and $OD = 4\sqrt{3}$, the area is $\frac{1}{2}(4\sqrt{3})(48) = 96\sqrt{3} \doteq 166.3$.

EXAMPLES

If each of the following gives data for a regular inscribed polygon where n is the number of sides, s is the length of a side, and a is the length of the apothem, find the measure of each of the angles in the figure, and then find the area and perimeter.

1. $n = 4, s = 2, a = 1$

2. $n = 8, s = 1, a = 2$

SOLUTIONS:

1. $90, A = 4, p = 8$

2. $67.5, A = 8, p = 8$

FORMALLY DEFINING CIRCUMFERENCE

[19] If an endless succession of regular polygons is inscribed in a circle, each polygon in turn having one more side than the one inscribed immediately preceding it, which of the following observations must be true?

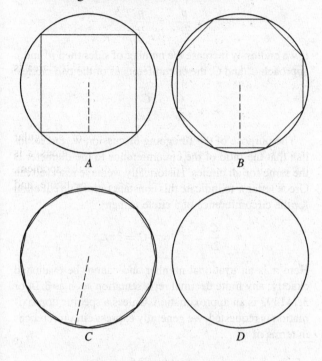

A   B

C   D

I. The length of a side decreases and gets closer and closer to zero.

II. The polygons more and more closely approximate the circle itself.

III. The length of the apothem increases but does NOT get closer and closer to any number.

(A) I only

(B) II only

(C) I and II only

(D) I, II, and III

(E) II and III only

A, *B*, and *C* depict regular inscribed polygons of 4, 8, and 16 sides, respectively. The dotted segment is the apothem in each case. Note that as the number of sides increases from 4 to 16, several important things happen:

1. The vertices get closer and closer together and the sides shorter and shorter. Though the sides can never

shrink to a length of zero (and still constitute a polygon) the lengths of the sides approach zero. We describe this situation by saying that the length of the sides approaches zero as a "limit."

2. The drawing of the polygon, though distinctly different from the drawing of the circle in diagram *A*, becomes less distinguishable from the sketch of the circle in *C*. Indeed, if we were to state that *D* was a picture of a million-sided polygon, anyone would be hard-pressed to prove us wrong. We are not suggesting for a moment that a circle is just a polygon with a large number of sides. But we are suggesting that a polygon more and more closely approximates a circle as the number of sides increases endlessly.

3. The apothems of the polygons more and more closely approximate the radius of the circle. We say that the apothem approaches the radius as a "limit" or more frequently that the radius is the "limit" of the apothem.

Using the ideas presented in these three observations, we can define "circumference of a circle." Since the polygons more and more closely approximate the circle as their number of sides increases, their perimeters more and more closely approximate "the distance around" the circle. Thus we will define *circumference* to mean the limit of the perimeters of the regular inscribed polygons as the number of sides of the polygons increases endlessly.

EXAMPLES

If a regular polygon has a perimeter of 10, what is the length of each side if the number of sides is:

1. 100

2. 1000

3. 100,000

4. 1,000,000

(Do you see that by increasing the number of sides we can make the length of each side as short as we please?)

SOLUTIONS:

1. .1

2. .01

3. .0001

4. .00001

WORKING WITH CIRCLES

[20] The accompanying figure shows a pair of circles that have the same center. The radius of the inner circle is r; the radius of the outer circle is 5. If the other segments have the lengths indicated, then $r = ?$

(A) 1

(B) 5

(C) 4

(D) 2

(E) $\frac{5}{2}$

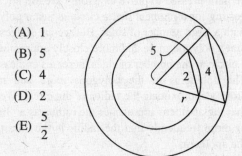

The multiple-choice question can be answered by comparing the sides of similar triangles. The numbers 2 and 4 are lengths of corresponding sides, as are r and 5:

$$\frac{r}{5} = \frac{2}{4} = \frac{1}{2},$$

$$r = \frac{5}{2}.$$

Though we have already answered the question, we will review a related concept leading to several important relationships between arcs, radii, and chords of a circle.

Suppose the question had asked for the circumference of the smaller circle. We'll develop the formula that relates the circumference to the radius.

In the two circles below, s and s' denote the lengths of segments that are sides of polygons P_1 and P (not shown) of the same number of sides. The two central angles θ and θ' have the same measure ($\frac{360}{n}$). The two sides of the triangles that include these angles are in the same ratio, so the triangles are similar by SAS. This means that:

$$\frac{r}{r'} = \frac{s}{s'}.$$

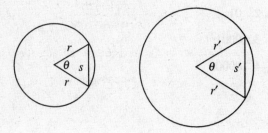

Multiplying the numerator and denominator of $\frac{r}{r'}$ by 2 and the numerator and denominator of $\frac{s}{s'}$ by n, we get:

$$\frac{2r}{2r'} = \frac{ns}{ns'}.$$

But ns and ns' are the perimeters of the given polygons. Substituting perimeter p for ns and p' for ns' we get:

$$\frac{2r}{2r'} = \frac{p}{p'},$$

$$\frac{p'}{2r'} = \frac{p}{2r}.$$

If we endlessly increase the number of sides then p' and p approach C' and C, the circumferences of the two circles:

$$\frac{C'}{2r'} = \frac{C}{2r}.$$

The purpose of the foregoing discussion was to establish that the ratio of the circumference to the diameter is the same for all circles. Historically we have reserved the Greek letter π to indicate this constant ratio. The equation for the circumference of a circle is then

$$\frac{C}{2r} = \pi \quad \text{or} \quad C = 2\pi r.$$

Here π is an irrational number and cannot be evaluated exactly; any finite decimal representation such as 3.14 or 3.141592 is an approximation. Unless a specific approximation is requested, we generally express circumferences in terms of π.

EXAMPLES

Find the missing elements of $\{C, r, d\}$, where C is the circumference, r is the radius, and d is the diameter. Express your answers as multiples of π, and not as approximations.

1. $C = 12\pi$

2. $C = 12$

3. $r = 2$

4. $d = 3$

SOLUTIONS:

1. $r = 6, d = 12$

2. $r = \dfrac{6}{\pi}, d = \dfrac{12}{\pi}$

3. $d = 4, C = 4\pi$

4. $r = 1.5, C = 3\pi$

[21] If the point of tangency of circles A and B is the center of the circular region that contains them, and if the diameter of this circular region is 10, what is the area of the shaded region?

(A) 39.3

(B) 78.5

(C) 62.8

(D) 19.0

(E) 157.1

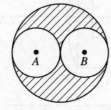

We have demonstrated the area of a polygon to be $\frac{1}{2}ap$, where a is the length of the apothem and p is the perimeter of the polygon. The limit of the apothem is the radius, and the limit of the perimeter is the circumference of the inscribing circle. If we let the number of sides of the polygonal regions increase endlessly, the area of the polygon will approach the *area of the circle* as a limit, and

$$A_c = \frac{1}{2}rC,$$

where A_c is the area of the circle, r is its radius, and C its circumference. Substituting $2\pi r$ for C, we get:

$$A_c = \frac{1}{2}r(2\pi r) = \pi r^2.$$

This formula will give us the area of any circle when the radius is known.

In the multiple-choice question, since the diameter of the greater circle is 10, its radius is 5 and the radius of each of the smaller circles is $\frac{5}{2}$. Therefore:

$$\text{Area of greater circle} = 5^2(\pi) = 25\pi,$$

$$\text{Area of each smaller circle} = \left(\frac{5}{2}\right)^2\pi = \frac{25}{4}\pi,$$

$$\text{Area of shaded region} = 25\pi - 2\left(\frac{25\pi}{4}\right),$$

$$25\pi - \frac{25\pi}{2} = \frac{25\pi}{2}$$

$$\doteq 39.3$$

EXAMPLES

Find the missing element of $\{A_c, r\}$:

1. $r = 2$

2. $A_c = 9\pi$

3. $r = \sqrt{2}$

4. $A_c = 9$

SOLUTIONS:

1. 4π

2. 3

3. 2π

4. $\frac{3}{\sqrt{\pi}} \doteq 1.69$

[22] If the area of the circle is 9π and the area of the shaded region is 6π, what is the measure of $\angle AOC$?

(A) 130

(B) 110

(C) 90

(D) 120

(E) 60

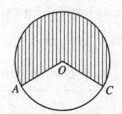

A "sector" of a circle is a region shaped like a pie slice or a combination of pie slices. More formally it is defined as the region of a circle bounded by two radii and that arc of the circle whose end points lie on the radii. In the sketches below, both the shaded and unshaded regions are sectors of the circles. The area of a sector is a fractional part of the area of the circle. Once we have found what fractional part it constitutes, we may use this fraction to compute the area. Depending on the given information, we can compute this fraction in one of two different ways:

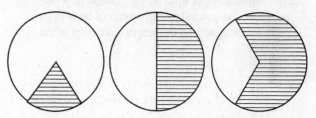

1. If we are given the length of the arc that bounds the sector and enough information to compute the circumference of the circle, then the fractional part, f, is given by

$$f = \frac{\text{arc length}}{\text{circumference}}.$$

2. If we are given the measure of the arc, then f is given by

$$f = \frac{\text{arc measure}}{360}$$

The area of the sector, A_s, is equal to f times the area of the circle, A_c.

In the multiple-choice question the sector constitutes $\frac{6\pi}{9\pi}$ or $\frac{2}{3}$ of the circle. The measure of $\angle AOC$ must then be $\frac{1}{3}$ of 360.

EXAMPLES

Find the fractional part of the circle, and the area of the sector, for each of the following:

1. $C = 4\pi$, arc length of sector $= \pi$

2. $r = 2$, arc measure of sector $= 30$

3. $r = 2$, arc length of sector $= 2$

SOLUTIONS:

1. $f = \dfrac{1}{4}$, circle is 4π, sector is π

2. $f = \dfrac{1}{12}$, circle is 4π, sector is $\dfrac{\pi}{3}$

3. $C = 4\pi$, $f = \dfrac{1}{2\pi}$, sector is 2

WORKING WITH PRISMS

[23] The number of units in the volume of a certain cube is equal to the number of units in its surface area. Find the length of an edge of the cube.

(A) 1

(B) 2

(C) 4

(D) 6

(E) 8

A cube is an example of a solid figure known as a prism. A *prism* is determined by a pair of congruent polygons, P and P', lying in a pair of parallel planes. If A and A' are corresponding vertices of polygons P and P', then the prism determined by P and P' is the union of all segments XX' such that (1) X lies in the region determined by P, (2) X' lies in the region determined by P', and (3) segment XX' is parallel to segment AA'.

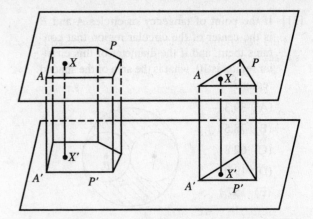

The polygonal regions P and P are called the *bases*. The segments connecting corresponding vertices are called *lateral edges*, and the sides of the polygons are called the *basal edges*. The region determined by a pair of basal edges and their connecting lateral edges is called a *lateral face*. A lateral face is always a parallelogram (and, when a lateral edge is perpendicular to a base, also a rectangle). The union of all lateral faces is called the *lateral surface*. The union of the lateral surface and the bases is the *total surface*.

If a lateral edge is perpendicular to the plane containing a base, the prism is a *right prism*—frequently referred to as a *rectangular solid*.

The distance between the two parallel planes is called the *altitude* of the prism.

The volume of a prism is given by the formula

$$(1) \qquad\qquad V = hB,$$

where h is the altitude of the solid and B is the area of the base. In the multiple-choice question we deal with a cube, which could be called a "right" (meaning the lateral edges are perpendicular to the base) "square" (meaning the defining polygonal bases are squares) "prism." Let e represent the length of an edge. All of the edges, lateral and basal, are equal in length. Thus formula (1) gives us $V = e^3$ for the volume of a cube.

The lateral surface area, S_L, of a prism is given by

$$(2) \qquad\qquad S_L = hp,$$

where h is the altitude of the solid and p is the perimeter of a base. If e represents the edge of a square, then $4e$ is the perimeter of its base and $S_L = 4e^2$.

The total surface area, S_T, of a prism is the lateral surface area plus the sum of the areas of the bases:

$$(3) \qquad\qquad S_T = hp + 2B.$$

If e represents the edge of a square, then $S_L = 4e^2$ and $2B = 2e^2$ so $S_T = 6e^2$.

Therefore, in the multiple-choice question, we are looking for e such that $e^3 = 6e^2$ Dividing each side by e^2, we get $e = 6$.

EXAMPLES

Find the volume, the lateral surface area, and the total surface area of each of the following:

1. A cube with edge of 2.

2. A rectangular solid with dimensions $1 \times 2 \times 3$.

3. The triangular prism shown at right.

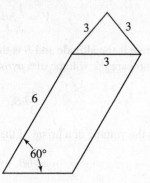

SOLUTIONS:

1. $V = 8$, $S_L = 16$, $S_T = 24$.

2. $V = 6$; any one of the six faces can be the base. We'll assume it is a 1×2 face; thus $S_L = 18$, $S_T = 22$.

3. $V = \dfrac{81}{4}$, $S_L = 27\sqrt{3}$, $S_T = \dfrac{63\sqrt{3}}{2}$.

WORKING WITH CIRCULAR CYLINDERS

[24] A certain toy block is a right circular cylinder 4 inches long with a volume of 154 cubic inches. A small can contains enough paint to cover an area of 1000 square inches. Approximately how many blocks can be painted completely with one can if you use $\dfrac{22}{7}$ for π?

(A) 1

(B) 2

(C) 4

(D) 6

(E) 8

A *circular cylinder* is determined by a pair of congruent circles, C and C', lying in a pair of parallel planes. The segment containing the centers, O and O', is called the *axis* of the cylinder. The cylinder determined by circles C and C' is the union of all segments XX' such that (1) X lies in the region determined by C, (2) X' lies in the region determined by C', and (3) segment XX' is parallel to the axis.

(Note the similarities between the definitions of "prism" and "cylinder.")

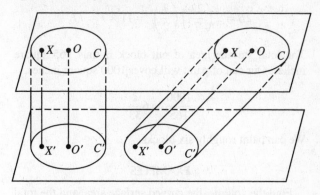

The circular regions are called the *bases*. The union of all segments connecting the circles (but not the circular regions) is called the *curved surface*. When the axis is perpendicular to the planes of the bases, the solid is a *right circular cylinder*. The distance between the parallel planes is called the *altitude* of the cylinder.

The formula for the volume of a cylinder is identical to that for a prism:

(1) $$V = hB,$$

where h is the altitude and B is the area of the base (B is, of course, figured differently for a cylinder and a prism).

In the multiple-choice question we can use the given length, 4, as h and compute the radius (approximately) by using the approximation $\frac{22}{7}$ for π:

$$154 = 4\left(\frac{22}{7}\right) r^2,$$

$$\frac{7}{88} \times 154 = r^2,$$

$$\frac{49}{4} = r^2,$$

$$\frac{7}{2} = r.$$

The formula for the curved surface area, S_c, is

(2) $$S_c = hC,$$

where C is the circumference of the base. (The circumference of a circle is analogous to the perimeter of a polygon—note the similarity between equation (2) of this section and equation (2) of section [23].)

For the multiple-choice question we have computed r to be $\frac{7}{2}$ so we can find C to be 7π using $C = 2\pi r$. Approximating π as $\frac{22}{7}$ gives us an approximation for C of 22. Thus the area of the curved surface of the block is hC or 88. But we will be painting the whole block, including the ends, so we need the formula for S_T, the total surface area.

(3) $$S_T = hC + 2B$$

The area B is πr^2 so we get

$$2B = 2\left(\frac{22}{7}\right)\left(\frac{7}{2}\right)^2 = 11 \times 7 = 77.$$

The total surface area of our block is thus 165 square inches. Our can of paint will cover 1000 square inches.

$$\frac{1000}{165} = 6\frac{2}{33}$$

We can paint roughly six blocks.

EXAMPLES

Find the volume, the curved surface area, and the total surface area for each of the following:

1. A right circular cylinder with radius of 5 and height of 1.

2. A right circular cylinder whose volume equals its curved surface area.

SOLUTIONS:

1. $V = 25\pi$, $S_c = 10\pi$, $S_T = 60\pi$.

2. The circular cylinder may be of any height as long as the radius of the base is 2 since $V = \pi r^2 h$ and $S_c = 2\pi rh$, yielding $\pi r^2 h = 2\pi rh$ and $r^2 = 2r$ so $r = 2$.

WORKING WITH PYRAMIDS

[25] A pyramid and a prism have equal altitudes and bases of equal area. What is the ratio of their volumes?

(A) $\frac{1}{2}$

(B) $\frac{1}{3}$

(C) $\frac{1}{4}$

(D) $\frac{1}{5}$

(E) $\frac{1}{6}$

Given: a plane containing a polygon P, and given a point X not contained in the plane. A *pyramid* is the union of all segments such that (1) X is an endpoint and (2) the other endpoint lies in the polygonal region determined by P. The polygonal region is the *base* of the pyramid, and the distance from X to the plane containing P is the *altitude*.

The formula for the volume V, is

$$V = \frac{1}{3}hB,$$

where h is the altitude and B is the area of the base.

Compare the volume of a *pyramid*,

$$\frac{1}{3}hB,$$

with the volume of a prism of the same altitude and base,

$$hB.$$

The ratio of the volumes is $\frac{1}{3}$, which is answer (B) of the multiple-choice question.

EXAMPLES

Find the volume of the following *pyramids*:

1. A square pyramid (meaning that the base is a square) with basal edge of 3 and height 4.

2. A rectangular pyramid with basal edges of 3 and 4 and a height of 5.

3. A pyramid all of whose faces are equilateral triangles with sides of length 6.

SOLUTIONS:

1. 12.

2. 20.

3. Area of base = $9\sqrt{3}$. Altitude of the pyramid is $2\sqrt{6}$. Volume is $18\sqrt{2}$.

WORKING WITH CONES

[26] If a solid brass cone with a height of 4 inches and a circular base of radius 4 inches is melted down and recast into two circular cones of height 2 inches and with circular bases of radius 4 inches, how many cubic inches of brass will be left over?

(A) There is exactly enough brass to do the job

(B) There is not enough brass

(C) 1

(D) π

(E) 4

Given: a plane containing a circle C, and a point X, not contained in the plane. A *cone* is the union of all segments such that (1) X is an endpoint and (2) the other endpoint lies in the circular region determined by C. The circular region is called the *base* of the cone, and the distance from X to the plane of the base is the *altitude*.

The volume formula is

$$V = \frac{1}{3}hB,$$

where h is the altitude and B is the area of the base.

In the multiple-choice question the original cone has volume V_1,

$$V_1 = \frac{1}{3}(4)(16\pi) = \frac{64\pi}{3} \text{ cubic inches.}$$

Each of the smaller cones has volume V_2,

$$V_2 = \frac{1}{3}(2)(16\pi) = \frac{32\pi}{3} \text{ cubic inches.}$$

Thus there is exactly enough metal to accomplish the recasting.

EXAMPLES

1. The volume of a right circular cone with altitude 6 and base of radius 2 is 8π.

2. The volume of a right circular cone with radius 4 for which the distance from the *vertex* of the cone (the point X of the definition) to any point of the circle that defines the base is 5 is 16π.

3. For a cone whose axis is not perpendicular to the base and for which the following are true: segment AB is a basal diameter of length 4, $XB \perp AB$ and $XA = 5$, the height is 3 and the volume is 4π.

WORKING WITH SPHERES

[27] An irregularly shaped chunk of metal is immersed in a pail that has been filled to the brim with water. The amount of water displaced by the immersion is 36π cubic inches. If the metal chunk were melted and recast in the shape of a spherical solid, what would the number of units be in the surface area of the new solid?

(A) 1

(B) 3

(C) 6

(D) 36

(E) 36π

Given a point O, and a positive number r, the set of all points in space that are r units from O is called a *sphere*. O is the center and r is the radius. The set of all points X such that $OX \leq r$ is called a *spherical solid*.

The volume V, of a spherical solid is given by the formula

$$V = \frac{4}{3}\pi r^3.$$

In the multiplication we find the radius of the sphere to be

$$36\pi = \frac{4}{3}\pi r^3,$$
$$27 = r^3,$$
$$3 = r.$$

The surface area of a sphere is given by

$$S = 4\pi r^2.$$

For the multiple-choice question the surface area is

$$47\pi(3)^2 = 36\pi.$$

EXAMPLES

Find the volume and the surface area of each of the following:

1. A sphere of radius 5.

2. A sphere for which the surface area equals the volume.

SOLUTIONS:

1. $V = \dfrac{500\pi}{3}$, $S = 100\pi$.

2. $\dfrac{4\pi r^3}{3} = 4\pi r^2$, so $r = 3$, $V = 36\pi = S$.

[28]   The area of the right triangle ABC is 72. X is the midpoint of AB. Y is the midpoint of BC. X' is the midpoint of AX and Y' is the midpoint of YC. Find the area of $\triangle PQR$.

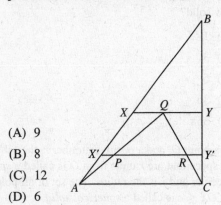

(A) 9

(B) 8

(C) 12

(D) 6

(E) Cannot be determined

This question combines three mathematical concepts involving parallel lines, similar triangles, and the areas of triangles. The guiding principle that will get you through the maze of ideas is the relationship between the areas of $\triangle ABC$ and $\triangle PQR$. That relationship, in turn, depends on the relationship between the altitudes of those two triangles and bases of a different pair of triangles, $\triangle PQR$ and $\triangle AQC$.

Let's begin with the altitudes. Because Y is the midpoint of BC and Y' is the midpoint of YC, YY' is one-fourth of BC. Because a set of parallel lines cuts all transversals into proportional parts, the altitude of $\triangle PQR$ is one-fourth of the altitude of $\triangle ABC$.

Now for the bases. $\triangle PQR$ is similar to $\triangle AQC$ because PR is parallel to AC. Because YY' is half of YC and XX' is half of XA, PR is half of AC.

Now you know that the altitude of $\triangle PQR$ is one-fourth the altitude $\triangle ABC$ and the base of $\triangle PQR$ is one-half the base $\triangle ABC$. That means the area of $\triangle PQR$ is $(\frac{1}{4})(\frac{1}{2})$ or $\frac{1}{8}$ times the area of $\triangle ABC$. Dividing 72 by 8 yields 9, answer (A).

Individually, none of these concepts is particularly challenging. It is because the question requires interconnecting three different concepts that it is pushed into the hard range of questions from 30 to 40 on the Level IC test. In fact, the most popular incorrect answer among our test group was (E).

Guessing, based on the figure alone, may not help. First, all of the numerical answer choices are factors of 72, so you can't eliminate any on that basis. Second, the size looks as much like one-ninth, one-sixth, or even one-twelfth as it does one-eighth.

[29]   Brandon leaves a cubical planter out in the rain. If the planter is one foot along each edge and the rainwater rises to 4 inches deep, what percent of the planter's volume is filled with water?

(A) 10%

(B) 25%

(C) $33\frac{1}{3}\%$

(D) 40%

(E) 50%

The volume of the empty planter is $1 \times 1 \times 1$ or 1 cubic foot. The height of the water is 4 inches or $\frac{1}{3}$ of a foot. Therefore, the volume of the water is $(\frac{1}{3}) \times 1 \times 1$ or $\frac{1}{3}$ cubic foot, which is $33\frac{1}{3}\%$ of the cubic container, answer (C).

[30]   If a cylinder is inscribed in a rectangular box with square base as shown, find its volume.

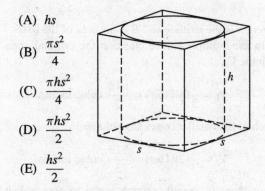

(A) hs

(B) $\dfrac{\pi s^2}{4}$

(C) $\dfrac{\pi h s^2}{4}$

(D) $\dfrac{\pi h s^2}{2}$

(E) $\dfrac{h s^2}{2}$

The dimensions are given in the figure rather than being stated in the question.

The radius of the circular base of the cylinder is $\frac{s}{2}$. Therefore, the area of the circular base is

$$\pi\left(\frac{s}{2}\right)^2 = \frac{\pi s^2}{4}.$$

But don't stop now just because you have an answer that looks like one of the choices (B). The volume of the cylinder is the product of the height and the area of the base. You still need to multiply by h to get $\frac{\pi h s^2}{4}$, choice (C).

[31] The ratio of the lengths of the sides of two squares is 1 to $\sqrt{x}$. What is the ratio of their areas?

(A) 1 to $\sqrt{x}$

(B) 1 to x

(C) 1 to x^2

(D) 1 to $2x$

(E) 1 to $4x$

You can find the answer by directly applying a principle of geometry: the ratio of the areas of two similar figures is the square of the ratio of the sides.

What do you do when you forget a principle such as this one? (After all, there really are a lot of principles of algebra, geometry, and trigonometry that are fair game for the Level IC test and you just might forget one—or two, or three.) You usually can go back to the basic ideas from which the principle was derived, as in this case. If the ratio of the lengths of the sides is 1 to $\sqrt{x}$, you can't say the sides of the squares must be 1 and $\sqrt{x}$. But you can say that squares with sides of 1 and $\sqrt{x}$ fit the given information so their areas must fit, too. These squares have areas 1 and x, which is the ratio given in (B).

[32] In the figure, the box has dimensions $3 \times 4 \times 5$. The edges are sealed by strips of tape that run from corner to corner and fold over each edge as shown. Which of the following best approximates the total length of tape used?

(A) 36

(B) 44

(C) 50

(D) 60

(E) 72

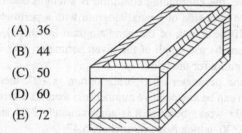

Sometimes the answer choices can help you understand and interpret a question that might not be clear to you. For example, the way the tape is folded over the edges in the diagram might make you think there are two strips going along each edge instead of one. There is no answer choice, however, that is close to the result you would get if you did seal the package with two strips of tape along each edge.

Further, you may know from your experience with wrapping packages that you don't always cut the tape to exact dimensions. But this question asks for the best approximation, which allows for small errors in cutting the tape. In fact, the answer you would get by cutting the tape exactly to specifications is not among the choices.

The figure shows three edges that are lengths, three widths, and three heights. There is one more unseen length, width and height. The exact amount of tape used would, therefore, be $4(3+4+5) = 48$. The closest number to that is 50, (C), which takes into consideration a bit of wastage. Misunderstanding the diagram to show two strips along each edge would take 96 or more, which is not among the choices. Always scan the answer choices for whatever guidance they may provide.

[33] In the figure, if $\angle AOB$ is $60°$, O is the center of the circle that defines arc AB, and r is the radius of circle O, then the area of sector AOB is ?

(A) $60\pi r$

(B) $6\pi r^2$

(C) $36\pi r^2$

(D) $\dfrac{\pi r^2}{3}$

(E) $\dfrac{\pi r^2}{6}$

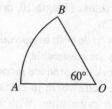

Some people have an easy time remembering formulas but others don't. By now you probably know which you are.

The formula folks do this problem by pulling something like the following from memory:

$$A = \frac{m\pi r^2}{360},$$

where $A =$ area of a sector of a circle, r is the radius of the circle, and m is the degree measure of the central angle.

We, the formula forgettors, don't do it that way. We see that the angle is $60°$ so the sector is a sixth of the circle. That means its area is $\frac{1}{6}$th of πr^2 (which just proves there is no escape from the memorization of *some* essential formulas).

[34] The figure is a rectangle separated into six squares. If the perimeter of the rectangle is 100, then what is the perimeter of each square?

(A) 10

(B) 20

(C) 40

(D) 50

(E) 400

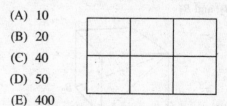

Some people approach math problems in a very formal and formulaic way. Others work them out informally and intuitively. The rest of us do both.

A formulaic and formal approach to this problem might look like this:

Let x be the length of one side of the square. Then the length of the rectangle would be $3x$, its width $2x$, and its perimeter $2(2x) + 2(3x) = 10x$. Because the perimeter is 100, it follows that

$$10x = 100$$
$$x = 10.$$

The perimeter of each square is $4x = 4(10) = 40$, (C).

An informal approach might be to start at one corner and count the sides of the squares as you work your way around the rectangle back to the corner. You should get ten sides, so each must be 10 units long to total 100. Each square has four sides of length 10, producing a perimeter of 40, answer (C).

Knowing how to do both helps you check your work to see if the results are reasonable.

Formulaic work can produce incorrect answers if you make a mistake somewhere in cranking out the answer or performing a calculation. With an intuitive backup method, you can make sure that an answer that should be 40 doesn't get recorded as 400 because you pushed the wrong button on your calculator or multiplied when you should have divided.

[35] A cube has a volume of 64. Point A is one corner and Point B is another. Which of the following could be the length of AB?

I.   4

II. $4\sqrt{2}$

III. $4\sqrt{3}$

(A) None

(B) I only

(C) I and II only

(D) II and III only

(E) All of I, II, and III

Draw a diagram. In the diagram shown, we have indicated Point A and the three possible locations for Point B as B_1, B_2, and B_3.

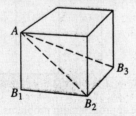

The volume is 64; therefore, the length of an edge is 4 because $4^3 = 64$. The edge is AB_1, so I is true.

$\triangle AB_1B_2$ is a 45-45-90 triangle. Therefore $AB_2 = 4\sqrt{2}$. That makes II true.

$\triangle AB_2B_3$ is a right triangle with legs of length 4 and $4\sqrt{2}$. Substitute those numbers into the Pythagorean Theorem and solve for the hypotenuse, $AB_3 = 4\sqrt{3}$. That makes three true so that the answer is (E).

In our test group, the most popular wrong answer was (C). Students who selected (C) said that III could not be true because $\sqrt{3}$ is the clue to the existence of a 30-60-90 triangle and there are no 30-60-90 triangles in the figure. That's faulty reasoning. In this case, $4\sqrt{3}$ is the length of the hypotenuse (not of one leg) of a triangle that lies in the plane defined by points A, B_2, and B_3. $\triangle AB_2B_3$ is not a 30-60-90 triangle.

[36] The perimeter of a parallelogram is 100. Which of the following could not be the length of a side?

(A) 1

(B) 10

(C) $\sqrt{30}$

(D) 10π

(E) 50

Don't be tempted to eliminate a number just because it looks unusual. In our test group, the most popular wrong answer was (D), 10π, just because numbers involving π are usually associated with circles and not parallelograms.

Here, the eliminating condition is a length that is too long to be a side of a parallelogram with a perimeter of 100. If the length of the parallelogram is 50, (E), then two lengths use up all of the given perimeter, 100, leaving nothing for the width.

If the perimeter of a parallelogram is 100, then the length can be any positive number less than 50. The number 10π works because it is approximately 31.4 and so does $\sqrt{30}$, which is approximately 5.47.

[37] In the figure, $AB \parallel OC$, the points have coordinates shown, and the measure of $\angle BOC$ is $30°$. What is the area of quadrilateral $ABCO$ to the nearest whole number?

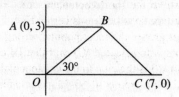

(A) 12

(B) 14

(C) 16

(D) 18

(E) Cannot be determined from the given information

The figure is a quadrilateral for which the area formula is

$$A = \left(\frac{h}{2}\right)(b_1 + b_2)$$

where b_1 and b_2 are the bases and h is the altitude. The altitude and one base can be read directly from the coordinates of the points. The altitude is 3 because point A is $(0,3)$. The lower base is 7 because point C is $(7,0)$.

The remaining base, AB, can be found by examining ABO as a 30-60-90 triangle. AB is opposite the 60° angle in a triangle for which the side opposite the 30°, AO, is 3. That makes $AB = 3\sqrt{3}$.

Substituting into the formula, we get:

$$\text{Area} = \left(\frac{3}{2}\right)(7 + 3\sqrt{3})$$

Because the answers are all in decimal form, we carry out the operation on a calculator to get 18.3. To the nearest whole number, that is (D).

[38] The ratio of the sides of a rectangular box is 1:1:2. Which of the following could be true?

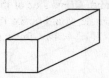

I. The number of edges equals the number of faces.

II. The number of units in the surface area equals the number of units in the volume.

III. Four faces have the same area.

(A) I only

(B) II only

(C) II and III only

(D) All of I, II and III

(E) None of I, II, or III

The three statements follow a pattern often used in constructing questions of this format.

Let's answer the question, then look at the pattern.

The number of edges is always eight and the number of faces is always six, regardless of the ratio. In other words, part of the given information (the part about the ratios of the sides), is irrelevant. Therefore, I is false.

If the ratio of the sides is 1:1:2, call the sides x, x, and $2x$, which covers all of the possibilities. The volume is found by multiplying the three dimensions, which produces $2x^3$ cubic units.

The surface area is found by adding the areas of the six faces. Two faces have areas x by x or x^2. The remaining four have areas x by $2x$ or $2x^2$, which gives $8x^2$. The total surface area is, then, $10x^2$.

Is it possible for the volume to equal the surface area?

Only if $10x^2 = 2x^3$ for some value of x (other than 0, which produces no box). Divide both sides of the equation by $2x^2$ and you get $5 = x$. In other words, when the box is 5 by 5 by 10, the volume and the surface area both equal 250. So II is true, regardless of how unlikely it seems. Remember that the question asks which statements *could* be true, not which statements must be true.

Statement III is true for the four faces with areas x by $2x$. Therefore the answer is (C). Note that the truth of statement III is part of the line of reasoning used in determining the truth of statement II.

All together now: (1) one statement does not require all of the given information, (2) one statement uses reasoning that is part of the reasoning in another statement, and (3) one statement is not true most of the time, but there is one case (not always obvious) for which it is true.

[39] Points $A, B, C,$ and D lie on a circle with area π. Which of the following is (are) true for quadrilateral $ABCD$?

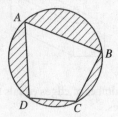

   I. Diagonal BD is always less than 2.
   II. The perimeter of quadrilateral $ABCD$ is always less than 2π.
   III. The area of the shaded region is always less than $\dfrac{\pi}{2}$.

   (A) I only

   (B) II only

   (C) II and III only

   (D) All of I, II, and III

   (E) None of I, II, or III

The three statements follow another pattern often used in constructing questions of this format.

Let's answer the question, then look at the pattern.

Because the area (πr^2) of the circle is π, its radius is 1 and its diameter is 2. Therefore, diagonal BD can be 2 if BD is a diameter. As a result, I is false. Statement I requires the straightforward application of a basic formula.

Because $ABCD$ is inscribed in the circle, its perimeter must be less than the circumference of the circle, $2\pi r = 2\pi$. Therefore, II is true. Statement II requires the straightforward application of a second basic formula, which then must be applied to a different situation (in this case, a different figure).

Also, because $ABCD$ is inscribed in the circle, its area plus the area of the shaded region is equal to π, the area of the circle. The way the figure is drawn, the quadrilateral takes up more than half of the circular region. It would be natural to assume that the area of the shaded region was less than $\frac{\pi}{2}$, half the area of the circle. But can you imagine the quadrilateral taking up less than half the circle? Do so by putting all of the points $A, B, C,$ and D in the same semicircle and then connecting them. Therefore, statement III is false and the answer is (B). The truth of the statement depends on visualizing a different situation from the one drawn, but a situation that still fits the given information.

All together now: (1) one statement involves the straightforward application of a basic principle, (2) a second statement involves the application of a different

basic principle to a second situation that also appears in the problem, and (3) the third statement requires re-interpreting the given information in terms of a situation allowed by the given information but not directly apparent in the way the information is presented (in this case, by a diagram that can be drawn in a different way).

[40] $ABCD$ is a square of side 1. The curved path is made up of 8 semicircles of equal diameter. What is the area of the shaded region?

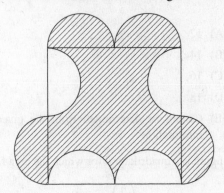

   (A) 1

   (B) 2

   (C) 2π

   (D) 4π

   (E) Cannot be determined

Though the figure looks very complicated, the question can be answered very easily with little or no calculation. The semicircles make four "bulges" and four "indentations" of equal area. The bulges and indentations exactly compensate for each other. In other words, if the bulges were cut off and moved to cover the indentations, the shaded area would cover the square exactly. The area of the square is 1, answer (A).

In our test group, a number of students immediately began calculating the areas of the semicircles without first developing an overall strategy. Before fully examining the figure, they were busily deciding that the radius of each semicircular piece was .25 (true) and then calculating the areas of the semicircles to be $\frac{\pi(.25)^2}{2}$ (true) and then adding and subtracting the results to the area of the square. Eventually, they got the right answer, but at a tremendous cost of time.

Always begin attacking a problem with the idea that there is something special about it that makes it a bit different from a standard textbook question. If you can discover that special difference, you can usually save yourself a lot of time in reaching the correct answer. You will also be more likely to understand why your answer is the correct one.

WHAT YOU SHOULD KNOW

KEY CONCEPTS

1. Congruent figures have equal areas.
2. Each region has one and only one area.
3. Two triangles with equal bases and equal altitudes have the same area.
4. The diagonal of a parallelogram forms two triangles of equal area with the sides.
5. A polygon is regular if it is convex, all of its sides are congruent, and all of its angles are congruent.
6. Volume is generally determined by using a memorized formula.
7. Surface area must by found by analyzing the shapes of the surfaces and choosing formulas that apply to these plane figures.
8. Prisms and cylinders are related forms and use similar formulas.
9. Pyramids and cones are related forms and use similar formulas.

KEY THEOREM AND RELATIONSHIP

1. A triangle is a right triangle if and only if the square of the length of its longest side is equal to the sum of the squares of the lengths of the remaining two sides. (Pythagorean Theorem)
2. In a triangle whose angle measures are 30, 60, and 90, the length of the side opposite the 30° angle is half the length of the hypotenuse and the length of the side opposite the 60° angle is $\sqrt{3}$ times the length of the side opposite the 30° angle. (30-60-90 Relationship)

KEY FORMULAS

1. To find the area A of a triangle, where b is the length of any side and h is the altitude to that side:

$$A = \frac{1}{2}bh.$$

2. To find the area A of a square, where s is the length of any side:

$$A = s^2.$$

3. To find the area A of a rectangle, where a is the length of any side and b is the length of an adjacent side:

$$A = ab.$$

4. To find the area A of a parallelogram, where b is the length of any side and h is the altitude to that side:

$$A = bh.$$

5. To find the area A of a right triangle, where a is the length of one leg and b is the length of the other:

$$A = \frac{1}{2}ab.$$

6. To find the area A of a trapezoid, where a is the length of one base, b is the length of the other base, and h is the altitude to the bases:

$$A = \frac{1}{2}h(a+b).$$

7. To find the area A of a rhombus, where a is the length of one diagonal and b is the length of the other:

$$A = \frac{ab}{2}.$$

8. To find the measure of any angle, A, of a regular polygon of n sides:

$$(\angle A)° = 180 - \frac{360}{n}.$$

9. To find the perimeter P of a regular polygon of n sides, each with length s:

$$P = ns.$$

10. To find the area A of a regular polygon with perimeter P and apothem a:

$$A = \frac{1}{2}ap.$$

11. To find the circumference C of a circle of radius r:

$$C = 2\pi r.$$

12. To find the area A of a circle of radius r:

$$A = \pi r^2.$$

13. *To find the volume of a prism:* If h is the altitude (the perpendicular distance between the planes containing the bases), and B is the area of a base, then

$$V = hB.$$

14. *To find the volume of a cube:* If e is the length of an edge, then
$$V = e^3.$$

15. *To find the volume of a cylinder:* If h is the altitude and B is the area of its base, then
$$V = hB.$$

16. *To find the volume of a pyramid:* If h is the altitude and B is the area of a base, then
$$V = \frac{1}{3}hB.$$

17. *To find the volume of a cone:* If h is the altitude and B is the area of a base, then
$$V = \frac{1}{3}hB.$$

18. *To find the volume of a sphere:* If r is the radius, then
$$V = \frac{4}{3}\pi r^3.$$

19. *To find the lateral surface area of a prism:* If h is the altitude and p is the perimeter of a base, then
$$S_L = hp.$$

20. *To find the total surface area of a prism:* If h is the altitude, p is the perimeter of a base, and B is the area of a base, then
$$S_T = hp + 2B.$$

21. *To find the total surface area of a cube:* If e is the length of an edge, then
$$A = 6e^2.$$

22. *To find the area of the curved surface of a cylinder:* If h is the altitude, and C is the circumference of the base, then
$$S_c = hC.$$

23. *To find the total surface area of a circular cylinder:* If h is the altitude, C is the circumference of the base, and B is the area of the base, then
$$S_T = hC + 2B.$$

24. *To find the surface area of a sphere:* If r is the radius, then
$$S = 4\pi r^2.$$

TEST-TAKING STRATEGIES

- Look for questions to which the Pythagorean Theorem applies.
- This theorem figures in more test questions than any other numerical law of geometry.
- Basic area formulas are not given on the test. Be prepared to supply them from your memory.
- When faced with a figure for which you have no area formula, try separating the figure up into composing triangles and (or) rectangles. Then calculate the areas of the composing pieces.
- Remember that an altitude can extend outside a figure. Don't limit yourself to the boundaries of the figure when drawing an altitude.
- Before attempting to answer a volume or surface area question, note carefully what solid figure is involved, and, if a diagram is given, identify the base, lateral and basal edges, altitude, and other relevant parts.

ANSWERS

[1] (B)	[8] (C)	[15] (A)	[22] (D)	[29] (C)	[36] (E)
[2] (C)	[9] (D)	[16] (D)	[23] (D)	[30] (C)	[37] (D)
[3] (D)	[10] (A)	[17] (A)	[24] (D)	[31] (B)	[38] (C)
[4] (A)	[11] (B)	[18] (A)	[25] (B)	[32] (C)	[39] (B)
[5] (E)	[12] (D)	[19] (C)	[26] (A)	[33] (E)	[40] (A)
[6] (E)	[13] (D)	[20] (E)	[27] (E)	[34] (C)	
[7] (E)	[14] (C)	[21] (A)	[28] (A)	[35] (E)	

COORDINATE GEOMETRY

CHAPTER

17

Questions relating to coordinate geometry make up nearly one fifth of the Level IC test. These concepts are the basis of many topics of intermediate and advanced math and their applications. In this chapter, we review the basics and provide a wide range of applications. This is the largest chapter in our review.

KEY TERMS

coordinate any of an ordered set of numbers used to specify the location of a point on a line, on a surface, or in space.

parabola the set of all points that are equidistant from a given line and a given point that is not on that line.

ellipse the set of all points such that the sum of the distances from each of these points to two given points never varies.

hyperbola a set of points such that the difference of the distances from each point to each of two fixed points never varies.

DEFINING COORDINATES

[1]   If p is the coordinate of point P and q is the coordinate of point Q, both on number line L, and $p < q$, then the distance from P to Q is:

(A) p

(B) $p + q$

(C) $p - q$

(D) $|p - q|$

(E) $|q|$

Let's review a few basic ideas about coordinate systems on a line.

Coordinate Postulate 1 *By first assigning 0 to a given point and 1 to a second point, both on a line L, a correspondence can be set up between the set of real numbers and the points on line L such that to every point on the line there corresponds a real number and to every real number there corresponds a point on L.*

The number assigned is called the *coordinate* of the point and the point is called the *graph* of the number. The point with coordinate 0 is the *origin*, and the point with coordinate 1 is the *unit point*. The positive integers are marked off on that ray of the line that contains the unit point, and the negative integers on the ray opposite to this. We assign integers in such a way that the distance between any two points associated with consecutive integers is the same as the distance between the origin and unit points. This, in fact, is where the "unit" point gets its name, since the distance between it and the origin becomes the unit of measure for laying off the other points.

The points associated with the rational numbers (the numbers of the form $\frac{p}{q}$, where p and q are integers and $q \neq 0$) are assigned by dividing the unit segment into q congruent parts and then assigning to $\frac{p}{q}$ the point at the end of the pth one of these parts (counting away from the origin).

The irrational numbers that are roots of prime numbers may be marked off via the *Pythagorean Theorem:*

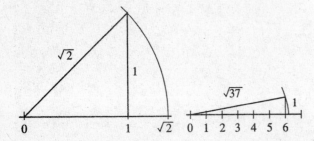

We will assume that all other irrational numbers have unique points of the line associated with them and that these can be approximated to any desired degree of accuracy by the use of rational approximations to the irrational number.

This correspondence is referred to as a *coordinate system on a line* or, more commonly, a *number line*.

The term *distance between two points* on a number line has no meaning until we define it. There are more obvious ways of accomplishing this than the one we are about to pursue, but it does have the virtue of brevity.

Coordinate Postulate 2 *The distance between two points on a number line is the absolute value of the difference of their coordinates.*

Note that, since the absolute value of $b - a$ is the same as the absolute value of $a - b$ (since $a - b$ is the negative of $b - a$ and each number has the same absolute value as its negative), the order of subtraction makes no difference. From this definition, the answer to the multiple-choice question is $|p - q|$. Answer (C) looks similar, but note that $p - q$ must be negative since $p < q$. If $q - p$ had been a choice, it would have been correct since $q - p$ is positive.

Does your calculator have an absolute value key? Look for the notation $\boxed{\text{abs}}$ or $\boxed{| \; |}$. You may have to access the function as a second or third function. You shouldn't need your calculator to find the absolute value of simple numerical expressions, but it might help you check your work. Be sure to enter any grouping symbols necessary. For example, to find $|5 - (-2)|$ on one of many scientific calculators, we entered $\boxed{\text{2nd}} \ \boxed{\text{abs}} \ \boxed{(}$ $5 \ \boxed{-} \ \boxed{(-)} \ 2 \ \boxed{)}$ and got 7.

EXAMPLES

If the following pairs of numbers are coordinates of points on a number line, find the distance between them (use your $\boxed{\text{abs}}$ key where appropriate).

1. 1 and 5

2. −4 and 4

3. −3 and 8

4. −7 and −3

5. $-p$ and q

6. p and $-q$

7. $-p$ and $-q$

SOLUTIONS:

1. 4

2. 8

3. 11

4. 4

5. $|q+p|$

6. $|p+q|$

7. $|q-p|$

ESTABLISHING A COORDINATE SYSTEM IN A PLANE

[2] If $P=(3,0)$, what is the second coordinate of the projection of P into the vertical axis?

(A) 3

(B) 0

(C) -3

(D) 4

(E) -4

The following postulate establishes a coordinate system in a plane.

Coordinate Postulate 3 *Given a plane determined by a pair of perpendicular number lines, L_1 and L_2, every point in the plane corresponds to an ordered pair of real numbers such that the first element of the ordered pair is the coordinate of the projection of the point into line L_1 and the second element of the ordered pair is the coordinate of the projection of the point into L_2.*

Though any pair of number lines intersecting at any point will do the job, we assist the application of this property a bit with a series of conventions. We will agree that:

1. The number lines intersect at the point that is the origin for both.
2. Line L_1, called the x-axis, is horizontal with its positive ray extending to the right.
3. Line L_2, called the y- axis, must then be vertical with its positive direction upward.
4. The unit for each number line is the same.

The *projection* of a point into a line L is the point of intersection of line L with the line containing P and perpendicular to L. In each of the following sketches the

point X is the projection of P into the x-axis and Y is the projection of P into the y-axis:

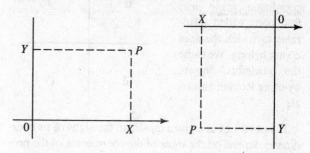

Note that, when P lies on one of the axes, the projection of P into the axis is P itself, whereas the projection of P into the other axis is the origin.

In the multiple-choice question, $P(3,0)$ is a point on the horizontal axis. Its projection into the vertical axis is the origin.

EXAMPLES

Draw a coordinate system in a plane and locate each of the following:

1. $A(3,5)$

2. $B\left(\dfrac{1}{2},\dfrac{1}{2}\right)$

3. $C(-2,1)$

4. $D(-3,-2)$

5. $E(8,-3)$

6. $F(0,0)$

SOLUTIONS:

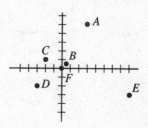

[3] If a point $A(-a,b)$ is in quadrant IV, then which of the following is correct?

(A) $a>0, b>0$

(B) $a>0, b<0$

(C) $a<0, b>0$

(D) $a<0, b<0$

(E) $a=0, b=0$

The axes separate the coordinate plane into four parts called quadrants to which the axes do not belong. We name the quadrants, shown, by using Roman numerals.

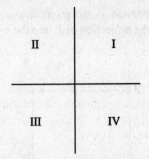

If a point lies in a given quadrant, the signs of its coordinates depend on the signs of the coordinates of the projections of the point into the axes. When (x, y) is in quadrant I, $x > 0$, $y > 0$; in quadrant II, $x < 0$, $y > 0$; quadrant III, $x < 0$, $y < 0$; and in quadrant IV, $x > 0$, $y < 0$.

In the multiple-choice question, since the point is in quadrant IV, the first coordinate, $-a$, is positive and the second coordinate, b, is negative.

If $-a > 0$ and $b < 0$, then $a < 0$ and $b < 0$.

EXAMPLES

Assuming a and b are both negative numbers:

1. (a, b) is in QIII.

2. $(-a, -b)$ is in QI.

3. $(-a, b)$ is is QIV.

4. $(a, -b)$ is in QII.

[4]   If $P = (3, 5)$ and $Q = (-1, 8)$, what is the length of the projection of segment PQ on the x-axis?

(A) 3

(B) 5

(C) −1

(D) 8

(E) 4

The projection of a segment AB into a line L is that segment of L whose endpoints are the projections of points A and B into L.

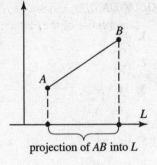

projection of AB into L

The length of the projection of a segment into a number line is the distance between the endpoints of the projection. By Coordinate Postulate 2, this distance is the absolute value of the difference of the coordinates on the number line.

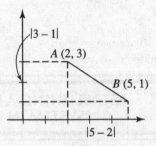

Note that the projection of a vertical segment into the horizontal axis is a point—thus the length of this projection is zero. The projection of a vertical segment into the vertical axis has the same length as the segment itself. Will the length of the projection of a segment ever be greater than the length of the segment itself? The projection will always be greater than or equal to 0 and less than or equal to the length of the segment itself.

The above definition of the projection of a segment into a line is still applicable when the segment and line intersect as at upper right. In each case segment PQ is the projection of segment AB.

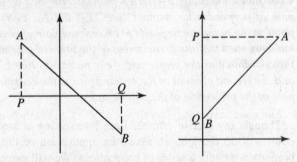

In the multiple-choice question, we note that the projections of $P(3, 5)$ and $Q(-1, 8)$ into the x-axis are, respectively, $(3, 0)$ and $(-1, 0)$. The distance between these points is 4.

[5] If $A = (a,b)$ and $B = (c,d)$, what is the second coordinate of the midpoint of segment AB?

(A) d

(B) b

(C) $\dfrac{b-d}{2}$

(D) $\dfrac{b+d}{2}$

(E) $\dfrac{d-b}{2}$

If segment AB with $A = (x_1, y_1)$ and $B = (x_1, y_2)$ has its midpoint at M with coordinates (x,y), we can use the following figure to show how to represent the coordinates of M in terms of the coordinates of A and B.

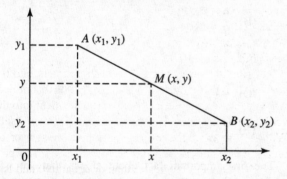

On the x-axis the point with coordinate x must be the midpoint of the segment with endpoints x_1 and x_2 since a set of parallel lines that cut off segments of equal length on one transversal (line AB) must cut off segments of equal length on any transversal (the x-axis in this case). The same will be true on the y-axis of the points with coordinates y, y_1, and y_2. Being the midpoint, x must separate the segment from x_1 to x_2 into two parts having the same length; thus

$$(1) \qquad |x - x_1| = |x_2 - x|.$$

Since we have been careful to arrange $x_2 > x > x_1$, we can state that

$$(2) \qquad |x - x_1| = x - x_1,$$

$$(3) \qquad |x_2 - x| = x_2 - x.$$

Accordingly, we can change (1) to

$$(4) \qquad x - x_1 = x_2 - x,$$

$$(5) \qquad 2x = x_2 + x_1,$$

$$(6) \qquad x = \frac{x_2 + x_1}{2}$$

You may verify that (6) is also true when $x_2 < x < x_1$. A similar line of reasoning yields

$$(7) \qquad y = \frac{y_2 + y_1}{2}.$$

The coordinates of M, the midpoint of segment AB, are thus

$$(8) \qquad \left(\frac{x_1 + x_2}{2}, \frac{y_1 + y_2}{2} \right)$$

Expression (8) is frequently called the "midpoint formula." Remember the formula as the "average of the coordinates," and you won't be confused over whether to add or subtract.

Applying this formula to the y-coordinate of points (a,b) and (c,d) of the multiple-choice question gives

$$\frac{b+d}{2}.$$

EXAMPLES

1. The midpoint of $A = (1,6)$, $B = (5,2)$ is $(3,4)$.

2. The midpoint of $A = (-1,-4)$, $B = (-3,0)$ is $(-2,-2)$.

3. The midpoint of $A = (-8,-1)$, $B = (-2,-3)$ is $(-5,-2)$.

4. The midpoint of $A = (5,-1)$, $B = (4,-2)$ is $(4.5,-1.5)$.

If the midpoint M and one endpoint A are given below, substitute in (6) and (7) to find the coordinates of B.

5. If $A(8,1)$, $M = (-2,-3)$, then $B = (-12,-7)$.

6. If $A(2,-5)$, $M = (-3,4)$, then $B = (-8,13)$.

DETERMINING SLOPES

[6] If the slope of segment AB is $\dfrac{1}{2}$ and $A = (-2,5)$, which of the following could be the coordinates of B?

(A) $(0,6)$

(B) $(2,6)$

(C) $\left(1, \dfrac{13}{4} \right)$

(D) $(6,4)$

(E) $(0,0)$

For many reasons it is useful to be able to indicate the relative degree of slant or tilt of a line in the coordinate plane with respect to the axes.

To enable us to do this, we define a certain number m to be the "slope" of a nonvertical segment AB, where $A = (x_1, y_1)$ and $B = (x_2, y_2)$. We define the slope, m, of line AB to be

$$(1) \qquad m = \frac{y_2 - y_1}{x_2 - x_1}.$$

A word of caution in determining slopes: note that we maintain a consistent order in the two subtractions involved in determining the slope of a segment. We are subtracting the coordinates of A from those of B. We will get the same slope if we reverse *both* subtractions since

$$y_2 - y_1 = -(y_1 - y_2) \text{ and } x_2 - x_1 = -(x_1 - x_2);$$

substitution of these in (1) above yields:

$$(2) \qquad m = \frac{y_2 - y_1}{x_2 - x_1} = \frac{-(y_1 - y_2)}{-(x_1 - x_2)} = \frac{y_1 - y_2}{x_1 - x_2}.$$

If, however, we had reversed the order of *only one* of the subtractions, we would *not* have gotten the same slope but rather its negative. *Use the same order in numerator as in denominator.* Check that you have used the same subtraction order by noting whether the y-coordinate of each point is above the x-coordinate of that point when the coordinates are substituted into the formula.

The multiple-choice question has many answers besides the correct choice of those given. All points on the line containing $(-2, 5)$ with slope $\frac{1}{2}$ would satisfy the conditions for B.

TEST-TAKING TIP

This is an example of a question that can probably be answered most quickly by checking the choices to see which is correct.

To do this quickly, you must be able to calculate slopes rapidly in your head. Since

$$\frac{6 - 5}{0 - (-2)} = \frac{1}{2},$$

the point $(0, 6)$ satisfies the conditions.

See Chapter 2 for a discussion of how to determine slopes with your calculator.

EXAMPLES

If A and B are as given in each of the following, find the slope of segment AB:

1. $A(1, 2), B(3, 4)$

2. $A(-1, -2), B(-3, -4)$

3. $A(-1, 2), B(-3, 4)$

4. $A(1, -2), B(-3, 4)$

SOLUTIONS:

1. 1

2. 1

3. -1

4. $-\dfrac{3}{2}$

[7] If A, B, and C are points on the same line and the slope of segment AB is $\dfrac{2}{3}$, what is the slope of segment BC?

(A) $\dfrac{3}{2}$

(B) $\dfrac{4}{9}$

(C) $\dfrac{2}{3}$

(D) $-\dfrac{3}{2}$

(E) $-\dfrac{2}{3}$

The first important fact about slopes that we will explore is that any two segments on the same nonvertical line will have the same slope.

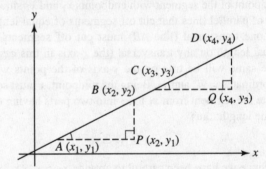

You may verify that the two triangles, ABP and CDQ, are similar by the Angle-Angle Similarity Theorem. Note that $DQ = y_4 - y_3$, $CQ = x_4 - x_3$, $BP = y_2 - y_1$, and $AP = x_2 - x_1$.

But similar triangles have corresponding sides in the same ratio, so

$$(1) \qquad \frac{y_2 - y_1}{y_4 - y_3} = \frac{x_2 - x_1}{x_4 - x_3}.$$

A little diligent application of algebra will transform (1) into

$$(2) \qquad \frac{y_2 - y_1}{x_2 - x_1} = \frac{y_4 - y_3}{x_4 - x_3}.$$

The two members of (2) are, respectively, the slopes of segments AB and CD. Though we have established this for only one of several possible cases, a similar argument will testify to the truth of the others. Thus it is meaningful to refer to *the* slope of a nonvertical line.

[8] If $A = (5,1)$, $B = (5,3)$, and $C = (2,3)$, what is the product of the slopes of line AB and line BC?

(A) 0

(B) 1

(C) 5

(D) 3

(E) Undefined

So far we have avoided comment on the slopes of vertical and horizontal lines.

The characteristic feature of two points, A and B, which are on the same horizontal line is that their projections into the y-axis are the same point P.

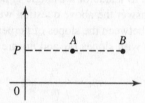

Thus any two points on the same horizontal line must have the same y-coordinate by definition of "y-coordinate." Let $A = (a,c)$ and $B = (b,c)$; the slope formula yields

$$\frac{c-c}{a-b} = \frac{0}{a-b} = 0 \quad (a \neq b).$$

Consequently, the slope of any *horizontal* line is zero.

Similarly, the chief property of two points, A and B, on the same vertical line is that they have the same x-coordinate. Let $A = (c,a)$ and $B = (c,b)$. The slope formula yields

$$\frac{a-b}{c-c} = \frac{a-b}{0} \quad (a \neq b).$$

But the division of a real number by zero does not define any real number as its quotient, so the slope of a vertical line is undefined. This does not handicap us too much since we can immediately recognize that any line with "undefined" slope is a vertical line.

In the multiple-choice question, line AB is vertical since points $A(5,1)$ and $B(5,3)$ have the same first coordinates. Therefore line AB has no slope. A product with a nonexistent factor is also undefined.

EXAMPLES

Indicate whether each of the lines that contain A and B below is horizontal or vertical by attempting to determine its slope.

1. $A(1,5)$, $B(1,9)$

2. $A\left(-2, -\frac{1}{2}\right)$, $B\left(-4, -\frac{1}{2}\right)$

3. $A(a,b)$, $B(c,b)$

4. $A(2,3)$, $B(3,2)$

SOLUTIONS:

1. Vertical (no slope)

2. Horizontal (zero slope)

3. Horizontal (zero slope)

4. Neither (slope is -1)

[9] If line AB is parallel to line CD and the slope of AB is -3, find the coordinates of D when $C = (2,0)$.

(A) No such point exists

(B) D exists but is not unique

(C) $(5, 2)$

(D) $\left(-\frac{1}{2}, \frac{1}{2}\right)$

(E) $(2, -3)$

Another argument based on similar triangles prvides us with a second major fact on slopes: two lines are parallel if and only if they have the same slope.

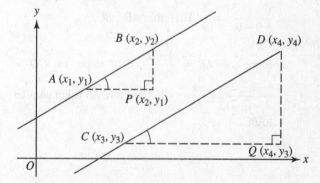

You may verify that triangles ABP and CDQ are similar by the Angle-Angle Similarity Theorem. Therefore, $AP = x_2 - x_1$, $BP = y_2 - y_1$, $CQ = x_4 - x_3$, and $DQ = y_4 - y_3$. Since similar triangles have proportional corresponding sides, then

(1) $$\frac{y_2 - y_1}{y_4 - y_3} = \frac{x_2 - x_1}{x_4 - x_3}.$$

Again, a little algebra will transform (1) into

(2)
$$\frac{y_2 - y_1}{x_2 - x_1} = \frac{y_4 - y_3}{x_4 - x_3}.$$

There are other cases, but a like argument will support these; and, in general, we conclude that nonvertical parallel lines have the same slope.

Conversely, two distinct lines that have the same slope are parallel.

In the multiple-choice question, lines AB and CD must have the same slope, -3, because they are parallel. Since C is the only point of CD that is given, D can be any other point of the line. Therefore D is not unique.

TEST-TAKING TIP

One approach to this problem is to try the suggested answers. Choices (C), (D), and (E) can be eliminated by direct calculations. If, upon eliminating three choices of a question, you still cannot decide between the remaining two, be sure to pick the choice that seems more reasonable—don't just leave the answer blank because you aren't sure.

EXAMPLES

■ Indicate whether lines AB and CD are parallel by finding their slopes (use your calculator where needed):

1. $A(-5,4)$, $B(4,9)$, $C(9,0)$, $D(0,-5)$

2. $A(0,0)$, $B(1,1)$, $C(-2,2)$, $D(2,-2)$

SOLUTIONS:

1. Slope of $AB = \dfrac{9-4}{4-(-5)} = \dfrac{5}{9}$, slope of $CD = \dfrac{0-(-5)}{9-0} = \dfrac{5}{9}$. Therefore $AB \parallel BC$.

2. Slope of $AB = \dfrac{1-0}{1-0} = 1$, slope of $CD = \dfrac{-2-2}{2-(-2)} = \dfrac{-4}{4} = -1$. Therefore AB is not parallel to BC.

RELATING THE SLOPES OF PERPENDICULAR LINES

[10] If the vertices of triangle ABC are $A = (15,1)$, $B = (9,3)$, and $C = (4,5)$, find the slope of the altitude to side AB.

(A) $-\dfrac{2}{3}$

(B) $\dfrac{2}{3}$

(C) $\dfrac{4}{9}$

(D) $-\dfrac{3}{2}$

(E) 3

The altitude to a side of a triangle is perpendicular to that side; to answer the above question we need to know a relationship between the slopes of perpendicular lines.

If two lines with slopes m_1 and m_2 are perpendicular, then

$$m_1 = -\frac{1}{m_2},$$

and conversely.

In the multiple-choice question, the slope of $A(15,1)$ and $B(9,3)$ is

$$\frac{3-1}{9-15} = \frac{2}{-6} = -\frac{1}{3}.$$

The slope of the altitude must be the negative reciprocal, 3.

■ To find the slope of the perpendicular on a calculator, enter the given slope, then press the reciprocal key followed by the negative key.

If the perpendicular lines are vertical and horizontal, the negative reciprocal rule does not work. A vertical line has no slope, so no product is possible. The horizontal line has slope 0.

EXAMPLES

If the number given is the slope of a line, find the slope of the line perpendicular to it by a mental calculation.

1. $-\dfrac{1}{2}$

2. 2

3. $\dfrac{1}{2}$

4. $-\dfrac{3}{4}$

SOLUTIONS: The slopes of the perpendiculars are:

1. 2

2. $-\dfrac{1}{2}$

3. -2

4. $\dfrac{4}{3}$

[11]   Which of the following most completely describes the figure with vertices: $A(-5,4)$, $B(4,9)$, $C(9,0)$, $D(0,-5)$.

   (A)   Quadrilateral

   (B)   Trapezoid

   (C)   Parallelogram

   (D)   Rectangle

   (E)   Square

By finding the slopes of the sides of a quadrilateral, we can tell which are parallel to each other, if any, and which are perpendicular, if any. The lengths of the sides can be determined by the distance formula.

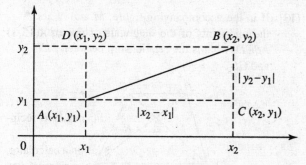

Verify that in the above figure, with lines BC and AD perpendicular to the x-axis and lines DB and AC perpendicular to the y-axis, triangle ABC is a right triangle. Verify, by noting their projections into the axes, that segment BC has length $|y_2 - y_1|$ and $AC = |x_2 - x_1|$. In the interest of a general proof we are *not* assuming $y_2 > y_1$ and $x_2 > x_1$, even though this is the way it appears in the figure.

The Pythagorean Theorem gives us

(1) $(AB)^2 = |x_2 - x_1|^2 + |y_2 - y_1|^2$.

Note that $|a| = a$ for $a \geq 0$ and $|a| = -a$ for $a < 0$, but both $(a)^2 = a^2$ and $(-a)^2 = a^2$ so $|a|^2 = a^2$ for all a. Using this fact we write equation (1) as

(2) $(AB)^2 = (x_2 - x_1)^2 + (y_2 - y_1)^2$,

(3) $AB = \sqrt{(x_2 - x_1)^2 + (y_2 - y_1)^2}$.

Equation (3) is referred to as the *distance formula* in a coordinate plane.

To answer the multiple-choice question, first plot the given points.

TEST-TAKING TIP

Whenever it is possible to draw a diagram illustrating the given information, the diagram is usually useful in answering the question.

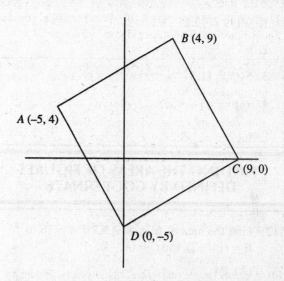

The above figure may suggest that all sides have the same length, but you may not be able to verify this solely from the sketch, since you will not have graph paper to use on the Level I and IC exams.

The distance formula should erase any doubts:

$$
\begin{aligned}
AD &= \sqrt{(-5-0)^2 + [4-(-5)]^2} \\
   &= \sqrt{25+81} \\
   &= \sqrt{106},
\end{aligned}
$$

$$
\begin{aligned}
CD &= \sqrt{(9-0)^2 + [0-(-5)]^2} \\
   &= \sqrt{81+25} \\
   &= \sqrt{106}. \\
   &\doteq 10.25
\end{aligned}
$$

From the diagram and the knowledge that adjacent sides are congruent, the figure can be judged to be a square.

EXAMPLES

For each of the following, first let $A = (x_1, y_1)$ and $B = (x_2, y_2)$ and compute the distance from A to B. Then let $B = (x_1, y_1)$ and $A = (x_2, y_2)$ and compute the distance from B to A. Does the distance formula give the same result regardless of the order of the points? (Use your calculator to approximate answers to the nearest tenth.)

1. $A(4, -5)$, $B(-6, 2)$

2. $A(-3, 5)$, $B(-3, -4)$

3. $A(6, -3)$, $B(-4, 2)$

4. $A(p, q)$, $B(0, 0)$

SOLUTIONS: The distances are as follows:

1. $\sqrt{149} \doteq 12.2$

2. 9

3. $5\sqrt{5} \doteq 11.2$

4. $\sqrt{p^2 + q^2}$

FINDING THE AREAS OF FIGURES DEFINED BY COORDINATES

[12]   Find the area of triangle ABC if $A = (6, 6)$, $B = (14, -2)$, and $C = (4, -4)$.

(A)   24

(B)   48

(C) $48\sqrt{2}$

(D)   96

(E)   None of these

Graphing the points suggests that the triangle is isosceles and possibly equilateral.

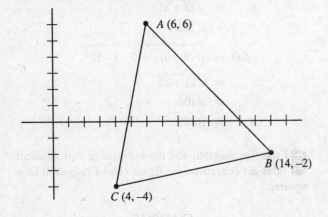

A (6, 6)

B (14, -2)

C (4, -4)

$$AB = \sqrt{(14-6)^2 + (-2-6)^2} = \sqrt{128} = 8\sqrt{2}$$

$$BC = \sqrt{(-14-4)^2 + [-2-(-4)]^2} = \sqrt{104} = 2\sqrt{26}$$

$$AC = \sqrt{(6-4)^2 + [6-(-4)]^2} = \sqrt{104} = 2\sqrt{26}$$

The distance formula applied to the sides of the above triangle proves it is isosceles. The altitude to the base (in this case, AB) of an isosceles triangle bisects the base. The midpoint formula will give the coordinates of the point of intersection of the altitude and the base, $(10, 2)$. The distance formula gives the length of the altitude, using the coordinates of the midpoint of the base and of C, the vertex of the angle included by the sides of equal length:

$$\sqrt{(-10-4)^2 + (2+4)^2} = \sqrt{72} = 6\sqrt{2}.$$

 Therefore the area is $\frac{1}{2}(6\sqrt{2})(8\sqrt{2}) = 48$.

USING COORDINATES TO COMPARE LENGTHS

[13]   If in the accompanying figure, M and N are the midpoints of the diagonals of trapezoid $ABCD$, what is the relationship between MN and CD?

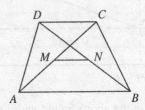

(A) $MN = .3(AB - CD)$

(B) $MN = .4(AB - CD)$

(C) $MN = .5(AB - CD)$

(D) $MN = .6(AB - CD)$

(E) $MN = .7(AB - CD)$

(Hint: first use the midpoint formula to represent the coordinates of M and N.)

The methods of coordinate geometry frequently provide efficient means for verifying statements of geometry. The above question is a case in point. Let us first put the given figure on a set of coordinate axes in such a way that one vertex is at the origin and one side is contained in an axis. Note that we have used the fact that the sides DC and AB are parallel to give points D and C the same y-coordinate.

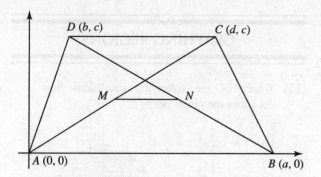

The midpoint formula gives us the coordinates of M and N.

$$M = \left(\frac{d}{2}, \frac{c}{2}\right) \qquad N = \left(\frac{b+a}{2}, \frac{c}{2}\right)$$

(Do you see that this proves segment MN to be parallel to both segments AB and CD since all have slopes of zero?) Thus the length of MN is

$$\sqrt{\left(\frac{b+a}{2} - \frac{d}{2}\right)^2 + \left(\frac{c}{2} - \frac{c}{2}\right)^2},$$

which simplifies to

$$\frac{b+a-d}{2} = \frac{a-(d-b)}{2}.$$

But the length of AB is a, and the length of DC is

$$\sqrt{(d-b)^2 + (c-c)^2} = d - b.$$

The length of MN is, therefore, half of $(AB - DC)$.

EXAMPLE

Using the following figure, verify that segment MN (M and N being the midpoints of the sides) is parallel to segment AB and has a length that is half the length of AB (Hint: use the midpoint formula to represent the coordinates of M and N.)

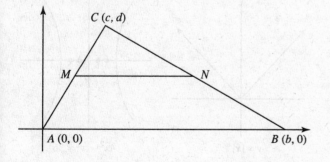

SOLUTION:

$$M = \left(\frac{c}{2}, \frac{d}{2}\right)$$

$$N = \left(\frac{b+c}{2}, \frac{d}{2}\right)$$

$$\text{slope of } MN = 0$$

$$MN = \frac{b}{2}$$

GRAPHING CURVES

[14] The figure below is part of the graph of which of the following conditions?

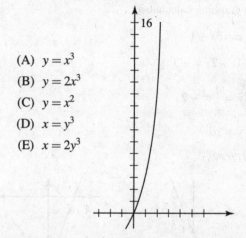

(A) $y = x^3$
(B) $y = 2x^3$
(C) $y = x^2$
(D) $x = y^3$
(E) $x = 2y^3$

The graph of an ordered pair, (x, y), is the point in the coordinate plane whose x- and y-coordinates are given by the ordered pair. The graph of a condition in x and y is the set of all points (and only those points) with ordered pairs (x, y) that make the condition true.

In graphing a condition it is seldom useful (or even possible) to write out all of the ordered pairs in its solution set first, since most of the conditions discussed have infinite solution sets. When the condition is specified by an equation such as

$$y = 2x^2 + 1,$$

the most elementary approach to graphing it is to plot several points of the graph by finding several ordered pairs of its solution set. These points can be obtained most readily by selecting arbitrary values for x and solving the equation to find the companion values for y.

The table (right) shows a few pairs.

x	y
-2	9
-1	3
0	1
1	3
2	9

When enough points have been determined to indicate the general pattern of the graph (and this number varies with the complexity of the graph), draw the simplest smooth curve that will contain all of the points, as shown at the right.

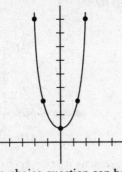

The graph in the multiple-choice question can be seen to contain points $(0,0)$, $(1,2)$, and $(2,16)$, all of which satisfy the condition $y = 2x^3$.

EXAMPLES

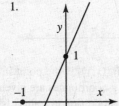
Plot at least six points for each of the following and draw the graph that contains them (check your work with a graphing calculator):

1. $y = 3x + 1$

2. $4x + 2y = -3$

3. $y = \frac{1}{2}x^4 - 2$

4. $y = |x|$

SOLUTIONS:

1.

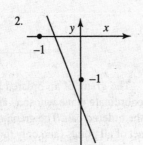

2.

3.

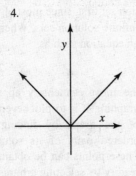

4.

1.

GRAPHING REGIONS

[15] Which of the following conditions best describes the graph below?

(A) $y = -\frac{1}{2}x^2 + 2$

(B) $y < -\frac{1}{2}x^2 + 2$

(C) $y > -\frac{1}{2}x^2 + 2$

(D) $y > -2x^2 + 2$

(E) $y < -2x^2 + 2$

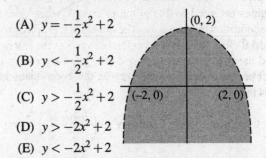

As we have seen, an equation in x and y has a graph that is a curve, a line, or a combination of curves or lines.

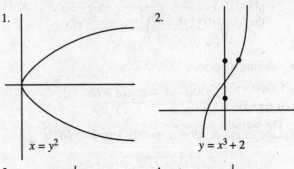

1. $x = y^2$

2. $y = x^3 + 2$

3. $4x^2 + y^2 = 36$

4. $y = 2x + 3$

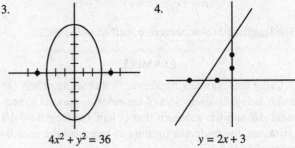

5. $y = |x|$

6. $4x^2 - y^2 = 36$

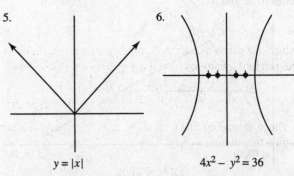

These curves or lines separate the plane into regions that lie on either side of them. For example, 1. determines one region that lies between its extensions and another that lies outside the extensions, 2. determines a region above it and one below it, 3. cuts off a region as its interior and another as its exterior, 4. is a line and thus separates the plane into two half-planes, 5. is an angle and thus separates the plane into its interior and exterior, and 6. determines a region between its branches and a pair of regions outside the branches. When $A = B$ is an equation in x and y, then $A > B$ is the condition that describes one of the regions bounded by the graph of $A = B$, while $A < B$ is the condition that describes the other. (The graph of 6. is a special case; think of the region between as the "interior" and the pair of separated regions as the "exterior.") This fact provides us with a simple way of graphing inequalities in x and y.

1. First graph the boundary condition as a dotted figure.

2. Select any point that is clearly on one side of the boundary condition, and test it in the inequality. If it satisfies the inequality, shade in the region of the plane that contains the point. If it does not satisfy the inequality, shade in the other region.

EXAMPLE 1

Graph $x < 3y^2 + 6y + 4$.

SOLUTION:

The boundary condition is

$$x = 3y^2 + 6y + 4,$$

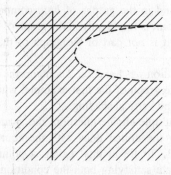

which we graph as a dotted curve. We then test $(0, 0)$ in the original inequality:

$$0 < 3(0)^2 + 6(0) + 4.$$

Since it makes the inequality true, we shade in the region that contains $(0,0)$.

EXAMPLE 2

Graph $y < |x|$.

SOLUTION: The boundary condition is

$$y = |x|.$$

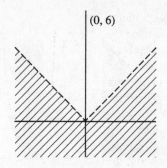

After graphing it as a pair of dotted rays, we test the point $(0, 6)$, which is clearly in the interior of the angle. Since $(0, 6)$ does *not* make the inequality true, we shade the region that does not contain it.

EXAMPLE 3

Graph $4x^2 - y^2 > 36$.

SOLUTION: The boundary condition is

$$4x^2 - y^2 = 36.$$

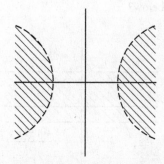

The graph of the inequality is either the region between the branches or the pair of regions outside the branches. We test $(0,0)$, which is clearly between the branches, but this point does not satisfy the inequality so we shade in the pair of regions that do not lie between the branches.

In the multiple-choice question, the labeled points $(-2,0), (0,2)$, and $(2,0)$ and the parabolic boundary show the dotted curve to be $y = -\frac{1}{2}x^2 + 2$. We can use $(0,0)$ as a test point to decide between answers (B) and (C).

EXAMPLES

Draw the graph of each of the following:

1. $y < x$

2. $y > 2x + 5$

3. $x^2 + y^2 < 9$

4. $y > x^3$

SOLUTIONS:

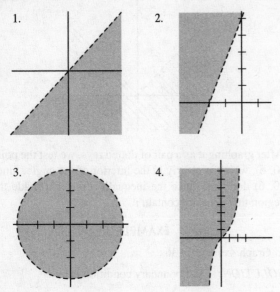

1.

2.

3.

4.

[16] Which of the following best describes the graph below?

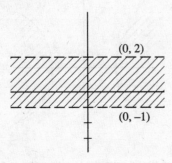

(0, 2)

(0, −1)

(A) $x < 2$ or $x > -1$

(B) $y < 2$ or $y > -1$

(C) $y > 2$ and $y < -1$

(D) $y < 2$ and $y > -1$

(E) None of these

When a condition is expressed as a compound statement using "or," the graph consists of all points that satisfy either part.

$y > 1$ or $x < 2$ consists of all points in the graph of $y > 1$ as well as all points in the graph of $x < 2$. In the graph (below) all points that have either vertical or horizontal shading are included.

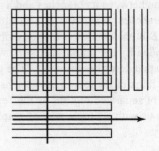

$y \geq 3x$ means $y > 3x$ or $y = 3x$ and thus consists of all points of the graph of $y > 3x$ as well as all points of the graph of $y = 3x$. The graph contains all points of the line and all points above the line.

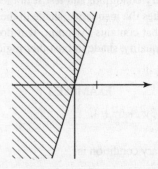

When a condition is expressed as a compound statement using "and," the graph consists of only those points that are found in the graphs of *both* composing conditions. If a point is found only in the graph of one of these conditions, it is *not* part of the graph of the compound condition.

The condition $y > 1$ and $x < 2$ contains the points in the region of the graph of the first example, which has both horizontal and vertical shading.

In the multiple-choice question, the shaded region is bounded by the dotted lines with the equations $y = 2$ and $y = -1$. To lie in this region, a point must have a y-coordinate satisfying both the conditions $y < 2$ and $y > -1$.

WRITING THE EQUATIONS OF LINES

[17] Which of the following is the point of intersection of the lines given by $y = 5$ and $x = -4$?

(A) $(5, -4)$

(B) $(4, -5)$

(C) $(-4, 5)$

(D) $(-4, -5)$

(E) The lines don't intersect

All points on the same vertical line have the same x-coordinate, since the projection of all of these points into the x-axis is the same point. Furthermore, no point that is *not* on the vertical line will have this x-coordinate. We can, therefore, give a complete description of any vertical line if we know what this common x-coordinate is.

If the x-coordinate is a, the condition

$$\{(x, y) : x = a\},$$

which is read "the set of ordered pairs (x, y) for which the x-coordinate is a," will be true for all points of the line and false for any point not on the line. As we saw in the preceding section, we usually take the $\{(x, y) : \quad\}$ notation for granted and write the condition without it.

This same situation exists for horizontal lines, which, in general, can be described by equations of the form $y = b$, where b is the common y-coordinate.

In the multiple-choice question, the point of intersection must lie on the vertical line $x = -4$ and the horizontal line $y = 5$. Its coordinates must, therefore, be $(-4, 5)$.

EXAMPLES

Note the equation for the line that contains the following points:

1. For $(3, 5)$, $(4, 5)$, the line is $y = 5$.

2. For $\left(-\frac{1}{2}, 3\right)$, $\left(-\frac{1}{2}, \frac{1}{2}\right)$, the line is $x = -\frac{1}{2}$.

3. For $(8, -4)$, $(-8, -4)$, the line is $y = -4$.

4. For $(\sqrt{2}, 3)$, $(\sqrt{2}, -\sqrt{2})$, the line is $x = \sqrt{2} \doteq 1.4$.

[18] If $A = (1, 3)$ and $B = (-2, 4)$, which of the following is not an equation of the line that contains A and B?

(A) $y - 3 = -\frac{1}{3}(x - 1)$

(B) $y - 4 = -\frac{1}{3}(x + 2)$

(C) $y - 1 = -\frac{1}{3}(x - 3)$

(D) $y = -\frac{1}{3}x + 3\frac{1}{3}$

(E) $3y + x - 10 = 0$

We have reviewed an important fact that will help us to describe any nonvertical line in the coordinate plane by an equation in x and y such as those in the above question. Recall that the slope of a given line is the same no matter what two points are used to compute it. Using this fact and given the points $A(a, b)$ and $B(m, n)$, we can write an equation in a and y such that the ordered pairs of numbers that make the sentence true are all of the ordered pairs (and only those ordered pairs) that represent points on the line that contains A and B. To accomplish this, we present the following argument.

Since x and y are variables that represent any real numbers, the symbol (x, y) is a variable that represents any ordered pair of real numbers, and, thereby, any point in the plane. Then

(1) $\qquad \dfrac{y - b}{x - a}$

represents the slope of any line in the plane that contains A, and

(2) $\qquad \dfrac{y - n}{x - m}$

represents the slope of any line in the plane that contains B. But we are interested only in the line that contains both A and B, and this will be the line for which (1) and (2) yield the same slope. Accordingly,

(3) $\qquad \dfrac{y - b}{x - a} = \dfrac{y - n}{x - m}$

will be true only for those ordered pairs (x, y) that determine points on the line that contains A and B.

EXAMPLE

Determine an equation of the line that contains $A(1,3)$ and $B(4,-2)$.

SOLUTION:

$$\frac{y-3}{x-1} = \frac{y-(-2)}{x-4}$$

We will develop other means for determining equations for lines and will not drill on this one.

In the multiple-choice question, the points $A(1,3)$ and $B(-2,4)$ can be used to determine the slope of line AB :

$$\frac{3-4}{1-(-2)} = -\frac{1}{3}.$$

But each of the five choices is a line having $-\frac{1}{3}$ as a slope. Answer (C) however, has the coordinates reversed, because in the slope formula the y-coordinates are subtracted from each other and the x-coordinates are subtracted from each other.

TEST-TAKING TIP

It would be easiest to solve this problem by inspection, as suggested above. A second method, though longer, involves the problem-solving technique of transformation. If each of the equations was simplified and changed to the same form, say that of choice (E), the maverick answer would readily stand out.

---

[19] If line L, with slope $\dfrac{1}{2}$, contains $(-1,4)$, which of the following is an equation of line L?

(A) $y+1 = \dfrac{1}{2}(x-4)$

(B) $y-4 = \dfrac{1}{2}(x+1)$

(C) $x+1 = \dfrac{1}{2}(y-4)$

(D) $x-4 = \dfrac{1}{2}(y+1)$

(E) None of these

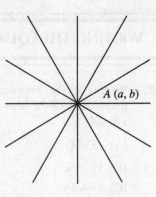

Given a point $A(a,b)$ in the plane, an infinite set of lines can be drawn that contain it. Some of these are shown in this figure. Each of these distinct lines must have a slope different from each of the others (two lines with the same slope would have to be parallel and, therefore, could not intersect at A). From this we can conclude that a given point, $A(a,b)$, and a given slope, m, determine one and only one line.

We can find the equation for this line in the following way:

Let (x,y) represent any point in the plane; then

(1) $$\frac{y-b}{x-a}$$

represents the slope of any line that passes through A. But we are interested only in the one line that has a slope of m. If we set m equal to (1) we get

(2) $$m = \frac{y-b}{x-a},$$

which is an equation that will be true only for those points such that their slope when computed with (a,b) is m. Thus the truth set of this equation is the set of all points of the given line except (a,b)—note that (a,b) leads to division by zero if we replace (x,y) by it. Hence we write (2) in the form:

(3) $$y-b = m(x-a),$$

since the truth set of (3) is the same as (2) except that (3) *includes* (a,b).

EXAMPLE 1

Write the equation of the line that contains $(4, 5)$ and has a slope of -2.

SOLUTION: $y-5 = -2(x-4)$ (In equation (3) we have replaced (a,b) by $(4,5)$ and m by -2.)

EXAMPLE 2

Write the equation of the line that contains $A(1,3)$ and $B(-2,4)$.

SOLUTION: First we use the slope formula to find the slope of line AB:

$$\frac{3-4}{1+2} = -\frac{1}{3}.$$

We then use equation (3) with *either A* or *B* to get an equation of the line:

$$y-3 = -\frac{1}{3}(x-1) \text{ or } y-4 = -\frac{1}{3}(x+2).$$

Verify that both equations can be transformed to:

$$x + 3y - 10 = 0.$$

The multiple-choice question can be answered directly by substituting $\frac{1}{2}$ for m and $(-1, 4)$ for (a, b) in equation (3), with (B) as the result.

EXAMPLES

Use equation (3) to write an equation of the line given by each of the following:

1. If the line contains $(1, -2)$, slope 3, the equation is $(y + 2) = 3(x - 1)$.

2. If the line contains $(0, 4)$, slope $-\frac{1}{3}$, the equation is
$$y - 4 = -\frac{1}{3}(x).$$

3. If the line contains $(1, -2)$ and $(0, 4)$, the equation is $y - 4 = -6x$.

[20] Which of the following is NOT an equation for the same line as each of the others?

(A) $\dfrac{y - 4}{x + 1} = \dfrac{1}{2}$

(B) $y - 4 = \dfrac{1}{2}(x + 1)$

(C) $y = \dfrac{1}{2}x + \dfrac{9}{2}$

(D) $x - 2y + 9 = 0$

(E) $x + 2y - 9 = 0$

Every line can be expressed by an equation of the form

(1) $\qquad Ax + By + C = 0,$

where *not both* $A = 0$ and $B = 0$. Furthermore, every equation of this form is an equation of a line. For this reason equations that can be transformed to form (1) are called *linear equations*.

All equations of the same line, when transformed to form (1), are identical as long as any common factors of A, B, and C are removed.

FINDING INTERCEPTS

[21] Which of the following choices lists *all* of the y-intercepts of $|x| + 12 = y$?

(A) There are none

(B) $\{12, -12\}$

(C) $\{12\}$

(D) $\{-12\}$

(E) $\{0\}$

The x-intercept of a graph is the x-coordinate of the point where the graph intersects the x-axis. It can be found most readily by substituting 0 for y in the graph of the condition and then solving for the values of x.

The y-intercept of a graph is the y-coordinate of the point where the graph intersects the y-axis. It can be found by substituting 0 for x in the condition and then solving for the values of y.

Intercepts are frequently the easiest points of a graph to find and, therefore, are ready aids to graphing.

The multiple-choice question is much simpler than it looks. Since you want the y-intercept, substitute 0 for x and solve the resulting equation for y:

$$|0| + 12 = y.$$

This provides the y-intercept, 12, directly.

EXAMPLES

Find the x- and y-intercepts for each of the following:

1. $\dfrac{x}{3} + \dfrac{y}{5} = 1$

2. $6x + 3y = 2$

3. $7 - 3y = 4x$

SOLUTIONS:

1. x-intercept is 3, y-intercept is 5

2. x-intercept is $\dfrac{1}{3}$, y-intercept is $\dfrac{2}{3}$

3. x-intercept is $\dfrac{7}{4}$, y-intercept is $\dfrac{7}{3}$

TESTING FOR SYMMETRY

[22] Which of the following completely describes the symmetry of the graph of $x^2 - 3y^2 = 3$?

(A) x-axis only

(B) y-axis only

(C) Both x- and y-axis

(D) x-axis, y-axis, and origin

(E) Origin only

By definition, two points A and B are symmetric with respect to a point M if and only if M is the midpoint of segment AB. A graph is therefore symmetric with respect to the origin if for every point A of the graph there is some point B of the graph such that the origin is the midpoint of segment AB. If (a,b) is any point of the graph, then the midpoint formula shows us that $(-a,-b)$ must also be on the graph when the graph has origin symmetry. To test for origin symmetry, substitute $(-a,-b)$ into the equation and then substitute (a,b); if the resulting equations are the same, then the graph is symmetric with respect to the origin.

By definition, two points A and B are symmetric with respect to a line L if and only if line L is the perpendicular bisector of segment AB.

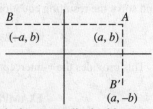

If $A = (a,b)$ and the y-axis is the perpendicular bisector of segment AB, then $B = (-a,b)$. (Verify this by plotting.) If $A = (a,b)$ and the x-axis is the perpendicular bisector of AB', then $B' = (a,-b)$.

To check for y-axis symmetry substitute in your equation both (a,b) and $(-a,b)$ in turn. If the two resulting equations are the same, the graph has y-axis symmetry. To check for x-axis symmetry, apply the same test using (a,b) and $(a,-b)$.

In the multiple-choice question, the resulting equation is:

$$a^2 - 3b^2 = 3.$$

This is the same equation that results from substituting $(a,-b)$, $(-a,b)$, or $(-a,-b)$, so the graph has all three types of symmetry.

[23] If points $(3,5)$ and (x,y) are symmetric to each other with respect to the origin, then $(x,y) =$?

(A) $(3,-5)$

(B) $(5,3)$

(C) $(-3,-5)$

(D) $(-5,-3)$

(E) $(-3,5)$

As noted earlier, two points, A and B, are symmetric to each other with respect to a third point M, if M is the midpoint of the segment AB. Symmetry questions can usually be solved algebraically. However, the concept of symmetry is very visual and many test questions can be more easily resolved by a simple graph than by creating an algebraic model.

In this case, locate the point $(3,5)$ and draw the segment connecting it to the origin. Copy a congruent segment on the opposite side of the origin on the same line as your original segment and locate the reflection of $(3,5)$ in the origin.

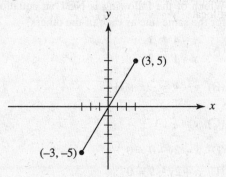

The concepts of symmetry, midpoint, and reflection are closely related to each other. The point $(-3,-5)$ is a *reflection* of the point $(3,5)$ in the origin because the origin is the midpoint of the segment connecting $(3,5)$ and $(-3,-5)$.

EXAMPLES

Use the ideas of symmetry and midpoint to locate the reflection of each of the following in the origin:

1. $(1,8)$

2. $(-2,-3)$

3. $(-7,2)$

4. $(-x,y)$

SOLUTIONS: The reflections in the origin are:

1. $(-1, -8)$

2. $(2, 3)$

3. $(7, -2)$

4. $(x, -y)$

[24] Which of the following is the equation of the perpendicular bisector of the segment AB if $A = (3, 3)$ and $B = (-3, -3)$?

(A) $y = 1$

(B) $x = 1$

(C) $y = x$

(D) $y = -x$

(E) $x = 0$

This is really another symmetry question even though it is not phrased as such. It can be solved through an elaborate algebraic model. However, you can readily visualize the answer with a sketch.

First locate the points $(3, 3)$ and $(-3, -3)$.

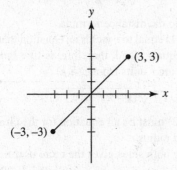

The perpendicular bisector of a segment is a line that is perpendicular to the segment and passes through its midpoint. You can see that the requested line is the one shown below and labeled ℓ.

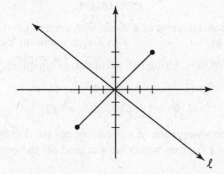

From your experience, you can probably tell that its equation is $y = -x$. If not, note that its slope is -1 and its y-intercept is 0. Then use the slope-intercept form of the equation of the line.

EXAMPLES

Write the equations of the perpendicular bisectors of the segments connecting each of the following pairs of points:

1. $(-2, 0), (2, 0)$

2. $(0, 5), (0, -5)$

3. $(1, 3), (7, 3)$

4. $(-3, 5), (5, -3)$

SOLUTIONS: The perpendicular bisectors are:

1. $x = 0$

2. $y = 0$

3. $x = 4$

4. $y = x$

[25] If quadrilateral $ABCD$ is a rhombus, the coordinates of C are what pair of values?

(A) $(1, \sqrt{3})$

(B) $(4, 1 + \sqrt{3})$

(C) $(3, 2)$

(D) $(3 + \sqrt{3}, 2)$

(E) $(3, 4)$

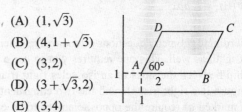

To answer the question you need to recall the relationship between the sides of a 30-60-90 triangle, which is summarized in the diagram for your reference.

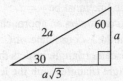

Because all sides of a rhombus are equal, $BC = 2$. In the figure below, we added the dotted lines parallel to the x- and y-axes. We used the 30-60-90 relationship to fill in the missing lengths.

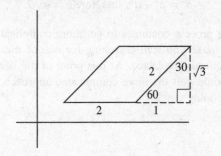

From resulting numbers shown in the diagram, you may now calculate the coordinates of C to be $(4, 1 + \sqrt{3})$.

[26] If $\angle C$ is a right angle, which of the following is the equation of the line containing 0 and C?

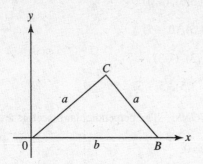

(A) $y = x$

(B) $y = \dfrac{a}{b} x$

(C) $y = \dfrac{b}{a} x$

(D) $y = \sqrt{a}\, x$

(E) $y = abx$

Coordinate geometry questions often involve other topics of math as well. This one requires you to use a relationship between the sides of an isosceles right triangle. The figure is a right triangle and the two congruent legs (both marked a) require the opposite angles to be equal. Therefore, m $\angle COB = 45$ because the sum of the measures of the angles of a triangle is 180.

You might, for example, remember that the slope of a line is the tangent of the angle it forms with the x-axis. Tan $45 = 1$, so the line must be $y = x$.

If, instead, you decide on an approach that uses b, you might realize that the x-coordinate of C is $\frac{b}{2}$ because the altitude of an isosceles triangle bisects the base. The altitude forms two right triangles with the legs marked a. As a result, the y-coordinate of C is also $\frac{b}{2}$. The slope of the line must be the quotient of the coordinates, 1.

You might also try an approach that begins with a and uses the Pythagorean Theorem:

$$b^2 = a^2 + a^2, \text{ therefore } b = a\sqrt{2}.$$

This process continues to get more complicated, and might make you start searching for one of the simpler ways already explained. At this point in the derivation, you would quit the more complicated approach, just as we are doing now!

[27] Which of the following is an equation of a circle with center at (3, -2) and radius 7?

(A) $x^2 + y^2 - 6x + 4y - 36 = 0$

(B) $x^2 + y^2 = 62$

(C) $x^2 - 6x + 9 + y^2 = 49$

(D) $x^2 + y^2 + 4y + 4 = 49$

(E) None of these

A *circle* is the set of all points that are at a given distance (the "radius") from a given point (the "center"). If we represent the center by $C(h, k)$ and the radius by r, and if $P(x, y)$ represents any point in the plane, then the distance from C to P is given by:

(1) $\qquad \sqrt{(x - h)^2 + (y - k)^2}$

according to the distance formula.

Setting (1) equal to r yields an equation that is true only when (1) equals r and, therefore, is true only for points $P(x, y)$ that are r units from $C(h, k)$:

(2) $\qquad \sqrt{(x - h)^2 + (y - k)^2} = r.$

Equation (2) must be an equation for the circle with center at C and radius r.

Squaring both sides gives the more useful form

(3) $\qquad (x - h)^2 + (y - k)^2 = r^2.$

We may readily write an equation for any circle, given the center and radius, by using (3).

EXAMPLE 1

Find an equation of a circle with center at $(-1, 4)$ and radius 11.

SOLUTION: Using (3), we obtain an equation:

$$[x - (-1)]^2 + (y - 4)^2 = (11)^2,$$
$$(x + 1)^2 + (y - 4)^2 = 121.$$

Given an equation of a circle, we can put it in the same form as (3), from which we can read off the center and radius.

EXAMPLE 2

Find the center and radius of:

$$x^2 + y^2 - 2x + 2y - 2 = 0.$$

SOLUTION: Completing the trinomial squares, we get:

$$x^2 - 2x + 1 + y^2 + 2y + 1 = 2 + 2,$$
$$(x-1)^2 + (y+1)^2 = 4,$$
$$\text{center, } (1, -1); \quad \text{radius, } 4.$$

Equation (3) also provides the key to identifying an equation as a circle: the equation must contain both an x^2 and a y^2 term, and both of these terms must have the same coefficient.

The equation of the circle in the multiple-choice question (center at $(3, -2)$ and radius 7) is:

$$(x-3)^2 + (y+2)^2 = 7^2,$$
$$x^2 - 6x + 9 + y^2 + 4y + 4 = 49,$$
$$x^2 + y^2 - 6x + 4y - 36 = 0.$$

TEST-TAKING TIP

The more experience you have with a concept or procedure, the quicker you can work through a problem and the more readily you can recognize a correct answer. If, for example, you've had lots of experience with the coordinate geometry of circles, the seemingly complicated question above can be answered in less than a minute without shortcuts. Beware of shortcuts that don't depend on sound mathematical principles. In this case, for example, you may be tempted to say that the constant must be 49, the square of the radius. As you can see from the process above, however, the number 49 is one of three constants in the equation, which, when combined, give the result -36.

Develop your skills and speed through practice, and avoid unsound shortcuts.

EXAMPLES

Given the following, note the equation of the circle:

1. Center $(-3, 4)$, radius 6, yields

$$(x+3)^2 + (y-4)^2 = 36.$$

2. Center $(-5, -2)$, radius 7, yields

$$(x+5)^2 + (y+2)^2 = 49.$$

Given the following equations, note the center and radius:

3. $x^2 + y^2 - 4x - 6y = 12$ has $C = (2, 3)$, $r = 5$.

4. $x^2 + y^2 + 16x - 10y = -25$ has $C = (-8, 5)$, $r = 8$.

[28] Which of the following is the graph of $x^2 = 1$?

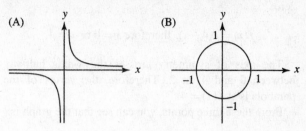

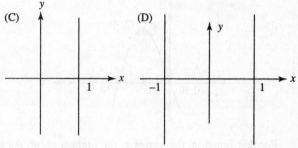

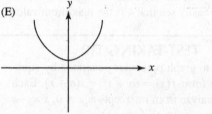

At first glance, you may have spotted the "x^2" term and thought the graph was a parabola or circle. However, the absence of a "y" term should have made you think again.

The equation $x^2 = 1$ is true whenever $x = 1$ or $x = -1$. Each of $x = 1$ and $x = -1$ is the equation of a vertical line; thus the answer is (D).

TEST-TAKING TIP

Beware of misleading "look-alikes." On each Level IC test, as the questions progress from easy to difficult, they tend to become more misleading to the unwary.

---

[29] The maximum value of the function $f(x) = 4x - x^2$ over the interval $0 \le x \le 5$ is:

(A) 0

(B) 4

(C) 5

(D) 6

(E) 2

The graph of a function of the form $f(x) = ax^2 + bx + c$ is a parabola with a vertical axis of symmetry. The simplest of these to graph and analyze are those for which $c = 0$. In such cases as $f(x) = 4x - x^2$, you can find the *x*-intercepts by factoring and setting each factor equal to zero:

$$f(x) = x(4 - x), \text{ therefore } x = 0 \text{ or } x = 4.$$

The axis of symmetry crosses the *x*-axis halfway between 0 and 4, at 2. Therefore, the vertex of the parabola is at $f(2) = 4$.

From these three points, you can see that the graph is:

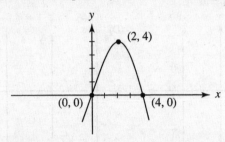

For this function, the vertex is the highest point. As a result, you can easily see that 4 is the maximum value.

TEST-TAKING TIP

Know how to graph parabolas generated by equations of the form $f(x) = ax + x^2 = x(a + x)$. Each is easy to analyze from intercepts at $x = 0$, $x = -a$ and a vertex at $\left(\dfrac{a}{-2}, f\left(\dfrac{a}{-2} \right) \right)$.

EXAMPLES

Graph each of the following by factoring and using its intercepts (check your results with a graphing calculator):

1. $f(x) = x^2 - x$

2. $f(x) = x - x^2$

3. $f(x) = 4x + x^2$

4. $f(x) = x^2 - 9x$

SOLUTIONS:

1. $x^2 - x = x(x - 1)$;
   $f\left(\dfrac{1}{2} \right) = -\dfrac{1}{4}$

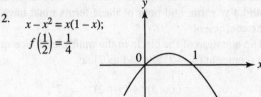

2. $x - x^2 = x(1 - x)$;
   $f\left(\dfrac{1}{2} \right) = \dfrac{1}{4}$

3. $4x + x^2 = x(4 + x)$;
   $f(-2) = -4$

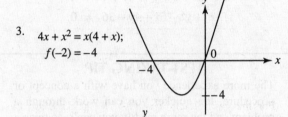

4. $x^2 - 9x = x(x - 9)$;
   $f\left(\dfrac{9}{2} \right) = -20\dfrac{1}{4}$

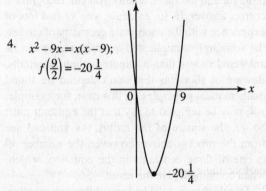

[30] If $f(x) = x^2 + 1$ for $-1 \le x \le 2$, then which of the following sets is the range of *f*?

(A) $\{y : 2 \le y \le 5\}$

(B) $\{y : 1 \le y \le 5\}$

(C) $\{y : -1 \le y \le 2\}$

(D) $\{y : 0 \le y \le 3\}$

(E) $\{y : 0 \le y \le 9\}$

Coordinate geometry is an essential tool in the analysis of many types of functions. We'll review functions in a later chapter. Our purpose here is to look further at parabolas, and in particular, a second very common algebraic form.

As previously noted, functions of the form $f(x) = ax^2 + bx + c$ have graphs that are parabolas with vertical axes of symmetry. If the function has no bx term, the axis of symmetry is the y-axis and the vertex is the point $(0, c)$.

The graph of $f(x) = x^2 + 1$ has a vertex at $(0, 1)$. Graph a second point by substituting another value for x. Choose 2, for example and you get $(2, 5)$. Because of the y-axis symmetry, $(-2, 5)$ is also a point. Therefore the graph of $f(x) = x^2 + 1$ looks like:

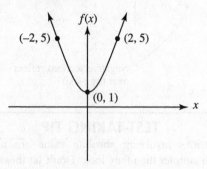

For the multiple-choice question, the function has a specified domain, $-1 \leq x \leq 2$.

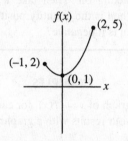

Therefore, the graph ends at $(2, 5)$ and $(-1, 2)$. The *range* is the set of y-values from least to greatest. The least value of y is 1 and occurs at the vertex. The greatest value is 5 and occurs at $(2, 5)$. Therefore the range is choice (B).

TEST-TAKING TIP

Know how to quickly and easily graph parabolas of the form $f(x) = ax^2 + c$. They are always symmetric with respect to the y-axis and cross the y-axis at $(0, c)$, a point that is also the vertex of the parabola. Substitute a convenient number to find a second (and by symmetry, a third) point. Most of the parabolic functions you will encounter on a Level IC test are selected from the simpler forms $f(x) = ax^2 + bx$ (reviewed previously) or $f(x) = ax^2 + c$. You will rarely see a question that requires a graph of $f(x) = ax^2 + bx + c$ where neither b nor c is 0.

EXAMPLES

Sketch the graphs of each of the following (check your results with a graphing calculator):

1. $f(x) = 1 - x^2$

2. $f(x) = 1 + x^2$

3. $f(x) = 4x^2 + 4$

4. $f(x) = -5x^2 - 25$

SOLUTIONS:

1. $f(0) = 1$;
   x-intercepts $= \pm 1$

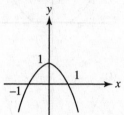

2. $f(0) = 1$;
   no x-intercepts

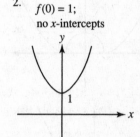

3. $f(0) = 4$;
   no x-intercepts

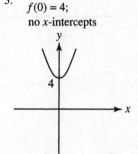

4. $f(0) = -25$;
   no x-intercepts

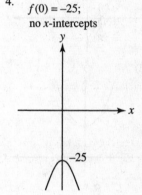

[31]   The graph of $f(x) = 1 - x^2$ is shown below. Which of the following is the graph of $y = |f(x)|$?

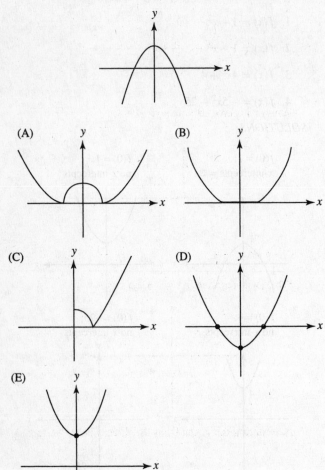

(A)

(B)

(C)

(D)

(E)

Absolute value bars make many students nervous enough to skip questions in which they appear—even relatively simple questions like this one. We've reviewed absolute value previously in a different context. The practice in this section and the next several sections should help increase your familiarity with applications of absolute value and help you reason your way to answers with less trepidation.

To answer questions involving the absolute value of $f(x)$, begin by graphing $f(x)$ if the graph is not given. Here, the graph is shown, which allows you to proceed to the next step, applying the absolute value operation.

Remember that the absolute value of a positive number is the number itself. As a result, all positive values of $f(x)$ remain exactly the way they are. In this case, all parts of $f(x)$ above the x-axis are unchanged. The absolute value of zero is also zero, so the x-intercepts remain unchanged.

On the other hand, the absolute value of a negative number is its opposite. Therefore, applying the absolute value operation to parts of the graph below the x-axis will

change the graph. The opposite of a y-value is its mirror image when reflected in the x-axis. You can accomplish this reflection merely by flipping the negative branches over the x-axis. The result looks like the following:

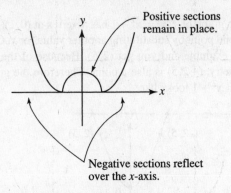

Positive sections remain in place.

Negative sections reflect over the x-axis.

TEST-TAKING TIP

Questions involving absolute value are usually much simpler than they look. Don't let those rigid vertical bars become mental blocks. Take a deep breath. Examine the quantity the absolute value operator is acting on. Then take a case-by-case approach. When is the quantity positive? When is it zero? When is it negative?

EXAMPLES

Sketch the graph of $y = |f(x)|$ for each of the following (check your results with a graphing calculator):

1. $f(x) = x^2 - 1$

2. $f(x) = x^2 - x$

3. $f(x) = x^3$

4. $f(x) = x^3 - 1$

SOLUTIONS: Dots show sections of $f(x)$ reflected upward for $|f(x)|$.

1.
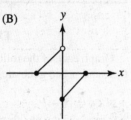

2.

3.
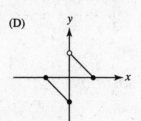

4.

[32] Which of the following is the graph of $y = |x| - 1$ on the interval $-1 \le x \le 1$?

(A)
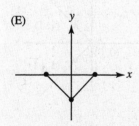

(B)

(C)

(D)

(E)

Here is more practice with visualizing the graphical effects of the absolute value operator. We'll use the case-by-case approach again. First, note that the absolute value bars are operating on x and then consider the outcomes when x is positive, then 0, then negative.

This case is complicated just a bit by the fact that a specific domain is given. As a result, we are limiting the graph to the values of x between -1 and 1, inclusive.

When x is positive, $|x| = x$, so $y = x - 1$.

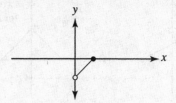

When x is zero, $|x| = 0$, so $y = -1$.

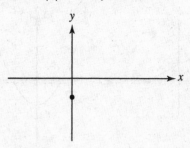

When x is negative, $|x| = -x$, so $y = -x - 1$.

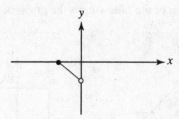

Assembling the graph from the three pieces, we get:

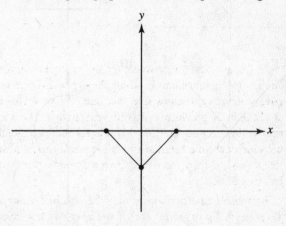

EXAMPLES

Graph each of the following on the interval $-1 \le x \le 1$. Check your results with a graphing calculator.

1. $y = |x - 1|$

2. $y = 1 - |x|$

3. $y = |1 - x|$

4. $y = |x^2| - 1$

SOLUTIONS:

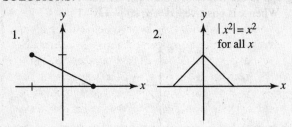

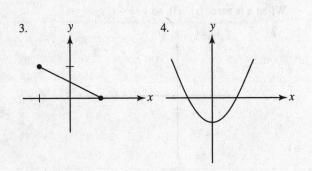

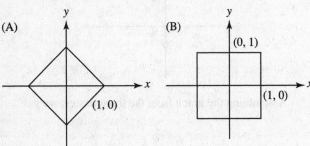

[33] Which of the following is the graph of $|x| = |y|$?

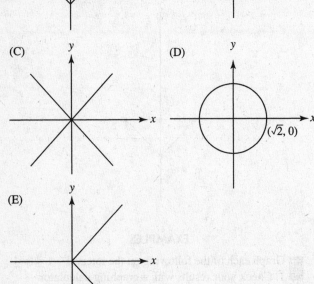

What can you do when a question seems very complicated and you don't have much faith in the answer you

have generated? Let's use this question as an example.

We'll begin by recognizing that $|x| = \pm x$ and $|y| = \pm y$ for appropriate values of x and y. As a result, we might conclude that $y = \pm x$ and choose answer (C) because it combines the graphs of the two lines $y = x$ and $y = -x$.

Perhaps the thought process above leaves us still a bit dissatisfied and doubtful. We can get just a bit more assurance by testing out some of the number pairs we can see to be on those lines. We can make the work easier by picking convenient pairs such as $(1, 1)$, $(-1, -1)$, $(1, -1)$, and $(-1, 1)$. Each of these satisfies the graph we have chosen, which may give us a bit more confidence.

On the other hand, the test points also satisfy choices (B) and (D). However, we can eliminate (B) and (D) by testing point $(0, 0)$, which lies on the graph of (C) but not on either (B) or (D).

TEST-TAKING TIP

Use test cases to verify or reject possible answer choices. Choose convenient numbers. Numbers like 0, 1, and −1 are easy to calculate with and often produce the desired results.

EXAMPLES

Graph each of the following. Verify your answers using 0, 1, and −1 to generate test points.

1. $y = |x|$

2. $x = |y|$

3. $y = |x^2|$

4. $|y| = x^2$

SOLUTIONS:

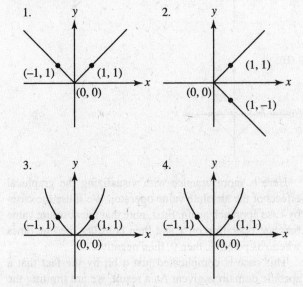

[34] If $f(x) = \sqrt{1-x}$ and $g(x) = x^2 + 1$, which of the following could be the graph of $y = g(f(x))$?

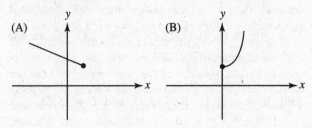

(A)   (B)

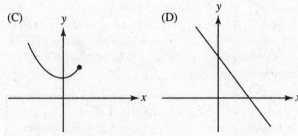

(C)   (D)

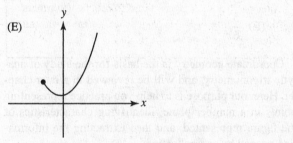

(E)

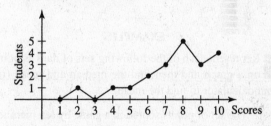

Coordinate geometry is a basic tool for the study of relations and functions. We will provide a detailed review of those topics in a later chapter. Our purpose here is to suggest part of the role coordinate geometry plays in analyzing functions.

The function $g(f(x))$ can be determined by substituting $f(x)$ for x in $g(x)$.

$$\begin{aligned} g(f(x))^2 &= (f(x))^2 + 1 \\ &= (\sqrt{1-x})^2 + 1 \\ &= 1 - x + 1 \\ &= 2 - x. \end{aligned}$$

In other words, performing the algebra produces the function determined by the equation $y = 2 - x$. You will recognize this as a line passing through $(0,2)$ with slope -1.

However, not all points on this line satisfy the original condition. In order for a number to be in the domain of $g(f(x))$, it must be in the domain of $f(x)$. But $f(x)$ will only accept values for which $1 - x \geq 0$, because $1 - x$ is under the radical sign. In the real number system, the radical sign may only operate on nonnegative numbers.

If $1 - x \geq 0$, then $1 \geq x$ and the line cannot extend past $(1,0)$.

EXAMPLES

For the following functions, determine the natural domains (the numbers that don't jam up the mechanism):

1. $f(x) = \sqrt{5x - 3}$

2. $g(x) = \sqrt{x^2 - 4}$

3. $h(x) = \dfrac{x - 1}{x^2 - 1}$

SOLUTIONS: The natural domains are:

1. $5x - 3 \geq 0$, $x \geq \dfrac{3}{5}$

2. $x^2 - 4 \geq 0$, $x \geq 2$ or $x \leq -2$

3. $x^2 - 1 \neq 0$, $x \neq 1$

[35] Twenty students took a ten-question true-false test. The graph below shows the number of students who earned each possible score from 0 to 10. To the nearest tenth, what is the positive difference between the median and the mean for the class?

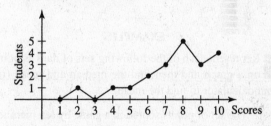

(A) .4

(B) 1

(C) 2

(D) 1.5

(E) 7.6

Statisticians use coordinate geometry to present data. We'll look further at probability and statistics in a later chapter. Here, we are offering this example as practice in seeing how coordinates represent data.

The graph is a visual summary of the information in the following table:

Score	Number of Students
10	4
9	3
8	5
7	3
6	2
5	1
4	1
3	0
2	1
1	0
0	0

In other words, the table indicates that the set of scores was $\{10, 10, 10, 10, 9, 9, 9, 8, 8, 8, 8, 8, 7, 7, 7, 6, 6, 5, 4, 2\}$. We have laboriously written them out so that you are better able to understand the next two steps.

The *mean* for a set of numbers is the common average you are accustomed to calculating. In other words, add up the twenty scores (you should get 151) and divide by 20. The mean is 7.55, rounded to the nearest tenth is 7.6.

See Chapter 2 for a discussion of how to calculate a mean.

The *median* is the number you get if you list all of the scores in order from highest to lowest and count down to the middle. Here, both the tenth and eleventh numbers from the top are 8, so the median is 8. (If the tenth and eleventh numbers had been different from each other, the median would be the average of the tenth and eleventh numbers.)

The difference between the mean and the median here is .4.

EXAMPLES

Represent each of the following sets of data as points on a graph and then find the median and mean (use your calculator to find the mean):

1. The set of points scored in a game by ten members of a basketball team were $\{28, 12, 12, 11, 6, 6, 6, 4, 4, 0\}$.

2. The number of heads showing when a pair of coins was tossed 12 times was $\{0, 2, 1, 2, 1, 0, 2, 2, 1, 0, 1, 1\}$.

3. The number of runs scored by a baseball team in the first eleven games of the season was $\{0, 3, 4, 2, 1, 3, 2, 0, 4, 5, 1\}$.

SOLUTIONS: The results are:

1. $\{(28, 1), (12, 2), (11, 1), (6, 3), (4, 2) (0, 1)\}$, median = 6, mean = $\frac{79}{10} = 7.9$.

2. $\{(0, 3), (1, 5) (2, 4)\}$, median = 1, mean = $\frac{16}{12} = \frac{4}{3} \doteq 1.3$.

3. $\{(0, 2), (1, 2), (2, 2), (3, 2), (4, 2), (5, 1)\}$, median = 2, mean = $\frac{25}{11} \doteq 2.3$.

[36]   If $A = (1,1)$, $B = (5,1)$, and $C = (5,6)$, $\tan \angle ACB = ?$

(A) $\dfrac{6}{5}$

(B) $\dfrac{5}{4}$

(C) $\dfrac{4}{5}$

(D) $\dfrac{2}{3}$

(E) $\dfrac{5}{6}$

Coordinate geometry is the basis for the study of analytic trigonometry, and will be reviewed in a later chapter. Here, our purpose is to help you practice representing points in a number plane, identifying characteristics of the figure represented, and then extracting the information needed by an application.

For this question, first graph the points:

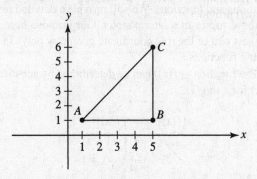

You should immediately recognize this as a right triangle because B and C are on the same vertical line, and A and B are on the same horizontal line. This makes the work of calculating the tangent much easier than otherwise. Because $\angle B$ is a right angle, $\tan \angle A = \frac{BC}{AB}$. From the coordinates of the points, you can see that $BC = 5$ and $AB = 4$. Therefore, $\tan \angle A = \frac{5}{4}$.

EXAMPLES

Using the given information for the question above note each of the following:

1. $AC = \sqrt{25 + 16} = \sqrt{41} \doteq 6.4$

2. $\sin \angle A = \dfrac{5}{\sqrt{41}} \doteq .78$

3. $\cos \angle A = \dfrac{4}{\sqrt{41}} \doteq .62$

4. $\sin \angle C = \dfrac{4}{\sqrt{41}} \doteq .62$

5. $\tan \angle C = \dfrac{4}{5} = .8$

STUDYING INVERSE VARIATION

[37] Which of the following is a vertex of the hyperbola $xy = -9$?

(A) $(3,0)$

(B) $(0,3)$

(C) $(3,3)$

(D) $(-3,3)$

(E) None of these

An equation important to the study of inverse variation (and the only conic we will study that has an xy term) is the rectangular hyperbola, $xy = k$, where the constant k is any real number. A study of a sample graph (for $xy = 1$, below) provides the required information.

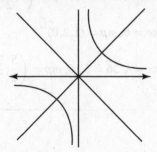

The axes of symmetry are the lines $y = \pm x$, and the asymptotes are the x and y axes. Since the vertices are the points of intersection of the hyperbola with the major axis, $y = x$, they can be found by substituting y for x in the equation and solving. We will not discuss the foci.

When k is negative, the asymptotes are still the coordinate axes, but the major axis is the line $y = -x$ and the vertices are found by substituting $-x$ for y in the equation and solving. The branches of these hyperbolas will lie in quadrants II and IV.

In the multiple-choice question,

$$xy = -9.$$

Replace y by $-x$ and solve for x:

$$-x^2 = -9,$$
$$x^2 = 9,$$
$$x = \pm 3.$$

Since $y = -x$, the vertices are $(3, -3)$ and $(-3, 3)$.

EXAMPLES

For each of the following find the vertices and indicate which quadrants the branches of the graph will lie in:

1. $xy = 16$

2. $xy = -1$

3. $xy = -12$

4. $xy = \dfrac{1}{4}$

SOLUTIONS: The results are:

1. $(4,4)$, $(-4,-4)$, I and III

2. $(1,-1)$, $(-1,1)$, II and IV

3. $(2\sqrt{3}, -2\sqrt{3})$, $(-2\sqrt{3}, 2\sqrt{3})$, II and IV

4. $\left(\dfrac{1}{2}, \dfrac{1}{2}\right)$, $\left(-\dfrac{1}{2}, -\dfrac{1}{2}\right)$, I and III

[38] The number of hours it takes to type a manuscript varies inversely with the number of typists assigned to the job. If it takes three typists 36 hours to complete a manuscript, how many hours will four typists take to do the job?

(A) 27

(B) 25

(C) 20

(D) 12

(E) 18

Inverse variation is part of our chapter on coordinate geometry only because problems involving it may be solved by using the equation $xy = k$, where x and y represent the: two quantities that vary inversely with respect to each other and k is the constant of variation.

In the given question let x represent the number of typists and y the number of hours; then

$$(1) \qquad\qquad xy = k$$

expresses the relationship between them. Once k is determined, equation (1) can be used to find the number of typists needed to do the job in a specified time or the number of hours the job will take for a given number of typists.

The constant k can be found by using the given information of three typists and 36 hours:

(2) $(3)(36) = k = 108,$

and equation (1) becomes

(3) $xy = 108.$

Let $x = 4$ and solve (3) to answer the question.

WORKING IN THREE-DIMENSIONAL COORDINATE GEOMETRY

[39] If point O is the origin and point P is (3, 4, 12), what is the distance between P and M, where M is the midpoint of segment OP?

(A) $6\frac{1}{2}$

(B) 4

(C) 9

(D) 7

(E) 3

Many of the formulas for plane coordinate geometry can be extended to space. In three-dimensional coordinate geometry, each point of space is represented by an ordered triple of numbers where each number is found in terms of the projected distance along each of three perpendicular axes as shown.

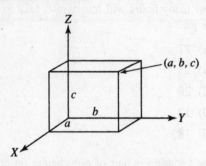

The distance between any two points (x_1, y_1, z_1) and (x_2, y_2, z_2) is given by

$$\sqrt{(x_1 - x_2)^2 + (y_1 - y_2)^2 + (z_1 - z_2)^2}.$$

The midpoint of the segment connecting them is

$$\left(\frac{x_1 + x_2}{2}, \frac{y_1 + y_2}{2}, \frac{z_1 + z_2}{2} \right).$$

If you compare these with the corresponding formulas in sections [11] and [5] of this chapter you will see the great similarity.

The question above can be answered quite simply without using the midpoint formula, however. Just find the distance between the origin and point P, then divide it by 2.

$$\begin{aligned} OP &= \sqrt{(3-0)^2 + (4-0)^2 + (12-0)^2} \\ &= \sqrt{9 + 16 + 144} \\ &= \sqrt{169} \\ &= 13 \end{aligned}$$

Therefore

$$OM = \frac{1}{2} \qquad OP = 6\frac{1}{2}.$$

EXAMPLES

Use your calculator to find the distance between the following pairs of points and the midpoints of the segments that contain them.

1. (1, 1, 2), (2, −1, 1)

2. (0, 1, 0), (0, 0, 1)

3. (1, 2, 3), (1, 2, −3)

4. (3, 4, 6), (2, −1, 6)

SOLUTIONS: The results are:

1. Distance $= \sqrt{6} \doteq 2.45$, $mp = \left(\frac{3}{2}, 0, \frac{3}{2} \right)$

2. Distance $= \sqrt{2} \doteq 1.41$, $mp = \left(0, \frac{1}{2}, \frac{1}{2} \right)$

3. Distance $= 6$, $mp = (1, 2, 0)$

4. Distance $= \sqrt{26} \doteq 5.10$, $mp = \left(\frac{5}{2}, \frac{3}{2}, 0 \right)$

[40] If the circle shown is tangent to the x- and y-axes, and (a,b) is the center, how is a related to b?

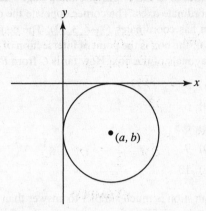

(A) $a = b$

(B) $a < b$

(C) $a = -b$

(D) $a + b = 1$

(E) $ab = 1$

The center of a circle is equidistant from all points of the circle, so (a,b) is the same distance from each point of tangency.

Therefore, a and b are equal in absolute value. Because (a,b) is in Quadrant IV, however, a is positive and b is negative. Therefore, a is the opposite of b, which is answer (C).

The most common wrong answer in our test group was (A), which fails to take into consideration that y-coordinates are negative in the fourth quadrant.

The problem many students have with a question like this is the realization that b can be negative without a negative sign in front of it. Because $b < 0$, the opposite of b, $-b$, is positive. The "$-$" sign in front does not make the number negative; for b in this question, the "$-$" sign makes $-b$ positive!

[41] If $\dfrac{x}{a} + \dfrac{y}{b} = 1$ contains the point $(-1, 0)$, which of the following must be true?

(A) $a = 0$

(B) $a = 1$

(C) $a = -1$

(D) $a = b$

(E) No value is possible

A true "SAT" question! Substitute and transform. Replace x with -1 and y with 0, the coordinates of the point $(-1, 0)$. That gives you $\dfrac{-1}{a} = 1$. Now transform by multiplying both sides by a to get $-1 = a$, answer (C).

Looks good, but that final choice, (E), makes you wonder if you have fallen into a trap because you know nothing about b yet. Suppose b turned out to be a number that made the equation impossible?

To allay your doubts, consider this an "SAT II" question—substitute and transform twice.

You've already done one substitution to find $a = -1$.

Now substitute $a = -1$ to get $-x + \dfrac{y}{b} = 1$ and then transform by solving for y. That gives you $y = b(x) + b$. From this form, you know that the given equation is actually a line for which both the slope and y-intercept are b. That means b can be any real number except 0 (to avoid division by 0 in the original equation). So the original equation is that of a line that passes through $(-1, 0)$ and $(b, 0)$, where b is any real number except 0.

In this case, examining choice (E) proved to be a waste of time.

[42] The parabola shown has V as its vertex and is the graph of which of the following?

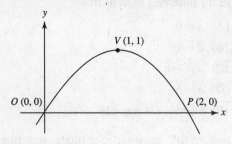

(A) $y = x^2 + 1$

(B) $y = x(2 - x)$

(C) $y = 1 - x^2$

(D) $y = 2 - x^2$

(E) $y = x^2 - 2x$

Equations of the form $y = x(a - x)$ are popular with test makers because they represent some types of real-world situations. They have graphs that go through the origin, which happens with many common applications for which the data begin with $x = 0$.

Furthermore, functions of this form rise from 0 to a highest point and then fall back to the intercept on the x-axis, as though following the path of a thrown ball (one of such applications).

Because this graph has intercepts at $x = 0$ and $x = 2$, the two factors of the function are x and either $(x - 2)$ or $(2 - x)$. Both (B) and (E) meet this condition. (Factor (E) into $x(x - 2)$ if this is not immediately apparent to you.)

The graph rises and falls, which only happens when the coefficient of x^2 in the product is negative. Therefore, we suspect that the correct answer is $y = x(2 - x)$, (B).

The only possible sticking point, however, is V. If V does not make the equation true, then $y = x(2 - x)$ can't be correct. Replacing x by 1 produces 1, so V is on the graph.

Note that the coordinates of V do not make answer choice (E) correct. Therefore, you would have been able to discard this choice even if you had not realized the need for the coefficient of x^2 to be negative.

[43] A rectangular box is positioned in a three-dimensional coordinate system so that one corner is at the origin and three edges lie in coordinate axes. The corner opposite the origin has coordinates $P(-4, 3, 12)$. The center, C, of the box is the point of intersection of the diagonals of the box. How far is C from P?

(A) 5

(B) 6

(C) 6.5

(D) 9

(E) 13

The question is much simpler to answer than it seems. From the given information, you can see that C is the midpoint of the diagonal. Therefore, PC is half the distance from P to the origin $(0, 0, 0)$.

Find PO by using the distance formula.

$$\sqrt{(-4 - 0)^2 + (3 - 0)^2 + (12 - 0)^2} = \sqrt{169} = 13.$$

Not so fast—don't choose (E) just because you have that answer staring you in the face. Remember that the question asks for the distance to the center, which is only half of 13 or 6.5, (C).

[44] Which of the following is the graph of $y = x - |x|$?

(A)

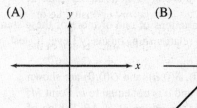

(B)

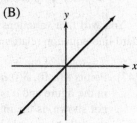

(C)

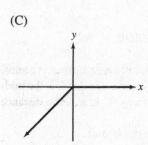

(D)

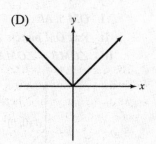

(E)

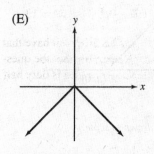

When confronted with a question involving $|x|$, use the definition of $|x|$.

$$|x| = \begin{cases} x, & \text{for } x \geq 0 \\ -x, & \text{for } x < 0 \end{cases}$$

For this function,

$$y = x - |x| = \begin{cases} x - x, & \text{for } x \geq 0 \\ x - (-x), & \text{for } x < 0 \end{cases} = \begin{cases} 0, & \text{for } x \geq 0 \\ 2x, & \text{for } x < 0 \end{cases}$$

Therefore, when $x \geq 0$, the graph is $x = 0$, which is the x-axis. At this point, the answer could be (A) or (C).

When $x < 0$, the graph is $y = 2x$, which eliminates (A). Because you don't have coordinates in (C), you may not be completely convinced that the ray on the left side of the graph satisfies the condition $y = 2x$. However, you have eliminated all other possibilities. Furthermore, there is no information given about the scale of the axis, so the left ray can really be the graph of any $y = kx$ as long as k is positive (which tells you the line is rising because the slope is positive).

[45] If k is any real number, the slope of $2x - 3y = k$ is ?

(A) Any real number

(B) 2

(C) -3

(D) $\dfrac{2}{3}$

(E) Cannot be determined

When the equation of a line is written in $y = mx + b$ form, the slope of the line is m and the y-intercept is b.

The given equation may be transformed to slope-intercept form by first subtracting $2x$ from both sides of the equation and then dividing each side by -3.

$$\begin{aligned} 2x - 3y &= k \\ -3y &= -2x + k \\ y &= \left(\frac{2}{3}\right)x + \left(\frac{-k}{3}\right) \end{aligned}$$

As you can see, the slope is $\frac{2}{3}$, (D).

Two of the five answer choices, (A) and (E), were distracters intended to make you think about the role of k, for which the value is unknown. Because k can be any real number, you might talk yourself into choosing (A). Further, because the value of k is unknown, you might be attracted to (E). However, the value of k is unrelated to the slope because it does not affect the coefficient of the x term in the $y = mx + b$ form of the equation.

[46]   If M is the midpoint of segment AB with coordinates shown in the diagram, which of the following is not the equation of a line containing two points of the set A, B, C, and M?

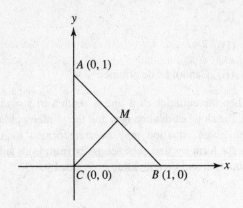

(A) $x = 0$

(B) $y = 0$

(C) $y = x$

(D) $y = 1 - x$

(E) $y = 1 + x$

In the figure, four lines go through pairs of points taken from among A, B, C, and M.

Line AC is a vertical line with equation $x = 0$; therefore (A) is true.

Line BC is a horizontal line with equation $y = 0$; therefore (B) is true.

Line MC goes through the midpoint of AB, so its coordinates are $(\frac{1}{2}, \frac{1}{2})$ from the midpoint formula. Its slope is 1 and y-intercept is 0. Therefore, the equation of MC is $y = x$, and (C) is true.

Line AB has slope -1 and y-intercept 1. Its equation is $y = -x + 1$ or $y = 1 - x$. Therefore, (D) is true.

The line with equation $y = 1 + x$ has slope 1 and y-intercept 1. It passes through $(0, 1)$ and rises to the right. No line in the figure has those characteristics. Therefore (E) is false, which makes it the correct answer.

The question uses facts you should have at your fingertips.

1. The equation of the y-axis is $x = 0$, and all vertical lines have equations $x = k$ where k is the x-intercept.

2. The equation of the x-axis is $y = 0$, and all horizontal lines have equations $y = k$, where k is the y-intercept.

3. The line with equation $y = x$ bisects the first and third quadrants, and all lines passing through the origin have equations of the form $y = kx$, except the vertical line $x = 0$.

4. The line with equation $y + x = 1$ has x-intercept 1 and y-intercept 1.

You will find variations of one or more of these standard line-equation relationships on every Level IC test.

[47]   Points $A(a, 0)$, $B(0, b)$, and $O(0, 0)$ are shown in the figure and a is not equal to b. Point M, not shown, is the midpoint of AB. Which of the following could be true?

   I. $OM \perp AB$

   II. Ray OM bisects $\angle AOB$

   III. $\angle OMB = \angle OMA$

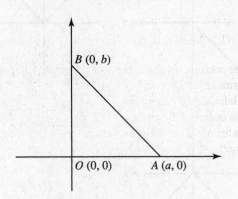

(Figure is not drawn to scale.)

(A) I only

(B) II only

(C) I and II only

(D) I and III only

(E) All of I, II, and III

Pay attention to the statement that the figure is not drawn to scale. It is drawn as though $a = b$, but you are given that a and b are not equal. If you position point M at the midpoint of segment AB, all of I, II, and III will look true.

What if statement I is true? Then $\triangle OMB$ is congruent to $\triangle OMA$ by side-angle-side. Therefore $OB = OA$ and $a = b$, which contradicts the given information.

What if statement II is true? Is $\triangle OMB$ congruent to $\triangle OMA$ by any theorem or postulate? The correspondence is SSA, which is not a congruence. Therefore OB does not have to equal OA and the given information is not contradicted.

What if statement III is true? Then $\triangle OMB$ is again congruent to $\triangle OMA$ by side-angle-side. Therefore $OB = OA$ and $a = b$, which contradicts the given information.

As a result, only II is true, (B).

Don't forget to play the what-if game, which is based on the principles of indirect proof you learned in your geometry course.

[48] If $(0,0)$ and $(6,8)$ are opposite ends of the diameter of a circle, which of the following must be true?

    I. The center of the circle is $(3,4)$.

    II. The radius of the circle is 5.

    III. The circle is tangent to the x-axis.

    (A) I only

    (B) II only

    (C) I and II only

    (D) I and III only

    (E) All of I, II, and III

The solution involves two straightforward applications of formulas and the ability to visualize the figure from a few defining characteristics.

The center of the circle is the midpoint of the diameter. From the midpoint formula, the center is $(3,4)$. Therefore, I is true.

The distance from the origin (one end of the diameter) to the center $(3,4)$ can be found using the distance formula.

$$\sqrt{(3-0)^2+(4-0)^2} = \sqrt{3^2+4^2}$$
$$= 5$$

(We hope you are now so familiar with 3-4-5 right triangles that you do not have to go through those steps!)

Therefore, II is true.

Statement III may look true for an instant because the circle passes through $(0, 0)$, which means it touches both the x- and y-axes. But it also intersects the axes at the points $(6,0)$ and $(0,8)$, which you can see by visualizing the similar triangles formed in the figure by the 3-4-5 and 6-8-10 triangles. Therefore, the answer is (C).

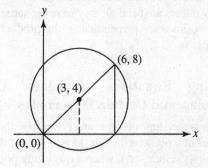

WHAT YOU SHOULD KNOW

KEY CONCEPTS

Handling Points and Lines

1. The distance between two points on a number line is the absolute value of the difference of their coordinates.
2. To every point in a plane there corresponds an ordered pair of numbers.
3. Every nonvertical line has exactly one slope.
4. If a line is vertical, it has no slope.
5. If a line is horizontal, its slope is zero.
6. If two lines are parallel, they have the same slope.
7. If two lines are perpendicular, the product of their slopes is -1.

Handling Equations of Lines, Circles, Parabolas, and Certain Hyperbolas

1. If m is the slope of a line and (x_1, y_1) are the coordinates of a point on the line, an equation of the line is $(y - y_1) = m(x - x_1)$, where (x, y) is any point of the line.
2. If m is the slope of a line and b is its y-intercept, an equation of the line is $y = mx + b$, where (x, y) is any point of the line.
3. If (h, k) is the center of a circle and r its radius, then $(x - h)^2 + (y - k)^2 = r^2$ is an equation of the circle, where (x, y) is any point of the circle.
4. The graph of $y = ax^2 + bx$ is a parabola. Factor and solve for x when $y = 0$ and you will find its intercepts at $(0, 0)$ and $\left(-\dfrac{b}{a}, 0\right)$. The axis of symmetry bisects the segment connecting the x-intercepts, producing $x = -\dfrac{b}{2a}$. To find the vertex, substitute $-\dfrac{b}{2a}$ for x.
5. The graph of $y = ax^2 + c$ is a parabola with y-axis symmetry and y-intercept at $(0, c)$. To find the x-intercepts, let $y = 0$ and solve for x to get $x = \pm\sqrt{\dfrac{-c}{a}}$. When the radicand, $\dfrac{-c}{a}$, is negative, the parabola has no x-intercepts.

Handling Graphs

1. To find the y-intercepts of the graph of an equation in x and y, replace x by zero and solve for y.
2. To find the x-intercepts of the graph of an equation in x and y, replace y by zero and solve for x.

KEY FORMULAS

If the endpoints of a segment are (x_1, y_1) and (x_2, y_2), then:

1. The midpoint $M = \left(\dfrac{x_1 + x_2}{2}, \dfrac{y_1 + y_2}{2}\right)$.
2. The slope m of the line $= \dfrac{y_2 - y_1}{x_2 - x_1}$.
3. The distance between the points $=$
$$\sqrt{(x_1 - x_2)^2 + (y_1 - y_2)^2}.$$

TEST-TAKING STRATEGIES

- Look for coordinate geometry questions that can be answered most quickly by:
  - checking each choice in turn to find the correct one,
  - eliminating some choices by direct calculation, *or*
  - using the technique of transformation, that is, putting all choices in the same form.
- Test questions involve both coordinate systems on a line and coordinate systems in a plane. Make sure you understand which is pertinent to the test question. You are likely to get confused when an equation in one variable is given. Such an equation can represent either a point on a line or a line (either vertical or horizontal) in a plane. Consult the given information to determine which is intended.
- Many beginning students are surprised to find that numbers in radical form represent finite lengths. Make sure you understand this so you don't discard a radical answer when the question asks for a length.
- Do not use decimal approximations for radicals unless the question specifically requests an approximation or the answer choices are in decimal form.
- When applying the slope formula, check yourself by asking four questions. Are both numbers in the numerator y-coordinates? Are both numbers in the denominator x-coordinates? Do the first numbers on top and bottom come from the same point? Do the second numbers on top and bottom come from the same point? The most common errors in applying the slope formula come from putting the numbers in the wrong places.

- To remember the midpoint formula, remember that the coordinates of the midpoint are the averages of the corresponding coordinates of the endpoints. The midpoint formula is the only formula in which the coordinates are added rather than subtracted.

CALCULATOR SKILLS

Learn how to use your absolute value key to find the absolute value of numerical expressions. Be sure to enter parentheses before and after the expression for which you wish to find the absolute value.

ANSWERS

[1] (D)	[9] (B)	[17] (C)	[25] (B)	[33] (C)	[41] (C)
[2] (B)	[10] (E)	[18] (C)	[26] (A)	[34] (A)	[42] (B)
[3] (D)	[11] (E)	[19] (B)	[27] (A)	[35] (A)	[43] (C)
[4] (E)	[12] (B)	[20] (E)	[28] (D)	[36] (B)	[44] (C)
[5] (D)	[13] (C)	[21] (C)	[29] (B)	[37] (D)	[45] (D)
[6] (A)	[14] (B)	[22] (D)	[30] (B)	[38] (A)	[46] (D)
[7] (C)	[15] (B)	[23] (C)	[31] (A)	[39] (A)	[47] (B)
[8] (E)	[16] (D)	[24] (D)	[32] (E)	[40] (C)	[48] (C)

QUADRATIC EQUATIONS

CHAPTER

18

KEY TERMS

quadratic equation   an equation of the form $ax^2 + bx + c = 0$, where $a \neq 0$.

trinomial square   the square of a linear binomial of the form $ax + b$.

FACTORING QUADRATICS

[1] For what value of k will the equation $x^2 - k = 0$ have the two solutions $\sqrt{2}$ and $\sqrt{-2}$?

(A) ± 2

(B) 2

(C) $\pm\sqrt{2}$

(D) $\sqrt{2}$

(E) $\pm\sqrt{-2}$

A *quadratic equation* is an equation of the form $ax^2 + bx + c = 0$, where $a \neq 0$. The equation above exemplifies the simplest type of quadratic:

$$x^2 + c = 0 \qquad (a = 1, b = 0).$$

The first step in understanding the solution of any quadratic is to realize the circumstances for which any statement of the form $mn = 0$ is true. It should be clear that no product of two numbers can ever equal zero unless one (or both) of the factors is zero.

Our procedure for finding solutions of quadratics, then, is to represent them as products of linear factors and then to discover which values of the variables cause these factors to equal zero.

The simple quadratic $x^2 + c = 0$ is factorable in the real number system only when c is negative.

EXAMPLE 1

Solve the equation $x^2 - 16 = 0$.

SOLUTION: The expression $x^2 - 16$ is the difference of squares and can be factored as follows:

$$(x - 4)(x + 4) = 0.$$

What values of x will make each of these factors equal zero? In other words, for which values of x is the statement

$$x - 4 = 0 \quad \text{or} \quad x + 4 = 0$$

true? The solutions must be 4 and -4. By similar reasoning we can state the following:

18-1 If $x^2 - k = 0$, where k is positive, then $(x - \sqrt{k})(x + \sqrt{k}) = 0$ and $x = \pm\sqrt{k}$.

EXAMPLE 2

Find x if $9x^2 - 36 = 0$.

SOLUTION: If $9x^2 - 36 = 0$, then $x^2 - 4 = 0$. Thus $x^2 = 4$ and $x = \pm 2$.

EXAMPLE 3

Find x if $3x^2 - 2 = 0$.

SOLUTION: Divide both sides of the equation by 3 to get

$$x^2 - \frac{2}{3} = 0.$$

Then

$$x^2 = \frac{2}{3}$$

and

$$x = \pm\sqrt{\frac{2}{3}} = \pm\frac{\sqrt{6}}{3} \qquad \text{(approximately .816)}.$$

[2] What is the value of b if the roots of the equation $x^2 - 5bx + 4b^2 = 0$ are 2 and 8?

(A) 1

(B) 2

(C) 3

(D) 4

(E) 5

Many trinomial quadratics (those for that $b \neq 0$) are also factorable into linear factors as we saw in section [7] of Chapter 8. To discover the circumstances under which this will occur, we will build a sample trinomial from the linear factors $x + m$ and $x + n$:

$$(x + m)(x + n) = x^2 + (m + n)x + mn.$$

The clue to factorization is thus to find a pair of numbers, m and n, such that their product is the constant term and their sum is the coefficient of the x term.

EXAMPLE 1

Find the solutions of $x^2 + 10x + 21 = 0$.

SOLUTION: We must find a pair of numbers whose product is 21 and whose sum is 10. Through trial and error (or insight developed with practice) we select 7 and 3. Thus

$$x^2 + 10x + 21 = 0,$$
$$(x + 7)(x + 3) = 0.$$

Since the product of two factors can be zero only when one of these factors is zero, we are interested in finding the values for which $(x + 7) = 0$ or $(x + 3) = 0$. Simple algebra indicates the solutions to be -7 and -3.

EXAMPLE 2

Solve the equation $2x^2 + 9x - 5 = 0$.

SOLUTION: Through practice in your Algebra I course you should have developed skills that will allow you to factor $2x^2 + 9x - 5^2$ in your head. If you do not have this facility, you can try dividing both sides of the equation by 2 to get

$$x^2 + \frac{9}{2}x - \frac{5}{2} = 0,$$

and attempt to discover two numbers with a product of $-\frac{5}{2}$ and a sum of $\frac{9}{2}$. Since the denominator of $\frac{9}{2}$ is 2, such a fraction must result from the addition of two fractions with denominators of 2 and such fractions will yield a product with denominator 4. With this in mind we change $-\frac{5}{2}$ to $-\frac{10}{4}$ and note from this the numbers $\frac{10}{2}$ and $-\frac{1}{2}$, which yield factors of

$$\left(x - \frac{1}{2}\right)\left(x + \frac{10}{2}\right) = 0$$

and roots of $\frac{1}{2}$ and $-\frac{10}{2} = -5$.

In the event that you are equally unable to master this method, this will prove little handicap in the solution of quadratics since we will review two other, more mechanical methods in later sections.

In the multiple-choice question the equation $x^2 - 5bx + 4b^2 = 0$ can be factored into $(x - 4b)(x - b) = 0$, with roots represented by $4b$ and b. If the values of these roots are 2 and 8, then $b = 2$.

USING TRINOMIAL SQUARES

[3]   For what value of k is $x^2 - \frac{4}{5}x + k$ a trinomial square?

(A) 5

(B) $-\frac{4}{9}$

(C) $\frac{4}{9}$

(D) $\frac{4}{25}$

(E) $-\frac{4}{25}$

The term *trinomial square* applies to expressions that are the squares of linear binomials of the form $(ax + b)$. The simplest of these is the expansion of $(x + b)^2$:

$$(x + b)^2 = x^2 + 2bx + b^2.$$

In the equation above, the coefficient of the x term is $2b$ and the constant is b^2. In other words, the constant term

is the square of half the coefficient of the x term, when the coefficient of the x^2 term is 1.

EXAMPLE 1

In each of the following replace the question mark with a constant making the trinomial a square:

1. $x^2 + 4x + ?$

2. $x^2 + ?x + 16$

3. $x^2 + 5x + ?$

4. $x^2 + ?x + 7$

SOLUTIONS:

1. The constant must be the square of half of 4 or $(2)^2$, giving $x^2 + 4x + 4$.

2. 16 is the square of half of the second coefficient, but 16 is the square of either 4 or -4. Hence the question mark is 8 or -8, giving $x^2 + 8x + 16$ or $x^2 - 8x + 16$.

3. Half of 5 is $\frac{5}{2}$, which when squared is $\frac{25}{4}$.

4. 7 is the square of either $\sqrt{7}$ or $\sqrt{-7}$, so the second coefficient can be either $2\sqrt{7}$ or $-2\sqrt{7}$.

EXAMPLE 2

Add a constant to both sides of $3x^2 + 4x + 5 = 0$ so that one side of the equation is a trinomial square.

SOLUTION: If $3x^2 + 4x + 5 = 0$, then $x^2 + \frac{4}{3}x + \frac{5}{3} = 0$. Thus:

$$x^2 + \frac{4}{3}x = -\frac{5}{3}$$

We complete the trinomial square on the left side by adding $\frac{4}{9}$ to both sides:

$$x^2 + \frac{4}{3}x + \frac{4}{9} = \frac{4}{9} - \frac{5}{3},$$
$$\left(x + \frac{2}{3}\right)^2 = -\frac{11}{9}.$$

Would you now be able to find the roots of this equation? There will be more about this in the next section.

In the multiple-choice question, the trinomial is a square if

$$k = \left(\frac{1}{2}\left(\frac{4}{5}\right)\right)^2$$
$$= \left(\frac{2}{5}\right)^2$$
$$= \frac{4}{25}.$$

EXAMPLES

Add a constant to both sides of each equation so that one side is a trinomial square.

1. If $x^2 + 2x = 8$, then $x^2 + 2x + 1 = 9$.

2. If $x^2 + 3x = 2$, then $x^2 + 3x + \dfrac{9}{4} = \dfrac{17}{4}$.

[4] Which of the following are the roots of the equation $(x+5)^2 - 3 = 0$?

(A) $\sqrt{3}$

(B) $\pm\sqrt{3}$

(C) -5

(D) ± 5

(E) $-5 \pm \sqrt{3}$

Any quadratic equation, whether readily factorable or not, can be solved by completing the square and using the fact that when $x^2 = k$, then $x = \pm\sqrt{k}$.

EXAMPLE 1

Find the roots of $x^2 + 9x - 10 = 0$.

SOLUTION: Though this quadratic is readily factorable, $(x + 10)(x - 1) = 0$, we will use it to show the method of completing the square. First transform the equation so that the constant term is the right member:

$$x^2 + 9x = 10.$$

Then add to both sides the number that makes the left side a square trinomial:

$$x^2 + 9x + \frac{81}{4} = 10 + \frac{81}{4},$$

$$\left(x + \frac{9}{2}\right)^2 = \frac{121}{4},$$

$$x + \frac{9}{2} = \pm\frac{11}{2},$$

$$x = -\frac{9}{2} \pm \frac{11}{2}.$$

Therefore $x = 1$ or -10.

EXAMPLE 2

Solve $4x^2 + 6x - 9 = 0$.

SOLUTION: Divide both members by 4

$$x^2 + \frac{3}{2}x - \frac{9}{4} = 0,$$

$$x^2 + \frac{3}{2}x = \frac{9}{4}.$$

Complete the square:

$$x^2 + \frac{3}{2}x + \frac{9}{16} = \frac{9}{4} + \frac{9}{16},$$

$$\left(x + \frac{3}{4}\right)^2 = \frac{45}{16},$$

$$x = -\frac{3}{4} \pm \frac{\sqrt{45}}{4}$$

$$(\doteq -.927 \text{ and } -2.427).$$

In the multiple-choice question, the process of solution is similar to several steps in the process of solving by completing the square:

$$(x+5)^2 - 3 = 0,$$

$$(x+5)^2 = 3,$$

$$x + 5 = \pm\sqrt{3},$$

$$x = -5 \pm \sqrt{3}$$

$$(\doteq -3.268 \text{ and } -6.732).$$

USING THE QUADRATIC FORMULA

[5] If $7x^2 - 12x + 3 = 0$, then $x = ?$

(A) Only 1.41

(B) 1.41 or .30

(C) Only $-.30$

(D) $\dfrac{-6 \pm \sqrt{15}}{7} - .30$ or -1.41

(E) No real number

In the preceding section we reviewed a method for solving any quadratic equation regardless of its factorability. The technique used provides the means for deriving a formula that will always yield the roots of a quadratic when the coefficients are known. We will state without proof:

18-2 If $ax^2 + bx + c = 0$ and $a \neq 0$, then

$$x = \frac{-b \pm \sqrt{b^2 - 4ac}}{2a}.$$

The above formula is called the "Quadratic Formula."

EXAMPLE

Find the roots of $x^2 - 8x + 6 = 0$.

SOLUTION: The coefficients are $a = 1$, $b = -8$, and $c = 6$. By formula:

$$x = \frac{-(-8) \pm \sqrt{64 - 24}}{2}$$

 $= 4 \pm \sqrt{10}$ (approximately 7.162 and .838).

In the multiple-choice question, since

$$7x^2 - 12x + 3 = 0,$$

$$x = \frac{-(-12) \pm \sqrt{(-12)^2 - 4(7)(3)}}{2(7)}$$

$$= \frac{12 \pm \sqrt{60}}{14}$$

$$= \frac{12 \pm 2\sqrt{15}}{14}$$

 $= \dfrac{6 \pm \sqrt{15}}{7}$ (approximately 1.410 and 304)

EXAMPLES

Use the Quadratic Formula to find the roots of the following. (Use your calculator to approximate your answers to the nearest tenth):

1. $2x^2 - x - 5 = 0$

2. $3x^2 + 10x - 4 = 0$

3. $x^2 - 5x + 6 = 0$

SOLUTIONS:

1. $\dfrac{1 \pm \sqrt{41}}{4}$ (approximately 3.702 and −2.702)

2. $\dfrac{-5 \pm \sqrt{37}}{3}$ (approximately −3.694 and .361)

3. $\{3, 2\}$

EXPRESSING INFORMATION AS A QUADRATIC EQUATION

[6]　If the length of a rectangle exceeds its width by 1 foot, and if its area is 2 square feet, find the dimensions of the rectangle.

(A) $1' \times 2'$

(B) $2' \times 3'$

(C) $\sqrt{2}' \times \sqrt{2}'$

(D) $\dfrac{3'}{2} \times 3'$

(E) No such rectangle is possible

Many common verbal problems can be resolved by first expressing the information given as a quadratic equation.

EXAMPLE 1

If the product of two numbers is 12 and the first exceeds the second by 1, find the numbers.

SOLUTION: Let x represent the smaller number; then $x + 1$ will represent the larger and $x(x + 1)$ will represent their product.

$$x(x + 1) = 12$$
$$x^2 + x - 12 = 0$$
$$(x + 4)(x - 3) = 0$$

Thus the smaller number can be either −4 or 3, and the larger −3 or 4.

EXAMPLE 2

An artist paints a picture that is 12 inches by 10 inches. He decides to put a uniform border around the picture that will have an area that is $\frac{4}{10}$ the area of the painting. What is the width of this border?

SOLUTION: Let x represent the width of the border. Then the total width of the painting and mounting will be $10 + 2x$ and the total length $12 + 2x$. The total area will be represented by $(10 + 2x)(12 + 2x)$. But the area of the painting is $12 \times 10 = 120$ and the area of the border is $\frac{4}{10}(120) = 48$. Therefore

$$(10 + 2x)(12 + 2x) = 120 + 48,$$

which simplifies to

$$(x + 12)(x - 1) = 0.$$

Since x is −12 or 1, the border must be 1 inch in width. The equation yields the root −12, but this answer is not applicable to the problem.

To answer the multiple-choice question, let x be the width. Then $x+1$ represents the length and $x(x+1)$ is the area. Therefore:

$$x(x+1) = 2,$$
$$x^2+x-2 = 0,$$
$$(x+2)(x-1) = 0,$$
$$x = -2 \text{ or } x = 1.$$

The solution -2 is extraneous since the width of a rectangle must be positive.

TEST-TAKING TIP

Checking the answer choices may be an even quicker way of selecting the correct answer than solving the equation. Choices (B) and (D) give the wrong area, (C) has the wrong relationship between length and width, (A) has the right area and the right length-width relationship—both can be seen by inspection.

SOLVING NONQUADRATIC EQUATIONS

[7] Find the values of x if

$$(x^2 - 3x)^2 - 2(x^2 - 3x) = 8.$$

(A) $\{-1,1\}$

(B) $\{2,1\}$

(C) $\{4,-1\}$

(D) $\{4,-1,2,1\}$

(E) $\{4,-1,-2,1\}$

Some equations, though not quadratic in themselves, can be solved by using the techniques developed for the solution of quadratic equations.

EXAMPLE 1

Find x if $x^4 - 3x^2 - 4 = 0$.

SOLUTION: Let $u = x^2$; then $x^4 - 3x^2 - 4 = 0$ can be rewritten as:

$$u^2 - 3u - 4 = 0,$$
$$(u-4)(u+1) = 0,$$
$$u = 4 \text{ or } u = -1.$$

But $u = x^2$, so

$$x^2 = 4 \text{ or } x^2 = -1,$$
$$x = \pm 2 \text{ or } x = \pm\sqrt{-1}.$$

The symbol $\sqrt{-1}$ should be familiar to students of intermediate math and would be an acceptable solution if the domain of the variable was the set of complex numbers. When, as in this case, no domain is specified, it is assumed to be the set of real numbers and thus excludes $\sqrt{-1}$. The required solution set is $\{2,-2\}$.

EXAMPLE 2

Solve $\left(\dfrac{1}{x}-2\right)^2 - 6\left(\dfrac{1}{x}-2\right)+5 = 0$.

SOLUTION: Let $u = \dfrac{1}{x} - 2$; then:

$$u^2 - 6u + 5 = 0,$$
$$(u-1)(u-5) = 0,$$
$$u = 1 \text{ or } u = 5.$$

But $u = \dfrac{1}{x} - 2$, so:

$$\frac{1}{x} - 2 = 1 \text{ or } \frac{1}{x} - 2 = 5.$$

The solution set for x is thus $\left\{\dfrac{1}{3}, \dfrac{1}{7}\right\}$.

In the multiple-choice question above, let $u = x^2 - 3x$; then:

$$u^2 - 2u - 8 = 0,$$
$$(u-4)(u+2) = 0,$$
$$u = 4 \text{ or } u = -2.$$

But $u = x^2 - 3x$, so:

$$x^2 - 3x = 4 \text{ or } x^2 - 3x = -2.$$

The solution set for x is thus $\{4,-1,2,1\}$.

SOLVING EQUATIONS WITH RADICAL TERMS

[8]   If $\sqrt{x} + \sqrt{x-4} + 2 = 0$, then $x = $?

(A) 4

(B) 4 or -4

(C) 16

(D) 8

(E) No solution

When both sides of an equation are squared, the resulting equation does not necessarily have the same roots as the original equation. For example, the equation $x = 3$ has only 3 as a root, but the equation whose members are its squares, $x^2 = 9$, has the two roots 3 and -3. Whatever the roots of the original equation are, however, they will be among the roots of the new equation. One technique for solving equations that have radical terms consists of squaring the equation as many times as necessary to remove the radicals and then checking the roots of the new equation in the original equation.

EXAMPLE 1

Find the roots of $\sqrt{x+1} = x - 1$.

SOLUTION: Squaring both sides, we get:

$$\begin{aligned} x + 1 &= x^2 - 2x + 1, \\ 0 &= x^2 - 3x, \\ 0 &= x(x - 3), \\ x &= 0 \text{ or } x = 3. \end{aligned}$$

These are the roots of $x^2 - 3x = 0$, but only one is a root of the original equation because substitution of 0 for x yields $\sqrt{1} = -1$.

EXAMPLE 2

We will solve the multiple-choice question.

SOLUTION: You may have recognized immediately that this equation has no solutions since all three terms represent positive numbers and the sum of three positive numbers can never be zero.

TEST-TAKING TIP

Level IC test questions rarely involve many steps or much calculation. Always consider the possibility of a direct and quick solution.

To pursue a mechanical solution, first isolate one radical:

$$\sqrt{x-4} = -\sqrt{x} - 2,$$

and then square both sides:

$$x - 4 = x + 4\sqrt{x} + 4.$$

(Note the square of the right side; remember that $(a + b)^2$ is $a^2 + 2ab + b^2$, not $a^2 + b^2$!) One radical remains, so we first simplify, isolate this radical, and then square both sides again:

$$\begin{aligned} -2 &= \sqrt{x}, \\ 4 &= x. \end{aligned}$$

We are tempted to say that the solution of the original equation is 4, but substituting 4 for x we get:

$$\begin{aligned} \sqrt{4} + \sqrt{4-4} + 2 &= 0, \\ 4 &= 0. \end{aligned}$$

A word of caution: to remove a radical by squaring you must first isolate it on one side of the equation. Suppose you did not do this for an equation such as $\sqrt{x} + x = 6$. Your result by squaring would be $x + 2x\sqrt{x} + x^2 = 36$ and the radical would still be there! Had you isolated it first, $\sqrt{x} = 6 - x$, you would have gotten $x = 36 - 12x + x^2$ with no radicals.

EXAMPLES

Solve each by the method of squaring:

1. $\sqrt{x-4} = 3$

2. $2\sqrt{x-5} + 4 = \sqrt{x-5}$

3. $x + \sqrt{x+1} = 1$

SOLUTIONS:

1. $\{13\}$

2. No solution, 21 doesn't work

3. $\{0\}$, 3 doesn't work

DETERMINING THE NATURE OF ROOTS

---

[9]   If $ax^2 + bx + c = 0$, $b > 1$, $b < 2\sqrt{ac}$, what is the nature of the roots of the quadratic equation?

(A) One real, rational root

(B) Two real, irrational roots

(C) Two real, rational roots

(D) One real, irrational root

(E) No real roots

The Quadratic Formula can be used to determine the nature of the roots of a quadratic without actually calculating them. Recall that the expression $\sqrt{b^2 - 4ac}$ appears in the formula. The number $b^2 - 4ac$ is called the *discriminant*. When the discriminant is negative, there can be no real roots for the equation since no negative number has a square root in the real number system. When the discriminant is zero,

$$\sqrt{b^2 - 4ac} = 0,$$

and the formula gives

$$\frac{-b \pm \sqrt{0}}{2a} = \frac{-b}{2a}.$$

Thus the equation has only the real number $\frac{-b}{2a}$ as a root. If the discriminant is positive and a perfect square, then the equation has two real, rational roots since $\sqrt{b^2 - 4ac}$ will be rational. If the discriminant is positive, but not a perfect square, then the equation has two real irrational roots since $\sqrt{b^2 - 4ac}$ will be irrational.

EXAMPLES

1. $x^2 - x + 1 = 0$; $b^2 - 4ac = -3$; no real roots

2. $4x^2 - 12x + 9 = 0$; $b^2 - 4ac = 0$; one real root

3. $x^2 - 5x + 6 = 0$; $b^2 - 4ac = 1$; two real rational roots

4. $x^2 + 3x - 1 = 0$; $b^2 - 4ac = 13$; two real irrational roots

In the multiple-choice question $b > 1$ and $b < 2\sqrt{ac}$, meaning that $b^2 < 4ac$ and $b^2 - 4ac < 0$, so the equation has no real roots. The condition that $b > 1$ assures us that b is positive, and, hence, squaring both sides involves multiplying both sides of our inequality by positive numbers; the direction of the inequality was thus preserved.

EXAMPLES

Without solving the equations below, indicate the nature of the roots:

1. $2x^2 - 4x - 7 = 0$

2. $21x^2 + 4x - 65 = 0$

3. $4x^2 - 36x + 81 = 0$

SOLUTIONS:

1. Discriminant: 72, two real irrational

2. Discriminant: 5476, which is 74^2, two real rational

3. Discriminant: 0, one real rational

[10] The roots of the equation $x^2 + 2bx + b^2 = 0$ are p and q. What can you conclude about b and q?

(A) Both are positive

(B) $b = q$

(C) $b = -q$

(D) $b > q$

(E) $b < q$

We have seen that the roots of a quadratic equation $ax^2 + bx + c = 0$ are

$$r_1 = \frac{-b + \sqrt{b^2 - 4ac}}{2a}$$

and

$$r_2 = \frac{-b - \sqrt{b^2 - 4ac}}{2a}$$

If we add r_1 and r_2 we get

$$(1) \qquad r_1 + r_2 = -\frac{b}{a}.$$

Multiplying r_1 by r_2 gives

$$(2) \qquad r_1 \cdot r_2 = \frac{c}{a}.$$

The two numbers found in (1) and (2) are recognizable as the coefficients of the equation we get when we divide our original equation by a to get a first coefficient of 1.

$$(3) \qquad x^2 + \frac{b}{a}x + \frac{c}{a} = 0$$

Thus we state that, when the leading coefficient of a quadratic equation is 1, the second coefficient is the negative of the sum of the roots, and the constant term is the product of the roots.

The equation $x^2 + 2bx + b^2 = 0$ involves a perfect square trinomial so its roots are equal and their sum is $-2b$ (the sum of the roots is the negative of the coefficient of the x-term). If the roots are p and q, then $p = q$. Thus $q + q = -2b$ and q and b are negatives of each other. We can draw no conclusion about which of the two, q or b, is positive; certainly both cannot be. Since one is positive and the other negative, then one of $q > b$ or $b > q$ must be true, but we can draw no conclusion about which relationship it is.

EXAMPLES

Without solving, indicate the sum and product of the roots of the equations given:

1. $x^2 - 4x + 2 = 0$

2. $x^2 = \frac{1}{3} - \frac{1}{2}x$

3. $3x^2 = 5x + 7$

SOLUTIONS:

1. $s = 4$, $p = 2$

2. $s = -\frac{1}{2}$, $p = -\frac{1}{3}$

3. $s = \frac{5}{3}$, $p = -\frac{7}{3}$

[11] If $x^2 = 15$ and $xy = 2\sqrt{15}$, then $y = ?$

    I. -2

    II. 2

    III. $\sqrt{15}$

(A) I only

(B) II only

(C) I and II only

(D) II and III only

(E) All of I, II, and III

Don't be tempted to begin by using your calculator to solve $x^2 = 15$ to find a value for $\sqrt{15}$.

Instead, square both sides of $xy = 2\sqrt{15}$ to get

$$x^2 y^2 = 4(15).$$

You were given $x^2 = 15$, so y^2 must be 4. If $y^2 = 4$, then $y = -2$ or 2.

At this point, it looks like I and II are true, but we need to be careful. Solutions that use squaring both sides of an equation are sometimes extraneous, meaning that they don't work in the unsquared equation even if they work in the squared result.

This time, both work, however. The value of y is -2 when x is $-\sqrt{15}$, and 2 works when x is $\sqrt{15}$.

Choice III is there only to fool the people who think that $\sqrt{15}$ times $\sqrt{15}$ is $2\sqrt{15}$.

Therefore, the answer is (C).

[12] If p is an integer and $3x^2 + px - 2$ can be written as factors with integers as coefficients, then p can be any of the following except?

(A) -5

(B) -2

(C) -1

(D) 1

(E) 5

If p must be an integer and the factors must involve only integers, the possible factorizations of $3x^2 + px - 2$ are:

$$(3x - 2)(x + 1) = 3x^2 + x - 2,$$
$$(3x + 2)(x - 1) = 3x^2 - x - 2,$$
$$(3x + 1)(x - 2) = 3x^2 - 5x - 2, \text{ or}$$
$$(3x - 1)(x + 2) = 3x^2 + 5x - 2.$$

Therefore, the middle term can only be -1, 1, -5, or 5. Among the choices offered, the only number that cannot be used for p is -2, answer (B).

You might argue that all second-degree polynomials can be factored but you must then consider factors that don't have integral coefficients. Those were excluded by the given information.

The Math Level IC test assumes complete mastery of the factoring of second-degree expressions where the coefficients are integers.

[13] If $x - y = 1$, then $x^2 - 2xy - y^2 = ?$

(A) 0

(B) 1

(C) 2

(D) 4

(E) Cannot be determined

From $x - y = 1$, the given information, neither x nor y can be determined, which makes choice (E) attractive.

It is not necessary to know either x or y, however, because $x^2 - 2xy - y^2 = (x - y)^2 = (1)^2 = 1$, (B).

The key to finding the answer is a common question-building device that is popular with test makers: the expression is readily factorable by a basic pattern introduced in elementary algebra.

In this case, the factoring pattern is based on the perfect square trinomial. Be sure to master the ability to recognize perfect square trinomials, which will fit either of the forms:

$$(a + b)^2 = a^2 + 2ab + b^2, \text{ or}$$
$$(a - b)^2 = a^2 - 2ab + b^2.$$

[14] If x satisfies the equation $x^2(x - 3)(3x + 1) = 0$, which of the following is (are) true?

    I. $x = 0$.

    II. The only positive value of x is 3.

    III. The only negative value of x is $\left(-\dfrac{1}{3}\right)$.

(A) I only

(B) II only

(C) I and II only

(D) II and III only

(E) All of I, II, and III

This is another question formulated on a fundamental and useful concept introduced early in algebra. A product can only be zero if one of its factors is zero. The concept is useful because it provides a direct way to solve higher-degree equations if they can be factored.

The equation in this question can only be true for values of x that make one or more factors equal zero. In other words,

$$x^2 = 0 \text{ or } x - 3 = 0 \text{ or } 3x + 1 = 0.$$

Therefore, $x = 0$, $x = 3$, or $x = -\frac{1}{3}$.

No other value of x makes a factor equal zero so no other values make the equation true. Hence all three statements are true and the correct answer is (E).

WHAT YOU SHOULD KNOW

KEY CONCEPTS

1. If $x^2 = k$ and $k > 0$, then $x = \pm\sqrt{k}$.
2. If $ax^2 + bx + c = 0$ and $ax^2 + bx + c$ can be factored into linear factors, then the solutions can be found by setting each factor equal to zero and solving for x.
3. To solve an equation of the form

$$\sqrt{ax + b} = c,$$

   square each side to eliminate the radical and solve the resulting equation. Be sure to check all roots to see whether extraneous roots have been introduced by squaring.
4. To solve an equation involving more than one radical expression, first solve for one radical and square both sides to eliminate this radical. If any radicals remain, solve for another radical and square both sides. Continue the process until all radicals have been eliminated.
5. The equation $ax^2 + bx + c = 0$ has:
   a. no real roots if $b^2 - 4ac < 0$,
   b. one real root if $b^2 - 4ac = 0$, and
   c. two real roots if $b^2 - 4ac > 0$.

KEY FORMULA

If $ax^2 + bx + c = 0$ and $a \neq 0$, then

$$x = \frac{-b \pm \sqrt{b^2 - 4ac}}{2a}$$

(Quadratic Formula)

TEST-TAKING STRATEGIES

- If a verbal problem involves finding one or more factors of a product when the numerical value of the product is given, the solution generally requires a quadratic equation—for example, when the area is given and the length and width are unknown, but are related to each other. Be thoroughly familiar with these equations and their application.
- The quadratic formula is a powerful tool for solving quadratic equations, but its use can be time-consuming. Before trying the formula, always check to see if the quadratic polynomial can be factored.
- Squaring both sides of an equation can introduce extraneous roots. (These are solutions of the squared equation that are not solutions of the original.) Always check your roots in the original equation.

ANSWERS

[1] (B)	[4] (E)	[7] (D)	[10] (C)	[13] (B)
[2] (B)	[5] (B)	[8] (E)	[11] (C)	[14] (E)
[3] (D)	[6] (A)	[9] (E)	[12] (B)	

RELATIONS AND FUNCTIONS

CHAPTER

19

KEY TERMS

relation   a set of ordered pairs.

function   a set of ordered pairs no two of which have the same first coordinate.

domain   of a relation (and, therefore, of a function), the set of first coordinates. When not specified, it includes all real numbers.

range   of a relation (and, therefore, of a function), the set of all second coordinates.

IDENTIFYING FUNCTIONS AND RELATIONS

[1]   Which of the following statements is (are) true?

    I.   A function is never a relation.

    II.   A function is always a relation.

    III.   All relations are functions.

    (A)   I only

    (B)   II only

    (C)   III only

    (D)   I and II only

    (E)   II and III only

It is frequently necessary in problem analysis to assign the elements of a set A to the elements of a second set B as directed by such rules as: (1) to every segment assign the positive real number that is its length, or (2) to every real number assign the number that is twice as great.

We are often concerned with pairings between sets of points and/or sets of numbers. Coordinate systems, for example, pair sets of points with sets of numbers or with sets of ordered pairs of numbers. Equations and inequalities in two variables pair a set of numbers with a second set of numbers. When we record the pairings of the elements of a set A with the elements of a set B, we generally use a fixed order that shows the sources of the entries of each pairing.

EXAMPLE

When we tabulate the ordered pairs of real numbers determined by an equation such as

$$y = 2x,$$

we always name the elements taken from the set of x values first. Some of these pairs are:

$$\left\{ (2,4), \left(\frac{1}{2},1\right), (-3,-6), \ldots \right\}.$$

The second entry in each case is, of course, the y value.

Any set of ordered pairs is called a *relation*. Relations are not necessarily sets of ordered pairs of real numbers, but we will deal primarily with those that are. The set of all first entries of the ordered pairs is called the *domain* of the relation. The set of all second entries is called the *range*. If a relation has the further characteristic that no two of its ordered pairs have the same first entry, then it is called a *function*. Thus a *function* is a set of ordered pairs for which no two ordered pairs have the same first

entry. Therefore a function is always a relation, but not all relations are functions.

RECOGNIZING FUNCTIONS

[2]   Which of the following statements does NOT describe a function?

    (A)   Assign to each triangle its area.

    (B)   Assign to each day its date.

    (C)   Assign to each book its number of pages.

    (D)   Assign to each hour the temperature at that hour.

    (E)   Assign to each positive number a number for which it is the absolute value.

Some of the possible answers above are examples of relations that do *not* assign numbers to numbers. Since all of them *do* establish ordered pairs by assigning the elements of one set to the elements of a second set, they are all relations. The set that is assigned is the range. The set that has the range elements assigned to it is the domain. In each of the relations except (E) each element of the domain has only one element of the range assigned to it. Note that in (E) every positive number has two numbers for which it is the absolute value. Since (E) contains such ordered pairs as

$$\left\{ (3,3), (3,-3), \left(\frac{1}{2},\frac{1}{2}\right), \left(\frac{1}{2},-\frac{1}{2}\right) \right\}$$

and more than one ordered pair has the same first element, (E) cannot be a function.

FINDING CARTESIAN PRODUCTS

[3]   If $A = \{1,2,3\}$ and $B = \{4,5\}$, which ordered pair is NOT an element of $A \times B$?

    (A) $(1,4)$

    (B) $(5,2)$

    (C) $(2,4)$

    (D) $(3,5)$

    (E) $(2,5)$

The symbol "$A \times B$" designates the result of assigning the elements of a set B to the elements of a set A. It is called the *Cartesian product* (sometimes the cross-product or the Cartesian cross-product) and consists of the set of all possible ordered pairs that have a member of A as first entry and a member of B as second entry. If $C = \{a,b,c\}$ and $D = \{x,y,z\}$, then $C \times D =$

$$\{(a,x), (a,y), (a,z), (b,x), (b,y), (b,z), (c,x), (c,y), (c,z)\}.$$

Each element of D is thus paired with each element of C.

The most commonly used cross-product is $R \times R$, the set of all possible ordered pairs that have both first and second entries in the real number system. The graph of $R \times R$ is the real number plane discussed in Chapter 17.

Representing information by means of a table can be helpful in many types of problems, for example, in determining cross-products. In the multiple-choice question:

$\times$	1	2	3
4	(1,4)	(2,4)	(3,4)
5	(1,5)	(2,5)	(3,5)

[4]   Which of the following are graphs of functions?

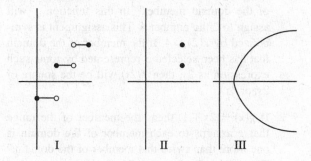

I   II   III

(A) I only

(B) II only

(C) III only

(D) I and III only

(E) II and III only

A function is a set of ordered pairs for which no two have the same first entry. A function can be graphed in the coordinate plane (as can a relation) by letting each first entry be the x-coordinate and each second entry be the y-coordinate. Since a function cannot have two ordered pairs with the same first coordinate, its graph cannot have two points on the same vertical line. A set of points, then, is the graph of a function if no vertical line intersects the graph in more than one point.

In the multiple-choice question, vertical lines strike more than one point of the graphs in both II and III; hence only I is a function.

[5]   Which of the following sets of ordered pairs is a function?

(A) $\{(x,y): y = x^3\}$

(B) $\{(x,y): x = |y|\}$

(C) $\{(x,y): y = \pm\sqrt{x}\}$

(D) $\{(x,y): y < x\}$

(E) All of these

The notation $\{(xy): \quad\}$ with the blank space containing some mathematical sentence, means "the set of ordered pairs such that [the mathematical sentence] is true." The mathematical sentence is generally an equation, an inequality, or a combination of equations and inequalities.

Intermediate math is primarily concerned with functions defined by equations. Other branches of math deal with other types of functions, but these are beyond the scope of our review.

No relation is completely specified unless its domain is established. The domain of a relation when not explicitly stated is the set of all real numbers except those that make the relation meaningless.

(A) $y = x^3$ defines a function, since no value of x yields more than one value for y. Since the domain is not explicitly stated, it is the set of all reals.

(B) $x = |y|$ must have a domain restricted to nonnegative real numbers, since negative real numbers cannot be absolute values. With the domain established we can determine that this is not a function, since each value of x yields two values for y. (Note that, when $x = 3$, $y = 3$ or -3.)

(C) $y = \pm\sqrt{x}$ has a domain also limited to nonnegative real numbers, because no negative number has a square root in the real number system. Yet it is not a function because it, too, yields two values of y for each value of x.

(D) $y < x$ yields infinitely many y values for each x value.

EXAMPLES

Each of the following equations will define a relation, the set of ordered pairs that make the equation true. Which of these will also define a function?

1. $y = x^2$

2. $y^2 = x$

3. $x^2 + y^2 = 4$

4. $x = 3$

SOLUTIONS:

Only 1. because 2., 3., and 4. all fail the vertical line test.

[6]   Which of the following statements describes the domain of the function defined as follows?

$$y = \frac{\sqrt{x-3}}{(x-2)(x-\sqrt{3})}$$

(A) All real numbers except 2 and $\sqrt{3}$

(B) All real numbers

(C) All positive real numbers

(D) All positive real numbers except 2 and $\sqrt{3}$

(E) All real numbers except those less than 3

When the domain of a function is not explicitly stated, it consists of all real numbers that are meaningful in the function. Among the common circumstances under which a real number will not be meaningful are (1) if it leads to division by zero, and (2) if it leads to the square root (fourth root, or any other even root) of a negative number. Both of these situations occur in the multiple-choice question. Note that 2 and $\sqrt{3}$ must be excluded from the domain because they lead to division by zero. Similarly, all real numbers less than 3 must be excluded because they yield negative values for $x-3$ and thus involve the square roots of negative numbers. Answer choice (E) does not specifically mention 2 and $\sqrt{3}$ but excludes them both since they *are* less than 3.

🖩 If you are using a graphing calculator, be sure you know how your display indicates domain exclusions for the graph of a function.

EXAMPLES

In each of the following indicate the values of x that must be excluded from the domain:

1. $y = \dfrac{2x}{x^2 - 2}$

2. $y = \dfrac{x^2 - 4}{x}$

3. $y = \sqrt{x - 4}$

4. $y = \sqrt{x^2 + 4}$

SOLUTIONS:

The excluded values are

1. $\sqrt{2}, -\sqrt{2}$

2. 0

3. All $x < 4$

4. None

USING FUNCTION NOTATION

[7]   If $f(x) = x^3 - 2x$, then $f(3t) = ?$

(A) $t^3 - 2t$

(B) $3t$

(C) $3t^3 - 6t$

(D) $27t^3 - 6t$

(E) $2t^3 - 6$

Three things are needed to specify a function: (1) a set called the domain, (2) a set called the range, and (3) a rule that assigns to each member of the domain exactly one member of the range.

The symbol "$f(x)$" means "the member of the range that the rule, f, assigns to the member, x, of the domain."

EXAMPLES

1. $f(x) = x^2$ means "the member of the range that f assigns to each member of its domain is the square of the domain member." In this function f will assign to 2 the number 4. This assignment is symbolized by $f(2) = 4$. If the member of the domain that has been selected is represented by some such expression as $2s$, then $f(2s)$ will be the square of $2s$, or $4s^2$.

2. If $g(x) = 2x + 1$, then "the member of the range that g assigns to each member of the domain is one more than twice that member of the domain." Thus $g(1) = 3$, $g(-4) = -7$, $g(2s) = 4s + 1$, $g(t^2) = 2t^2 + 1$, $g(3t^2) = 6t^2 + 1$.

In the multiple-choice question, $f(3t) = (3t)^3 - 2(3t) = 27t^3 - 6t$.

EXAMPLES

If $f(x) = |x - 1|$, $g(x) = 1 - x^2$, and $h(x) = 2x^2 - x + 3$, note each of the following:

1. $f(-3) + g(-3) = -4$

2. $g(a^2) + h(a^2) = a^4 - a^2 + 4$

3. $g(0) \div h(0) = \dfrac{1}{3}$

4. $3f(2) + 4g(-3) - 2h(1) = -37$

IDENTIFYING ZERO, CONSTANT, AND IDENTITY FUNCTIONS

[8] Which of the following terms describe(s) $f(x) = 0$?

   I. The zero function

   II. The constant function

   III. The identity function

  (A) I and III only

  (B) II and III only

  (C) I and II only

  (D) All of I, II, and III

  (E) I only

The *zero function* assigns 0 to every member of its domain. It consists of such ordered pairs as $\{(3,0), (-2,0), (\frac{1}{2},0), \ldots\}$ and is usually symbolized by $y = 0$ or $f(x) = 0$. Its graph is the y-axis.

Any function that assigns the same constant, c, to every member of its domain is a *constant function*. It is usually symbolized by an equation such as $f(x) = c$ or $y = c$. The graph of any constant function is a horizontal line. Since 0 is a constant, the zero function is a constant function.

The *identity function* is the function that assigns every member to itself. It is usually symbolized by $y = x$ or $f(x) = x$. Its graph is the line that bisects the first and third quadrants.

[9] If $f(x) = 2x$, $g(x) = \frac{1}{2}x$, and $f(g(x)) = 6$, what is x?

  (A) 4

  (B) 12

  (C) 6

  (D) 3

  (E) 2

$f(g(x))$ is called "the composition of f with g." Using the functional notation described in the preceding section, we interpret $f(g(x))$ to mean "the value that f assigns to the value that g assigns to x."

In the multiple-choice question g assigns $\frac{1}{2}x$ to x and f assigns $2x$ to x. Thus $f(g(x))$ is $2(\frac{1}{2}x)$ or x, since f must assign $2(\frac{1}{2}x)$ to $\frac{1}{2}x$ For this case we see that $f(g(x)) = x$ so $f(g(6)) = 6$ and x must be 6.

In general, to evaluate $f(g(x))$ substitute the expression which represents $g(x)$ for x in $f(x)$.

EXAMPLES

1. If $f(x) = x^2$ and $g(x) = \dfrac{x}{3}$, then $f(g(x)) = [g(x)]^2 = \left(\dfrac{x}{3}\right)^2 = \dfrac{x^2}{9}$.

2. If $f(x) = x + 2$ and $g(x) = x^3$, then $f(g(x)) = g(x) + 2 = x^3 + 2$.

3. If $f(x) = \dfrac{(8x + 1)}{4}$ and $g(x) = 3x$, then $f(g(x)) = \dfrac{[8\,g(x) + 1]}{4} = \dfrac{(24x + 1)}{4}$.

4. If $f(x) = x^2$ and $g(x) = x - 3$ then:

$$f(g(x)) = x^2 - 6x + 9$$
$$f(f(-1)) = 1$$
$$g(f(x)) = x^2 - 3$$
$$g(f(3a)) = 9a^2 - 3$$

FINDING THE INVERSE OF A FUNCTION

[10] If $f(x) = 3x + 2$, what is the inverse of f?

  (A) $g(x) = -3x - 2$

  (B) $g(x) = 3x - 2$

  (C) $g(x) = \dfrac{1}{3}x - \dfrac{2}{3}$

  (D) $g(x) = \dfrac{1}{3}x + \dfrac{2}{3}$

  (E) $g(x) = -\dfrac{1}{3}x - \dfrac{2}{3}$

Two functions, f and g, are inverses if and only if for every (a,b) in f, (b,a) belongs to g and for every (b,a) in g, (a,b) belongs to f. It follows that the domain of f is the range of g and the range of f is the domain of g.

It also follows that $f(a) = b$ and $g(b) = a$. Substituting $g(b)$ for a in $f(a)$, we get

(1) $$f(g(b)) = b.$$

If we substitute $f(a)$ for b in $g(b)$, we get

(2) $$g(f(a)) = a.$$

Therefore for all x in the domain of both f and g,

(3) $$f(g(x)) = g(f(x)) = x,$$

if and only if f and g are inverses. We can use (3) to derive the inverse (if it exists) of any given function.

EXAMPLE

Find the inverse of $f(x) = 4x - 7$.

SOLUTION:

Find an expression for the value that f assigns to $g(x)$ by substituting $g(x)$ for x in the given function:

$$f(g(x)) = 4g(x) - 7.$$

But $f(g(x)) = x$ by equation (3), so:

$$x = 4g(x) - 7,$$
$$\frac{x+7}{4} = g(x).$$

We can generalize the method to save a few steps. To find the inverse $g(x)$ of a function $f(x)$ replace every x with $g(x)$ and replace $f(x)$ with x; then solve for $g(x)$.

For example, in the multiple-choice question:

$$f(x) = 3x + 2,$$
$$x = 3(g(x)) + 2,$$
$$\frac{x-2}{3} = g(x),$$
$$\frac{1}{3}x - \frac{2}{3} = g(x).$$

EXAMPLES

In each case find $g(x)$ if g is to be the inverse of f:

1. $f(x) = \dfrac{1}{2}x - 1$

2. $f(x) = \sqrt{x}$

3. $f(x) = x^3$

4. $f(x) = \dfrac{1}{x}$

SOLUTIONS:

The inverses are:

1. $g(x) = 2x + 2$

2. $g(x) = x^2$ with domain $x \geq 0$

3. $g(x) = x^{\frac{1}{3}}$

4. $g(x) = \dfrac{1}{x}$

[11] If the figure below is the graph of a function, which of the following is the graph of its inverse?

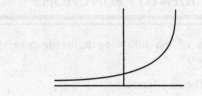

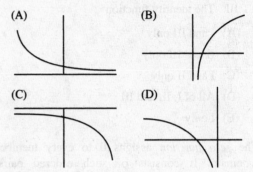

(A)   (B)

(C)   (D)

(E) None of these

The definition of inverse functions provides the basis for discovering an important relationship between the graphs of a function f and its inverse, g. If the ordered pair $F(a,b)$ belongs to f, the ordered pair $G(b,a)$ must belong to g. The configuration of these points in the plane suggests that a search for a line of symmetry between them might be fruitful. The line of symmetry between two points is the perpendicular bisector of the segment for which the given points are endpoints. The perpendicular bisector of a segment is the set of all points equidistant from the endpoints of the segment. If $P(x,y)$ is any point in the plane, then the distance from P to F is given by:

$$(1) \qquad \sqrt{(x-a)^2 + (y-b)^2},$$

and the distance from P to G by:

$$(2) \qquad \sqrt{(x-b)^2 + (y-a)^2}.$$

The line of symmetry is the set of points (x,y) for which $(1) = (2)$. If we set $(1) = (2)$ and simplify (we'll leave the details to the energetic reader) we get

$$(3) \qquad x = y.$$

We conclude that every function f is symmetric to its inverse g, with respect to the line $y = x$. The following graphs show examples of this symmetry:

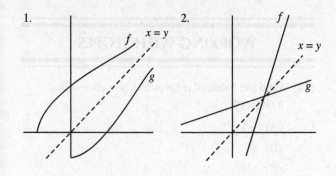

1.   2.

[12] Which of the following functions does NOT have an inverse?

(A) $y = \sqrt{x}$

(B) $y = 3x$

(C) $y = x^3$

(D) $y = -2x + 5$

(E) $y = x^2$

The inverse of a function must be a function. But the set of ordered pairs, g, for which $f(g(x)) = g(f(x)) = x$ is *not* always a function:

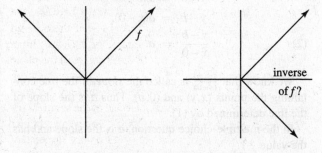

inverse of f?

If g is not a function, then our definition of inverse excludes g from being the inverse of f and we say that f has no inverse.

How do you determine when a function has no inverse? When $F(a, b)$ is a point on the graph of a function, $G(b, a)$ is a point on the graph of its inverse. This means that the y-coordinates of f are the x-coordinates of g. By definition of function, g cannot be a function if two of its points have the same x-coordinate and this means no two points of f can have the same y-coordinate. Any two points of f that had the same y-coordinate would lie on the same horizontal line. Thus, if any horizontal line intersects the graph of a function in more than one point, the function can have no inverse.

Therefore, if a function has an inverse, for each x there is exactly one y and for each y there is exactly one x. Answer choice (E) is the only equation that gives multiple values of x for each value of y (when $y = 4$, for example, $x = \pm 2$), which prevents it from representing a function with an inverse.

EXAMPLES

Sketch the graph of each of the following and then indicate whether or not it has an inverse:

1. $y = 2$

2. $y = 3x + 2$

3. $y = 3x^2 + 2$

4. $y = |x|$

SOLUTIONS: The graphs and the answers are:

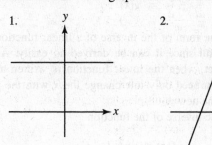

1.   2.

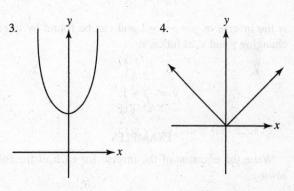

3.   4.

1. No inverse

2. Has an inverse

3. No inverse

4. No inverse

[13] Which of the following is the inverse of the linear function $f(x) = -x - 1$?

(A) $g(x) = x + 1$

(B) $y = x + 1$

(C) $g(x) = -x - 1$

(D) $y = x - 1$

(E) $y = -x + 1$

A linear function is any function of the form $f(x) = ax + b$; $a \neq 0$. We have continued to use the notation $f(x)$ here to help make it familiar to you. Note that the ordered pairs of f are $(x, f(x))$, thus making $y = f(x)$. You may choose to think of the linear function as being defined by any equation of the form $y = ax + b$. Indeed, we will use the two interchangeably from now on.

The term "linear" refers to the facts that (1) the graph of every linear function is a line and (2) every nonvertical line has an equation that can be written in this form.

To find the inverse, g, of the linear function $f(x) = ax + b$, we will substitute $g(x)$ for x and x for $f(x)$:

$$x = a(g(x)) + b,$$
$$x - b = a(g(x)),$$
$$\frac{1}{a}x - \frac{b}{a} = g(x).$$

Memorizing the form of the inverse of a linear function is seldom useful since it can be derived so easily. As a matter of fact, when the linear function is written as $y = ax + b$, you need only interchange the x with the y and solve for the new y.

Therefore the inverse of the function

$$f(x) = -x - 1$$

is the inverse of $y = -x - 1$ and can be found by interchanging y and x, as follows:

$$x = -y - 1,$$
$$y = -x - 1.$$

EXAMPLES

Write the equation of the inverse for each of the following:

1. $y = x$

2. $f(x) = 3x + 4$

3. $y = \frac{1}{3}x - \frac{4}{3}$

4. $f(x) = 2$

SOLUTIONS: The inverses are:

1. $y = x$

2. $g(x) = \frac{1}{3}x - \frac{4}{3}$

3. $y = 3x + 4$

4. No inverse

WORKING WITH SLOPES

[14] Find the value of a for which $y = ax + 4$ has a slope of -1.

(A) -1

(B) 4

(C) -4

(D) $\frac{1}{4}$

(E) $-\frac{1}{4}$

Since the equation $y = ax + b$ is true for $x = 0$, and $y = b$, one point on the line must be $P(0, b)$. Because the x-coordinate of P is 0, P will be the point of intersection of the line determined by $y = ax + b$ with the y-axis. For this reason, b is called the y-*intercept* of the function.

The equation $y = ax + b$ can be transformed as follows:

(1)
$$y = ax + b,$$
$$y - b = ax,$$
$$y - b = a(x - 0),$$

(2)
$$\frac{y - b}{x - 0} = a.$$

We know that $\frac{(y-b)}{(x-0)}$ is called the *slope* of the line containing the points (x, y) and $(0, b)$. Thus a is the slope of the line determined by (1).

In the multiple-choice question, a is the slope and has the value -1.

To summarize: In the equation $y = ax + b$, the number a is the slope of the line and the number b is the y-intercept (the y-coordinate of the point where the line intersects the y-axis).

EXAMPLES

Each of the following defines a linear function. Write each in slope-intercept form and then indicate the slope and y-intercept:

1. $6x + 3y = 2$

2. $\frac{x}{2} + \frac{y}{3} = 1$

3. $2x + y = 0$

4. $5 - 4x = 20y$

SOLUTIONS:

1. $y = -2x + \dfrac{2}{3}$, slope: -2, y-intercept: $\dfrac{2}{3}$

2. $y = -\dfrac{3}{2}x + 3$, slope: $-\dfrac{3}{2}$, y-intercept: 3

3. Slope: -2, y-intercept: 0

4. Slope: $-\dfrac{1}{5}$, y-intercept: $\dfrac{1}{4}$

[15] If $f(z) = az + b$, what is the value of $\dfrac{f(b) - f(a)}{b - a}$?

(A) z

(B) b

(C) az

(D) a

(E) $az + b$

We have included this question as further practice in using $f(x)$ notation:

$$
\begin{aligned}
f(b) &= ab + b, \\
f(a) &= a^2 + b, \\
f(b) - f(a) &= ab - a^2, \\
&= a(b - a), \\
\frac{f(b) - f(a)}{b - a} &= \frac{a(b - a)}{(b - a)} = a.
\end{aligned}
$$

We could, of course, have predicted this outcome without any calculation since $(b, f(b))$ and $(a, f(a))$ are the coordinates of points on the graph of the given linear function. Hence the expression to simplify must be the slope of the line containing these points.

EXAMPLES

If $f(2) = az + b$, evaluate:

1. $f(2) + f(4)$

2. $f(x + 1) - f(x - 1)$

3. $f(3t) - f(-3t)$

4. $[f(2x)]\left[f\left(\dfrac{1}{2}x\right)\right]$

SOLUTIONS: The values are:

1. $6a + 2b$

2. $2a$

3. $6ta$

4. $a^2x^2 + \dfrac{5}{2}abx + b^2$

FINDING THE AXIS OF SYMMETRY

[16] The quadratic function $f(x) = 3x^2 - 12x + 16$ is symmetric with respect to which of the following lines?

(A) $x = 2$

(B) $x = 12$

(C) $x = 16$

(D) $y = x$

(E) $x = 0$

A graphing calculator will display the graph, from which the axis could be determined by inspection.

A quadratic function is a function of the form $f(x) = ax^2 + bx + c$, where a, b, and c are real numbers and $a \neq 0$. The graph of every quadratic function is a parabola whose line of symmetry is parallel to the y-axis. This line of symmetry can be readily determined by changing the equation to the form

$$f(x) = a(x - k)^2 + p.$$

The axis of symmetry will be the line $x = k$. Then:

$$
\begin{aligned}
f(x) &= 3x^2 - 12x + 16 \\
&= 3(x^2 - 4x) + 16 \\
&= 3(x^2 - 4x + 4) + 16 - 3(4) \\
&= 3(x - 2)^2 + 4.
\end{aligned}
$$

Therefore the axis of the parabola given in the multiple-choice question is $x = 2$.

EXAMPLES

Find the axis of symmetry:

1. $y = x^2$

2. $y = 3x^2 + 2$

3. $y = -2x^2 + 4x + 1$

4. $y = x^2 + 4x + 4$

SOLUTIONS: The axes of symmetry are:

1. $y = (x - 0)^2 + 0$, $x = 0$

2. $y = 3(x - 0)^2 + 2$, $x = 0$

3. $y = -2(x - 1)^2 + 3$, $x = 1$

4. $y = (x + 2)^2 + 0$, $x = -2$

FINDING MAXIMA OR MINIMA

[17] What is the minimum value that $f(x)$ can attain if $f(x) = 2x^2 + 8x - 1$?

(A) -1

(B) -8

(C) 9

(D) -9

(E) 7

The point of intersection of the axis of symmetry of a parabola with the parabola itself is called the *vertex*. For a parabola that opens upward ($a > 0$) the vertex is the lowest point of the graph. Similarly the vertex is the highest point on the graph of a parabola that opens downward ($a < 0$).

Recall that the axis of symmetry is $x = k$ for a parabola where $f(x) = a(x - k)^2 + p$. The x-coordinate of the vertex must be k, which when substituted for x yields p as the y-coordinate. Thus the value of p is either the maximum or the minimum value of the function depending on whether the graph opens up or down.

To find the minimum value of the function

$$f(x) = 2x^2 + 8x - 1,$$

transform it to

$$\begin{aligned} f(x) &= 2(x^2 + 4x) - 1 \\ &= 2(x^2 + 4x + 4) - 1 - 2(4) \\ &= 2(x + 2)^2 - 9. \end{aligned}$$

The minimum value occurs at the vertex of the parabola, which is the intersection of $f(x)$ with the axis, $x = -2$, of the parabola:

$$f(-2) = -9.$$

▥ Note that graphing calculators are programmed to find maximum and minimum values. From the graphs, you can also determine the range and domain of a function.

EXAMPLES

Find any maximum or minimum values for each of the following:

1. $y = -x^2 - 10x + 24$

2. $y = x^2 + x + 4$

3. $y = 2 + 10x - 10x^2$

SOLUTIONS:

First change the equation. Then find the max or min.

1. $\begin{aligned} y = -x^2 - 10x + 24 &= -(x^2 + 10x) + 24 \\ &= -(x + 5)^2 + 49 \end{aligned}$

$\therefore$ max is 49

2. $\begin{aligned} y = x^2 + x + 4 &= \left(x^2 + x + \frac{1}{4}\right) + \frac{15}{4} \\ &= \left(x + \frac{1}{2}\right)^2 + \frac{15}{4} \end{aligned}$

$\therefore$ min is $\dfrac{15}{4}$

3. $\begin{aligned} y &= -10x^2 + 10x + 2 \\ &= -10(x^2 - x) + 2 \\ &= -10\left(x^2 - x + \frac{1}{4}\right) + \frac{9}{2} \\ &= -10\left(x - \frac{1}{2}\right)^2 + \frac{9}{2} \end{aligned}$

$\therefore$ max is $\dfrac{9}{2}$

[18] A rectangular field is bordered on one side by a straight canal. If the total length of fencing used on the other three sides is 240 feet and the dimensions of the field are chosen so that the maximum area is enclosed, what are these dimensions?

(A) $60' \times 60'$

(B) $60' \times 120'$

(C) $90' \times 90'$

(D) $80' \times 80'$

(E) $120' \times 2'$

A frequent problem in many diverse fields is that of finding the maximum or minimum results, given certain conditions. The solutions of most of these problems lie beyond the scope of intermediate math (usually requiring the calculus), but some can be found through the use of quadratic functions. The procedure is to express the desired value as a quadratic function and then find the vertex of the corresponding parabola.

EXAMPLE

Find the greatest rectangular region (in area) that can be enclosed by a string of length 48 inches.

SOLUTION: Let x be the length of the rectangle; then $24 - x$ will be the width and the following function represents the area:

$$A(x) = x(24 - x)$$
$$= -1(x - 12)^2 + 144,$$

the second quotation being the $a(x - k)^2 + p$ form of the first. The graph is a parabola that opens downward and has a vertex of (12, 144). Thus the maximum area that can be enclosed is 144, and this occurs when the length is 12.

To work the original problem, let w represent the width; then the length is $240 - 2w$ and the area function is:

$$A(w) = w(240 - 2w)$$
$$= -2(w - 60)^2 + 7200.$$

The vertex is (60, 7200), and the maximum area is 7200, which will occur when the width is 60.

WORKING WITH FUNCTIONS

[19] The function $f(x)$ has the value 0 if and only if x is a member of the set $\{-3, 0, 1\}$. For what values of x is $f(x - 3) = 0$?

(A) $\{-3, 0, 1\}$

(B) $\{0, 1\}$

(C) $\{0, 3, 4\}$

(D) $\{-6, 0, -2\}$

(E) $\{3, 0, -2\}$

The symbol $f(a) = b$ represents the fact that f is a rule that results in b when it works on a. In the given information about the function f, above, we discover that f can result in 0 only when it works on $-3, 0$, or 1. This means that when f works on $x - 3$, it is the $x - 3$ that must be $-3, 0$, or 1 in order to yield 0. Thus

$$x - 3 = -3 \rightarrow x = 0$$
$$= 1 \rightarrow x = 4$$
$$= 0 \rightarrow x = 3.$$

[20] If $f(x) = \dfrac{3x - 2}{4}$, where $x > 0$, for what values of x is $f(x) < 0$?

(A) $0 < x < \dfrac{2}{3}$

(B) $0 < x < 2$

(C) $-2 < x < 4$

(D) $0 < x < 3$

(E) No value of x

Students often misinterpret $f(x) < 0$ to mean $x < 0$. Remember that a function is a set of ordered pairs whose members can be represented by the ordered pair

$$(x, f(x)),$$

where the rule, f tells how $f(x)$ is derived from x. Thus x and $f(x)$ represent two different quantities.

Therefore, in the question above, $f(x) < 0$ means

$$\dfrac{3x - 2}{4} < 0.$$

To solve this inequality, first multiply each side by 4 (there is no change in the direction of the inequality because the multiplier is positive).

$$3x - 2 < 0$$
$$3x < 2$$
$$x < \dfrac{2}{3}$$

There was, however, an initial restriction that x was to be positive. Combining the restrictions, we get

$$0 < x < \dfrac{2}{3}.$$

Decimal approximations can be tricky when you are working with inequalities. Here, for example, you might be tempted to round off to the nearest hundredth and think of this inequality as $0 < x < 0.67$. However, there are numbers between $\frac{2}{3}$ and .67 that do not make the inequality true. For example, x could be .667 or .668 or any other number greater than .666 but still less than .67. Avoid these rounding-off errors when using your calculator to approximate the values represented by an inequality. In this case, the best hundredths decimal equivalent to $0 < x < \frac{2}{3}$ is $0 < x < .66$. The latter excludes some numbers that make the original inequality true, but it does not include any numbers that make it false.

[21] If $f(x) + \dfrac{1}{x} + x + \dfrac{1}{x} + x$, for all real numbers, which of the following will be true?

(A) $f(0) = 0$

(B) $f(x) = f\left(\dfrac{1}{x}\right)$

(C) $f(x) = f(-x)$

(D) $f(x) = x$

(E) $f(x) = \dfrac{1}{f(x)}$

This question illustrates several different aspects of functions, which we will review by discussing each of the choices given. First, however, note that $f(x)$ can be simplified:

$$f(x) = 2\left(\dfrac{1}{x}\right) + 2x$$
$$= 2\left(\dfrac{1}{x} + x\right).$$

(A) Since no domain is specified, the values that may be used for x include all real numbers except those that produce meaningless operations. The number 0 is the only one that causes complications, since it cannot be used as a divisor. Hence $f(0)$ is meaningless.

(B) To find $f(\frac{1}{x})$, replace x by $\frac{1}{x}$ wherever x occurs. Therefore

$$f\left(\dfrac{1}{x}\right) = 2\left(\dfrac{1}{\frac{1}{x}} + \dfrac{1}{x}\right)$$
$$= 2\left(x + \dfrac{1}{x}\right)$$
$$= 2\left(\dfrac{1}{x} + x\right).$$

The latter is, of course, $f(x)$.

(C) To find $f(-x)$, replace x by $(-x)$:

$$f(-x) = 2\left(\dfrac{1}{-x} + (-x)\right) = -2\left(\dfrac{1}{x} + x\right).$$

The latter is not $f(x)$, but is $-f(x)$. Any function for which $f(-x)$ is $-f(x)$ is referred to as an "odd function." If $f(-x) = f(x)$, it is an "even function."

(D) $f(x) \neq x$, since $2(\frac{1}{x} + x) \neq x$.

(E)
$$\dfrac{1}{f(x)} = \dfrac{1}{2(\frac{1}{x} + x)}$$
$$= \dfrac{1(x)}{2(\frac{1}{x} + x)(x)}$$
$$= \dfrac{x}{2(1 + x^2)}$$
$$\neq 2\left(\dfrac{1}{x} + x\right).$$

EXAMPLES

For each of the following find $f\left(\dfrac{1}{x}\right)$ and $f(-x)$:

1. $f(x) = \dfrac{1}{x}$

2. $f(x) = \dfrac{1}{x^2}$

3. $f(x) = \dfrac{-1}{x-1}$

SOLUTIONS:

1. $f\left(\dfrac{1}{x}\right) = x,\ f(-x) = -\dfrac{1}{x}$

2. $f\left(\dfrac{1}{x}\right) = x^2\ f(-x) = \dfrac{1}{x^2}$

3. $f\left(\dfrac{1}{x}\right) = \dfrac{-x}{1-x} = \dfrac{x}{x-1}$

$\ f(-x) = \dfrac{-x}{-x-1} = \dfrac{x}{x+1}$

[22] For which of the following is $f(3) = f\left(\dfrac{1}{3}\right)$?

(A) $f(x) = x^2$

(B) $f(x) = 1 + \dfrac{1}{x}$

(C) $f(x) = \dfrac{(x+1)}{x}$

(D) $f(x) = \dfrac{1}{x} + x + \dfrac{1}{x} + x$

(E) $f(x) = \dfrac{1}{x}$

The algebra in this question looks as though it could be complicated, which means you might want to try finding the answer by testing the answer choices. Test them by alternately substituting $\frac{1}{3}$ and then 3 for x.

But don't begin substituting until you have scanned answers to eliminate any that obviously won't work.

For example, you can immediately eliminate (B) and (C) because the two algebraic expressions are equal to each other. Thus, if (B) were true, (C) would have to be, too.

Now look at (A) and (E), because they are simpler and, therefore, make substitution easier. Squaring 3 produces a result different from squaring $\frac{1}{3}$, so (A) is eliminated.

Taking the reciprocal of a number produces a different number for all numbers except 1. Therefore (E) is eliminated.

Only (D), the most complicated expression, is left, so it must be the correct choice.

[23] If $f(x)$ is a linear function for which $f(2) = 1.2$ and $f(4) = 3.6$. If $f(a) = 0$, $a = ?$

(A) −1

(B) 0

(C) 1

(D) 1.2

(E) 2.4

The method you would most likely choose for a question like this would be to first find the equation of the line in $f(x) = mx + b$ form. Then substitute a for x and 0 for $f(x)$. Finally, solve for a.

Find the slope from the two given points:

$$\frac{3.6 - 1.2}{4 - 2} = \frac{2.4}{2} = 1.2$$

Now the equation looks like this:

$$f(x) = 1.2x + b.$$

To find b, substitute 2 for x and 1.2 for $f(x)$.

$$1.2 = 2(1.2) + b$$
$$b = -1.2.$$

Therefore, $f(x) = 1.2x - 1.2$. Substitute 0 for $f(x)$ and a for x to get

$$0 = 1.2a - 1.2.$$

From this, $a = 1$, (C).

Once you have the slope, however, you could find a directly by using the fact that the slope is constant for all pairs of points on the line.

$$1.2 = \frac{1.2 - 0}{2 - a}$$

$$2 - a = 1$$
$$a = 1.$$

[24] If $f(x) = 3x - \dfrac{9}{5}$, then $\dfrac{f(a) - f(b)}{a - b} = ?$

(A) −3

(B) −1

(C) 0

(D) 1

(E) 3

Make the substitutions indicated and carry out the algebra to simplify the expression.

$$\frac{f(a) - f(b)}{a - b} = \frac{(3a - \frac{9}{5}) - (3b - \frac{9}{5})}{a - b}$$

$$= \frac{3a - 3b}{a - b}$$

$$= \frac{3(a - b)}{a - b}$$

$$= 3, \text{ (E)}.$$

If you have studied calculus, this problem may remind you of steps in doing a calculus problem. However, no calculus questions appear on the Math Level IC test and this problem can be done easily by a student with no calculus experience.

Furthermore, you may have recognized

$$\frac{f(a) - f(b)}{a - b}$$

as the formula for the slope of the line containing the points $(a, f(a))$ and $(b, f(b))$. From the given equation for $f(x)$, that slope can easily be seen to be 3, without calculation.

Though no calculus or other higher math is required, the more experience you have with advanced topics, concepts, and techniques, the more quickly and easily you can work through the procedures of elementary and intermediate math.

[25] The functions $f(x)$ and $g(x)$ are defined by values from the following table:

x	$f(x)$	$g(x)$
0	−2	2
2	4	0
4	8	−2

Which of the following is (are) true?

 I. $f(0) = g(4)$

 II. $f(g(2)) = -2$

 III. $g(f(2)) = -2$

(A) I only

(B) I and II only

(C) I and III only

(D) II and III only

(E) I, II, and III

The question tests your ability to interpret information presented in a table and to use functional notation.

From the table, $f(0) = -2$ (line one) and $g(4) = -2$ (line three). Therefore I is true.

For statement II, you first need to know $g(2) = 0$, from line two of the table. Therefore, $f(g(2)) = f(0) = -2$ from line one. Therefore, statement II is true.

For statement III, you need to know that $f(2) = 4$, from line one and then $g(f(2)) = f(4) = -2$ from line three.

All three statements are true, so the answer is (E).

[26] If $f(x) = 16x^2 - 16x + 4$, then $f(.25) = ?$

    (A) -6.25

    (B) -1

    (C) $.25$

    (D) 1

    (E) 6.25

Perhaps you saw the decimal, .25, and reached immediately for your calculator.

Remember that test makers never create a question merely to be an excuse to plug and chug.

First, look for a mathematical principle, concept, or fact illustrated by the question.

In this case, $f(x) = (4x-2)^2$ because $f(x)$ is a trinomial square.

That expression will make substituting for x much easier, even if you do decide to proceed with your calculator from here on.

Now check to see if there is a more convenient form of the number with which you are working.

Note that $.25 = \frac{1}{4}$.

You can now find the result in your head, though we will write the steps below:

$$\left(4\left(\frac{1}{4}\right) - 2\right)^2 = (1-2)^2 = 1, \text{ answer (D)}.$$

If you have not already done so, commit to memory these basic number facts:

$$\frac{1}{2} = .5 \qquad \frac{1}{6} = .1666\ldots$$

$$\frac{1}{3} = .3333\ldots \qquad \frac{1}{8} = .125$$

$$\frac{1}{4} = .25 \qquad \frac{2}{3} = .666\ldots$$

$$\frac{1}{5} = .2 \qquad \frac{3}{4} = .75$$

[27] $F(x) = 0$ only if x is -3, 0, or 1. $F(x+3) = 0$ if and only if $x = ?$

    (A) $-6, 0$, or 1

    (B) $-6, -3$, or -2

    (C) $-3, 0$, or 1

    (D) $3, 0$, or -1

    (E) $0, 3$, or 4

Think of the function $F(x)$ as changing the numbers $-3, 0$, and 1 into 0. Therefore, $F(x+3) = 0$ if and only if $x + 3$ is either $-3, 0$, or 1.

In other words,

$$x+3 = -3, \text{ so } x = -6,$$

$$x+3 = 0, \text{ so } x = -3, \text{ and}$$

$$x+3 = 1, \text{ so } x = -2.$$

These results, -6, -3, and -2, comprise the values listed in answer (B).

Such a line of reasoning may not work well for you if you think we are telling you that x can only be $-3, 0$, or 1 and then, without blinking an eye, telling you the values are really something else, namely $-6, -3$, or -2.

Your skepticism might be eased by approaching the problem from the opposite direction, namely trying values presented in the answers. First, interpret the given information as saying that $F(-3) = 0$, $F(0) = 0$, and $F(1) = 0$. Furthermore, understand that $F(?)$ can only be 0 if you replace the question mark with one of those three numbers.

Now, substitute some values from among the answer choices. Use 0 for x in $F(x+3)$ and you now have $F(3)$. But $F(3)$ is not 0 because only $F(-3)$, $F(0)$, and $F(1)$ produce 0. Then use -6 for x, which gives you $F(-6+3) = F(-3)$. The given information tells you that $F(-3) = 0$, so -6 produces the desired result.

WHAT YOU SHOULD KNOW

KEY CONCEPTS

1. The expression $f(x)$ represents the value of the function at x.
2. The expression $f(g(x))$ represents the value that f assigns to the value that g assigns to x.
3. The graph of a function is symmetric to the graph of its inverse with respect to the line $y = x$.
4. To find an equation of the inverse of a function, substitute x for y and y for x; then solve for y.
5. If a quadratic function is in the form

$$f(x) = a(x - p)^2 + k,$$

then $x = p$ is its axis and (p, k) is its vertex.

TEST-TAKING STRATEGIES

- For appropriate problems, such as determining cross-products, clarify information by representing it in the form of a table.
- Most questions about functions require the use of function notation—that is, $f(x) =$ an algebraic expression involving x. Be sure you understand the use of this notation in calculations and finding ranges.

KEY EQUATIONS

1. For the zero function:

$$y = 0 \quad \text{or} \quad f(x) = 0.$$

2. For the constant function:

$$f(x) = c \quad \text{or} \quad y = c.$$

3. For the identity function:

$$y = x \quad \text{or} \quad f(x) = x.$$

ANSWERS

[1] (B)	[6] (E)	[11] (B)	[16] (A)	[21] (B)	[26] (D)
[2] (E)	[7] (D)	[12] (E)	[17] (D)	[22] (D)	[27] (B)
[3] (B)	[8] (C)	[13] (C)	[18] (B)	[23] (C)	
[4] (A)	[9] (C)	[14] (A)	[19] (C)	[24] (E)	
[5] (A)	[10] (C)	[15] (D)	[20] (A)	[25] (E)	

COMPLEX NUMBERS

CHAPTER

20

KEY TERMS

imaginary number   a unit defined by the equation $i^2 = -1$; in other words, $i = \sqrt{-1}$.

Complex Number System (C)   the set of all numbers $a + bi$ in which a and b are real numbers and $i^2 = -1$.

DEFINING COMPLEX NUMBERS

[1] Which of the following equations has (have) solutions in the complex number system?

I. $x^2 - 1 = 0$

II. $x^2 - 2 = 0$

III. $x^2 + 2 = 0$

(A) I and II only

(B) II and III only

(C) I and III only

(D) All of these

(E) None of these

The extension of the number system from the integers to the rational numbers to the real numbers is motivated by the search for a number system that is "closed." A system is *closed* when every equation that has all of its coefficients in the system has all of its roots in the system.

The set of integers is not closed since it has no solution for $2x + 3 = 0$. The rational numbers fail to provide solutions for $x^2 - 3 = 0$. The extension of the number system to the real numbers incorporates additional elements (the irrationals), but these still don't provide solutions for $x^2 + 3 = 0$ since the square of no real number is negative. To produce a number system that is closed, we need introduce only one additional number and then define a system based on combinations of this new number with the real numbers.

The additional number, i, is termed the *imaginary unit* and is defined by the relation $i^2 = -1$. The extended system is called the *Complex Number System* (designated by C) and consists of the set of all numbers $a + bi$ in which a and b are real numbers and $i^2 = -1$. The $a + bi$ form is called the *standard* form of a complex number with a termed the *real part* and b the *imaginary part*. Note that the imaginary part is actualy a real number.

The complex number system contains three categories of numbers: the reals, the imaginaries, and the "pure" imaginaries. The reals are the numbers for which $b = 0$, such as $3 + 0i$, $-2 + 0i$, $\frac{1}{2} + 0i$, and $\pi + 0i$. These are, of course, the same real numbers we have studied throughout and differ only in form.

The *pure imaginaries* occur when $a = 0$ and $b \neq 0$: $0 + 3i$, $0 + (-2)i$, $0 + \frac{1}{2}i$, $0 + \pi i$, etc. The *imaginaries* are complex numbers for which $a \neq 0$ and $b \neq 0$, such as $3 + 2i$, $5 + (-2)i$, and $\frac{1}{2} + \pi i$.

We define two complex numbers, $a + bi$ and $c + di$, to be *equal* if and only if $a = c$ and $b = d$.

Every equation that has coefficients in the complex number system has roots in the complex number system. Equations I, II, and III have real coefficients, and (as noted above) all real numbers are complex numbers.

■ Check to see how your calculator represents even roots of negative numbers. Most devices provide only an error message, leaving you to do all calculations algebraically. Odd roots of negative numbers should be no problem. They exist and your calculator will find them for you. For example, $\sqrt[3]{-27} = -3$.

TEST-TAKING TIP

The word "complex" may have misled you into thinking the roots are imaginary (since most students do not encounter the term "complex number" until they are introduced to imaginary numbers). Always be sure to read a problem carefully enough to guarantee that you are answering the question asked and not a different one that was suggested by it.

---

[2] If $2x + 3yi = 1 + 4i^2$, then $y = ?$

(A) $\dfrac{4i^2}{3}$

(B) 0

(C) $\dfrac{4}{3}$

(D) 4

(E) $\dfrac{1}{2}$

Since two complex numbers in standard form are equal if and only if their real parts are equal and their imaginary parts are equal, the best way to solve a first-degree equation in two variables that involves the real and imaginary parts of complex numbers is to put both sides of the equation into standard form and set the real parts equal and the imaginary parts equal:

$$\begin{aligned} 2x + 3yi &= 1 + 4i^2 \\ &= 1 + 4(-1) \\ &= -3 \\ &= -3 + (0)i. \end{aligned}$$

Therefore $2x = -3$ and $3y = 0$, so $x = -\frac{3}{2}$ and $y = 0$.

FINDING SOME POWERS OF i

[3] Which of the following has the same value as i^{63}?

(A) i

(B) -1

(C) $-i$

(D) 1

(E) None of these

We have defined i by the relation $i^2 = -1$. This leads to:

$$i^0 = 1, \qquad i^5 = i^4 i = i,$$
$$i^1 = i, \qquad i^6 = i^4 i^2 = 1,$$
$$1^2 = -1, \qquad i^7 = i^4 i^3 = -i,$$
$$i^3 = i^2 i = -i, \qquad i^8 = i^4 i^4 = 1.$$
$$i^4 = i^2 i^2 = 1,$$

You may verify for yourself that successive powers of i take on the values $i, -1, -i, 1$, which continue to repeat in the same order. Thus the higher powers of i can be found by breaking up the power of i into factors of i^4 times whatever power of i remains.

EXAMPLES

$$i^{11} = i^4 i^4 i^3 = 1 \times 1 \times i^3 = -i$$

$$i^{113} = \underbrace{i^4 i^4 \ldots i^4}_{28 \text{ factors}} i = i$$

$$i^{63} = (i^4)^{15}(i^3)$$
$$= (1)^{15}(-1)$$
$$= -1$$

EXAMPLES

1. $i^7 = -i$

2. $i^{19} = -i$

3. $i^{99} = -i$

4. $i^{4m+1} = i$

ADDING COMPLEX NUMBERS

[4] Express the sum of $\sqrt{-36} + \sqrt{-25} + \sqrt{-16}$ as a pure imaginary.

(A) 15

(B) -15

(C) $15i$

(D) $-15i$

(E) $5i$

When a is positive the symbol $\sqrt{a}$ stands for the positive number that when squared is a. When a is negative we define $\sqrt{a}$ to mean $i\sqrt{|a|}$. Thus $\sqrt{-36} = i\sqrt{36}$ or $6i$.

To answer the given question we must use some elementary facts about adding complex numbers. But remember that the real numbers are elements of C. Any laws we establish in C must in no way produce results for the real numbers in C that differ from the results we established for the reals before defining C. One way to help guarantee this uniformity is to accept as postulates for C the same laws we postulated for the reals. From here on we will assume that the properties postulated for the reals will hold true for C. Furthermore, we will make no definition that contradicts the established behavior of the reals.

Since, when $b = 0$ and $d = 0$, the numbers $a + bi$ and $c + di$ are real, we want the result of addition in C to accomplish

$$(a + 0i) + (c + 0i) = (a + c) + 0i.$$

We will, therefore, define addition in C to be

$$(a + bi) + (c + di) = (a + c) + (b + d)i.$$

$$\sqrt{-36} + \sqrt{-25} + \sqrt{-16}$$
$$= i\sqrt{36} + i\sqrt{25} + i\sqrt{16}$$
$$= 6i + 5i + 4i$$
$$= 15i.$$

EXAMPLES

Add the following (put them in standard form and use the definition above):

1. $\sqrt{-4} + \sqrt{-12} = 0 + (2 + 2\sqrt{3})i$

2. $4i + (3 - 9i) = 3 + (-5)i$

3. $(2 + 3i) + (4 + 5i) = 6 + 8i$

4. $6 + (10i - 6) = 0 + 10i$

SUBTRACTING AND MULTIPLYING COMPLEX NUMBERS

[5] If $z_1 = 3 + (-6)i$, $z_2 = 4 + 5i$, and $z_3 = 42 + (-9)i$, the operation that results in z_3 from z_1 and z_2 is:

(A) Addition

(B) Subtraction

(C) Multiplication

(D) Division

(E) None of these

The following definitions for subtraction and multiplication are consistent with the same operations in the reals:

$$(a+bi)-(c+di) \ = \ (a-c)+(b-d)i,$$
$$(a+bi)(c+di) \ = \ (ac-bd)+(bc+ad)i.$$

The second definition may appear complicated but is motivated by the application of familiar procedures.

$$(a+bi)(c+di) \ = \ (a+bi)c+(a+bi)di$$
$$= \ ac+bci+adi+bdi^2$$

Since $i^2 = -1$ this becomes

$$= \ ac+bci+adi-bd$$
$$= \ (ac-bd)+(bc+ad)i.$$

Indeed you may find it easier to ignore the definition above and just repeat the procedure that motivates it. Note that the correct application of the definition necessitates that the numbers be in standard form.

We will postpone our review of division until the next section.

$$(z_1)(z_2) \ = \ (3-6i)(4+5i)$$
$$= \ 12-24i+15i-30i^2$$
$$= \ 12-9i+30$$
$$= \ 42-9i$$

EXAMPLES

Carry out the indicated multiplications and express the products in standard form:

1. $(3-i)(6+i)$

2. $i(1+2i)$

3. $(-6+3i)(6+3i)$

4. $(a-b)(a+bi)$

SOLUTIONS: The simplified products are:

1. $19+(-3)i$

2. $-2+1$

3. $-45+(0)i$

4. $(a^2-ab)+(ab-b^2)i$

FINDING ADDITIVE INVERSES, RECIPROCALS, AND CONJUGATES

[6] If $z_1 = 6 + 2i$ and $z_2 = \dfrac{3}{20} + \dfrac{-1}{20}i$, then the term that best describes the relation between z_1 and z_2 is:

(A) Additive inverses

(B) Reciprocals

(C) Conjugates

(D) z_2 is the absolute value of z_1

(E) No relation

The additive inverse of a number is defined to be the number that when added to the given number yields zero. We designate the additive inverse of z by $-z$. Since zero in standard form is $0+0i$, we can prove that $-(a+bi)$ is $-a+(-b)i$. You may verify this by showing that $-a+(-b)i$ when added to $a+bi$ gives zero.

The reciprocal, or multiplicative inverse, of z is the number that when multiplied by z yields 1. We designate the reciprocal of z by $\frac{1}{z}$. If the standard form of z is $a+bi$, the following discussion derives the standard form of $\frac{1}{(a+bi)}$.

Let $x+yi$ be the reciprocal of $a+bi$; then

$$(a+bi)(x+yi) = 1+0i,$$

by definition of reciprocal. Also,

$$(ax-by)+(ay+bx)i = 1+0i,$$

by definition of multiplication. And

$$(ax-by) = 1 \quad \text{and} \quad (ay+bx) = 0,$$

by definition of "equal" for complex numbers. Solving the last two equations for x and y, simultaneously, produces

$$x = \frac{a}{a^2+b^2} \quad \text{and} \quad y = \frac{-b}{a^2+b^2}$$

The *conjugate* of $a + bi$ is defined to be the number $a + (-b)i$ and could have been used to find the reciprocal. In fact the use of the conjugate of the divisor will simplify the division process in general. Note that the product of a complex number and its conjugate is real:

$$(a+bi)(a+(-b)i) = (a^2+b^2) + (ab-ab)i$$
$$= a^2 + b^2.$$

We will use this fact to change the denominator of $\frac{1}{(a+bi)}$ into a real number and put it in standard form in relatively few steps.

$$\frac{1}{a+bi} \times \frac{a+(-b)i}{a+(-b)i} = \frac{a+(-b)i}{a^2+b^2}$$
$$= \frac{a}{a^2+b^2} + \frac{-b}{a^2+b^2}i$$

In the multiple-choice question,

$$z_1 = 6+2i,$$
$$\frac{1}{z_1} = \frac{1}{6+2i} = \frac{1}{6+2i}\left(\frac{6-2i}{6-2i}\right)$$
$$= \frac{6-2i}{36+12i-12i-4i^2}$$
$$= \frac{6-2i}{40}$$
$$= \frac{3-i}{20} = \frac{3}{20} - \frac{1}{20}i.$$

Therefore z_2 is the reciprocal of z_1.

We will postpone our review of "absolute value" until a later section.

EXAMPLES

For each of the following find its additive inverse, its reciprocal, and its conjugate:

1. $7 - i$

2. $2i$

3. $-i$

4. $a - bi$

SOLUTIONS: The requested expressions are:

1. $-7+i$; $\frac{7}{50} + \frac{1}{50}i$; $7+i$

2. $-2i$; $-\frac{1}{2}i$; $-2i$

3. i; i; i

4. $-a+bi$; $\frac{a}{a^2+b^2} + \frac{b}{a^2+b^2}i$; $b+bi$

DIVIDING COMPLEX NUMBERS

[7] Evaluate $\frac{2-i}{1+i}$ and put it in standard form.

(A) $\left(\frac{1}{2} - \frac{3}{2}\right)i$

(B) $\frac{1}{2} + \left(-\frac{3}{2}\right)i$

(C) $2 - \frac{1}{i}$

(D) None of these

(E) All of these

If z_1 and z_2 are complex numbers, then $\frac{z_1}{z_2}$ is that number z such that $z_2 \cdot z = z_1$. We could use this definition to divide complex numbers, but the process is a lengthy one and involves the solution of a pair of simultaneous equations in two variables. Instead we will multiply the numerator and denominator by the conjugate of the denominator. The resulting fraction will have a real denominator, and the complex number it represents can then be easily expressed in standard form.

EXAMPLE

Evaluate $\frac{5+2i}{6+4i}$.

SOLUTION: Multiply the numerator and denominator by the conjugate of the denominator:

$$\frac{5+2i}{6+4i} \times \frac{6-4i}{6-4i} = \frac{38-8i}{52}$$
$$= \frac{38}{52} + \frac{-8}{52}i$$
$$= \frac{19}{26} + \frac{-2}{13}i$$

To evaluate the expression in the multiple-choice question,

$$\frac{2-i}{1+i} = \left(\frac{2-i}{1+i}\right)\left(\frac{1-i}{1-i}\right)$$
$$= \frac{2-i-2i+i^2}{1+1}$$
$$= \frac{1-3i}{2}$$

EXAMPLES

Perform the following divisions by the method of conjugates:

1. $1 \div (3 + 2i)$

2. $(2 + 3i) \div (5 + 4i)$

3. $3i \div (8 + 3i)$

4. $(3 + \sqrt{2i}) \div (3 - \sqrt{2i})$

SOLUTIONS: The quotients are:

1. $\dfrac{3}{13} + \dfrac{-2}{13}i$

2. $\dfrac{22}{41} + \dfrac{7}{41}i$

3. $\dfrac{9}{73} + \dfrac{24}{73}i$

4. $\dfrac{7}{11} + \dfrac{6\sqrt{2}}{11}i$

USING THE QUADRATIC FORMULA

[8]   If $r + si$ is a solution of $ax^3 + bx^2 + cx + d = 0$, where a, b, c, and d are real, then another solution is:

(A) $r - si$

(B) $-r + si$

(C) $-(r + si)$

(D) All of these

(E) None of these

Let us begin the discussion of the complex roots of a polynomial equation with a simpler situation than the one aoove and then extend our results.

When the domain of x for $ax^2 + bx + c = 0$ is the set of real numbers, we can derive the values of x by the

Quadratic Formula. We state without proof that the same formula produces the solutions for $ax^2 + bx + c = 0$ when the domain of x is C and all of a, b, and c are real.

When the discriminant $b^2 - 4ac$ is negative, the solution set contains the two imaginary numbers:

$$\frac{-b \pm i\sqrt{|b2 - 4ac|}}{2a}$$

You may verify that the two solutions above are conjugates of each other.

If the roots of a polynomial with *real* coefficients are imaginary, then these imaginary roots come in *conjugate* pairs.

In the multiple-choice question, $r + si$ is given as a root of an equation with real coefficients, so $r - si$ must also be a root.

EXAMPLES

Use the Quadratic Formula to find the roots of:

1. $3x^2 + x + 2 = 0$

2. $x^2 + 2x + 1 = 0$

3. $x^2 - 3x + 8 = 0$

If one of the roots of $ax^5 + bx^4 + cx^3 + dx^2 + ex + f = 0$, where a, b, c, d, e, and f are real, is given in each of the following, find another root:

4. $3 + i$

5. $-5i$

6. $i + 1$

SOLUTIONS: The requested values are:

1. $-\dfrac{1}{6} \pm \dfrac{\sqrt{23}}{6}i$

2. -1

3. $\dfrac{3}{2} \pm \dfrac{\sqrt{23}}{2}i$

4. $3 - i$

5. $5i$

6. $1 - i$

[9] The solution set of $x^6 - 64 = 0$, with the set of complex numbers as its domain, contains:

(A) $-1 + \sqrt{3}i$

(B) 2 only

(C) 2 and -2 only

(D) No more than 4 distinct roots

(E) No roots

We can use the Quadratic Formula to find the roots of equations of higher degree when these equations have members that can be factored into linear and quadratic factors. For example, the expression in the question above can be factored as follows:

$$x^6 - 64 = 0,$$
$$(x^3 - 8)(x^3 + 8) = 0,$$
$$(x - 2)(x^2 + 2x + 4)(x + 2)(x^2 - 2x + 4) = 0.$$

The linear factors yield the roots 2 and -2. The quadratic factors yield the roots $-1 \pm i\sqrt{3}$ and $1 \pm i\sqrt{3}$ from the Quadratic Formula.

MULTIPLYING THE ROOTS OF NEGATIVE NUMBERS

[10] If a and b are real numbers, then under which of the following conditions is $\sqrt{a}\sqrt{b} = \sqrt{ab}$ NOT true?

(A) $a > 0, b > 0$

(B) $a < 0, b > 0$

(C) $a < 0, b < 0$

(D) $a > 0, b < 0$

(E) $a = 0, b = 0$

When $x > 0$, we define $\sqrt{x}$ to be the nonnegative number that when squared is x. From this we may derive the statement $\sqrt{x}\sqrt{y} = \sqrt{xy}$ when x and y are positive by showing that $\sqrt{x}\sqrt{y}$ is the nonnegative number that when squared is xy. The rule can be extended if only one of x or y is negative, as in

$$\sqrt{-2}\sqrt{18} = \sqrt{-36} = 6i.$$

But it does lead to a contradiction when both $x < 0$ and $y < 0$. If the rule were applicable to the latter situation, then

$$\sqrt{-2}\sqrt{-2} = \sqrt{(-2)(-2)} = \sqrt{4} = 2.$$

The latter statement contradicts the meaning of $\sqrt{-2}$ since we want the square of $\sqrt{-2}$ to be -2.

Thus $\sqrt{a}\sqrt{b} = \sqrt{ab}$ is inconsistent with the definition of $\sqrt{}$ when both a and b are negative. This does not, however, leave us without a formula for the multiplication of the roots of negative numbers—our definition. Therefore

$$\sqrt{a} = i\sqrt{|a|} \text{ when } a < 0$$

provides the clue:

If $a < 0$ and $b < 0$, then

$$\begin{aligned} \sqrt{a}\sqrt{b} &= i\sqrt{|a|}\,i\sqrt{|b|} \\ &= i^2\sqrt{|a|}\sqrt{|b|} \\ &= -\sqrt{|a|}\sqrt{|b|}. \end{aligned}$$

But $|a|$ and $|b|$ are positive real numbers, so

$$-\sqrt{|a|}\sqrt{|b|} = -\sqrt{|a|\,|b|}$$

EXAMPLES

Carry out each of the following multiplications:

1. $\sqrt{-3}\sqrt{-4}$

2. $\sqrt{4}\sqrt{-3}$

3. $\sqrt{-4}\sqrt{3}$

4. $\sqrt{4}\sqrt{3}$

SOLUTIONS: The results are:

1. $\begin{aligned} \sqrt{-3}\sqrt{-4} &= (i\sqrt{3})(i\sqrt{4}) \\ &= -(\sqrt{3})(2) \\ &= -2\sqrt{3} \end{aligned}$

2. $\sqrt{4}\sqrt{-3} = 2i\sqrt{3}$

3. $2i\sqrt{3}$

4. $2\sqrt{3}$

FINDING THE ABSOLUTE VALUE OF A COMPLEX NUMBER

[11] In the complex plane, which of the following does NOT determine a point on a circle of radius 1 with center at the origin?

(A) 1

(B) i

(C) $\dfrac{1}{2} - \dfrac{\sqrt{3}}{2}i$

(D) $1 - i$

(E) $-\dfrac{\sqrt{2}}{2} - \dfrac{\sqrt{2}}{2}i$

Recall that two complex numbers in standard form are equal if and only if the real parts are equal and the imaginary parts are equal. Thus, if $a \neq b$, then $a + bi \neq b + ai$. In other words, each complex number determines a pair of real numbers for which the order makes a difference. The complex number $a + bi$ determines the ordered pair (a, b) and the number $b + ai$ determines (b, a). Our experience with ordered pairs suggests that we can form a coordinate plane with points determined by complex numbers, a complex number plane. We establish the horizontal axis as the *axis of reals* and agree that our x-coordinates shall be the real parts of the complex numbers. The vertical axis is the *axis of imaginaries*, and we shall let the y-coordinates be the imaginary parts of the complex numbers.

A reminder: the imaginary part of a complex number is a real number—the definition of "imaginary part" excludes the i.

To graph a point that corresponds to a given complex number, put the number in standard form, find the ordered pair it determines, and then plot the ordered pair in the manner already established for the real number plane.

We define the *absolute value* of the complex number $a + bi$ to be its distance from the origin. Using the Pythagorean Theorem, we can demonstrate this distance to be $\sqrt{a^2 + b^2}$ and write the following:

$$|a + bi| = \sqrt{a^2 + b^2}.$$

(A) $|1| = \sqrt{1^2 + 0^2} = \sqrt{1} = 1.$

(B) $|i| = |0 + 1i| = \sqrt{0^2 + 1^2} = \sqrt{1} = 1.$

(C) $\left|\dfrac{1}{2} - \dfrac{\sqrt{3}}{2}i\right| = \sqrt{\left(\dfrac{1}{2}\right)^2 + \left(\dfrac{\sqrt{3}}{2}\right)^2} = \sqrt{1} = 1.$

(D) $|1 - i| = \sqrt{1^2 + 1^2} = \sqrt{2}.$

(E) $\left|-\dfrac{\sqrt{2}}{2} - \dfrac{\sqrt{2}}{2}i\right| = \sqrt{\left(\dfrac{\sqrt{2}}{2}\right)^2 + \left(\dfrac{\sqrt{2}}{2}\right)^2} = 1.$

EXAMPLES

Find the absolute value of each of the following:

1. $2 + 4i$

2. 0

3. $5i - 2$

4. $3 - i$

SOLUTIONS: The absolute values are:

1. $\sqrt{2^2 + 4^2} = \sqrt{20} = 2\sqrt{5}$

2. $\sqrt{0^2 + 0^2} = 0$

3. $\sqrt{5^2 + 2^2} = \sqrt{25 + 4} = \sqrt{29}$

4. $\sqrt{3^2 + 1^2} = \sqrt{9 + 1} = \sqrt{10}$

FACTORING OVER COMPLEX NUMBERS

[12] One of the factors of $4a^2 + 16y^2$ over the complex numbers is:

(A) $2a + 4y$

(B) $2a - 4y$

(C) $4a + yi$

(D) $a + 4yi$

(E) $2a - 4yi$

Recall that $a^2 - b^2$ can be factored over the reals (not to mention the integers, rationals, etc.) since it is the difference of squares:

(1) $$a^2 - b^2 = (a - b)(a + b).$$

Recall also that $a^2 + b^2$ cannot be factored over the reals. But it can be factored over the complex numbers since it can be represented by

(2) $$a^2 - (ib)^2.$$

Expression (2) follows from $(ib)^2 = -b^2$. Thus

(3) $$a^2 + b^2 = a^2 - (ib)^2 = (a + ib)(a - ib).$$

In the multiple-choice question we can represent the given expression by $(2a)^2 - (4yi)^2$. The factors are, therefore:

$$(2a - 4yi)(2a + 4yi).$$

EXAMPLES

Note the factor of each of the following over C:

1. $x^2 + y^2 = (x - yi)(x + yi)$

2. $x^2 - y^2 = (x + y)(x - y)$

3. $2a^2 + 3b^2 = (a\sqrt{2} + bi\sqrt{3})(a\sqrt{2} - bi\sqrt{3})$

SOLVING OTHER COMPLEX NUMBER PROBLEMS

[13] Which of the following statements is (are) true?

    I. The product of any two complex numbers that are conjugates of each other is a real number.

    II. The sum of any two complex numbers that are conjugates of each other is imaginary.

    III. The conjugate of i equals the reciprocal of i.

    (A) I and II only

    (B) II and III only

    (C) I only

    (D) III only

    (E) I and III only

  I. If $z = a + bi$, then the conjugate of z (designated by $\bar{z}$) has been defined to be $a - bi$ for every z in C. Thus:

$$\begin{aligned} z \cdot \bar{z} &= (a + bi)(a - bi) \\ &= a^2 + b^2 + (ab - ab)i \\ &= a^2 + b^2 + (0)i. \end{aligned}$$

Since a and b are both real, $a^2 + b^2$ is real and $z \cdot \bar{z}$ is real.

  II. Similarly,

$$\begin{aligned} z + \bar{z} &= a + bi + a - bi \\ &= 2a + (0)i. \end{aligned}$$

Since a is real, $2a$ is real and $z + \bar{z}$ is real.

III. Finally, the conjugate of i is $-i$. The reciprocal of i is $\frac{1}{i}$. But

$$\frac{1}{i} = \frac{1(i)}{i \cdot i} = \frac{i}{-1} = -i.$$

Thus $\bar{i} = \frac{1}{i}$.

[14] If z is a complex number and $\bar{z} = \frac{1}{z}$, then a possible value for z is:

    (A) $1 + i$

    (B) 0

    (C) $2 + 2i$

    (D) $-1 + i$

    (E) 1

When a single variable such as z is used to represent a complex number, it is sometimes preferable to express the number in standard form. In other words, let $z = x + yi$, where x and y are real numbers. This conversion allows you to use the familiar rules of the real numbers as well as those of the complex.

To solve the multiple-choice question let $z = x + yi$; then

$$\bar{z} = \frac{1}{z},$$

$$x - yi = \frac{1}{x + yi},$$

$$x^2 + y^2 = 1.$$

In coordinate geometry the last equation defines a circle of radius 1 with center at the origin. Any complex number whose real part and imaginary part satisfy this equation will answer the question.

For choice (E), $1 + 0i$, $x = 1$ and $y = 0$, so

$$x^2 + y^2 = 1.$$

TEST-TAKING TIP

The method of testing each choice to see whether it satisfies the original conditions can be a lengthy and tedious process—a fact you will recognize immediately on trying it. The best method to use here was to transform the given condition into one that provided a simpler means of checking. Test-takers must be skilled in a great number of problem-solving strategies if they are to be consistently successful. No one method will always work best—or even work at all.

[15] If $i = \sqrt{-1}$ and $x - xi = 2$, then $x = ?$

(A) $1 - i$

(B) $1 + i$

(C) i

(D) $2i$

(E) $-2i$

Factor $x - xi$ to rewrite the equation as

$$(1 - i)x = 2.$$

Now divide both sides by $1 - i$.

$$x = \frac{2}{1 - i}$$

The value shown for x is correct, but it is not in a form that is recognizable among the answer choices.

What do you do to transform it?

Note that none of the choices has a denominator. Your job, then, is to find a way to eliminate the denominator of $\frac{2}{(1-i)}$.

Multiply the fraction by $\frac{(1+i)}{(1+i)}$.

$$\frac{2(1+i)}{(1-i)(1+i)} = \frac{2(1+i)}{1-i^2} = \frac{2(1+i)}{2} = 1+i, \text{ (B)}.$$

Note that trying the choices in the original equation might have been a tedious option unless you hit the correct answer early in the process.

Here's what it looks like when you try $1 + i$ for x in $x - xi$:

$$\begin{aligned}(1+i) - (1+i)i &= 1+i-i-i^2 \\ &= 1+i-i+1 \\ &= 2.\end{aligned}$$

[16] If $i = \sqrt{-1}$ and the solutions of $x^2 - 2x + 2 = 0$ are r and $1 + i$, then $r = ?$

(A) $1 + 2i$

(B) 2

(C) $-i$

(D) $1 - i$

(E) $2 + i$

Test makers like questions that can be answered using several approaches that differ in complexity.

The answer to this question can be found very simply if you know that the imaginary solutions of equations with real coefficients must come in conjugate pairs. In other words, when $a + bi$ is a solution, $a - bi$ is also a solution if the coefficients are real. The coefficients of the given equation are 1, -2, and 2, all real numbers, so the solution $1 + i$ will be matched with the solution $1 - i$, choice (D).

If you had forgotten that fact, you could still find the answer by solving the equation using the quadratic formula.

Here,

$$\frac{-b \pm \sqrt{b^2 = 4ac}}{2a} = \frac{2 \pm \sqrt{2^2 - 8}}{2} = 1 \pm i.$$

By not knowing the simpler concept, you pay the price in time that might otherwise have been spent answering additional questions, but you eventually gain the points for answering this one.

WHAT YOU SHOULD KNOW

KEY CONCEPTS

1. The standard form of a complex number is $a + bi$, where a and b are real.
2. To find the value of i^n, where n is a positive integer, divide n by 4 to get the remainder, r. The value of i^n is i^r.
3. For $a < 0$, $\sqrt{a} = i\sqrt{|a|}$.
4. If a, b, c, and d are real numbers, then:
    a. $(a+bi)+(c+di) = (a+c)+(b+d)i$,
    b. $(a+bi)-(c+di) = (a-c)+(b-d)i$,
    c. $(a+bi)(c+di) = (ac-bd)+(ad+bc)i$.
5. To find the value of $\dfrac{a+bi}{c+di}$, multiply by $\dfrac{c-di}{c-di}$ and simplify the result.
6. If $a + bi$ is a root of an equation with real coefficients, then $a - bi$ is also a root.
7. If $a < 0$ and $b < 0$, then
$$\sqrt{a}\sqrt{b} = -1\sqrt{|ab|}.$$
8. In the complex number plane, the graph of $a + bi$ is the point whose coordinates are (a, b).

KEY FORMULA

If $ax^2 + bx + c = 0$ and $a \neq 0$, then
$$x = \frac{-b \pm \sqrt{b^2 - 4ac}}{2a}.$$
(Quadratic Formula)

TEST-TAKING STRATEGIES

- If, in solving a complex number problem, you realize that the first method you try will be a lengthy process, abandon it in favor of another logical approach, and then if necessary try a third, since test questions rarely require long, tedious procedures.
- In dealing with high powers of i, look for cyclical patterns; for example,
$$i^2 = i^6 = i^{10} = i^{14} = \ldots = -1.$$
- In operating with complex numbers, i can be treated as though it were a variable like x. When the result involves a power of i, calculate the power from the cyclical pattern of powers of i.

CALCULATOR TIP

Know how your calculator represents the roots of a negative number. For even roots, most calculators will display an error message of some form. For odd roots, the calculator should find the correct value.

ANSWERS

[1] (D)	[4] (C)	[7] (B)	[10] (C)	[13] (E)	[16] (D)
[2] (B)	[5] (C)	[8] (A)	[11] (D)	[14] (E)	
[3] (C)	[6] (B)	[9] (A)	[12] (E)	[15] (B)	

SYSTEMS OF EQUATIONS

CHAPTER

21

KEY TERMS

linear equation	any equation of the form $ax + by + c = 0$, where a, b, and c are real numbers and not both of a and b are zero.
solution set of a linear equation	the set of ordered pairs, (x, y), that satisfy the equation.
system of linear equations	a set of two (or more) linear equations.
solution set of a system	the set of ordered pairs that satisfy the two equations of the system.
equivalent systems of equations	two systems that have the same solution set.

SOLVING A SYSTEM OF EQUATIONS BY GRAPHING

[1]   Which of the following best describes the graph of the solution set of the system:

$$\begin{vmatrix} 2x+y=4 \\ 2x-y=-8 \end{vmatrix} ?$$

(A) A pair of intersecting lines

(B) A pair of parallel lines

(C) A point

(D) A single line

(E) The graph of the solution set contains no points

The *solution set of a system* is the set of ordered pairs that satisfy both equations—in other words, the intersection of the solution sets of the two equations of the system. When the graphs of the two linear equations are intersecting lines, the graph of the solution set of the system is a point; when the lines are parallel, the graph of the solution set of the system contains *no* points. If the two linear equations are different equations for the same line, the solution set of the system is the set of all points on this line.

An elementary method of solving a system is to graph the composing lines and find the solution set by inspection.

EXAMPLE

Graph the system containing

$$2x+y=4$$

and

$$2x-y=-8.$$

SOLUTION: The point of intersection has coordinates $(-1,6)$. A common error is to consider the graph of the solution set to mean the same thing as the graph of the system. The graph of this system is the pair of intersecting lines, but the graph of its solution set is only the point $(-1,6)$.

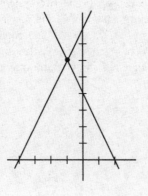

Using a graphing calculator, you can enter the equations, display the graphs of the lines, and then locate the points of intersection. With most graphing calculators, the equations must first be converted to $y =$ form. These calculators also have programs that determine the points of intersection.

Solving a system by graphing has only limited practical value, because coordinates that are not integers are hard to determine. In the next few sections we will review algebraic methods.

TEST-TAKING TIP
Diagrams can be useful in suggesting relationships between algebraic quantities and parts of geometric figures. Diagrams can also suggest problem-solving approaches. Rarely, however, can precise information about lengths, measures, and coordinates be judged accurately from a sketch. Don't rely solely on a sketch for precise information about lengths and measures.

EXAMPLES

Solve the following systems graphically:

1. $\begin{vmatrix} x-y=5 \\ x+2y=2 \end{vmatrix}$

2. $\begin{vmatrix} x+2y=2 \\ 3x-4y=6 \end{vmatrix}$

3. $\begin{vmatrix} 5x+2y=13 \\ 4x+3y=9 \end{vmatrix}$

SOLUTIONS: The lines cross at the following points:

1. $(4,-1)$

2. $(2,0)$

3. $(3,-1)$

DETERMINING EQUIVALENT SYSTEMS

[2] Which of the following systems is equivalent to:
$$\begin{vmatrix} x+y=6 \\ x-2y=-6 \end{vmatrix} ?$$

(A) $\begin{vmatrix} x=2 \\ y=4 \end{vmatrix}$

(B) $\begin{vmatrix} y=2 \\ x=4 \end{vmatrix}$

(C) $\begin{vmatrix} x=6 \\ y=-6 \end{vmatrix}$

(D) $\begin{vmatrix} x=2 \\ y=2 \end{vmatrix}$

(E) $\begin{vmatrix} x=4 \\ y=4 \end{vmatrix}$

Two systems of equations are *equivalent* if and only if they have the same solution set. Algebraic methods of solving systems (sometimes called "simultaneous" equations) are procedures that transform a system into a simpler equivalent system. The simplest type of system is that which consists of a horizontal and vertical line, and its form is
$$\begin{vmatrix} x=h \\ y=k. \end{vmatrix}$$

Its solution set can be determined by inspection as follows: every point on the vertical line $x=h$ must have h as its x-coordinate and every point on $y=k$ must have k as its y-coordinate. In order for a point to lie on both, its coordinates must be (h,k).

To answer the multiple-choice question, find the solution of the system of simultaneous equations by any of the methods in the next two sections. Then represent the vertical and horizontal lines through the points.

EXAMPLES

Graph each of the following systems, and determine from your graph an equivalent system consisting of a horizontal and a vertical line:

1. $\begin{vmatrix} 3x-2y=19 \\ x+y=23 \end{vmatrix}$

2. $\begin{vmatrix} x+2y=3 \\ 3y+4x=2 \end{vmatrix}$

SOLUTIONS: The pairs of vertical and horizontal lines are:

1. $x=3$ and $y=10$

2. $x=-1$ and $y=2$

SOLVING A SYSTEM OF EQUATIONS BY SUBSTITUTION

[3] Which of the following systems are equivalent?

I. $\begin{vmatrix} y=5x-4 \\ y=-3x+2 \end{vmatrix}$

II. $\begin{vmatrix} y=5x-4 \\ 5x-4=-3x+2 \end{vmatrix}$

III. $\begin{vmatrix} y=-3x+2 \\ -3x+2=5x-4 \end{vmatrix}$

(A) All are equivalent

(B) I and II only

(C) II and III only

(D) I and III only

(E) No one is equivalent to any other

The method of substitution provides a way of solving a system and is based on the fact that the following two systems are equivalent:

21-1
$$\begin{vmatrix} ax+by+c=0 \\ y=mx+k \end{vmatrix} \leftrightarrow \begin{vmatrix} ax+b(mx+k)+c=0 \\ y=mx+k \end{vmatrix}$$

We will use the symbol $\leftrightarrow$ to mean "is equivalent to." This equivalence may be verified by noting that the lower equations in the two systems are the same and that the only alteration in the upper equation is the substitution for y of the expression equal to y from the lower equation. The value to us lies in the fact that the new upper equation now contains only the variable x.

EXAMPLE 1

Solve the system:

$$\left|\begin{array}{l} 3x - y = 15 \\ 2x + y = 10. \end{array}\right.$$

SOLUTION: We solve one equation (either one) for y, which transforms the system to:

$$\left|\begin{array}{l} 3x - y = 15 \\ y = -2x + 10. \end{array}\right.$$

We then substitute $-2x + 10$ for y in the upper equation to get the equivalent system:

$$\left|\begin{array}{l} 3x - (-2x + 10) = 15 \\ y = -2x + 10. \end{array}\right.$$

The latter system simplifies to:

$$\left|\begin{array}{l} x = 5 \\ y = -2x + 10. \end{array}\right.$$

The solution set can now be determined by inspection, since any ordered pair that satisfies it must have an x-coordinate of 5. The second equation gives us the companion y-value, $y = -2(5) + 10 = 0$.

EXAMPLE 2

Solve the system:

$$\left|\begin{array}{l} 6m - 2n = 1 \\ 3m + 10n = 6. \end{array}\right.$$

SOLUTION: Applying the same procedure as in the preceding example, we first solve one equation for a variable, set up an equivalent system resulting from a substitution, and then simplify.

$$\left|\begin{array}{l} 6m - 2n = 1 \\ 3m + 10n = 6 \end{array}\right. \leftrightarrow \left|\begin{array}{l} n = 3m - \dfrac{1}{2} \\ 3m + 10\left(3m - \dfrac{1}{2}\right) = 6 \end{array}\right.$$

$$\leftrightarrow \left|\begin{array}{l} n = 3m - \dfrac{1}{2} \\ m = \dfrac{1}{3} \end{array}\right.$$

Since $m = \frac{1}{3}$ and $n = 3m - \frac{1}{2}$, $n = 3(\frac{1}{3}) - \frac{1}{2} = \frac{1}{2}$ and the solution set contains only the ordered pair $(\frac{1}{3}, \frac{1}{2})$.

In the multiple-choice question, systems II and III are based on substitutions using the equations of system I. Each contains one equation from system I and a second equation that replaces y by its equivalent algebraic expression from the other equation in I.

SOLVING A SYSTEM OF EQUATIONS BY ELIMINATING A VARIABLE

[4]   A system contains the equations $ax + by + c = 0$ and $dx + ey + f = 0$, whose graphs are a pair of intersecting lines. A second system contains the equations $ax + by + c = 0$ and $p(ax + by + c) + q(dx + ey + f) = 0$. For what values of p and q will the systems be equivalent?

(A) $p = 0$ and $q = 0$ only

(B) $q = 0$ only

(C)   All values of p and q

(D)   No values of p and q

(E) $p \neq 0$ or $q \neq 0$

If the original system,

$$(1) \qquad \left|\begin{array}{l} ax + by + c = 0 \\ dx + ey + f = 0, \end{array}\right.$$

is a pair of intersecting lines, then their intersection is some point (m, n). Thus (m, n) satisfies both equations. In other words:

$$(2) \qquad am + bn + c = 0 \quad \text{and} \quad dm + en + f = 0.$$

The second system,

$$(3) \qquad \left|\begin{array}{l} ax + by + c = 0 \\ p(ax + by + c) + q(dx + ey + f) = 0, \end{array}\right.$$

must also be satisfied by (m, n) from the following argument. We have already concluded that (m, n) satisfies the equations of the original system (see (2)). Thus

$$(4) \qquad \begin{aligned} p(am + bn + c) &+ q(dm + en + f) \\ &= p(0) + q(0) = 0. \end{aligned}$$

But if both p and q are zero, then

$$(5) \qquad p(ax + by + c) + q(dx + ey + f) = 0$$

is not a linear equation, so the second system, (3), would consist of only one linear equation as well as the identity $0 = 0$. If only $q = 0$, we get a system containing two different equations for the same line:

$$(6) \qquad \left|\begin{array}{l} ax + by + c = 0 \\ p(ax + by + c) = 0. \end{array}\right.$$

If only $p = 0$, then we get the original system, except that the second equation has been multiplied by a constant.

You may have noted that we are already well on the way to solving the system, but we will postpone our review of this until the next section.

SOLVING WORD PROBLEMS

[5]   A boat takes two trips on a river. On the first trip it travels upstream for 5 hours and returns in 2 hours. On the second trip it goes downstream for 3 hours, turns around and heads back upstream. After spending 7 hours on the return trip it is still 2 miles from its starting point. Which of the following is the speed of the current in miles per hour?

(A) 3

(B) 4

(C) 5

(D) 6

(E) 7

An important application of systems of equations is to the solution of word problems. We will review the method of solution through elimination by solving a few systems derived from word problems.

As with the majority of such problems, we let our variables represent the quantities asked for: b = rate of the boat exclusive of any effects of current (sometimes called its rate in still water) and s = rate of stream. Its speed going upstream is thus $b - s$ and going downstream is $b + s$. Since it takes 5 hours to cover the upstream leg of the first trip and $b - s$ miles is covered each hour, the distance upstream must be $5(b - s)$. By similar reasoning we find the distance back down to be $2(b + s)$. But these two distances must be the same. In other words,

$$5(b - s) = 2(b + s),$$

which becomes

(1) $3b - 7s = 0.$

For the second trip the first leg takes 3 hours downstream so the distance traveled is $3(b + s)$. When the boat comes back upstream for 7 hours, it covers a distance of $7(b - s)$ miles, but this is 2 miles short of the downstream distance. In other words,

$$3(b + s) - 2 = 7(b - s),$$

which becomes

(2) $2b - 5s + 1 = 0.$

From equations (1) and (2) we get the following system to solve:

(3) $\begin{vmatrix} 3b - 7s = 0 \\ 2b - 5s + 1 = 0. \end{vmatrix}$

System (3) is equivalent to

(4) $\begin{vmatrix} 3b - 7s = 0 \\ m(3b - 7s) + n(2b - 5s + 1) = 0. \end{vmatrix}$

We select values for m and n that will eliminate the b variable: $m = 2$, $n = 3$, and system (4) becomes

(5) $\begin{vmatrix} 3b - 7s = 0 \\ s = 3. \end{vmatrix}$

Since $s = 3$ and $3b = 7s$, then $b = 7$. The rate of the boat is thus 7 miles per hour and of the stream is 3 miles per hour.

EXAMPLE

We have two containers of sugar solution; the first is 4 percent and the second 8 percent. How much of each should we combine to get 40 gallons of a 5 percent solution?

SOLUTION: Let x represent the number of gallons of 4 percent solution and y the number of gallons of 8 percent solution in the *final* mixture. Then

$$x + y = 40.$$

To get a second equation we note that the amount of sugar contributed by the 4 percent solution, 4 percent of x, when added to the amount of sugar contributed by the 8 percent solution, 8 percent of y, must yield the amount of sugar in the final solution, 5 percent of 40. In other words,

$$.04x + .08y = .05(40).$$

From these two equations we get the system:

$$\begin{vmatrix} x + y = 40 \\ .04x + .08y = 2. \end{vmatrix}$$

We multiply both sides of the lower equation by 100 to remove the decimals and then transform each equation until the right member is 0.

$$\begin{vmatrix} x + y - 40 = 0 \\ 4x + 8y - 200 = 0 \end{vmatrix}$$

This latter system is equivalent to

$$\begin{vmatrix} x + y - 40 = 0 \\ p(x + y - 40) + q(4x + 8y - 200) = 0. \end{vmatrix}$$

We choose $p = -4$ and $q = 1$ to get

$$\begin{vmatrix} x + y - 40 = 0 \\ y = 10. \end{vmatrix}$$

The proper solutions are 10 gallons of 8 percent solution and 30 gallons of 4 percent solution.

EXAMPLES

Solve each of the systems by elimination:

1. $\begin{vmatrix} 4x + 5y - 6 = 0 \\ 2x + 3y - 4 = 0 \end{vmatrix}$

2. $\begin{vmatrix} 4x - 8y = 17 \\ 12x + 16y = -9 \end{vmatrix}$

3. $\begin{vmatrix} 2x + 5y - 19 = 0 \\ 3x = -4y - 6 \end{vmatrix}$

SOLUTIONS: The points of intersection are:

1. $(-1, 2)$

2. $\left(\dfrac{5}{4}, -\dfrac{3}{2} \right)$

3. $(2, -3)$

[6] A father is 4 times as old as his son. Five years ago he was 9 times as old as his son was then. What is the son's present age in years?

(A) 6

(B) 7

(C) 8

(D) 9

(E) 10

In section [5] we began an exploration of the use of systems of equations to solve certain types of word problems. We will continue by analyzing the above question and several other examples.

Let f be the father's age now and s be the son's age. Since the father's age is 4 times the son's,

(1) $\qquad\qquad f = 4s.$

Five years ago, the father's age was $f - 5$ and the son's age was $s - 5$. Since the father was 9 times as old as the son, $f - 5 = 9(s - 5)$, and

(2) $\qquad\qquad f - 9s = -40.$

Which of the two methods, substitution or elimination, would you choose to solve the system containing (1) and (2)? Though both, of course, give the same answer, substitution is probably easier:

(3) $\qquad 4s - 9s = -40$ (Substitution of $4s$ for f in (2)),

$\qquad\qquad -5s = -40,$

$\qquad\qquad\quad s = 8.$

EXAMPLE

A certain two-digit number has the following characteristics: (1) the tens digit when multiplied by 3 equals the sum of the digits, and (2) the number that is obtained by reversing the digits is 54 less than the product of 4 and the original number. Find the number.

SOLUTION: Let t equal the tens digit and u equal the units digit. A common error is to conclude from this that the number itself must then be $t + u$. Note, however, that a two-digit number, say 37, is equal to ten times the tens digit plus the units digit: $37 = 3 \times 10 + 7$. We conclude that the original number is $10t + u$ and the number obtained by reversing the digits is $10u + t$. We translate characteristic (1) to

(1) $\qquad\qquad 3t = t + u,$

and characteristic (2) to

(2) $\qquad\qquad 10u + t = 4(10t + u) - 54.$

Simplifying (1) and (2), we get

(3) $\begin{vmatrix} 2t - u = 0 \\ 6u - 39t + 54 = 0. \end{vmatrix}$

Since $2t - u = 0$, $u = 2t$. By the substitution method, $t = 2$ and $u = 4$, so the number is 24.

EXAMPLES

1. The sum of two numbers is 10 and their difference is 4. Find the two numbers.

2. If the perimeter of a certain square is increased by 100 inches, the area of the square becomes 325 more than three times its original area. Find the original dimensions.

SOLUTIONS:

1. $x + y = 0$

$\quad x - y = 4$

$\quad\ 2x = 14$

$\qquad x = 7$

$\qquad y = 3$

2. Let P = the original perimeter and A = original area; then

$$\left(\frac{P}{4} \right)^2 = A \ \text{ and } \ \left(\frac{P + 100}{4} \right)^2$$
$$= 325 + 3A.$$

As with many simple problems susceptible to solution by systems of equations, this one is more easily done by solving a single equation in one unknown. The square has a side of 30 inches.

GRAPHING LINEAR INEQUALITIES

[7]   Which geometric figure best describes the graph of the solution set of the system:

$$\begin{vmatrix} x+y>7 \\ 2x-y>3 \end{vmatrix} ?$$

(A) An angle

(B) The exterior of an angle

(C) The interior of an angle

(D) The exterior of a triangle

(E) The interior of a triangle

If a given line, L, has the equation $ax+by+c=0$, then the inequalities $ax+by+c>0$ and $ax+by+c<0$ determine the regions on either side of L. L is called the boundary condition of the regions and provides a ready method for graphing them.

EXAMPLE 1

Draw the graph of $3x-4y+12>0$.

SOLUTION: The graph is one side of the line $3x-4y+12=0$. First graph the boundary condition, but indicate it as a dotted line since no point of the line satisfies the inequality. To discover which side of the line is the one in question, substitute the coordinates of some point that can be easily located on one side of the line. In this case we will choose the origin:

$$3(0)-4(0)+12>0.$$

Since this point clearly satisfies the inequality, the graph in question must be the region determined by the line and containing the origin.

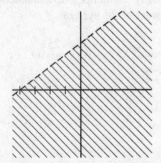

Had the coordinates of our trial point not satisfied the inequality, we would have known just as assuredly that the graph was the other side of the line.

EXAMPLE 2

Represent graphically the solution set of the system:

$$\begin{vmatrix} x+2y\le 3 \\ 3y+x>2. \end{vmatrix}$$

SOLUTION: Using the procedure of Example 1, we first graph $x+2y=3$ as a solid line and then check to see which side contains the origin.

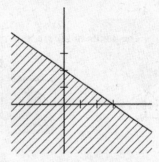

$(0,0)$ satisfies $x+2y\le 3$, so the region is the one shown above.

We then graph (dotted line) $3y+x=2$.

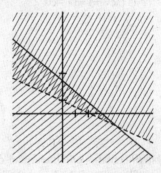

But $(0,0)$ does not satisfy $3y+x>2$, so we shade in the region above the line. The graph of the system is the cross-hatched region and includes the solid line.

In the multiple-choice question, the cross-hatched region at right shows the graph of the solution set of the system of equations. Note that the region is the interior of an angle.

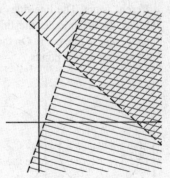

EXAMPLES

Represent graphically the solution sets of the systems given:

1. $\begin{vmatrix} x-y-2<0 \\ x+2y-8>0 \end{vmatrix}$

2. $\begin{vmatrix} x+2y<3 \\ 3y-2x\leq 6 \end{vmatrix}$

SOLUTIONS:

(1) 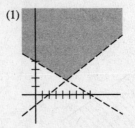   (2)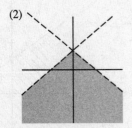

[8] How many points are in the graph of the solution set of the system

$$\begin{vmatrix} 2x-y-1=0 \\ x^2+y^2=9 \end{vmatrix} ?$$

(A) 0

(B) 1

(C) 2

(D) 3

(E) 4

When a system contains one linear and one quadratic equation, the number of possible points of intersection is 0, 1, or 2. The equations in the multiple-choice question, for example, represent a line and a circle. Each of the following drawings shows a circle and line intersecting in different ways. The line does not intersect the circle on the left. In the middle, the line is tangent to the circle, intersecting in one point. On the right, the line is a secant, intersecting in two points.

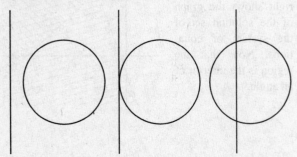

This question does not ask us to find the points of intersection but merely to tell how many points there are. We can readily answer the question from a quick sketch.

Graph the line using its intercepts at $(\frac{1}{2},0)$ and $(0,1)$. Graph the circle by recognizing that its center is at $(0,0)$ and radius is 3.

The usual procedure for solving such a system is the method of substitution: solve the linear equation for y and substitute in the second-degree equation.

EXAMPLE 1

Solve the system:

$$\begin{vmatrix} 3x+2y-6=0 \\ 9x^2=36-4y^2 \end{vmatrix}$$

SOLUTION: From the first equation we get $y=-\frac{3}{2}x+3$. Substituting for y, we get:

$$9x^2=36-4\left(-\frac{3}{2}x+3\right)^2.$$

If we simplify and solve we get $x=0$ or $x=2$. Substituting these values for x in the linear equation, we get $(0,3)$ and $(2,0)$.

EXAMPLE 2

Solve the following system:

$$\begin{vmatrix} y=-x+7 \\ y^2=25-x^2 \end{vmatrix}$$

SOLUTION:

$$
\begin{aligned}
(-x+7)^2 &= 25-x^2 \\
x^2-14x+49 &= 25-x^2 \\
2x^2-14x+24 &= 0 \\
x^2-7x+12 &= 0 \\
(x-3)(x-4) &= 0 \\
x &= 3 \text{ or } 4
\end{aligned}
$$

Points of intersection are $(3,4)$ and $(4,3)$.

[9] How many elements are contained in the solution set of the system

$$\begin{vmatrix} x^2+y^2=25 \\ x^2-y^2=7 \end{vmatrix} ?$$

(A) 0

(B) 1

(C) 2

(D) 3

(E) 4

Though the method of substitution is the more general procedure for solving quadratic-quadratic systems, the method of elimination sometimes produces quick results. If we add the two equations, the y^2 terms drop out and we get

$$2x^2 = 32$$
$$x^2 = 16$$
$$x = \pm 4$$

At this point, you may think there are only two solutions. However, substituting 4 for x in $x^2 + y^2 = 25$ produces $y = \pm 3$. Now you have four points: $(4, 3)$, $(-4, 3)$, $(4, -3)$, and $(-4, -3)$, and all four work in both equations.

EXAMPLE

Solve the system:

$$\begin{vmatrix} x^2 + y^2 - 1 = 0 \\ x^2 - y - 1 = 0. \end{vmatrix}$$

SOLUTION: This system can be solved by elimination, but again we will use the more general method of substitution. From the lower equation we see that

$$x^2 = y + 1.$$

If we substitute $y + 1$ for x^2 in the upper equation, we find:

$$y + 1 + y^2 - 1 = 0,$$
$$y^2 + y = 0,$$
$$y = 0 \quad \text{or} \quad y = -1.$$

Substituting the two values for y gives the companion values of x.

DETERMINING INTEGRAL SOLUTIONS TO EQUATIONS IN TWO VARIABLES

---

[10] If $9x + 3y = 25$ and x and y are positive integers less than 25, how many ordered pairs (x, y) are solutions of the equation?

(A) 0

(B) 1

(C) 2

(D) 3

(E) 4

A moment's study will show that there are no methods for "solving" this equation since it involves two unknowns and only one equation. Can you work it out just by trial and error? In other words, can you just pick positive integers that will satisfy the equation? Trying all possible pairs of integers from 1 to 25 would certainly be a lengthy process, and subject test questions rarely require lengthy solutions.

Do you see that the left side, $9x + 3y$, has a factor of 3? Thus,

$$3(3x + y) = 25,$$
$$3x + y = \frac{25}{3}$$
$$= 8\frac{1}{3}.$$

But addition and multiplication involving integers must always result in an integer. Thus, the left side can never result in $8\frac{1}{3}$. The equation can never be true for a pair of integers.

EXAMPLES

Indicate which of the following can have integral solutions:

1. $2x + 3y = 15$

2. $5x - 10y = 3$

3. $2x - 6y = 1$

SOLUTIONS:

1. Yes, for example, $(3, 3)$

2. No, because $x - 3y = \frac{3}{5}$

3. No, because $x - 3y = \frac{1}{2}$

[11] If $x + y = 12$ and $x - y = 4$, $x = ?$

(A) 6

(B) 8

(C) 10

(D) 12

(E) 16

You may have sized up this question instantly by realizing it asks for two numbers that add up to 12 and subtract to produce 4. With no work, you can immediately choose 8 and 4 because $8 + 4 = 12$ and $8 - 4 = 4$.

There is no good reason to spend any more time or effort on a question than circumstances require.

On the other hand, if your intuition abandoned you when you read this question, do the algebra.

By adding the two equations, you will make the y terms drop out so you get $2x = 16$. From that, $x = 8$, (B).

Wasn't it lucky that the y terms dropped out so simply? Not at all. That eventuality was built into the question. If the test makers did not want the y terms to drop out easily, they would have given them complicated coefficients. Take advantage of the patterns and structures the test makers have provided.

WHAT YOU SHOULD KNOW

KEY CONCEPTS

1. *To solve a system of equations by graphing*, graph each equation and estimate the coordinates of the point of intersection.
2. *To solve a system of two equations by substitution*, solve one equation for a variable and substitute the resulting expression for that variable into the other equation. Then solve for the value of the second variable.
3. *To solve a system of two equations by addition*, eliminate a variable (we'll use x as an example) by the following steps:
   a. multiply the first equation by the coefficient of x in the second equation, then
   b. multiply the second equation by the negative of the coefficient of x in the first equation, then
   c. add the two equations, then
   d. solve for the value of y, then
   e. substitute the value of y for y in one of the original equations to find x.

KEY RELATIONSHIP

Equivalent Systems:

$$\begin{vmatrix} ax+by+c=0 \\ y=mx+k \end{vmatrix} \leftrightarrow \begin{vmatrix} ax+b(mx+k)+c=0 \\ y=mx+k \end{vmatrix}$$

TEST-TAKING STRATEGY

- When you encounter a word problem with two unknowns, set up a system of equations in which the variables represent the quantities the question asks for, then solve through elimination of a variable.

CALCULATOR TIP

If you are using a graphing calculator, know how to enter equations as functions and how to access the intersection feature.

ANSWERS

[1] (C)	[3] (A)	[5] (A)	[7] (C)	[9] (E)	[11] (B)
[2] (A)	[4] (E)	[6] (C)	[8] (C)	[10] (A)	

EXPONENTS AND LOGARITHMS

CHAPTER

22

In this chapter, several topics are more typical of those tested on the Mathematics Level IIC exam than of those on the Level IC exam. We have denoted these with an asterisk (*). Review of such topics may assist you in answering Level IC questions, however, because it increases your general knowledge of mathematical ideas, methods, and skills.

KEY TERMS

exponent a number or letter written above and to the right of a mathematical expression (the *base*) to indicate that it is to be raised to a certain power.
Example: x^5 means that x is to be used as a factor 5 times.

logarithm an exponent that indicates to what power a base must be raised to produce a given number. Example: The logarithm of 25 to the base 5 is 2.

exponential function a function of the form $\{(x, y) : y = a^x\}$, where a is any positive number except 1.

characteristic the integer part of a common logarithm.

mantissa the decimal part of a common logarithm.

APPLYING FIVE LAWS OF EXPONENTS

[1]   Which of the following (where all exponents are integers) is NOT equal to xy?

(A) $(xy^2)y^{-1}$

(B) $\dfrac{12^0 x^{12}}{x^{11}y^{-1}}$

(C) $\dfrac{1}{x^{-1}y^{-1}}$

(D) $(x^n y)x^{1-n}$

(E) $(xy)^2(xy)^{-2}$

TEST-TAKING TIP

The type of question used here—given five statements, select the incorrect one—will be used repeatedly throughout the chapter because it allows the presentation and resolution of many examples.

▣ Before proceeding, make sure you know how to use your calculator to raise numbers to positive and negative powers.

In our review of exponents we will present five laws. Our intention will be primarily the development of manipulative skills.

To answer the given question we may use the following law:

EX-1   If a is a real number and m and n are integers, then

$$a^m a^n = a^{m+n}.$$

EX-1   has no meaning, however, until the following definitions are understood.

Definition 1 *If a is a real number and m is a positive integer, then*

$$a^m = \underbrace{a \cdot a \cdot a \cdot \ldots a}_{m \text{ factors}}.$$

Definition 2 *If a is a real number (except zero) and m = 0, then*

$$a^m = 1.$$

(In other words, $a^0 = 1$.)

Definition 3 *If a is a real number and m = 1, then*

$$a^m = a.$$

(In other words, $a^1 = a$.)

Definition 4 *If a is a real number and m is any integer $(a \neq 0)$, then*

$$a^m = \frac{1}{a^{-m}}.$$

EXAMPLES

$$a^{-1} = \frac{1}{a}, \qquad a^{-3} = \frac{1}{a^3}, \qquad \left(\frac{1}{2}\right)^{-2} = 4$$

Law EX-1 can be used to simplify each of the answer selections.

(A) $(xy^2)y^{-1} = x(y^2 y^{-1})$ (Recognize the Associative Law of Multiplication?)

$= xy^{2+(-1)}$ EX-1 with $a = y$, $m = 2$, and $n = -1$

$= xy^1$

$= xy$ Definition 3

(B) $\dfrac{12^0 x^{12}}{x^{11}y^{-1}} = \dfrac{x^{12}}{x^{11}y^{-1}}$ Definition 3

$= \dfrac{x^{12}}{\frac{1}{x^{-11}}y^{-1}}$ Definition 4, $x^{11} = \dfrac{1}{x^{-11}}$

$= \dfrac{x^{12}}{\frac{1}{x^{-11}} \cdot \frac{1}{y}}$ Definition 4

$= \dfrac{x^{12}}{\frac{1}{x^{-11}y}}$

$= x^{12}x^{-11}y$

$= x^1 y$ By EX-1, with $a = x$, $m = 11$, $n = -11$.

$= xy$

(C) $\dfrac{1}{x^{-1}y^{-1}} = \dfrac{1}{\frac{1}{x}\frac{1}{y}}$ Definition 4

$= \dfrac{1}{\frac{1}{xy}}$

$= xy$

(D) $(x^n y)x^{1-n} = x^{1-n}(x^n y)$ (Recognize the Commutative Law of Multiplication?)

$= (x^{1-n}x^n)y$ (And the Associative Law?)

$= x^{1-n+n}y$ EX-1 with $a = x$, $m = 1 - n$, $n = n$

$= xy$

(E) $(xy)^2(xy)^{-2} = (xy)^{2+(-2)}$ EX-1 with $a = xy$, $m = 2$, $n = -2$

$= (xy)^0$

$= 1$ Definition 3

EXAMPLES

Use EX-1 and the definitions to simplify each of the following where all exponents are integers:

1. $y^2 y^4 = y^6$

2. $a^{2n}a = a^{2n+1}$

3. $x^a x^b = x^{a+b}$

4. $a^x a^x = a^{2x}$

5. $y^{n-2}y^2 y^n = y^{2n}$

6. $(-x^{m+1})(-x^{m-1}) = x^{2m}$

[2] Which of the following (where all exponents are integers) is NOT equal to w?

(A) $\dfrac{3w^2}{(3w)^2(3w)^{-1}}$

(B) $\dfrac{w^2 x^6}{(wx^2)x^4}$

(C) $\dfrac{w^{-2}}{w^{-3}}$

(D) $\dfrac{w^{-3}}{w^{-2}}$

(E) $\dfrac{w^{n-2}}{w^{n-3}}$

We could have used EX-1 to simplify each of these, but it is more expedient to introduce a second law to handle expressions that involve division.

EX-2 If a is a real number ($a \neq 0$) and m and n are integers, then

$$\frac{a^m}{a^n} = a^{m-n}.$$

As examples of the use of EX-2 we will simplify each of the answer selections.

(A) $\dfrac{3w^2}{(3w)^2(3w)^{-1}} = \dfrac{3w^2}{3w}$ EX-1 with $a = 3w$, $m = 2, n = -1$

     $= \dfrac{w^2}{w}$

     $= \dfrac{w^2}{w^1}$ Definition 3

     $= w^1$ EX-2 with $a = w$, $m = 2, n = 1$

(B) $\dfrac{w^2 x^6}{(wx^2)x^4} = \dfrac{w^2 x^6}{w(x^2 x^4)}$

     $= \dfrac{w^2 x^6}{wx^6}$

     $= \dfrac{w^2}{w} \cdot \dfrac{x^6}{x^6}$

     $= wx^0$ EX-2

     $= w$

(C) $\dfrac{w^{-2}}{w^{-3}} = w^{-2-(-3)}$ EX-2

     $= w$

(D) $\dfrac{w^{-3}}{w^{-2}} = w^{-3-(-2)}$ EX-2

     $= w^{-1}$

     $= \dfrac{1}{w}$ Definition 4

(E) $\dfrac{w^{n-2}}{w^{n-3}} = w^{(n-2)-(n-3)}$ EX-2

     $= w$

EXAMPLES

Simplify:

1. $x^{12} \div x^4 = x^{12-3} = x^9$

2. $y^{2n} \div y = y^{2n-1}$

3. $2^8 \div 2^4 = 2^{8-4} = 2^4$

4. $12m^3 n^2 \div 2mn = \dfrac{12}{2}m^2 n$

5. $(y-4)^3 \div (y-4) = (y-4)^2$

[3] Which of the following (where all exponents are integers) is NOT true?

(A) $(2^2)^3 = 32$

(B) $(x^3)^p = x^{3p}$

(C) $(-b^{p+1})^2 = b^{2p+2}$

(D) $(b^x)^{x+1} = b^{x^2+x}$

(E) $(x^3)^0 = 1$

Again, we could have used EX-1 to simplify each of these, but we will introduce a third law to expedite the raising of a power to a power.

EX-3 If a is a real number and m and n are integers, then
$$(a^m)^n = a^{mn}.$$

(A) $(2^2)^3 = 2^{2\times3}$ EX-3
$$= 2^6$$
$$= 64 \quad \text{(By direct multiplication)}$$

(B) $(x^3)^p = x^{3p}$ EX-3

(C) $(-b^{p+1})^2 = (b^{p+1})^2$ Since the square of every real number equals the square of its negative.
$$= b^{(p+1)2} \quad \text{EX-3 with } a = b,$$
$$m = p+1, n = 2$$
$$= b^{2p+2} \quad \text{(Recognize the Distributive Law?)}$$

(D) $(b^x)^{x+1} = b^{x(x+1)}$ EX-3 with $a = b$, $m = x, n = x+1$
$$= b^{x^2+x} \quad \text{(The Distributive Law again)}$$

(E) $(x^3)^0 = x^{3\times0}$ EX-3
$$= x^0$$
$$= 1 \quad \text{Definition 2}$$

EXAMPLES

Simplify:

1. $(b^2)^5 = b^{10}$

2. $(b^{2p})^2 = b^{4p}$

3. $(-c^3)^4 = c^{12}$

4. $(d^p)^q = d^{pq}$

5. $(-2^2)^3 = -2^6$

[4] Which of the following (where all exponents are integers) is NOT true?

(A) $(x^2y)^3 = x^6y^3$

(B) $(2r^2s)^p = 2^p r^{2p} s^p$

(C) $(3x)^2(2x^3) = 6x^5$

(D) $(xy^2z^3)^4 = x^4y^8x^{12}$

(E) $(x^3y^2)^3 \div x^3y = x^6y^5$

We introduce the next law to simplify the raising of a product to a power.

EX-4 If a and b are real numbers and m is an integer, then:
$$(ab)^m = a^m b^m.$$

The following argument shows EX-4 to be applicable to the product of three factors raised to a power.

$$(xya)^p = (xy)^p z^p \quad \text{EX-4 with } a = xy,$$
$$b = z, m = p$$
$$= x^p y^p z^p \quad \text{EX-4}$$

In general, the power of a product equals the product of the powers of its factors regardless of the number of factors.

(A) $(x^2y)^3 = (x^2)^3 y^3$ EX-4
$$= x^{2\times3} y^3 \quad \text{EX-3}$$
$$= x^6 y^3$$

(B) $(2r^2s)^p = (2r^2)^p s^p$ EX-4
$$= 2^p (r^2)^p s^p \quad \text{EX-4}$$
$$= 2^p r^{2p} s^p \quad \text{EX-3}$$

(C) $(3x)^2(2x^3) = 3^2 x^2 2x^3$ EX-4
$$= 9x^2 2x^3$$
$$= 18x^2 x^3$$
$$= 18x^5 \quad \text{EX-1}$$

(D) $(xy^2z^3)^4 = x^4(y^2)^4(z^3)^4$ EX-4
$$= x^4 y^8 z^{12} \quad \text{EX-3}$$

(E) $(x^3y^2)^3 \div x^3y = (x^3)^3(y^2)^3 \div x^3y$ EX-4
$$= x^9 y^6 \div x^3 y \quad \text{EX-3}$$
$$= x^6 y^5 \quad \text{EX-2}$$

EXAMPLES

Simplify:

1. $(2x^3)(3x^2) = 6x^5$

2. $(-3x^4)^2 = 9x^8$

3. $(2y)^3 \div (2y)^2 = 2y$

4. $\left(\dfrac{1}{2}x^{4p}\right)^2 = \dfrac{1}{4}x^{8p}$

5. $(3x^{-1}y^{-2})^{-3} = \dfrac{1}{27}x^3y^6$

6. $(x^{-1}+2y)^{-1} = \dfrac{1}{\frac{1}{x}+2y}$
$$= \dfrac{x}{1+2xy}$$

[5] Which of the following (where all exponents are integers) is NOT true?

(A) $\left(-\dfrac{2}{p}\right)^3 = -\dfrac{8}{p^3}$

(B) $\left(\dfrac{3x^2}{y^4}\right)^3 = \dfrac{27x^6}{y^{12}}$

(C) $\left(\dfrac{x^{-2}y^{-3}}{w^{-4}z^{-5}}\right)^{-1} = \dfrac{x^2y^3}{w^4z^5}$

(D) $\dfrac{1}{\left(\frac{2}{3}\right)^{-1}} = \dfrac{3}{2}$

(E) $\left(\dfrac{x^{-1}}{y^{-1}}\right)^{-1} = \dfrac{x}{y}$

EX-5 If a and b are real numbers ($b \neq 0$) and m is an integer, then

$$\left(\frac{a}{b}\right)^m = \frac{a^m}{b^m}.$$

(A) $\left(-\dfrac{2}{p}\right)^3 = \left(\dfrac{-2}{p}\right)^3$

$= \dfrac{(-2)^3}{p^3}$ EX-5

$= \dfrac{-8}{p^3}$

$= -\dfrac{8}{p^3}$

(B) $\left(\dfrac{3x^2}{y^4}\right)^3 = \dfrac{(3x^2)^3}{(y^4)^3}$ EX-5

$= \dfrac{3^3(x^2)^3}{y^{12}}$ EX-4

$= \dfrac{27x^6}{y^{12}}$

(C) $\left(\dfrac{x^{-2}y^{-3}}{w^{-4}z^{-5}}\right)^{-1} = \dfrac{(x^{-2}y^{-3})^{-1}}{(w^{-4}z^{-5})^{-1}}$ EX-5

$= \dfrac{(x^{-2})^{-1}(y^{-3})^{-1}}{(w^{-4})^{-1}(z^{-5})^{-1}}$ EX-4

$= \dfrac{x^2y^3}{w^4z^5}$

(D) $\dfrac{1}{\left(\frac{2}{3}\right)^{-1}} = \dfrac{2}{3}$ Definition 4 with $a = \dfrac{2}{3}$

(E) $\left(\dfrac{x^{-1}}{y^{-1}}\right)^{-1} = \dfrac{(x^{-1})^{-1}}{(y^{-1})^{-1}}$ EX-5

$= \dfrac{x^{(-1)(-1)}}{y^{(-1)(-1)}}$ EX-3

$= \dfrac{x}{y}$

EXAMPLES

Simplify:

1. $\left(\dfrac{3x^2}{y}\right)^3 = \dfrac{27x^6}{y^3}$

2. $\left(\dfrac{2}{3}\right)^3 = \dfrac{2^3}{3^3} = \dfrac{8}{27}$

3. $\left(\dfrac{x^{-1}}{y^{-2}}\right)^{-3} = \dfrac{x^3}{y^6}$

4. $\left(\dfrac{x^2y}{z}\right)^{-2} = \dfrac{x^{-4}y^{-2}}{z^{-2}} = \dfrac{z^2}{x^4y^2}$

AVOIDING IMPROPER APPLICATIONS

[6] Which of the following (where all exponents are integers) is NOT true? ($x \neq 0$)

(A) $\dfrac{1}{x^m} \cdot \dfrac{1}{x^n} = x^{-m-n}$

(B) $\dfrac{x^m}{x^{-n}} = x^{m+n}$

(C) $x^m + x^n = x^{m+n}$

(D) $(x^m + x^n)^{-1} = \dfrac{1}{x^m + x^n}$

(E) $\left(\dfrac{x^{-1} + y^{-1}}{x^{-1}}\right)(x+y)^{-1} = \dfrac{1}{y}$

No new information is needed here; our purpose is to review errors frequently made by intermediate math students.

(A) $\dfrac{1}{x^m} \cdot \dfrac{1}{x^n} = x^{-m}x^{-n}$ Definition 4

$= x^{-m+(-n)}$ EX-1

$= x^{-m-n}$

Error to avoid: multiplying exponents in a product,

$$x^{-m} \cdot x^{-n} \neq x^{(-m)(-n)}.$$

(B) $\dfrac{x^m}{x^{-n}} = x^{m-(-n)}$ EX-2

$\qquad\qquad = x^{m+n}$

Error to avoid: adding exponents in a quotient,

$$\dfrac{x^m}{x^{-n}} \neq x^{m+(-n)}.$$

(C) $x^{m+n} = x^m \cdot x^n$ EX-1

Error to avoid: adding exponents in a sum,

$$x^{m+n} \neq x^m + x^n.$$

(D) $(x^m + x^n)^{-1} = \dfrac{1}{x^m + x^n}$ Definition 4

Error to avoid: raising each term of a sum to a power when the sum is raised to the power,

$$(x^m + x^n)^{-1} \neq x^{-m} + x^{-n}.$$

(E) $\left(\dfrac{x^{-1} + y^{-1}}{x^{-1}}\right)(x+y)^{-1}$

$\qquad = \dfrac{\frac{1}{x} + \frac{1}{y}}{\frac{1}{x}} \cdot \dfrac{1}{x+y}$ Definition 4

$\qquad = \dfrac{\frac{y+x}{xy}}{\frac{1}{x}} \cdot \dfrac{1}{x+y}$

$\qquad = \dfrac{y+x}{xy} \cdot \dfrac{x}{1} \cdot \dfrac{1}{x+y}$

$\qquad = \dfrac{1}{y}$

Errors to avoid:

$$x^{-1} + y^{-1} \neq \dfrac{1}{x+y}$$

and

$$(x+y)^{-1} \neq (x^{-1} + y^{-1}).$$

---

[7]   Which of the following is NOT true?

(A) $X^{-1/3} = \dfrac{1}{\sqrt[3]{X}}$

(B) $5^{2/3} = \sqrt[3]{5^2}$

(C) $(3X)^{-1/2} = \dfrac{1}{\sqrt{3X}}$

(D) $64^{3/2} = 512$

(E) $\dfrac{1}{2X^{-1/3}} = \sqrt[3]{2X}$

We have reviewed, so far, only expressions in which the exponents were integers. Our purpose in this section will be to give meaning to rational exponents. We will be guided by a desire to define these exponents in such a way as to preserve the laws of exponents already assumed.

Definition 5 *If a is a real number and q is any positive integer, then*

$$a^{1/q} = \sqrt[q]{a} \quad (\textit{read: the principal qth root of a}).$$

In other words, $a^{1/q}$ is the number such that $(a^{1/q})^q = a$, with the following restrictions:

1. *If q is an even number and $a \geq 0$, then $a^{1/q}$ is the positive qth root.*
2. *If q is an even number and $a \leq 0$, then $a^{1/q}$ defines no real number.*
3. *If q is an odd number and $a \geq 0$, then*

$$a^{1/q} \geq 0.$$

4. *If q is an odd number and $a < 0$, then*

$$a^{1/q} < 0.$$

Definition 6 *If a is a real number and p and q are integers $(q \neq 0)$, then*

$$a^{p/q} = (a^{1/q})^p = (a^p)^{1/q} = \sqrt[q]{a^p} = \left(\sqrt[q]{a}\right)^p.$$

We will agree that all of the preceding definitions and laws of exponents will hold true when the domain of the exponents is all rationals.

(A) $X^{-1/3} = \dfrac{1}{X^{1/3}}$ Definition 4

$\qquad\quad = \dfrac{1}{\sqrt[3]{X}}$ Definition 5

(B) $5^{2/3}$ equals all of the following by Definition 6:

$$(5^{1/3})^2 = (5^2)^{1/3} = \sqrt[3]{5^2} = \left(\sqrt[3]{5}\right)^2.$$

(C) $(3X)^{-1/2} = \dfrac{1}{(3X)^{1/2}}$ Definition 4

$\qquad\qquad = \dfrac{1}{\sqrt[2]{3X}}$ Definition 6

(D) $64^{3/2} = \left(\sqrt[2]{64}\right)^3$ Definition 6

       $= 8^3$

       $= 512$

(E) $\dfrac{1}{2X^{-1/3}} = \dfrac{1}{2\left(\frac{1}{X^{1/3}}\right)}$ Definition 4

       $= \dfrac{\frac{1}{2}}{\sqrt[3]{X}}$ Definition 5

       $= \dfrac{\sqrt[3]{X}}{2}$

EXAMPLES

Write each of the following in radical form and then simplify:

1. $3^{1/2} \times 4^{1/2} \times 3^{1/2} = \sqrt{3}\sqrt{4}\sqrt{3}$

                            $= 3 \times 2$

                            $= 6$

2. $5^{1/3} \times 2^{5/2} \times 5^{2/3} = \sqrt[3]{5}\sqrt{2^5}\sqrt[3]{5^2}$

                            $= 5 \times 4\sqrt{2}$

                            $= 20\sqrt{2}$

CONVERTING RADICALS TO EXPONENTS

[8]   Which of the following is not ALWAYS true?

     (A) $\sqrt{x^2y^6} = xy^3$

     (B) $\left(\sqrt[5]{\sqrt[6]{2}}\right)^{30} = 2$

     (C) $\sqrt[5]{128} = 2\sqrt[3]{4}$

     (D) $\sqrt[6]{x^4}\sqrt[6]{x^4} = x^{4/3}$

     (E) $\sqrt{45} = 3\sqrt{5}$

We have agreed that EX-1 through EX-5, as well as their accompanying definitions, will apply as long as the domain of each exponent variable is the set of rational numbers.

(A) $\sqrt{x^2y^6} = (x^2y^6)^{1/2}$ Definition 5

           $= (x^2)^{1/2}(y^6)^{1/2}$ EX-4

           $= |x|\,|y^3|$ Definition 5 and EX-3

(Note that we have introduced the absolute value bars because x and y represent any real numbers, positive or negative, but the exponent $\frac{1}{2}$ indicates the *principal* square root *only*, which is positive. Without these absolute value bars, the statement is false.)

(B) $\left(\sqrt[5]{\sqrt[6]{2}}\right)^{30} = \left[(2^{1/6})^{1/5}\right]^{30}$ Definition 5

           $= (2^{1/30})^{30}$ EX-3

           $= 2$

(C) $\sqrt[5]{128} = (128)^{1/5}$ Definition 5

           $= (32 \times 4)^{1/5}$

           $= 32^{1/5} \times 4^{1/5}$ EX-4

           $= (2^5)^{1/5} \times (4)^{1/5}$

           $= 2(4)^{1/5}$ EX-3

           $= 2\sqrt[5]{4}$ Definition 5

(D) $\sqrt[6]{x^4}\sqrt[6]{x^4} = x^{4/6} \times x^{4/6}$ Definition 6

              $= x^{2/3} \times x^{2/3}$

              $= x^{4/3}$ EX-1

(E) $\sqrt{45} = (45)^{1/2}$ Definition 5

          $= (9 \times 5)^{1/2}$

          $= 9^{1/2} \times 5^{1/2}$ EX-4

          $= 3\sqrt{5}$ Definition 5

EXAMPLES

1. $\left(\sqrt[3]{7}\right)^5 = \left(\sqrt[3]{7}\right)^3\left(\sqrt[3]{7}\right)^2$

            $= 7\sqrt[3]{49}$

2. $\sqrt[3]{2}\sqrt[3]{4} = \sqrt[3]{8} = 2$

3. $\left(\sqrt[3]{9}\right)^6 = \left(\sqrt[3]{9}\right)^3\left(\sqrt[3]{9}\right)^3$

            $= 9 \times 9$

            $= 81$

4. $\sqrt{7}\sqrt{3} = \sqrt{21}$

5. $\sqrt{a^3} \div \sqrt{a} = \sqrt{a^2} = a$

6. $\sqrt{75} = \sqrt{25}\sqrt{3} = 5\sqrt{3}$

SIMPLIFYING FRACTIONAL EXPONENTS

[9]   Which of the following is NOT true?

(A) $(xy)^{-2/5} = \left(\dfrac{1}{\sqrt[5]{xy}}\right)^2$

(B) $y^{1/2}(y^{1/2} + y^{-1/2}) = y$

(C) $y^{3/2} \times y^{1/2} \times y^{-3} = \dfrac{1}{y}$

(D) $y^{1/2} \div y^{-1/2} = y$

(E) $\sqrt[3]{\dfrac{y^6}{x^3}} = \dfrac{y^2}{x}$

We have included this problem as further review of topics already discussed.

(A) $(xy)^{-2/5} = \left((xy)^{-1/5}\right)^2$ Definition 6

$= \left(\dfrac{1}{(xy)^{1/5}}\right)^2$ Definition 1

$= \left(\dfrac{1}{\sqrt[5]{xy}}\right)^2$ Definition 5

(B) $y^{1/2}(y^{1/2} + y^{-1/2})$
$= y^{1/2} \cdot y^{1/2} + y^{1/2} \cdot y^{-1/2}$
$= y^1 + y^0$ EX-1
$= y + 1$ Definitions 2 and 3

(C) $y^{3/2} \times y^{1/2} \times y^{-3} = y^{3/2 + 1/2 - 3}$ EX-1
$= y^{-1}$
$= \dfrac{1}{y}$

(D) $y^{1/2} \div y^{-1/2} = y^{1/2 - (-1/2)}$ EX-2
$= y$

(E) $\sqrt[3]{\dfrac{y^6}{x^3}} = \left(\dfrac{y^6}{x^3}\right)^{1/3}$ Definition 5

$= \dfrac{y^2}{x}$ EX-5 and EX-3

GRAPHING EXPONENTIAL FUNCTIONS

*[10] Which of the following could be the equation for the graph below?

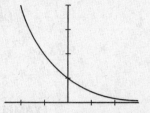

(A) $y = 2^x$

(B) $y = -2^x$

(C) $y = 2^{-x}$

(D) $y = (-2)^x$

(E) $y = (-2)^{-x}$

An *exponential function* is a function of the form $\{(x,y) : y = a^x\}$, *where a is any positive number except 1*. Its domain is the set of real numbers, and its range is the set of positive real numbers.

Two of the above answer selections define exponential functions, and we will discuss their graphs.

(A) $y = 2^x$ is an exponential function for which $a = 2$. The domain of this function is defined to be the set of all real numbers, but we have not yet reviewed the meaning of irrational exponent.

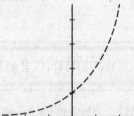

The graph at right shows the curve we might expect when the values of x are limited to the rationals and $y = 2x$. The curve actually is not solid but, rather, full of holes. The holes are the points that have irrational first coordinates. The holes suggest a meaning for irrational exponents. We define the ordered pairs $(x, 2^x)$, where x is irrational, to be the coordinates of the points on the graph necessary to complete the curve. We rely heavily on your intuition, as we usually do in intermediate math, because a more rigorous approach necessitates the development of aspects of limit theory that are beyond the scope of this review.

(B) By our definition, $y = -2^x$ is not an exponential function, but its graph is based on the graph in (A). The table on p. 317 shows the corresponding values of $y = -2^x$ and $y = 2^x$ and gives the information necessary to produce the graph shown.

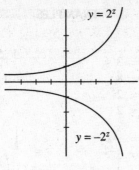

$y = 2^z$

$y = -2^z$

x	2^x	-2^x
-2	$\dfrac{1}{4}$	$-\dfrac{1}{4}$
-1	$\dfrac{1}{2}$	$-\dfrac{1}{2}$
0	1	-1
1	2	-2
2	4	-4

(C) $y = 2^{-x}$ does not, at first, appear to fit the definition of "exponential function," but recall that $2^{-x} = (2^{-1})^x$ by EX-3 (we have here made the assumption that the laws EX-1 through EX-5 hold for *all* reals). Thus we are dealing with $y = \left(\frac{1}{2}\right)^x$, whose graph is the one given in the multiple-choice question.

Neither (D) nor (E) is an exponential function, so we will not discuss them. Verify that neither could fit the given graph by taking some value such as $x = 1$ and showing that this does not yield a point on the curve. Try plotting these graphs by taking such sample values of x as 1, 2, 3, 4, $\frac{1}{2}$, and $\frac{1}{4}$ and note the complications that arise.

*[11] Which of the following is NOT true?

(A) $\left(3^{\sqrt{3}}\right)^{\sqrt{3}} = 27$

(B) $\left(10^{\sqrt{2}}\right)\left(10^{\sqrt{2}}\right) = 100^{\sqrt{2}}$

(C) $\left(3^{1/\sqrt{2}}\right)^{\sqrt{2}} = 3$

(D) $\left(9^{1/\sqrt{2}}\right) = 3^{\sqrt{2}}$

(E) $(\pi)^{\pi} = 1$

EX-1 through EX-5 as well as their accompanying definitions are true for all real exponents.

▦ The expressions can be easily simplified using the laws of exponents. Some can be done on the calculator with care and patience.

(A) $\left(3^{\sqrt{3}}\right)^{\sqrt{3}} = 3^3 = 27$ EX-3 and definition of $\sqrt{3}$

(B) $\left(10^{\sqrt{2}}\right)\left(10^{\sqrt{2}}\right) = 10^{(\sqrt{2}+\sqrt{2})}$ EX-1
$= 10^{2\sqrt{2}}$
$= (10^2)^{\sqrt{2}}$ EX-3
$= 100^{\sqrt{2}}$

(C) $\left(3^{1/\sqrt{2}}\right)^{\sqrt{2}} = 3^{(1/\sqrt{2})\sqrt{2}}$ EX-3
$= 3$

(D) $\left(9^{1/\sqrt{2}}\right) = 9^{1/\sqrt{2} \times \sqrt{2}/\sqrt{2}}$
$= 9^{\sqrt{2}/2}$
$= (9^{1/2})^{\sqrt{2}}$ EX-3
$= 3^{\sqrt{2}}$

(E) We know that $\pi^0 = 1$ by Definition 2. π^{π} would equal π only if the exponent, π, equaled the exponent, 0. But $\pi = 3.14159\ldots \neq 0$.

RECOGNIZING THAT "LOGARITHM" AND "EXPONENT" ARE SYNONYMOUS

*[12] Which of the following is the inverse of $y = 2^x$?

(A) $y = \left(\dfrac{1}{2}\right)^{-x}$

(B) $y = \left(\dfrac{1}{2}\right)^{x}$

(C) $x = \log_2 y$

(D) $y = \log_2 x$

(E) $x = 2^{-y}$

An exponential function is of the form

(1) $\qquad y = a^x;\ a > 0,\ a \neq 1.$

A simple procedure for finding the inverse of a function is to interchange the range and domain variables. The inverse of $y = a^x$ is, therefore,

(2) $\qquad x = a^y;\ a > 0,\ a \neq 1.$

In defining functions we find it most expedient to express y in terms of x. No amount of algebraic manipulation, however, will allow us to do this with equation (2). To enable us to solve the inverse of an exponential function for y, we introduce the symbol *log* and make the following agreement:

(3) $\qquad \log_b N = m$ means $b^m = N.$

Applying (3) to equation (2), we get

(4) $\qquad\qquad y = \log_a x.$

Thus equations (1) and (4) define functions that are the inverses of each other.

The statement "$\log_b N = m$" is read "the logarithm to the base b of N is m." If you read this carefully, you will see that we are saying that m is a "logarithm." But m is also the exponent. Our agreement, then, is that the terms "logarithm" and "exponent" have the same meaning.

In summary: the table below is arranged so that the two statements in the same column are equivalent, whereas any two statements connected by line segments are inverses.

$$y = a^x \qquad\Longleftrightarrow\qquad x = a^y$$
$$x = \log_a y \qquad\Longleftrightarrow\qquad y = \log_a x$$

[13] Which of the following equations has 9 as a solution?

    (A) $\log_{10}(1+y) = 2$

    (B) $\log_2(3y-5) = 3$

    (C) $\log_3(1+y)^2 = 2$

    (D) $x = 10^{\log_{10} 9}$

    (E) $x = \log_2 \sqrt{2}$

We have included this question to review the conversion from equations in exponential form to equations in logarithmic form. Do not fail to memorize the following statement (introduced in the preceding section):

$$\log_b N = m \text{ means } b^m = N.$$

(A) $\log_{10}(1+y) = 2$ means
$$\begin{aligned} 10^2 &= 1+y, \\ 100 &= (1+y), \\ 99 &= y. \end{aligned}$$

(B) $\log_2(3y-5) = 3$ means
$$\begin{aligned} 2^3 &= 3y-5, \\ 8 &= 3y-5, \\ 13 &= 3y \\ \frac{13}{3} &= y. \end{aligned}$$

(C) $\log_3(1+y)^2 = 2$ means
$$\begin{aligned} 3^2 &= (1+y)^2, \\ 9 &= y^2+2y+1, \\ 0 &= y^2+2y-8, \\ 0 &= (y+4)(y-2), \\ y = -4 &\text{ or } y = 2. \end{aligned}$$

(D) $x = 10^{\log_{10} 9}$ means $\log_{10} x = \log_{10} 9,$
$$\qquad\qquad\qquad\qquad x = 9.$$

(E) $x = \log_2 \sqrt{2}$ means
$$\begin{aligned} 2^x &= \sqrt{2}, \\ 2^x &= 2^{1/2}, \\ x &= \frac{1}{2}. \end{aligned}$$

Solve:

1. $\log_a 8 = 3$
$$\begin{aligned} a^3 &= 8 \\ &= 2^3 \\ a &= 2 \end{aligned}$$

2. $\log_3 a = -2$
$$\begin{aligned} a &= 3^{-2} \\ &= \frac{1}{9} \end{aligned}$$

3. $\log_3 \dfrac{1}{9} = a$
$$\begin{aligned} 3^a &= \frac{1}{9} \\ &= 3^{-2} \\ a &= -2 \end{aligned}$$

APPLYING EIGHT LAWS OF LOGARITHMS

[14] Which of the following is NOT true?

    (A) $\log 6 = \log 3 + \log 2$

    (B) $\log 12 - \log 2 = \log 6$

    (C) $\log 6 = (\log 3)(\log 2)$

    (D) $\log 6 = \log \dfrac{12}{2}$

    (E) $\log 6 = \dfrac{1}{2} \log 36$

A calculator solution is possible but tedious. Use your knowledge of the laws of logs.

We will review two laws of logs in this section.

LG-1   If $M > 0, N > 0, a > 0, a \neq 1$, then
$$\log_a(MN) = \log_a M + \log_a N.$$

LG-2   If $M > 0, N > 0, a > 0, a \neq 1$, then
$$\log_a \frac{M}{N} = \log_a M - \log_a N.$$

Applying these laws to the answer choices in question [14], we get:

$$\log_a \frac{M}{N} = y - x \qquad \text{Definition of log}$$

$$\log_a \frac{M}{N} = \log_a M - \log_a N \qquad \text{Substitution}$$

(A) $\quad \log 6 \;=\; \log(3 \times 2)$
$\qquad\qquad = \; \log 3 + \log 2 \quad$ LG-1

(B) $\quad \log 6 \;=\; \log(12 \div 2)$
$\qquad\qquad = \; \log 12 - \log 2 \quad$ LG-2

(C) This statement contradicts what we just demonstrated for answer (A).

(D) This is true since $\dfrac{12}{2} = 6$.

(E) $\quad \log 36 \;=\; \log(6 \times 6)$
$\qquad\qquad = \; \log 6 + \log 6 \quad$ LG-1
$\qquad\qquad = \; 2\log 6$

$\quad \dfrac{1}{2}\log 36 \;=\; \log 6$

EXAMPLES

Use LG-1 and LG-2 to express each of the following as the logarithm of a single number (where possible, check your result with your calculator):

1. $\log_a^4 + \log_a^8 = \log_a^{32}$

2. $\log_6 16 - \log_6 4 = \log_6 4$

3. $2\log_2 8 - \log_2 7 \;=\; \log_2 64 - \log_2 7$
$\qquad\qquad\qquad\qquad = \; \log_2 \dfrac{64}{7}$

4. $\log_2 8 - \log_2 8 \;=\; 0$
$\qquad\qquad\qquad = \; \log_2 1$

[15] Which of the following is NOT equal to 1?

(A) $\log_3 3$

(B) $\log_{10} 10$

(C) $\log_2 1$

(D) $2^{\log_2 1}$

(E) $3^{\log_4 1}$

LG-3 If $a > 0$, $a \neq 1$, then
$$\log_a a = 1.$$

By LG-3 we can conclude that (A) and (B) are true.

LG-4 If $a > 0$, $a \neq 1$, then
$$\log_a 1 = 0.$$

By LG-4 the logarithm of 1 is always zero regardless of the base of the logarithm—a consequence of this law is that the graph of every function $y = \log_a x$ contains the point $(1,0)$.

From LG-4 we conclude that the expression in (C) as well as the exponents in (D) and (E) must equal zero. We could now make our conclusion that (D) and (E) both equal 1 by Definition 2. However, another law relates to expressions of the type shown in (D).

LG-5 If $p > 0$, $p \neq 1$, then
$$p^{\log_p q} = q.$$

EXAMPLES

Simplify:

1. $\log_2 4 \;=\; \log_2 + \log_2 2$
$\qquad\qquad = \; 1 + 1$
$\qquad\qquad = \; 2$

2. $\log_e 1 = 0$

3. $e^{\log_e e} = e$

4. $16^{\log_4 2} \;=\; 4^{2\log_4 2}$
$\qquad\qquad = \; 4^{\log_4 4}$
$\qquad\qquad = \; 4$

[16] Which of the following Is NOT true?

(A) $\log_2 8 = 3$

(B) $\log_3 81 = 4$

(C) $\log_2 \left(\dfrac{1}{2}\right) = -1$

(D) $-\log_3 \left(\dfrac{1}{3}\right) = \log_3 3$

(E) $\log_{10} 3^{-1} = \dfrac{1}{3}$

Each of the above answer selections can be tested by the preceding laws of logs, but we will review two additional laws that are directly applicable.

LG-6   If a is a positive real number, $n \geq 0$ and $b > 0$ but $b \neq 1$, then

$$\log_b a^n = n \log_b a.$$

LG-7   If $a \geq 0, b > 0, b \neq 1$, then

$$\log_b \left(\frac{1}{a} \right) = -\log_b a.$$

(A) $\log_2 8 = \log_2 2^3$
$\qquad = 3 \log_2 2 \quad$ LG-6
$\qquad = 3 \qquad\quad$ LG-3

(B) $\log_3 81 = \log_3 3^4$
$\qquad = 4 \log_3 3 \quad$ LG-6
$\qquad = 4 \qquad\quad$ LG-3

(C) $\log_2 \left(\frac{1}{2} \right) = -\log_2 2 \quad$ LG-7
$\qquad\qquad = -1 \qquad\quad$ LG-3

(D) $-\log_3 \left(\frac{1}{3} \right) = -(-\log_3 3) \quad$ LG-7
$\qquad\qquad\quad = \log_3 3$
$\qquad\qquad\quad = 1 \qquad\quad$ LG-3

(E) $\log_{10} 3^{-1} = \log_{10} \left(\frac{1}{3} \right)$

But $\log_{10} \left(\frac{1}{3} \right) \neq \frac{1}{3}$ since $\frac{1}{3} = \log_{10} 10^{1/3}$ by LG-5.

EXAMPLES

Evaluate:

1. $\log_2 \sqrt{8} = \log_2 2^{3/2}$
$\qquad\qquad = \frac{3}{2}$

2. $\log_6 \left(\frac{36}{\sqrt[3]{6}} \right) = \log_6 6^{5/3}$
$\qquad\qquad\quad = \frac{5}{3}$

3. $\log_5 \left(\frac{\sqrt[3]{5}}{125} \right) = \log_5 \frac{5^{1/3}}{5^3}$
$\qquad\qquad\quad = \log_5 5^{-8/3}$
$\qquad\qquad\quad = \frac{-8}{3}$

*[17] If $\log_3 x = 5$ and $\log_3 y = 2$, which of the following is $\log_y x$?

(A)   3

(B) $2\frac{1}{2}$

(C) $\frac{2}{5}$

(D)   10

(E)   7

It is sometimes useful to be able to express logarithms of one base as logarithms of a different base.

LG-8   If $a > 0, a \neq 1, b > 0, b \neq 1, N \geq 0$, then

$$\log_a N = \frac{\log_b N}{\log_b a}.$$

EXAMPLE

Show that $\log_3 5 = \frac{1}{\log_5 3}$.

SOLUTION: $\log_3 5 = \dfrac{\log_b 5}{\log_b 3} \quad$ LG-8

Since the statement above will be true no matter what base is selected for b, let $b = 5$.

$$\log_3 5 = \frac{\log_5 5}{\log_5 3}$$
$$= \frac{1}{\log_5 3} \quad \text{LG-3}$$

In the multiple-choice question,

$$\log_y x = \frac{\log_3 x}{\log_3 y} = \frac{5}{2}.$$

EXAMPLES

Use your calculator and LG-8 to find each of the following:

1. $\log_2 3 = \dfrac{\log 3}{\log 2} = \dfrac{.4771}{.3010} = 1.5850$

2. $\log_3 2 = \dfrac{\log 2}{\log 3} = \dfrac{.3010}{.4771} = .6309$

3. $\log_5 6 = \dfrac{\log 6}{\log 5} = \dfrac{.7781}{.6990} = 3.9073$

WORKING WITH EQUAL EXPONENTIAL EXPRESSIONS

[18] Find the value of x if $4^x = 8$.

(A) 2

(B) $\dfrac{1}{2}$

(C) $\dfrac{3}{2}$

(D) 3

(E) Cannot be determined

If two exponential expressions are equal and have the same base, then the exponents must be equal. Thus the procedure for working out the question above is to express each side of the equation as an exponential form with the same base. Do you see that both 4 and 8 are powers of 2? Since $4 = 2^2$ and $8 = 2^3$, it follows that

$$4^x = 8$$

is the same as

$$(2^2)^x = 2^3.$$

Applying the laws of exponents gives

$$2^{2x} = 2^3.$$

Since the expressions are equal and the bases are equal, the exponents must be equal.

$$2x = 3$$
$$x = \dfrac{3}{2}$$

TEST-TAKING TIP
One of the advantages to the student of a multiple-choice test is that the correct answer is given. Thus a student who did not know the procedure for finding x directly could probably get the answer just as quickly by trying each of the choices.

EXAMPLES

Refer to Chapter 2 for a calculator procedure that solves for exponents. Solve each of the following for x algebraically and by calculator.

1. $\quad 2^{x-1} = 16$
$$= 2^4$$
$$\therefore x - 1 = 4$$
$$x = 5$$

2. $\quad 3^{-x} = \dfrac{1}{27}$
$$= 3^{-3}$$
$$\therefore -x = -3$$
$$x = 3$$

3. $\quad 8^x = \dfrac{1}{2}$
$$2^{3x} = 2^{-1}$$
$$3x = -1$$
$$x = \dfrac{-1}{3}$$

[19] If $\dfrac{a^{x-y}}{a^{x+y}} = a^2$, then $y = ?$

(A) -1

(B) 0

(C) 1

(D) 2

(E) 4

Because the left member of the equation is a quotient, subtract the exponents and rewrite the result as

$$a^{-2y} = a^2$$

The two expressions can only be equal if $-2y = 2$. Therefore, $y = -1$, (A),

WHAT YOU SHOULD KNOW

KEY CONCEPTS

Handling Exponents

If a, b, m, and n are real numbers, then:

1. $a^m \cdot a^n = a^{m+n}$,

2. $\dfrac{a^m}{a^n} = a^{m-n}$,

3. $(a^m)^n = a^{mn}$,

4. $(ab)^m = a^m b^m$,

5. $a^{-m} = \dfrac{1}{a^m}$,

6. $\left(\dfrac{a}{b}\right)^m = \dfrac{a^m}{b^m}$,

7. $a^{1/n} = \sqrt[n]{a}$, and

8. $a^{m/n} = \sqrt[n]{a^m} = \left(\sqrt[n]{a}\right)^m$, $a > 0$.

Handling Logarithms

If $M > 0$, $N > 0$, $b > 0$, $b \neq 1$, $a > 0$ and $a \neq 1$, then:

1. $\log_b(MN) = \log_b M + \log_b N$,

2. $\log_b\left(\dfrac{M}{N}\right) = \log_b M - \log_b N$,

3. $\log_b N^x = x\log_b N$,

4. $\log_b b = 1$,

5. $\log_b 1 = 0$,

6. $\log_b\left(\dfrac{1}{N}\right) = -\log_b N$, and

7. $\log_b N = \dfrac{\log_a N}{\log_a b}$.

KEY STATEMENT

To convert an equation in exponential form to an equation in logarithmic form: If $N = b^m$, then $\log_b N = m$.

TEST-TAKING STRATEGIES

- Keep in mind that the terms "logarithm" and "exponent" are synonymous, and that the laws of logarithms are the same as the laws of exponents.
- Knowing the laws of exponents is critical to working successfully and quickly with exponential expressions. However, when exponents are numerals, you can often check your work by going back to the two very simplest principles. These are a^m means a is used as a factor m times and $a^{-m} = \dfrac{1}{a^m}$. These allow you to write out the expressions as a succession of factors, thereby working with elementary algebraic principles. The method can be laborious, but remember that it also suggests a result when no other idea occurs to you.

CALCULATOR TIP

Know how to use your calculator to raise a number to a positive or negative power.

ANSWERS

[1] (E)	[5] (D)	[9] (B)	[13] (D)	[17] (B)
[2] (D)	[6] (C)	[10] (C)	[14] (C)	[18] (C)
[3] (A)	[7] (E)	[11] (E)	[15] (C)	[19] (A)
[4] (C)	[8] (A)	[12] (D)	[16] (E)	

TRIGONOMETRY

CHAPTER

23

In this chapter, some of the topics are more typical of those tested on the Mathematics Level IIC test than of those on the Level IC test. We have denoted these with an asterisk (*). Review of such topics may assist you in answering Level IC questions, however, because it increases your general knowledge of mathematical ideas, methods, and skills.

🖩 A calculator can take a lot of the drudgery out of trigonometric calculations. However, you must still be familiar with the fundamental principles of the subject.

KEY TERMS

angle
the union of two noncollinear rays (the *initial* and the *terminal* rays) that have a common endpoint with its degree measure defined as a number between 0 and 180.

degree measure
the number of degrees of rotation through which the initial ray would have to be turned to coincide with the terminal ray. The degree measure may be any real number.

straight angle
an angle with the degree measure of 180, formed when two rays lie on the same line but point in opposite directions.

angle in standard position
an angle that has its vertex at the origin and its initial side coincident with the positive ray of the x-axis.

reference angle
the smallest nonnegative angle between the terminal side of a given angle in standard position and the x-axis.

DEFINING TRIGONOMETRIC ANGLES AND THEIR MEASURES

[1]   Which of the following statements is NOT true?

(A)   The term "angle" is defined the same way in geometry as it is in trigonometry.

(B)   In trigonometry an angle has an initial ray and a terminal ray.

(C)   The measure of an angle in trigonometry is not unique.

(D)   The measure of an angle in trigonometry may be either positive or negative.

(E)   The measure of an angle in trigonometry can be zero.

In geometry, we define an *angle* to be the union of two noncollinear rays that have a common endpoint with its degree measure defined as a number between 0 and 180. In trigonometry the definition is extended with the designation of one of the rays as the "initial" ray and the other as the "terminal" ray. The *degree measure* is then defined as the number of degrees of rotation through which the initial ray would have to be turned to coincide with the terminal ray. If this rotation is counterclockwise, the measure is positive. If the rotation is clockwise, the measure is negative. There are times when it is valuable to consider the two rays as coincident; in such cases the measure is defined as zero. If the two rays lie on the same line but point in opposite directions (forming "opposite rays"), the angle thus formed is termed a *straight angle* and has a degree measure of 180.

Considered in these terms, an angle has an infinite set of possible measures, since the rotation of the terminal ray may be either positive or negative and is not even restricted to a single revolution. The figures below show three possible measures for the same angle:

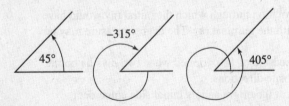

▦ Your calculator accepts the measures of angles in degree mode or in radian mode. Before continuing, make sure you know how to change your calculator setup from one mode to the other. Also, get in the habit of checking the mode setting each time you work a trig problem. On Level IC, all angles will be in degrees.

FINDING THE RADIAN MEASURES OF ANGLES

[2]   Which of the following is the radian measure of an angle whose degree measure is 135?

(A) $-\dfrac{\pi}{4}$

(B) $\dfrac{\pi}{4}$

(C) $\dfrac{3\pi}{4}$

(D) $\dfrac{3}{4}$

(E) $-\dfrac{3\pi}{4}$

Though the degree measure of an angle is useful, it is often more valuable to use a measure defined in terms of arc length. If an angle is a central angle of a circle of radius 1 unit (termed a "unit" circle), and the arc which it cuts off is also of length 1 unit, the measure of the angle is 1 *radian*. Since the circumference of this unit circle is 2π, such an arc (of length 1) can be laid off 2π times on the circle. In other words, a measure of 360° is equivalent to a measure of 2π radians, or

(1) π radians $= 180°$.

This yields the two equations most useful in converting from one unit to the other. Dividing both sides of (1) by π produces

(2) ▦   1 radian $= \left(\dfrac{180}{\pi}\right)^{\circ} =$ approximately $57.3°$

Dividing both sides of (1) by 180 produces

(3) $\dfrac{\pi}{180}$ radians $= 1°$.

To convert from radians to degrees, multiply the given number of radians times both sides of (2) and then simplify. To convert from degrees to radians, multiply the given number of degrees times both sides of (3) and then simplify.

Since $1° = \dfrac{\pi}{180}$ radians, it follows that

$$135(1°) = 135\left(\dfrac{\pi}{180}\right) \text{ radians,}$$

$$135° = 3(45)\left(\dfrac{\pi}{4(45)}\right) \text{ radians}$$

$$= \dfrac{3\pi}{4} \text{ radians. (approximately 2.36).}$$

Note that your calculator will display radian measure in decimal form rather than in terms of the π symbol.

[3] If a central angle of a circle of radius 4 cuts off an arc of length 8, what is the radian measure of the angle?

(A) 2π

(B) 2

(C) 8

(D) 4

(E) 8π

As we have noted, the radian measure of an angle is determined by the length of the arc it cuts off on a unit circle. A theorem from geometry, however, states that arcs subtending central angles that have the same measure are in the same ratio as are their radii. Thus, if s and r are the respective lengths of arc and radius of one circle and s' and r' are the lengths of arc and radius of another circle, then

$$\frac{s}{r} = \frac{s'}{r'}$$

when the defining central angles have the same measure. In the unit circle where $r' = 1$ and $s' = \theta$ in radians, we get

$$\frac{s}{r} = \frac{\theta}{1}.$$

In short we can find the radian measure of an angle by dividing the subtended arc length by the radius. The latter formula may be used, of course, to find either the arc length or the radius of the circle when the other two of $\{s, r, \theta\}$ are known.

If $r = 4$ and $s = 8$, then

$$\theta = \frac{s}{r} = \frac{8}{4} = 2 \text{ radians.}$$

EXAMPLES

Find the radian measure of the angle that subtends arc s on a circle of radius r:

1. $s = 4, r = 5$

2. $s = 2\pi, r = 2$

3. $s = \pi, r = 1$

Now find the arc length of

4. $\theta = \frac{\pi}{2}$ and $r = 2$

SOLUTIONS:

1. $\dfrac{s}{r} = \dfrac{4}{5}$

2. $\dfrac{s}{r} = \dfrac{2\pi}{2} = \pi$

3. $\dfrac{s}{r} = \dfrac{\pi}{1} = \pi$

4. $r\theta = \left(\dfrac{\pi}{2}\right)(2) = \pi$

[4] If an angle is in standard position and the point $(-1, 0)$ is a point on the terminal side, in what quadrant does the terminal side lie?

(A) I

(B) II

(C) III

(D) IV

(E) None of these

The coordinate axes are a pair of perpendicular lines that separate the plane into four regions called *quadrants,* and no point of either axis belongs to any quadrant.

An angle in *standard position* is one that has its vertex at the origin and its initial side coincident with the positive ray of the x-axis. The angle is said to *lie* in the quadrant through which the terminal ray passes, even though the interior of the angle may contain points of several quadrants. Two angles in standard position are referred to as *coterminal* when they have the same terminal side. Any angle that is coterminal with either ray of either axis does not lie in any quadrant and is called a *quadrantal angle.*

Since the point $(-1, 0)$ is on the negative ray of the x-axis, the angle defined is a quadrantal angle and does not lie in any quadrant.

[5] If an angle has a radian measure of $\dfrac{5\pi}{4}$, what is the radian measure of its reference angle?

(A) $\dfrac{5\pi}{4}$

(B) $-\dfrac{5\pi}{4}$

(C) $\dfrac{3\pi}{4}$

(D) $\dfrac{\pi}{4}$

(E) $-\dfrac{\pi}{4}$

The concept of "reference angle" is useful in cutting down the size of trigonometric tables. Every angle in standard position has a *reference* angle (except for the quadrantal angles), which is defined to be the smallest nonnegative angle between the terminal side of the given angle and the x-axis. The ray of the x-axis you choose is the one that yields the smaller nonnegative angle.

The angle $\frac{5\pi}{4}$ terminates in the third quadrant, as you can see from the fact that $\frac{4\pi}{4}$ terminates on the negative ray of the x-axis. The angle formed by the negative ray of the x-axis and $\frac{5\pi}{4}$ is $\frac{\pi}{4}$.

FINDING THE COORDINATES OF A POINT ON THE TERMINAL SIDE

[6]   If the x-coordinate of a point is -3 and its distance from the origin is 5, then its y-coordinate is?

(A) 4 or -4

(B) 4

(C) -4

(D) $\sqrt{34}$

(E) $\sqrt{34}$ or $-\sqrt{34}$

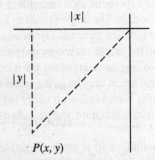

The absolute value of a coordinate of a point is the distance from that point to an axis. If a point $P(x,y)$ is r units from the origin, then the line segment from P to the x-axis completes a right triangle whose sides have length $|x|$, $|y|$, and r. Note that r, a distance, is always positive.

The Pythagorean Theorem yields

(1) $|x|^2 + |y|^2 = r^2$.

Since $|x| = x$ when $x \geq 0$ and $-x$ when $x < 0$ and since both of $(x)^2$ and $(-x)^2$ are equal to x^2, we rewrite (1) as

(2) $x^2 + y^2 = r^2$.

When two elements of $\{x, y, r\}$ are given, the other can be found by substituting for the known variables and solving for the third in (2). Whenever r is given with either x or y, the equation yields two values for the third unknown.

EXAMPLE

If $y = 2$ and $r = 3$, find x.

SOLUTION:
$$x^2 + (2)^2 = (3)^2$$
$$x^2 = 5$$
$$x = \pm\sqrt{5}$$

This would indicate that two different angles satisfy the given conditions as in the figure below for which $y = 2$, $r = 3$. When x and y are given, however, only one value is meaningful for r.

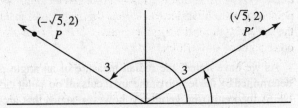

In the multiple-choice question, $x = -3$ and $r = 5$. Then:

$$x^2 + y^2 = r^2,$$
$$(-3)^2 + y^2 = 5^2,$$
$$9 + y^2 = 25,$$
$$y^2 = 16,$$
$$y = \pm 4.$$

WORKING WITH TRIGONOMETRIC FUNCTIONS

[7]   If the terminal side of θ contains the point $(3,7)$, which of the following is NOT true?

(A) $\sin\theta = \dfrac{7}{\sqrt{58}}$

(B) $\cos\theta = \dfrac{3}{\sqrt{58}}$

(C) $\tan\theta = \dfrac{7}{3}$

(D) $\cot\theta = \dfrac{3}{7}$

(E) $\sec\theta = \dfrac{\sqrt{58}}{7}$

The trigonometric functions of an angle in standard position are defined as follows.

If $P(x,y)$ is a point on the terminal side of an angle θ and is r units from the origin ($r \neq 0$), then:

$$\sin\theta = \frac{y}{r}, \quad \cos\theta = \frac{x}{r}, \quad \tan\theta = \frac{y}{x},$$

$$\csc\theta = \frac{r}{y}, \quad \sec\theta = \frac{r}{x}, \quad \cot\theta = \frac{x}{y},$$

You may verify for yourself (using similar triangles) that the values of the functions do not depend on the point of the terminal side that is chosen. For a given angle, any point on the terminal side (other than the origin) will yield the same values for the trig functions of that angle as any other point on the terminal side.

The term "function" is used here properly, since the sets of ordered pairs of the form $(\theta, \sin\theta)$, $(\theta, \cos\theta)$, etc., satisfy the definition of function. Note also that any two angles that are coterminal must have the same values for their trig functions, since their terminal sides contain exactly the same points. Thus $\sin 45° = \sin 405°$ and $\cos(-120°) = \cos 240°$.

To apply the definition of the trigonometric functions to the multiple-choice question, we must first find r. We are given $(x,y) = (3,7)$. Then:

$$x^2 + y^2 = r^2,$$
$$9 + 49 = r^2,$$
$$58 = r^2,$$
$$\sqrt{58} = r.$$

Using $x = 3$, $y = 7$, $r = \sqrt{58}$ and the formulas for $\sin\theta$, $\cos\theta$, $\tan\theta$, $\cot\theta$ and $\sec\theta$, we see that

$$\sec\theta = \frac{\sqrt{58}}{3},$$

which disagrees with answer (E), while all of the others agree with the corresponding choices.

EXAMPLES

If each of the following is a point on the terminal side of an angle in standard position, find the value of the requested function:

1. $(3, -2)$; $\sin\theta = \dfrac{-2}{\sqrt{13}}$

2. $(-\sqrt{2}, 4)$; $\csc\theta = \dfrac{3\sqrt{2}}{4}$

3. $(-4, -2)$; $\tan\theta = \dfrac{1}{2}$

[8] $\triangle ABC$ is a right triangle with right angle at B Find the cotangent of $\angle C$.

(A) $\dfrac{1}{2}$

(B) 2

(C) $\sqrt{3}$

(D) $\dfrac{2}{\sqrt{3}}$

(E) $\dfrac{\sqrt{3}}{2}$

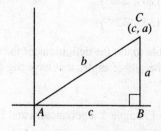

Two of the angles of a right triangle must be acute. If we position a right triangle in the coordinate plane so that one of the acute angles is in standard position, this angle will lie in the first quadrant. The lengths of the legs of the triangle tell us the coordinates of a point on the terminal side and the hypotenuse indicates the distance of this point from the origin.

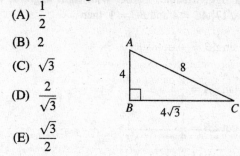

If θ is an angle of a right triangle, then:

$$\sin\theta = \frac{\text{opposite leg}}{\text{hypotenuse}}, \quad \cos\theta = \frac{\text{adjacent leg}}{\text{hypotenuse}},$$

$$\tan\theta = \frac{\text{opposite leg}}{\text{adjacent leg}}, \quad \cot\theta = \frac{\text{adjacent leg}}{\text{opposite leg}},$$

$$\csc\theta = \frac{\text{hypotenuse}}{\text{opposite leg}}, \quad \sec\theta = \frac{\text{hypotenuse}}{\text{adjacent leg}}$$

From the above equations we can find the values of the trig functions of the angles of a right triangle.

In the multiple-choice question, the adjacent leg for $\angle C$ is $BC = 4\sqrt{3}$, and the opposite leg is $AB = 4$. Therefore:

$$\cot\angle C = \frac{\text{adjacent leg}}{\text{opposite leg}}$$
$$= \frac{BC}{AB}$$
$$= \frac{4\sqrt{3}}{4}$$
$$= \sqrt{3}.$$

EXAMPLES

In a right triangle, $\triangle ABC$ with right angle at C, if $AB = \sqrt{17}$, $AC = 4$ and $BC = 1$, then

1. $\sin \angle B = \dfrac{4}{\sqrt{17}}$

2. $\tan \angle A = \dfrac{1}{4}$

3. $\cot \angle B = \dfrac{1}{4}$

[9]   If $\cos\theta = -\dfrac{1}{2}$ and $0 \le \theta < 360°$ then the set of possible values for θ is:

    (A) $\{60°, 300°\}$

    (B) $\{210°, 330°\}$

    (C) $\{240°, 300°\}$

    (D) $\{120°, 240°\}$

    (E) $\{135°, 225°\}$

It is possible to use the definitions of the trig functions to discover the sets of angles that have trig functions of a given value.

We'll do Example 1 algebraically and Example 2 by calculator.

EXAMPLE 1

If $\sin\theta = \dfrac{\sqrt{3}}{2}$ and $0 \le \theta < 2\pi$, find θ.

SOLUTION: We conclude from the definition of sine that

(1) $\qquad\qquad\qquad \dfrac{y}{r} = \dfrac{\sqrt{3}}{2}.$

This, of course, does *not* mean that y must be $\sqrt{3}$ and r must be 2. As a matter of fact, *any* two numbers whose ratio is $\sqrt{3} : 2$ will satisfy equation (1). Indeed, we may choose any value for r that we please, since any point on the terminal side—whatever its distance, r, from the origin—will produce the same values for the trig functions as any other point. Once we have selected our arbitrary value for r, equation (1) tells us the value of y and $x^2 + y^2 = r^2$ yields the value of x.

For simplicity we let $r = 2$; then $y = \sqrt{3}$ and

$$x^2 + (\sqrt{3})^2 = 4,$$
$$x^2 = 1,$$
$$x = \pm 1.$$

The points $P(1, \sqrt{3})$ and $P'(-1, \sqrt{3})$ lie on the terminal sides of angles that satisfy the given information, as shown in the figure:

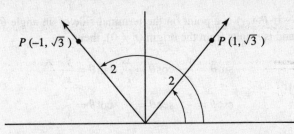

By dropping perpendiculars to the x-axis from points P and P', we form triangles with sides having the familiar ratios of the special 30-60-90 triangles (Chapter 18, section [15]):

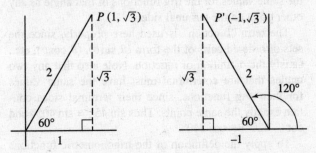

The angles between 0 and 2π, then, that satisfy the given information are, in radian measure, $\dfrac{\pi}{3}$ and $\dfrac{2\pi}{3}$ (from 60° and 120°).

EXAMPLE 2

If $\tan\theta = -1$ and $\cos\theta > 0$, find θ.

SOLUTION:

Set the mode of your calculator to degrees before proceeding.

If $\tan\theta = -1$, then

$$\theta = \tan^{-1}(-1)$$

Enter $\tan^{-1}(-1)$ according to the procedure indicated in your calculator manual. Your calculator will then display -45, which is in quadrant IV. Note that in quadrant IV, the value of $\cos\theta$ is positive, which satisfies the second piece of given information.

In the multiple-choice question, $\cos\theta$ is negative so θ represents angles terminating in quadrants II and III. From the 30-60-90 triangle, we see that $0 = 60°$ gives a cosine of $\dfrac{1}{2}$. The angles in quadrants II and III with reference angle of 60 are

$$180 - 60 = 120 \quad \text{and} \quad 180 + 60 = 240.$$

USING COFUNCTIONS

[10] If $\cot\theta = \tan 15°$, then $\theta = $?

(A) 65°

(B) 75°

(C) 15°

(D) −15°

(E) None of these

Because the acute angles of a right triangle are complementary, we can state for the triangle at right that

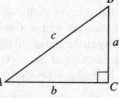

(1) $(\angle A)° + (\angle B)° = 90.$

Thus

(2) $(\angle B)° = 90 - (\angle A)°$ and

(3) $(\angle A)° = 90 - (\angle B)°.$

But the sine of $\angle A$ is $\frac{a}{c}$, which is also the cosine of $\angle B$. Similarly, $\frac{a}{b}$ is the tangent of $\angle A$ as well as the cotangent of $\angle B$, while the secant of $\angle A$ is the cosecant of $\angle B$. Thus, if two angles, $\angle A$ and $\angle B$, are complementary, then

$$\sin \angle A = \cos \angle B,$$
$$\tan \angle A = \cot \angle B,$$
$$\sec \angle A = \csc \angle B.$$

Substituting the relations of (2) and (3) in each of the above produces

$$\sin \angle A = \cos (90 - \angle A),$$
$$\tan \angle A = \cot (90 - \angle A),$$
$$\sec \angle A = \csc (90 - \angle A).$$

We call the sine and cosine, tangent and cotangent, secant and cosecant, "cofunctions." Indeed, the prefix "co" serves to remind us of the complementary nature of the sine-cosine, etc., relationships.

In the multiple-choice question,

$$\cot\theta = \tan(90 - \theta) = \tan 15°.$$

Therefore:

$$90 - \theta = 15,$$
$$-\theta = -75,$$
$$\theta = 75.$$

EXAMPLE

Express each of the following as a cofunction of a complementary angle:

1. $\sin 45 = \cos 45$

2. $\tan 13 = \cot 77$

3. $\csc 53 = \sec 37$

4. $\cot 42 = \tan 48$

USING REFERENCE ANGLES

[11] Which of the following is (are) true?

   I. $\sin 45° = \sin 135°$

  II. $\cos 83° = -\cos 263°$

 III. $\tan 16° = -\tan 344°$

(A) I only

(B) II only

(C) I, II, and III

(D) I and II only

(E) None

The equations can be checked by calculator. However, it is very useful to know the algebraic relationships between angles and their reference angles.

Quadrant I The reference angle of every first quadrant angle is the angle itself. Thus the functions of the angles are the same as the functions of the reference angles.

Quadrant II The reference angle of an angle, θ, in the second quadrant has measure $180 - \theta$. In the figure at upper right we constructed both θ and the angle in the first quadrant with measure $180 - \theta$. On the terminal sides we selected points P and P' to be r units from the origin and have dropped perpendiculars from these points to the x-axis. The two triangles thus formed are congruent by SAA and thus the pairs of corresponding legs must have the same length. Since we have chosen the lengths of the corresponding legs to be a and b, the point P is $(-a, b)$ and P' is (ab).

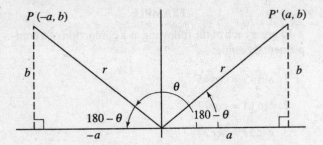

We draw the following conclusions from the figure:

(1) $\sin\theta = \dfrac{b}{r}$ and $\sin(180-\theta) = \dfrac{b}{r}$,

so $\sin\theta = \sin(180-\theta)$;

(2) $\cos\theta = \dfrac{a}{r}$ and $\cos(180-\theta) = \dfrac{-a}{r}$,

so $\cos\theta = -\cos(180-\theta)$;

(3) $\tan\theta = \dfrac{b}{a}$ and $\tan(180-\theta) = \dfrac{-b}{a}$,

so $\tan\theta = -\tan(180-\theta)$.

Quadrant III   Let θ be the reference angle for an angle terminating in the third quadrant. Then the angle itself can be designated as $180+\theta$. From the figure below we see that

(4) $\sin\theta = -\sin(180+\theta)$,

(5) $\cos\theta = -\cos(180+\theta)$,

(6) $\tan\theta = \tan(180+\theta)$.

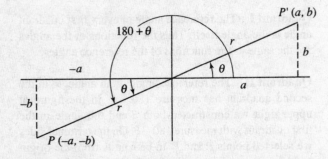

Quadrant IV   Let θ be the reference angle for an angle terminating in the fourth quadrant. Then the angle itself can be designated as $360-\theta$. From the figure following we see that

(7) $\sin\theta = -\sin(360-\theta)$,

(8) $\cos\theta = \cos(360-\theta)$,

(9) $\tan\theta = -\tan(360-\theta)$.

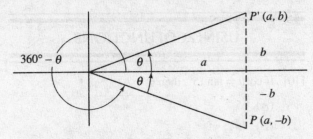

There is little value in memorizing equations (1) through (9). You should, instead, make a sketch of the given angle and its reference angle as positioned in quadrant I. Then compare the signs of the coordinates of the points at some fixed distance r from the origin on the terminal sides of both angles—the absolute values of these coordinates will not differ, of course. The relationship between the signs will be the desired relationship between the function of the angle and its reference angle.

In the multiple-choice question,

I. The reference angle for $135°$ is $45°$, and $135°$ is in quadrant II, where sine is positive. Therefore $\sin 45° = \sin 135°$.

II. The reference angle for $263°$ is $263° - 180° = 83°$, and $263°$ is in quadrant III, where cosine is negative. Therefore $\cos 83° = -\cos 263°$.

III. The reference angle for $344°$ is $360° - 344° = 16°$, and $344°$ is in quadrant IV, where tangent is negative. Therefore $\tan 16° = -\tan 344°$.

Hence all are true.

EXAMPLES

Express each of the following as the same function of its reference angle:

1. $\sin 340° = -\sin 20°$

2. $\cos 192° = -\cos 12°$

3. $\csc 92° = \csc 88°$

USING SPECIAL TRIANGLES

[12]   Which of the following is NOT true?

(A) $\sin\dfrac{\pi}{6} = \dfrac{1}{2}$

(B) $\cos 45° = \dfrac{\sqrt{2}}{2}$

(C) $\tan 135° = -1$

(D) $\sin 270° = -1$

(E) $\cos 0° = 0$

The answer choices can be checked by calculator. However, you should also know how to determine the trigonometric values of special angles through geometry.

Let us begin by reviewing some facts from geometry and then answer the question in [12] directly. Two right triangles received special attention in geometry: the 30°-60°-90° triangle and the 45°-45°-90° triangle. Their significance stems from the simple ratios of their sides.

From the special triangles it is possible to determine the trig functions of angles of 30°, 45°, 60°, and, through the application of the techniques of section [11], any other angles that have 30°, 45°, or 60° as reference angles. We will use the answer selections (A) to (E) under [12] as examples.

(A) Because $\frac{\pi}{6}$ radians $= 30°$, $\sin \frac{\pi}{6} = \sin 30°$.

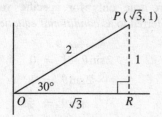

Because we are interested in a method that is as general as possible, we will construct a 30° angle in standard position and then select a point P on the terminal side such that $OP = 2$. (P may be any point on the terminal side, so we have selected a point that will simplify our calculations.) If segment PR is perpendicular to the x-axis, then $PR = 1$, and $OR = \sqrt{3}$ by the 30°-60°-90° triangle ratios. Thus the coordinates of P are $(\sqrt{3}, 1)$ and $\sin \frac{\pi}{6} = \frac{1}{2}$.

(B) Construct a 45° angle in standard position and choose a point P such that $OP = 1$ (another reminder that P may be any point on the terminal side and we have selected $OP = 1$ merely for simplicity).

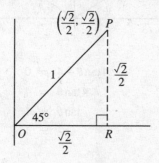

Then, if PR is perpendicular to the x-axis, $PR = \frac{\sqrt{2}}{2}$ and $OR = \frac{\sqrt{2}}{2}$ by the 45°-45°-90° triangle ratios. Thus the coordinates of P are $\left(\frac{\sqrt{2}}{2}, \frac{\sqrt{2}}{2}\right)$ and

$$\cos 45° = \frac{\sqrt{2}}{2}.$$

(C) Construct an angle of 135° in standard position and choose a point P on the terminal side such that $OP = 1$.

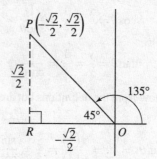

Then $PR = \frac{\sqrt{2}}{2}$ and $OR = \frac{\sqrt{2}}{2}$. But the x-coordinate of any point in quadrant II is negative, so $P = \left(-\frac{\sqrt{2}}{2}, \frac{\sqrt{2}}{2}\right)$ and

$$\tan 135° = \frac{\frac{\sqrt{2}}{2}}{-\frac{\sqrt{2}}{2}} = -1.$$

(D) An angle of 270° is coterminal with the negative ray of the y-axis. Select $OP = 1$. Then $P = (0, -1)$ and $\sin 270° = -1$.

(E) 0° is coterminal with the positive ray of the x-axis. Select $OP = 1$. Then $P = (1, 0)$ and $\cos 0° = 1$.

USING IDENTITIES

[13] Which of the following statements is NOT true for all values of the variable for which the function is defined?

(A) $\cos^2 \theta + \sin^2 \theta = 1$

(B) $\sec^2 \theta = 1 - \tan^2 \theta$

(C) $\tan \theta = \dfrac{\sin \theta}{\cos \theta}$

(D) $1 + \csc \theta = \dfrac{1 + \sin \theta}{\sin \theta}$

(E) $(\cos^2 \theta)(\tan^2 \theta + 1) = 1$

Equations that are true for all values in the domain of the variable are referred to as *identities*. Such equations form an important part of trigonometry, since they allow the transformation of an expression involving one or more functions into an expression involving other functions that may be more useful in a given problem.

Some of these are obvious, such as those suggested by the definitions of the functions themselves.

(1) $$\sin\theta = \frac{y}{r} = \frac{1}{\frac{r}{y}} = \frac{1}{\csc\theta}$$

(2) $$\cos\theta = \frac{x}{r} = \frac{1}{\frac{r}{x}} = \frac{1}{\sec\theta}$$

(3) $$\tan\theta = \frac{y}{x} = \frac{1}{\frac{x}{y}} = \frac{1}{\cot\theta}$$

Others follow from the definitions but are less obvious.

(4) $$\tan\theta = \frac{y}{x} = \frac{y\left(\frac{1}{r}\right)}{x\left(\frac{1}{r}\right)} = \frac{\frac{y}{r}}{\frac{x}{r}} = \frac{\sin\theta}{\cos\theta}$$
$$\text{(answer (C))}$$

(5) $$x^2 + y^2 = r^2, \text{ so } \frac{x^2}{r^2} + \frac{y^2}{r^2} = 1.$$

Therefore,

$$\cos^2\theta + \sin^2\theta = 1. \quad \text{(answer A)}$$

Identities (1) through (5), which should be memorized, lead immediately to others through various substitutions.

$$\cos^2\theta + \sin^2\theta = 1$$
$$\frac{\cos^2\theta}{\cos^2\theta} + \frac{\sin^2\theta}{\cos^2\theta} = \frac{1}{\cos^2\theta}$$
$$1 + \tan^2\theta = \frac{1}{\cos^2\theta} \quad \text{Identity (4)}$$

(6) $$1 + \tan^2\theta = \sec^2\theta \quad \text{Identity (2)}$$

(Note: compare (6) with answer (B)).

They can also be used to prove the truth of others, as is demonstrated here for answers (D) and (E).

(D) $$1 + \csc\theta = 1 + \frac{1}{\sin\theta} \quad \text{Identity (1)}$$
$$= \frac{\sin\theta}{\sin\theta} + \frac{1}{\sin\theta}$$
$$= \frac{(\sin\theta) + 1}{\sin\theta}$$

(E) $$(\cos^2\theta)(\tan^2\theta + 1)$$
$$= (\cos^2\theta)\left(\frac{\sin^2\theta}{\cos^2\theta} + 1\right) \quad \text{Identity (4)}$$
$$= \sin^2\theta + \cos^2\theta$$
$$= 1 \quad \text{Identity (5)}$$

USING CONDITIONAL EQUATIONS

[14]   The set $\{150°, 30°\}$ is the set of solutions for which of the following equations? (Assume the domain of the variable to be $0 \le \theta < 360$.)

(A) $2\sin\theta - 1 = 0$

(B) $4\tan\theta - 4 = 0$

(C) $(\cos\theta)(\sin\theta) = 0$

(D) $\sin^2\theta + 1 = 3$

(E) $\sin^2\theta - 1 = 0$

In this section we will consider trigonometric equations that are true only for specific values of the variables—referred to as *conditional equations*.

(A)

$$2\sin\theta - 1 = 0$$
$$2\sin\theta = 1$$
$$\sin\theta = \frac{1}{2}$$
$$\frac{y}{r} = \frac{1}{2}$$

Using the method shown in section [9], we let $r = 2$, then $y = 1$. Since $x^2 + y^2 = r^2$, we conclude $x = \pm\sqrt{3}$. If we plot the points and use the 30-60-90 triangle relations as in the figure below, we get 30° and 150° for θ.

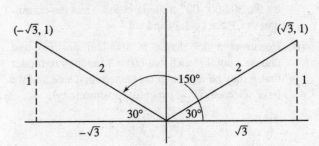

(B)

$$4\tan\theta - 4 = 0$$
$$4\tan\theta = 4$$
$$\tan\theta = 1$$
$$\frac{y}{x} = 1$$

If we let $x = 1$, then $y = 1$ and $r = \sqrt{2}$. Plotting the point and applying the 45°-45°-90° triangle information, we get θ to be 45°. But we may also let $x = -1$, for which $y = -1$ and $r = \sqrt{2}$. From the latter information we find θ to be 225°.

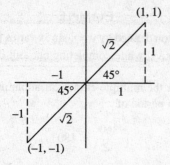

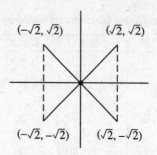

(C) $(\cos\theta)(\sin\theta) = 0$

An important algebraic theorem states that $ab = 0$ if and only if $a = 0$ or $b = 0$. If we apply this fact to the equation in (C), we get

$$\cos\theta = 0 \quad \text{or} \quad \sin\theta = 0.$$

Because any angle that satisfies either part of this compound statement will satisfy the original equation, the solution set is

$$\{190°, 270°, 0°, 180°\}.$$

The first two elements are solutions of $\cos\theta = 0$; the second two are solutions of $\sin\theta = 0$.

(D)
$$\sin^2\theta + 2\sin\theta = 3$$
$$\sin^2\theta + 2\sin\theta - 3 = 0$$
$$(\sin\theta + 3)(\sin\theta - 1) = 0$$
$$\sin\theta + 3 = 0 \quad \text{or} \quad \sin\theta - 1 = 0$$
$$\sin\theta = -3 \quad \text{or} \quad \sin\theta = 1$$

(E) Because no angle may have a sine less than -1, $\sin\theta = -3$ has no solutions, but $\sin\theta = -1$ is satisfied by 90°.

(F)
$$2\sin^2\theta - 1 = 0$$
$$2\sin^2\theta = 1$$
$$\sin^2\theta = \frac{1}{2}$$
$$\sin\theta = \pm\sqrt{\frac{1}{2}}$$
$$= \pm\frac{\sqrt{2}}{2}$$
$$\frac{y}{r} = \pm\frac{\sqrt{2}}{2}$$

Let $r = 2$; then $y = \pm\sqrt{2}$ and $x = \pm\sqrt{2}$ (from $x^2 + y^2 = r^2$). Note that the absolute values of the x- and y-coordinates are the same, so the triangles formed are isosceles right triangles (45°-45°-90°) and the solutions are $\{45°, 135°, 225°, 315°\}$.

FINDING PERIODS AND AMPLITUDES

*[15] The graph below is part of $y = 2\sin 2x$.

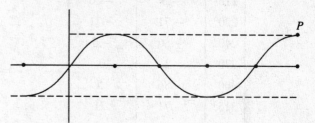

What are the coordinates of P?

(A) $\left(180°, \dfrac{1}{2}\right)$

(B) $(180°, 2)$

(C) $(360°, 1)$

(D) $(450°, 2)$

(E) $(225°, 2)$

For a trig function, though no two ordered pairs have the same first coordinate, an infinite set of ordered pairs have each of the possible second coordinates. The complete graph of a trig function is an infinite series of identical sections, each beginning where the last left off. Such functions are termed "periodic." A function, $f(x)$, is *periodic* if and only if there is some number p such that:

$$f(x) = f(x+p) \quad \text{for all } x.$$

The smallest number p that indicates the distance between the points at the beginning and end of each cycle is called the *period* of the function. The table and the graphs on the next page show the functions defined by $y = \sin x$ (solid line) and $y = \cos x$ (dotted line) from 0° to 360°.

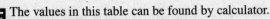 The values in this table can be found by calculator.

x	$\sin x$	$\cos x$
0	0	1
30°	.5	$\frac{\sqrt{3}}{2}$ or .86
45°	$\frac{\sqrt{2}}{2}$ or .71	$\frac{\sqrt{2}}{2}$ or .71
60°	$\frac{\sqrt{3}}{2}$ or .86	.5
90°	1	0
120°	.86	−.5
135°	.71	−.71
150°	.5	−.86
180°	0	1
210°	−.5	−.86
220°	−.71	−.71
240°	−.86	−.5
270°	−1	0
300°	−.86	.5
315°	−.71	.71
330°	−.5	.86
360°	0	1

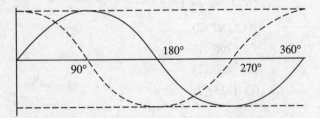

Since the terminal sides of θ, $\theta + 360°$, $\theta + 720°\ldots$, $\theta + k \cdot 360°$ are coincident, the graph to the right of 360° is a series of repetitions of the section drawn below.

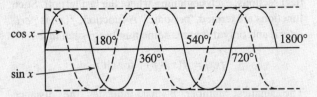

Note that no matter how great θ becomes, neither $\sin\theta$ nor $\cos\theta$ takes values greater than 1 or less than −1.

The *amplitude* of the function is $\frac{1}{2}(p - q)$, where p is the maximum value of the function and q is the minimum value.

Many curves are based on the sine and cosine curves. Some of these are defined by equations of the form $y = A\sin Bx$ and $y = A\cos Bx$. In such cases the amplitude is $|A|$ and the period is $\frac{360°}{B}$.

EXAMPLE

The function defined by $y = \frac{1}{4}\sin 3x$ varies between $-\frac{1}{4}$ and $\frac{1}{4}$, inclusive, while completing one full cycle from 0 to 120°.

To answer the multiple-choice question, note that $y = 2\sin 2x$ has a period of

$$\frac{360°}{2} = 180°$$

and an amplitude of 2. The period tells us that a cycle begins at 0 and ends at 180°. Point P is a quarter-cycle past 180°, so the first coordinate of P is

 $$180 + \frac{1}{4}180° = \frac{5}{4}180° = 225°$$

Since the amplitude is 2, the second coordinate of P is 2.

USING THE LAW OF COSINES

*[16] If the lengths of two sides of a triangle are 5 and 6 while the measure of their included angle is 60, what is the length of the third side?

(A) $\sqrt{31}$

(B) $\sqrt{91}$

(C) $\sqrt{61}$

(D) $\sqrt{11}$

(E) None of these

LAW OF COSINES

If a, b, and c are the lengths of the sides of a triangle and $\angle C$ is the included angle of the sides having length a and b, then

$$c^2 = a^2 + b^2 - 2ab \cos \angle C.$$

We can apply the Law of Cosines directly to the multiple-choice question, allowing a to be 5, b to be 6. The cosine of $\angle C$ must be $\frac{1}{2}$ since $\angle C$ has a measure of 60. We'll leave the rest to you.

Because the given information for this question is side-angle-side, there is no ambiguity about the third side; you will recall that SAS is a congruence relation and thereby determines a triangle uniquely.

Third-side ambiguity sometimes arises when the given information comprises two sides and an angle that is not included between them. In such cases, the third side may not be unique. You will recall the absence from geometry of a side-side-angle congruence relation. (Indeed, the third side may not even exist, a situation we will review last.) The following figures show the two possible triangles based on the given information that m $\angle C = 60$ with $a = 5$ and $c = 6$.

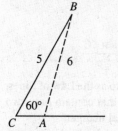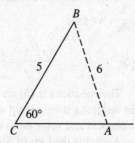

When applied to this situation, the Law of Cosines yields

$$36 = 25 + b^2 - 2 \cdot 5 \cdot b \cdot \frac{1}{2},$$
$$36 = 25 + b^2 - 5b,$$
$$0 = b^2 - 5b - 11.$$

Therefore, by formula,

$$b = \frac{5 \pm \sqrt{80}}{2}$$
$$= \frac{5 \pm 2\sqrt{5}}{2}.$$

The two solutions provide the lengths of the sides for both possible cases.

We can use the Law of Cosines to find the length of the missing side and the measures of the missing angles whenever the given information is two sides and an angle. If all three sides are given, we can use the same law to find the three missing angles. This process of finding the missing parts is called *solving* the triangle.

In order to be solved, the triangle must, of course, exist. The figure at right shows a situation under which the triangle would not exist.

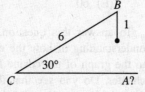

Given m $\angle C = 30$, $a = 6$, and $c = 1$.

The side opposite angle C must be at least as long as the distance from point B to line AC in order for the triangle to exist.

FINDING THE AREA OF A TRIANGLE

*[17] In $\triangle ABC$, if the area is $\frac{21}{2}$, $AC = 6$, and $BA = 7$, then which of the following can be the measure of $\angle A$?

(A) $45°$

(B) $60°$

(C) $30°$

(D) $40°$

(E) $22\frac{1}{2}°$

The area of a triangle is $\frac{1}{2}ab$, where b is the length of a side and a is the length of the altitude to that side. A formula for the area of a triangle can be derived based on the lengths of any two sides and the sine of their included angle.

Given acute $\triangle ABC$ with altitude h, $AB = c$ and $AC = b$. The area as indicated by the base-height formula is

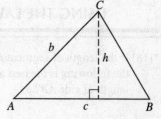

(1) $\qquad\qquad \frac{1}{2}ch.$

But $\sin \angle A = \frac{h}{b}$, so

(2) $\qquad\qquad h = b\sin\angle A.$

Substituting (2) in (1), we get

(3) $\qquad\qquad \text{Area} = \frac{1}{2}cb\sin\angle A.$

A similar argument produces the same formula for the area of an obtuse triangle.

If we rearrange (3) to apply directly to the multiple-choice question, we get

$$\sin\angle A = \frac{2 \times \text{Area}}{bc}.$$

Applying this formula to the multiple-choice question gives

$$\sin\angle A = \frac{2(\frac{21}{2})}{6(7)} = \frac{21}{42} = \frac{1}{2}.$$

If $\sin\angle A = \frac{1}{2}$, then $\angle A = 30°$.

EXAMPLES

Find the area of $\triangle ABC$, given the following:

1. $AB = 12$, $AC = 4$, $(\angle A)^\circ = 45$

2. $AC = 2$, $BC = 5$, $(\angle C)^\circ = 150$

SOLUTIONS:

1. Area $= \dfrac{1}{2}(AB)(AC)\sin 45$

   $= 6\sqrt{2}$

   $\doteq 8.49$

2. Area $= \dfrac{1}{2}(AC)(BC)\sin \angle C$

   $= \dfrac{1}{2}(2)(5)(\sin 150)$

   $= 2.5$

USING THE LAW OF SINES

*[18] If the length of segment BC is 24.6, which of the following is the best approximation to the length of side AB?

(A) 18

(B) 50

(C) 45

(D) 31

(E) 29

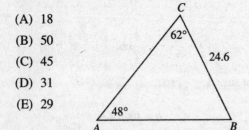

The Law of Cosines is a formula for solving a triangle when two sides and an angle (or all three sides) are given. Here we will review a formula for solving a triangle when two sides and an angle opposite one of them or two angles and a side are given.

The area of a triangle is one-half the product of the lengths of two sides and the sine of the included angle. If we apply this area formula to a triangle, $\triangle ABC$, we get the following three equations by exhausting the possible combinations of two sides and their included angle:

(1) $\qquad A = \dfrac{1}{2}ab \sin \angle C,$

(2) $\qquad A = \dfrac{1}{2}ac \sin \angle B,$

(3) $\qquad A = \dfrac{1}{2}bc \sin \angle A.$

But each of the formulas must give exactly the same area since the area of a triangle is unique, so

(4) $\qquad \dfrac{1}{2}ab \sin \angle C = \dfrac{1}{2}ac \sin \angle B = \dfrac{1}{2}bc \sin \angle A.$

If we multiply each member of the equations in (4) by $\dfrac{2}{abc}$, we get

(5) $\qquad \dfrac{\sin \angle A}{a} = \dfrac{\sin \angle B}{b} = \dfrac{\sin \angle C}{c}$

The equations in (5) are referred to as the Law of Sines. In applying it we set up equations that contain only two members and solve them in the usual manner.

Applying the Law of Sines to the multiple-choice question gives

$$\frac{\sin 48}{24.6} = \frac{\sin 62}{AB}$$

Therefore

$$AB = \left(\frac{\sin 62}{\sin 48}\right)(24.6)$$

$$= \frac{.8829}{.7431}(24.6).$$

WORKING WITH SINES AND COSINES

[19] If x is positive but less than 90, what is the least value of x for which $\cos(x + 30) = 0$?

(A) -30

(B) 30

(C) 0

(D) 90

(E) 60

To answer this question, you need to have a basic understanding of how the cosine function varies. Refer to the graph of the cosine found in section [15] of this chapter. Do you see that the smallest positive number that yields a cosine of 0 is 90? Since $\cos 90 = 0$ and $\cos(x + 30) = 0$, it follows that

$$\cos(x + 30) = \cos 90.$$

Therefore

$$x + 30 = 90,$$
$$x = 90 - 30$$
$$= 60.$$

[20] What is the least positive number x for which $\cos(30° - x) = \sin(45° + 2x)$?

(A) 30

(B) 20

(C) 60

(D) 15

(E) 12

The sine and cosine functions are cofunctions, meaning that the cosine of an angle is the sine of its complement. This may be stated in either of two ways:

$$\sin x = \cos(90° - x)$$

or

$$\cos x = \sin(90° - x).$$

The same is true, of course, for secant and cosecant as well as for tangent and cotangent. In other words, when cofunctions are equal, the sum of the angle measures is 90°.

Applying this information to the question above, we get

(1) $\qquad (30° - x) + (45° + 2x) = 90°,$

(2) $\qquad 75 + x = 90°$

(3) $\qquad x = 15°$

A common mistake made in approaching a question like this is to say that sine and cosine are equal for 45° only on the domain specified so that both

(4) $\qquad 30° - x = 45°$ and $45° + 2x = 45°,$

but the two equations given in (4) result in two different values for x! In fact, there is no basis to assume that the cosine and sine are operating on the same number.

[21] Let $a = \cos \dfrac{p}{2}$, let $b = \cos p$ and let $c = \cos 2p$, where $0 < p < 45°$. Arrange a, b, and c in order from least to greatest.

(A) a, b, c

(B) a, c, b

(C) b, c, a

(D) b, a, c

(E) c, b, a

The cosine of x is a decreasing function as x increases from 0 to π. You can clearly see this from the graph of cosine in section [15]. This means that the cosine gets smaller as x gets larger on this interval. In the question above, the number of which we are taking the cosine progresses from least at $\frac{p}{2}$ to greatest at $2p$. This means that

the cosine is *decreasing* from $\frac{p}{2}$ through p to $2p$. Thus the corresponding values of cosine, a, b, and c are decreasing. The order must be reversed to cause them to go from least to greatest.

[22] Suppose θ is a number between 0 and 90° for which $\sin\theta = \dfrac{120}{169}$ and $\cos\theta = \dfrac{119}{169}$. Which of the following would be the closest approximation to the value of θ?

(A) 15°

(B) 30°

(C) 45°

(D) 60°

(E) 90°

Students frequently pass up easy questions like this one because they look much more complex than they are. The most important information given is that $\sin\theta$ and $\cos\theta$ are nearly equal, differing only by $\frac{1}{169}$. At what point do the graphs of $y = \cos\theta$ and $y = \sin\theta$ cross? Expressed in another way, under what circumstances will the ratio of the opposite side of an acute angle of a right triangle to the hypotenuse be equal to the ratio of the adjacent side to the hypotenuse? The latter question is answered by noting that this can occur when adjacent and opposite are equal, thus making the triangle an isosceles right triangle with angles of 45°. The former question (where do the graphs cross?) can be answered directly by referring to the graphs in section [15] of this chapter.

The given information that θ is between 0 and 90° actually reduces the complexity of the problem by eliminating the alternatives.

[23] If the diagram shows a portion of the graph of $y = \sin x$, then $|a| + |b| = ?$

(A) 1

(B) 2

(C) π

(D) 2π

(E) $\dfrac{\pi}{2}$

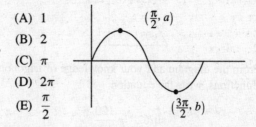

The sine function ranges from -1 to 1. Therefore, the difference between the maximum and minimum values is $1 - (-1) = 2$, (B).

The ranges of the three basic trigonometric functions, sine, cosine, and tangent, are among the facts you should have at your fingertips. The sine and cosine functions are defined for all real numbers and vary between -1 and 1.

The tangent function is defined for all real numbers except odd multiples of $\frac{\pi}{2}$, and its range is all real numbers.

These facts are easily remembered by visualizing their graphs, which you should study until they come readily to mind.

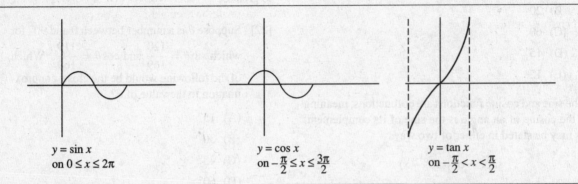

$y = \sin x$
on $0 \le x \le 2\pi$

$y = \cos x$
on $-\frac{\pi}{2} \le x \le \frac{3\pi}{2}$

$y = \tan x$
on $-\frac{\pi}{2} < x < \frac{\pi}{2}$

[24] A ladder must reach a window sill 10 feet above the ground. Safety specifications for the conditions on this job say that the angle the ladder makes with the ground cannot be greater than 62°. To the nearest inch, what is the length of the shortest ladder possible?

(A) 11

(B) 12

(C) 120

(D) 136

(E) 148

First, change 10 feet to 120 inches so that your answer will be in the units specified.

Then, draw a diagram and label it with the given information.

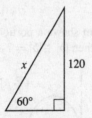

From the diagram and your knowledge of trigonometric functions, write the equation

$$\sin 62° = \frac{120}{x}.$$

To aid in solving the equation, convert it to

$$x = \frac{120}{\sin 62°}.$$

Be sure your calculator is set to degree mode before continuing. The way you proceed from here depends on the type of calculator you have and your skill in using it.

On the simplest scientific calculator, you may have to proceed backward by first finding $\sin 62°$ (which your calculator will display as .8829475), recording your results on your paper (or in the memory of your calculator) and then re-entering the result as a step in dividing 120 by $\sin 62°$.

If you are using a more advanced calculator, such as a graphing calculator, you can enter your steps in algebraic order by keying in 120, then the keys for division, sin, and 62.

Whatever your method, your calculator should now display 135.90842. Rounding off to the nearest inch, your result is 136 inches, (D).

You might have chosen to write your original equation as

$$\csc 62° = \frac{x}{120}$$

and then changed it to

$$x = 120 \csc 62°.$$

This equation also produces the correct answer, of course. We did not set up the equation this way because Level IC does not directly test the cosecant, cotangent, and secant functions. As in this case, knowledge of these functions could prove useful.

[25] If A is an angle with vertex at the origin and $(x, 3)$ is a point on one side of $\angle A$ (as shown), find x when $\sin \angle A = \frac{1}{3}$.

(A) $\frac{2}{3}$

(B) 4

(C) 6

(D) $\sqrt{\frac{2}{3}}$

(E) $6\sqrt{2}$

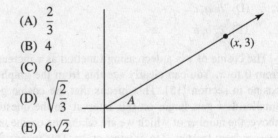

If (x, y) is a point on the terminal side of an angle in standard position, and r is the distance between the point and the origin, then the sine of the angle is $\frac{y}{r}$ and $r = \sqrt{x^2 + y^2}$.

Therefore, in this problem,

$$\sin \angle A = \frac{1}{3} = 3\sqrt{x^2 + 9}.$$

Cross multiply and solve for x.

$$\sqrt{x^2 + 9} = 9$$
$$x^2 + 9 = 81$$
$$x = \pm\sqrt{72}$$

If you have not already done so, now is the time to check the form of the answer choices. If the choices were in decimals, you might tap out a decimal approximation on your calculator. In this case, the correct answer is in simplified radical form. Therefore, you would factor 72 into 2(36) and write the result as $6\sqrt{2}$. (Note that we did not consider a negative result because the angle is in the first quadrant).

If you were rusty with radicals and tapped out an answer on your calculator, you would now be looking at 8.4852814 on your display. All of the choices except (E) can readily be seen to be less than 8, which means your calculator answer gave you the information you needed.

[26] If $\angle A$ is the greater acute angle of a triangle with sides 5, 12, and 13, then $\cos \angle A = ?$

(A) $\dfrac{5}{13}$

(B) $\dfrac{5}{12}$

(C) $\dfrac{12}{13}$

(D) $\dfrac{12}{5}$

(E) $\dfrac{13}{5}$

The numbers 5, 12, and 13 are a Pythagorean triple because $5^2 + 12^2 = 13^2$. Therefore, the triangle is a right triangle and the cosine of each acute angle will be the length of the adjacent side over the hypotenuse.

As a result, your two choices are $\frac{5}{13}$ and $\frac{12}{13}$. Don't be tempted to select $\frac{12}{13}$ because the question asks for the greater angle and $\frac{12}{13}$ is greater than $\frac{5}{13}$. The cosine is a decreasing function for acute angles, which means the cosine of the greater angle is less than the cosine of the lesser angle.

A diagram makes this information clear. Draw a right triangle that roughly approximates the given information.

Do you see that the greater angle is opposite the side of length 12? Its adjacent side is 5, so its cosine is $\frac{5}{13}$, (A).

[27] If $1 - 2\sin x = 0$, which of the following could be a value of x?

   I.   30°

  II.   60°

 III.   150°

 IV.   −30°

(A) I and IV only

(B) II only

(C) I and III only

(D) II, III, and IV only

(E) II and III only

The classic classroom solution would be to solve the equation in order to write all possible values of x. The plug-and-chug-only way would be to substitute each choice in the equation with your calculator.

A combination of the two might be something you like better than either.

Transform the equation

$$1 - 2\sin x = 0,$$

by subtracting 1 from each side and then dividing by −2. The result,

$$\sin x = \frac{1}{2}$$

is a much easier equation in which to test the choices, either with your calculator or with your knowledge of the trigonometric function values of special angles. Among the choices offered, the sine is $\frac{1}{2}$ for 30 and 150, but not the others, (C).

[28]   If $\dfrac{(\sin A)}{(\sin B)} = 1$ and $AB = 2\sqrt{2}$ for the triangle shown, which of the following are true?

   I. $a = b$

   II. $\angle A = \angle B$

   III. $a^2 + b^2 = c^2$

   IV. $c > a + b$

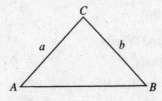

(Figure is not drawn to scale.)

(A) I and IV only

(B) I and II only

(C) I and III only

(D) I, II, and III only

(E) All of I, II, III, and IV

Let's see if there is a statement that can be easily eliminated. Statement IV cannot possibly be true because the sum of the lengths of two sides of a triangle must always exceed the length of the third.

Now our choices are (B), (C), and (D). If statement I is true, then II must be true by the Isosceles Triangle Theorem, which means we can eliminate (C).

So it comes down to the truth or falsity of $a^2 + b^2 = c^2$. In other words, is this a right triangle? It looks as though it is, but looks don't count—especially when the diagram is labeled "figure not drawn to scale." The $\sqrt{2}$ in the given information for AB is prodding us on into thinking the triangle is an isosceles right triangle.

The test makers have set a trap for the lazy.

From the given information we know that $\angle A = \angle B$ because their sines are equal. Therefore, $a = b$ by the Isosceles Triangle Theorem, as already stated.

Because $a = b$, the perpendicular line segment introduced into the figure below creates two congruent right triangles and bisects side AB. But now we have reached a dead end. Everything said so far could be true even if the figure is not a right triangle. So (B) it is.

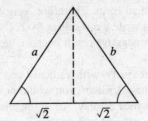

WHAT YOU SHOULD KNOW

KEY CONCEPTS

Handling Angles

1. In trigonometry, an angle is a rotation; therefore any real number (positive, negative, or zero) may be the measure of an angle.
2. An angle in standard position has the origin as its vertex and the positive ray of the x-axis as its initial ray. If the rotation to the terminal side is clockwise, the measure is negative. If it is counterclockwise, the measure is positive.
3. Since π radians $= 180°$,
   a. *to convert from radians to degrees,* multiply each side of the equation
   $$1 \text{ radian } = \frac{180}{\pi}$$
   degrees by the given number of radians and simplify;
   b. *to convert from degrees to radians,* multiply each side of the equation
   $$1 \text{ degree } = \frac{\pi}{180}$$
   radians by the given number of degrees and simplify.
4. If r is the radius of a circle, θ the measure of a central angle in radians, and s the length of its interceptedd arc, then
   $$\theta = \frac{s}{r}.$$
5. If θ is an angle in standard position, its reference angle is the smallest positive angle between its terminal side and the nearer ray of the x-axis.
6. If (x, y) is a point r units from the origin, then
   $$x^2 + y^2 = r^2.$$

Defining Trigonometric Functions

1. If (x, y) is a point on the terminal side of an angle θ in standard position and (x, y) is r units from the origin, then:
   $$\sin \theta = \frac{y}{r}, \quad \csc \theta = \frac{r}{y},$$
   $$\cos \theta = \frac{x}{r}, \quad \sec \theta = \frac{r}{x},$$
   $$\tan \theta = \frac{y}{x}, \quad \cot \theta = \frac{x}{y}.$$

2. If θ is an acute angle of a right triangle, then:
   $$\sin \theta = \frac{\text{opposite side}}{\text{hypotenuse}}, \quad \csc \theta = \frac{\text{hypotenuse}}{\text{opposite side}},$$
   $$\cos \theta = \frac{\text{adjacent side}}{\text{hypotenuse}}, \quad \sec \theta = \frac{\text{hypotenuse}}{\text{adjacent side}},$$
   $$\tan \theta = \frac{\text{opposite side}}{\text{adjacent side}}, \quad \cot \theta = \frac{\text{adjacent side}}{\text{opposite side}}$$

3. If $\angle A$ and $\angle B$ are complementary, then:
   $$\sin \angle A = \cos \angle B,$$
   $$\sec \angle A = \csc \angle B,$$
   $$\tan \angle A = \cot \angle B.$$

4. For all values of θ:
   $$\sin^2 \theta + \cos^2 \theta = 1,$$
   $$\tan \theta = \frac{\sin \theta}{\cos \theta},$$
   $$\sin \theta = \frac{1}{\csc \theta},$$
   $$\cos \theta = \frac{1}{\sec \theta},$$
   $$\tan \theta = \frac{1}{\cot \theta}.$$

Finding Values of Trigonometric Functions of Angles

1. *To find values of trigonometric functions of angles with reference angle of 30° or 60° use the 30°-60°-90° triangle:*

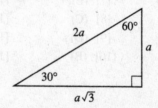

2. *To find values of trigonometric functions of angles with reference angle 45°, use the isosceles right triangle:*

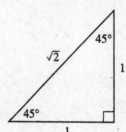

3. *To find values of trigonometric functions of quadrantal angles (0, 90, 180, 270, 360 . . .),* use the diagram below with (x, y) the values given and $r = 1$ for each point.

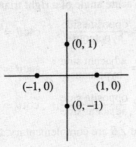

KEY LAWS

1. If a, b, and c are *any* sides of *any* triangle and $\angle C$ is the angle opposite side c, then

$$c^2 = a^2 + b^2 - 2ab \cos \angle C.$$

(Law of Cosines)

2. If a, b, and c are the sides of any triangle and $\angle A$, $\angle B$, and $\angle C$ are, respectively, the angles opposite these sides, then

$$\frac{\sin \angle A}{a} = \frac{\sin \angle B}{b} = \frac{\sin \angle C}{c}.$$

(Law of Sines)

TEST-TAKING STRATEGIES

- Apply your knowledge of the ratios of the sides of 30-60-90 and 45-45-90 right triangles to find the trig functions of 30°, 45°, and 60° angles.
- Know how to set your calculator at radian mode or degree mode and get into the habit of checking the mode when doing trigonometry problems.
- Know how to use your calculator to find the values of sine, cosine, and tangent.
- Know how to use your calculator to find values of $\sin^{-1}$, $\cos^{-1}$, $\tan^{-1}$. Know the ranges of these inverse functions so that you can properly interpret the values your calculator displays.
- Know the significance of obtaining a negative value for the measure of an angle.

ANSWERS

[1] (A)	[6] (A)	[11] (C)	[16] (A)	[21] (E)	[26] (A)
[2] (C)	[7] (E)	[12] (E)	[17] (C)	[22] (C)	[27] (B)
[3] (B)	[8] (C)	[13] (B)	[18] (E)	[23] (B)	
[4] (E)	[9] (D)	[14] (A)	[19] (E)	[24] (D)	
[5] (D)	[10] (B)	[15] (E)	[20] (D)	[25] (E)	

SEQUENCES AND SERIES

CHAPTER

24

In this chapter, some of the topics are more typical of those tested on the Mathematics Level IIC test than of those on the Level IC test. We have denoted these with an asterisk (*). Review of such topics may assist you in answering Level IC questions, however, because it increases your general knowledge of mathematical ideas, methods, and skills.

KEY TERMS

sequence	a set of numbers that have a prescribed order.
arithmetic sequence (arithmetic progression, A. P.)	a sequence that progresses by the addition to each term of some constant d. Example: 3, 6, 9, 12, where $d = 3$.
geometric sequence (geometric progression, G. P.)	a sequence in which each term is the product of some number r (called the *common ratio*) and the preceding term. Example: $\frac{1}{4}$, 1, 4, where $r = 4$.
arithmetic series	the indicated sum of the terms of an arithmetic sequence. Example: $3 + 6 + 9 + 12$.
geometric series	the indicated sum of the terms of a geometric sequence. Example: $\frac{1}{4} + 1 + 4 + 16$.
infinite geometric sequence	a geometric sequence that continues without end.
arithmetic means	in an arithmetic sequence, terms other than the first and last.
geometric means	in a geometric sequence, terms other than the first and last.

RECOGNIZING AN ARITHMETIC SEQUENCE

[1] From which of the following can we conclude that a, b, c is an arithmetic sequence?

(A) $a + b = b + c$

(B) $a + b = 2c$

(C) $b - a = c - b$

(D) $\dfrac{b}{a} = \dfrac{c}{b}$

(E) $\dfrac{a}{b} = c$

A *sequence* is a set of numbers that have a prescribed order. Every sequence is a function that associates with each positive integer n the number a_n. a_n is called a *term* and n is the *number of the term*. For example, in the sequence

$$2, 4, 6, 8, \ldots$$

the fifth term is 10, the sixth is 12, and the function associates with each positive integer n the number $2n$. The majority of sequences dealt with in intermediate math have some such algebraic relationship between n and a_n.

The simplest is the *arithmetic sequence*, which progresses by the addition to each term of some constant d resulting in the succeeding term.

The sequence

(1) $3, 7, 11, 15 \ldots$

is arithmetic since each term is four more than its predecessor. The relationship between each term in an arithmetic sequence, and the number of that term, is not obvious but can be found by a formula that we will develop in the next section. You may be able to guess by looking at sequence (1) that this relationship is $4n - 1$.

We can recognize an arithmetic sequence (sometimes called an "arithmetic progression" and hence symbolized by "A. P.") by noting that the difference between any two consecutive terms is always the same as the difference between the next two terms.

For the multiple-choice question, this means that

$$b - a = c - b.$$

Indicate whether each of the following is an A. P.

1. $1, 2, 3, 4, 5, \ldots$

2. $2, 4, 8, 16, \ldots$

3. $\dfrac{1}{2}, \dfrac{1}{4}, 1, \dfrac{5}{4}, \ldots$

4. $-3, 0, 3, 6, \ldots$

SOLUTIONS:

1. yes, $d = 1$

2. no

3. no

4. yes, $d = 3$

FINDING A TERM IN AN ARITHMETIC SEQUENCE

[2] Which of the following expressions is the general term of the sequence $-2, 1, 4, 7 \ldots$?

(A) $n + 3$

(B) $-2 + n$

(C) $-2 + 3$

(D) $-2 + 3n$

(E) $-2 + (n - 1)3$

The *general term* of a sequence is a formula for deriving each term from n, the number of the term. We may readily discover this formula for an A. P. by observing the following pattern, where a_1 is the first term, n is the number of the term, and d is the difference between any two consecutive terms:

$$
\begin{aligned}
a_1 &= a_1 + (0)d & &= a_1 + (1-1)d, \\
a_2 &= a_1 + (1)d & &= a_1 + (2-1)d, \\
a_3 &= (a_1 + d) + d & &= a_1 + (3-1)d, \\
a_4 &= [(a_1 + d) + d] + d & &= a_1 + (4-1)d.
\end{aligned}
$$

We conclude:

24-1   If $a_1, a_2, \ldots, a_n$ is an arithmetic sequence, then
$$a_n = a_1 + (n - 1)d.$$

We can use 24-1 to compute any term of an A. P. when several terms are given.

No matter how rapidly you can punch the keys of your calculator, you will need algebraic methods to find answers in a reasonable amount of time.

EXAMPLE 1

Find the 50th term of $\frac{1}{3}, \frac{2}{3}, 1, \ldots$

SOLUTION: $a_1 = \frac{1}{3}, d = \frac{1}{3}, n = 50$; therefore:

$$a_n = \frac{1}{3} + (50-1)\frac{1}{3} = \frac{1}{3} + \frac{49}{3} = \frac{50}{3}$$

EXAMPLE 2

If the 10th term of an A. P. is 6 and the common difference between terms is -2, find the first term.

SOLUTION: $6 = a_1 + (10-1)(-2),$
$24 = a_1.$

EXAMPLE 3

If the third term of an A. P. is -9 and the 20th term is 59, find the first term.

SOLUTION: Since $a_3 = -9$,

(1) $-9 = a_1 + 2d.$

Since $a_{20} = 59$,

(2) $59 = a_1 + 19d.$

Solving (2) and (3) simultaneously, we get:

(3) $d = 4$ and $a_1 = -17.$

In the multiple-choice question, the first term is -2 and the common difference is 3 (found by subtracting any term from the next term).
Therefore:
$$a_n = -2 + 3(n-1).$$

FINDING THE SUM OF AN ARITHMETIC SERIES

*[3]   Which of the following series has 35 as its sum?

(A) $\displaystyle\sum_{k=3}^{k=7} (k+2)$

(B) $\displaystyle\sum_{k=1}^{k=4} \left(k^2 + \frac{1}{k}\right)$

(C) $\displaystyle\sum_{k=2}^{k=8} \left(k + \frac{k}{2}\right)$

(D) $\displaystyle\sum_{k=3}^{k=5} \left(\frac{k-2}{3}\right)$

(E)   None of these

A *series* is the indicated sum of the terms of a sequence (caution: do not confuse the series with its sum). Given the sequence 5, 6, 7, 8, 9, its corresponding series is $5+6+7+8+9$ and its sum is 35.

We frequently use summation notation (Σ being the Greek letter corresponding to the first letter of "sum") as a shorthand for series. The following table (which expands the possible answers above) exemplifies this use. The numbers above and below the Σ are the initial and terminal values of k; k also takes each integral value in between them.

Σ notation (see above)	Series	Sum
(A)	$5+6+7+8+9$	35
(B)	$2 + 4\frac{1}{2} + 9\frac{1}{3} + 16\frac{1}{4}$	$32\frac{1}{12}$
(C)	$3 + 4\frac{1}{2} + 6 + 7\frac{1}{2} + 9 + 10\frac{1}{2} + 12$	$52\frac{1}{2}$
(D)	$\frac{1}{3} + \frac{2}{3} + 1$	2

In the Σ notation k does not necessarily represent the number of the term (as, indeed, it does not in any of the examples above).

When the series is infinite, we note this by placing the symbol ∞ above the Σ.

$$\sum_{k=1}^{\infty} \frac{1}{k^2} = 1 + \frac{1}{4} + \frac{1}{9} + \frac{1}{16} + \frac{1}{25} + \ldots$$

The three dots at the end of the indicated part of the series above tells us that it continues endlessly.

*[4] Which of the following is an arithmetic series of 21 terms with a sum of $10\frac{1}{2}$ and a common difference of -3?

(A) $30.5 + 27.5 + 24.5 + \ldots + (-29.5)$

(B) $(-29.5) + (-32.5) + (-35.5) + \ldots + 30.5$

(C) $24.5 + 27.5 + 30.5 + \ldots + (-29.5)$

(D) $24.5 + 21.5 + 18.5 + \ldots + (-30.5)$

(E) None of these

The sum of a finite arithmetic series can be found by a simple formula that is intuitively appealing. It is the average of the first and last terms times the number of terms.

24-2   The sum of the first n terms of an arithmetic sequence, symbolized by S_n, is given by:

$$S_n = n\left(\frac{a_1 + a_n}{2}\right).$$

Applying this formula to the above question yields the sum 10.5 for both (A) and (B), but (B) could not be an arithmetic series if its last term is 30.5 while all other terms are negative.

By recalling that $a_n = a_1 + (n-1)d$, we can transform 24-2 into

---

24-3
$$S_n = n\left(\frac{a_1 + a_1 + (n-1)d}{2}\right)$$
$$= \frac{n}{2}[2a_1 + (n-1)d].$$

Both 24-2 and 24-3 are useful; you should memorize the former and learn the substitution needed to get the latter.

EXAMPLE 1

Find the sum of the positive multiples of 3 that are less than 300.

SOLUTION: The series in question is:

$$3 + 6 + 9 + \ldots + 297.$$

Since 297 is 3(99), there are 99 terms in this arithmetic series. Applying 24-2, we get

$$S_{99} = 99\left[\frac{(3 + 297)}{2}\right] = 14{,}850.$$

EXAMPLE 2

How many terms are there in the series with a sum of 435 if the first term is -13 and the common difference is 6?

SOLUTION: Since the given information is S_n, a_1, and d, we will use 24-3:

$$435 = \frac{n}{2}[2(-13) + (n-1)6]$$
$$= -16n + 3n^2,$$
$$0 = 3n^2 - 16n - 435.$$

Therefore $n = 15$ ($n = \dfrac{-29}{3}$ is meaningless).

RECOGNIZING A GEOMETRIC SEQUENCE

---

[5]   What is the value of a if $2a - 1$, $4a + 1$, $15a - 3$ is a geometric sequence?

(A) 1

(B) 2

(C) 3

(D) 4

(E) -1

A sequence is *geometric* if each term is the product of some number r (called the *common ratio*) and the preceding term. For example, the sequence

$$\frac{1}{3},\ 1,\ 3,\ldots$$

is geometric with $r = 3$. The common ratio can be found by dividing any term by the one preceding it. Since this number r must remain constant throughout the sequence, the answer to the above question is the solution of the equation

$$\frac{4a + 1}{2a - 1} = \frac{15a - 3}{4a + 1}.$$

We have

$$(4a + 1)(4a + 1) = (2a - 1)(15a - 3),$$
$$16a^2 + 8a + 1 = 30a^2 - 21a + 3,$$
$$0 = 14a^2 - 29a + 2$$
$$= (14a - 1)(a - 2),$$

$$14a - 1 = 0 \quad \text{or} \quad a - 2 = 0,$$
$$a = \frac{1}{14} \quad \text{or} \quad a = 2.$$

EXAMPLES

Indicate which of the following are geometric sequences and find the common ratio:

1. $2, 4, 6, 8, \ldots$

2. $\dfrac{1}{2}, \dfrac{1}{4}, \dfrac{1}{8}, \ldots$

3. $-4, 20, -100, \ldots$

4. $1, 2x, 4x^2, \ldots$

SOLUTIONS:

1. no

2. yes, $r = \dfrac{1}{2}$

3. yes, $r = -5$

4. yes, $r = 2x$

FINDING A TERM IN A GEOMETRIC SEQUENCE

[6] Which of the following is the eighth term of the sequence $1, \dfrac{\sqrt{3}}{2}, \dfrac{3}{4}, \ldots$?

(A) $\dfrac{2 + 7\sqrt{3}}{2}$

(B) $\dfrac{3\sqrt{3}}{8}$

(C) $\dfrac{27}{64}$

(D) $\dfrac{27\sqrt{3}}{128}$

(E) $\dfrac{81}{256}$

The general term of a geometric sequence (or geometric progression and hence the abbreviation, G. P.) is a formula that relates each term to the number of that term. This formula for a G. P. can be derived by observing the way a G. P. develops as follows:

$$a_1 = a_1 r^0 = a_1 r^{1-1},$$
$$a_2 = a_1 r^1 = a_1 r^{2-1},$$
$$a_3 = a_1 r^2 = a_1 r^{3-1},$$
$$a_4 = a_1 r^3 = a_1 r^{4-1}.$$

We conclude:

> 24-4   If $a_1, a_2, a_3, \ldots a_n$ is a geometric sequence, then
> $$a_n = a_1 r^{n-1}.$$

EXAMPLE 1

Find the eighth term of $5, 10, 20, \ldots$.

 SOLUTION:

$$a_1 = 5, \, r = 2, \, n = 8$$
$$a_8 = 5(2^7) = 640$$

EXAMPLE 2

How many terms are there in the sequence $64, 32, 16, \ldots, \dfrac{1}{128}$?

SOLUTION: $a_1 = 64$ and $r = \dfrac{1}{2}$.

$$\dfrac{1}{128} = 64\left(\dfrac{1}{2}\right)^{n-1}$$
$$\dfrac{1}{8192} = \left(\dfrac{1}{2}\right)^{n-1}$$
$$\left(\dfrac{1}{2}\right)^{13} = \left(\dfrac{1}{2}\right)^{n-1}$$
$$13 = n - 1$$
$$14 = n$$

EXAMPLE 3

The fifth term of a G. P. is $32\sqrt{2}$, while the common ratio is $-\sqrt{2}$. What is the first term?

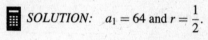 *SOLUTION:* $a_n = 32\sqrt{2}, r = -\sqrt{2}, n = 5$

$$32\sqrt{2} = a_1(-\sqrt{2})^4$$
$$= a_1(4)$$
$$8\sqrt{2} = a_1.$$

In the multiple-choice question,

$$a_1 = 1,$$
$$r = \dfrac{\sqrt{3}}{2},$$
$$a_8 = a_1 r^7 = 1\left(\dfrac{\sqrt{3}}{2}\right)^7$$
$$= \dfrac{27\sqrt{3}}{128}.$$

FINDING THE SUM OF A GEOMETRIC SERIES

*[7]   Each of the following represents a geometric series. Which one has $\dfrac{40}{81}$ as its sum?

(A) $\displaystyle\sum_{k=1}^{k=10} (-1)^k$

(B) $\displaystyle\sum_{k=1}^{k=10} (-2)^{k-1}$

(C) $\displaystyle\sum_{k=0}^{k=9} \dfrac{1}{3^k}$

(D) $\displaystyle\sum_{k=2}^{k=5} 3\left(\dfrac{1}{3}\right)^k$

(E)   None of these

We will introduce a formula and then answer this question directly.

> **24-5**   For a geometric series, the sum S_n is given by
> $$S_n = \frac{a_1 - a_1 r^n}{1 - r}.$$

(A)   In expanded form: $-1 + 1 + (-1) + \ldots + 1$. Therefore $a_1 = -1$, $r = -1$ and $n = 10$,

$$S_{10} = \frac{-1 - (-1)(-1)^{10}}{1 - (-1)} = 0.$$

(B)   In expanded form: $1 + (-2) + 4 + \ldots + (-512)$. Therefore $a_1 = 1$, $r = 2$ and $n = 10$,

$$S_{10} = \frac{1 - 1(-2)^{10}}{1 - (-2)} = \frac{1 - 1024}{3} = \frac{-1023}{3}.$$

(C)   Though the initial and terminal values of k are different from those in (A) and (B), you may verify that this series also has 10 terms. In expanded form:

$$1 + \frac{1}{3} + \frac{1}{9} + \cdots \frac{1}{19,683}.$$

Therefore $a_1 = 1$, $r = \frac{1}{3}$, $n = 10$,

$$S_{10} = \frac{1 - 1\left(\dfrac{1}{3}\right)^{10}}{1 - \left(\dfrac{1}{3}\right)} = \frac{1 - \left(\dfrac{1}{59,049}\right)}{\dfrac{2}{3}}$$

$$= \frac{59,048}{59,049} \times \frac{3}{2}$$

$$= \frac{29,524}{19,683}$$

(D)   In expanded form: $\dfrac{1}{3} + \dfrac{1}{9} + \dfrac{1}{27} + \dfrac{1}{81}$.
Therefore $a_1 = \dfrac{1}{3}$, $r = \dfrac{1}{3}$, and $n = 4$,

$$S_4 = \frac{\dfrac{1}{3} - \dfrac{1}{3}\left(\dfrac{1}{3}\right)^4}{1 - \dfrac{1}{3}} = \frac{40}{81}.$$

*[8]   If a rubber ball is dropped from a height of 1 yard and continues to rebound to a height that is $\dfrac{9}{10}$ of its previous fall, find the total distance in yards that it travels on falls only.

(A) $\dfrac{81}{100}$

(B)   1

(C)   9

(D)   10

(E)   Impossible to determine

As we add more terms to a finite series, the sum gets greater and greater. Accordingly it may at first seem impossible to find the sum of any infinite series, but we can attach a meaning to the term "sum" when the series is geometric and when the common ratio is between 1 and -1. Recall that the sum of the first n terms of any geometric series is given by:

> **24-6** $S_n = \dfrac{a_1 - a_1 r^n}{1 - r}$, which can be written as:
> $$S_n = \frac{a_1}{1 - r} - \frac{a_1 r^n}{1 - r}.$$

If we were to allow the number n to increase endlessly for a series such that $-1 < r < 1$, the value of r^n would approach zero and hence the value of $\dfrac{a_1 r^n}{(1 - r)}$ would also approach zero. With this in mind we define S_∞, the sum of an infinite geometric series with $|r| < 1$, to be:

24-7
$$S_\infty = \frac{a_1}{1-r}.$$

EXAMPLE

Find the sum of the infinite series

$$1 + \frac{9}{10} + \frac{81}{100} + \dots.$$

SOLUTION: $S_\infty = \dfrac{1}{1 - \frac{9}{10}} = 10$

(Note that this is the geometric series given by the falls of the ball in the above question.)

FINDING THE FRACTIONAL EQUIVALENT OF A REPEATING DECIMAL

[9]   Which of the following is a fractional expression equal to $1.\overline{45}$ (the bar over the digits indicates that they repeat endlessly)?

(A) $1\dfrac{45}{100}$

(B) $\dfrac{5}{11}$

(C) $1\dfrac{5}{110}$

(D) $1\dfrac{9}{20}$

(E) $1\dfrac{5}{11}$

Recall that every rational number can be expressed as a repeating or terminating decimal. But a repeating decimal can be written as an infinite geometric series, and its fractional equivalent can be found by using formula 24-7.

EXAMPLE 1

Find the fractional equivalent of $.\overline{6}$ (remember that $.\overline{6} = .66666666\dots$ with the digit 6 repeating endlessly).

SOLUTION: $.\overline{6} = .6 + .06 + .006 + .0006 + \dots$
Therefore $a_1 = .6$ and $r = .1$.

$$S_\infty = \frac{.6}{1 - .1} = \frac{.6}{.9} = \frac{2}{3}$$

EXAMPLE 2

(Example 2 is the multiple-choice question.)
What fraction represents $1.\overline{45}$?

SOLUTION: $1.\overline{45} = 1 + .45 + .0045 + .000045 + \dots$

Beginning with the second term, this is an infinite geometric series. We must first find the value of $.\overline{45}$ and then add it to 1.

$$S = \frac{.45}{1 - .01} = \frac{.45}{.99} = \frac{5}{11}$$

Therefore $1.\overline{45} = 1\dfrac{5}{11}$.

INSERTING ARITHMETIC MEANS

*[10] If nine arithmetic means are to be inserted between 6 and 20, one of them will be:

(A) 10

(B) 10.2

(C) $7\dfrac{3}{11}$

(D) 7

(E) 11

In a finite arithmetic progression the first and last terms are called the *extremes* and the remaining terms, the *means*. To insert k arithmetic means between two numbers means to construct an A. P. with the given numbers as extremes and with k numbers in between. Such an A. P. will have $k + 2$ terms. To do this we use the formula for a_n, allowing a_1 and a_n to be the extremes and $n = k + 2$. In this way we find d, which we can then use to complete the A. P.

EXAMPLE

Insert 10 arithmetic means between -5 and 72.

SOLUTION: Let $a_1 = -5$, $n = 12$ (the 10 means plus the two extreme terms, -5 and 72), $a_n = 72$. Accordingly,

$$72 = -5 + (12 - 1)d,$$
$$7 = d.$$

The required sequence is

$$-5, 2, 9, 16, 23, 30, 37, 44, 51, 58, 65, 72.$$

In the multiple-choice question, the sequence will have 11 terms (the two given terms and nine means), the 11th term of which is 20. Therefore:

$$20 = 6 + (11 - 1)d,$$
$$14 = 10d,$$
$$1.4 = d.$$

Hence the sequence is

$$6, 7.4, 8.8, 10.2, 11.6, \ldots, 20.$$

INSERTING GEOMETRIC MEANS

*[11] If two geometric means were inserted between 128 and -2, their sum could be:

    (A) -24

    (B) 24

    (C) 12

    (D) -12

    (E) None of these

In a finite G. P. the intermediate terms between the first and last are called *geometric means*. To insert k geometric means between two numbers is to construct a G. P. of $k+2$ terms for which the two given numbers are a_1 and a_{k+2}. With this given information, we may use formula 24-4 to find the values of r. In general, we restrict such values of r to exclude imaginary numbers unless otherwise requested. Note that geometric means need not be numerically between the extremes. For 2, -4, 8, -16, 32, neither the -4 nor the -16 is numerically between the 2 and 32.

EXAMPLE

Insert four geometric means between 192 and 6.

SOLUTION: Let $a_n = 6$, $n = 6$, and $a_1 = 192$.
    Therefore

$$6 = 192(r)^5,$$
$$\frac{1}{32} = r^5,$$
$$r = \frac{1}{2},$$

and the requested progression is

$$192, 96, 48, 24, 12, 6.$$

In the multiple-choice question, the sequence must be of the form

$$128, 128r, 128r^2, 128r^3,$$

where

$$128r^3 = -2,$$
$$r^3 = -\frac{2}{128}$$
$$= -\frac{1}{64}$$
$$r = -\frac{1}{4}.$$

Therefore the terms are

$$128, -32, 8, -2.$$

The sum of the inserted means is $-32 + 8 = -24$.

SOLVING WORD PROBLEMS

*[12] If \$900 is invested at 5 percent annual interest and this interest is compounded semiannually, find the total amount payable to the investor to the nearest dollar after $1\frac{1}{2}$ years.

    (A) \$945

    (B) \$968

    (C) \$969

    (D) \$990

    (E) \$970

If i is the interest rate for each unit period of time and P is the principal (or amount of money invested), the interest earned for the first unit of time is $P \times i$ and the amount due the investor at the end of this period is $P + Pi$ or $P(1 + i)$. When interest is compounded, the amount of money earned, $P \times i$, is added to the principal at the end of each time period to form the new principal for the next period. This process continues from period to period to form the G. P. which follows:

$$P, P(1+i), P(1+i)^2, P(1+i)^3, \ldots,$$

for which the general term, P_n, is

$$P_n - P(1+i)^n,$$

where n is the number of periods of time.

For the question above, $P = \$900$, $i = 2.5$ percent (since the interest is compounded each half-year and $\frac{1}{2}(5 \text{ percent}) = 2.5 \text{ percent}$) and $n = 3$ (since there are 3 half-year periods in $1\frac{1}{2}$ years). Note that 2.5 percent is .025 when expressed as a decimal.

$$P_3 = 900(1 + .025)^3 = 900(1.077) = \$969.30$$

EXAMPLE

A ranch had a herd of 8,000 steers. The herd increased at the rate of 6 percent per year. How many steers were in the herd after 9 years?

SOLUTION:

$$S = 8,000(1 + .06)^9 \doteq 13,515$$

[13] If the average of the sequence $1, \dfrac{1}{2}, \dfrac{1}{3}, \dfrac{1}{4}, x$, is $1, x = ?$

(A) $\dfrac{1}{5}$

(B) $\dfrac{2}{3}$

(C) $\dfrac{11}{5}$

(D) $\dfrac{25}{12}$

(E) $\dfrac{35}{12}$

This question tests whether you are paying attention. If you aren't, you will pick $\dfrac{1}{5}$ because it fits the pattern set by the first four numbers. However, x must make the average of the five numbers 1.

Therefore,

$$\frac{1 + \frac{1}{2} + \frac{1}{3} + \frac{1}{4} + x}{5} = 1$$

Multiply both sides by 5 and then subtract

$$1 + \frac{1}{2} + \frac{1}{3} + \frac{1}{4}.$$

$$x = 5 - \left(1 + \frac{1}{2} + \frac{1}{3} + \frac{1}{4}\right).$$

Don't begin immediately by changing all the fractions to lowest common denominators. See what you can do easily first. In your head, you can combine $\frac{1}{2}$ and $\frac{1}{4}$ to get $\frac{3}{4}$. In your head, subtract $5 - 1 = 4$ then $4 - \frac{3}{4} = 3\frac{1}{4} = \frac{13}{4}$. Your subtraction now is

$$\frac{13}{4} - \frac{1}{3} = \frac{39}{12} - \frac{4}{12} = \frac{35}{12}, \text{ (E)}.$$

WHAT YOU SHOULD KNOW

KEY CONCEPTS

1. An *arithmetic sequence* follows the pattern

$$a, a+d, a+2d, a+3d, \ldots, a+(n-1)d,$$

where n is the number of the term.

2. A *geometric sequence* follows the pattern

$$a, ar, ar^2, ar^3, ar^4, \ldots, ar^{n-1},$$

where n is the number of the term and r is the ratio of any two consecutive terms.

KEY FORMULAS

Handling Arithmetic Sequences

1. *To find a general term* in an arithmetic sequence where a_n is the nth term, a_1 is the first term, n is the number of the term, and d is the difference between two consecutive terms:

$$a_n = a_1 + (n-1)d.$$

2. *To find the sum of the first n terms* of an arithmetic sequence, symbolized by S_n:

$$S_n = n\left(\frac{a_1 + a_n}{2}\right)$$

or

$$S_n = \frac{n}{2}(2a_1 + (n-2)d).$$

Handling Geometric Sequences

1. *To find a general term* in a geometric sequence where a_1 is the first term, r is the ratio between two consecutive terms, n is the number of the term, and a_n is the nth term:

$$a_n = a_1 r^{n-1}.$$

2. *To find the sum of the first n terms* of a geometric series, symbolized by S_n:

$$S_n = \frac{a_1 - a_1 r^n}{1 - r}.$$

3. *To find the sum of an infinite geometric series* with $|r| < 1$, symbolized by S_∞:

$$S_\infty = \frac{a}{1-r}.$$

TEST-TAKING STRATEGY

- If a question requires you to find the next term in a sequence, first determine the relationship between the consecutive terms given in order to identify the progression as arithmetic or geometric.

ANSWERS

[1] (C)   [4] (A)   [7] (D)   [10] (B)   [13] (E)
[2] (E)   [5] (B)   [8] (D)   [11] (A)
[3] (A)   [6] (D)   [9] (E)   [12] (C)

COUNTING PROBLEMS

CHAPTER
25

KEY TERMS

permutation	any ordered arrangement of all the elements of a finite set. Example: b, a, c and b, c, a are two different permutations of the letters a, b, c.
combination	a set of elements; a collection of elements in which the order makes no difference. Example: a committee consisting of the combination Alice, Bill, and Carol is the same as the committee consisting of Bill, Carol, and Alice.
factorial notation	the use of the exclamation point to indicate the product of a sequence of descending integers. Example: $5! = 5 \cdot 4 \cdot 3 \cdot 2 \cdot 1$.
mutually exclusive events	events that cannot occur simultaneously. Example: when a coin is flipped, "heads" and "tails" are mutually exclusive.

[1] The expression $\dfrac{6!}{3!2!}$ is equal to which of the following?

(A) 1!

(B) 1

(C) 0!

(D) 60

(E) 60!

In this chapter we will review some of the elementary techniques of counting and their applications. We will frequently use factorial notation to simplify long products and define it here.

For every positive integer n the notation $n!$ represents the product of the first n integers.

$$n! = n(n-1)(n-2)(n-3)\ldots 3 \times 2 \times 1.$$

For example,

$$3! = 3 \times 2 \times 1 = 6,$$
$$6! = 6 \times 5 \times 4 \times 3 \times 2 \times 1 = 720.$$

Furthermore, we define

$$0! = 1$$

in order to be consistent with formulas we will develop later.

EXAMPLE 1

Find the value of $\dfrac{12!}{10!}$

SOLUTION:

$$\frac{12!}{10!} = \frac{12 \times 11 \times 10 \times 9 \times 8 \times 7 \times 6 \times 5 \times 4 \times 3 \times 2 \times 1}{10 \times 9 \times 8 \times 7 \times 6 \times 5 \times 4 \times 3 \times 2 \times 1}$$

$$= 12 \times 11$$

$$= 132$$

From the meaning of 12! and 10!, you can easily simplify the expression in your head. Think, but don't write, the expanded fraction.

Once you realize the 10! cancels, you can see that your answer is simply 12 times $11 = 132$.

A calculator with a factorial key can do this quickly. Depending on your calculator model, the factorial calculation might be done by either the first, second or third function (check your manual) or be accessed through a special menu.

EXAMPLE 2

$$\frac{(k+1)!}{k!} = \frac{(k+1)k!}{k!} = k+1$$

EXAMPLE 3

Simplify $\dfrac{8!(k+1)!k}{7!(k-1)!}$

SOLUTION: This expression in expanded form is:

$$\frac{(8 \times 7 \times 6 \times 5 \times 4 \times 3 \times 2 \times 1)(k+1)(k)(k-1)!(k)}{(7 \times 6 \times 5 \times 4 \times 3 \times 2 \times 1)(k-1)!}$$

$$= 8k^2(k+1) = 8k^3 + 8k^2.$$

In the multiple-choice question,

$$\frac{6!}{3!2!} = \frac{6 \times 5 \times 4 \times 3 \times 2 \times 1}{3 \times 2 \times 1 \times 2 \times 1}.$$

Removing common factors, we obtain

$$6 \times 5 \times 2 = 60.$$

TEST-TAKING TIP

Note that answers (A), (B), and (C) are different in form only. The numbers 1!, 1, and 0! are all equal. Since only one choice can be correct, all three can be eliminated. Answer (E) can be eliminated simply because it is far too great to be correct. Thus, even if you can readily simplify the given expression, you can more quickly determine the answer by scanning the choices first.

USING THE FUNDAMENTAL PRINCIPLE OF COUNTING

[2] In how many ways can a three-digit number be formed from the set of digits $\{1, 2, 3, 4, 5, 6, 8\}$ if no digit may appear twice?

(A) 8

(B) 210

(C) 336

(D) 27

(E) 343

Suppose 16 boys and 15 girls attend a dance, and the host, in order to assure that no one is left out, rotates the couples so that every boy dances with every girl. How many different couples can he make up? He can select the boy in 16 different ways, and for each boy he can choose

15 different girls. This means that each boy will be part of 15 different couples. Since there are 16 boys, the total number of couples is $16 \times 15 = 240$. (Some dance!)

The analysis of this example illustrates the *Fundamental Principle of Counting*:

> 25-1   If the first of two actions can be done in m ways and the second done in n ways, the number of ways the two actions can be done in order is $m \times n$.

In the multiple-choice question three actions are being performed: the actions of selecting digits. There are seven ways to select the first digit. The second digit can be selected in only six ways, since no digit may appear more than once. The last digit may be selected in five ways, so the total number of ways of forming the three-digit number is

$$7 \times 6 \times 5 = 210.$$

EXAMPLE 1

If a customer buys lunch at a restaurant that offers four kinds of soups, seven kinds of sandwiches, and three kinds of pies, how many different soup-sandwich-pie lunches can she choose?

SOLUTION: The three possible actions are the selections of a soup, a sandwich, and a pie.

$$4 \times 7 \times 3 = 84.$$

EXAMPLE 2

If a bag contains eight marbles, each of different color, how many different pairs of marbles can be chosen from the bag?

SOLUTION: The action of selecting the first marble can be done in eight different ways. Once the first marble is selected, the second can be selected in seven ways.

$$8 \times 7 = 56.$$

[3]   How many different three-digit even numbers can be formed from the set of integers from 1 to 9 inclusive if no repetitions are allowed?

(A) 224

(B) 504

(C) 84

(D) 104

(E) 94

This is an example of a problem in which a restriction is placed on the way in which one or more actions can

take place. It is usually easiest to analyze such a case by performing the restricted action(s) first. In the above the restricted action is that of selecting the final digit; it may be only a 2, 4, 6 or 8, yielding four ways. Once this digit is selected, the next can be chosen from the remaining ones in eight ways and the first in seven ways.

$$4 \times 8 \times 7 = 224.$$

EXAMPLE 1

Mr. Haddick selects a baseball squad from among nine men. Each player except the pitcher and catcher can play any position. How many different fielding arrangements can Mr. Haddick make?

SOLUTION: There are nine actions (the actions of selecting nine positions for nine men) that are to be performed. By selecting the pitcher and catcher first we get

$$1 \times 1 \times 7 \times 6 \times 5 \times 4 \times 3 \times 2 \times 1.$$

EXAMPLE 2

In how many ways may six boys be seated around a table if two specific boys are not allowed to sit next to each other?

SOLUTION: We seat the antagonists first. There are six ways in which the first boy may be seated, but only three ways in which the second boy may be seated so that he is not sitting next to the first boy. There are four remaining seats to be filled yielding four ways for the third boy, three ways for the fourth, two ways for the fifth, and one way for the sixth.

   $$6 \times 3 \times 4 \times 3 \times 2 \times 1 = 432.$$

Had we construed the problem to make a difference only in the order of seating rather than in the actual selection of seats, then the first boy's choice is in effect only that of selecting a reference point for the remaining boys. Each of the six choices for a reference point is no different from the others so that he is, in effect, making one choice rather than six different choices. The answer under these circumstances is

$$1 \times 3 \times 4 \times 3 \times 2 \times 1 = 72.$$

This problem admits of at least one other method of solution. First find the total number of ways in which six boys could be arranged and then subtract from this the total number of ways that the two specific boys would be seated next to each other.

   $$6 \times 5 \times 4 \times 3 \times 2 \times 1 - 6 \times 2 \times 4 \times 3 \times 2 \times 1$$
$$= 720 - 288$$
$$= 432$$

WORKING WITH PERMUTATIONS

[4] How many different seating arrangements can be made for eight students in a row of eight chairs?

(A) 8

(B) 64

(C) 10,080

(D) 40,320

(E) 10,000

Any ordered arrangement of all the elements of a finite set is called a *permutation*. Since the process of selecting the n elements in each permutation of a set involves n actions, and since the first action can be done in n ways with the next done in $n-1$ ways and the next in $n-2$ ways, etc., until all elements have been used, we conclude the following:

25-2 The number of possible permutations or orderings of a finite set of n elements is always $n!$

EXAMPLE 1

How many different orderings are possible of the letters in the word "SOME"?

SOLUTION: There are four elements in the set of letters in the word "some" so the number of different permutations is $4! = 24$.

EXAMPLE 2

How many different football lineups can Mr. Beebe choose from his 11 players if every player can play any position?

SOLUTION: We are after the number of permutations of 11 things taken all at a time.

$$11! = 11 \times 10 \times 9 \times 8 \times 7 \times 6 \times 5 \times 4 \times 3 \times 2 \times 1$$
$$= 39,916,800$$

In the multiple-choice question, the number of possible arrangements of 8 different objects in a row is $8!$.

[5] How many different six-letter arrangements can be made using the letters of the name of a Hawaiian fish, POOPAA?

(A) 6

(B) 720

(C) 120

(D) 6

(E) 90

The repetitions of letters that appear in the word above cause some permutations to be identical with others. For example, the geological term for a type of lava is "aa." Whereas the usual two-letter word has two permutations, both permutations of "aa" are identical and thus we say the word has only one permutation. If a letter appears p times, then the number of identical permutations is $p!$ In general:

25-3 The number of distinct permutations of n things, a of which are alike of one kind, b of which are alike of another kind, etc., is given by:
$$\frac{n!}{a!b!\dots}$$

EXAMPLE 1

How many distinct permutations are there of the letters of the word "STRUCTURE"?

SOLUTION: The nine-letter word "structure" has two "t's," two "r's," and two "u's."

$$\frac{9!}{2!2!2!} = \frac{9 \times 8 \times 7 \times 6 \times 5 \times 4 \times 3 \times 2 \times 1}{2 \times 2 \times 2}$$
$$= 45,360$$

Our Hawaiian fish name has six letters, but three pairs are identical.

$$\frac{6!}{2!2!2!} = \frac{6 \times 5 \times 4 \times 3 \times 2 \times 1}{2 \times 2 \times 2}$$
$$= 90$$

EXAMPLE 2

In how many ways may seven books be arranged on a shelf if three are identical algebra books, two are identical geometry books, one is a chemistry book, and the remaining one is a history book?

SOLUTION:
$$\frac{7!}{3!2!} = 420$$

[6] If you were to pick a three-letter name for a college fraternity from among the 24 letters of the Greek alphabet and no name could have the same letter appearing twice, how many possible names could you choose?

(A) 2160

(B) 216

(C) 72

(D) 8

(E) 12,144

In this problem we are asked to find the number of possible permutations of a set of 24 elements taken three at a time. To do this we must analyze three actions, the first performed in 24 ways, the next in 23, and the last in 22. Thus the answer is

$$\underbrace{24 \times 23 \times 22}_{\text{3 factors.}}$$

In general, when we are finding the number of permutations of an n-element set taken r at a time, we start the factorial representation of n but carry it down only to r factors:

$$\underbrace{n(n-1)(n-2)\ldots}_{r \text{ factors}} = n(n-1)(n-2)\ldots$$
$$[n-(r-1)].$$

A simpler notation for the right member of the above equation is

$$\frac{n!}{(n-r)!}.$$

25-4 The number of possible permutations of a set of n elements taken r at a time is indicated by the symbol $_nP_r$ (other symbols sometimes used are $P\begin{pmatrix} n \\ r \end{pmatrix}$ and $P(n,r)$) and is equal to

$$\frac{n!}{(n-r)!}.$$

🖩 Your calculator may be able to find the number of permutations or combinations directly through built-in formulas and functions. These may be accessed through the first, second, or third function keys or through a special menu. If you do not have $_nP_r$ or $_nC_r$ capabilities, you can still get answers quickly with the factorial key, $x!$.

EXAMPLE 1

In how many different arrangements may four people seat themselves in six seats at the theater?

SOLUTION: Our problem is to find the number of permutations of six chairs taken four at a time:

$$_6P_4 = \frac{6!}{(6-4)!} = 6 \times 5 \times 4 \times 3 = 360.$$

EXAMPLE 2

In how many ways can a five-digit number be written from the digits 1 to 8 inclusive if no repetitions of digits are allowed?

Our problem is to find the number of permutations of eight digits taken five at a time:

$$_8P_5 = \frac{8!}{3!} = 8 \times 7 \times 6 \times 5 \times 4 = 6720.$$

EXAMPLE 3

If $_nP_4 = 6(_nP_3)$, find n.

SOLUTION:

$$_nP_4 = \frac{n!}{(n-4)!} \text{ and } _nP_3 = \frac{n!}{(n-3)!}$$

Therefore the given information can be written as:

$$\frac{n!}{(n-4)!} = 6\left(\frac{n!}{(n-3)!}\right),$$
$$(n-3)!n! = 6n!(n-4)!,$$
$$(n-3)! = 6(n-4)!,$$
$$(n-3)(n-4)! = 6(n-4)! \text{ because}$$
$$(n-3)! = (n-3)(n-4)!,$$
$$n-3 = 6,$$
$$n = 9.$$

[7] In how many different ways can six keys be arranged on a key ring?

(A) 720

(B) 120

(C) 24

(D) 60

(E) 180

We briefly touched on an idea in [3] to which we will return now. Most of our work so far has been with *linear* permutations, arrangements of objects lined up in a row. Arranging the same elements in a circle changes the number of permutations possible.

For example, if the letters of $\{A, B, C\}$ were arranged in a row, then the order ABC is different from the order BCA. But if these were arranged in a circle, the order ABC is identical to BCA.

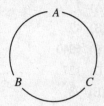

25-5 The number of circular permutations in a plane of n objects taken n at a time is

$$\frac{n!}{n} = (n-1)!$$

EXAMPLE 1

In how many different arrangements can seven guests be seated at a circular dining table?

 SOLUTION: This is an example of circular permutations in a plane, so the number of arrangements possible is $(7-1)! = 6! = 720$.

EXAMPLE 2

In how many ways may eight differently colored beads be arranged on a bracelet?

SOLUTION: In any situation where the circular arrangement may be meaningfully flipped over, a given clockwise permutation and its counterclockwise reflection are considered the same. Note that they were considered to be different for circular permutations in a plane. We must then modify our formula, since we now have half the number of permutations. The new formula is $\frac{(n-1)!}{2}$. Such a situation is given in this problem and is referred to as a "cyclic permutation in space."

$$\frac{(8-1)!}{2} = \frac{7!}{2} = 2520$$

Since a key ring can be turned over, we use this concept to answer the multiple-choice question. The six keys can be arranged in

$$\frac{(6-1)!}{2} = \frac{5!}{2} = 60 \text{ ways.}$$

WORKING WITH COMBINATIONS

[8] How many possible committees can be formed from a group of seven people if each committee can have any number of members from one to seven?

(A) 7

(B) 49

(C) 5040

(D) 127

(E) 98

A *combination* of elements is a set of elements; in other words, it is a collection of elements in which the order makes no difference. For example, though the arrangements *ABC* and *BAC* are different permutations of these three elements, they are the same combination because they consist of the same three elements.

25-6 The total number of combinations of a set of n elements is the total number of its subsets which contain at least one element, and this number is:

$$2^n - 1.$$

The committees in the above problem would be combinations rather than permutations, since the order of the people in the committees does not alter them. For example, a committee containing Rod, Jim, Tony and Chester is the same committee as the one composed of Jim, Chester, Tony and Rod. Remember: order is the determining factor in deciding whether you use a permutations or combinations formula for a particular counting problem.

The answer to the multiple-choice question would, therefore, be

$$2^7 - 1 = 128 - 1 = 127.$$

EXAMPLE 1

In how many ways may I make up a theater party from one, two, or all three of my friends, if I go along, too?

SOLUTION: The question asks for the total number of one-, two-, or three-element subsets that can be made from the set of three friends. (Since taking Larry and Harry is the same as taking Harry and Larry, these are combinations.) Because $n = 3$,

$$2^n - 1 = 7.$$

EXAMPLE 2

If I have one penny, one nickel, one dime, one quarter, and one half-dollar, how many different sums of money can I make up?

SOLUTION: There are five different coins so the answer is $2^5 - 1 = 31$ (assuming 0 ¢ is not allowed).

[9] How many lines can be drawn such that each contains two points of a set of nine points, and no three of the points of this set are collinear?

(A) 224

(B) 7560

(C) 27

(D) 84

(E) 36

Each combination of r elements has $r!$ permutations. Therefore

$$({}_nC_r)(r!) = {}_nP_r,$$

where ${}_nC_r$ represents the number of combinations of n things taken r at a time. Hence:

25-7
$$ {}_nC_r = \frac{{}_nP_r}{r!} = \frac{n!}{r!(n-r)!}. $$

Your calculator may be able to find the number of permutations or combinations directly through built-in formulas and functions. These may be accessed through the first, second, or third function keys or through a special menu. If you do not have ${}_nP_r$ or ${}_nC_r$ capabilities, you can still get answers quickly with the factorial key, $x!$.

In the question above, we are interested in learning the number of two-point subsets there are in a set of nine points. This is a combinations problem since line AB is identical to line BA.

$$ {}_9C_2 = \frac{9!}{7!2!} = \frac{9 \times 8}{2} = 36 $$

EXAMPLE 1

Find the number of different five-card hands a poker player can draw from a deck of 52 cards.

SOLUTION: We are interested in the number of five-element subsets of a set of 52 cards.

$$ {}_{52}C_5 = \frac{52!}{5!47!} = 2,598,960 $$

EXAMPLE 2

From a group of eight men and ten women in how many ways may a game of tennis "doubles" be set up involving two men and two women?

SOLUTION: There are ${}_8C_2 = 28$ ways of selecting the men and ${}_{10}C_2 = 45$ ways of selecting the women. By 24-1, there are 28×45 ways of making up the game.

$$ 28 \times 45 = 1260 $$

[10] In how many ways can we select a collection of three red or three white marbles from a bag of six white marbles and four red marbles?

(A) 80

(B) 210

(C) 24

(D) 5040

(E) 5

Two events are *mutually exclusive* if they do not occur simultaneously.

25-8   If two events are mutually exclusive and the first of these can occur in m ways while the second can occur in n ways, then one or the other event can occur in $m+n$ ways.

In the question above the number of ways we can select three red marbles from among four red marbles is ${}_4C_3 = 4$, and the number of ways of selecting three white marbles from six white marbles is ${}_6C_3 = 20$. Then the number of ways of accomplishing one selection *or* the other selection is 24. Note that this is a far different problem from one that asks the number of ways of accomplishing a first selection *and* a second selection. Had we been asked the number of ways of selecting three reds and three whites, six marbles altogether, we would have gotten 4×20 or 80 by 24-1; such actions would not be mutually exclusive.

EXAMPLE 1

A man has seven foxes and twelve chickens that he must take from their cages and ferry across a river. His boat can hold four animals (for obvious reasons, this means four chickens *or* four foxes). In how many different ways can he select the first load?

SOLUTION: He can select four foxes in ${}_7C_4 = 35$ ways, and four chickens in ${}_{12}C_4 = 495$ ways. This means that he can select four foxes *or* four chickens in $495 + 35 = 530$ ways.

EXAMPLE 2

In how many ways can a committee of five be made up from a group of twelve men and nine women if the committee must be all men or all women?

SOLUTION:

$$ {}_{12}C_5 = 792 \text{ if all men} $$
$$ {}_9C_5 = 126 \text{ if all women} $$

$$ 792 + 126 = 918 $$

WHAT YOU SHOULD KNOW

KEY CONCEPTS

Handling Permutations and Combinations

1. The value of the expression $n!$, where n is any positive integer, is given by

$$n! = n(n-1)(n-2)\ldots 3 \times 2 \times 1.$$

2. The number of distinct permutations of n things, a of which are alike of one kind, b of which are alike of another kind, etc., is given by

$$\frac{n!}{a!b!c!\ldots}$$

3. The number of possible permutations of a set of n elements, taken r at a time, is indicated by the symbol $_nP_r$ and is equal to

$$\frac{n!}{(n-r)!}.$$

4. The number of ways that r things can be chosen from a set containing n different things is

$$_nC_r = \frac{n!}{r!(n-r)!}.$$

Handling Mutually Exclusive Events

1. Two events are mutually exclusive if they cannot both occur at the same time.
2. If two events are mutually exclusive and the first of these can occur in m ways while the second can occur in n ways, then one or the other event can occur in $m + n$ ways.

KEY PRINCIPLES

1. If the first of two actions can be done in m ways and the second done in n ways, the number of ways the two actions can be done in order is mn. (Fundamental Principle of Counting).
2. The number of possible permutations or orderings of a finite set of n elements is always $n!$ (Principle of Permutation).
3. The total number of combinations of a set of n elements is the total number of its subsets that contain at least one element, and this number is $2^n - 1$. (Principle of Combination).

TEST-TAKING STRATEGY

- Use the criterion of order (Does it matter in which order the objects or people occur or are placed?) to decide whether to use a permutations or a combinations formula to solve a counting problem.

CALCULATOR TIPS

- Check to see if your calculator has a factorial key (often indicated by $\boxed{x!}$). If so, learn how to use it to answer counting problems.
- Does your calculator have a key or a built-in program to calculate combinations or permutations of sets? If so, learn how to use these features to answer basic problems involving selection and ordering.

ANSWERS

[1] (D)	[3] (A)	[5] (E)	[7] (D)	[9] (E)
[2] (B)	[4] (D)	[6] (E)	[8] (D)	[10] (C)

PROBABILITY AND STATISTICS

CHAPTER

26

KEY TERMS

probability	analysis of the chances an event will occur.
statistical probability	a method of analysis based on observed occurrences by actual count.
a priori probability	a method of analysis based on determining equally likely outcomes from the circumstances of an event.
sample space	the set of all possible outcomes of an experiment.
sample point	any of the possible outcomes that comprise the sample space.
event	any subset of a sample space.

[1]   A golfer concludes that the chances of a hole-in-one are one out of two and cites the laws of probability as her reason, since the outcome can happen in only one of two ways: the ball either goes into the cup or it doesn't. What is wrong with her argument?

(A) There is a third outcome: the golf club could miss the ball entirely.

(B) The golfer did not consider the length of the grass on the green.

(C) The argument does not reflect the skill of the golfer.

(D) A hole-in-one is really impossible.

(E) The two events are not equally likely.

The sporting nature of this question is not limited to the subject discussed; you may rightly conclude that this is not a case of figures lying but of liars figuring.

Probability is an analysis of the different ways an event may occur based on the assumption that all outcomes are equally likely. This golfer could have come to a better understanding of her chances through statistical probability from the accumulated evidence of her past record of driving balls from the tee she could figure her total past outcomes and the number of these that were holes-in-one. *Statistical probability* bases its analysis on observed occurrences by actual count and is used by insurance companies and others.

When the number of possible outcomes can be calculated in advance, we use *a priori probability*. For example, the number of ways in which a perfect cubical block of wood can come to rest on a different face is easily reckoned to be six. If five of these faces are painted green and one red, the chances that the block will land on a green face are five out of six.

EXAMPLES

For each of the following decide whether the probability can be figured by *a priori* or whether it must be computed through statistical methods. If *a priori*, indicate the total possible outcomes.

1. The chances of drawing a red marble from a bag containing eight marbles of different colors, one of which is red.

2. The probability that a baseball player will get a hit at his next time at bat.

3. The probability that a machine part put out by a specific worker will be defective.

4. The probability that a hexagonal pencil when rolled on a flat table will come to rest with the manufacturer's name on the top face.

SOLUTIONS:

1. *a priori*, 8 ways.

2. requires statistical analysis based on number of hits in past games.

3. requires statistical analysis of number of defects put out in the past.

4. *a priori*, there are 6 faces, so there are 6 outcomes.

FINDING THE SAMPLE SPACE

[2]   Four cards in a pile are labeled *A*, *B*, *C*, and *D*. Prior to figuring the probability that the first two drawn will be an *A* and a *C*, we must determine a sample space of the experiment. Which of the following is a sample space for the selection?

(A) $\{(A,B), (A,C), (A,D), (B,C), (B,D), (C,D)\}$

(B) $\{(A,B)\}$

(C) $\{(A,B), (B,A)\}$

(D) $\{(C,D)\}$

(E) $\{(A,B), (B,A), (A,C), (C,A), (A,D), (D,A), (B,C), (C,B), (B,D), (D,B), (C,D), (D,C)\}$

A *sample space* of an experiment is a set of all possible outcomes. We frequently designate a sample space by a set of ordered pairs, triples, etc., as in the above question. In this case the order of each pair represents the order in which the cards are drawn. Each outcome is represented by an element of the sample space and is called a *sample point*.

EXAMPLE

Find a sample space for an experiment in which three coins are tossed.

SOLUTION: Each of the three actions of flipping a coin can turn out in two ways. By 25-1 we can expect the sample space to have $2 \times 2 \times 2 = 8$ outcomes.

The branching diagram below indicates how these outcomes can be ascertained:

First Coin   Second Coin   Third Coin   Sample Point

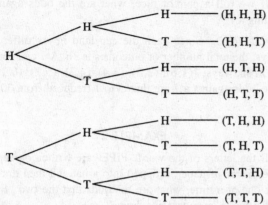

In the multiple-choice question, a sample space is the set of all ordered pairs for which the first entry is A, B, C, or D and the second entry is different from the first. Choice (E) fits this description.

[3]   Two boys choose blind dates at random from among a group of three girls. How many elements are there in the "event" that is the set of all sample points for which a specific girl does not have a date?

(A) 1

(B) 2

(C) 3

(D) 4

(E) 6

An *event* is any subset of a sample space. Label the boys A and B. Label the girls X, Y, and Z, with Z being the girl in question. We want to find that subset of the set of matchings that contains all the sample points for which Z is dateless. We set up the sample space by means of the following table (dl stands for "dateless"):

	X	Y	Z
(1)	A	B	dl
(2)	B	A	dl
(3)	A	dl	B
(4)	B	dl	A
(5)	dl	A	B
(6)	dl	B	A

Each sample point is a set of three elements, for example $\{AX, BY, \text{dateless } Z\}$, rather than an ordered triple. This is so because the ordered triples: $(BY, AX, \text{dateless } Z)$, $(AX, \text{dateless } Z, BY)$, and $(AX, BY, \text{dateless } Z)$, etc., all result in the same dating couples.

The event in question is the set that contains the first two rows of the table above.

Event: $\{\{AX, BY, \text{dateless } Z\}, \{BX, AY, \text{dateless } Z\}\}$

EXAMPLE

A bag contains a red ball, a blue ball, and a white ball. Each of the three balls is drawn in turn from the bag and not replaced. Set up the sample space for the experiment and the event for which the first ball drawn is white.

SOLUTION: The sample space will be a set of ordered triples, since the order of the drawing is specified in the action of the experiment. In the table below the numbers represent the order of the draw:

Red	White	Blue	Sample Point
1	2	3	(R, W, B)
1	3	2	(R, B, W)
2	1	3	(W, R, B)
2	3	1	(B, R, W)
3	1	2	(W, B, R)
3	2	1	(B, W, R)

The sample space is the set of ordered triples in the column on the right, and the event is the subset $\{(W,R,B), (W,B,R)\}$.

FINDING THE PROBABILITY OF AN EVENT

[4]   A chewing gum vending machine contains red, yellow, and green gum-balls. The number of red is the same as the number of green but is half the number of yellow. If the balls were placed in the machine at random when it was loaded, what is the probability that a customer will get a red one on a given purchase?

(A) $\dfrac{1}{4}$

(B) $\dfrac{1}{2}$

(C) 1

(D) 2

(E) 4

Probability may be defined as follows:

Suppose a sample space contains n sample points (outcomes), each equally likely (no outcome occurring more frequently than any other), and suppose that a certain event E, having e possible outcomes, is a subset of the sample space. Then the probability of the event E is $\frac{e}{n}$ and is designated by $P(E)$.

In the question above let n represent the total number of gum-balls (this will be the number of sample points) in the machine. Then $\left(\frac{1}{4}\right)n$ is the number of red ones. By the definition of probability the answer is

$$\frac{\left(\frac{1}{4}\right)n}{n} = \frac{1}{4}$$

EXAMPLE

If we take the spades from a pinochle deck, we get 12 cards, two each of 9, 10, J, K, Q, and A. If after shuffling these cards and placing them facedown on the table we draw a card, what is the probability that it will be an ace?

SOLUTION: The sample space contains 12 sample points (the 12 different cards that can be drawn). The event in question contains two sample points, the two aces.

$$P(E) = \frac{2}{12} = \frac{1}{6}$$

[5] Before the start of a horse race, and based on the past performances of the horses entered, the spectators are told that the chances are 4 to 1 that "Old Rosebud" will lose. What is the probability that Old Rosebud will win?

(A) $\frac{1}{4}$

(B) 4

(C) 5

(D) $\frac{1}{5}$

(E) $\frac{4}{5}$

The probability of the occurrence of an event ranges from 0 (impossible) to 1 (certainty) because the number of sample points in the event can range from 0 to n, where n is the total number of possible outcomes. If the event of occurrence contains e elements, then the event of nonoccurrence contains $n - e$ elements. The probability of occurrence is defined to be $\frac{e}{n}$ and of nonoccurrence to be

$$\frac{n-e}{n} = 1 - \frac{e}{n}.$$

Thus, when the probability of an event is $\frac{2}{7}$, the probability of nonoccurrence is $\frac{5}{7}$.

When we express probability as "chances for" or as "odds on," we use the ratio of the probability of occurrence to the probability of nonoccurrence. When we say

that the chances of losing for Old Rosebud are 4 to 1, we mean that the probability of loss is $\frac{4}{5}$ and of victory is $\frac{1}{5}$.

EXAMPLE 1

If we roll a pair of dice, what are the odds against rolling a 7?

SOLUTION: Since each die can land in six different ways, the total number of outcomes is 36. A 7 can come up in six ways: $\{(1,6), (2,5), (3,4), (4,3), (5,2), (6,1)\}$. The odds against a 7 are thus 5 to 1 (reduced from 30 to 6).

EXAMPLE 2

If the letters of the word "PIPE" are written on separate pieces of paper, dropped into a hat and then drawn out one at a time, what are the odds that the two "P's" will emerge on successive draws?

SOLUTION: There are 6 ways the letters can be next to each other and an equal number of ways they will be separated, so the odds are 1 to 1.

FINDING THE PROBABILITY OF MUTUALLY EXCLUSIVE EVENTS

[6] A bag contains 12 marbles; six are red, four are blue, and two are white. If one marble is drawn from the bag, what is the probability that it is either white or blue?

(A) $\frac{1}{6}$

(B) $\frac{1}{18}$

(C) $\frac{1}{2}$

(D) 2

(E) 1

Two or more events are mutually exclusive if success in one event necessitates failure for the others. For example, if a die is rolled on a flat table, each outcome excludes all of the others (the die cannot turn up with both a 2 and a 4 at the same time). The outcome of selecting a marble of one color from the bag above excludes each of the other colors.

26-1 If two events are mutually exclusive and a is the probability of the first event while b is the probability of the second event, then the probability of either one or the other event is $a + b$.

The probability of selecting a white marble is $\frac{2}{12}$; of selecting a blue marble, $\frac{4}{12}$. The probability of selecting one *or* the other is

$$\frac{2}{12} + \frac{4}{12} = \frac{6}{12} = \frac{1}{2}.$$

EXAMPLE

If the letters of the word "STATISTICS" are written on separate cards, shuffled and dropped into a hat, and if a card is drawn at random, what is the probability it will be either an "S" or a "T"?

SOLUTION: The events are mutually exclusive, since drawing a given letter indicates failure at drawing any other letter. The probability of an "S" is $\frac{3}{10}$ and of a "T" is $\frac{3}{10}$, so the probability of "S" or "T" is

$$\frac{6}{10} = \frac{3}{5}.$$

FINDING THE PROBABILITY OF INDEPENDENT EVENTS

[7] The six faces of a perfect cubical wooden block are painted so that four are red and two are green. If the block is rolled twice, what is the probability that it will come to rest on a green face both times?

(A) $\frac{2}{3}$

(B) $\frac{1}{9}$

(C) $\frac{1}{2}$

(D) $\frac{1}{18}$

(E) $\frac{1}{3}$

Two or more events are *independent* if success on one has no bearing on the success of any other. In the question above the first roll does not influence the second roll in any way.

> 26-2 When two events are independent and if the probability of the occurrence of the first is a while the probability of the second is b, then the probability that both will occur is ab.

EXAMPLE

A coin is tossed three times. What is the probability that all three will be "heads"? All three "tails"? All three the same?

SOLUTION: Each flip is independent of any other flip. The probability of "heads" for a given flip is $\frac{1}{2}$. The probability of "tails" on a given flip is also $\frac{1}{2}$, so the probability of all "tails" is $\frac{1}{8}$. The probability of all being the same means that all are "heads" or all are "tails." Since these two events are mutually exclusive, the probability of all coins the same is

$$\frac{1}{8} + \frac{1}{8} = \frac{1}{4}.$$

In the multiple-choice question, the result of the second toss is independent of the result of the first toss. The probability of landing with a green facedown on one toss is $\frac{1}{3}$, two faces out of six, and on both tosses is

$$\left(\frac{1}{3}\right)\left(\frac{1}{3}\right) = \frac{1}{9}.$$

[8] Two cards are drawn at random from a standard deck of 52 cards containing four different suits of 13 cards each. If the first card is not replaced before the second card is drawn, what is the probability that both cards will be of a given suit?

(A) $\frac{12}{51}$

(B) $\frac{3}{51}$

(C) $\frac{1}{16}$

(D) $\frac{1}{2}$

(E) $\frac{1}{4}$

In this problem, the outcome of the first draw changes the experiment and alters the probability of the second. In such a case the probability of *both* outcomes happening is, again, the product of the probabilities, but the probability of the second trial is based on the assumption that the first trial was successful. Do you see that if we assumed the first trial to be unsuccessful, the probability of *both* events occurring would be 0? The probability of the first card drawn is $\frac{13}{52}$ or $\frac{1}{4}$, and, if this trial was successful, then the second probability is $\frac{12}{51}$ and the compound probability is

$$\left(\frac{1}{4}\right)\left(\frac{12}{51}\right) = \frac{3}{51}.$$

This problem could, of course, have been worked directly from the definition of probability. The number of outcomes in the event is the number of permutations of the 13 cards in a suit taken two at a time or 13×12. The number of outcomes in the sample space is the number of permutations of the whole deck taken two at a time or 52×51. The probability is therefore:

$$\frac{13 \times 12}{52 \times 51} = \frac{3}{51}.$$

Another way to approach this is to say that, since any card is a satisfactory first card, its probability is 1. In order to get a second card of the same suit, the probability is $\frac{12}{51}$.

$$1 \cdot \frac{12}{51} = \frac{12}{51}$$

Suppose the question had asked for the probability that the cards would be of the *same* suit rather than one given suit. This means both are hearts or both clubs, etc. Since these are mutually exclusive and the probability has just been figured at $\frac{3}{51}$, the total probability is

$$\frac{3}{51} + \frac{3}{51} + \frac{3}{51} + \frac{3}{51} = \frac{12}{51}.$$

EXAMPLE

A box contains four red marbles and four white marbles. If two marbles are drawn at random and the first is *not* replaced before the second is drawn, what is the probability that both are white?

SOLUTION: The probability is $\frac{1}{2}$ on the first draw and $\frac{3}{7}$ on the second.

$$\therefore \frac{1}{2} \times \frac{3}{7} = \frac{3}{14} \text{ is the probability that both are white.}$$

[9]   The lengths of three edges of a rectangular box are x, $3x$, and $6x$. What is the mean length (to the nearest hundredth) of the set of 12 edges?

(A) .83x

(B) 3.00x

(C) 2.5x

(D) .75x

(E) 3.33x

The *mean* of a set of numbers is the result derived by adding all members of the set and dividing by the number of members in the set. This is the number you are accustomed to finding when asked for the "average." The term average, however, may have other meanings, as well, which we will review after answering this question.

The box has four edges of length x, four more of length $3x$, and four more of length $6x$. You could do it by working with all twelve edges:

$$\frac{4(x) + 4(3x) + 4(6x)}{12} = \frac{40x}{12}$$
$$= \frac{10x}{3}$$
$$= 3.33x \text{ (approximately).}$$

Or you could recognize that the duplication of the edges has no effect on the outcome and work with a single set of edges:

$$\frac{x + 3x + 6x}{3} = \frac{10x}{3}$$
$$= 3.33x \text{ (approximately).}$$

Let's change the problem a bit and review the other "averages" you might need to know.

EXAMPLE

A triangular prism has edges x, $3x$, and $6x$ as shown in the diagram. For the set of lengths of sides, which difference is greater, mean minus median or median minus mode?

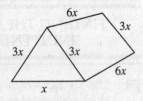

We calculate the mean from the equation:

$$\frac{2(x) + 4(3x) + 3(6x)}{9} = \frac{32x}{9}$$
$$= 3.56x \text{ (approximately).}$$

The *median* of a set of numbers is the number you reach when you arrange the set in order from greatest to least and count down to the middle from the top. There are nine edges ($6x$, $6x$, $6x$, $3x$, $3x$, $3x$, $3x$, x, x) and the median is $3x$.

The *mode* of a set is the number that occurs most often, which is $3x$ in this case.

Therefore, the difference between median and mode is 0 and the difference between mean and median is .56x.

[10] The Wildcats basketball team averaged 81 points per game for the first 15 games of its season. How many points did it average in its last 10 games if its average for the 25 games was 82.6?

(A) 83

(B) 84.2

(C) 85

(D) 85.2

(E) 86.2

When the term "average" is used in familiar circumstances, such as these, you may assume the mean is implied. To answer this question, you must understand that the final average is made up of two parts that are weighted differently. The first 15 games represent more of the total and will count more.

If the team averaged 81 points in its first 15 games, then $15(81) = 1215$ is the total number of points scored in those 15 games. Let x be the average of the 10 games left. Then $10x$ is the total number of points scored in the concluding games.

$$\frac{15(81) + 10x}{25} = 82.6.$$

Therefore, $x = 85$.

EXAMPLES

Use the concept of weighted average to answer each of the following questions:

1. If a team averages 50 points in its first 10 games and 55 points in its next 20 games, what is its 30-game average?

2. If a student averages 80 points on the first 5 tests of the semester, what must the average be on the remaining 2 tests to raise the grade to 85?

SOLUTIONS:

1. $\dfrac{(50)(10) + (55)(20)}{30} = 53.3$

2. $\dfrac{(80)(5) + 2x}{7} = 85$

$$400 + 2x = 595$$
$$2x = 195$$
$$x = 97.5$$

[11] The graph shows the number of students at a college who are involved in each of four sports: swimming, S, rowing, R, basketball, B, and track, T. If the number of rowers increases by x and the others remain the same, the average number of athletes in a sport changes by 10. How many rowers are there after the increase?

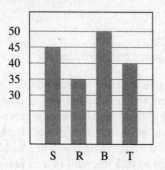

(A) 40

(B) 45

(C) 55

(D) 60

(E) 75

From the graph, there are 45 swimmers, 35 rowers, 50 basketball players, and 40 track athletes. Therefore, the average number of athletes per sport is 42.5.

If the average changes by 10, the new average is 52.5.

If the number of rowers increases by x, the new number is $35 + x$. With this information, the equation representing the new average is:

$$\frac{35 + x + 45 + 50 + 40}{4} = 52.5$$

Multiply both sides by 4, combine the numbers and the resulting equation is $x + 35 = 75$, which is the new number of rowers, (E).

Can you trust your intuition in a problem that seems as complicated as this? Your intuition may tell you that an average change of 10 people in four sports means a total change of 40. Since only one sport, rowing, is changing, all of the change happens to that number. Here's a case where number sense is really all you need.

[12] For every 5 two-point field goals a basketball team shoots, it sinks 2 three-point field goals and 3 one-point foul shots. If a team scores 57 points in one game, what is its ratio of two-point field goals to three-point field goals?

(A) 5 : 2

(B) 3 : 2

(C) 2 : 5

(D) 3 : 5

(E) Cannot be determined

This problem contains information that appears to be merely descriptive and seems not to contribute to the solution. Why would the number of points scored and the number of one-point foul shots matter? Both would affect the answer if the combination was impossible to attain.

You are given that the ratio of two-pointers to three-pointers is 5:2, which is choice (A). But because of choice (E), we cannot just settle for that result without eliminating the possibility that the actual score, 57 points, is impossible. Can you score points in the given ratios and reach 57 points?

With 15 two-pointers (30 points), 6 three-pointers (18 points) and 9 one-pointers (9 points) you get exactly 57 points. How did we guess those numbers?

Remember that the shot-ratios were 5:2:3. That means that the point ratios were 10:6:3 (multiplying each number in the shot ratio by its corresponding point value).

The sum $10 + 6 + 3 = 18$. Therefore, the scores must be multiples of 18. The result of this game, 57, is 3 times 18.

So, the answer is (A), but the test-maker could just as easily have made it (E) simply by choosing a total score that was not a multiple of 18.

[13] The table shows the highest high tide and lowest low tide at Hilo Bay for each of five months. Which month had the greatest range of tide heights?

Month	lowest low tide	highest high tide
January	−.3	2.4
March	−.2	2.0
May	−.4	2.1
July	−.2	2.6
September	.1	2.7

(A) January

(B) March

(C) May

(D) July

(E) September

This question tests little more than your ability to read a table and subtract signed numbers in decimal form. It is also designed to waste your time if you must resort to a calculator to do simple computations you should be able to do in your head.

To find the range for each month, subtract the lowest low tide from the highest high tide. For the months shown, the monthly ranges are:

January	$2.4 - (-.3)$	=	2.7
March	$2.0 - (-.2)$	=	2.2
May	$2.1 - (-.4)$	=	2.5
July	$2.6 - (-.2)$	=	2.8
September	$2.7 - (.1)$	=	2.6

Therefore, (D) July had the greatest range in the height of the tide. (And, yes, the difference in high and low tides at coastal points in Hawaii really is less than 3 feet year-round. The huge surfing swells off Hawaii beaches are generated by storms, not tides. And the killer waves at Hilo Bay in 1946 and 1960, called "tsunamis," were caused by undersea earthquakes. Be sure to visit the Tsunami Museum if you ever get to Hilo.)

[14] The table shows the distribution of term grades for a class of 500 seniors. If every senior received exactly one grade, what is the maximum value of y?

Grade	Number of grades awarded
A	73
B	150
C	194
D	x
F	y

(A) 0

(B) 43

(C) 83

(D) 194

(E) Cannot be determined

Add all numbers of grades. The result must be 500.

$$x + y + 194 + 150 + 73 = 500$$
$$x + y = 83$$

Because every senior was graded, the values for each of x and y range from 0 to 83. In other words, if x is 0, y must be 83. If y is 0, then x must be 83. Each of x and y can, of course, be any number from 0 to 83 inclusive. Therefore, the maximum possible value of y is 83, (C).

In a test group, the most common wrong answers for this question were (B) and (E). Because y is unknown, its value cannot be determined. But that value cannot be greater than 83, which is what the question asked. Those who chose answer (B) made the assumption that the remaining grades had to be somewhat evenly distributed among the remaining students. Do not bring your own assumptions to the problems you face on the Level IC test.

[15] Each of the first six prime numbers is written on a card. The six cards are shuffled and two are dealt. If p is the probability that the sum of the numbers on the two cards is prime, then $p = ?$

(A) $\frac{1}{5}$

(B) $\frac{1}{4}$

(C) $\frac{1}{3}$

(D) $\frac{1}{2}$

(E) $\frac{2}{3}$

The first six prime numbers are 2, 3, 5, 7, 11, and 13. The number of ways you can select two cards from six is given by the formula

$$C(6,2) = \frac{6!}{2!4!} = 15.$$

Therefore, there are 15 possible sums.

Ignore any sums that result from adding odd numbers—the sum of two odds is always even and, therefore, not prime.

The sums you need to consider just involve 2, so they are:

$$2 + 3 = 5 \text{ (prime)}$$
$$2 + 5 = 7 \text{ (prime)}$$
$$2 + 7 = 9 \text{ (not prime)}$$
$$2 + 11 = 13 \text{ (prime)}$$
$$2 + 13 = 15 \text{ (not prime)}$$

Therefore, the probability is $\frac{3}{15} = \frac{1}{5}$, (A).

[16] A number is drawn at random from the set of factors of 144. What is the probability that the number selected is a perfect square?

(A) $\frac{2}{5}$

(B) $\frac{1}{6}$

(C) $\frac{4}{15}$

(D) $\frac{1}{3}$

(E) $\frac{1}{2}$

The set of factors of 144 is

1, 2, 3, 4, 6, 8, 9, 12, 16, 18, 24, 36, 48, 72, 144.

You might find these by repeated divisions, beginning with 1, then 2, then 3, etc. until you had progressed to 12. When you reach 12, you can quit because 12 is the square root of 144. Therefore, you have already found all factors that are greater than 12 when you found the ones less than 12 and divided them into 144.

Or you might find all factors by writing the prime factorization of 144, or $3^2 \times 2^4$ and then building the factors by pairing up all possibilities using 3, 3^2, 2, 2^2, 2^3, and 2^4.

Either way, you see that there are 15 factors, of which six are perfect squares. (The squares are 1, 4, 9, 16, 3 6, and 144.)

Therefore, the probability is $\frac{6}{15}$, which reduces to $\frac{2}{5}$, (A).

WHAT YOU SHOULD KNOW

KEY CONCEPTS

1. If an event E can occur in e possible, equally likely ways out of a sample space containing n equally likely outcomes and $0 \leq e \leq n$, then the probability of E is $\dfrac{e}{n}$.
2. Two or more events are *mutually exclusive* if success in one event must result in failure for the other(s).
3. Two or more events are *independent* if success in one event has no bearing on the success or failure of th other(s).

KEY PRINCIPLES

1. For *mutually exclusive* events: If two events are mutually exclusive and a is the probability of the first event while b is the probability of the second event, then the probability of either one or the other event is $a + b$.
2. For *independent* events: If two events are independent and the probability of the first is a while the probability of the second is b, then the probability that both will occur is ab.

TEST-TAKING STRATEGIES

- To find the sample space for a given experiment or other situation, set up a table showing the elements that comprise each sample point.
- Be clear on when probabilities are multiplied (independent events) and when they are added (mutually exclusive events).

ANSWERS

[1] The question is purposely facetious; read the section. The best answer is (E).

[2] (E)

[3] (B)

[4] (A)

[5] (D)

[6] (C)

[7] (B)

[8] (B)

[9] (A)

[10] (C)

[11] (E)

[12] (A)

[13] (D)

[14] (C)

[15] (A)

[16] (A)

MODEL TESTS

PART

3

Six Practice Model Tests

With Answers Explained and Analyzed

Each Model Test Includes:

✓ **Answer Key**

✓ **Answer Explanations**

In Level IC Tests, both calculator-active and calculator-inactive answers are explained.

✓ **Self-Evaluation Chart**

Analyze your strengths and weaknesses by subject area

✓ **Determining Your College Board Scaled Score**

A conversion chart allows you to convert your raw score on the model test to the equivalent College Board Scaled Score

SOME FACTS ABOUT THE MODEL TESTS

Directions for the Model Tests

Each SAT II: Mathematics Level IC test is composed of 50 multiple-choice questions with a time limit of 1 hour. Thus the candidate who completes the test (80% of the test-takers do) average 1 minute and 12 seconds per question. Though it is unrealistic for most students to expect to answer every question accurately, you should not let yourself get bogged down—obviously, the more questions you answer correctly, the better your final score. An announcement of elapsed time is made every 20 minutes, but you would do well to bring your own watch. A good guideline is to spend no more than 2 minutes on a given question.

In general the questions get progressively more difficult; this is tempered somewhat by your preparation. For example, if you have a thorough grounding in trigonometry but your experience with radicals is negligible, you might find question 44 of Test 1, which follows, to be easier than question 1.

The most important thing you can learn from taking practice achievement tests is how to pace yourself without getting bogged down. When taking these tests try to approximate testing conditions as closely as possible—arrange for an undistracted hour with no other materials than several sharpened pencils and the test itself. You may want to use scratch paper, but all scratchwork on the SAT II: Level IC Math test must be done in the test booklet. No scratchwork counts toward your score; only the answer recorded on the answer sheet is graded.

When you grade your model test, give yourself 1 point for each correct answer and $-\frac{1}{4}$ for each incorrect answer. Note that there is a difference between an incorrect answer and an answer left blank. No points are added or subtracted for an answer left blank. The $-\frac{1}{4}$ point for each incorrect answer is computed as a penalty for indiscriminant guessing. If you were to guess at five questions that you knew nothing at all about, the probability is that you would guess one correctly and four incorrectly. Adding together the 1 point for the one correct answer and the $4\left(-\frac{1}{4}\right)$ points for the four incorrect answers gives you a net score of 0.

Thus the probability is that indiscriminate guessing will not help your score and may actually hurt it. If, however, you knew enough about each question to be able to eliminate at least one of the choices given, the probability would be in your favor, and you might aid your score by selecting for each question the one among the remaining answers that seemed most likely.

In general, you should not guess unless you can definitely eliminate at least one of the possible answers given for a particular question. By doing this, you are in no way attemping to "beat" the test, but are just trying to get credit for knowing something about the question.

Most SAT II: Mathematics Level IC tests contain approximately 15 questions of an elementary nature, questions that seem quite easy to a person who is well prepared. Among such easy questions might be:

[1]   If $2x = 5$, which of the following is $4x$?

(A) $\frac{5}{2}$

(B) 10

(C) 20

(D) $\frac{5}{4}$

(E) $\frac{4}{5}$

or

[2] $\sin^2 x + \cos^2 x = ?$

(A) -1

(B) 0

(C) 1

(D) $\sin 2x$

(E) No answer is possible unless x is known.

The answer to [1] can be readily found by doubling both sides, and the answer to [2] should be recognized easily as the result of a basic fact of trigonometry. You should have quickly arrived at (B) and (C) in a matter of seconds.

In order to make the most efficient use of your review time, we have replaced the easy questions normally found on the Level IC tests with others that are slightly more difficult. The result is that our model tests, with one exception, will seem quite a bit harder than the actual Level IC test that you will eventually take on examination day. The practice you get by taking more difficult model tests should sharpen your ability to work quickly on the test that counts. Do not let the more difficult nature of our model tests scare you away from taking the Level IC test. It will be easier than any of the model tests that follow. You will probably not finish any of our model tests in the one-hour time limit, but the actual tests are designed to allow the majority of students (80%) to finish them, while all students complete at least 37 or 38 questions.

Model Test 6, however, is only slightly more difficult than the actual Level IC test and should give you a good idea of the degree of difficulty of these tests.

All geometric figures are drawn as accurately as possible except when a specific problem states that its figure is not drawn to scale. Unless otherwise specified, all figures lie in a plane.

You may assume that the domain of a function f is the set of all real numbers x for which $f(x)$ is a real number, unless the question indicates otherwise.

Self-Evaluation Charts

Each model test is followed by a self-evaluation chart on which to monitor your progress. Each test question is assigned to an appropriate subject matter category on each chart.

To monitor your progress, place a check ($\checkmark$) in the box below each question that you have answered correctly. Use an X to mark each question you have answered incorrectly. Leave the box blank below every question you have not answered.

The chart enables you to compute not only your total score for the test, but also a separate score for each topic that will appear on the Level IC test, such as algebra, coordinate geometry, or functions. In this way you can easily spot the areas in which you are weak and need further review before taking the next test.

The number of questions selected from each subject area varies slightly from test to test, just as it does on the actual SAT II: Math Level IC test.

After completing each test, calculate your score using the formula:

Number of correct answers

$$-\frac{1}{4} \text{ the number of incorrect answers}$$
$$= \text{ score}$$

Then record your score on page 395 by placing a dot opposite the nearest value on the vertical axis and above the appropriate test number on the horizontal axis. As you progress from one test to the next, the graph of your progress should show a steady rise from Test 1 to Test 5 and a marked jump for Test 6, which, you will recall, is less difficult than the others.

ANSWER SHEET FOR MODEL TEST 1

Determine the correct answer for each question. Then, using a No. 2 pencil, blacken completely the oval containing the letter of your choice.

1. Ⓐ Ⓑ Ⓒ Ⓓ Ⓔ   18. Ⓐ Ⓑ Ⓒ Ⓓ Ⓔ   35. Ⓐ Ⓑ Ⓒ Ⓓ Ⓔ

2. Ⓐ Ⓑ Ⓒ Ⓓ Ⓔ   19. Ⓐ Ⓑ Ⓒ Ⓓ Ⓔ   36. Ⓐ Ⓑ Ⓒ Ⓓ Ⓔ

3. Ⓐ Ⓑ Ⓒ Ⓓ Ⓔ   20. Ⓐ Ⓑ Ⓒ Ⓓ Ⓔ   37. Ⓐ Ⓑ Ⓒ Ⓓ Ⓔ

4. Ⓐ Ⓑ Ⓒ Ⓓ Ⓔ   21. Ⓐ Ⓑ Ⓒ Ⓓ Ⓔ   38. Ⓐ Ⓑ Ⓒ Ⓓ Ⓔ

5. Ⓐ Ⓑ Ⓒ Ⓓ Ⓔ   22. Ⓐ Ⓑ Ⓒ Ⓓ Ⓔ   39. Ⓐ Ⓑ Ⓒ Ⓓ Ⓔ

6. Ⓐ Ⓑ Ⓒ Ⓓ Ⓔ   23. Ⓐ Ⓑ Ⓒ Ⓓ Ⓔ   40. Ⓐ Ⓑ Ⓒ Ⓓ Ⓔ

7. Ⓐ Ⓑ Ⓒ Ⓓ Ⓔ   24. Ⓐ Ⓑ Ⓒ Ⓓ Ⓔ   41. Ⓐ Ⓑ Ⓒ Ⓓ Ⓔ

8. Ⓐ Ⓑ Ⓒ Ⓓ Ⓔ   25. Ⓐ Ⓑ Ⓒ Ⓓ Ⓔ   42. Ⓐ Ⓑ Ⓒ Ⓓ Ⓔ

9. Ⓐ Ⓑ Ⓒ Ⓓ Ⓔ   26. Ⓐ Ⓑ Ⓒ Ⓓ Ⓔ   43. Ⓐ Ⓑ Ⓒ Ⓓ Ⓔ

10. Ⓐ Ⓑ Ⓒ Ⓓ Ⓔ   27. Ⓐ Ⓑ Ⓒ Ⓓ Ⓔ   44. Ⓐ Ⓑ Ⓒ Ⓓ Ⓔ

11. Ⓐ Ⓑ Ⓒ Ⓓ Ⓔ   28. Ⓐ Ⓑ Ⓒ Ⓓ Ⓔ   45. Ⓐ Ⓑ Ⓒ Ⓓ Ⓔ

12. Ⓐ Ⓑ Ⓒ Ⓓ Ⓔ   29. Ⓐ Ⓑ Ⓒ Ⓓ Ⓔ   46. Ⓐ Ⓑ Ⓒ Ⓓ Ⓔ

13. Ⓐ Ⓑ Ⓒ Ⓓ Ⓔ   30. Ⓐ Ⓑ Ⓒ Ⓓ Ⓔ   47. Ⓐ Ⓑ Ⓒ Ⓓ Ⓔ

14. Ⓐ Ⓑ Ⓒ Ⓓ Ⓔ   31. Ⓐ Ⓑ Ⓒ Ⓓ Ⓔ   48. Ⓐ Ⓑ Ⓒ Ⓓ Ⓔ

15. Ⓐ Ⓑ Ⓒ Ⓓ Ⓔ   32. Ⓐ Ⓑ Ⓒ Ⓓ Ⓔ   49. Ⓐ Ⓑ Ⓒ Ⓓ Ⓔ

16. Ⓐ Ⓑ Ⓒ Ⓓ Ⓔ   33. Ⓐ Ⓑ Ⓒ Ⓓ Ⓔ   50. Ⓐ Ⓑ Ⓒ Ⓓ Ⓔ

17. Ⓐ Ⓑ Ⓒ Ⓓ Ⓔ   34. Ⓐ Ⓑ Ⓒ Ⓓ Ⓔ

Model Test Score Conversion Table							
Raw Score	Scaled Score	Raw Score	Scaled Score	Raw Score	Scaled Score	Raw Score	Scaled Score
50	800	34	630	18	500	2	370
49	790	33	620	17	490	1	360
48	780	32	610	16	480	0	360
47	770	31	600	15	480	−1	350
46	760	30	590	14	470	−2	340
45	750	29	580	13	460	−3	330
44	740	28	580	12	450	−4	330
43	730	27	570	11	440	−5	320
42	720	26	560	10	440	−6	310
41	710	25	550	9	430	−7	300
40	700	24	540	8	420	−8	300
39	690	23	540	7	410	−9	290
38	680	22	530	6	400	−10	280
37	660	21	520	5	390	−11	270
36	650	20	510	4	390	−12	270
35	640	19	510	3	380		

MODEL TEST 1

Directions: For each of the 50 multiple-choice test questions, select the BEST answer among the five choices given. When the exact numerical value is not one of the choices, select the best approximation to the exact value. Mark your choice on the answer sheet by filling in the corresponding oval.

Notes:

1. Some questions (but not all) will require the use of at least a scientific calculator. Programmable and graphing calculators are also permitted. Calculator questions are not marked as such, so you will have to decide whether or not to use one on each question.

2. All angle measures are in degrees. Set your calculator to degree mode.

3. Some problems are accompanied by figures, which provide information useful in solving the problem. Figures are drawn accurately unless marked "Figure not drawn to scale." All figures lie in a plane unless the diagram clearly shows otherwise.

4. Except when stated otherwise, the domain of a function f is the set of real number values of x for which $f(x)$ is a real number.

5. Reference information consisting of volume and surface area formulas that may be useful in answering some questions on this test can be found below:

REFERENCE INFORMATION

- Sphere with radius r.   Volume: $V = \frac{4}{3}\pi r^3$ Surface Area: $S = 4\pi r^2$
- Right circular cone with radius r and height h.   Volume: $V = \frac{1}{3}\pi r^2 h$
- Right circular cone with circumference of base c and slant height L.
  Lateral Area: $S = \frac{1}{2}cL$
- Pyramid with base area B and height h.   Volume: $V = \frac{1}{3}Bh$

1. $\dfrac{\sqrt{10}\sqrt{2}}{\sqrt{15}} =$

   (A) $\dfrac{2}{5}$

   (B) $\dfrac{2\sqrt{5}}{5}$

   (C) $\dfrac{\sqrt{3}}{6}$

   (D) $\dfrac{2\sqrt{3}}{3}$

   (E) $\dfrac{\sqrt{6}}{3}$

2. What is the relationship between the areas of $\triangle ABC$ and $\triangle DBC$ in Figure 1 at right?

   (A) Equal

   (B) Area $\triangle ABC = \dfrac{1}{2}$ Area of $\triangle DBC$

   (C) Area of $\triangle ABC >$ Area $of \triangle BDC$

   (D) Area of $\triangle ABC + 1 =$ Area of $\triangle BDC$

   (E) Area of $\triangle ABC = \dfrac{1}{3}$ Area of $\triangle DBC$

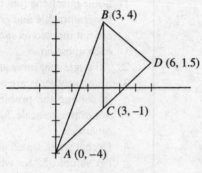

Figure 1

3. If $a \ne -b$, then $\dfrac{a-b}{a+b} - 1 =$

   (A) 0

   (B) $\dfrac{a-b-1}{a+b}$

   (C) $\dfrac{-2b}{a+b}$

   (D) $\dfrac{2a}{a+b}$

   (E) $\dfrac{a^2+b^2}{a+b}$

4. If the given angles have the measures indicated in Figure 2, what are the measures of x and y?

   (A) $x = 100°, y = 90°$

   (B) $x = 120°, y = 85°$

   (C) $x = 120°, y = 90°$

   (D) $x = 100°, y = 85°$

   (E) $x = 110°, y = 90°$

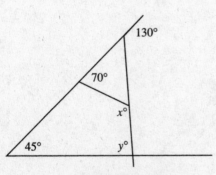

Figure 2

GO ON TO THE NEXT PAGE

5. If $3+y=a$ and $3-y=a$, then

    (A) $a=5, y=2$

    (B) $a=1, y=-1$

    (C) $a=2, y=-1$

    (D) $a=3, y=1$

    (E) $a=3, y=0$

6. If 250 quadles = 1 dorple and 1750 septles = 1 dorple, how many septles = 1 quadle?

    (A) 3

    (B) 7

    (C) 17

    (D) 30

    (E) 70

7. If $\dfrac{x-1}{x+1}=\dfrac{2}{3}$. then $x=$

    (A) 3

    (B) 2

    (C) No value possible

    (D) 4

    (E) 5

8. In Figure 3, if ray OA is perpendicular to line BD and $\angle AOE$ has degree measure of 15, then the measure of $\angle COD$ is

    (A) 75

    (B) 95

    (C) 100

    (D) 105

    (E) 100

9. If $4^{x/2}=16$, then $x=$

    (A) -2

    (B) 1

    (C) 2

    (D) 4

    (E) -4

USE THIS SPACE FOR SCRATCH WORK

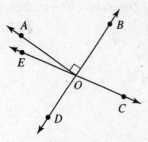

Figure 3

GO ON TO THE NEXT PAGE

10. If $\dfrac{x^2-1}{3} = 5$ and $y\left(\dfrac{x^2-1}{3}\right) = 15$, then $y =$

   (A) 5

   (B) 3

   (C) $\sqrt{3}$

   (D) 15

   (E) Cannot be determined

11. $\cos x - (\sin(90° - x)) =$

   (A) 0

   (B) 1

   (C) -1

   (D) .87

   (E) .5

12. In Figure 4, arc CD is a semicircle. $AB \perp CD$, $BC = 3$, $BD = 4$. Then the length of $AB =$

   (A) 3.46

   (B) 4.42

   (C) 3

   (D) 4

   (E) 5

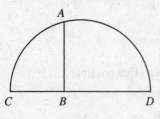

Figure 4

13. If $(b+c)(ab-ac) = b^2 - c^2$, then $a =$

   (A) 0

   (B) 1

   (C) -1

   (D) b

   (E) c

14. If $x = 2$, $y = 3$, and $z = 4$, then $\dfrac{x^3 + yz^2}{-2(2-3y)} =$

   (A) 5

   (B) -5.6

   (C) -5

   (D) 5.6

   (E) 4

GO ON TO THE NEXT PAGE

15. If the radii of the circles in Figure 5 are 5 and 3, the centers are *A* and *B* and both ∠*GAF* and ∠*DBC* are right angles, what is the perimeter of △*CEG*?

    (A) 32

    (B) 38.63

    (C) 30

    (D) 30.14

    (E) Cannot be determined

16. If *ABCD* in Figure 6 is a parallelogram and is positioned in the coordinate plane so that $A = (1,1)$, $B = (4,2)$, and $E = (3,3)$, then *D* is

    (A) $(-4,-2)$

    (B) $(-4,2)$

    (C) $(2,4)$

    (D) $(2,-4)$

    (E) $(-2,-4)$

17. In Figure 7, if *AD* = 2 and *DB* = 3, then the ratio

    $$\frac{\text{area } \triangle ADC}{\text{area } \triangle ABC}$$

    is

    (A) $\dfrac{2}{3}$

    (B) $\dfrac{3}{2}$

    (C) $\dfrac{2}{5}$

    (D) $\dfrac{3}{5}$

    (E) $\dfrac{5}{3}$

18. If $f\left(\dfrac{1}{x}\right) = 2x$, what is $f(x)$?

    (A) $\dfrac{2}{x}$

    (B) $\dfrac{x}{2}$

    (C) $\dfrac{1}{2x}$

    (D) 2

    (E) Cannot be determined

USE THIS SPACE FOR SCRATCH WORK

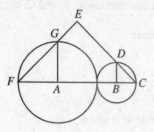

Figure 5

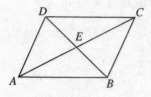

Figure 6

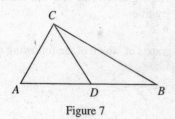

Figure 7

GO ON TO THE NEXT PAGE

19. In Figure 8, $\angle D$ and $\angle B$ are right angles. $AD = AB$, $BC = DC$, and $AB \neq BC$. How many circles can be drawn that contain A, B, and C, but not D?

(A) None

(B) 1

(C) 2

(D) 3

(E) Infinitely many

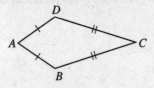

Figure 8

20. If $\left(x - \dfrac{1}{2}\right)\left(x - \dfrac{3}{2}\right) < 0$, then the greatest negative value for x is

(A) -1

(B) $-\dfrac{1}{2}$

(C) $-\dfrac{3}{2}$

(D) 0

(E) No negative value of x will make the inequality true

21. The graphs of which of the following are the same?

I. $y = \dfrac{1}{2}x + \dfrac{1}{2}$

II. $y + 1 = \dfrac{1}{2}(x + 3)$

III. $y - 2 = \dfrac{1}{2}(x - 3)$

(A) I and II only

(B) None

(C) II and III only

(D) I and III only

(E) I, II, and III

GO ON TO THE NEXT PAGE

22. In 10 minutes, the number of degrees the hour hand of a clock rotates is

   (A) 1
   (B) 6
   (C) $6\frac{2}{3}$
   (D) 5
   (E) 10

USE THIS SPACE FOR SCRATCH WORK

23. If $\dfrac{1}{x} + \dfrac{1}{\sqrt{x}} = 0$, then $x =$

   (A) 0
   (B) 1
   (C) −1
   (D) 111
   (E) No real value possible

24. $(\sin x)(\csc x) = 1$ when $x =$

   I. 0
   II. $\dfrac{\pi}{4}$
   III. All real numbers

   (A) I only
   (B) II only
   (C) I and II only
   (D) none
   (E) all

25. If $\dfrac{1}{x} < \dfrac{1}{2}$, then

   (A) $x > 2$
   (B) $x > 2$ or $x < 2$
   (C) $x > 2$ and $x < 2$
   (D) $x > 2$ or $x < 0$
   (E) x is any real number except zero

GO ON TO THE NEXT PAGE

26. If $k+1$ represents a given odd integer, which of the following must also be an odd integer?

(A) $2(k+1)$

(B) $k(k+1)$

(C) $(k+1)(k+2)$

(D) $(k+1)(k-1)$

(E) $(k+1)^2 - 1$

27. If $(a^2 - 3a)(a+3) = 0$ then $a =$

(A) $\{3\}$

(B) $\{-3\}$

(C) $\{3, -3\}$

(D) $\{0, 3, -3\}$

(E) $\{0, -1, 3, -3\}$

28. If the right angles and sides are as marked in Figure 9, the area of trapezoid $ABCD$ is 18, and $a = 2b$, then $c =$

(A) 4.47

(B) 8.94

(C) 4

(D) 2

(E) Cannot be determined

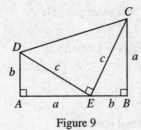

Figure 9

29. If $f(x) = -\dfrac{1}{x^3}$ and x takes on successive values from -10 to $-\dfrac{1}{10}$, then

(A) $f(x)$ increases throughout

(B) $f(x)$ decreases throughout

(C) $f(x)$ increases, then decreases

(D) $f(x)$ decreases, then increases

(E) $f(x)$ remains constant throughout

GO ON TO THE NEXT PAGE

30. If in a $\triangle ABC$, $\angle C$ is a right angle, $BC = 1$, and $\tan \angle B = p$, then $\cos \angle A =$

(A) $\dfrac{1}{\sqrt{p^2+1}}$

(B) $\dfrac{p}{p+1}$

(C) $\dfrac{p}{\sqrt{p^2+1}}$

(D) $\dfrac{\sqrt{p^2+1}}{p}$

(E) p^2+1

31. A gold bar with dimensions $2' \times 3' \times 4'$ has all of its faces rectangular. If it is melted and recast into three cubes of equal volumes, what is the length of an edge of each cube?

(A) 1

(B) 2

(C) 3

(D) 4

(E) 5

32. If $\dfrac{n!}{2} = (n-2)!$ then $n =$

(A) 1

(B) 2

(C) 3

(D) 4

(E) 5

33. If $\log x = \dfrac{1}{2}\log a - \log b$ and $a = 4b^2$, then $x =$

(A) 1

(B) 2

(C) 4

(D) 8

(E) 16

GO ON TO THE NEXT PAGE

34. If p, m, and n are prime numbers, none of which is equal to the other two, what is the greatest common factor of $24pm^2n^2$, $9pmn^2$, and $36p(mn)^3$?

    (A) $3pmn$

    (B) $3p^2m^2n^2$

    (C) $3pmn^2$

    (D) $3pmn^2n^2$

    (E) $3pmn^3n^3$

35. If the perpendicular bisector of the segment with endpoints $A\,(1,2)$ and $B\,(2,4)$ contains the point $(4,c)$, then the value of c is

    (A) 7

    (B) $\dfrac{7}{4}$

    (C) -7

    (D) 4

    (E) -4

36. If $f(x) = \dfrac{1}{x}$ and $f[f(x)] = f(x)$, then x is

    (A) 1 only

    (B) -1 only

    (C) 1 or -1

    (D) no real number

    (E) any real number

37. If in Figure 10, line DE is parallel to line AB, and $CD = 3$ while $DA = 6$, which of the following must be true?

    I. $\triangle CDE \sim \triangle CAB$

    II. $\dfrac{\text{Area } \triangle CDE}{\text{Area } \triangle CAB} = \left(\dfrac{CD}{CA}\right)^2$

    III. If $AB = 4$, then $DE = 2$

    (A) I only

    (B) II only

    (C) III only

    (D) II and III only

    (E) I and II only

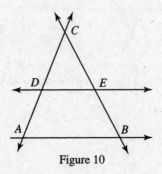

Figure 10

GO ON TO THE NEXT PAGE

38. If $x = 3i$, $y = 2i$, and $z = 1 + i$, then $xy^2z =$

   (A) 0
   (B) -1
   (C) $1 - i$
   (D) $12 - 12i$
   (E) $6 - 6i$

39. If $a < b$, then each of the following is true for all a and b EXCEPT

   (A) $-a < |b|$
   (B) $-a > -b$
   (C) $-b^2 < a^2$
   (D) $-a^2 < b^2$
   (E) $0 < b - a$

40. A singer has memorized 12 different songs. If every time he performs he sings any three of these songs, how many different performances can he give?

   (A) 4
   (B) 12
   (C) 110
   (D) 220
   (E) 440

41. In Figure 11, the measure of $\angle AOD$ and $\angle BOY$ is 90, and the measure of $\angle DOY$ is between 40 and 50. What is the range of possible values of the measure of $\angle AOC$?

   (A) 30 to 40
   (B) 40 to 50
   (C) 50 to 60
   (D) 40 to 60
   (E) Cannot be determined

42. If a circle is tangent to both the x- and y-axis and has a radius of 1, then its equation is

   (A) $(x - 1)^2 + (y + 1)^2 = 1$
   (B) $x^2 + y^2 = 1$
   (C) $x^2 + (y + 1)^2 = 1$
   (D) $(x + 1)^2 + y^2 = 1$
   (E) $(x - 1)^2 + y^2 = 1$

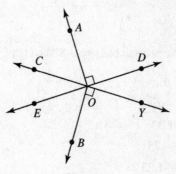

Figure 11

GO ON TO THE NEXT PAGE

43. If two planes, P_1, and $P_2 2$, are parallel, then

   (A) Any line in P_1 is parallel to any line in P_2.

   (B) $AB = CD$ whenever A and C are in P_1, and B and D are in P_2.

   (C) Any line that intersects P_1 in exactly one point will intersect P_2 in exactly one point.

   (D) Any line parallel to P_1 will intersect P_2.

   (E) Any line that intersects P_1 in more than one point must intersect P_2 in more than one point.

44. If $\tan \frac{y}{2} = \sin \frac{y}{2}$ and $0 \le \frac{y}{2} \le \frac{\pi}{2}$, then $\cos y = ?$

   (A) 0

   (B) 1

   (C) -1

   (D) $\frac{1}{2}$

   (E) $-\frac{\sqrt{2}}{2}$

45. The number of points in the intersection of the graphs of $y = |x+2|$ and $y = -|x| + 2$ is

   (A) Infinitely many

   (B) A finite but indeterminable number

   (C) 3

   (D) 2

   (E) 0

46. If $\sin x > 0$ and $\cos x = -.8$, then $\tan x =$

   (A) .6

   (B) $-.6$

   (C) 1.33

   (D) $-.75$

   (E) -1.33

GO ON TO THE NEXT PAGE

47. If $x = \sqrt{yz}$, $x > 0$, $y > 0$, and $z > 0$, then $\log y =$

(A) $\dfrac{x^2}{z}$

(B) $\dfrac{\log x^2}{\log z}$

(C) $\dfrac{2\log x}{\log z}$

(D) $2\log x - \log z$

(E) $2(\log x - \log z)$

USE THIS SPACE FOR SCRATCH WORK

48. A parallelogram has an area of 36 square feet and two sides of lengths 6 feet and 9 feet. Which of the following is the sine of an angle of the parallelogram?

(A) $\dfrac{2}{3}$

(B) $\dfrac{3}{2}$

(C) $\dfrac{4}{9}$

(D) $\dfrac{5}{9}$

(E) $-\dfrac{5}{6}$

49. Three cards, Card One, Card Two, and Card Three, are drawn from a deck. One of these is a queen, one an ace, and one a king. One and only one of the following statements is true.

I. Card Two is NOT a queen.
II. Card Three IS a queen.
III. Card One is NOT an ace.

Based on this information, which of the following is true?

(A) Card One is a queen.
(B) Card One is an ace.
(C) Card Two is a king.
(D) Card Three is an ace.
(E) Card Three is a queen.

GO ON TO THE NEXT PAGE

50. If a cube has an edge of length 10, then the length of the segment connecting the center of a face of the cube to any vertex not contained in the plane of that face is

(A) $\sqrt{6}$

(B) $5\sqrt{6}$

(C) $6\sqrt{5}$

(D) $3\sqrt{5}$

(E) $10\sqrt{6}$

USE THIS SPACE FOR SCRATCH WORK

STOP
IF YOU FINISH BEFORE TIME IS CALLED, YOU MAY CHECK YOUR WORK ON THIS TEST ONLY.
DO NOT WORK ON ANY OTHER TEST IN THIS BOOK.

ANSWER KEY

1. D	11. A	21. E	31. B	41. B
2. A	12. A	22. D	32. B	42. A
3. C	13. B	23. E	33. B	43. C
4. B	14. E	24. B	34. C	44. B
5. E	15. B	25. D	35. B	45. A
6. B	16. C	26. D	36. C	46. D
7. E	17. C	27. D	37. E	47. D
8. D	18. A	28. A	38. D	48. A
9. D	19. A	29. A	39. A	49. D
10. B	20. E	30. C	40. D	50. B

ANSWER EXPLANATIONS

1. (D)
$$\frac{\sqrt{10}\sqrt{2}}{\sqrt{15}} = \frac{\sqrt{5}\sqrt{2}\sqrt{2}}{\sqrt{5}\sqrt{3}}$$
$$= \frac{2}{\sqrt{3}}$$
$$= \frac{2\sqrt{3}}{\sqrt{3}\sqrt{3}}$$
$$= \frac{2\sqrt{3}}{3}$$

Or use your calculator to find a decimal value and check the answer choices.

Alternate solution: Compare answer choices with 1.1547...

2. (A) Altitude from A to segment BC is 3 and $BC = 5$, so area of $\triangle ABC = \frac{1}{2} \times 5 \times 3 = 15$. Altitude from D to segment BC is 3 and $BC = 5$, so area of $\triangle BCD = \frac{1}{2} \times 5 \times 3 = \frac{15}{2}$.

3. (C)
$$\frac{a-b}{a+b} - 1 = \frac{a-b}{a+b} - \frac{a+b}{a+b}$$
$$= \frac{(a-b)-(a+b)}{a+b}$$
$$= \frac{-2b}{a+b}$$

Alternate solution: Test values of a and b such as $a = 3$ and $b = 2$.

4. (B) Angle adjacent to $130°$ is $50°$ and $x = 70 + 50 = 120$, since the measure of an exterior angle $\angle x$ of a triangle equals the sum of the measures of its remote interior angles. Also $50 + 45 + y = 180$, since the sum of the measures of the angles of a triangle is 180. Therefore $y = 180 - 95 = 85$.

Comment: When angle measurements involve more complicated numbers (such as decimals), you might use your calculator to check your work.

5. (E) If $x = 3$, then $3 + y = a$ and $3 - y = a$, so $3 + y = 3 - y$ and $y = 0$. Thus $3 + 0 = a$, using the first equation given.

6. (B)
$$250 \text{ quadles} = 1750 \text{ septles}$$
$$1 \text{ quadle} = \frac{1750}{250} \text{ septles}$$
$$\frac{1750}{250} = 7 \text{ septles}$$

7. (E) $\frac{x-1}{x+1} = \frac{2}{3}$, so $3(x-1) = 2(x+1)$, and $3x - 3 = 2x + 2$; $x = 5$.

8. (D) m$\angle COD = $ m$\angle BOE$ since they are vertical angles. m$\angle BOE = $ m$\angle EOA + $ m$\angle AOB = 15 + 90 = 105$.

Comment: When angle measures involve more complicated numbers, you might use your calculator to check your work.

9. (D) $16 = 4^2$, so $4^{x/2} = 4^2$ and $\frac{1}{2}x = 2$. Thus $x = 4$.

Or $\log 4^{x/2} = \log 16$, $\frac{x}{2}\log 4 = \log 16$, $\frac{x}{2} = \frac{\log 16}{\log 4}$, $\frac{x}{2} = \frac{\log 16}{\log 4}$, $\frac{x}{2} = 2$. Thus $x = 4$.

10. (B) Since $\frac{x^2 - 1}{3} = 5$, then $y(5) = 15$ and $y = 3$.

11. (A) x and $90 - x$ are complementary, so any trigonometric cofunctions are equal.

12. (A) There are at least three different ways of doing this question using areas, similar triangles, or special relationships such as the following: The altitude to the hypotenuse is the geometric mean of the segments of the hypotenuse. Join C and A; A and D. $\triangle CAD$ is a right $\triangle$ because $\angle CAD$ is inscribed in a semicircle.

$$AB = \sqrt{(CB)(BD)}$$
$$= \sqrt{3 \times 4}$$
$$= 2\sqrt{3}$$
$$\doteq 3.46$$

13. (B) The left member can be transformed as follows: $(b+c)(ab - ac) = (b+c)(b-c)a = (b^2 - c^2)a$.

It is thus a times the right member so $a = 1$.

14. (E) $\dfrac{(2)^3+(3)(4)^2}{-2(2-3.3)} = \dfrac{8+48}{14} = \dfrac{56}{14} = 4$

🖩 If you use your calculator, be sure to insert parentheses before and after the numerator and denominator.

15. (B) $\triangle GEC$ is an isosceles right triangle since $m\angle G = m\angle C = 45$. GC is composed of two radii from each triangle, so $GC = 16$. From the special triangle relations $GE = EC = \dfrac{16}{\sqrt{2}} = 8\sqrt{2}$.

🖩 The sum is $16 + 16\sqrt{2} \doteq 38.63$.

16. (C) Diagonals of a parallelogram bisect each other, so E is the midpoint. Using the midpoint formula to find $D(xy)$:

$\dfrac{x+4}{2} = 3$ and $\dfrac{y+2}{2} = 3$, so $x = 2$ and $y = 4$.

17. (C) Altitudes are equal, so ratio of areas is ratio of bases. $AB = 2 + 3 - 5$.

18. (A) Replace x with $\dfrac{1}{\frac{1}{x}}$ so $f(x) = f\left(\dfrac{1}{\frac{1}{x}}\right) = 2\left(\dfrac{1}{x}\right)$.

19. (A) AC is the hypotenuse of both $\triangle ADC$ and $\triangle ABC$. The midpoint, M, of AC must be equidistant from the vertices of the right triangles. M must be the center of any circle containing A, B, and C, and this circle must contain D since $MD = MA = MB = MC$.

20. (E) Any negative values of x will make *both* factors negative and thus give a positive product.

21. (E) Solve II and III for y and simplify; you will get equation I in both cases.

Alternate solution:

🖩 With a graphing calculator, you could enter each function and compare the graphs.

22. (D) In 1 hour the hour hand will rotate $\dfrac{1}{12}$ of a revolution, or $\dfrac{1}{12}$ of $360° = 30°$. In 10 minutes it will rotate $\dfrac{1}{6}$ of this distance, or $\dfrac{1}{6}$ of $30° = 5°$.

23. (E) If $\dfrac{1}{x} + \dfrac{1}{\sqrt{x}} = 0$, then $\dfrac{1}{x} = \dfrac{-1}{\sqrt{x}}$ and $\sqrt{x} = -x$. But $x > 0$ for $\sqrt{x}$ to exist ($x = 0$ leads to division by 0) and "$\sqrt{}$" is defined to be positive. $-x$ is negative.

24. (B) I and III are false since $\sin x = 0$ and $\csc x$ is undefined when $x = n\pi$ where n is an integer.

25. (D) There are two cases to consider: $x > 0$ and $x < 0$ ($x = 0$ leads to division by 0).

Case I, $x > 0$

If $\dfrac{1}{x} < \dfrac{1}{2}$, then $2 < x$.

Case II, $x < 0$

If $\dfrac{1}{x} < \dfrac{1}{2}$ then $2 > x$, but $2 > x$ for all x in this case, which includes only $x < 0$.

Thus $x > 2$ or $x < 0$.

26. (D) If $k + 1$ is odd, then k is even, and k^2 is even. $(k+1)(k-1) = k^2 - 1$ and $k^2 - 1$ is odd.

27. (D) If $(a^2 - 3a)(a+3) = 0$, then $a(a-3)(a+3) = 0$. But the latter equation is true for any number that makes a factor equal to zero.

Thus $a = 0$ or $a - 3 = 0$ or $a + 3 = 0$.

28. (A) Replace a by $2b$ wherever it occurs. Using the formula for the area of a trapezoid:

$$18 = \dfrac{1}{2}(3b)(b + 2b)$$

from which

$$b = 2 \text{ and } a = 4 \text{ (since } a = 2b).$$

But

$$\begin{aligned} c^2 &= a^2 + b^2 \\ c^2 &= 20 \\ c &= 2\sqrt{5} \\ &\doteq 4.47 \end{aligned}$$

🖩

29. (A)

$$f(-10) = -\dfrac{1}{(-10)^3} = \dfrac{1}{1000}$$

$$f(-5) = -\dfrac{1}{(-5)^3} = \dfrac{1}{125}$$

$$f(-1) = -\dfrac{1}{(-1)^3} = 1$$

Alternate solution:

🖩 Graphing calculator: graph the function on the interval from -10 to $-.1$ and note that the graph always rises.

$$f\left(-\dfrac{1}{10}\right) = \dfrac{1}{(-\frac{1}{10})^3} = 1000$$

The representative values of $f(x)$ shown above suggest that $f(x)$ increases throughout the interval.

30. (C) Tan $\angle B = \dfrac{AC}{BC} = \dfrac{AC}{1} = p$; therefore $AC = p$.

By the Pythagorean Theorem:

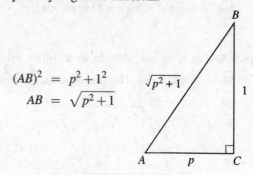

$$(AB)^2 = p^2 + 1^2$$
$$AB = \sqrt{p^2 + 1}$$

Thus $\cos \angle A = \dfrac{AC}{AB} = \dfrac{p}{\sqrt{p^2 + 1}}$.

31. (B) Volume of bar $= 2 \times 3 \times 4 = 24$

Volume of cube $= e^3 = \dfrac{1}{3}(24) = 8$

Therefore $e = 2$.

32. (B)

$$\frac{n!}{2} = \frac{n(n-1)(n-2)(n-3)\ldots 3 \times 2 \times 1}{2}$$

$$(n-2)! = (n-2)(n-3)\ldots 3 \times 2 \times 1$$

Thus, if we divide both sides of the given equation by $(n-2)!$, we get:

$$\frac{n(n-1)}{2} = 1$$
$$n^2 - n - 2 = 0$$
$$(n-2)(n+1) = 0$$

$\{2, -1\}$ But $n!$ is not defined for -1.

Alternate solution:

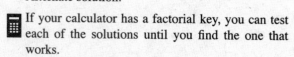 If your calculator has a factorial key, you can test each of the solutions until you find the one that works.

33. (B) If $\log x = \dfrac{1}{2} \log a - \log b$, then

$$\log x = \log \frac{\sqrt{a}}{b} \text{ and } x = \frac{\sqrt{a}}{b}$$

But $a = 4b^2$ so $\sqrt{a} = 2b$ and $x = \dfrac{2b}{b} = 2$

34. (C)

$$24pm^2n^2 = (3pmn^2)(8m)$$
$$9pmn^2 = (3pmn^2)(3)$$
$$36p(mn)^3 = (3pmn^2)(12m^2n).$$

35. (B) $(4, c)$ must be equidistant from A and B so:

$$\sqrt{(4-1)^2 + (c-2)^2} = \sqrt{(4-2)^2 + (c-4)^2}$$
$$\sqrt{9 + c^2 - 4c + 4} = \sqrt{4 + c^2 - 8c + 16}$$
$$c^2 - 4c + 13 = c^2 - 8c + 20$$
$$4c = 7$$
$$c = \frac{7}{4}$$

36. (C) $f[f(x)] = f\left(\dfrac{1}{x}\right) = x$ and $f(x) = \dfrac{1}{x}$, so $x = \dfrac{1}{x}$.
Thus $x^2 = 1$ and $x = 1$ or $x = -1$.

37. (E)

   I. True by angle-angle since the parallel lines form congruent corresponding angles.
   II. True because the ratio of the areas of similar triangles is the square of the ratio of the corresponding sides.
   III. False because $CA = CD + DA = 3 + 6 = 9$.

$$\frac{CD}{CA} = \frac{DE}{AB} \text{ so } \frac{3}{9} = \frac{DE}{4} \text{ and } DE = \frac{12}{9} = \frac{4}{3}$$

38. (D)

$$(3i)(2i)^2(1+i) = (3i)(-4)(1+i) = -12i$$

$$(1+i) = -12i - 12i^2 = 12 - 12i$$

39. (A) Let $a = -5$ and $b = -4$. Thus $-a = 5$ and $|b| = 4$ so $-a > |b|$ in contradiction to (A).

40. (D) The question asks for the number of combinations of 12 songs taken three at a time, which is (by formula):

$$\frac{12!}{9!3!} = 220$$

41. (B) $m\angle AOC + m\angle COE = 90$ and $m\angle COE = m\angle DOY$. Thus $m\angle AOC = 90 - m\angle DOY$. When $m\angle DOY = 40$, then $m\angle AOC = 50$ and when $m\angle DOY = 50$, then $m\angle AOC = 40$.

42. (A) Since the radius to the point of tangency is always $\perp$ to the tangent, and since this radius is 1, the center of any such circle is one of the points $\{(1,1), (1,-1), (-1,1), (-1,-1)\}$. The center of the circle in (A) is $(1,-1)$.

43. (C) The two planes are parallel, so that a line which pierces P_1 cannot bypass P_2.

44. **(B)** Let $\dfrac{y}{2} = \theta$; then $\tan\theta = \sin\theta$ is given. But

$\tan = \dfrac{\sin\theta}{\cos\theta}$ for any θ whose cosine is defined, so

$\cos\theta = 1$ and $\theta = 0$. Since $\dfrac{y}{2} = \theta$, we conclude that

$\dfrac{y}{2} = 0$, so $y = 0$, and $\cos y = 1$.

45. **(A)** From the graph below, the intersection is a segment (which contains infinitely many points).

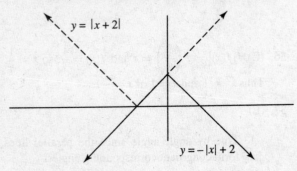

$y = |x + 2|$

$y = -|x| + 2$

Alternate solution:

📇 Graphing calculator: graph each function and compare the graphs.

46. **(D)** $\sin^2 x + \cos^2 x = 1$

$\sin^2 x + \dfrac{16}{25} = 1$

$\sin^2 x = \dfrac{9}{25}$

$\sin x = \pm\dfrac{3}{5}$

$\doteq \pm.6$

But $\sin x$ was given as positive, so $\sin x \doteq .6$.

$\tan x = \dfrac{\sin x}{\cos x} = \dfrac{.6}{-.8} = \dfrac{-.75}{25}$

47. **(D)** If $x\sqrt{yz}$, then $x^2 = yz$ and $y = \dfrac{x^2}{z}$. Thus $\log y = \log\dfrac{x^2}{z} = \log x^2 - \log z = 2\log x - \log z$.

48. **(A)** Let h be the altitude to a 9-foot side; then $9h = 36$ and $h = 4$. The sine of $\angle A$ is $\dfrac{4}{6} = \dfrac{2}{3}$.

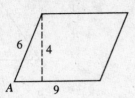

49. **(D)** By trial and error, let each statement be true and the others false. Each such trial will lead to a contradiction except III true and both I and II false.

50. **(B)** $AB = 10$ (given), $AC = 10\sqrt{2}$ (Pythagorean Theorem), $AM = 5\sqrt{2}$ (M is midpoint as given). $(BM)^2 - (AB)^2 + (AM)^2$ (Pythagorean Theorem)

$BM = \sqrt{100 + 50}$
$= \sqrt{150}$
$= 5\sqrt{6}$

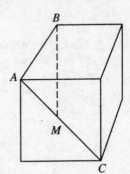

SELF-EVALUATION CHART FOR MODEL TEST 1

SUBJECT AREA	QUESTIONS ANSWERED CORRECTLY	NUMBER OF CORRECT ANSWERS
Algebra (15 questions)	1 3 5 7 9 10 13 14 20 23 25 27 32 39 47	_____
Plane geometry (10 questions)	4 8 12 15 17 19 28 35 37 41	_____
Solid geometry (3 questions)	31 43 50	_____
Coordinate geometry (5 questions)	2 16 21 42 45	_____
Trigonometry (7 questions)	11 22 24 30 44 46 48	_____
Functions (5 questions)	14 18 29 33 36	_____
Miscellaneous (7 questions)	6 26 32 34 38 40 49	_____

Total number of correct answers _____

Total number of incorrect answers _____

Total score = total number of correct answers _____

minus $\frac{1}{4}$ number of incorrect answers − _____

(Reminder: Answers left blank are not counted as correct or incorrect)

Raw score = (number correct) $-\frac{1}{4}$ (number incorrect)

To evaluate your performance, compare your raw score with the table below.

Evaluate Your Performance
Model Test 1

Excellent	760–800	46–50
Very Good	700–750	40–45
Good	610–690	32–39
Above Average	560–600	26–31
Average	500–550	18–25
Below Average	270–490	17 or less

ANSWER SHEET FOR MODEL TEST 2

Determine the correct answer for each question. Then, using a No. 2 pencil, blacken completely the oval containing the letter of your choice.

1. Ⓐ Ⓑ Ⓒ Ⓓ Ⓔ   18. Ⓐ Ⓑ Ⓒ Ⓓ Ⓔ   35. Ⓐ Ⓑ Ⓒ Ⓓ Ⓔ
2. Ⓐ Ⓑ Ⓒ Ⓓ Ⓔ   19. Ⓐ Ⓑ Ⓒ Ⓓ Ⓔ   36. Ⓐ Ⓑ Ⓒ Ⓓ Ⓔ
3. Ⓐ Ⓑ Ⓒ Ⓓ Ⓔ   20. Ⓐ Ⓑ Ⓒ Ⓓ Ⓔ   37. Ⓐ Ⓑ Ⓒ Ⓓ Ⓔ
4. Ⓐ Ⓑ Ⓒ Ⓓ Ⓔ   21. Ⓐ Ⓑ Ⓒ Ⓓ Ⓔ   38. Ⓐ Ⓑ Ⓒ Ⓓ Ⓔ
5. Ⓐ Ⓑ Ⓒ Ⓓ Ⓔ   22. Ⓐ Ⓑ Ⓒ Ⓓ Ⓔ   39. Ⓐ Ⓑ Ⓒ Ⓓ Ⓔ
6. Ⓐ Ⓑ Ⓒ Ⓓ Ⓔ   23. Ⓐ Ⓑ Ⓒ Ⓓ Ⓔ   40. Ⓐ Ⓑ Ⓒ Ⓓ Ⓔ
7. Ⓐ Ⓑ Ⓒ Ⓓ Ⓔ   24. Ⓐ Ⓑ Ⓒ Ⓓ Ⓔ   41. Ⓐ Ⓑ Ⓒ Ⓓ Ⓔ
8. Ⓐ Ⓑ Ⓒ Ⓓ Ⓔ   25. Ⓐ Ⓑ Ⓒ Ⓓ Ⓔ   42. Ⓐ Ⓑ Ⓒ Ⓓ Ⓔ
9. Ⓐ Ⓑ Ⓒ Ⓓ Ⓔ   26. Ⓐ Ⓑ Ⓒ Ⓓ Ⓔ   43. Ⓐ Ⓑ Ⓒ Ⓓ Ⓔ
10. Ⓐ Ⓑ Ⓒ Ⓓ Ⓔ   27. Ⓐ Ⓑ Ⓒ Ⓓ Ⓔ   44. Ⓐ Ⓑ Ⓒ Ⓓ Ⓔ
11. Ⓐ Ⓑ Ⓒ Ⓓ Ⓔ   28. Ⓐ Ⓑ Ⓒ Ⓓ Ⓔ   45. Ⓐ Ⓑ Ⓒ Ⓓ Ⓔ
12. Ⓐ Ⓑ Ⓒ Ⓓ Ⓔ   29. Ⓐ Ⓑ Ⓒ Ⓓ Ⓔ   46. Ⓐ Ⓑ Ⓒ Ⓓ Ⓔ
13. Ⓐ Ⓑ Ⓒ Ⓓ Ⓔ   30. Ⓐ Ⓑ Ⓒ Ⓓ Ⓔ   47. Ⓐ Ⓑ Ⓒ Ⓓ Ⓔ
14. Ⓐ Ⓑ Ⓒ Ⓓ Ⓔ   31. Ⓐ Ⓑ Ⓒ Ⓓ Ⓔ   48. Ⓐ Ⓑ Ⓒ Ⓓ Ⓔ
15. Ⓐ Ⓑ Ⓒ Ⓓ Ⓔ   32. Ⓐ Ⓑ Ⓒ Ⓓ Ⓔ   49. Ⓐ Ⓑ Ⓒ Ⓓ Ⓔ
16. Ⓐ Ⓑ Ⓒ Ⓓ Ⓔ   33. Ⓐ Ⓑ Ⓒ Ⓓ Ⓔ   50. Ⓐ Ⓑ Ⓒ Ⓓ Ⓔ
17. Ⓐ Ⓑ Ⓒ Ⓓ Ⓔ   34. Ⓐ Ⓑ Ⓒ Ⓓ Ⓔ

Model Test Score Conversion Table

Raw Score	Scaled Score	Raw Score	Scaled Score	Raw Score	Scaled Score	Raw Score	Scaled Score
50	800	34	630	18	500	2	370
49	790	33	620	17	490	1	360
48	780	32	610	16	480	0	360
47	770	31	600	15	480	−1	350
46	760	30	590	14	470	−2	340
45	750	29	580	13	460	−3	330
44	740	28	580	12	450	−4	330
43	730	27	570	11	440	−5	320
42	720	26	560	10	440	−6	310
41	710	25	550	9	430	−7	300
40	700	24	540	8	420	−8	300
39	690	23	540	7	410	−9	290
38	680	22	530	6	400	−10	280
37	660	21	520	5	390	−11	270
36	650	20	510	4	390	−12	270
35	640	19	510	3	380		

MODEL TEST 2

Directions: For each of the 50 multiple-choice test questions, select the BEST answer among the five choices given. When the exact numerical value is not one of the choices, select the best approximation to the exact value. Mark your choice on the answer sheet by filling in the corresponding oval.

Notes:

1. Some questions (but not all) will require the use of at least a scientific calculator. Programmable and graphing calculators are also permitted. Calculator questions are not marked as such, so you will have to decide whether or not to use one on each question.

2. All angle measures are in degrees. Set your calculator to degree mode.

3. Some problems are accompanied by figures, which provide information useful in solving the problem. Figures are drawn accurately unless marked "Figure not drawn to scale." All figures lie in a plane unless the diagram clearly shows otherwise.

4. Except when stated otherwise, the domain of a function f is the set of real number values of x for which $f(x)$ is a real number.

5. Reference information consisting of volume and surface area formulas that may be useful in answering some questions on this test can be found below:

REFERENCE INFORMATION

- Sphere with radius r.   Volume: $V = \frac{4}{3}\pi r^3$ Surface Area: $S = 4\pi r^2$
- Right circular cone with radius r and height h.   Volume: $V = \frac{1}{3}\pi r^2 h$
- Right circular cone with circumference of base c and slant height L. Lateral Area: $S = \frac{1}{2}cL$
- Pyramid with base area B and height h.   Volume: $V = \frac{1}{3}Bh$

1. If $a = 3b + 5$ and $c = 3a$, then $c =$

   (A) $9b + 15$

   (B) $3b + 5$

   (C) $b + \dfrac{2}{3}$

   (D) $9b$

   (E) $3b + \dfrac{5}{3}$

2. In Figure 1, the length of arc AC is twice the length of arc BC. Each of the following is true EXCEPT

   (A) the degree measure of $\angle AOC$ is twice the degree measure of $\angle BOC$

   (B) the degree measure of arc AC is twice the degree measure of arc BC

   (C) the radian measure of $\angle AOC$ is twice the radian measure of $\angle BOC$

   (D) the radius of arc AC is equal to the radius of arc BC

   (E) the length of line segment AC is twice the length of line segment BC

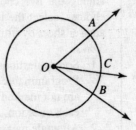

Figure 1

3. If $a = 3^2$, $b = \dfrac{1}{a}$, and $c = b^4$, then

   (A) $a > b > c$

   (B) $a < b < c$

   (C) $a < c < b$

   (D) $c < a < b$

   (E) $b < c < a$

4. If $\dfrac{x-2}{y} = 4$ and $y - 1 = 0$, what is the value of x?

   (A) No value possible

   (B) 6

   (C) 5

   (D) 4

   (E) 3

GO ON TO THE NEXT PAGE

5. In Figure 2, lines L_1 and L_2 are NOT parallel and will intersect at some point to the right of the page. Which of the following must be true?

   I. $c = e$
   II. $b > d$
   III. $a = c$

   (A) I only
   (B) II only
   (C) III only
   (D) I and II only
   (E) II and III only

6. If $A = (-1, 2)$ and $B = (2, -1)$, where A and B are two points in the coordinate plane, then what is the length of segment AB?

   (A) 1
   (B) 2
   (C) 3
   (D) 4.24
   (E) 3.46

7. An operation, $\circ$, on the numbers a and b is defined by the formula $a \circ b = 2(a + 2b)$. For what values of x and y is $x \circ y = y \circ x$?

   (A) All real values
   (B) Only when $x = y$
   (C) Only when both x and y are 0
   (D) Only when $x = -y$
   (E) Only when x and y are both 1

8. If the area of a square is 1.44 square feet, its perimeter is

   (A) 1.2
   (B) 4.8
   (C) 14.4
   (D) 12
   (E) 14

USE THIS SPACE FOR SCRATCH WORK

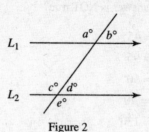

Figure 2

GO ON TO THE NEXT PAGE

9. In Figure 3, the arc measures are as shown, $L_1 \parallel L_2$ and L_1 is tangent to the circle whose center is O. Which answer is NOT true?

(A) $z = 45°$

(B) $x = 95°$

(C) $y = 50°$

(D) $w = 70°$

(E) $v = 130°$

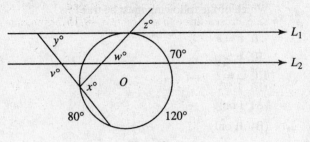

Figure 3

10. If $\sqrt{x^2 - 6x + 9} = x - 3$, then $x =$

(A) No real number

(B) Any real number

(C) 3 or -3 only

(D) 3 only

(E) $x \geq 3$

11. If $a = 5$, which of the following must be true?

  I. a cannot be zero.

  II. a and b cannot both be integers.

  III. a and b must both have the same sign.

(A) I only

(B) I and II only

(C) I and III only

(D) II only

(E) II and III only

12. What is the simplified form of

$$\frac{\dfrac{m+n}{m-1} + n}{\dfrac{m+n}{m-1} - 1}$$

(A) $\dfrac{m+n}{m-1}$

(B) 1

(C) m

(D) -1

(E) $m^2 - n^2$

GO ON TO THE NEXT PAGE

13. If $\angle A$ is positioned on a set of coordinate axes so that its vertex is at the origin and one of its sides is the nonnegative ray of the x-axis, and if its other side passes through the point $(-8, 15)$, then sine $\angle A =$

(A) $-.53$

(B) 1.88

(C) $.53$

(D) $.88$

(E) $-.47$

14. If $a = -\dfrac{1}{2}$ and $b = -8$, then $\dfrac{a^2}{b} + b =$

(A) -8

(B) -8.03

(C) -6

(D) $.03$

(E) -10

15. If, in $\triangle ABC$ in Figure 4, $AB = 4$, $\angle A = 44°$, and $AC = 10$, what is the area of $\triangle ABC$?

(A) 13.9

(B) 12.9

(C) 14.9

(D) 27.8

(E) 25.8

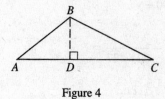

Figure 4

16. If $f(x) = 2 - |x| + x^2$, then $f(-2) =$

(A) 0

(B) 4

(C) 2

(D) -2

(E) -4

17. If $x - 1, x, x - 1$ is a geometric sequence, then $x =$

(A) $-\dfrac{1}{2}$

(B) $\dfrac{1}{2}$

(C) 2

(D) 1

(E) -1

GO ON TO THE NEXT PAGE

18. A circle with center $(-3, 4)$ is tangent to the x-axis. Which of the following is a point of intersection of the circle with the y-axis?

    (A) $(0, -4 - \sqrt{7})$

    (B) $(0, 9)$

    (C) $(0, +4 - \sqrt{7})$

    (D) $(0, 1)$

    (E) $(0, -1)$

19. In Figure 5, ray AD is the bisector of $\angle CAB$, and the measure of $\angle ACD$ is y. What must be the measure of $\angle ADC$ in order for line AB to be parallel to line CD?

    (A) $90 - y$

    (B) $90 - \dfrac{y}{2}$

    (C) $180 - \dfrac{y}{2}$

    (D) $180 - y$

    (E) $90 + y$

20. $\sqrt{108} - \dfrac{2}{3 - \sqrt{27}} =$

    (A) 11.3

    (B) 8.2

    (C) -2

    (D) 16.39

    (E) 41.57

21. If $|x|^2 - |x| - 6 = 0$, then $x =$

    (A) $\{3, 2\}$

    (B) $\{-3, 2\}$

    (C) $\{3, -3\}$

    (D) $\{\pm 3, \pm 2\}$

    (E) $\{-3, -2\}$

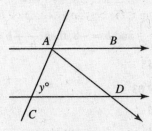

Figure 5

GO ON TO THE NEXT PAGE

22. The radius of the circle in Figure 6 is 4, and the measure of ∠AOC is 120. What is the length of chord AC?

   (A) 5
   (B) 2.83
   (C) 5.66
   (D) 8
   (E) 6.93

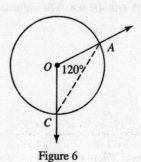

USE THIS SPACE FOR SCRATCH WORK

Figure 6

23. If $\tan x° = .727$ and $\tan(x+1)° = .754$, which of the following is the best approximation to $\tan(x+.8)°$?

   (A) .734
   (B) .745
   (C) .736
   (D) .737
   (E) .749

24. For what value of c will $2x^2 - 3x + c = 0$ have one and only one real root?

   (A) 4
   (B) 1
   (C) −4
   (D) $\dfrac{9}{8}$
   (E) 0

25. If $f(x) = x+1$ and $g(x) = x^2 - 1$, for what value(s) of x does $g(f(x)) = 0$?

   (A) 0 only
   (B) 1 and −1 only
   (C) 1 only
   (D) −2 only
   (E) 0 and −2

26. If $(a^x)^{2/3} = \dfrac{1}{a^2}$, then $x =$

   (A) −1
   (B) −2
   (C) −3
   (D) 2
   (E) 1

GO ON TO THE NEXT PAGE

27. In Figure 7, a rectangular box is inscribed in a cylinder of height 5 and with a circular base of radius 2.5 and $AB = 4$. The volume of the box is

    (A) 20
    (B) 45
    (C) 15
    (D) 30
    (E) 60

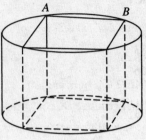

Figure 7

28. If $x^2 - 2x - 3 > 0$, then

    (A) $x > 2$
    (B) $1 < x < 3$
    (C) $-1 < x < 3$
    (D) $x > 3$ or $x < 1$
    (E) $x > 3$ or $x < -1$

29. If $f(x) = \dfrac{3x + 1}{x}$, and $f(2b) = 2f(b)$, then b is

    (A) Any real number
    (B) Any real number except 0
    (C) $-\dfrac{1}{2}$ only
    (D) No real number
    (E) 0 and $-\dfrac{1}{2}$ only

30. The points of intersection of the line $y = 3x$ and the hyperbola $y^2 - x^2 = 2$ are

    (A) $\left(\pm\dfrac{1}{4}, \pm\dfrac{3}{4} \right)$
    (B) $\left(\pm\dfrac{1}{2}, \pm\dfrac{3}{2} \right)$
    (C) $(\pm 1, \pm 3)$
    (D) $(\pm 2, \pm 6)$
    (E) $(0, 0)$

GO ON TO THE NEXT PAGE

31. In Figure 8, if the cosine of each of $\angle A$, $\angle B$, $\angle C$, and $\angle D$ is $-.5$ which of the following can be concluded?

   (A) Points A, E, and D are collinear

   (B) $\cos \angle E = \dfrac{1}{2}$

   (C) $\angle AED$ is a right angle

   (D) $\angle AED$ and $\angle EDC$ are complementary

   (E) the given information is self-contradictory

USE THIS SPACE FOR SCRATCH WORK

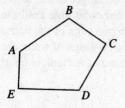

Figure 8

32. The probability that a lightbulb is defective is .05 and the probability that its socket is defective is .02. A lightbulb and socket are chosen at random. What is the probability that the bulb is good but the socket isn't?

   (A) .05

   (B) .02

   (C) .95

   (D) .98

   (E) .019

33. If, in $\triangle ABC$, $AB = 12$, $AC = 14$, and $BC = 16$, then $\cos \angle A =$

   (A) .8571

   (B) .6875

   (C) .8750

   (D) .2500

   (E) .7500

34. Which of the following statements about the values of $f(x)$ will lead to the conclusion that f does NOT define a function?

   I. There exists some a such that $f(a) = f(-a)$.

   II. There exists some a such that $f(a) = f\left(\dfrac{1}{a}\right)$.

   III. There exists some a and b such that $f(a) \neq f(b)$ but $a = b$.

   (A) I only

   (B) II only

   (C) I and II only

   (D) III only

   (E) II and III only

GO ON TO THE NEXT PAGE

35. A rectangular aquarium is $\frac{2}{3}$ filled with water and then is tilted on its side until the water level coincides with one edge of the bottom. During the tilting process, 6 quarts of water are poured out. What is the volume of the tank in quarts?

(A) 12

(B) 24

(C) 36

(D) 48

(E) 64

36. If $\log_{10}(x+4) + \log_{10}(x-4) = 1$, then $x =$

(A) -2.45

(B) 5.1

(C) 5

(D) 2.45

(E) 1.25

37. An equation for the line containing the point $(-2, 1)$ and parallel to $4x - 2y = 3$ is

(A) $y = 2x + 5$

(B) $y = 2x - 1$

(C) $y = x - 2$

(D) $y = \frac{1}{2}x$

(E) $y = 2x - 2$

38. Point O is the center of the circle in Figure 9. The measure of arc XB is $\frac{1}{3}$ the measure of arc AB, and the measure of arc YC is $\frac{1}{2}$ the measure of arc DC. If the measure of $\angle AXB$ is 140, then the measure of $\angle DYC$ is

(A) 120

(B) 140

(C) 135

(D) 145

(E) $137\frac{1}{2}$

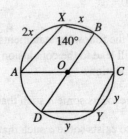

Figure 9

GO ON TO THE NEXT PAGE

39. If $f(a) = 2^a$, then $\log_2 f(a) =$

    (A) 2

    (B) $f(a)$

    (C) a

    (D) $\dfrac{1}{2^a}$

    (E) a^2

40. Which of the following is the set of all points in space that are equidistant from two given points?

    (A) A sphere

    (B) An ellipse

    (C) A parabola

    (D) A plane

    (E) A line

41. Which term in the expansion of $\left(\dfrac{1}{x} + x^2\right)$ contains no power of x?

    (A) No term

    (B) Sixth

    (C) Fifth

    (D) Third

    (E) Fourth

42. In Figure 10, both $\angle XAB$ and $\angle XYZ$ are right angles, $XB = 6$, $BY = 2$, and $AB = 4$. The ratio of $\dfrac{\text{area of } \triangle XAB}{\text{area of } \triangle XYZ}$ is

    (A) $\dfrac{3}{5}$

    (B) $\dfrac{5}{16}$

    (C) $\dfrac{9}{25}$

    (D) $\dfrac{4}{5}$

    (E) $\dfrac{3}{25}$

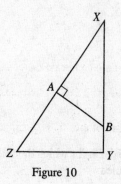

Figure 10

GO ON TO THE NEXT PAGE

43. The range of $f(x) = -\dfrac{1}{4}\sin 4x$ is

    (A) $-.25 \le y \le 0$
    (B) $-.25 \le y \le .25$
    (C) $0 \le y \le .25$
    (D) $-1 \le y \le 1$
    (E) $-4 \le y \le 4$

44. Three planes, E, F, and G, intersect so that each is perpendicular to the other two. A segment AB is positioned so that the length of its projection on the intersection of E and F is 1, on the intersection of F and G is 2, and on the intersection of E and G is 3. What is the length of AB?

    (A) 3.74
    (B) 4
    (C) 5
    (D) 6
    (E) 3.46

45. A bag contains seven marbles, three red and four green. If three marbles are drawn from the bag at random, what is the probability that all three will be red?

    (A) $\dfrac{3}{35}$
    (B) $\dfrac{3}{7}$
    (C) $\dfrac{1}{35}$
    (D) $\dfrac{3}{4}$
    (E) $\dfrac{4}{7}$

46. The values of m for which the following has no real value defined:
    $$\frac{1}{\dfrac{m^2 - m - 2}{m^2 - 4}}$$
    are

    (A) $\{-2, -1\}$
    (B) $\{-1, 2, -2\}$
    (C) $\{2, -2\}$
    (D) $\{-1, 2\}$
    (E) $\{1, -1, 2, -2\}$

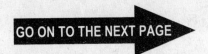
GO ON TO THE NEXT PAGE

47. If $\log_{10}(x-5) > 0$, then

    USE THIS SPACE FOR SCRATCH WORK

    (A) $x > 5$

    (B) $x > 6$

    (C) $x > 1$

    (D) $x > 0$

    (E) $x < 5$

48. If one solution for $x^3 + 2x^2 + x + 2$ is i, where $i = \sqrt{-1}$, which of the following sets contains all other solutions?

    (A) $\{-i\}$

    (B) $\{-i, 2\}$

    (C) $\{-i, -2\}$

    (D) $\{2, -2\}$

    (E) $\{2\}$

49. If $f(x) = -\sqrt{x}$ and g is the inverse of f, which of the following describes the domain of g?

    (A) $y \neq 0$

    (B) All rational numbers

    (C) All real numbers

    (D) $y \geq 0$

    (E) $y \leq 0$

50. If $0 \leq x \leq 360$ and $4\sin^2 x + 4\cos x - 1 = 0$, which of the following sets contains all values of x?

    (A) $\{30, 60\}$

    (B) $\{60, 120\}$

    (C) $\{120, -120\}$

    (D) $\{60, -60\}$

    (E) $\{120, 240\}$

STOP

IF YOU FINISH BEFORE TIME IS CALLED, YOU MAY CHECK YOUR WORK ON THIS TEST ONLY.
DO NOT WORK ON ANY OTHER TEST IN THIS BOOK.

ANSWER KEY

1. A	11. C	21. C	31. B	41. E
2. E	12. C	22. E	32. E	42. B
3. A	13. D	23. E	33. D	43. B
4. B	14. B	24. D	34. D	44. A
5. D	15. A	25. E	35. C	45. C
6. D	16. B	26. C	36. B	46. B
7. B	17. B	27. E	37. A	47. B
8. B	18. C	28. E	38. B	48. C
9. D	19. B	29. C	39. C	49. E
10. E	20. A	30. B	40. D	50. E

ANSWER EXPLANATIONS

1. (A) If $c = 3a$, then $a = \dfrac{c}{3}$ and $\dfrac{c}{3} = 3b + 5$.

$$c = 3(3b + 5) = 9b + 15$$

2. (E) Arc length, arc measure, and angle measure are all directly proportional. To see that (E) is not true, note the figure (below) showing a similar situation for which OX bisects $\angle ZOY$. $\angle ZOY = 2\angle XOY$, but if $ZY = 2XY$, then $ZX + XY = ZY$, which is impossible.

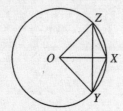

3. (A) $a = 3^2$
$$= 9$$

$b = \dfrac{1}{a}$

$$= \dfrac{1}{9}$$

$c = b^4$

$$= \left(\dfrac{1}{9}\right)^4$$

$$= \dfrac{1}{6561}$$

4. (B) If $y - 1 = 0$, then $y = 1$. Thus:

$$\dfrac{x-2}{1} = 4$$

$$x - 2 = 4$$

$$x = 6$$

5. (D)

I. $c = e$ because vertical angles are congruent.

II. $b > d$ because the intersecting lines form a triangle with b measuring an exterior angle.

III. If $a = c$ then the lines must be parallel, since a pair of corresponding angles are equal in measure.

6. (D) $AB = \sqrt{(-1-2)^2 + (2+1)^2}$
$$= \sqrt{9+9}$$
$$= \sqrt{9 \times 2}$$
$$= 3\sqrt{2}$$
$$\doteq 4.24$$

7. (B) If $x \circ y = y \circ x$, then $2(x + 2y) = 2(y + 2x)$ and $x + 2y = y + 2x$ so $y = x$.

8. (B) Let $x = $ length of a side, then

$$x^2 = 1.44$$
$$= (1.2)^2$$
$$x = 1.2$$
$$\text{Perimeter} = 4x$$
$$= 4(1.2)$$
$$= 4.8$$

9. (D) $\angle x$ is an inscribed angle and is thus $\dfrac{1}{2}$ the measure of its intercepted arc:

$$x = \dfrac{1}{2}(70 + 120) = \dfrac{1}{2}(190) = 95.$$

The angle adjacent to $\angle z$ is a secant-tangent angle and is thus $\dfrac{1}{2}$ the measure of its intercepted arc:

$$\dfrac{1}{2}(70 + 120 + 80) = \dfrac{1}{2}(270) = 135, \text{ so}$$

$$z = 45.$$

$\angle w$ and $\angle z$ are corresponding angles, so $w = 45$.

The remaining arc in the figure is:

$$360 - (70 + 120 + 80) = 90.$$

$\angle y$ has a measure equal to $\frac{1}{2}$ the difference of the measures of its intercepted arcs:

$$\frac{1}{2}(190 - 90) = 50.$$

$\angle v$ and $\angle y$ are supplementary, so $v = 130$.

Verify your answer by using your calculator to assist the additions, subtractions, and divisions.

10. (E) $\sqrt{x^2 - 6x + 9} = \sqrt{(x-3)^2} = x - 3$ only when $x - 3 \geq 0$ by definition of "$\sqrt{}$."

11. (C) I.   If a were 0, then $\frac{a}{b} = 0$.

To see why II is false, let $a = 10$ and $b = 2$.

III is true because $\dfrac{+}{+} = \dfrac{-}{-} = +$.

12. (C)
$$\frac{\dfrac{m+n}{m-1} + n}{\dfrac{m+n}{m-1} - 1} = \frac{\dfrac{m+n}{m-1} + \dfrac{n(m-1)}{m-1}}{\dfrac{m+n}{m-1} - \dfrac{m-1}{m-1}}$$

$$= \frac{\dfrac{m+n+mn-n}{m-1}}{\dfrac{m+n-m+1}{m-1}}$$

$$\frac{m+n+mn-n}{m+n-m+1} = \frac{m+mn}{n+1}$$

$$= \frac{m(1+n)}{1+n}$$

$$= m$$

13. (D) Sin $\angle A = \dfrac{y}{r}$, where r is the distance of the point (x, y) from the vertex and (x, y) is on the terminal side. The point $(-8, 15)$ is at a distance of $\sqrt{(8-0)^2 + (15-0)^2} = 17$ units from the origin so

$\sin \angle A = \dfrac{15}{17} = .8824$

14. (B) Rewrite as $\dfrac{a^2 + b^2}{b}$, substitute and calculate $\doteq -8.03$.

Alternate solution:

Rewrite as $\dfrac{a^2 + b^2}{b}$, substitute values and use your calculator to simplify.

15. (A)

$$\sin 44 = \frac{BD}{AB}$$

$$.695 = \frac{BD}{4}$$

$$2.78 = BD$$

$$\text{Area} = \frac{1}{2}(BD)(AC)$$

$$= \frac{1}{2}(2.78)(10)$$

$$\text{or, Area} = \frac{1}{2}(AB)(AC)\sin(\angle A)$$

$$= \frac{1}{2} \cdot 4 \cdot 10 \cdot (.695)$$

$$= 13.9$$

16. (B) $f(-2) = 2 - |-2| + (-2)^2 = 2 - 2 + 4 = 4$

17. (B)
$$\frac{x}{x-1} = \frac{x-1}{x}$$
$$x^2 = (x-1)^2$$
$$x^2 = x^2 - 2x + 1$$
$$0 = -2x + 1$$
$$\frac{1}{2} = x$$

18. (C)

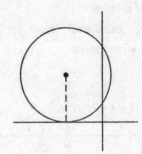

From the figure the radius is 4, so the equation of the circle is:

$$(x+3)^2 + (y-4)^2 = 4^2$$

Let $x = 0$ to find the y-intercept.

$$9 + y^2 - 8y + 16 = 16$$
$$y^2 - 8y + 9 = 0$$

By quadratic formula:

$$y = \frac{8 \pm \sqrt{28}}{2}$$
$$= \frac{8 \pm 2\sqrt{7}}{2}$$
$$= 4 \pm \sqrt{7}$$

Alternate solution:

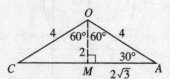 Graphing calculator: solve $y = x^2 - 8x + 9$ and check against the answer choices.

19. **(B)** For $AB \parallel CD$, $\angle ACD$ and $\angle CAB$ must be supplementary, so m $\angle CAB = 180 - y$. Thus:

$$\text{m} \angle BAD = \frac{1}{2}(180 - y) = 90 - \frac{y}{2}$$

by definition of angle bisector and m $\angle ADC =$ m $\angle BAD$, since parallel lines must have pairs of alternate interior angles equal in measure.

20. **(A)** $\sqrt{108} - \dfrac{2}{3 - \sqrt{27}} \doteq 11.3$.

At the start or any point later, enter the values and continue to a decimal answer.

21. **(C)** Let $u = |x|$; then

$$u^2 - u - 6 = 0$$
$$(u + 3)(u + 2) = 0$$
$$u = 3 \text{ or } u = -2$$

Replace u with $|x|$:

$$|x| = 3 \quad \text{or} \quad |x| = -2$$

$x = \pm 3$, but $|x| = -2$ has no solutions.

Alternate solution:

Graphing calculator: enter $y = \boxed{\text{abs}}(x^2) - \boxed{\text{abs}}(x) - 6$ and solve.

22. **(E)**

The figure shows the given triangle with a segment from O and $\perp$ to AC. M must be the midpoint of AC, so $OM = 2$, $AM = 2\sqrt{3}$, by the 30-60-90 triangle relations.

$$\therefore AC = 4\sqrt{3}$$
$$\doteq 6.9$$

23. **(E)** The necessary interpolation is shown below:

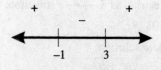

$$\frac{.8}{1.0} = \frac{d}{.027}$$

$$.8(.027) = d = .0216 \doteq .022$$

$$\tan x + .8 = .727 + .022 = .749$$

24. **(D)** The equation will have one and only one real root when the discriminant, $b^2 - 4ac$, equals 0.

$$b^2 - 4ac = 9 - 4(2)(c) = 9 - 8c.$$

If $9 - 8c = 0$, then $c = \dfrac{9}{8}$.

25. **(E)**

$$g(x) = x^2 - 1$$
$$g(f(x)) = [f(x)]^2 - 1$$
$$= [x + 1]^2 - 1$$
$$= x^2 + 2x + 1 - 1$$
$$= x^2 + 2x$$

If $x^2 + 2x = 0$, then $x(x + 2) = 0$ and $x = 0$ or -2.

26. **(C)** $(a^x)^{2/3} = a^{2x/3}$ and $\dfrac{1}{a^2} = a^{-2}$.

So, $\dfrac{2}{3}x = -2$ and $x = -2\left(\dfrac{3}{2}\right)$ giving $x = -3$.

27. **(E)** Volume of box equals the height, 5, times the area of the base, which is the rectangle shown.

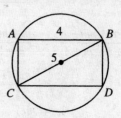

Since $AB = 4$ and $BC = 5$, then $AC = 3$ by the Pythagorean Theorem so the area is 12 and the volume is $5(12) = 60$.

28. **(E)** If $x^2 - 2x - 3 > 0$, then $(x - 3)(x + 1) > 0$, which is true when both factors are positive or when both are negative. By testing values,

$$x < -1 \text{ or } x > 3$$

Alternate solution:

Graphing calculator: enter $y = x^2 - 2x - 3$ and identify the values of x for which the graph is above the x-axis.

29. (C) $f(2b) = 2\dfrac{3(2b)+1}{2b} = \dfrac{6b+1}{2b}$

$2f(b) = 2\left(\dfrac{3b+1}{b}\right) = \dfrac{6b+2}{b}$

$\dfrac{6b+1}{2b} = \dfrac{6b+2}{b}$

$6b+1 = 12b+4 \quad (b \neq 0)$

$-3 = 6b$

$-\dfrac{1}{2} = b$

30. (B) Replace y by $3x$ in $y^2 - x^2 = 2$ to get:

$$(3x)^2 - x^2 = 2$$
$$9x^2 - x^2 = 2$$
$$8x^2 = 2$$
$$x^2 = \dfrac{1}{4}$$
$$x = \pm\dfrac{1}{2}$$
$$y = 3x$$
$$\text{so } y = \pm\dfrac{3}{2}$$

Alternate solution:

Graphing calculator: enter $y = \sqrt{2+x^2}$, $y = -\sqrt{2+x^2}$, and $y = 3x$. Graph and trace to points of intersection.

31. (B) The diagonals of a pentagon form three triangles with the sides of the pentagon, so the sum of the measures of its angles is $3(180) = 540$. If the cosine of an angle of a polygon is $-\dfrac{1}{2}$, then its measure is 120 and the four angles, $\angle A$, $\angle B$, $\angle C$, and $\angle D$, total 480, so the remaining angle is 60 with a cosine of $\dfrac{1}{2}$.

32. (E)

$P(\text{bulb is good}) \times P(\text{socket is defective})$

$= (95)(.02)$

$= .019$

33. (D) By the "Law of Cosines"

$$(BC)^2 = (AC)^2 + (AB)^2$$
$$-2(AC)(AB)\cos\angle A$$
$$(16)^2 = (14)^2 + (12)^2 - 2(14)(12)\cos\angle A$$
$$256 = 196 + 144 - 336\cos\angle A$$
$$\dfrac{256-340}{-336} = \cos\angle A$$

$.25 = \cos\angle A$

34. (D) I and II.   In a function, two points with different first coordinates $\left(\text{for example: } a, -a, \text{ or } \dfrac{1}{a}\right)$ may have the same second coordinate.

III.   If $a = b$ and $f(a) \neq f(b)$, then $(a, f(a))$ and $(b, f(b))$ are coordinates of two different points on the same vertical line.

35. (C) In the diagram below the dotted line indicates the water level. Note that the volume remaining must be half of that of the aquarium.

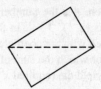

Thus, if V = the volume of the aquarium, then

$$\dfrac{2}{3}V - \dfrac{1}{2}V = 6$$
$$\dfrac{4}{6}V - \dfrac{3}{6}V = 6$$
$$\dfrac{1}{6}V = 6$$
$$V = 36$$

36. (B) $\log_{10}(x+4) + \log_{10}(x-4) = 1$

$\log_{10}(x+4)(x-4) = 1$

$\log_{10}(x^2 - 16) = 1$

$10^1 = x^2 - 16$

$26 = x^2$

$\sqrt{26} = x$

$5.2 \doteq x^2$

37. (A) In the slope-intercept form (found by solving the equation for y) the equation $4x - 2y = 3$ is $y = 2x - \dfrac{3}{2}$ so the slope is 2. The slope of any line $\parallel$ to it must also be 2. Thus the equation requested is:

$$y - 1 = 2(x+2)$$
$$= 2x + 4$$
$$y = 2x + 5$$

38. (B) m∠AOB = m∠DOC since they are vertical angles, so m arc AB = m arc DC because they are cut off by central angles having the same measure. Thus ∠AXB and ∠DYC are inscribed in arcs of equal measure in the same circle, so they in turn must be equal in measure.

39. (C) By definition $\log_b x = y$ means $b^y = x$. Thus $f(a) = 2^a$ means $\log_2 f(a) = a$.

40. (D) The set of all points in space equidistant from the points X and Y is the perpendicular bisecting plane of segment XY.

41. (E) Each term in the expansion of $(x^{-1} + x^2)^9$ is the product of some coefficient, C, and a factor that is $(x^2)^{r-1}$, where r is the number of the term, and a factor that is $(x^{-1})^{9-(r-1)}$. In this question we are not concerned with the coefficient but must find the value of r for which the sum of the exponents is 0, which will yield the required $x^0 = 1$.

$$(x^2)^{r-1} = x^{2r-2}$$
$$(x^{-1})^{9-(r-1)} = x^{-9+r-1}$$
$$= x^{r-10}$$
$$2r - 2 + r - 10 = 0$$
$$3r = 12$$
$$r = 4$$

42. (B) $\triangle XAB \sim \triangle XYZ$ by AA with the corresponding vertices indicated by the order of listing. Since the triangles are similar, the ratio of the areas is the square of the ratio of a pair of corresponding sides or

$$\left(\frac{XA}{XY}\right)^2.$$ By Pythagorean Theorem.

$$XA = 2\sqrt{5}. \qquad XY = 8.$$

$$\left(\frac{2\sqrt{5}}{8}\right)^2 = 4 \times \frac{5}{64} = \frac{5}{16} \doteq .31$$

43. (B) The range of a function of the form $y = A\sin Bx$ is determined by A, the amplitude. Since $y = \sin Bx$ varies between -1 and 1, then $y = -\frac{1}{4}\sin Bx$ varies between $-.25$ and $.25$.

44. (A) Segment AB will be the diagonal of a box with the given projection lengths equal to the lengths of the edges of the box. By repeated use of the Pythagorean Theorem we get:

$$AB = \sqrt{1^2 + 2^2 + 3^2} = \sqrt{14}$$
$$\doteq 3.74$$

45. (C) The total number of ways three marbles can be drawn from a bag of seven is the number of combinations of seven marbles taken three at a time.

$$\frac{7!}{4!3!} = 35.$$

Only one of these is the desired combination.

46. (B) The complex fraction will be undefined whenever the denominator, $\frac{(m^2 - m - 2)}{(m^2 - 4)}$, is either undefined or zero. This occurs when

$$m^2 - m - 2 = 0 \quad \text{or} \quad m^2 - 4 = 0.$$

$m^2 - m - 2 = 0$	$m^2 - 4 = 0$
$(m-2)(m+1) = 0$	$(m-2)(m+2) = 0$
$\{2, -1\}$	$\{2, -2\}$

47. (B) Log $A > 0$ for all $A > 1$. Thus $x - 5 > 1$ and $x > 6$.

Alternate solution:

Graphing calculator: graph $y = \log(x - 1)$ and trace to intercepts.

48. (C) Since the coefficients are real, any imaginary roots must come in conjugate pairs, so $-i$ is also a root and $(x + i)$, $(x - i)$ are factors.

$$(x + i)(x - i) = x^2 + 1$$

$$\begin{array}{r} x + 2 \\ x^2 + 1 \overline{\smash{)}\ x^3 + 2x^2 + x + 2} \\ \underline{x^3 \qquad\quad + x} \\ 2x^2 \qquad + 2 \\ \underline{2x^2 \qquad + 2} \\ 0 \end{array}$$

Thus $x + 2$ is the remaining factor and -2 the remaining root.

Alternate solution:

Graphing calculator: graph $y = x^3 + 2x^2 + x + 2$ and solve.

49. (E) If f and g are inverses, the domain of g is the range of f that is the set of all $y \le 0$.

Alternate solution:

Graphing calculator: in parametric mode, with $t > 0$, graph $y = t$, $x = \sqrt{t}$, and determine domain from graph.

50. (E) $4\sin^2 x + 4\cos^2 x - 1 = 0$. Since $\sin^2 x + \cos^2 x = 1$, we replace $\sin^2 x$ with $1 - \cos^2 x$ to get:

$$4(1 - \cos^2 x) + 4\cos x - 1 = 0$$
$$-4\cos^2 x + 4\cos x + 3 = 0$$
$$4\cos x^2 - 4\cos x - 3 = 0$$
$$(2\cos x - 3)(2\cos x + 1) = 0$$

$$\cos x = \frac{3}{2} \text{ or } \cos x = -\frac{1}{2}$$

But $\cos x = \frac{3}{2}$ has no root since $\cos x$ cannot be greater than 1. $\cos x = \frac{1}{2}$ is true for $120°$ and $240°$. Although $\{120°, -120°\}$ are solutions, (C) is not correct because $-120°$ is not between 0 and $360°$.

By graphing calculator, enter $y = 4\sin^2 x + 4\cos x - 1 = 0$. Use the "solve" feature. Test all solutions between 0 and 360.

SELF-EVALUATION CHART FOR MODEL TEST 2

SUBJECT AREA	QUESTIONS ANSWERED CORRECTLY	NUMBER OF CORRECT ANSWERS

Algebra
(14 questions)

1	3	4	7	10	11	12	14	20	21	24	26	28	46

_____

Plane geometry
(8 questions)

2	5	8	9	19	22	38	42

_____

Solid geometry
(4 questions)

27	35	40	44

_____

Coordinate geometry
(5 questions)

6	13	18	30	37

_____

Trigonometry
(6 questions)

15	23	31	33	43	50

_____

Functions
(7 questions)

16	25	29	34	36	39	49

_____

Miscellaneous
(6 questions)

17	32	41	45	47	48

_____

Total number of correct answers _____

Total number of incorrect answers _____

Total score = total number of correct answers _____

minus $\frac{1}{4}$ number of incorrect answers − _____

_____

(Reminder: Answers left blank are not counted as correct or incorrect)

Raw score = (number correct) $-\frac{1}{4}$ (number incorrect)

To evaluate your performance, compare your raw score with the table below.

Evaluate Your Performance
Model Test 2

Excellent	760–800	46–50
Very Good	700–750	40–45
Good	610–690	32–39
Above Average	560–600	26–31
Average	500–550	18–25
Below Average	270–490	17 or less

ANSWER SHEET FOR MODEL TEST 3

Determine the correct answer for each question. Then, using a No. 2 pencil, blacken completely the oval containing the letter of your choice.

1. Ⓐ Ⓑ Ⓒ Ⓓ Ⓔ   18. Ⓐ Ⓑ Ⓒ Ⓓ Ⓔ   35. Ⓐ Ⓑ Ⓒ Ⓓ Ⓔ

2. Ⓐ Ⓑ Ⓒ Ⓓ Ⓔ   19. Ⓐ Ⓑ Ⓒ Ⓓ Ⓔ   36. Ⓐ Ⓑ Ⓒ Ⓓ Ⓔ

3. Ⓐ Ⓑ Ⓒ Ⓓ Ⓔ   20. Ⓐ Ⓑ Ⓒ Ⓓ Ⓔ   37. Ⓐ Ⓑ Ⓒ Ⓓ Ⓔ

4. Ⓐ Ⓑ Ⓒ Ⓓ Ⓔ   21. Ⓐ Ⓑ Ⓒ Ⓓ Ⓔ   38. Ⓐ Ⓑ Ⓒ Ⓓ Ⓔ

5. Ⓐ Ⓑ Ⓒ Ⓓ Ⓔ   22. Ⓐ Ⓑ Ⓒ Ⓓ Ⓔ   39. Ⓐ Ⓑ Ⓒ Ⓓ Ⓔ

6. Ⓐ Ⓑ Ⓒ Ⓓ Ⓔ   23. Ⓐ Ⓑ Ⓒ Ⓓ Ⓔ   40. Ⓐ Ⓑ Ⓒ Ⓓ Ⓔ

7. Ⓐ Ⓑ Ⓒ Ⓓ Ⓔ   24. Ⓐ Ⓑ Ⓒ Ⓓ Ⓔ   41. Ⓐ Ⓑ Ⓒ Ⓓ Ⓔ

8. Ⓐ Ⓑ Ⓒ Ⓓ Ⓔ   25. Ⓐ Ⓑ Ⓒ Ⓓ Ⓔ   42. Ⓐ Ⓑ Ⓒ Ⓓ Ⓔ

9. Ⓐ Ⓑ Ⓒ Ⓓ Ⓔ   26. Ⓐ Ⓑ Ⓒ Ⓓ Ⓔ   43. Ⓐ Ⓑ Ⓒ Ⓓ Ⓔ

10. Ⓐ Ⓑ Ⓒ Ⓓ Ⓔ   27. Ⓐ Ⓑ Ⓒ Ⓓ Ⓔ   44. Ⓐ Ⓑ Ⓒ Ⓓ Ⓔ

11. Ⓐ Ⓑ Ⓒ Ⓓ Ⓔ   28. Ⓐ Ⓑ Ⓒ Ⓓ Ⓔ   45. Ⓐ Ⓑ Ⓒ Ⓓ Ⓔ

12. Ⓐ Ⓑ Ⓒ Ⓓ Ⓔ   29. Ⓐ Ⓑ Ⓒ Ⓓ Ⓔ   46. Ⓐ Ⓑ Ⓒ Ⓓ Ⓔ

13. Ⓐ Ⓑ Ⓒ Ⓓ Ⓔ   30. Ⓐ Ⓑ Ⓒ Ⓓ Ⓔ   47. Ⓐ Ⓑ Ⓒ Ⓓ Ⓔ

14. Ⓐ Ⓑ Ⓒ Ⓓ Ⓔ   31. Ⓐ Ⓑ Ⓒ Ⓓ Ⓔ   48. Ⓐ Ⓑ Ⓒ Ⓓ Ⓔ

15. Ⓐ Ⓑ Ⓒ Ⓓ Ⓔ   32. Ⓐ Ⓑ Ⓒ Ⓓ Ⓔ   49. Ⓐ Ⓑ Ⓒ Ⓓ Ⓔ

16. Ⓐ Ⓑ Ⓒ Ⓓ Ⓔ   33. Ⓐ Ⓑ Ⓒ Ⓓ Ⓔ   50. Ⓐ Ⓑ Ⓒ Ⓓ Ⓔ

17. Ⓐ Ⓑ Ⓒ Ⓓ Ⓔ   34. Ⓐ Ⓑ Ⓒ Ⓓ Ⓔ

Model Test Score Conversion Table

Raw Score	Scaled Score	Raw Score	Scaled Score	Raw Score	Scaled Score	Raw Score	Scaled Score
50	800	34	630	18	500	2	370
49	790	33	620	17	490	1	360
48	780	32	610	16	480	0	360
47	770	31	600	15	480	−1	350
46	760	30	590	14	470	−2	340
45	750	29	580	13	460	−3	330
44	740	28	580	12	450	−4	330
43	730	27	570	11	440	−5	320
42	720	26	560	10	440	−6	310
41	710	25	550	9	430	−7	300
40	700	24	540	8	420	−8	300
39	690	23	540	7	410	−9	290
38	680	22	530	6	400	−10	280
37	660	21	520	5	390	−11	270
36	650	20	510	4	390	−12	270
35	640	19	510	3	380		

MODEL TEST 3

Directions: For each of the 50 multiple-choice test questions, select the BEST answer among the five choices given. When the exact numerical value is not one of the choices, select the best approximation to the exact value. Mark your choice on the answer sheet by filling in the corresponding oval.

Notes:

1. Some questions (but not all) will require the use of at least a scientific calculator. Programmable and graphing calculators are also permitted. Calculator questions are not marked as such, so you will have to decide whether or not to use one on each question.

2. All angle measures are in degrees. Set your calculator to degree mode.

3. Some problems are accompanied by figures, which provide information useful in solving the problem. Figures are drawn accurately unless marked "Figure not drawn to scale." All figures lie in a plane unless the diagram clearly shows otherwise.

4. Except when stated otherwise, the domain of a function f is the set of real number values of x for which $f(x)$ is a real number.

5. Reference information consisting of volume and surface area formulas that may be useful in answering some questions on this test can be found below:

REFERENCE INFORMATION

- Sphere with radius r.   Volume: $V = \frac{4}{3}\pi r^3$ Surface Area: $S = 4\pi r^2$
- Right circular cone with radius r and height h.   Volume: $V = \frac{1}{3}\pi r^2 h$
- Right circular cone with circumference of base c and slant height L.
  Lateral Area: $S = \frac{1}{2}cL$
- Pyramid with base area B and height h.   Volume: $V = \frac{1}{3}Bh$

1. Which of the following is the simplified form of $x - [2x - (3 - x)]$?

   (A) x

   (B) 3

   (C) $3 - 2x$

   (D) $2x - 3$

   (E) $4x + 3$

2. If $a - b > 0$, which of the following must equal $|a - b|$?

   I. $a - b$

   II. $-(a - b)$

   III. $|b - a|$

   (A) III only

   (B) I and III only

   (C) II and III only

   (D) I and II only

   (E) I, II, and III

3. $\sqrt{\dfrac{2}{3}}\sqrt{\dfrac{15}{4}} =$

   (A) $\dfrac{\sqrt{30}}{6}$

   (B) $\dfrac{\sqrt{10}}{2}$

   (C) $\sqrt{30}$

   (D) $\sqrt{5}$

   (E) $\dfrac{\sqrt{10}}{3}$

4. If $x - y = 0$, then each of the following is equal to xy EXCEPT

   (A) yx

   (B) $-y^2$

   (C) $(-x)(-y)$

   (D) x^2

   (E) y^2

GO ON TO THE NEXT PAGE

5. If $x < -x$, then

(A) $x > 0$

(B) $x < 0$

(C) $x = 0$

(D) $\dfrac{1}{x} > 0$

(E) $x^2 < 0$

USE THIS SPACE FOR SCRATCH WORK

6. The first and last terms of a perfect square trinomial are $36x^2$ and $4y^2z^2$. Which of the following could be the middle term?

(A) $24xyz$

(B) $2xyz$

(C) $12x^2y^2z^2$

(D) $12xyz$

(E) $24x^2y^2z^2$

7. What number of pennies is equivalent to $4x$ nickels plus $2x$ dimes?

(A) $6x$

(B) $8x^2$

(C) $15x$

(D) $40x$

(E) $30x$

8. If $x - 2y - z = 2$, $x - y + 2z = 9$ and $2x + y + z = 3$, then $z =$

(A) -1

(B) 0

(C) 1

(D) 2

(E) 3

GO ON TO THE NEXT PAGE

9. Which of the following is the reciprocal of $\dfrac{a}{b} + \dfrac{b}{a}$?

(A) $\dfrac{ab}{a+b}$

(B) $\dfrac{b}{a} + \dfrac{a}{b}$

(C) $ab^{-1} + ba^{-1}$

(D) $\dfrac{1}{a^2 + b^2}$

(E) $\dfrac{ab}{a^2 + b^2}$

10. Which of the following can never be zero, if x is a real number?

(A) $x^2 - 1$

(B) $|x|$

(C) $\dfrac{x}{4}$

(D) $x^3 + 1$

(E) $2x^2 + 2$

11. If the diagonal of a square is 20, the length of a side is

(A) 21.21

(B) 1.41

(C) 7.07

(D) 14.14

(E) 28.28

12. If $f(x) = 3x^2 + kx - 2$ and $f(-2) = 2$, then $k =$

(A) 1

(B) 2

(C) 3

(D) 4

(E) 5

13. Which of the following is the completely factored form of $5x^4 - 20$ in the real number system?

(A) $5(x^4 - 4)$

(B) $5(x^2 - 2)(x^2 + 2)$

(C) $(x^2 - 2)(5x + 10)$

(D) $5(x - \sqrt{2})(x + \sqrt{2})(x^2 + 2)$

(E) $(x - \sqrt{2})(x + \sqrt{2})(5x + 10)$

GO ON TO THE NEXT PAGE

14. If the sides of a right triangle have lengths of $x - 7$, x, and $x + 1$, then $x =$

    (A) $\{1, 7\}$

    (B) $\{7, -1\}$

    (C) $\{7, 4\}$

    (D) $\{7, 12\}$

    (E) $\{4, 12\}$

15. Which of the following must be true for all real numbers x, y, and z?

    I. $x(y + z) = xy + xz$

    II. $x(y + z) = x(z + y)$

    III. $x(y + z) = (y + z)x$

    (A) I and II only

    (B) I and III only

    (C) II and III only

    (D) I, II, and III

    (E) None

16. If $\dfrac{3a}{a-1} = 1 + \dfrac{2a}{a+1}$ then $a =$

    (A) $\{1, -1\}$

    (B) $\left\{-\dfrac{1}{5}, 1, -1\right\}$

    (C) $\left\{-\dfrac{1}{5}\right\}$

    (D) $\{-5\}$

    (E) $\left\{-\dfrac{1}{5}, 0\right\}$

17. What is the greatest integer x for which $-6x - 1 > 12$?

    (A) -2

    (B) -3

    (C) 3

    (D) 2

    (E) -1

USE THIS SPACE FOR SCRATCH WORK

GO ON TO THE NEXT PAGE

18. The sum of two numbers is 21, and the difference of their squares is 63. The numbers are

(A) $\{10,11\}$

(B) $\{8,13\}$

(C) $\{9,12\}$

(D) $\{14,7\}$

(E) $\{6,15\}$

19. If $(a+1)(2-a) < 0$, then

(A) $-2 < a < 1$

(B) $a < -2$ or $a > 1$

(C) $a < -2$ or $a < 1$

(D) $-1 < a < 2$

(E) $a > 2$ or $a < -1$

20. If a student's first two test grades are 100 and 91, what grade must she make on her third test for the average of the three to be 90?

(A) 79

(B) 78

(C) 77

(D) 76

(E) 75

21. The volume of Cube A is three times the volume of Cube B. If the sum of the areas of all of the faces of Cube B is 18, then the volume of Cube A is

(A) $\sqrt{3}$

(B) 3

(C) $3\sqrt{3}$

(D) 9

(E) $9\sqrt{3}$

22. If $f(x) = x^2 + 3x - 4$, then $f(x+1) =$

(A) $x^2 + 3x - 3$

(B) $x(x+5)$

(C) $x^2 + 5x - 3$

(D) $x^2 + 3x - 1$

(E) $3x + 1$

USE THIS SPACE FOR SCRATCH WORK

GO ON TO THE NEXT PAGE

23. The ratio of the length of a rectangle to its width is 5 to 4. If the perimeter of the rectangle is 36, the length is

(A) 10
(B) 3
(C) 4
(D) 5
(E) 6

24. If $P = (4,1)$, $O = (0,0)$ and $Q = (0,-2)$, then $\sin \angle POQ =$

(A) .75
(B) $-.8$
(C) $-.75$
(D) .8
(E) .97

25. Given that $\angle A$ in Figure 1 is a right angle and $AB = AC$, which of the following constructions will yield the bisector of $\angle A$?

  I. Construct a perpendicular from A to segment BC.
 II. Construct a line containing any two points equidistant from B and C.
III. Construct a line containing the midpoint of BC and any point equidistant from all three vertices.

(A) I only
(B) II only
(C) III only
(D) I and II only
(E) II and III only

26. Which of the following is equal to $\tan \theta + \cot \theta$?

(A) $\dfrac{1}{\cot \theta + \tan \theta}$

(B) $\dfrac{\sin \theta + \cos \theta}{(\sin \theta)(\cos \theta)}$

(C) $\tan^2 \theta + 1$

(D) $(\sec \theta)(\csc \theta)$

(E) $\sec^2 \theta$

USE THIS SPACE FOR SCRATCH WORK

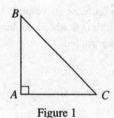

Figure 1

GO ON TO THE NEXT PAGE

27. In Figure 2, $BC \parallel AD, CE \perp AD, CF = FE, AF = 8$, $FD = 2, BC = 6$. The area of pentagon $ABCDE$ is

   (A) 24

   (B) 30

   (C) 36

   (D) 52

   (E) 64

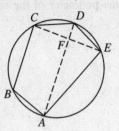

Figure 2

28. Which of the following is a quadratic equation with roots of $-\dfrac{3}{4}$ and $\dfrac{1}{2}$?

   (A) $8x^2 + 5x - 3 = 0$

   (B) $8x^2 - 5x - 3 = 0$

   (C) $8x^2 + 5x + 3 = 0$

   (D) $8x^2 - 2x - 3 = 0$

   (E) $8x^2 + 2x - 3 = 0$

29. What is the increase in volume V of a rectangular box if its width is doubled, its length is tripled, and its height quadrupled?

   (A) $23V$

   (B) $8V$

   (C) $9V$

   (D) $16V$

   (E) $12V$

30. If $f(x) = 4^{-x}$, then $f\left(\dfrac{a}{2}\right) =$

   (A) 2

   (B) 1

   (C) $2^{1/a}$

   (D) $\dfrac{1}{2^a}$

   (E) 2^a

31. $\triangle BCD$ in Figure 3 is equilateral with $BC = 4$. AE is perpendicular to plane F. $AE = 4$. The volume of the pyramid is

   (A) 48

   (B) 5.33

   (C) 27.71

   (D) 16

   (E) 9.24

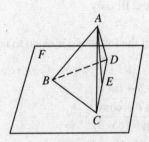

Figure 3

GO ON TO THE NEXT PAGE

32. If $6a - 2$, $3a$ and $a + 2$ are in arithmetic progression, then $a =$

    (A) 0
    (B) 1
    (C) 2
    (D) 3
    (E) 4

33. Each of the following sets of lines will determine a plane EXCEPT

    (A) a pair of parallel lines
    (B) a pair of perpendicular lines
    (C) two lines perpendicular to the same plane
    (D) any two nonintersecting lines
    (E) any two intersecting lines

34. What is the range of the function defined by $y = \dfrac{|x|}{x}$?

    (A) $y > 0$
    (B) $\{1, -1\}$
    (C) $y < 0$
    (D) All real numbers except zero
    (E) No real numbers

35. If the sum of the measures of the angles of a polygon is 1440, how many sides does the polygon have?

    (A) 14
    (B) 8
    (C) 12
    (D) 10
    (E) 16

36. Which of the following has the greatest y-intercept?

    (A) $x + 2y = 3$
    (B) $2x + 3y = 4$
    (C) $3x + 4y = 5$
    (D) $4x + 5y = 6$
    (E) $5x + 6y = 7$

GO ON TO THE NEXT PAGE

37. In Figure 4, $DF \parallel AB$, $BC \perp AB$, $BC = 5$, $BG = 4$, $BA = 12$, $DA = 3$. $CE =$

(A) 5.44

(B) .54

(C) 1.09

(D) .42

(E) 4.93

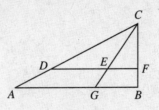

Figure 4

38. The axis of symmetry of $y = -3x^2 + 12x - 9$ is

(A) $x = 3$

(B) $x = -3$

(C) $x = 6$

(D) $x = -2$

(E) $x = 2$

39. If $z = 7 - 24i$, then $|z| =$

(A) 5

(B) 17

(C) 31

(D) 168

(E) 25

40. The expression $\dfrac{a^{-1} - b^{-1}}{a^{-2} - b^{-2}} =$

(A) $\dfrac{b - a}{ab}$

(B) $\dfrac{b + a}{ab}$

(C) $\dfrac{ab}{b + a}$

(D) $\dfrac{a^2 - b^2}{a - b}$

(E) $a - b$

41. The radian measure of an angle of $16°$ is

(A) .0889

(B) 50.27

(C) .2793

(D) 35.34

(E) 11.25

GO ON TO THE NEXT PAGE

42. For what real values of x and y is the following true?

$$x - y + 2i = 6 + (x + y)i$$

(A) $(4, -2)$

(B) $(1, 2)$

(C) $(2, 4)$

(D) $(3, 1)$

(E) $(3, 2)$

43. If $x > 0$ and $\log_{3x} 27 = 1$, then $x =$

(A) 9

(B) $-\dfrac{1}{3}$

(C) -3

(D) $\dfrac{1}{3}$

(E) 3

44. Which of the following is a point in the intersection of $x^2 + y^2 < 4$ and $x - 3y < -3$?

(A) $(0, 1)$

(B) $(1, -1)$

(C) $(1, 0)$

(D) $(-1, 1)$

(E) $(0, 0)$

45. If n is the number of any term, then the nth term of the geometric sequence $2\sqrt{2}, 8, 16\sqrt{2}, \ldots$ is

(A) $n\sqrt{2}$

(B) $(n\sqrt{2})^2$

(C) $(2\sqrt{2})^n$

(D) $(2\sqrt{2})^{n+1}$

(E) $(2\sqrt{2})^{n-1}$

46. In how many different ways can the letters of the word "WINDOW" be arranged?

(A) 720

(B) 360

(C) 180

(D) 90

(E) 45

GO ON TO THE NEXT PAGE

47. Which of the following is a point of intersection of the graphs of $y = \frac{1}{2} \sin 2x$ and $y = \frac{1}{2}$?

(A) $\left(45°, \frac{1}{2}\right)$

(B) $\left(60°, \frac{1}{2}\right)$

(C) $\left(90°, \frac{1}{2}\right)$

(D) $\left(180°, \frac{1}{2}\right)$

(E) $\left(360°, \frac{1}{2}\right)$

48. The graph of $xy = 0$ is

(A) a point

(B) a line

(C) a pair of intersecting lines

(D) a pair of parallel lines

(E) a hyperbola

49. If 40 percent of a 20-gallon solution is alcohol, how many QUARTS of water must be added to make a new solution that is 25 percent alcohol?

(A) 60

(B) 48

(C) 36

(D) 24

(E) 12

50. If $y^2 - 9x^2 = 25$, then the maximum negative value of y is

(A) -25

(B) -1

(C) -5

(D) $-\frac{5}{3}$

(E) The maximum negative value cannot be determined

USE THIS SPACE FOR SCRATCH WORK

STOP
IF YOU FINISH BEFORE TIME IS CALLED, YOU MAY CHECK YOUR WORK ON THIS TEST ONLY.
DO NOT WORK ON ANY OTHER TEST IN THIS BOOK.

ANSWER KEY

1. C	11. D	21. E	31. E	41. C
2. B	12. D	22. B	32. A	42. A
3. B	13. D	23. A	33. D	43. A
4. B	14. E	24. E	34. B	44. D
5. B	15. D	25. D	35. D	45. C
6. A	16. C	26. D	36. A	46. B
7. D	17. B	27. D	37. E	47. A
8. E	18. C	28. E	38. E	48. C
9. E	19. E	29. A	39. E	49. B
10. E	20. A	30. D	40. C	50. C

ANSWER EXPLANATIONS

1. (C)
$$\begin{aligned} x - [2x - (3 - x)] &= x - [2x - 3 + x] \\ &= x - 2x + 3 - x \\ &= -2x + 3 \\ &= 3 - 2x \end{aligned}$$

2. (B) Trying $a = 5$ and $b = 3$ will help you see that I and III are true while II is false.

   I. $|5 - 3| = 5 - 3 = 2$
   II. $-(5 - 3) = -2$
   III. $|3 - 5| = |-2| = 2$

3. (B)
$$\begin{aligned} \sqrt{\frac{2}{3}}\sqrt{\frac{15}{4}} &= \sqrt{\frac{2 \cdot 15}{3 \cdot 4}} \\ &= \sqrt{\frac{2 \cdot 5}{4}} \\ &= \frac{\sqrt{10}}{\sqrt{4}} \\ &= \frac{\sqrt{10}}{2} \end{aligned}$$

🖩 If you forget your radical rules, convert to decimals and check the answer choices with your calculator.

4. (B) If $x - y = 0$ then $x = y$. Thus $xy = y^2$ when x is replaced by y, and $xy = x^2$ when y is replaced by x. Each answer except $-y^2$ simplifies to either x^2 or y^2.

5. (B) If $x < -x$, then $0 < -2x$.
$$-\frac{1}{2} \cdot 0 > -\frac{1}{2}(-2x)$$
$$0 > x$$

6. (A) The perfect square trinomial is the square of a binomial. The first term of the trinomial is thus the square of the first term of the binomial and the last term of the trinomial is the square of the last term of the binomial. Thus the trinomial in question is either
$$(6x + 2yz)^2 = 36x^2 + 24xyz + 4y^2z^2$$
or
$$(6x - 2yz)^2 = 36x^2 - 24xyz + 4y^2z^2$$

7. (D) Each nickel is equivalent to 5 pennies, so $4x$ nickels equals $4x(5) = 20x$ pennies. Each dime is equivalent to 10 pennies, so $2x$ dimes equals $2x(10) = 20x$ pennies; $20x + 20x = 40x$.

8. (E) In the following system:

   (1) $\qquad x - 2y - z = 2$
   (2) $\qquad x - y + 2z = 9$
   (3) $\qquad 2x + y + z = 3$

   if we subtract equation (2) from equation (1) to get a new equation (2)′ and then subtract twice equation (1) from equation (3) to get a new equation (3)′, we get the following equivalent system:

   (1) $\qquad x - 2y - z = 2$
   (2)′ $\qquad -y - 3z = -7$
   (3)′ $\qquad 5y + 3z = -1$

   In this new system we will add five times equation (2)′ to equation (3)′ to get a new equation (3)″:

   (3)″ $\qquad -12z = -36.$

   Thus $z = 3$.

9. (E)
$$\frac{1}{\dfrac{a}{b} + \dfrac{b}{a}} = \frac{1}{\dfrac{a^2}{ab} + \dfrac{b^2}{ab}} = \frac{1}{\dfrac{a^2 + b^2}{ab}} = \frac{ab}{a^2 + b^2}$$

10. (E) If $2x^2 + 2 = 0$, then $2x^2 = -2$ and $x^2 = -1$. No root for this equation exists in the real number system.

11. (D) Let $s =$ one side; then the diagonal forms a right triangle with two adjacent sides so that:
$$\begin{aligned} s^2 + s^2 &= (20)^2 \\ 2s^2 &= 400 \\ s^2 &= 200 \\ s &= \sqrt{200} \\ &\doteq 14.14 \end{aligned}$$

12. (D) $f(-2) = 3(-2)^2 + k(-2) - 2$
$$= 12 - 2k - 2$$
$$= 10 - 2k$$
If $f(-2) = 2$, then
$$2 = 10 - 2k$$
$$2k = 8$$
$$k = 4$$

13. (D) $5x^4 - 20 = 5(x^4 - 4)$
$$= 5(x^2 - 2)(x^2 + 2)$$
$$= 5(x - \sqrt{2})(x + \sqrt{2})(x^2 + 2)$$

14. (E) x must be positive for these to be sides of a triangle, so $x + 1$ is the longest side and:
$$(x+1)^2 = (x-7)^2 + x^2$$
$$x^2 + 2x + 1 = x^2 - 14x + 49 + x^2$$
$$0 = x^2 - 16x + 48$$
$$= (x - 4)(x - 12)$$

The values of x are $\{4, 12\}$, but 4 makes $x - 7 = -3$.

15. (D) Each statement follows from a fundamental law of real number operations.

  I. Distributive law
  II. Commutative law of addition
  III. Commutative law of multiplication

16. (C) $\dfrac{3a}{a-1} = 1 + \dfrac{2a}{a+1}$; LCD $= (a-1)(a+1)$.

Therefore:
$$\frac{3a(a+1)}{(a-1)(a+1)}$$
$$= \frac{(a-1)(a+1)}{(a-1)(a+1)} + \frac{(a-1)(2a)}{(a-1)(a+1)}$$

Multiply both sides by the LCD to get:
$$3a(a+1) = (a-1)(a+1) + (a-1)(2a)$$
$$3a + 3a = a^2 - 1 + 2a^2 - 2a$$
$$3a = -1 - 2a$$
$$5a = -1$$
$$a = -\frac{1}{5}$$

Alternate solution:

Graphing calculator: enter $y = 1 + (2x)/(x+1) - (3x)/(x-1)$ and solve.

17. (B) If $-6x - 1 > 12$, then
$$-6x > 13$$
$$x < -\frac{13}{6}$$
$$x < -2.17$$

The greatest integer less than -2.17 is -3.

18. (C) Let $x =$ the smaller; then $21 - x$ is the larger and
$$(21 - x)^2 - x^2 = 63$$
$$441 - 42x + x^2 - x^2 = 63$$
$$-42x = 63 - 441$$
$$-42x = -378$$
$$x = 9$$
$$21 - x = 12$$

19. (E) If $(a+1)(2-a) < 0$, then one factor is negative while the other is positive, so:
$$(a + 1 < 0 \text{ and } 2 - a > 0)$$
$$\text{or } (a + 1 > 0 \text{ and } 2 - a < 0)$$
$$(a < -1 \text{ and } 2 > a) \text{ or } (a > -1 \text{ and } 2 < a)$$
$$(a < -1) \text{ or } (a > 2)$$

Alternate solution:

Graphing calculator: graph $y = (x+1)(2-x)$ and identify the points for which the graph is below the x-axis.

20. (A) Let x be the third grade; then:
$$\frac{100 + 91 + x}{3} = 90$$
$$191 + x = 270$$
$$x = 79$$

21. (E) Each face of Cube B is a square of side b with an area of b^2. The total surface is composed of six such faces.
$$6b^2 = 18$$
$$b^2 = 3$$
$$b = \sqrt{3}$$

The volume of Cube B is $(\sqrt{3})^3 = 3\sqrt{3}$, so the volume of Cube A is $3(3\sqrt{3}) = 9\sqrt{3}$.

22. (B) $f(x+1) = (x+1)^2 + 3(x+1) - 4$
$$= x^2 + 2x + 1 + 3x + 3 - 4$$
$$= x^2 + 5x$$
$$= x(x + 5)$$

23. (A) If the ratio is 5 to 4, then the length is $5x$ and the width is $4x$, where x is the common factor (if any) removed in the reduction to $\dfrac{5}{4}$. The perimeter contains two lengths and two widths, so:

$$2(5x) + 2(4x) = 36$$
$$18x = 36$$
$$x = 2$$

Thus the length is $5(2) = 10$ and the width is $4(2) = 8$.

24. (E) The graph of the points is shown at right. To find the sine of the angle, put the angle in standard position by choosing segment OQ to lie on the positive ray of the x-axis and adjusting the coordinates (you can visualize this by turning the page so that OQ of the upper diagram is to your right).

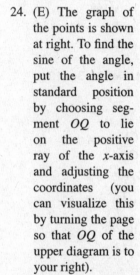

The sine of $\angle POQ$ is the y-coordinate of P, 4, over the distance of P to the origin, $\sqrt{17}$.

$$\boxed{\blacksquare}\quad \sin \angle POQ = \frac{4}{\sqrt{17}} \doteq .97$$

25. (D) The midpoint of BC is the only point equidistant from the vertices of the right triangle. Thus only one point is specified by III, and this point will not determine a line.

26. (D) $\tan \theta + \cot \theta = \dfrac{\sin \theta}{\cos \theta} + \dfrac{\cos \theta}{\sin \theta}$

$$= \frac{\sin^2 \theta}{\cos \theta \sin \theta} + \frac{\cos^2 \theta}{\cos \theta \sin \theta}$$

$$= \frac{\sin^2 \theta + \cos^2 \theta}{\cos \theta \sin \theta}$$

$$= \frac{1}{\cos \theta \sin \theta}$$

$$= \frac{1}{\cos \theta} \cdot \frac{1}{\sin \theta}$$

$$= \sec \theta \csc \theta$$

Alternate solution:

$\boxed{\blacksquare}$ Graphing calculator: graph $y = \tan x + \cot x$ and compare with the graph of each choice.

27. (D) $CF = EF$ and $(CF)(FE) = (AF)(FD)$, so:

$$(CF)^2 = 8 \cdot 2 = 16$$
$$CF = 4 = FE$$

$$\text{Area } \triangle CFD = \frac{1}{2}(CF)(FD) = \frac{1}{2}(4)(2) = 4$$

$$\text{Area } \triangle DFE = \frac{1}{2}(FE)(FD) = \frac{1}{2}(4)(2) = 4$$

$$\text{Area } \triangle AFE = \frac{1}{2}(FE)(AF) = \frac{1}{2}(4)(8) = 16$$

$$\text{Area trapezoid } AFCB = \frac{1}{2}(FC)(BC + AF)$$

$$= \frac{1}{2}(4)(6 + 8) = 28$$

Total area $= 52$

or, alternative method:

$$\text{Area trapezoid } ABCD = \frac{1}{2}(FC)(BC + AD)$$

$$= \frac{1}{2}(4)(6 + 10) = 32$$

$$\text{Area } \triangle AED = \frac{1}{2}(AD)(FE) = \frac{1}{2}(10)(4) = 20$$

$\therefore$ Total area $= 32 + 20 = 52$

28. (E) If the roots are $-\dfrac{3}{4}$ and $\dfrac{1}{2}$, then the factors are $\left(x + \dfrac{3}{4}\right)$ and $\left(x - \dfrac{1}{2}\right)$.

$$\left(x + \frac{3}{4}\right)\left(x - \frac{1}{2}\right) = x^2 + \frac{3}{4}x - \frac{1}{2}x - \frac{3}{8}$$

$$= x^2 + \frac{1}{4}x - \frac{3}{8}$$

An equation with these roots then is:

$$x^2 + \frac{1}{4}x - \frac{3}{8} = 0$$

Multiply both sides by 8 and you will get:

$$8x^2 + 2x - 3 = 0$$

29. (A) Let $V = lwh$ be the original volume. Then the new volume is

$$V' = (2w)(3l)(4h) = 24lwh.$$

$$V' - V = 24lwh - lwh = 23lwh.$$

30. (D) $f\left(\dfrac{a}{2}\right) = 4^{-a/2} = (2^2)^{-a/2} = 2^{-a} = \dfrac{1}{2^a}$

31. (E) Pyramid volume $= \frac{1}{3}$(area $\triangle BCD$)$\times$ (height of pyramid). Using the 30-60-90 triangle relations on $\triangle BDC$, we get the figure below.

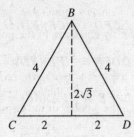

So, area $\triangle BCD = \frac{1}{2}(2\sqrt{3})(4) = 4\sqrt{3}$. Height of pyramid is $AE = 4$.

$$V = \frac{1}{3}(4\sqrt{3})(4) \doteq 9.24$$

32. (A) If the progression is arithmetic, then:

$$3a - (6a - 2) = (a + 2) - 3a$$
$$-3a + 2 = -2a + 2$$
$$0 = a$$

33. (D) No plane will contain both L_1 and L_2 below:

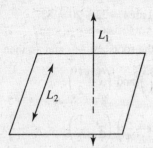

34. (B) If $x > 0$, then $|x| = x$ and $y = \frac{|x|}{x} = \frac{x}{x} = 1$.

If $x < 0$, then $|x| = -x$ and $y = \frac{|x|}{x} = \frac{-x}{x} = -1$.

If $x = 0$, then $|x|$ is undefined.

Alternate solution:

Graphing calculator: graph $y = (abs(x))/x$. The graph breaks at 0, so check $x = 0$ and you will recognize that it is undefined.

35. (D) If n is the number of sides of a polygon, then $(n - 2)180$ is the sum of the measures of its angles.

$$(n - 2)180 = 1440$$
$$n - 2 = 8$$
$$n = 10$$

36. (A) To find the y-intercept, let $x = 0$ and solve for y.

37. (E) By the Pythagorean Theorem:

$$(GC)^2 = (BC)^2 + (GB)^2$$
$$= 25 + 16 = 41$$
$$GC = \sqrt{41}$$
$$(AC)^2 = (BC)^2 + (AB)^2$$
$$= 24 + 144$$
$$= 169$$
$$AC = \sqrt{169}$$
$$= 13$$

$$DC = AC - AD = 13 - 3 = 10$$

$\triangle DEC \sim \triangle AGC$ so:

$$\frac{DC}{AC} = \frac{CE}{GC}$$
$$\frac{10}{13} = \frac{CE}{\sqrt{41}}$$
$$CE = \frac{10\sqrt{41}}{13} = 4.9$$

38. (E)
$$y = -3x^2 + 12x - 9$$
$$= -3(x^2 - 4x) - 9$$
$$= -3(x^2 - 4x + 4) - 9 + 12$$
$$= -3(x - 2)^2 + 3$$

Thus the axis of symmetry is $x = 2$.

Alternate solution:

Graphing calculator: graph $y = -3x^2 + 12x - 9$ and trace to the highest point.

39. (E) By definition, $|a + bi| = \sqrt{a^2 + b^2}$

$$|7 + (-24)i| = \sqrt{49 + 576} = \sqrt{625} = 25$$

40. (C)

$$\frac{a^{-1}-b^{-1}}{a^{-2}-b^{-2}} = \frac{\dfrac{1}{a}-\dfrac{1}{b}}{\dfrac{1}{a^2}-\dfrac{1}{b^2}}$$

$$= \frac{\dfrac{b}{ab}-\dfrac{a}{ab}}{\dfrac{b^2}{a^2b^2}-\dfrac{a^2}{a^2b^2}}$$

$$= \frac{\dfrac{b-a}{ab}}{\dfrac{b^2-a^2}{a^2b^2}}$$

$$= \frac{b-a}{ab} \times \frac{a^2b^2}{b^2-a^2}$$

$$= \frac{(b-a)}{ab} \times \frac{(ab)(ab)}{(b-a)(b+a)}$$

$$= \frac{ab}{b+a}$$

41. (C) $1° = \left(\dfrac{\pi}{180}\right) \doteq .017$ radians, so

$(16)1° = 16(.017)$ radians $= .279$ radians

Alternate solution:

With your calculator in degree mode, find $\sin 16 = .2756$. Change to radian mode and find $\sin^{-1} .2756 = .2793$.

42. (A) When two complex numbers in standard form are equal, their real parts are equal and their imaginary parts are equal. Thus:

$$\begin{vmatrix} x-y=6 \\ x+y=2 \end{vmatrix}$$

Adding the two equations gives:

$$\begin{aligned} 2x &= 8 \\ x &= 4 \end{aligned}$$

By substitution of 4 for x in one of the equations above we find $y = -2$.

43. (A) $\log_{3x} 27 = 1$ means $3x^1 = 27$ so $x = 9$.

Alternate solution:

Graphing calculator: graph

$$y = 1 - (\log 27)/(\log 3x)$$

and solve.

44. (D) The point $(-1, 1)$ is in the intersection since it satisfies both inequalities.

Alternate solution:

Graphing calculator: graph $y = \dfrac{1}{2}\sin 2x$ and $y = \dfrac{1}{2}$ simultaneously and trace to the points of intersection.

45. (C) Each term of a geometric sequence is of the form ar^{n-1}, where a is the first term, r the common ratio, and n the number of the term.

$$a = 2\sqrt{2}$$

$$r = \frac{8}{2\sqrt{2}} = \frac{4}{\sqrt{2}} = \frac{4\sqrt{2}}{\sqrt{2}\sqrt{2}} = \frac{4\sqrt{2}}{2} = 2\sqrt{2}$$

Thus:

$$ar^{n-1} = (2\sqrt{2})(2\sqrt{2})^{(n-1)} = (2\sqrt{2})^n$$

46. (B) The question asks for the number of permutations of six letters taken all at a time, two of which are identical. By formula:

$$\frac{6!}{2!} = 360$$

47. (A) $y = \sin\theta$ varies between -1 and 1, so $y = \dfrac{1}{2}\sin\theta$ varies between $-\dfrac{1}{2}$ and $\dfrac{1}{2}$. Thus $y = \dfrac{1}{2}$ when $\sin\theta = 1$.

Since $\sin\theta = 1$ when $0 = 90°$,

$$2x = 90 \text{ and } x = 45$$

48. (C) $xy = 0$ if and only if $x = 0$ or $y = 0$. All points for which $x = 0$ lie on the y-axis and for which $y = 0$ lie on the x-axis. The graph is thus the union of the coordinate axes.

49. (B) 20 gallons $= 4(20) = 80$ quarts. 40 percent of $80 = .40(80) = 32$ quarts of alcohol. Let $x =$ amount of water added. Then $80 + x$ is the total amount of the new, 25 percent solution, and $.25(80 + x)$ is the amount of alcohol in this solution. But the number of quarts of alcohol is unchanged, so $.25(80 + x) = 32$.

$$\begin{aligned} .25(80) + .25(x) &= 32 \\ 20 + .25(x) &= 32 \\ .25(x) &= 12 \\ 25(x) &= 1200 \\ x &= 48. \end{aligned}$$

50. (C) $y^2 - 9x^2 = 25$ is the equation of a hyperbola with intercepts on the y-axis.

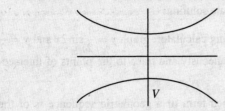

The maximum negative value occurs at V in the diagram above. Let $x = 0$, then $y^2 = 25$; $y = \pm 5$.

SELF-EVALUATION CHART FOR MODEL TEST 3

SUBJECT AREA	QUESTIONS ANSWERED CORRECTLY	NUMBER OF CORRECT ANSWERS
Algebra (17 questions)	1 2 3 4 5 6 7 8 9 10 13 15 16 18 19 20 28	_____
Plane geometry (8 questions)	11 14 23 25 27 33 35 37	_____
Solid geometry (3 questions)	21 29 31	_____
Coordinate geometry (6 questions)	34 38 44 47 48 50	_____
Trigonometry (3 questions)	24 26 41	_____
Functions (6 questions)	10 12 22 30 34 43	_____
Miscellaneous (8 questions)	17 32 39 40 42 45 46 49	_____

Total number of correct answers _____

Total number of incorrect answers _____

Total score = total number of correct answers _____

$\quad$ minus $\dfrac{1}{4}$ number of incorrect answers − _____

_____

(Reminder: Answers left blank are not counted as correct or incorrect)

Raw score = (number correct) $-\dfrac{1}{4}$ (number incorrect)

To evaluate your performance, compare your raw score with the table below.

Evaluate Your Performance
Model Test 3

Excellent	760–800	46–50
Very Good	700–750	40–45
Good	610–690	32–39
Above Average	560–600	26–31
Average	500–550	18–25
Below Average	270–490	17 or less

ANSWER SHEET FOR MODEL TEST 4

Determine the correct answer for each question. Then, using a No. 2 pencil, blacken completely the oval containing the letter of your choice.

1. (A)(B)(C)(D)(E)
2. (A)(B)(C)(D)(E)
3. (A)(B)(C)(D)(E)
4. (A)(B)(C)(D)(E)
5. (A)(B)(C)(D)(E)
6. (A)(B)(C)(D)(E)
7. (A)(B)(C)(D)(E)
8. (A)(B)(C)(D)(E)
9. (A)(B)(C)(D)(E)
10. (A)(B)(C)(D)(E)
11. (A)(B)(C)(D)(E)
12. (A)(B)(C)(D)(E)
13. (A)(B)(C)(D)(E)
14. (A)(B)(C)(D)(E)
15. (A)(B)(C)(D)(E)
16. (A)(B)(C)(D)(E)
17. (A)(B)(C)(D)(E)

18. (A)(B)(C)(D)(E)
19. (A)(B)(C)(D)(E)
20. (A)(B)(C)(D)(E)
21. (A)(B)(C)(D)(E)
22. (A)(B)(C)(D)(E)
23. (A)(B)(C)(D)(E)
24. (A)(B)(C)(D)(E)
25. (A)(B)(C)(D)(E)
26. (A)(B)(C)(D)(E)
27. (A)(B)(C)(D)(E)
28. (A)(B)(C)(D)(E)
29. (A)(B)(C)(D)(E)
30. (A)(B)(C)(D)(E)
31. (A)(B)(C)(D)(E)
32. (A)(B)(C)(D)(E)
33. (A)(B)(C)(D)(E)
34. (A)(B)(C)(D)(E)

35. (A)(B)(C)(D)(E)
36. (A)(B)(C)(D)(E)
37. (A)(B)(C)(D)(E)
38. (A)(B)(C)(D)(E)
39. (A)(B)(C)(D)(E)
40. (A)(B)(C)(D)(E)
41. (A)(B)(C)(D)(E)
42. (A)(B)(C)(D)(E)
43. (A)(B)(C)(D)(E)
44. (A)(B)(C)(D)(E)
45. (A)(B)(C)(D)(E)
46. (A)(B)(C)(D)(E)
47. (A)(B)(C)(D)(E)
48. (A)(B)(C)(D)(E)
49. (A)(B)(C)(D)(E)
50. (A)(B)(C)(D)(E)

Model Test Score Conversion Table

Raw Score	Scaled Score	Raw Score	Scaled Score	Raw Score	Scaled Score	Raw Score	Scaled Score
50	800	34	630	18	500	2	370
49	790	33	620	17	490	1	360
48	780	32	610	16	480	0	360
47	770	31	600	15	480	−1	350
46	760	30	590	14	470	−2	340
45	750	29	580	13	460	−3	330
44	740	28	580	12	450	−4	330
43	730	27	570	11	440	−5	320
42	720	26	560	10	440	−6	310
41	710	25	550	9	430	−7	300
40	700	24	540	8	420	−8	300
39	690	23	540	7	410	−9	290
38	680	22	530	6	400	−10	280
37	660	21	520	5	390	−11	270
36	650	20	510	4	390	−12	270
35	640	19	510	3	380		

MODEL TEST 4

Directions: For each of the 50 multiple-choice test questions, select the BEST answer among the five choices given. When the exact numerical value is not one of the choices, select the best approximation to the exact value. Mark your choice on the answer sheet by filling in the corresponding oval.

Notes:

1. Some questions (but not all) will require the use of at least a scientific calculator. Programmable and graphing calculators are also permitted. Calculator questions are not marked as such, so you will have to decide whether or not to use one on each question.

2. All angle measures are in degrees. Set your calculator to degree mode.

3. Some problems are accompanied by figures, which provide information useful in solving the problem. Figures are drawn accurately unless marked "Figure not drawn to scale." All figures lie in a plane unless the diagram clearly shows otherwise.

4. Except when stated otherwise, the domain of a function f is the set of real number values of x for which $f(x)$ is a real number.

5. Reference information consisting of volume and surface area formulas that may be useful in answering some questions on this test can be found below:

REFERENCE INFORMATION

- Sphere with radius r.   Volume: $V = \frac{4}{3}\pi r^3$ Surface Area: $S = 4\pi r^2$
- Right circular cone with radius r and height h.   Volume: $V = \frac{1}{3}\pi r^2 h$
- Right circular cone with circumference of base c and slant height L. Lateral Area: $S = \frac{1}{2}cL$
- Pyramid with base area B and height h.   Volume: $V = \frac{1}{3}Bh$

1. If a is positive and b negative, which of the following is negative?

   (A) $|ab|$

   (B) $a|b|$

   (C) $|a|b$

   (D) $a+|b|$

   (E) $|a|-b$

2. If the sum of $x-6y+2z$ and $3x-4y+2z$ is subtracted from $3y-4z+x$, the result is

   (A) $13y-8z-3x$

   (B) $7y+5x$

   (C) $4x-10y+4z$

   (D) $x-6y+2z$

   (E) $3x+8z-13y$

3. If the equation of a circle is $x^2+y^2=3$, which of the following is an x-intercept?

   (A) 0

   (B) $-\sqrt{3}$

   (C) 3

   (D) -3

   (E) Cannot be determined

4. If $\dfrac{8a+1}{2}=\dfrac{8a+6}{4}+5$ then $a=$

   (A) 0

   (B) 1

   (C) 2

   (D) 3

   (E) 4

5. Together Mr. Haddick and Mr. Beebe have $20.25. Mr. Haddick has only dimes, and Mr. Beebe only quarters. If Mr. Haddick has twice as many coins as Mr. Beebe, how many does Mr. Beebe have?

   (A) 45

   (B) 40

   (C) 35

   (D) 30

   (E) 25

USE THIS SPACE FOR SCRATCH WORK

GO ON TO THE NEXT PAGE

6. If $a = 3b - 5$ and $b = 4a - 2$, then $a =$

(A) 1

(B) 2

(C) 3

(D) −1

(E) 0

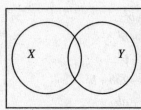

7. $\dfrac{\sqrt{x-y}}{\sqrt{x+y}} =$

(A) $\dfrac{x-y}{x+y}$

(B) $\dfrac{\sqrt{x^2 - y^2}}{x+y}$

(C) $\sqrt{x-y}$

(D) $x-y$

(E) $x+y$

8. In Figure 1, X and Y are the sets of all points contained in the circular regions. Which of the following must be true?

I. $(X \cup Y)$ is a subset of Y.
II. $X \cap Y = \emptyset$.
III. If a point is not in $X \cup Y$, then it is not in X.

(A) I only

(B) I and II only

(C) II only

(D) III only

(E) II and III only

Figure 1

9. If two angles of a quadrilateral are equal in measure, then the other two must be

(A) equal in measure

(B) obtuse

(C) acute

(D) supplementary

(E) no conclusion possible

GO ON TO THE NEXT PAGE

10. Which of the following is true?

    (A) $(13^2)^4 = 13^6$

    (B) $3^2 + 3^3 = 3^5$

    (C) $4^{-4} \times 4^3 = \dfrac{1}{4}$

    (D) $(36)^{1/2} = 18$

    (E) $7\sqrt{11} = 11\sqrt{7}$

11. If $x = -\dfrac{1}{4}$, then $4[(x+4)(4x-1)] =$

    (A) -120

    (B) 0

    (C) 30

    (D) -15

    (E) -30

12. If $2a^3 - ab^2 + b^3$ is divided by $a+b$, the result is

    (A) $a^2 - b^2$

    (B) $2a^2 - b^2$

    (C) $2a^2 + b^2$

    (D) $2a^2 - 2ab + b^2$

    (E) $2a^2 + ab$

13. In $\triangle ABC$ in Figure 2, $AC = AB$, ray BD bisects $\angle ABC$, m$\angle ACB = 50°$. What is the degree measure of $\angle ABD$?

    (A) $50°$

    (B) $75°$

    (C) $25°$

    (D) $60°$

    (E) $30°$

14. Each of the following is a term in the product of $x^2 - x + 2$ and $x^2 + x + 1$ EXCEPT

    (A) x^4

    (B) x^3

    (C) $2x^2$

    (D) x

    (E) 2

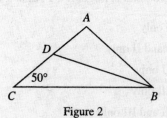

Figure 2

GO ON TO THE NEXT PAGE

15. Which of the following equations must be true?

I. $(a+b)+c = a+(b+c)$
II. $a+(b+c) = a+(c+b)$
III. $a+(c+b) = (a+c)+b$

(A) I only

(B) II only

(C) I and III only

(D) all

(E) II and III only

USE THIS SPACE FOR SCRATCH WORK

16. If $2 \le 8x - 1 \le -6$, then

(A) $-\dfrac{5}{8} \le x \le \dfrac{3}{8}$

(B) $x \ge 0$

(C) $x \le 0$

(D) $-\dfrac{7}{8} \le x \le \dfrac{1}{8}$

(E) There are no values for x

17. In Figure 3, $\angle COE$ and $\angle BOD$ are right angles. If the measure of $\angle BOC$ is four times the measure of $\angle COD$, what is the measure of $\angle AOB$?

(A) $16°$

(B) $17°$

(C) $18°$

(D) $19°$

(E) $20°$

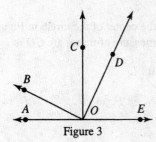

Figure 3

18. The measure of the positive angle formed by the nonnegative ray of the x-axis and the line defined by $y = -\sqrt{3}x$ is

(A) $30°$

(B) $120°$

(C) $90°$

(D) $45°$

(E) $150°$

GO ON TO THE NEXT PAGE

19. The simplified form of

$$\frac{\frac{1}{a}+1}{a+1}$$

is

(A) 1

(B) $\dfrac{1}{a}$

(C) a

(D) $a+1$

(E) $(a+1)^2$

20. Which of the following is a factor of $x^2-(y+1)^2$?

(A) $x-y-1$

(B) $y+1$

(C) $x-1$

(D) $x-y$

(E) $x-y+1$

21. If O is the center of the circle in Figure 4, then the degree measure of minor arc CD is

(A) 180

(B) 45

(C) 90

(D) 135

(E) 75

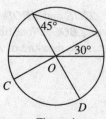

Figure 4

22. The intersection of a line and a circle may contain how many points?

  I. 0

  II. 1 or 2

  III. 3

(A) I only

(B) None of I, II, or III

(C) I and II only

(D) All of I, II, and III

(E) II only

GO ON TO THE NEXT PAGE

23. If p and q are the coordinates of points on the number line, the distance between the points will always be

   (A) $p - q$
   (B) $q - p$
   (C) $-(p - q)$
   (D) $|p - q|$
   (E) $\sqrt{p^2 + q^2}$

24. If $f(x) = |x - 1|$ and $g(x) = 1 - x^2$, then $3f(-2) + 4g(-3) =$

   (A) -23
   (B) -5
   (C) 13
   (D) 32
   (E) -13

25. Which of the following is the degree measure of an angle in standard position and coterminal with an angle of $-8°$?

   I. $352°$
   II. $8°$
   III. $-368°$

   (A) I only
   (B) I and III only
   (C) II only
   (D) Il and III only
   (E) I, II, and III

26. Assuming that a and b are both NEGATIVE numbers, in which quadrant does the point $(a, -b)$ lie?

   (A) I
   (B) II
   (C) III
   (D) IV
   (E) Cannot be determined

GO ON TO THE NEXT PAGE

27. The product of $(-x^{m+1})$ and $(-x^{m-1})$ is

(A) x^{2m}

(B) $-x^{2m}$

(C) x^{m-1}

(D) x^{m^2-1}

(E) $\dfrac{1}{x^{2m}}$

28. What is the radian measure of a central angle that cuts off an arc n inches long on a circle of radius 2 inches?

(A) $\dfrac{1}{2}$

(B) $\dfrac{\pi}{2}$

(C) $\dfrac{\pi}{4}$

(D) π

(E) 2

29. Which of the following is equal to

$$y^{1/2}(y^{1/2}+y^{-1/2})?$$

(A) $y+1$

(B) y

(C) 1

(D) 0

(E) $\dfrac{1}{y}$

30. If $\log_3(1+y)^2 = 2$, then $y =$

(A) 1

(B) 2

(C) 3

(D) 4

(E) 5

31. Which of the following is equal to $(\tan\theta)(\csc\theta)$?

(A) $\sin\theta$

(B) $\cos\theta$

(C) $\sec\theta$

(D) $\csc\theta$

(E) $\cot\theta$

GO ON TO THE NEXT PAGE

32. If a solid metal sphere of radius 1 foot is melted and recast to form spheres of radius 1 inch, how many of these smaller spheres can be made?

   (A) 12
   (B) 36
   (C) 144
   (D) 432
   (E) 1728

33. The average (arithmetic mean) score of the two forwards on a basketball team was 21 pts. The average scores of the remaining three players was 11. What was the average score of all 5 players on the team?

   (A) 15
   (B) 16
   (C) 5
   (D) 15.5
   (E) 14.5

34. In $\triangle ABC$, if $AB = 6$, $AC = 4$, and the degree measure of $\angle A$ is 30, the area of the triangle is

   (A) 2
   (B) 3
   (C) 6
   (D) 12
   (E) The area cannot be determined

35. If $\log a = .4771$ and $\log b = .3010$, then $\log ab =$

   (A) .7781
   (B) .1761
   (C) .6532
   (D) .6990
   (E) .5229

36. What is the number of square inches in the area of the base of a right circular cone with a volume of 40π cubic inches and a height of 6 inches?

   (A) 40π
   (B) 20π
   (C) 10π
   (D) 5π
   (E) π

GO ON TO THE NEXT PAGE

37. In Figure 5, line *AB* is tangent to the circle at *T*. Radius *ED* has length 6. *TE* ⊥ *CD* and ray *ET* bisects ∠*AEB*, *AB* =

(A) 6

(B) 5

(C) 12

(D) 9

(E) Cannot be determined

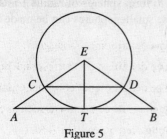

Figure 5

38. If a polygon is inscribed in a circle, then

(A) It is equilateral.

(B) It is equiangular.

(C) It is BOTH equiangular and equilateral.

(D) It has a finite number of sides.

(E) It has at least one right angle.

39. Which of the following is the equation of a line that is neither parallel nor perpendicular to the line defined by $y + x = 0$?

(A) $y = x$

(B) $y = x + 2$

(C) $y - x + 2 = 0$

(D) $2y - 2x = 1$

(E) $2y = 4x + 1$

40. If *t* can represent any positive integer, then

(A) $\sqrt{t}$ is always irrational.

(B) $\sqrt{t}$ is not always real.

(C) t^2 is always an even integer.

(D) $2t + 1$ is always an odd integer.

(E) $\dfrac{t}{3}$ is never an even integer.

41. If a point *X* lies in the interior of △*ABC* in Figure 6, then which of the following must be true?

(A) $BX < BA$

(B) $BX > BA$

(C) $BX = BA$

(D) $BX \leq BA$

(E) $BX < BC$

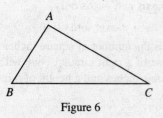

Figure 6

GO ON TO THE NEXT PAGE

42. In a geometric proof the reason "corresponding parts of congruent triangles are congruent" refers to

    (A) The definition of "triangle."
    (B) The definition of "correspondence."
    (C) The definition of "congruent triangles."
    (D) A congruence postulate such as SAS.
    (E) A theorem already proved.

43. If the measures of the exterior angles of a certain polygon are added and this sum is divided by the number of sides of the polygon, the result is 18. How many sides does the polygon have?

    (A) 36
    (B) 24
    (C) 20
    (D) 12
    (E) 10

44. What is the middle term in the expansion of

$$(2x - \frac{1}{2}y)^6?$$

    (A) $-20x^3y^3$
    (B) $-80x^2y^4$
    (C) $-20x^2y^4$
    (D) $-80x^3y^3$
    (E) $-20x^4y^4$

45. Which of the following completely describes the symmetry of $\{(x,y) : |x| = 2\}$?

    (A) x-axis only
    (B) y-axis only
    (C) x-axis and y-axis only
    (D) Origin, x-axis, and y-axis
    (E) Origin only

USE THIS SPACE FOR SCRATCH WORK

GO ON TO THE NEXT PAGE

46. The domain of the function defined by

$$f(x) = \frac{x}{\sqrt{x}}$$

is

(A) All reals.

(B) All positive reals.

(C) All nonnegative reals.

(D) All reals except zero.

(E) All negative reals.

47. The graph of one cycle of $y = 3\sin\frac{1}{2}x$ is given in Figure 7. What is the x-coordinate of P?

(A) 90°

(B) 180°

(C) 360°

(D) 720°

(E) 1080°

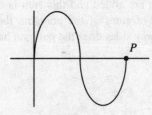

Figure 7

48. Which of the following is the general term of the sequence $11, 9, 7, \ldots$, where n is the number of the term?

(A) n

(B) $11 + n$

(C) $11 - 2n$

(D) $11 - 2(n-1)$

(E) $n - 2$

49. The minimum value of $f(x) = x^2 + x + 4$ is

(A) 2

(B) −2

(C) 4

(D) $\frac{15}{4}$

(E) $\frac{17}{4}$

GO ON TO THE NEXT PAGE

50. If $\cos x = -.9287$, then $\cos(x + 180°) =$

    (A) $-.9287$

    (B) $.9287$

    (C) $.0713$

    (D) $-.0713$

    (E) -1.8574

USE THIS SPACE FOR SCRATCH WORK

STOP

IF YOU FINISH BEFORE TIME IS CALLED, YOU MAY CHECK YOUR WORK ON THIS TEST ONLY.
DO NOT WORK ON ANY OTHER TEST IN THIS BOOK.

ANSWER KEY

1.	C	11.	E	21.	C	31.	C	41.	E
2.	A	12.	D	22.	C	32.	E	42.	C
3.	B	13.	C	23.	D	33.	A	43.	C
4.	D	14.	B	24.	A	34.	C	44.	A
5.	A	15.	D	25.	B	35.	A	45.	D
6.	A	16.	E	26.	B	36.	B	46.	B
7.	B	17.	C	27.	A	37.	E	47.	D
8.	D	18.	B	28.	B	38.	D	48.	D
9.	E	19.	B	29.	A	39.	E	49.	D
10.	C	20.	A	30.	B	40.	D	50.	B

ANSWER EXPLANATIONS

1. (C) $|a|$ is positive and b negative, so their product is negative.

2. (A)

$$(3y - 4z + x) - [(x - 6y + 2z) + (3x - 4y + 2z)]$$
$$= (3y - 4z + x) - [4x - 10y + 4z]$$
$$= 3y - 4z + x - 4x - 10y - 4z$$
$$= 13y - 8z - 3x$$

3. (B) Let $y = 0$, then $x^2 = 3$ and $x = \pm\sqrt{3}$. Thus $+\sqrt{3}$ and $-\sqrt{3}$ both qualify as x-intercepts.

4. (D) Multiply both sides of the equation by 4 to get:

$$2(8a + 1) = 8a + 6 + 4(5)$$
$$16a + 2 = 8a + 6 + 20$$
$$8a = 24$$
$$a = 3$$

5. (A) Let $x =$ the number of quarters; then $.25x =$ the total value of the quarters, $2x =$ the number of dimes, and $.10(2x)$ the total value of the dimes.

$$.25x + .10(2x) = 20.25$$
$$.25x + .20x = 20.25$$
$$.45x = 20.25$$
$$x = \frac{20.25}{.45}$$
$$45$$

6. (A) Substitute $4a - 2$ for b in the first equation:

$$a = 3(4a - 2) - 5$$
$$= 12a - 6 - 5$$
$$-11a = -11$$
$$a = 1$$

7. (B)

$$\frac{\sqrt{x-y}}{\sqrt{x+y}} = \frac{\sqrt{x-y}}{\sqrt{x+y}} \cdot \frac{\sqrt{x+y}}{\sqrt{x+y}}$$
$$= \frac{\sqrt{(x-y)(x+y)}}{x+y}$$
$$= \frac{\sqrt{x^2 - y^2}}{x+y}$$

8. (D)

I. $X \cup Y$ contains points not in Y.

II. $X \cap Y$ contains the points in the overlapping region.

III. $X \cup Y$ is the set of all points that belong to at least one of the regions X and Y. Thus a point cannot be in either X or Y if it doesn't belong to their union.

9. (E) No restriction exists on the measures of the angles of a quadrilateral except that their sum be 360.

10. (C) $4^{-4} \times 4^3 = 4^{-4+3} = 4^{-1} = \frac{1}{4}$

Testing each answer choice with a calculator works, but is tedious. Use your knowledge of the laws of exponents.

11. (E) Replace x with $-\frac{1}{4}$ to get:

$$4\left[\left(-\frac{1}{4} + 4\right)\left(4\left(-\frac{1}{4}\right) - 1\right)\right]$$
$$= 4\left[\left(-\frac{1}{4} + \frac{16}{4}\right)(-1 - 1)\right]$$
$$= 4\left[\left(\frac{15}{4}\right)(-2)\right]$$
$$= 15(-2)$$
$$= -30$$

Or use $x = .25$ and substitute with your calculator.

12. (D)

$$
a + b \overline{) \begin{array}{l} \; 2a^2 - 2ab + b^2 \\ 2a^3 - ab^2 + b^3 \\ \underline{2a^3 + 2a^2b} \\ -2a^2b - ab^2 \\ \underline{-2a^2b - 2ab^2} \\ ab^2 + b^3 \\ \underline{ab^2 + b^3} \\ 0 \end{array}}
$$

13. (C) Since $AC = AB$, then $\angle ABC = 50$ by the Isosceles Triangle Theorem. $\angle ABD = \dfrac{1}{2}(50) = 25$ by definition of angle bisector.

14. (B)

$$
\begin{array}{l} x^2 + x + 1 \\ x^2 - x + 2 \\ \underline{x^4 + x^3 + x^2} \\ -x^3 - x^2 - x \\ \underline{+ 2x^2 + 2x + 2} \\ x^4 + 2x^2 + x + 2 \end{array}
$$

15. (D) Steps I and III are by the Associative Law, and step II by the Commutative Law.

16. (E) If $2 \le 8x - 1 \le -6$, add 1 to each member to get $3 \le 8x \le -5$. Divide each member by 8 to get $\dfrac{3}{8} \le x \le -\dfrac{5}{8}$. Since no real number is both less than a negative number and greater than a positive number, there is no solution.

17. (C) Let $\angle COD = x$; then $m\angle COB = 4x$ and $m\angle BOD = 4x + x = 5x = 90°$. Thus $x = \dfrac{90°}{5} = 18°$. $\angle COD$ and $\angle AOB$ are complements of the same angle, $\angle BOC$, and thus have the same measure.

18. (B) In the diagram let P be the point on the line $y = -\sqrt{3}x$ for which $x = -1$.

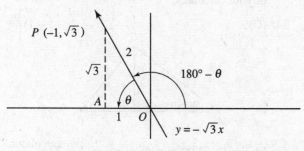

Thus $y = -\sqrt{3}(-1) = \sqrt{3}$ and

$$
OP = \sqrt{(\sqrt{3})^2 + (-1)^2} = \sqrt{3 + 1} = 2
$$

$\triangle OPA$ is therefore a 30°-60°-90° triangle with $\theta = 60°$ so the angle in question is 120°.

Alternate solution:

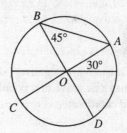 $\theta = \tan^{-1}\sqrt{3}$, so $\theta = 60°$ and $180 - \theta = 120°$.

19. (B)

$$
\frac{\dfrac{1}{a} + 1}{a + 1} = \frac{\dfrac{1}{a} + \dfrac{a}{a}}{a + 1}
$$

$$
= \frac{\dfrac{1 + a}{a}}{a + 1}
$$

$$
= \frac{1 + a}{a} \cdot \frac{1}{a + 1}
$$

$$
= \frac{1}{a}
$$

Graphing calculator: graph $y = ((1/x) + 1)/(x + 1)$ and you will get a hyperbola. Choices (A), (C), and (D) are lines. (E) is a parabola.

20. (A) The given expression is the difference of two squares:

$$
\begin{aligned}
x^2 - (y + 1)^2 &= [x - (y + 1)][x + (y + 1)] \\
&= [x - y - 1][x + y + 1]
\end{aligned}
$$

21. (C) Since $m\angle ABD = 45$, arc $AD = 90° = m\angle AOD$. AC is a diameter, so $\angle AOD$ is supplementary to $\angle COD$, which must also be 90°. Hence arc $CD = 90°$.

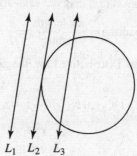

22. (C) The possibilities are shown by L_1, L_2, and L_3. If you chose (D), you probably made the mistake of assuming that the center of a circle is a point of the circle.

23. (D)　(D) satisfies the definition of "distance" on the number line.

24. (A)

$$3f(x)+4g(x) = 3|x-1|+4(1-x^2)$$
$$3f(-2)+4g(-3) = 3|-2-1|+4[1-(-3)^2]$$
$$= 3|-3|+4(-8)$$
$$= 9+(-32)$$

$$= -23.$$

25. (B)

I

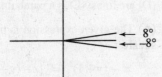
352°
← -8°

II

8°
← -8°

III

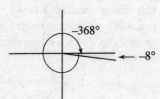
-368°
← -8°

26. (B) Since a and b are negative, $-b$ is positive and the point has a negative first coordinate with positive second coordinate.

27. (A)

$$(-x^{m+1})(-x^{m-1}) = (-1)(x^{m+1})(-1)(x^{m-1})$$
$$= (-1)(-1)(x^{m+1+m+1})$$
$$= x^{2m}$$

28. (B) θ in radians $= \dfrac{\text{arc length}}{\text{radius}} = \dfrac{\pi}{2}$

29. (A) By the Distributive Law, the given expression equals:

$$y^{1/2}(y^{1/2}+y^{1/2}) = y^{1/2+1/2}+y^{1/2-1/2}$$
$$= y^1+y^0$$
$$= y+1$$

30. (B) $\log_3(1+y)^2 = 2$ means

$$3^2 = (1+y)^2$$
$$9 = 1+2y+y^2$$
$$0 = y^2+2y-8$$
$$= (y+4)(y-2)$$

$$y=-4 \text{ or } y=2$$

Alternate solution:

Graphing calculator: graph $y = 2 - (\log(x+1)^2)\boxed{/}(\log 3)$ and solve for x.

31. (C) $\tan\theta = \dfrac{\sin\theta}{\cos\theta}$ and $\csc\theta = \dfrac{1}{\sin\theta}$

Thus:

$$(\tan\theta)(\csc\theta) = \dfrac{\sin\theta}{\cos\theta}\cdot\dfrac{1}{\sin\theta}$$
$$= \dfrac{1}{\cos\theta}$$
$$= \sec\theta$$

Alternate solution:

Graphing calculator: graph $y = (\tan x)(1\boxed{/}\sin x)$ and compare with known graphs of answer choices.

32. (E) $V = \dfrac{4}{3}\pi r^3$. Let $r = 1$ foot $= 12$ inches, then:

$$\left\{V = \dfrac{4}{3}\pi(12)^3 = \dfrac{4}{3}\pi(1728).\right\}$$

Let $r = 1$ inch, then:

$$V' = \dfrac{4}{3}\pi(1).$$

Thus $V = (1728)V'$.

33. (A) Total score $= 2(21)+3(11) = 75$.

Average $= \dfrac{75}{5} = 15$.

Weighted averages are more easily calculated directly rather than by using the averaging program of your calculator.

34. (C)

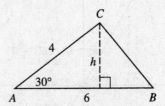

By the 30-60-90 triangle relations, $h = 2$ so

$$\text{Area } \triangle ABC = \dfrac{1}{2}(2)(6)$$
$$= 6.$$

35. (A)
$$\log_{10} ab = \log_{10} a + \log_{10} b$$
$$= .7781$$

36. (B) $V = \frac{1}{3}hA$, where A = area of base and h = height of cone.
$$40\pi = \frac{1}{3}(6)A$$
$$40\pi = 2A$$
$$20\pi = A$$

37. (E) The given figure and information are not contradicted regardless of the length of AB.

38. (D) No restriction on angle measure or length of side is implied by inscribing the polygon; by definition of "polygon," the number of sides is finite.

39. (E) In slope-intercept form the line $y + x = 0$ is $y = -x$, giving a slope of -1. Any parallel line has a slope of -1 and any perpendicular a slope of 1. The equation in (E) is $y = 2x + \frac{1}{2}$ when in slope-intercept form and thus has a slope of 2.

40. (D) For any integer t, $2t$ will always be even (since it has a factor of 2), so $2t + 1$ will always be odd.

41. (E) Trial and error will demonstrate this.

42. (C) Definition of congruent triangles.

43. (C) The sum of the measures of the exterior angles of a polygon is always 360. Let n = the number of sides (hence the number of exterior angles—counting one to a vertex). Then $\frac{360}{n}$ = the measure of each angle and:
$$\frac{360}{n} = 18$$
$$360 = 18n$$
$$\frac{360}{18} = n$$

$$20 = n$$

44. (A) There are seven terms, so the middle term is the fourth. By formula:
$${}_6C_3(2x)^3\left(-\frac{1}{2}y\right)^3 = \frac{6!}{3!3!}(8x^3)\left(-\frac{1}{8}y^3\right)$$
$$= 20(-1)(x^3)(y^3)$$
$$= -20x^3y^3$$

Use your calculator to find $\frac{6!}{3!3!}$.

45. (D) Note the graph.

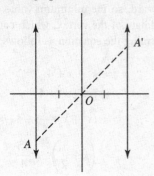

The x- and y-axis symmetry are obvious. For origin symmetry note that each nonvertical line through the origin intercepts the graph in two points, A and A', such that $OA = OA'$.

46. (B) $x = 0$ leads to division by zero. $x < 0$ leads to the square root of a negative number.

Alternate solution:

Graphing calculator: graph $y = x\boxed{/}\sqrt{x}$. Determine domain by inspection. Be sure to check endpoint at $x = 0$.

47. (D) Since the y-coordinate of P is 0,
$$0 = 3\sin\frac{1}{2}x$$

Divide both sides by 3:
$$0 = \sin\frac{1}{2}x$$

The smallest positive angle whose sine is zero has radian measure 360, so:
$$\frac{1}{2}x = 360$$
$$x = 720$$

With a graphing calculator, graph the function and trace a point until it reaches the intercept.

48. (D) The sequence is arithmetic with $a = 11$ and $d = -2$, so, by formula, the general term, a_n, is given by:
$$a_n = 11 + (n-1)(-2)$$
$$= 11 - 2(n-1)$$

49. (D) The graph of $y = x^2 + x + 4$ is a parabola opening upward, so the minimum value of $f(x)$ is the y-coordinate of the vertex, which can be found by transforming the equation as follows:

$$\begin{aligned} y &= x^2 + x + 4 \\ &= (x^2 + x) + 4 \\ &= (x^2 + x + \frac{1}{4}) + 4 - \frac{1}{4} \\ &= \left(x + \frac{1}{2}\right)^2 + \frac{15}{4} \end{aligned}$$

Thus the vertex is $\left(-\frac{1}{2}, \frac{15}{4}\right)$.

With a graphing calculator, enter the function and use the "minimum" finding feature.

50. (B) The two diagrams show unit circles that have possible arcs of length x and $x + \pi$, respectively, marked off:

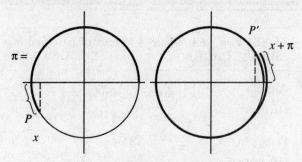

As you can see from the symmetry, points P and P' have x-coordinates that differ only in sign. The cosine of each arc (which is the x-coordinate in each case) then must differ only in sign.

SELF-EVALUATION CHART FOR MODEL TEST 4

SUBJECT AREA	QUESTIONS ANSWERED CORRECTLY	NUMBER OF CORRECT ANSWERS

Algebra
(16 questions)

1	2	4	5	6	7	10	12	14	15	16	19	20	27	29	30

_____

Plane geometry
(10 questions)

9	13	17	21	22	37	38	41	42	43

_____

Solid geometry
(2 questions)

22	36

_____

Coordinate geometry
(6 questions)

3	18	23	26	39	45

_____

Trigonometry
(6 questions)

25	28	31	34	47	50

_____

Functions
(5 questions)

11	24	35	46	49

_____

Miscellaneous
(5 questions)

8	33	40	44	48

_____

Total number of correct answers   _____

Total number of incorrect answers   _____

Total score = total number of correct answers   _____

minus $\frac{1}{4}$ number of incorrect answers $-$ _____

_____

(Reminder: Answers left blank are not counted as correct or incorrect)

Raw score = (number correct) $-\frac{1}{4}$ (number incorrect)

To evaluate your performance, compare your raw score with the table below.

**Evaluate Your Performance
Model Test 4**

Excellent	760–800	46–50
Very Good	700–750	40–45
Good	610–690	32–39
Above Average	560–600	26–31
Average	500–550	18–25
Below Average	270–490	17 or less

ANSWER SHEET FOR MODEL TEST 5

Determine the correct answer for each question. Then, using a No. 2 pencil, blacken completely the oval containing the letter of your choice.

1. Ⓐ Ⓑ Ⓒ Ⓓ Ⓔ	18. Ⓐ Ⓑ Ⓒ Ⓓ Ⓔ	35. Ⓐ Ⓑ Ⓒ Ⓓ Ⓔ
2. Ⓐ Ⓑ Ⓒ Ⓓ Ⓔ	19. Ⓐ Ⓑ Ⓒ Ⓓ Ⓔ	36. Ⓐ Ⓑ Ⓒ Ⓓ Ⓔ
3. Ⓐ Ⓑ Ⓒ Ⓓ Ⓔ	20. Ⓐ Ⓑ Ⓒ Ⓓ Ⓔ	37. Ⓐ Ⓑ Ⓒ Ⓓ Ⓔ
4. Ⓐ Ⓑ Ⓒ Ⓓ Ⓔ	21. Ⓐ Ⓑ Ⓒ Ⓓ Ⓔ	38. Ⓐ Ⓑ Ⓒ Ⓓ Ⓔ
5. Ⓐ Ⓑ Ⓒ Ⓓ Ⓔ	22. Ⓐ Ⓑ Ⓒ Ⓓ Ⓔ	39. Ⓐ Ⓑ Ⓒ Ⓓ Ⓔ
6. Ⓐ Ⓑ Ⓒ Ⓓ Ⓔ	23. Ⓐ Ⓑ Ⓒ Ⓓ Ⓔ	40. Ⓐ Ⓑ Ⓒ Ⓓ Ⓔ
7. Ⓐ Ⓑ Ⓒ Ⓓ Ⓔ	24. Ⓐ Ⓑ Ⓒ Ⓓ Ⓔ	41. Ⓐ Ⓑ Ⓒ Ⓓ Ⓔ
8. Ⓐ Ⓑ Ⓒ Ⓓ Ⓔ	25. Ⓐ Ⓑ Ⓒ Ⓓ Ⓔ	42. Ⓐ Ⓑ Ⓒ Ⓓ Ⓔ
9. Ⓐ Ⓑ Ⓒ Ⓓ Ⓔ	26. Ⓐ Ⓑ Ⓒ Ⓓ Ⓔ	43. Ⓐ Ⓑ Ⓒ Ⓓ Ⓔ
10. Ⓐ Ⓑ Ⓒ Ⓓ Ⓔ	27. Ⓐ Ⓑ Ⓒ Ⓓ Ⓔ	44. Ⓐ Ⓑ Ⓒ Ⓓ Ⓔ
11. Ⓐ Ⓑ Ⓒ Ⓓ Ⓔ	28. Ⓐ Ⓑ Ⓒ Ⓓ Ⓔ	45. Ⓐ Ⓑ Ⓒ Ⓓ Ⓔ
12. Ⓐ Ⓑ Ⓒ Ⓓ Ⓔ	29. Ⓐ Ⓑ Ⓒ Ⓓ Ⓔ	46. Ⓐ Ⓑ Ⓒ Ⓓ Ⓔ
13. Ⓐ Ⓑ Ⓒ Ⓓ Ⓔ	30. Ⓐ Ⓑ Ⓒ Ⓓ Ⓔ	47. Ⓐ Ⓑ Ⓒ Ⓓ Ⓔ
14. Ⓐ Ⓑ Ⓒ Ⓓ Ⓔ	31. Ⓐ Ⓑ Ⓒ Ⓓ Ⓔ	48. Ⓐ Ⓑ Ⓒ Ⓓ Ⓔ
15. Ⓐ Ⓑ Ⓒ Ⓓ Ⓔ	32. Ⓐ Ⓑ Ⓒ Ⓓ Ⓔ	49. Ⓐ Ⓑ Ⓒ Ⓓ Ⓔ
16. Ⓐ Ⓑ Ⓒ Ⓓ Ⓔ	33. Ⓐ Ⓑ Ⓒ Ⓓ Ⓔ	50. Ⓐ Ⓑ Ⓒ Ⓓ Ⓔ
17. Ⓐ Ⓑ Ⓒ Ⓓ Ⓔ	34. Ⓐ Ⓑ Ⓒ Ⓓ Ⓔ	

Model Test Score Conversion Table

Raw Score	Scaled Score	Raw Score	Scaled Score	Raw Score	Scaled Score	Raw Score	Scaled Score
50	800	34	630	18	500	2	370
49	790	33	620	17	490	1	360
48	780	32	610	16	480	0	360
47	770	31	600	15	480	−1	350
46	760	30	590	14	470	−2	340
45	750	29	580	13	460	−3	330
44	740	28	580	12	450	−4	330
43	730	27	570	11	440	−5	320
42	720	26	560	10	440	−6	310
41	710	25	550	9	430	−7	300
40	700	24	540	8	420	−8	300
39	690	23	540	7	410	−9	290
38	680	22	530	6	400	−10	280
37	660	21	520	5	390	−11	270
36	650	20	510	4	390	−12	270
35	640	19	510	3	380		

MODEL TEST 5

Directions: For each of the 50 multiple-choice test questions, select the BEST answer among the five choices given. When the exact numerical value is not one of the choices, select the best approximation to the exact value. Mark your choice on the answer sheet by filling in the corresponding oval.

Notes:

1. Some questions (but not all) will require the use of at least a scientific calculator. Programmable and graphing calculators are also permitted. Calculator questions are not marked as such, so you will have to decide whether or not to use one on each question.

2. All angle measures are in degrees. Set your calculator to degree mode.

3. Some problems are accompanied by figures, which provide information useful in solving the problem. Figures are drawn accurately unless marked "Figure not drawn to scale." All figures lie in a plane unless the diagram clearly shows otherwise.

4. Except when stated otherwise, the domain of a function f is the set of real number values of x for which $f(x)$ is a real number.

5. Reference information consisting of volume and surface area formulas that may be useful in answering some questions on this test can be found below:

REFERENCE INFORMATION

- Sphere with radius r.   Volume: $V = \frac{4}{3}\pi r^3$ Surface Area: $S = 4\pi r^2$
- Right circular cone with radius r and height h.   Volume: $V = \frac{1}{3}\pi r^2 h$
- Right circular cone with circumference of base c and slant height L.
  Lateral Area: $S = \frac{1}{2}cL$
- Pyramid with base area B and height h.   Volume: $V = \frac{1}{3}Bh$

1. The number of oranges in 8 crates of 24 each is the same as the number of oranges in

   (A) 4 crates of 48 each

   (B) 2 crates of 36 each

   (C) 6 crates of 12 each

   (D) 3 crates of 75 each

   (E) 7 crates of 10 each

2. $\dfrac{4}{7} \times \dfrac{8}{7} =$

   (A) $\dfrac{1}{2}$

   (B) $\dfrac{56}{28}$

   (C) $\dfrac{32}{7}$

   (D) $\dfrac{16}{7}$

   (E) $\dfrac{32}{49}$

3. Which of the following sets of numbers could be the degree measures of the three angles of an isosceles triangle?

     I. 50, 50, 60
    II. 30, 60, 90
   III. 45, 45, 90

   (A) I only

   (B) II only

   (C) III only

   (D) I and II only

   (E) II and III only

4. $(3b)^2 =$

   (A) $6b$

   (B) $6b^2$

   (C) $3b^2$

   (D) $9b^2$

   (E) $9b$

USE THIS SPACE FOR SCRATCH WORK

GO ON TO THE NEXT PAGE

5. If $\dfrac{x}{5} = 2$, then $x =$

(A) $\dfrac{5}{2}$

(B) $\dfrac{2}{5}$

(C) 10

(D) 5^2

(E) 7

USE THIS SPACE FOR SCRATCH WORK

6. If $D = RT$, then, when $D = 6$ and $T = \dfrac{1}{2}$, $R =$

(A) 12

(B) 3

(C) 6

(D) $6\dfrac{1}{2}$

(E) 15

7. Which of the following statements about the diagonals of a rectangle must be true?

  I. The diagonals always have the same length.
 II. The diagonals always are perpendicular
III. The diagonals always bisect each other.

(A) I only

(B) I and II only

(C) I and III only

(D) II and III only

(E) I, II, and III

8. $\dfrac{9a^2 + 3a}{3a} =$

(A) $4a$

(B) $6a$

(C) $9a^2$

(D) $3a + 1$

(E) $9a^{2+1}$

GO ON TO THE NEXT PAGE

9. If A is an angle in standard position, $\sin A$ is positive and $\cos A$ is negative, in what quadrant is the terminal side of angle A?

(A) I

(B) II or III

(C) II

(D) IV

(E) III or IV

10. If $\dfrac{x+5}{x-1} = \dfrac{x}{x-5}$, then $x =$

(A) -5

(B) 25

(C) 0

(D) 1

(E) 10

11. $\sin a =$

(A) $\cos a$

(B) $\sin(90° - a)$

(C) $1 + \cos(90° - a)$

(D) $\sin 90° - \sin(90° - a)$

(E) $\cos(90° - a)$

12. If $5x - 4 = 2x + 8$, what does $3x = $?

(A) 12

(B) 4

(C) 8

(D) -4

(E) 2

13. If you are given that each of two angles of a triangle is acute, what conclusion can you draw about the third?

(A) It is obtuse.

(B) It is a right angle.

(C) It is acute.

(D) It cannot exist since the triangle is impossible.

(E) It can have any measure between 0 and 180.

GO ON TO THE NEXT PAGE

14. In quadrilateral *ABCD* in Figure 1, if angles *A* and *D* are right angles, what is the value of *y* in terms of *x*?

(A) $\dfrac{x}{2}$

(B) $180° - x$

(C) $\dfrac{x}{3}$

(D) $x - 90°$

(E) $\dfrac{180° - x}{2}$

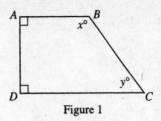

Figure 1

15. If the area of the square in Figure 2 is 9, then the area of the circle is

(A) 28.3

(B) 9.4

(C) 7.1

(D) 4.7

(E) 18.8

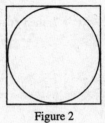

Figure 2

16. In decimal form, 15% of $\dfrac{1}{2}$ is

(A) .025

(B) .075

(C) 7.5

(D) .30

(E) .75

17. If *DE* is parallel to *AB*, and the length of the sides are as shown in Figure 3, what is the length of *DE*?

(A) 3

(B) $\dfrac{4}{5}$

(C) $1\dfrac{1}{4}$

(D) $2\dfrac{1}{2}$

(E) 2

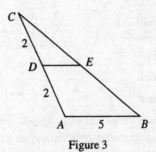

Figure 3

GO ON TO THE NEXT PAGE

18. $\dfrac{x}{yz} + y =$

(A) $\dfrac{x}{z}$

(B) $\dfrac{y^2 z}{x}$

(C) $\dfrac{xy}{z}$

(D) $\dfrac{x}{y^2 z}$

(E) $\dfrac{z}{x}$

19. If $f(x) = x^3 - 5x^2 + 7$, then $f(-2) - f(2) =$

(A) -26

(B) -16

(C) 8

(D) -6

(E) -7

20. If $\log_a 25 - \log_a 2 = \log_a x$, then $x =$

(A) 23

(B) 50

(C) 5

(D) 27

(E) $12\dfrac{1}{2}$

21. $\dfrac{\cot \theta}{\cos \theta} =$

(A) $\sin \theta$

(B) $\sec \theta$

(C) $\tan \theta$

(D) $\csc \theta$

(E) 1

22. Which of the following is a value of x for which $1 + \cos x + \sin^2 x = 0$ is true?

(A) $90°$

(B) $100°$

(C) $60°$

(D) $360°$

(E) 0

GO ON TO THE NEXT PAGE

23. If x is a positive number, which of the following has the greatest value?

(A) $\dfrac{x}{x}$

(B) $\dfrac{x+1}{x}$

(C) $\dfrac{x}{x+1}$

(D) $\dfrac{x+1}{x-1}$

(E) $\dfrac{x+2}{x+3}$

24. Which of the following points is in the graph of the solution set of the system

$$x+y < 7$$
$$x-y < 3$$

(A) $(7,0)$

(B) $(3,-3)$

(C) $(7,7)$

(D) $(7,3)$

(E) $(0,0)$

25. If $3(x+4) = 9$, then $x =$

(A) $\dfrac{5}{3}$

(B) -1

(C) 3

(D) 7

(E) 2

26. A rectangle has a width of 9 and a diagonal of 15. What is its length?

(A) 12

(B) 10

(C) 11

(D) 13

(E) 14

USE THIS SPACE FOR SCRATCH WORK

GO ON TO THE NEXT PAGE

27. If the point $(b, -2)$ is on the graph of the equation $2x + y = 7$, then $b =$

(A) -3

(B) 3

(C) $2\frac{1}{2}$

(D) -5

(E) $4\frac{1}{2}$

28. $3\sqrt{3a} =$

(A) $\sqrt{12a}$

(B) $\sqrt{9a}$

(C) $\sqrt{27a}$

(D) $\sqrt{6a}$

(E) $\sqrt{15a}$

29. For the triangles in Figure 4, each set of given information leads to the conclusion that $\triangle ABC \cong \triangle XYZ$ EXCEPT

(A) $AB = XY, AC = YZ$, and $\angle C = \angle Z$

(B) $AB = XY, \angle B = \angle Y$, and $\angle C = \angle Z$

(C) $AB = XY, AC = XZ$, and $\angle A = \angle X$

(D) $AB = XY, \angle B = \angle Y$, and $\angle A = \angle X$

(E) $AB = XY, BC = YZ$, and $AC = XZ$

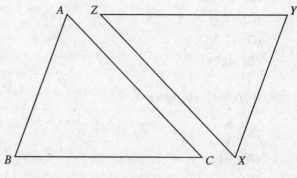

Figure 4

30. The area of a certain triangle is one-quarter the area of a certain rectangle. If the two figures have equal heights, the ratio $\dfrac{\text{base of rectangle}}{\text{base of triangle}}$ is

(A) 4

(B) 1

(C) 8

(D) 2

(E) $\dfrac{1}{4}$

GO ON TO THE NEXT PAGE

31. If $\dfrac{4^x}{4^2} = 4^8$, then $x =$

    (A) 6

    (B) 16

    (C) 4

    (D) 10

    (E) 64

32. A cup is in the shape of a cone with a circular lip. The radius of the lip is 2 inches, and the height of the cone is 4 inches. When the cup is filled to half its volume, the height of the liquid, h, is

    (A) $2h^2 = 5$

    (B) $3h = 4$

    (C) $\dfrac{h}{3} = 12$

    (D) $h^2 = 16$

    (E) $h^3 = 32$

33. In Figure 5, if $\dfrac{AB}{AC} = \dfrac{1}{2}$, then $\sin \angle A =$

    (A) $\dfrac{1}{3}$

    (B) $\dfrac{1}{2}$

    (C) $\dfrac{\sqrt{3}}{2}$

    (D) $\sqrt{3}$

    (E) 2

34. Which of the following is an expression for $\sqrt{-81} - \sqrt{-36}$ in the form $x + yi$, where x and y are real?

    (A) $0 + (\sqrt{117})i$

    (B) $0 + 3i$

    (C) $3 + 0i$

    (D) $0 + 45i$

    (E) $0 + (\sqrt{45})i$

USE THIS SPACE FOR SCRATCH WORK

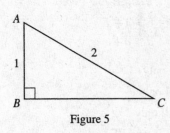

Figure 5

GO ON TO THE NEXT PAGE

35. If $y = x + 3$, then $|x - y| + |y - x| =$

   (A) 0

   (B) 6

   (C) −6

   (D) 3

   (E) Cannot be determined

36. What is the smallest value of x such that $0 < x < 90°$ and $\tan(45° + 2x) = \cot(30° - x)$?

   (A) 15°

   (B) 20°

   (C) 60°

   (D) 18°

   (E) 12°

37. If a, b, c, and d are positive numbers, $d > a$ and $b > c$, which of the following must be true?

   I. $a + b > c + d$
   II. $b + c > a + d$
   III. $b + d > a + c$

   (A) I only

   (B) II only

   (C) III only

   (D) I, II, and III

   (E) None

38. The base of an isosceles triangle lies on the x-axis. What is the sum of the slopes of the three sides?

   (A) 0

   (B) 1

   (C) −1

   (D) $2\sqrt{3}$

   (E) Cannot be determined

39. Which of the following is the set of all real numbers x such that $|x| - 6 \leq |x - 6|$?

   (A) $\{6\}$

   (B) $\{-6\}$

   (C) $\{x : x \geq 0\}$

   (D) $\{x : x \leq 0\}$

   (E) All real numbers

USE THIS SPACE FOR SCRATCH WORK

GO ON TO THE NEXT PAGE

40. If $\dfrac{x}{x+1} \geq 1$, then

(A) $-1 < x < 0$

(B) $x > -1$

(C) $x \geq -1$

(D) $x < -1$

(E) $-1 \leq x < 0$

41. $\dfrac{\csc x}{\sec(90 - x)} =$

(A) 0

(B) $\tan x$

(C) $\cot x$

(D) 1

(E) -1

42. If three numbers are added in pairs, the sums equal 5, 16, and 27. The greatest of the three numbers is

(A) 15

(B) 17

(C) 19

(D) 21

(E) 23

43. Two planes, P and Q, are perpendicular to each other. If S is the set of all points that are 5 inches from P and 3 inches from Q, which of the following describes S?

(A) Two parallel lines

(B) Two intersecting lines

(C) Two points

(D) Four points

(E) Four parallel lines

44. The area of a square is 81, and the coordinates of one corner are $(5, -4)$. The coordinates of an adjacent corner are

(A) $(-3.49, 1)$

(B) $(-8, 4.49)$

(C) $(2, 4.49)$

(D) $(4.49, -1)$

(E) $(8, -4.49)$

GO ON TO THE NEXT PAGE

USE THIS SPACE FOR SCRATCH WORK

45. If f and g are inverse functions and if $(2, -3)$ is a point on the graph on $y = g(x)$, then f is

(A) $f(x) = 2x + 8$

(B) $f(x) = 4x - 11$

(C) $f(x) = x^2 - 1$

(D) $f(x) = 5x - 7$

(E) $f(x) = x - 5$

46. A rectangular solid has length 4, width 3, and height 5. If AB is a diagonal of the base and AC is a diagonal of the solid, then $\tan \angle BAC =$

(A) .75

(B) 1

(C) .8

(D) .6

(E) 1.33

47. In rectangle $XYZW$, in Figure 6, $YZ = 2$ and $YW = 2\sqrt{5}$. How long is the side of a square whose area is the same as the area of $XYZW$?

(A) 3.16

(B) 6.32

(C) 12

(D) 2.83

(E) 3.46

48. In the graph in Figure 7, an equation of the given line is

(A) $y = 2x + 1$

(B) $y = 2.5x - 1$

(C) $y = \dfrac{1}{2}x + 1$

(D) $y = \dfrac{1}{2}x - \dfrac{1}{2}$

(E) $y = -2x + 1$

USE THIS SPACE FOR SCRATCH WORK

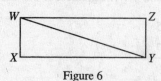

Figure 6

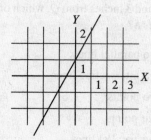

Figure 7

49. If $\log_2 k^3 = 6$, then $k =$

(A) $3\dfrac{1}{3}$

(B) $6\dfrac{1}{3}$

(C) 1

(D) 4

(E) 8

50. When simplified,

$$\dfrac{2 - \dfrac{1-2x}{x-2}}{\dfrac{x^2+4x+4}{x^2-4}} =$$

(A) $\dfrac{2x+1}{x+2}$

(B) $\dfrac{4x-3}{x+2}$

(C) $-\dfrac{5}{x+2}$

(D) $\dfrac{(x-2)(4x-5)}{x+2}$

(E) $\dfrac{4x-5}{x+2}$

USE THIS SPACE FOR SCRATCH WORK

STOP
IF YOU FINISH BEFORE TIME IS CALLED, YOU MAY CHECK YOUR WORK ON THIS TEST ONLY.
DO NOT WORK ON ANY OTHER TEST IN THIS BOOK.

ANSWER KEY

1. A	11. E	21. D	31. D	41. D
2. E	12. A	22. B	32. E	42. C
3. C	13. E	23. D	33. C	43. E
4. D	14. B	24. E	34. B	44. C
5. C	15. C	25. B	35. B	45. A
6. A	16. B	26. A	36. A	46. B
7. C	17. D	27. E	37. C	47. D
8. D	18. D	28. C	38. A	48. A
9. C	19. B	29. A	39. E	49. D
10. B	20. E	30. D	40. D	50. E

ANSWER EXPLANATIONS

---

1. (A) $8 \times 24 = 4 \times 2 \times 24$
$$= 4 \times 48.$$

Alternate solution:

Test each choice by multiplying.

2. (E) $\dfrac{4}{7} \times \dfrac{8}{7} = \dfrac{4 \times 8}{7 \times 7}$
$$= \dfrac{32}{49}$$

3. (C) Two angles must have the same measure (since the triangle is isosceles), and their sum must be 180.

4. (D) $(3b)^2 = (3b)(3b) = 9b^2$

5. (C) $\dfrac{x}{5} = 2$ so $x = 5\left(\dfrac{x}{5}\right) = 5 \cdot 2 = 10$

6. (A) $6 = R \times \dfrac{1}{2}$. Multiply each side by 2 to get $12 = R$.

7. (C)

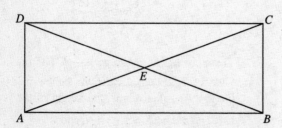

For a rectangle such as $ABCD$, $\triangle DBA \cong \triangle CAB$ by SAS so $DB = AC$ by CP. Also, $\triangle DEA \cong \triangle CEB$ by ASA so $DE = EB$ and $CE = EA$ by CP. DB and CA are clearly not perpendicular.

8. (D)
$$\dfrac{9a^2 + 3a}{3a} = \dfrac{9a^2}{3a} + \dfrac{3a}{3a}$$
$$= 3a + 1$$

9. (C) A device for remembering the quadrants for which the basic trig functions (sin, cos, tan) are positive is

ALL	Seniors	Turn	Crazy
I	II	III	IV

10. (B) Cross-multiply:
$$(x+5)(x-5) = x(x-1)$$
$$x^2 - 25 = x^2 - x$$
$$-25 = -x$$
$$25 = x$$

11. (E) Sine and cosine are cofunctions, meaning $\sin A = \cos(90 - A)$.

12. (A) $(5x - 4) - 2x = (2x + 8) - 2x$.
$$3x - 4 = 8$$
$$3x = 12$$

13. (E) Every triangle must have at least two acute angles.

14. (B) Since AB is parallel to CD, $\angle B$ and $\angle C$ are supplementary, so $x + y = 180$.

15. (C) Area of square is 3^2 so side is 3. Radius of circle must be $\dfrac{3}{2}$. Area is $\pi r^2 = \pi \left(\dfrac{3}{2}\right)^2$.

16. (B)
$$15\% = .15$$
$$\tfrac{1}{2} = .5$$
$$(.5)(.15) = 0.75$$

17. (D)
$$\triangle CDE \cong \triangle CAB$$
$$\dfrac{CD}{CA} = \dfrac{DE}{AB}$$
$$\dfrac{2}{4} = \dfrac{DE}{5}$$
$$\dfrac{5}{2} = DE$$

18. (D) $\dfrac{x}{yz} + y = \dfrac{x}{yz} \cdot \dfrac{1}{y} = \dfrac{x}{y^2 z}$

19. (B)
$$f(-2) = (-2)^3 - 5(-2)^3 + 7$$

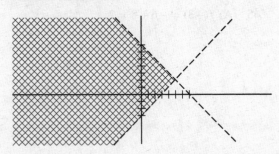 $= -21$

$$f(2) = (2)^3 - 5(2)^2 + 7$$

$$= -5$$

$$(-21) - (-5) = -16$$

20. (E) $\log_a 25 - \log_a 2 = \log_a \dfrac{25}{2}$

$$\dfrac{25}{2} = x = 12\dfrac{1}{2}$$

21. (D) $\dfrac{\cot \theta}{\cos \theta} = \dfrac{\cos \theta}{\sin \theta} \cdot \dfrac{1}{\cos \theta}$

$$= \dfrac{1}{\sin \theta}$$

$$= \csc \theta$$

22. (B)
$$1 + \cos x + \sin^2 x = 0$$

$$1 + \cos x + (1 - \cos^2 x) = 0$$

$$2 + \cos x - \cos^2 x = 0$$

$$\cos x = 2 \text{ or } \cos x = -1$$

$$\cos x = 2 \text{ is impossible}$$

$$\cos x = -1 \text{ at } 180°$$

With a graphing calculator, enter the function and use the "solve" feature.

23. (D) Greatest value occurs when the ratio of numerator to denominator is greatest. Denominators are greater than numerators in (A), (C), and (E), so they are eliminated. In (B) the numerator is only one unit more than its denominator as compared with two units in (D).

24. (E) The cross-hatched region of the graph below contains all solutions.

25. (B)
$$\dfrac{3(x+4)}{3} = \dfrac{9}{3}$$

$$x + 4 = 3$$

$$x = -1$$

26. (A) If length $= x$ then $x^2 + 9^2 = 15^2$ by the Pythagorean Theorem and

$$x^2 = 225 - 81$$

$$= 144$$

$$x = 12$$

27. (E) Substitute $(b, -2)$ for (x, y) in the equation.

$$2b - 2 = 7$$

$$2b = 9$$

$$b = \dfrac{9}{2}$$

28. (C) $3\sqrt{3a} = \sqrt{9}\sqrt{3a} = \sqrt{9 \cdot 3a} = \sqrt{27a}$

29. (A) Correspondence in (A) is SSA, which is not a congruence.

30. (D)
$$\dfrac{A_t}{A_r} = \dfrac{1}{4} = \dfrac{\frac{1}{2} b_t \cdot h}{b_r \cdot h} = \dfrac{b_t}{2 b_r}$$

Therefore $4b_t = 2b_r$, so $\dfrac{b_r}{b_t} = 2$.

31. (D)
$$x - 2 = 8$$

$$x = 10$$

32. (E) The volume of the cone is

$$\dfrac{1}{3} \pi r^2 h = \dfrac{16}{3} \pi$$

Therefore half the volume is $\dfrac{8}{3} \pi$. The liquid contents form a second cone in the same proportion as the first; in other words, the height of the cone is twice its radius. Since $r = \dfrac{1}{2} h$ and $V = \dfrac{8}{3} \pi$.

$$\dfrac{8}{3} \pi = \dfrac{1}{3} \pi \left(\dfrac{1}{2} h \right)^2 h$$

$$32 = h^3$$

33. (C) $BC = \sqrt{3}$ by the Pythagorean Theorem.

$$\sin \angle A = \frac{\text{opposite side}}{\text{hypotenuse}} = \frac{\sqrt{3}}{2}$$

34. (B)
$$\sqrt{-81} = 9i,$$
$$\sqrt{-36} = 6i$$
$$9i - 6i = 3i.$$

 Note: your calculator gives you an error message when you enter $\sqrt{-81}$.

35. (B) Substitute $x + 3$ for y.

$$|x - x - 3| + |x + 3 - x| = 3 + 3 = 6.$$

36. (A) Since cofunctions of complementary angles are equal,

$$(45° + 2x) + (30° - x) = 90°$$
$$x = 90° - (30° + 45°)$$
$$= 15$$

37. (C) By addition of the given inequalities $b + d > a + c$, so III is correct. If a, b, c, and $d = 1, 3, 2$, and 4, respectively, it can be seen that I and II are false.

38. (A) Situate the triangle on a coordinate system as shown.

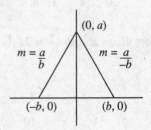

Slope of base $= 0$. Therefore

$$\text{sum of slopes } = 0 + \frac{a}{b} - \frac{a}{b} = 0$$

39. (E) If $x \geq 6$, both sides of inequality are equal. If $-6 < x < 6$, the left side is negative and the right side is positive, so inequality is true.

If $x \leq -6$, both sides are positive but left side is always less than the right side. Therefore inequality is always true.

Alternate solution:

Graphing calculator: graph $y = \boxed{\text{abs}}(x - 6) + 6 - \boxed{\text{abs}}(x)$ and determine where the graph is above the x-axis.

40. (D) If $x + 1 > 0$, $x > x + 1$, which is never true. If $x + 1 < 0$, inequality is reversed when multiplying through, so $x \leq x + 1$. Therefore, when $x < -1$, $0 \leq 1$, so inequality is true for all $x < -1$.

Alternate solution:

Graphing calculator: graph $y = 1 - (x/(x + 1))$ and determine where the graph is below the x-axis.

41. (D) Since cofunctions of complementary angles are equal, $\sec x = \csc(90 - x)$.

$$\frac{\csc x}{\sec(90 - x)} = \frac{\csc x}{\csc x} = 1$$

42. (C)
$$x + y = 5$$
$$y + z = 16$$
$$x + z = 27$$

z is largest.

Subtract first from second, and add result to third to get

$$2z = 38$$
$$z = 19$$

43. (E) The set of all points 5 inches from P is a pair of parallel planes (call them M and N), one on each side of P. Likewise, the set of all points 3 inches from Q is a pair of parallel planes (call them R and S). Planes M and N are both perpendicular to planes R and S. The four planes intersect in pairs to form four parallel lines.

44. (C) The other corner must lie on a circle with center $(5, -4)$ and radius 9. The equation is $(x - 5)^2 + (y + 4)^2 = 81$.

(D) and (E) can be ruled out because the radical does not drop out when substituted and squared.

Trying the others:

$$
\begin{aligned}
\text{(A)} \quad & 72 + 25 \neq 81 \\
\text{(B)} \quad & 169 + 72 \neq 81 \\
\text{(C)} \quad & 9 + 72 = 81.
\end{aligned}
$$

45. (A) $f(-3) = -6 + 8 = 2$.

46. (B) Refer to the diagram:

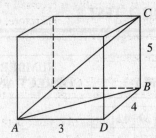

If the dimensions of the base are 3 by 4, diagonal $AB = 5$ by the Pythagorean Theorem. $\triangle ABC$ is a right triangle. Therefore

$$\tan \angle CAB = \frac{BC}{AB} = \frac{5}{5} = 1$$

47. (D) $WZ = 4$ by Pythagorean Theorem.

Area $= 8$.

Therefore, the side of the square with area of 8 is $\sqrt{8} = 2.83$.

48. (A)

$$m = \frac{\text{change in } y\text{-coordinates}}{\text{change in } x\text{-coordinates}} = \frac{2}{1}$$

y-intercept $= 1$

$y = 2x + 1$.

49. (D) By definition of logs,

$$2^6 = k^3$$
$$2^6 = (2^2)^3$$
$$= k^3$$

Therefore $2^2 = k = 4$.

Alternate solution:

Graphing calculator: graph

$$y = 6 - ((\log x^3)/(\log 2))$$

and solve.

Or enter $k = \sqrt[3]{2^6}$ to find $k = 4$.

50. (E) Multiply top and bottom of original fraction by $x^2 - 4$:

$$\frac{2(x^2 - 4) - (1 - 2x)(x + 2)}{x^2 + 4x + 4}$$

$$= \frac{2x^2 - 8 - x - 2 + 2x^2 + 4x}{x^2 + 4x + 4}$$

$$= \frac{4x^2 + 3x - 10}{x^2 + 4x + 4}$$

$$= \frac{(x + 2)(4x - 5)}{(x + 2)(x + 2)}$$

SELF-EVALUATION CHART FOR MODEL TEST 5

SUBJECT AREA	QUESTIONS ANSWERED CORRECTLY															NUMBER OF CORRECT ANSWERS
Algebra (15 questions)	4	5	6	8	10	12	18	25	28	31	35	37	39	42	50	_____
Plane geometry (10 questions)				3	7	13	14	15	17	26	29	30	32			_____
Solid geometry (3 questions)										32	43	46				_____
Coordinate geometry (5 questions)									24	27	38	44	48			_____
Trigonometry (7 questions)								9	11	21	22	33	36	41		_____
Functions (5 questions)									19	20	23	40	45			_____
Miscellaneous (5 questions)									1	2	16	34	39			_____

Total number of correct answers	_____
Total number of incorrect answers	_____
Total score = total number of correct answers	_____
minus $\frac{1}{4}$ number of incorrect answers	$-$ _____
	_____

(Reminder: Answers left blank are not counted as correct or incorrect)

Raw score = (number correct) $- \frac{1}{4}$ (number incorrect)

To evaluate your performance, compare your raw score with the table below.

Evaluate Your Performance
Model Test 5

Excellent	760–800	46–50
Very Good	700–750	40–45
Good	610–690	32–39
Above Average	560–600	26–31
Average	500–550	18–25
Below Average	270–490	17 or less

ANSWER SHEET FOR DIAGNOSTIC TEST

Determine the correct answer for each question. Then, using a No. 2 pencil, blacken completely the oval containing the letter of your choice.

1. Ⓐ Ⓑ Ⓒ Ⓓ Ⓔ
2. Ⓐ Ⓑ Ⓒ Ⓓ Ⓔ
3. Ⓐ Ⓑ Ⓒ Ⓓ Ⓔ
4. Ⓐ Ⓑ Ⓒ Ⓓ Ⓔ
5. Ⓐ Ⓑ Ⓒ Ⓓ Ⓔ
6. Ⓐ Ⓑ Ⓒ Ⓓ Ⓔ
7. Ⓐ Ⓑ Ⓒ Ⓓ Ⓔ
8. Ⓐ Ⓑ Ⓒ Ⓓ Ⓔ
9. Ⓐ Ⓑ Ⓒ Ⓓ Ⓔ
10. Ⓐ Ⓑ Ⓒ Ⓓ Ⓔ
11. Ⓐ Ⓑ Ⓒ Ⓓ Ⓔ
12. Ⓐ Ⓑ Ⓒ Ⓓ Ⓔ
13. Ⓐ Ⓑ Ⓒ Ⓓ Ⓔ
14. Ⓐ Ⓑ Ⓒ Ⓓ Ⓔ
15. Ⓐ Ⓑ Ⓒ Ⓓ Ⓔ
16. Ⓐ Ⓑ Ⓒ Ⓓ Ⓔ
17. Ⓐ Ⓑ Ⓒ Ⓓ Ⓔ

18. Ⓐ Ⓑ Ⓒ Ⓓ Ⓔ
19. Ⓐ Ⓑ Ⓒ Ⓓ Ⓔ
20. Ⓐ Ⓑ Ⓒ Ⓓ Ⓔ
21. Ⓐ Ⓑ Ⓒ Ⓓ Ⓔ
22. Ⓐ Ⓑ Ⓒ Ⓓ Ⓔ
23. Ⓐ Ⓑ Ⓒ Ⓓ Ⓔ
24. Ⓐ Ⓑ Ⓒ Ⓓ Ⓔ
25. Ⓐ Ⓑ Ⓒ Ⓓ Ⓔ
26. Ⓐ Ⓑ Ⓒ Ⓓ Ⓔ
27. Ⓐ Ⓑ Ⓒ Ⓓ Ⓔ
28. Ⓐ Ⓑ Ⓒ Ⓓ Ⓔ
29. Ⓐ Ⓑ Ⓒ Ⓓ Ⓔ
30. Ⓐ Ⓑ Ⓒ Ⓓ Ⓔ
31. Ⓐ Ⓑ Ⓒ Ⓓ Ⓔ
32. Ⓐ Ⓑ Ⓒ Ⓓ Ⓔ
33. Ⓐ Ⓑ Ⓒ Ⓓ Ⓔ
34. Ⓐ Ⓑ Ⓒ Ⓓ Ⓔ

35. Ⓐ Ⓑ Ⓒ Ⓓ Ⓔ
36. Ⓐ Ⓑ Ⓒ Ⓓ Ⓔ
37. Ⓐ Ⓑ Ⓒ Ⓓ Ⓔ
38. Ⓐ Ⓑ Ⓒ Ⓓ Ⓔ
39. Ⓐ Ⓑ Ⓒ Ⓓ Ⓔ
40. Ⓐ Ⓑ Ⓒ Ⓓ Ⓔ
41. Ⓐ Ⓑ Ⓒ Ⓓ Ⓔ
42. Ⓐ Ⓑ Ⓒ Ⓓ Ⓔ
43. Ⓐ Ⓑ Ⓒ Ⓓ Ⓔ
44. Ⓐ Ⓑ Ⓒ Ⓓ Ⓔ
45. Ⓐ Ⓑ Ⓒ Ⓓ Ⓔ
46. Ⓐ Ⓑ Ⓒ Ⓓ Ⓔ
47. Ⓐ Ⓑ Ⓒ Ⓓ Ⓔ
48. Ⓐ Ⓑ Ⓒ Ⓓ Ⓔ
49. Ⓐ Ⓑ Ⓒ Ⓓ Ⓔ
50. Ⓐ Ⓑ Ⓒ Ⓓ Ⓔ

Model Test Score Conversion Table							
Raw Score	Scaled Score	Raw Score	Scaled Score	Raw Score	Scaled Score	Raw Score	Scaled Score
50	800	34	630	18	500	2	370
49	790	33	620	17	490	1	360
48	780	32	610	16	480	0	360
47	770	31	600	15	480	−1	350
46	760	30	590	14	470	−2	340
45	750	29	580	13	460	−3	330
44	740	28	580	12	450	−4	330
43	730	27	570	11	440	−5	320
42	720	26	560	10	440	−6	310
41	710	25	550	9	430	−7	300
40	700	24	540	8	420	−8	300
39	690	23	540	7	410	−9	290
38	680	22	530	6	400	−10	280
37	660	21	520	5	390	−11	270
36	650	20	510	4	390	−12	270
35	640	19	510	3	380		

MODEL TEST 6

Directions: For each of the 50 multiple-choice test questions, select the BEST answer among the five choices given. When the exact numerical value is not one of the choices, select the best approximation to the exact value. Mark your choice on the answer sheet by filling in the corresponding oval.

Notes:

1. All angle measures are in degrees.

2. Some problems are accompanied by figures, which provide information useful in solving the problem. Figures are drawn accurately unless marked "Figure not drawn to scale." All figures lie in a plane unless the diagram clearly shows otherwise.

3. Except when stated otherwise, the domain of a function f is the set of real number values of x for which $f(x)$ is a real number.

4. Reference information consisting of volume and surface area formulas that may be useful in answering some questions on this test can be found below:

REFERENCE INFORMATION

- Sphere with radius r.　　Volume: $V = \frac{4}{3}\pi r^3$　　Surface Area: $S = 4\pi r^2$
- Right circular cone with radius r and height h.　　Volume: $V = \frac{1}{3}\pi r^2 h$
- Right circular cone with circumference of base c and slant height L.
  Lateral Area: $S = \frac{1}{2}cL$
- Pyramid with base area B and height h.　　Volume: $V = \frac{1}{3}Bh$

NOTE TO STUDENTS:

By taking the first five model tests with your calculator, you have now had lots of chances to practice when to use it and when not to. On this final test, there are about ten questions for which you will be tempted to start punching buttons right off the bat. Hold off. Remember that your success on the Math Level IC test will depend most on your knowledge of mathematical principles and your skill in applying them. When taking this final practice test, set your calculator aside to see how well you can do without it. You should be able to answer every question without your electronic aid. All of the explanations at the end of the test will be noncalculator solutions.

1. If .2 of a cup of liquid weighs 3 ounces, how many ounces will .6 of a cup of the same liquid weigh?

   (A) 10
   (B) 6
   (C) 1
   (D) 15
   (E) 9

2. If ray R_1 and ray R_2 are parallel in Figure 1, then $a+b+c = ?$

   (A) 180°
   (B) 200°
   (C) 300°
   (D) 270°
   (E) 360°

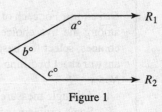

Figure 1

3. If a point (x,y) is in the third quadrant, which of the following must be true?

   I. $x+y < 0$
   II. $x > y$
   III. $xy < 0$

   (A) I only
   (B) I and II only
   (C) II only
   (D) III only
   (E) II and III only

4. In Figure 2, the coordinates of A are

   (A) $(-8,2)$
   (B) $(-4,2)$
   (C) $(-4,4)$
   (D) $(-2,-2)$
   (E) $(-4,-4)$

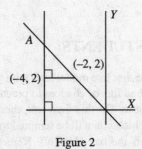

Figure 2

GO ON TO THE NEXT PAGE

5. What is the area of the triangle formed by the x-axis and the lines $x - y = 4$ and $x + y = 12$?

(A) 48

(B) 8

(C) 16

(D) 3

(E) 20

6. If a is a positive number, then $\dfrac{a^{1/3}}{a^{-2/3}} =$

(A) $-a$

(B) $-\dfrac{1}{2}$

(C) $a^{-1/3}$

(D) a

(E) -2

7. Which of the following is the relationship between x and y if the circles in Figure 3 are tangent to each other and to the sides of the rectangle?

(A) $x = \dfrac{1}{4}y$

(B) $x = \dfrac{y}{\pi}$

(C) $x = \pi y^2$

(D) $x = 2\pi y$

(E) $x = 4y$

8. If $m = 2b$ for the linear function $f(x) = mx + b$, and $f(1) = 12$, then $b =$

(A) 6

(B) 3

(C) -6

(D) 8

(E) 4

USE THIS SPACE FOR SCRATCH WORK

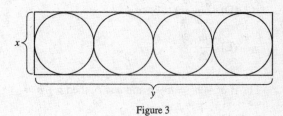

Figure 3

GO ON TO THE NEXT PAGE

9. If $x^{-1} = 2^{-1} + 3^{-1}$, then $x =$

(A) 5

(B) $\dfrac{6}{5}$

(C) -5

(D) $\dfrac{2}{3}$

(E) $\dfrac{1}{5}$

10. If $p + q = a$ and $p \cdot q = b$, then the average of p and q is

(A) $a + \dfrac{b}{2}$

(B) $\dfrac{a}{2}$

(C) $\dfrac{a+b}{2}$

(D) $\dfrac{a-b}{2}$

(E) $\dfrac{ab}{2}$

11. If $a^2 - b^2 = a - b$ and $a \neq b$, then $a + b =$

(A) 0

(B) 3

(C) 1

(D) -2

(E) Cannot be determined

12. If in Figure 4, $WXYZ$ is a square inscribed in a circle for which C is the circumference, XY is the length of one side and XZ is the length of the diagonal, then

(A) $4XY < C < 4XZ$

(B) $C < 4XY < 4XZ$

(C) $4XY < 4XZ < C$

(D) $C < 4XZ < 4XY$

(E) $4XZ < 4XY < C$

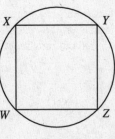

Figure 4

GO ON TO THE NEXT PAGE

13. If in Figure 5, θ is the angle formed by the x-axis and a ray of the line $y = 2x$, then $\sin\theta =$

(A) .5

(B) 2

(C) .33

(D) .89

(E) .45

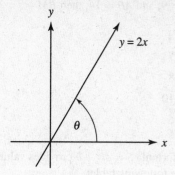

Figure 5

14. If p is a number between 0 and 30°, which of the following is an arrangement of I, II, and III in order from least to greatest?

I. $\cos p$

II. $\cos\dfrac{p}{2}$

III. $\cos 2p$

(A) III, I, II

(B) II, I, III

(C) I, II, III

(D) III, II, I

(E) II, III, I

15. If x is an integer greater than -10 but less than 10, and $|x - 2| < 3$, then the values of x are

(A) $-10, -9, -8, -7, -6, -5, -4, -3, -2, -1,$
    $0, 1, 2, 3, 4$

(B) $0, 1, 2, 3, 4, 5, 6, 7, 8, 9, 10$

(C) $0, 1, 2, 3, 4$

(D) $-4, -3, -2, -1, 0, 1, 2, 3, 4$

(E) $-1, 0, 1$

16. If a and b are both positive integers divisible by 5 without remainder, then each of the following is divisible by 5 without remainder EXCEPT

(A) ab

(B) $a + b$

(C) $a - b$

(D) $a^2 + b^2$

(E) $\dfrac{a}{b}$

GO ON TO THE NEXT PAGE

17. If MN in Figure 6 is parallel to AC, $BC = 21$, $NC = 9$, and $AB = 14$, then $BM =$

   (A) 9

   (B) 7

   (C) 8

   (D) 10

   (E) 6

USE THIS SPACE FOR SCRATCH WORK

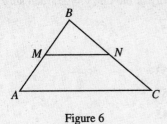

Figure 6

18. The formula $S = at^2 + b$ provides values according to the following table:

t	S
0	3
2	11

   The values of a and b are

   (A) $a = -1, b = 3$

   (B) $a = 0, b = 11$

   (C) $a = 3, b = 8$

   (D) $a = 2, b = 14$

   (E) $a = 2, b = 3$

19. If $8x = 25$, then $\frac{2}{5}x =$

   (A) $\frac{5}{4}$

   (B) $\frac{4}{5}$

   (C) $\frac{125}{4}$

   (D) $\frac{125}{16}$

   (E) $\frac{16}{25}$

20. If $y = \log_{10} 5$, then

   (A) $y = \frac{1}{2}$

   (B) $y = 2$

   (C) $10^y = 5$

   (D) $5^y = 10$

   (E) $y^5 = 10$

GO ON TO THE NEXT PAGE

21. $\dfrac{4}{2-2i} =$

(A) $1-i$

(B) $1+i$

(C) i

(D) $2i$

(E) $-2i$

22. $\sqrt{\cos^2 4\theta + \sin^2 4\theta} =$

(A) $\cos 4\theta + \sin 4\theta$

(B) $\cos 2\theta + \sin 2\theta$

(C) 1

(D) $\sec^2 4\theta$

(E) $\sec 2\theta$

23. If $(a, \sin a)$ and $(b, \sin b)$ are any two points on the graph of $y = \sin x$, then the greatest value of $\sin a - \sin b$ is

(A) 1

(B) 2

(C) 0

(D) 180°

(E) 360°

24. If $\log_a(x+2) - \log_a(x-1) = \log_a 4$, then what is x?

(A) -2

(B) 2

(C) 1

(D) -1

(E) 4

25. In triangle ABC in Figure 7, M and N are the midpoints of sides AB and BC, respectively.

If $MN = 3x - 2$ and $AC = 5x + 7$, then $x =$

(A) 11

(B) 10

(C) 6

(D) 31

(E) 24

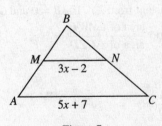

Figure 7

GO ON TO THE NEXT PAGE

26. In Figure 8, $AB = BC$ and $AD = CD$. Which of the following must be true?

    I. BD bisects $\angle ABC$.

    II. BD bisects AC.

    III. AC bisects BD.

(A) I only

(B) II only

(C) II and III only

(D) I and II only

(E) I and III only

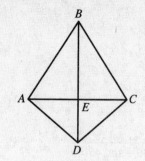

Figure 8

27. In Figure 9, $ABCD$ is a parallelogram. If the measures of the angles are represented in terms of x as shown, then $x =$

(A) 45°

(B) 30°

(C) 60°

(D) 50°

(E) 55°

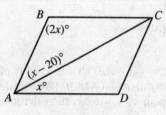

Figure 9

28. If $f(x) = \dfrac{1}{\sin x}$, then

(A) $f(x) = \dfrac{1}{f(x)}$

(B) $-f(x) = f(-x)$

(C) $f(x) = -f(x)$

(D) $f(-x) = f\left(\dfrac{1}{x}\right)$

(E) $f\left(\dfrac{1}{x}\right) = -f(x)$

29. In Figure 10, $CD \parallel XY$ and $AB \parallel XY$. W and Z are equidistant from XY. If $AB = a$ and $CD = 3a$, then the ratio $\dfrac{\text{area of } \triangle AWB}{\text{area of } \triangle CZD} =$

(A) a^2

(B) $\dfrac{1}{9}a^2$

(C) $\dfrac{1}{9}$

(D) $\dfrac{1}{3}$

(E) $\dfrac{1}{3}a$

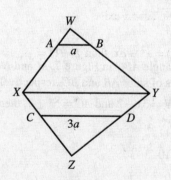

Figure 10

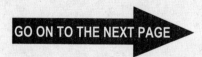

GO ON TO THE NEXT PAGE

30. If $2\sin^2 x = \sin x$, then a value of x is

   (A) 30°

   (B) 45°

   (C) 60°

   (D) 120°

   (E) 360°

31. If $x * (x - y) = x^2 + y^2$, then $5 * 3 =$

   (A) 34

   (B) 8

   (C) 64

   (D) 16

   (E) 29

32. In Figure 11, $\triangle ABD$ has a point C of side AD for which $AB = BC = CD$. If the measure of $\angle BCD$ is 110°, then the measure of $\triangle ABD =$

   (A) 90

   (B) 80

   (C) 75

   (D) 100

   (E) 95

33. If $3^x < 0$, then

   (A) $0 < x < 1$

   (B) $-1 < x < 0$

   (C) $x > 1$

   (D) $x < -1$

   (E) No such x exists

34. If $f(x) = x^2 - ax$, then $f(-1) =$

   (A) $-1 - a$

   (B) a

   (C) $1 - a$

   (D) $a + 1$

   (E) 1

USE THIS SPACE FOR SCRATCH WORK

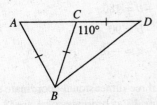

(The figure is not drawn to scale.)

Figure 11

GO ON TO THE NEXT PAGE

35. $\dfrac{\sin 30° + \cos 30°}{\sqrt{3}\tan 30°} =$

(A) $\dfrac{1}{\sqrt{3}}$

(B) 2

(C) $\sqrt{3}+1$

(D) $\dfrac{1}{2}+\sqrt{3}$

(E) $\dfrac{1+\sqrt{3}}{2}$

36. If in Figure 12, $PQ = PR$, then

(A) $a = 120$

(B) $b = 40$

(C) $a+b = 180$

(D) $a-b = 90$

(E) $b-a = -10$

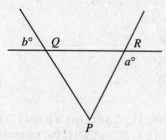

Figure 12

37. In the three-dimensional coordinate system shown in Figure 13, coordinates of A are $(3,0,5)$ and of C are $(0,4,5)$. How far is B from D?

(A) 5

(B) 25

(C) $5\sqrt{2}$

(D) 3

(E) 4

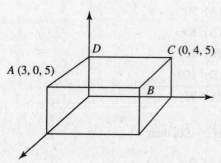

Figure 13

38. For the parabola that is the graph of $y = x(a - x)$, which of the following must be true?

    I. the x-intercepts are 0 and a

    II. the vertex is $\left(\dfrac{a}{2}, \dfrac{a^2}{4}\right)$

    III. the axis of symmetry is $x = a$

(A) I and II only

(B) II and III only

(C) I and III only

(D) all

(E) none

GO ON TO THE NEXT PAGE

39. If in Figure 14, $AB = DB$, $\angle A = 70°$, $\angle DBC = 20°$, and $\angle C = x°$, then $x =$

(A) 70

(B) 60

(C) 45

(D) 50

(E) 65

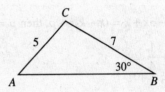

Figure 14

40. In $\triangle ABC$ in Figure 15, if the parts have the measures shown, then $\sin A =$

(A) .60

(B) .70

(C) .80

(D) .50

(E) .75

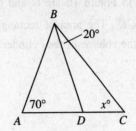

Figure 15

41. Which of the following is not equal to

$$(x+2)(3x-3)?$$

(A) $3(x+2)(x-1)$

(B) $(2+x)(3x-3)$

(C) $-(2+x)(3-3x)$

(D) $(2+x)(3-3x)$

(E) $3x^2 + 3x - 6$

42. Which of the following is the solution set of

$$7x^2 - 7x - 14 = 0?$$

(A) $\{1,2\}$

(B) $\{7,-2\}$

(C) $\{2,-7\}$

(D) $\{-14,1\}$

(E) $\{-1,2\}$

43. If $\dfrac{\sqrt{5}+x}{\sqrt{5}-x} = 1$, then $x =$

(A) $\sqrt{5}$

(B) $-\sqrt{5}$

(C) 5

(D) $\dfrac{1}{\sqrt{5}}$

(E) 0

GO ON TO THE NEXT PAGE

44. The centers of the upper and lower bases of the cylinder in Figure 16 are C and C', respectively. $AC = \frac{1}{2}CC'$. The area of rectangle $ACC'A'$ is 2. What is the volume of the cylinder?

    (A) 2π
    (B) 4π
    (C) π
    (D) 2
    (E) 4

45. If $x^2 - 3x + 2 = (x - k)^2 + p$, then $p =$

    (A) $-\dfrac{1}{4}$
    (B) 2
    (C) 3
    (D) -2
    (E) -1

46. If S is a set of six distinct points of a circle, how many chords can be drawn if any pair of elements of S can be endpoints?

    (A) 6
    (B) 20
    (C) 10
    (D) 15
    (E) 36

47. $\sqrt{16 + 16x^2} - \sqrt{9 + 9x^2} =$

    (A) $1 + x^2$
    (B) $7 + x^2$
    (C) $\sqrt{7 + 7x^2}$
    (D) $1 + x$
    (E) $\sqrt{1 + x^2}$

48. If $f(x)$ is a function for which $f(2 + k) = f(2 - k)$ and $f(-3) = 0$, for which of the following is $f(x)$ also equal to zero?

    (A) $x = 3$
    (B) $x = 5$
    (C) $x = -1$
    (D) $x = 6$
    (E) $x = 7$

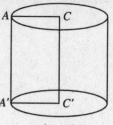

Figure 16

GO ON TO THE NEXT PAGE

49. If $\dfrac{1}{x+1} + \dfrac{1}{x-1} = \dfrac{a}{x^2-1}$, then $a =$

    (A) $2x$

    (B) x

    (C) 2

    (D) x^2

    (E) $2x+2$

50. If $f(x) = x+3$, then the equation of the graph in Figure 17 is

    (A) $y = f(x)$

    (B) $y = |f(x)|$

    (C) $y = f(|x|)$

    (D) $y = \dfrac{1}{f(x)}$

    (E) $y = -|f(x)|$

USE THIS SPACE FOR SCRATCH WORK

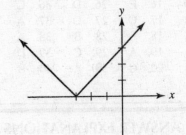

Figure 17

STOP
**IF YOU FINISH BEFORE TIME IS CALLED, YOU MAY CHECK YOUR WORK ON THIS TEST ONLY.
DO NOT WORK ON ANY OTHER TEST IN THIS BOOK.**

ANSWER KEY

1. E	11. C	21. B	31. E	41. D
2. E	12. A	22. C	32. C	42. E
3. A	13. D	23. B	33. E	43. E
4. C	14. A	24. B	34. D	44. A
5. C	15. C	25. A	35. E	45. A
6. D	16. E	26. D	36. C	46. D
7. A	17. C	27. D	37. A	47. E
8. E	18. E	28. B	38. A	48. E
9. B	19. A	29. C	39. D	49. A
10. B	20. C	30. A	40. B	50. B

ANSWER EXPLANATIONS

1. (E) Since .6 is three times .2, the number of ounces is three times 3 ounces.

2. (E) Draw line XY as shown.

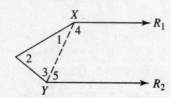

The sum of angles 1, 2, and 3 is 180. Angles 4 and 5 are supplementary since R_1 and R_2 are parallel. The sum of the measures of all five angles is 360.

3. (A)

   I. In the third quadrant, both x and y are negative, so $x+y$ is negative.

   II. The point $(-3,-2)$, is in the third quadrant.

   III. The product of two negative numbers is positive.

4. (C) First coordinate must be -4 because all points on the same vertical line must have the same first coordinate. Second coordinate must be 4 since the line through the points A, $(-2,2)$ and the origin must be $y = -x$.

5. (C) Lines $x - y = 4$ and $x + y = 12$ intersect at $(8,4)$. The equations can be solved simultaneously by adding the left sides and the right sides:

$$(x-y)+(x+y) = 4+12$$
$$2x = 16$$
$$x = 8$$

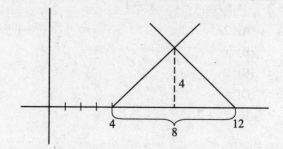

Since $x - y = 4$, $y = 4$. From the diagram, the triangle has altitude 4 and base 8. Therefore the area is

$$\frac{1}{2}(4)(8) = 16.$$

6. (D) $\dfrac{a^{1/3}}{a^{-2/3}} = a^{(1/3)-(-2/3)} = a^{3/3} = a$

7. (A) x is the diameter of one circle; y is the diameter of four circles, all having the same size.

8. (E) Since $m = 2b$, $f(x) = 2bx + b$. Since $f(1) = 12$,

$$12 = 2b+b$$
$$4 = b$$

9. (B) $x^{-1} = 2^{-1} + 3^{-1}$
$$\frac{1}{x} = \frac{1}{2}+\frac{1}{3}$$
$$\frac{1}{x} = \frac{5}{6}$$
$$x = \frac{6}{5}$$

10. (B) The average is found by adding p and q, then dividing by 2. Since $p+q = a$, the result is $\dfrac{a}{2}$. Note that the fact $p \cdot q = b$ is not needed.

11. (C) $a^2 - b^2 = (a-b)(a+b)$
Since $a^2 - b^2 = a - b$, $a+b = 1$.

12. (A) $4XY$ is the perimeter of the square, which can be easily seen to be less than the circumference, C. Since $C = \pi D$, C is approximately 3.14 (XZ). Therefore $4XZ > C$.

13. (D) Pick any point on line $y = 2x$, say, $(1,2)$. Its distance r from the origin is $\sqrt{5}$. Therefore

$$\sin\theta = \frac{1}{\sqrt{5}} = \frac{2\sqrt{5}}{5}$$

$\sqrt{5}$ is between $\sqrt{4} = 2$ and $\sqrt{9} = 3$, so $\frac{2}{5}\sqrt{5}$ is between .8 and 1.2.

14. (A) Cosine is a decreasing function from 0 to 90° meaning that the function decreases as the angle increases. To put cosine θ in increasing order, put θ in the decreasing order $2p$, p, $\dfrac{p}{2}$.

15. (C) If $|x - 2| < 3$, then

$$
\begin{array}{cccc}
-3 & < & x-2 & < 3 \\
-1 & < & x & < 5
\end{array}
$$

16. (E) If 5 is a factor of a and b, it will also be a factor of ab, $a+b$, $a-b$, and a^2+b^2, but not of $\dfrac{a}{b}$. To test the latter, try $a = 10$ and $b = 5$, for example. In this case, $\dfrac{a}{b} = 2$.

17. (C) Since $\triangle BMN \cong \triangle BAC$,

$$\frac{BM}{AB} = \frac{BN}{BC}\frac{BM}{BC} = \frac{12}{21} = \frac{4}{7}$$

$$BM = 14\left(\frac{4}{7}\right) = 8$$

18. (E) Substituting $t = 0$ and $s = 3$ gives

$$
\begin{aligned}
3 &= a(0)^2 + b \\
3 &= b
\end{aligned}
$$

Substituting $t = 2$, $s = 11$ and $b = 3$ gives

$$
\begin{aligned}
11 &= a(4) + 3 \\
8 &= 4a \\
2 &= a
\end{aligned}
$$

19. (A) To find $\dfrac{2}{5}x$, divide each side of $8x = 25$ by 20 (since 20 is 4 times 5):

$$
\begin{aligned}
\frac{8x}{20} &= \frac{25}{20} \\
\frac{2}{5}x &= \frac{5}{4}
\end{aligned}
$$

20. (C) $y = \log_{10} 5$ means $10^y = 5$ by definition.

21. (B)
$$
\begin{aligned}
\frac{4}{2-2i} &= \frac{2(2)}{2(1-i)} \\
&= \frac{2}{1-i} \\
&= \frac{2(1+i)}{(1-i)(1+i)} \\
&= \frac{2(1+i)}{1-i^2} \\
&= \frac{2(1+i)}{2} \\
&= 1+i
\end{aligned}
$$

22. (C) $\sqrt{\cos^2 4\theta + \sin^2 4\theta} = \sqrt{1} = 1$

23. (B) The greatest value of $\sin x$ is 1, and the least value is -1. Therefore the greatest difference between two values is $1 - (-1) = 2$.

24. (B) $\log(x+2) - \log(x-1) = \log\dfrac{x+2}{x-1}$. Since

$$\log\frac{x+2}{x-1} = \log 4, \frac{x+2}{x-1} = 4.$$

Therefore $x + 2 = 4x - 4$ by cross-multiplying, and $x = 2$.

25. (A) Because M and N are midpoints,

$$
\begin{aligned}
MN &= \frac{1}{2}AC \\
3x - 2 &= \frac{1}{2}(5x + 7) \\
6x - 4 &= 5x + 7 \\
x &= 11
\end{aligned}
$$

26. (D)
$$
\begin{aligned}
\triangle ABD &\cong \triangle CBD \text{ by SSS} \\
\therefore \angle ABD &\cong \angle CBD \text{ by CPCTC (I)}
\end{aligned}
$$

$$
\begin{aligned}
\triangle ABE &\cong \triangle CBE \text{ by SAS} \\
AE &= CE \text{ by CPCTC (II)}
\end{aligned}
$$

III is false since $BE \neq ED$ (refer to original diagram)

27. (D) Because $BC \parallel AD$, $\angle ABC$ and $\angle BAD$ are supplementary.

$$
\begin{aligned}
2x + x - 20 + x &= 180 \\
4x - 20 &= 180 \\
4x &= 200 \\
x &= 50
\end{aligned}
$$

28. (B) Since $\sin(-x) = -\sin x$, $-f(x) = f(x) = f(-x)$.

29. (C) $\triangle XWY$ and $\triangle XYZ$ have equal altitudes and equal bases, so they have equal areas. Since $AB \parallel XY$,

$$\frac{\text{area of } \triangle AWB}{\text{area of } \triangle XWY} = \left(\frac{AB}{XY}\right)^2 = \frac{a^2}{XY^2}$$

Since $CD \parallel XY$,

$$\frac{\text{area of } \triangle ZCD}{\text{area of } \triangle XYZ} = \left(\frac{CD}{XY}\right)^2 = \frac{9a^2}{XY^2}$$

$$\frac{\text{area of } \triangle AWB}{\text{area of } \triangle XWY} \cdot \frac{\text{area of } \triangle XYZ}{\text{area of } \triangle ZCD}$$

$$= \frac{a^2}{XY^2} \cdot \frac{XY^2}{9a^2}$$

$$= \frac{1}{9}$$

30. (A) $2\sin^2 x = \sin x$.

When $\sin x \neq 0$, $2\sin x = 1$.

$$\sin x = \frac{1}{2}$$

$$x = 30°$$

31. (E) $5 * 3 = 5 * (5-2) = 5^2 + 5^2 + 2^2 = 29$

32. (C)

$$x + x + 110 = 180$$
$$2x = 70$$
$$x = 35$$

$$2y + z = 180$$
$$y = 70$$
$$140 + z = 180$$
$$z = 40$$
$$x + z = 75$$

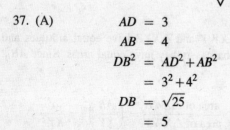

33. (E) Regardless of the value of x, 3^x is positive.

34. (D) $f(-1) = (-1)^2 - a(-1) = 1 + a$

35. (E) $\sin 30 = \frac{1}{2}$, $\cos 30 = \frac{\sqrt{3}}{2}$, $\tan 30 = \frac{1}{\sqrt{3}}$. Substitute the values into the given expression and simplify.

36. (C) From the figure at right,

$$b + a = 180$$

37. (A)
$$AD = 3$$
$$AB = 4$$
$$DB^2 = AD^2 + AB^2$$
$$= 3^2 + 4^2$$
$$DB = \sqrt{25}$$
$$= 5$$

38. (A) The diagram at right shows the parabola, its intercepts, and its axis of symmetry. The first coordinate of the vertex of the parabola can be easily seen from the sketch. The second coordinate is found by substituting into the equation.

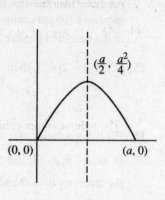

39. (D) Since $AB = DB$, $\angle BDA \cong \angle A$, so $\angle BDA$ is 70°. Since $\angle BDA$ is an exterior angle of $\triangle BDC$, its measure is the sum of the measures of $\angle B$ and $\angle C$.

$$70 = 20 + x$$
$$50 = x$$

40. (B) By the Law of Sines,

$$\frac{BC}{\sin A} = \frac{AC}{\sin B}$$

$$\frac{7}{\sin A} = \frac{5}{\frac{1}{2}}$$

$$5\sin A = \frac{1}{2}(7)$$

$$\sin A = \frac{1}{2}(7)\left(\frac{1}{5}\right)$$

$$= \frac{7}{10}$$

41. (D) $3x - 3 = -1(3 - 3x)$. The factor -1 is missing in (D), but it appears in (C) as the opposite of the quantity.

42. (E)
$$7x^2 - 7x - 14 = 0$$
$$7(x^2 - x - 2) = 0$$
$$7(x - 2)(x + 1) = 0,$$
$$\text{so } x - 2 = 0 \text{ or } x + 1 = 0.$$
$$\text{Therefore } x = 2 \text{ or } x = -1.$$

43. (E) Cross-multiply to get $\sqrt{5}+x = \sqrt{5}-x$, $x = -x$, so $2x = 0$ and $x = 0$.

44. (A)
$$
\begin{aligned}
\text{Area of } ACC'A' &= (AC)(CC') \\
2 &= (AC)(2AC) \\
1 &= AC^2 \\
1 &= AC
\end{aligned}
$$

The volume of the cylinder is
$$
\begin{aligned}
h(\pi r^2) &= 2(\pi \cdot 1^2) \\
&= 2\pi
\end{aligned}
$$

45. (A) $x^2 - 3x + 2 = \left(x^2 - 3x + \dfrac{9}{4}\right) + 2 - \dfrac{9}{4}$

$$
= \left(x - \dfrac{3}{2}\right)^2 - \dfrac{1}{4}
$$

46. (D) From any point A, there are five chords that have the other five points as endpoints.

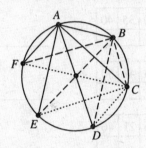

From B, there are four chords since AB has already been drawn. From C, there are three chords since AC and BC have already been drawn. From D, two (not drawn) remain. From E, one (not drawn) remains. From F, none remains.

47. (E)
$$
\begin{aligned}
&\sqrt{16 + 16x^2} - \sqrt{9 + 9x^2} \\
&= 4\sqrt{1 + x^2} - 3\sqrt{1 + x^2} \\
&= \sqrt{1 + x^2}
\end{aligned}
$$

48. (E) Since $f(2+k) = f(2-k)$, $x = 2$ is an axis of symmetry for $f(x)$. Since $x = -3$ is 5 units to the left of $x = 2$, its reflection is $x = 7$, which is 5 units to the right of $x = 2$.

49. (A) The lowest common denominator is $(x+1)(x-1) = x^2 - 1$, so

$$
\begin{aligned}
\frac{1}{x+1} + \frac{1}{x-1} &= \frac{x-1+x+1}{x^2-1} \\
&= \frac{2x}{x^2-1}
\end{aligned}
$$

50. (B) The graph of $f(x) = x + 3$ is as follows:

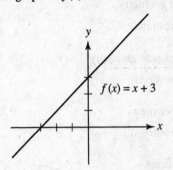

The graph of $|f(x)|$ is the same for $x \geq -3$, but when $x < -3$, $|f(x)|$ is $-f(x) = -(x+3)$, which is graphed below:

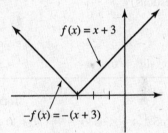

SELF-EVALUATION CHART FOR MODEL TEST 6

SUBJECT AREA	QUESTIONS ANSWERED CORRECTLY	NUMBER OF CORRECT ANSWERS

Algebra
(14 questions)

1	6	11	15	19	20	24	31	33	41	42	43	47	49

_____

Plane geometry
(10 questions)

2	7	12	17	25	26	27	32	36	39

_____

Solid geometry
(3 questions)

29	31	44

_____

Coordinate geometry
(6 questions)

3	4	5	23	38	45

_____

Trigonometry
(5 questions)

13	22	30	35	40

_____

Functions
(6 questions)

8	18	28	34	48	50

_____

Miscellaneous
(6 questions)

9	10	14	16	21	46

_____

Total number of correct answers _____

Total number of incorrect answers _____

Total score = total number of correct answers _____

minus $\frac{1}{4}$ number of incorrect answers − _____

_____

(Reminder: Answers left blank are not counted as correct or incorrect)

Raw score = (number correct) $-\frac{1}{4}$ (number incorrect)

To evaluate your performance, compare your raw score with the table below.

Evaluate Your Performance
Model Test 6

Excellent	760–800	46–50
Very Good	700–750	40–45
Good	610–690	32–39
Above Average	560–600	26–31
Average	500–550	18–25
Below Average	270–490	17 or less

APPENDIX

PART
4

REVIEW OF CONCEPTS AND FORMULAS

ALGEBRA

25 IMPORTANT CONCEPTS

1. The term *set* designates a collection of objects named in such a way as to provide a test that will indicate whether or not some particular object belongs to (symbolized as "ϵ") the set.

2. Objects belonging to a set are called *elements* or *members* of the set.

3. A square root of a number x is a number y for which $y^2 = x$.

4. Two terms of a polynomial are like terms if they have the same variables and each variable has the same exponent.

5. The first step in factoring a polynomial is to look for a common factor and remove it by using the generalized Distributive Law:

$$ab + ac + ad + \ldots = a(b + c + d + \ldots).$$

6. If a and b are any real numbers and if

$$a < b \text{ and } b < c, \text{ then } a < c.$$

7. A rational expression is a fraction whose numerator and denominator are polynomials.

8. To solve an equation involving rational expressions, it is necessary to clear fractions by multiplying all terms by the lowest common denominator (LCD).

9. If $ax^2 + bx + c = 0$ and $ax^2 + bx + c$ can be factored into linear factors, then the solutions can be found by setting each factor equal to zero and solving for x.

10. A relation is a set of ordered pairs.

11. A function is a set of ordered pairs no two of which have the same first coordinate. Therefore a function is always a relation, but not all relations are functions.

12. The imaginary number i is defined by the equation $i^2 = -1$; in other words, $i = \sqrt{-1}$.

13. The standard form of a complex number is $a + bi$, where a and b are real.

14. In the complex number plane, the graph of $a + bi$ is the point whose coordinates are (a, b).

15. A system of equations can be solved in three ways:
    a. by graphing,
    b. by substitution, and
    c. by addition, which involves eliminating a variable.

16. The terms *logarithm* and *exponent* are synonymous.

17. The common logarithm of a positive number can be expressed as the sum of an integer (called the *characteristic*) and the common log of a number (called the *mantissa*) between 1 and 0.

18. The values of a polynomial can be calculated quickly by synthetic division.

19. The number of linear factors of a polynomial of degree n is n.

20. An arithmetic sequence follows the pattern

$$a, a+d, a+2d, a+3d, \ldots, a+(n-1)d,$$

    where n is the number of the term.

21. A geometric sequence follows the pattern

$$a, ar, ar^2, ar^3, ar^4, \ldots, ar^{n-1},$$

    where n is the number of the term and r is the ratio of any two consecutive terms.

22. If the first of two actions can be done in m ways and the second done in n ways, the number of ways the two actions can be done in order is $m \times n$.

23. The value of the expression $n!$, where n is any positive integer, is given by

$$n! = n(n-1)(n-2)\ldots3 \cdot 2 \cdot 1.$$

24. The total number of combinations of a set of n elements is the total number of those subsets that contain at least one element, and this number is

$$2^n - 1.$$

25. If two events are mutually exclusive (i.e., they cannot both occur at the same time), and the first event can occur in m ways while the second can occur in n ways, then one or the other event can occur in $m + n$ ways.

25 FREQUENTLY USED ALGEBRA FORMULAS

1. $a^2 - b^2 = (a+b)(a-b)$.

2. If $ax^2 + bx + c = 0$, then

$$x = \frac{-b \pm \sqrt{b^2 - 4ac}}{2a}$$

3. $x^m \cdot x^n = x^{m+n}$.

4. $\dfrac{x^m}{x^n} = x^{m-n}$.

5. $(x^m)^n = x^{mn}$.

6. $(xy)^m = x^m y^m$.

7. $\left(\dfrac{x}{y}\right)^m = \dfrac{x^m}{y^m}$.

8. $x^{-m} = \dfrac{1}{x^m}$.

9. $x^{m/n} = \sqrt[n]{x^m}$ or $(\sqrt[n]{x})^m$.

10. $\log MN = \log M + \log N$.

11. $\log \dfrac{M}{N} = \log M - \log N$.

12. $\log M^n = n \log M$.

13. $\log \dfrac{1}{M} = -\log M$.

14. If $P(x_1, y_1)$ and $Q(x_2, y_2)$ are two points in a plane, then

   a. the slope of line $PQ = \dfrac{y_1 - y_2}{x_1 - x_2}$,

   b. the midpoint of segment $PQ =$

   $$\left(\frac{x_1 + x_2}{2}, \frac{y_1 + y_2}{2}\right),$$

   c. the length of segment $PQ =$

   $$\sqrt{(x_1 - x_2)^2 + (y_1 - y_2)^2},$$

   d. an equation of line PQ is

   $$y - y_1 = \frac{y_1 - y_2}{x_1 - x_2}(x - x_1).$$

15. If m is the slope of a line and $(0, b)$ is the point at which it intersects the y-axis, then

$$y = mx + b$$

is the equation of the line.

16. If (h, k) is the center of a circle and r is its radius, then

$$(x - h)^2 + (y - k)^2 = r^2$$

is the equation of the circle. When the center is the origin, then $x^2 + y^2 = r^2$ is the equation.

17. If $f(x)$ is a second-degree function, then its graph is a parabola with equation

$$f(x) = ax^2 + bx + c$$

with vertex at the point $\left(\dfrac{-b}{2a}, \dfrac{4ac - b^2}{4a}\right)$.

18. The equation of an ellipse with center at the origin is

$$\frac{x^2}{a^2} + \frac{y^2}{b^2} = 1$$

with axial intersections at the points $(\pm a, 0)$ and $(0, \pm b)$.

19. The equation of an hyperbola whose asymptotes intersect at the origin is

$$\frac{x^2}{a^2} - \frac{y^2}{b^2} = 1 \quad \text{(intercepts on the x-axis),}$$

or

$$\frac{y^2}{b^2} - \frac{x^2}{a^2} = 1 \quad \text{(intercepts on the y-axis).}$$

The asymptotes are found by factoring the left side according to the difference of squares, then equating each factor with zero.

20. $a^2 - b^2 = (a + b)(a - b)$.

21. If a_n is any term of an arithmetic sequence, then

$$a_n = a_1 + (n - 1)d,$$

where a_1 is the first term, n is the number of terms, and d is the difference between any term and its successor.

22. If S_n is the sum of the first n terms of an arithmetic sequence, then

$$S_n = \frac{(a_1 + a_n)}{2}n.$$

23. If a_n is any term of a geometric sequence, then

$$a_n = a_1 r^{n-1},$$

where a_1 is the first term, n the number of terms, and r the quotient found by dividing any term into its successor.

24. For a geometric series, the sum S_n is given by

$$S_n = \frac{a_1 - a_1 r^n}{1 - r}$$

where the variables have the same meaning as in 23.

25. For an infinite geometric series, the sum S_∞ is given by

$$S_\infty = \frac{a_1}{1 - r}$$

where the variables have the same meaning as in 23.

GEOMETRY

23 IMPORTANT CONCEPTS

1. A point has no width or thickness, only position.
2. A line is a set of points, has no thickness, is straight, and continues infinitely in two directions.
3. A plane is a set of points, is flat, has no depth (thickness), and continues infinitely in all directions.
4. The midpoint of a right triangle is equidistant from its vertices.
5. The sum of the measures of the angles of a triangle is 180.
6. The sum of the measures of the angles (interior) of any polygon is $180(n-2)$, where n is the number of sides.
7. The sum of the measures of the exterior angles of a regular polygon is 360.
8. The measure of an angle inscribed in a circle is half the measure of the intercepted arc.
9. An angle inscribed in a semicircle is a right angle.
10. A triangle is a right triangle if and only if the square of the length of its longest side is equal to the sum of the squares of the lengths of the remaining two sides.
11. A right angle has degree measure 90.
12. An obtuse angle has a measure greater than 90.
13. An acute angle has a measure less than 90.
14. The measure of an exterior angle of a triangle is equal to the sum of the measures of its remote interior angles.
15. An altitude of a triangle is a segment containing the vertex of one angle of the triangle and is perpendicular to the opposite side.

16. In any 45-45-90 triangle, the sides are proportional to those shown at right.

17. In any 30-60-90 triangle, the sides are proportional to those shown at right.

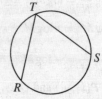

18. Triangles with sides having lengths 3-4-5, 5-12-13, and 8-15-17 are right triangles and so are triangles with sides in the same proportion (for example, 6-8-10, 15-36-39, 32-60-68).
19. Two lines are parallel if and only if they lie in the same plane and do not intersect.
20. Parallel lines are everywhere equidistant.

21. If R, S, and T are three distinct points of a circle, then the measure of $\angle RTS$ is half the measure of arc RS.

22. The intersection of two sets, $A \cap B$, consists of all elements that belong to both sets.
23. The union of two sets, $A \cup B$, consists of all elements that belong to one or both of the sets.

STANDARD ABBREVIATIONS FOR 10 GEOMETRIC LAWS

CP (or CPCT): All pairs of corresponding parts of triangles are congruent if and only if the triangles are congruent. This is the definition of "congruent" triangles.

ITT: Two sides of a triangle are congruent if and only if the angles opposite them are congruent. The Isosceles Triangle Theorem.

SAS: If two sides and the included angle of one triangle are each congruent to the corresponding parts of a second triangle, then the triangles are congruent. The Side-Angle-Side Postulate.

ASA: If two angles and the included side of one triangle are each congruent to the corresponding parts of a second triangle, then the triangles are congruent. The Angle-Side-Angle Postulate. (This is actually a theorem, but the proof is generally beyond the scope of elementary geometry students, so the law is just postulated.)

SSS: If the three sides of one triangle are each congruent to the corresponding sides of a second triangle, then the triangles are congruent. The Side-Side-Side Postulate. (Again, though the law is postulated for simplicity, it can be proved.)

AAS: If two angles and a side opposite one of the angles are each congruent to the corresponding parts of a second triangle, the triangles are congruent. The Side-Angle-Angle Theorem, also commonly abbreviated SAA.

HL: If the hypotenuse and one leg of a right triangle are congruent to the corresponding parts of a second right triangle, the two triangles are congruent. The Hypotenuse-Leg Theorem.

HA: If the hypotenuse and one acute angle of a right triangle are congruent to the corresponding parts of a second right triangle, the two triangles are congruent. The Hypotenuse-Angle Theorem.

SSS Similarity: A correspondence between two triangles is a similarity if the lengths of all three pairs of corresponding sides are proportional.

AA Similarity: A correspondence between two triangles is a similarity if any two pairs of corresponding angles are congruent.

SAS Similarity: A correspondence between two triangles is a similarity if two pairs of corresponding sides are in proportion and their included legs are congruent.

---

20 FREQUENTLY USED GEOMETRY FORMULAS

1. The area of a circle, A, is related to the radius by

$$A = \pi r^2.$$

2. The circumference of a circle, C, is related to the radius by

$$C = 2\pi r,$$

and to the diameter by

$$C = \pi d.$$

3. If A is the area of a square and s is the length of one side, then

$$A = s^2.$$

The perimeter, P, is $4s$.

4. If A is the area of a rectangle, l is its length and w its width, then

$$A = lw.$$

The perimeter, P, is

$$2l + 2w.$$

5. The area, A, of any triangle is related to the length, b, of any base and the altitude, a, to that base by

$$A = \frac{1}{2}ab.$$

6. If A and B are the midpoints of the sides of a triangle, then

$$AB = \frac{1}{2}CD$$

and

$$AB \parallel CA.$$

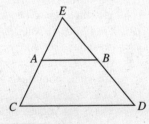

7. If $GH \parallel IJ$ and E and F are the midpoints of the sides of a parallelogram, then

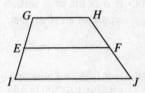

$$EF = \frac{1}{2}(GH + IJ) \quad \text{and} \quad EF \parallel GH \parallel IJ.$$

8. In right triangle ABC with $BD \perp AC$,

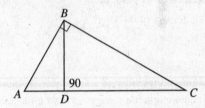

$$\frac{AD}{AB} = \frac{AB}{AC} \text{ or } \frac{DC}{BC} = \frac{BC}{AC} \text{ and } \frac{AD}{BD} = \frac{BD}{DC}.$$

9.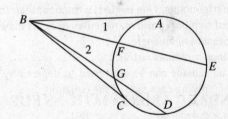

If AB and BC are tangents, then $AB = BC$, $(BE) \cdot (BF) = (BD) \cdot (BG) = (BA)^2 = (BC)^2$. $\angle 1 = \frac{1}{2}(AE - AF)$. $\angle 2 = \frac{1}{2}(DE - FG)$.

10. If XW and YT are chords intersecting at point Z in the interior of a circle, then $(XZ)(ZW) = (YZ)(ZT)$ and

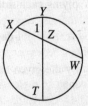

$$\angle 1 = \frac{1}{2}(XY + TW).$$

11. If V is the volume of a prism, h is the altitude (the perpendicular distance between the planes containing the bases), and B is the area of a base, then

$$V = hB.$$

12. If S_L is the lateral surface area of a prism, h is its altitude, and p is the perimeter of a base, then

$$S_L = hp.$$

13. If S_T is the total surface area of a prism, then

$$S_T = hp + 2B.$$

14. If A is the total surface area of a cube and e is the length of an edge, then

$$A = 6e^2.$$

15. If V is the volume of a cube and e is the length of an edge, then
$$V = e^3.$$

16. If V is the volume of a cylinder, h is its altitude, and B the area of its base, then

$$V = hB.$$

17. If S_c is the area of the curved surface of a cylinder, h is its altitude, and C is the circumference of the base, then

$$S_c + hC.$$

If S_T is the total surface area, then

$$S_T = hC = 2B.$$

18. If V is the volume of a pyramid, h its altitude, and B is the area of a base, then

$$V = \frac{1}{3}hB.$$

19. If V is the volume of a cone, h is its altitude, and B is the area of a base, then

$$V = \frac{1}{3}hB.$$

20. If V is the volume of a sphere, S is its surface, and r is its radius, then

$$V = \frac{4}{3}\pi r^2 \text{ and } S = 4\pi r^2.$$

TRIGONOMETRY

5 IMPORTANT CONCEPTS

1. In trigonometry, an angle is a rotation; therefore any real number (positive, negative, or zero) may be the measure of an angle.
2. Since π radians $= 180°$:
   a. radians can be converted to degrees by multiplying each side of the equation

   $$1 \text{ radian} = \frac{180}{\pi} \text{ degrees}$$

   by the given number of radians and simplifying;
   b. degrees can be converted to radians by multiplying each side of the equation

   $$1 \text{ degree} = \frac{\pi}{180} \text{ radians}$$

   by the given number of degrees and simplifying.

3. To find values of trigonometric functions of angles with a reference angles of 30 or 60, the 30-60-90 triangle is used:

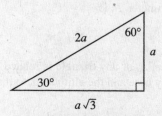

4. To find values of trigonometric functions of angles with reference angle 45, the isosceles right triangle is used:

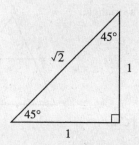

5. To find values of trigonometric functions of quadrantal angles (0, 90, 180, 270, 360, ...), the diagram at right, with (x,y) the values given and $r = 1$ for each point, is used:

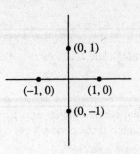

5 FREQUENTLY USED TRIGONOMETRY FORMULAS

1. If $\angle X$ is an acute angle of a right triangle, then

$$\sin \angle X = \frac{\text{opposite leg}}{\text{hypotenuse}}, \quad \tan \angle X = \frac{1}{\cot \angle X}$$

$$\cos \angle X = \frac{\text{adjacent leg}}{\text{hypotenuse}}, \quad \cot \angle X = \frac{\text{adjacent leg}}{\text{opposite leg}},$$

$$\tan \angle X = \frac{\text{opposite leg}}{\text{adjacent leg}}, \quad \sec \angle X = \frac{\text{hypotenuse}}{\text{adjacent leg}},$$

$$\sin \angle X = \frac{1}{\csc \angle X} \quad \csc \angle X = \frac{\text{hypotenuse}}{\text{opposite leg}},$$

$$\cos \angle X = \frac{1}{\sec \angle X}$$

2. If θ is an angle in standard position and (x,y) is a point on its terminal side at a distance r units from the origin, then

$$\sin \theta = \frac{y}{r}, \quad \csc \theta = \frac{r}{y} \quad \cos \theta = \frac{x}{r},$$

$$\sec \theta = \frac{r}{x}, \quad \tan \theta = \frac{y}{x} \quad \cot \theta = \frac{x}{y}.$$

3. For any $\angle X$, the following must be true:

$$(\sin \angle X)(\csc \angle X) = 1,$$

$$\sin \angle X = \frac{1}{\csc \angle X},$$

$$\csc \angle X = \frac{1}{\sin \angle X};$$

$$(\cos \angle X)(\sec \angle X) = 1,$$

$$\cos \angle X = \frac{1}{\sec \angle X},$$

$$\sec \angle X = \frac{1}{\cos \angle X};$$

$$(\tan \angle X)(\cot \angle X) = 1,$$

$$\tan \angle X = \frac{1}{\cot \angle X},$$

$$\cot \angle X = \frac{1}{\tan \angle X}.$$

4. For any angle X,

$$\sin^2 \angle X + \cos^2 \angle X = 1,$$

$$\tan^2 \angle X + 1 = \sec^2 \angle X;$$

$$\cot^2 \angle X + 1 = \csc^2 \angle X,$$

$$\tan \angle X = \frac{\sin \angle X}{\cos \angle X},$$

$$\cot \angle X = \frac{\cos \angle X}{\sin \angle X}.$$

5. In any triangle with vertices X, Y, and Z,

$$\frac{YZ}{\sin \angle X} = \frac{XY}{\sin \angle Z} = \frac{XZ}{\sin \angle Y}$$

(Law of Sines),

$$XY^2 = YZ^2 + XZ^2 - 2(YZ)(XZ) \cos \angle Z$$

(Law of Cosines).

3 MEASURES OF CENTRAL TENDENCY FOR A SET OF QUANTITIES

1. The arithmetic *mean* is the result obtained by adding the quantities and dividing by the number of quantities.

2. The *median* is the middle quantity when the set is listed from greatest to least. If the set has an even number of quantities, the median is the average of the two middle quantities.

3. The *mode* is the quantity that occurs most frequently.

INDEX

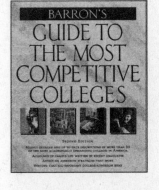

Success on Advanced Placement Tests Starts with Help from Barron's

Each May, thousands of college-bound students take one or more Advanced Placement Exams to earn college credits—and for many years, they've looked to Barron's, the leader in Advanced Placement test preparation. You can get Barron's user-friendly manuals for eleven different AP subjects. That includes two—in French and Spanish—that come with audiocassettes to improve your listening comprehension skills. Every Barron's AP manual gives you—

- **Diagnostic tests**
- **Extensive subject review**
- **Full-length model AP exams**
- **Study help and test-taking advice**

Model exams are designed to reflect the actual AP exams in question types, subject matter, length, and degree of difficulty. All questions come with answers and explanations. All books are paperback.

AP: Biology, 6th Ed.
0-7641-1375-5, 430 pp., $14.95, Can$21.00

AP: Calculus, 7th Ed.
0-7641-1790-4, 624 pp., $16.95, Can$23.95

AP: Chemistry, 2nd Ed.
0-7641-0474-8, 672 pp., $14.95, Can$19.95

AP: Computer Science
0-7641-0546-9, 600 pp., $14.95, Can$21.00

AP: English, 7th Ed.
0-7641-1230-9, 464 pp., $14.95, Can$21.00

AP: Environmental Science
0-7641-2161-8, 688 pp., $16.95, Can$23.95

AP: European History, 2nd Ed.
0-7641-0458-6, 240 pp., $14.95, Can$21.00

AP: French with Two Cassettes, 2nd Ed.
0-7641-7159-3, 450 pp.,
cassettes 90-min. each, $24.95, Can$32.50

AP: Macroeconomics/ Microeconomics
0-7641-1164-7, 496 pp., $14.95, Can$21.00

AP: Physics B, 2nd Ed.
0-7641-0475-6, 460 pp., $15.95, Can$22.50

AP: Physics C
0-7641-1802-1, 500 pp., $16.95, Can$23.95

AP: Psychology
0-7641-0959-6, 320 pp., $16.95, Can$23.95

AP: Spanish with Three CDs, 3rd Ed.
0-7641-7397-9, 480 pp., cassettes 90-min. each, $24.95, Can$34.95

AP: Statistics, 2nd Ed.
0-7641-1091-8, 432 pp., $14.95, Can$21.00

AP: U.S. Government and Politics, 3rd Ed.
0-7641-1651-7, 512 pp., $16.95, Can$23.95

AP: U.S. History, 6th Ed.
0-7641-1157-4, 336 pp., $15.95, Can$22.50

AP: World History
0-7641-1816-1, 512 pp., $16.95, Can$23.95

Barron's Educational Series, Inc.
250 Wireless Blvd.
Hauppauge, NY 11788
Call toll-free: 1-800-645-3476
Order by fax: 1-631-434-3217

Visit our website at:
www.barronseduc.com

In Canada:
Georgetown Book Warehouse
34 Armstrong Ave.
Georgetown, Ontario L7G 4R9
Canadian orders: 1-800-247-7160
Order by fax: 1-800-887-1594

(#93) R8/02